AN EXPLORER'S GUIDE

The Hudson Valley & Catskill Mountains

Includes Saratoga Springs & Albany

Ulster County Tourism

AN EXPLORER'S GUIDE

The Hudson Valley & Catskill Mountains

Includes Saratoga Springs & Albany

Joanne Michaels

EIGHTH EDITION

The Countryman Press * Woodstock, Vermont

We welcome your comments and suggestions. Please contact Explorer's Guide Editor, The Countryman Press, P.O. Box 748, Woodstock, VT 05091, or by e-mail at countrymanpress@wwnorton.com.

Eighth Edition

Explorer's Guide Hudson Valley & Catskill Mountains
ISBN 978-1-58157-151-6

Cover photo Bear Mountain Bridge, © Hardie Truesdale, www.hardietruesdale.com
Interior photographs by the author unless otherwise specified
Maps by Moore Creative Design, © The Countryman Press
Cover and interior design by Bodenweber Design
Composition by PerfecType, Nashville, TN

Published by The Countryman Press, P.O. Box 748, Woodstock, VT 05091
Distributed by W. W. Norton & Company, Inc., 500 Fifth Avenue, New York, NY 10110
Printed in the United States of America

10 9 8 7 6 5 4 3 2 1

To the people in my life who have supported, loved, and believed in me through
the years, particularly Renee, Lawrence, Nancy, and Erik.
I have been very fortunate in my family and friends.

A NOTE TO THE READER

No entries for any of the establishments appearing in the Explorer's Guide series have been solicited or paid for. I have selected lodging and dining places for mention in this book based on their merits alone. There is no charge to innkeepers or restaurant owners for inclusion. The decision to include a place here has to do with quality alone: The book is the best of the Hudson Valley and Catskill Mountains.

PRICES

Please do not hold me or the owners of various establishments mentioned responsible for any prices listed as of press time in 2013. Some changes are inevitable. State and local taxes should be added to all prices, as well.

The price rating system is simple and provides general guidelines to travelers. By their nature, restaurants included in the Eating Out group are generally inexpensive. For entrées in the Dining Out and Eating Out sections, in general:

$ means most entrées are $15 and under
$$ means $15–25
$$$ means above $25

For inns and bed & breakfasts (per room before tax):

$ means most rooms run $125 and under
$$ means $125–200
$$$ means above $200

SMOKING

All B&Bs, inns, and restaurants are now smoke-free. If this is an issue for you, do inquire when you call. Assume that all establishments do not permit smoking anywhere.

READER RESPONSE

Over the 25 years that this book has been in print, I have received many letters from readers throughout the country. If you would like to share any of your experiences, please contact me at P.O. Box 425, Woodstock, NY 12498, or e-mail jmichaels2@hvc.rr.com.

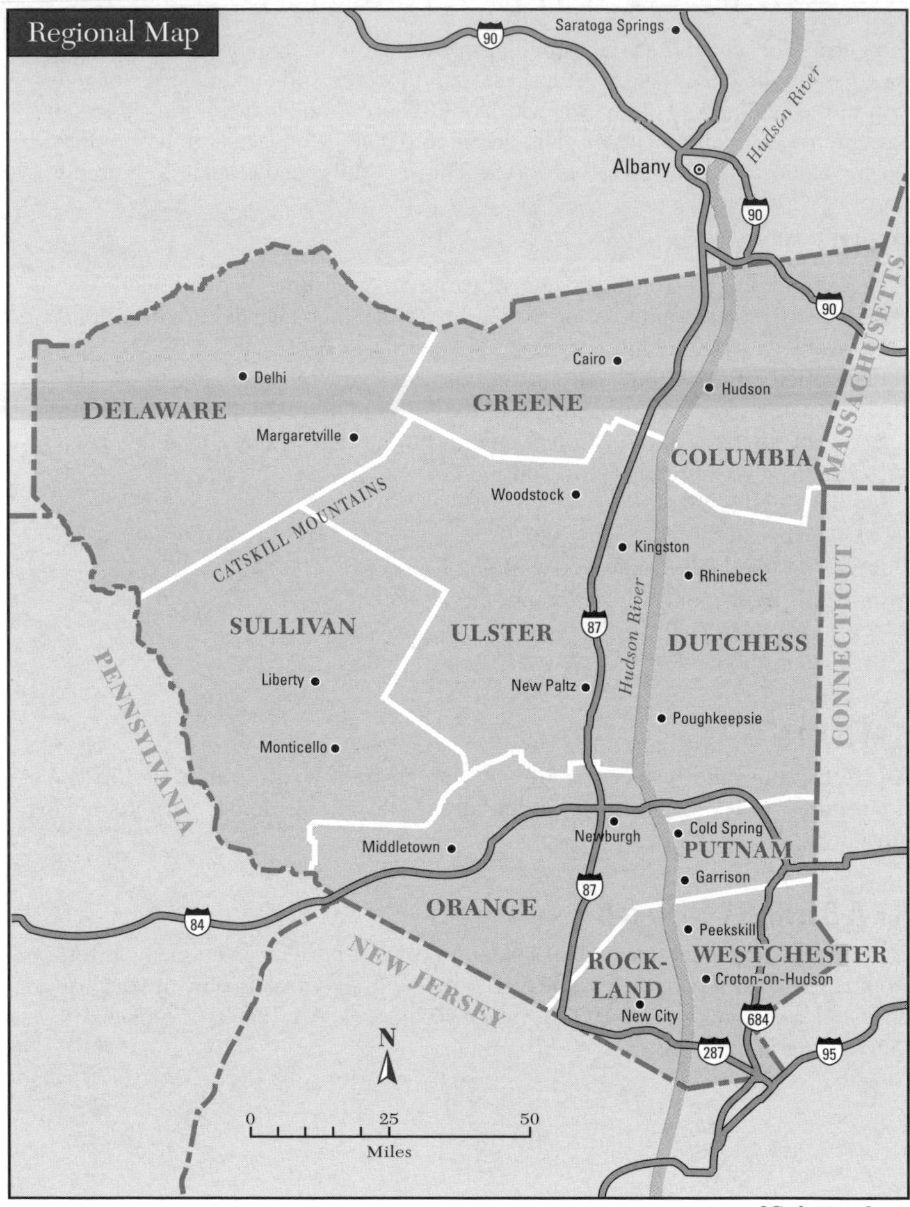

Regional Map
Saratoga Springs
90
Hudson River
Albany
90
90
Cairo
Delhi
Hudson
DELAWARE
GREENE
Margaretville
COLUMBIA
MASSACHUSETTS
Woodstock
CATSKILL MOUNTAINS
Kingston
Rhinebeck
CONNECTICUT
SULLIVAN
ULSTER
87
Hudson River
DUTCHESS
PENNSYLVANIA
Liberty
New Paltz
Poughkeepsie
Monticello
Newburgh
Cold Spring
Middletown
PUTNAM
Garrison
87
ORANGE
84
Peekskill
WESTCHESTER
NEW JERSEY
ROCK-
LAND
Croton-on-Hudson
New City
684
N
287
95
0
25
50
Miles

CONTENTS

10 MAPS
11 ACKNOWLEDGMENTS
13 INTRODUCTION

1 Rockland County / 15

2 Orange County / 37

3 Sullivan County / 79

4 Ulster County / 111

5 Delaware County / 191

6 Greene County / 221

7 Albany / 253

8 Saratoga Springs and Environs / 281

9 Columbia County / 311

10 Dutchess County / 349

11 Putnam County / 417

12 Westchester County / 435

495 INDEX

MAPS

8 REGIONAL MAP
16 ROCKLAND COUNTY
38 ORANGE COUNTY
80 SULLIVAN COUNTY
112 ULSTER COUNTY
192 DELAWARE COUNTY
222 GREENE COUNTY
254 ALBANY
282 SARATOGA SPRINGS AND ENVIRONS
312 COLUMBIA COUNTY
350 DUTCHESS COUNTY
418 PUTNAM COUNTY
436 WESTCHESTER COUNTY

ACKNOWLEDGMENTS

It is never possible to thank everyone who helps a book of this kind come to life; for every person I mention, several more were behind the scenes, answering questions, mailing brochures, offering suggestions, and opening their homes to me.

I want to particularly thank the members of the county tourism departments and chambers of commerce throughout the region who assisted me tremendously on my travels: Nancy Lutz of Dutchess County Tourism, Natasha Caputo of Westchester County Tourism, Patty Cullen of Delaware County Chamber of Commerce, Nancy Petramale of Greene County Tourism, Annie Cooper and Ann Marie Schaumann of Columbia County Tourism, Schuyler Bull of the Albany County Convention & Visitors Bureau, and Roberta Byron Lockwood of Sullivan County Tourism. Ann Marie Bellantoni at the Saratoga County Chamber of Commerce and Candace Bergman of the Gideon Putnam Resort were both enormously helpful as well.

The following people, who regularly travel throughout the Hudson Valley and Catskills, gave me excellent recommendations and support: Betsy Bergman, John and Nancy Bruno, Mark Cuddy, Helen Hosking, Nancy Michaels, Babs Moley, Bruce Moor, Gail and Alan Paley, Heather Rolland, and Michael Silfen. I sincerely appreciate their input. Hardie Truesdale did a wonderful job on the cover photograph. I would also like to thank Kermit Hummel and Lisa Sacks for their guidance through the publishing process—and willingness to consider new ideas. Justine Rathbun paid enormous attention to details, and I'm grateful to her. Tom Haushalter was exceedingly efficient in handling publicity for the book.

Many people gave their opinions and the names of their favorite spots, based on years of growing up and living in their respective towns. They probably didn't realize at the time how helpful they were. These locals got me off the beaten track, and I discovered charming neighborhood restaurants, tranquil back roads, and a swimming spot or hiking area I probably never would have found on my own. So this book, aside from being the best guide to this phenomenal region, is also a gift to all the people of the Hudson Valley and Catskills.

INTRODUCTION

Although I am certainly not the first traveler to recognize the scenic wonders of the Hudson Valley and Catskills, I am proud to say that I have remained at the forefront of reminding people that some of the most beautiful sights in the world are, literally, at their back doors. A close friend once commented that by writing about these regional treasures, I am causing them to be overrun with tourists; he suggested I keep these special places to myself, or they will risk being ruined. I cannot deny that there are times when I have the impulse not to include a deserted swimming place I frequent in the summer or an "undiscovered" eatery on a back road I stopped at one day, but I know that sharing this information is what makes my book the best one available.

For more than 25 years, various editions of this guide have enriched the travels of tens of thousands of people visiting the region. Once in a while readers take the time to write a letter, sharing their experience of a particular inn or historic site. I have never heard anything but praise for the beauty of the Hudson Valley and Catskills—even if, on occasion, a particular restaurant didn't live up to their expectations.

When people think of this area, many imagine mysterious mountains where Rip Van Winkle slept away the years or lush valleys where bobcats roamed or even huge hotels where the entertainment and food never stopped. True, these are part of the region's story, but after traveling hundreds of thousands of miles on back roads and main roads, in snow, fog, sun, and rain, I have come to the conclusion that practically nowhere else in this country can one enjoy the startling beauty, the rich history, and the culture that can be found here.

And because there is so much to see and do, I chose to include only what I consider the best—be it food, inns, parks, or history. At historic sites or places of interest, I looked for unusual exhibits or special events. When evaluating restaurants, inns, hotels, and B&Bs, I looked for value, distinctiveness, quality, cleanliness, and courtesy. Farm stands, whether large or small, had to show pride in their produce. I traveled the area in all seasons, talked to hundreds of people, and visited every historic and cultural site. In a few cases, if I couldn't experience a place myself, I talked to experts whose judgment I relied on to ensure that you are getting the recommendations of the best people, as well.

I know that there are many different types of travelers, so this book offers a large number of places for visiting and dining. I have tried to select a wide variety of places to please people of all ages, all backgrounds, and all budgets. Some places are free while others are rather expensive, but all are the best of their type.

I have to emphasize, however, that dollar ratings sometimes change between the time when a book is written and the time when it appears in the bookstore. Remember that lunches may cost considerably less than dinners, single-lodging rates may be higher or lower depending on the establishment, and in some places special rates are available for groups, senior citizens, and midweek. If a site or restaurant does not appear in this book, this omission does not reflect a negative review. Perhaps I didn't know about it, or it may only recently have opened, or I might just have missed it. Tell me about it so that future editions of this guidebook will be as complete and as accurate as possible.

All the sites included in this book are within a day's drive of New York City and New Jersey, and many are a few hours by car from Boston and Philadelphia. The book is arranged by county, beginning with those on the west side of the Hudson River, heading north to Albany and Saratoga, and continuing south of Albany on the east side of the Hudson. You can be where the action is or be utterly alone. You can consume crunchy apples and creamy goat cheese, hike, kayak, or just take a walk. The climate is temperate, and the views are extraordinary.

Many places of interest are seasonal, as are the outdoor activities, but many sites throughout the region are open year-round. Summer events in particular are often held rain or shine, but I strongly suggest that you plan ahead and check schedules before taking a long trip. At the beginning of each chapter, I have listed phone numbers and websites for tourism departments in every county.

The Hudson Valley and Catskills offer such a range of sights and activities, virtually all visitors will enjoy their stay here. Take your time exploring my favorite region—my childhood home, and where I have returned to live since 1980. And remember to send your suggestions and discoveries to me at **P.O. Box 425, Woodstock, NY 12498** or e-mail jmichaels2@hvc.rr.com. Keep this book in your car to assist you while traveling through this special place on the planet!

—Joanne Michaels, Woodstock, NY
2013

Rockland County

1

Joanne Michaels

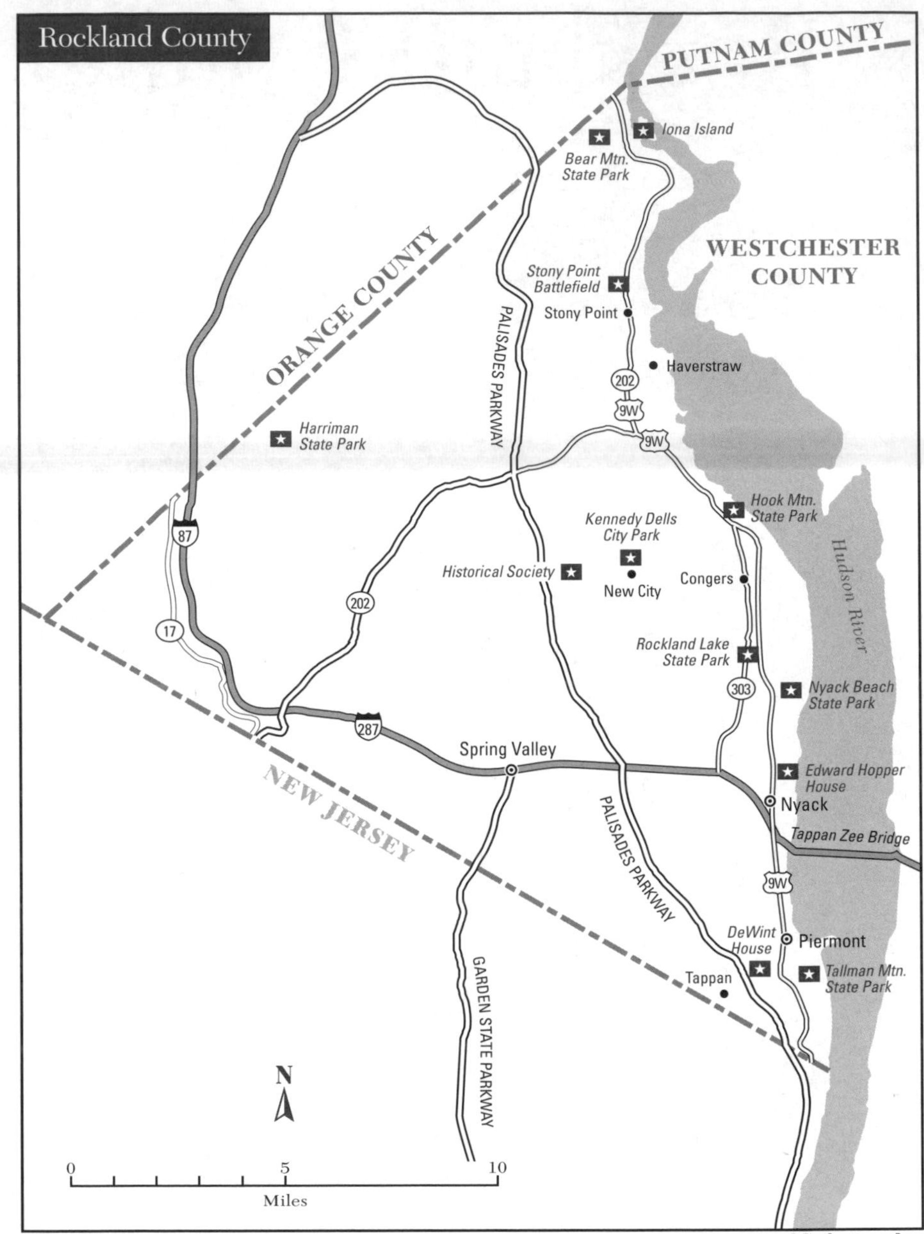
Rockland County
PUTNAM COUNTY
ORANGE COUNTY
WESTCHESTER COUNTY
NEW JERSEY
Iona Island
Bear Mtn. State Park
Stony Point Battlefield
Stony Point
Haverstraw
Harriman State Park
PALISADES PARKWAY
Hook Mtn. State Park
Kennedy Dells City Park
Historical Society
New City
Congers
Hudson River
Rockland Lake State Park
Nyack Beach State Park
Spring Valley
Edward Hopper House
Nyack
Tappan Zee Bridge
PALISADES PARKWAY
DeWint House
Piermont
Tappan
Tallman Mtn. State Park
GARDEN STATE PARKWAY
202
9W
87
202
17
287
303
N
0
5
10
Miles

ROCKLAND COUNTY

Only 176 square miles in size, Rockland County packs a lot into its area. It seems that everywhere you look in Rockland there is a park, from the tiny vest-pocket squares of green in towns and villages to the great spaces of Bear Mountain. Only 30 miles north of New York City, Rockland has preserved many of its forests, wetlands, mountains, and historic sites and still offers residents and visitors 32,000 acres of parkland. Wealthy patrons, civic leaders, and citizen activists joined forces to prevent Bear Mountain and High Tor from becoming a prison site and a quarry, respectively. Today, the fruits of those early environmental battles are seen and enjoyed by all. Hundreds of miles of hiking and biking trails wind through estuarine marshes, along the Hudson River, and up over dramatic peaks. Lakes and streams teem with wildlife, and plant lovers will delight in the explosion of color and scent that marks the spring wildflower season. Stony Point Battlefield, the mountaintop meadow where American troops defeated the British redcoats, is very much as it was more than 200 years ago.

In small towns and villages throughout the county, houses have been preserved with such care and such a sense of history that visitors feel as if they have stepped back in time. While touring Rockland, you will hear again and again the names of those who made history and are still remembered in ceremonies and festivals throughout the county: George Washington, Benedict Arnold, John André, and even Captain Kidd!

GUIDANCE Rockland County Tourism (845-708-7300; 1-800-295-5723), 18 New Hempstead Road, New City 10956; www.rocktourism.com.

Chamber of Commerce of the Nyacks (845-353-2221), P.O. Box 677, Nyack 10960; http://nyackchamber.org.

Arts Council of Rockland County (845-426-3660), 185 North Main Street, Spring Valley 10977; www.artscouncilofrockland.org.

Historical Society of Rockland County (845-634-9629), 20 Zukor Road, New City 10956; www.rocklandhistory.org.

GETTING THERE *By car:* From the upper deck of the George Washington Bridge, follow signs to the Palisades Parkway. Take exit 9E, the New York State Thruway, which leads into I-287 South to I-87 South. Get off at exit 11, Nyack, the last exit before the Tappan Zee Bridge. Make a left off the exit onto Route 59, which becomes Main Street.

By bus: **Rockland Coaches** (845-356-0877) operates buses that travel daily from the Port Authority in Manhattan at 20 minutes past the hour, to Route 9W in Nyack. **Transport of Rockland** (845-364-3333; www.co.rockland.ny.us/Public Trans) operates a bus line that services 10 routes within Rockland County and offers service to the Westchester towns of Tarrytown and White Plains. Some of these buses stop at the Metro North train station, where travelers can make connections to Manhattan.

MEDICAL EMERGENCY **Nyack Hospital** (845-348-2000), North Midland Avenue, Nyack.

Good Samaritan Hospital (845-368-5000), 255 Lafayette Avenue, Suffern.

Poison Control Center (1-800-222-1222); Rabies Information (845-364-2594).

✷ Villages

Nyack. Located off the NYS Thruway at exit 11, the last exit before the Tappan Zee Bridge. First settled by the Nyack Indians, who moved there from Brooklyn, Nyack soon became home to the Dutch, who began to farm the region. When steamboats arrived, making river travel easier, Nyack became a center for shipping and boatbuilding. The town is now known as an antiques and arts center, home to dozens of shops that offer the finest furniture, jewelry, crafts, and artwork (see *Selective Shopping*).

To see Nyack's charming architectural heritage, begin at South Broadway near the **Nyack Public Library,** one of the libraries built with funds from the Carnegie Foundation at the turn of the 20th century. Next to the library is a Queen Anne–style house with a tower and fine shingle work. Heading north, at 46 South Broadway, **Couch Court** is an unusual late-19th-century building that sports a towerlike cupola. The Presbyterian church was built in 1838 in the Greek Revival style, in which columns and symmetry were used in an effort to capture what was considered the ancient purity of Greece. Down the street a little farther, look for the **Tappan Zee Theatre,** built when movies were silent and vaudeville shows were the rage. Across the street, the Reformed church has a clock tower that dates from 1850. On Burd Street a plaque on the bank tells a little of the history of Nyack. On North Broadway you'll see the **Congregation of the Sons of Israel,** a synagogue founded in 1870. A side trip down and around Van Houten Road (it turns into Castle Heights) runs past riverfront homes and offers a magnificent view of the Hudson. Continue your drive up North Broadway, passing splendid mansions and lovely 18th-century homes, to **Hook Mountain State Park.**

The village of Nyack sponsors special events throughout the year, including a farmers' market every Thursday 8:30–2:30, May through November, in the municipal lot at Main and Cedar streets, rain or shine; there are arts and antiques street fairs during the spring and fall, a Halloween parade, and other happenings. A series of spring walking tours includes a guided walk through Oak Hill Cemetery, which contains the burial sites of Helen Hayes, Edward Hopper, Ben Hecht, Carson McCullers, and many other fascinating people who made Nyack their home. For information regarding dates and times, check the website www.friendsofthenyacks.org.

Piermont. Many travelers neglect to take a detour to this charming village, located about 4 miles south of Nyack. It is one of my favorite places in Rockland County. Just follow Piermont Avenue from Nyack, which takes you along the Hudson River right into town; 9W South is an alternate route. The village became somewhat renowned after Woody Allen filmed *The Purple Rose of Cairo* here. **The Piermont Flywheel Gallery** on the pier is just one of many intriguing places to see fine art and photography. The best way to experience Piermont is to park the car and wander along Piermont Avenue and the waterfront; the village is chock-full of interesting shops and galleries.

Haverstraw. The brickworks that lined the Hudson in the 19th century made this town, located north of Nyack, known as the brick-making capital of the world. At the time, barges carried the bricks to New York City. Then cement became a more popular building material, and the town deteriorated, like many places with economies based around changing industries. Today, however, Haverstraw is in the midst of an exciting renaissance. Upscale businesses and restaurants are moving into newly renovated storefronts. A downtown walking tour offers a sample of some fine Central American cuisine. At 91 Broadway a restored brick firehouse is now the **Arts Alliance of Haverstraw** (845-786-0253), open Monday through Friday 10–5; Saturday and Sunday by appointment only. Don't miss the **Garnerville Arts and Industrial Center** (845-947-1155), 55 West Railroad Avenue, a renovated factory complex filled with an array of art galleries, crafts shops, and cabinetmakers. **The Haverstraw Brick Museum** (845-947-3505), at 12 Main Street, gives a detailed overview of the town's past, when it was home to more than 40 brickyards. **Emeline Park,** at the foot of Main Street, is the perfect place to rest after strolling; you will be treated to wonderful river views. Traveling by ferry is also an option for commuters in Haverstraw. A direct ferry service is available between Haverstraw and Ossining. For schedule information, check www.nywaterway.com.

Tappan. The local government here was the first in New York State to establish by ordinance a historic district. A walk down Main Street in Tappan will reveal the result, with many 18th- and 19th-century structures still standing tall. The **Tappan Library,** a frame house dating from the mid-18th century boasts a restored colonial garden. John André was imprisoned in the **Yoast Mabie Tavern,** built in 1755, although Washington's instructions were that André be treated civilly. Just beyond the tavern look for the **Killoran House,** a town house built in 1835 with the bricks taken from a dismantled church. In the middle of Main Street, where it meets Old Tappan Road, the village green was the site of the public stocks and the liberty pole, depending on the mood of the townspeople at the time. The nearby **Reformed Church of Tappan** stands on the site where André was tried and convicted of spying. Although André requested that he be shot as a soldier, the tribunal ordered him hanged as a spy, since to do otherwise would have been to cast doubt upon his guilt. In the nearby burying grounds you will find many old tombstones. Farther up the road is the **Demming-Latrelle House,** best known as the home of the man who manufactured the first canned baby food.

✱ To See

Edward Hopper House and Edward Hopper House Art Center (845-358-0774; www.edwardhopperhouse.org), 82 North Broadway, Nyack. Open Thursday through Sunday 1–5. Admission fee. The American realist painter Edward Hopper was born in Nyack in 1882 and as a youth spent much of his time in the village. Several of his paintings feature local landmarks, and he taught painting classes at the house, which was built by his grandfather. When he died in 1967, Hopper was buried in the Oak Hill Cemetery. His boyhood home was rescued from demolition not long after his death, and today it is a community arts and cultural center. Exhibits include works by Hopper and other American painters, and concerts are given in the gardens of the Hopper House each summer. There are art classes and workshops for both adults and children, so call for an updated schedule.

HISTORIC HOME **DeWint House National Shrine and George Washington Masonic Historic Site** (845-359-1359; www.dewinthouse.com), 20 Livingston Avenue, near Oak Tree Road, in Tappan. Open year-round, daily, except Monday, 10–4. Free. Constructed in 1700 of Holland brick and sandstone, the DeWint House boasts the pitched roof and tile fireplace common in well-to-do Dutch homes of the period. Although the house is important architecturally, it is best known as George Washington's headquarters and as a shrine to Washington's participation in the fraternal organization known as the Masons. It was also here that Washington—after refusing to commute the sentence—stayed the day that British spy Maj. John André was hanged. It is recorded that Washington asked that the shutters to his room be closed—the same shutters that cover the window today. When the house was purchased by the Masons, the owner said family tradition held that several of the items in the house were there at the time of Washington's visits. Today the house offers a look into Washington's day-to-day life during the war, along with the story of his participation in the Masons. A small carriage-house museum also contains period artifacts and exhibits, and trees around the site have been marked with identification tags. Information on a self-guided walking tour of Tappan is also available at the carriage house.

HISTORIC SITES **Camp Shanks World War II Museum** (845-638-5419; www.rockvets.com), South Greenbush Street, Orangeburg. Open Memorial Day weekend through Labor Day, Saturday and Sunday noon–4. Free. This site was the processing center for more than a million soldiers who shipped overseas from the Piermont Pier to Normandy. Now a small museum, it tells the story of military life at the camp through exhibits and a visit to a barracks.

Historical Society of Rockland County (845-634-9629; www.rocklandhistory.org), 20 Zukor Road, New City. Open Wednesday through Sunday noon–4. Jacob Blauvelt House is open by appointment only. Admission fee. This site features a history museum and the 1832 Jacob Blauvelt House. Rotating exhibits and programs throughout the year display the history of Rockland County. Special events include the Miniature Dollhouse and Art Exhibition and History Month Events in October, including a Fall Family Festival. The museum shop offers a large selection of local history publications and maps.

Holocaust Museum & Study Center (845-356-2700), 17 South Madison Avenue, Spring Valley. Open Monday through Thursday 10–4; Sunday noon–4; closed on national and Jewish holidays. Free. Visitors to this small museum will be humbled and moved by powerful images of the Holocaust and the strength shown by its survivors. A permanent exhibit examines the history and effects of the Holocaust, while videos and artwork bring home the personal horrors of this period. A research library is available for public use.

Stony Point Battlefield (845-786-2521; www.palisadesparksconservancy.org), 44 Battlefield Road, Stony Point; located on Park Road, off Route 9W. Open mid-April through October 31, Wednesday through Saturday 10–4:30; Sunday noon–4:30. Grounds open Monday through Saturday 10–5; Sunday noon–5. Free, but there is a parking fee on weekends and a charge for special events. When George Washington felt he had to demonstrate that American troops were determined to stand up to the superior British forces in the Hudson Highlands, he sent in General Wayne to prove the point. In July 1779, Wayne led the elite troops of the Corps of Light Infantry in an attack on the British at Stony Point. During a midnight raid, the Americans routed the British from their beds and challenged their reputation as an invincible fighting force. A self-guided walking tour of the battlefield takes visitors through a wildly beautiful park where remnants of British fortifications still survive. Trails are marked with plaques explaining the battle, and you will pass the 1826 Stony Point Lighthouse, used for more than a century to aid ships on the Hudson; it was restored in 1995. The museum offers exhibits and original memorabilia illustrating the tactics and strategies that brought victory to the Americans. Dogwoods bloom along the paths, and special events, like military encampments and holiday celebrations, are held in the spring, summer, and fall.

✷ To Do

BASEBALL **Provident Bank Park/Home of the Rockland Boulders** (845-364-0009; www.rocklandboulders.com), 1 Provident Bank Drive, Pomona. This impressive stadium opened in 2011 and overlooks the scenic Ramapo Mountains. Home to the Rockland Boulders (an independent professional minor league baseball team), the ballpark features extra-wide seats, a large food court, a special kids' zone, and an exciting atmosphere. If you are a baseball fan, make sure to take in a game when you are in the area. The season runs from mid-May through early September, and the prices are exceedingly reasonable. Check the website for a full schedule of games.

BICYCLING Both Bear Mountain State Park and Harriman State Park offer a number of challenging bike routes. However, both of these areas can get extremely congested on weekends. You might want to try Rockland Lake and Tallman State Park, which both have paved bicycle paths. Another option is Nyack Beach State Park, located off Route 9W with access from Broadway in Upper Nyack. This park runs along the river, and the paths are flat, with fine views of the Hudson. Hook Mountain State Park also has biking paths with scenic views of the Hudson. To get there, go east on North Broadway in Nyack; the park is located at the end of the road. Bike Route 9 starts in Manhattan, then crosses the George Washington Bridge and goes north along the Hudson River, crossing back over the river at the Bear Mountain Bridge. Bike Route 9 is part of the Hudson Valley Greenway.

FARM STANDS AND PICK-YOUR-OWN FARMS Even though Rockland County is small, you can still discover some terrific outlets for local fruits and vegetables.

Auntie El's Farm Market (845-753-2122), 171 Route 17, Sloatsburg. Open year-round, daily 8–7; close at 6 on Monday and Tuesday. This market offers an enormous array of fruits and vegetables from Rockland County farms.

Dr. Davies Farm (845-268-7020), Route 9W, Congers; Route 304, Congers. Both locations open July through November, daily 9–5:30. You can pick your own apples in the fall and then select from a wide variety of berries, pumpkins, plums, and other goodies at the farm stand. This farm is the oldest one in the county, dating back to 1836, and one of the last that is independently owned. Niles and Jan Davies are wonderful people who are involved in the arts in the county. The produce here is excellent, and the farm is well worth a stop. Dr. Davies was Niles's grandmother, by the way!

The Hand and Hoe, at the Fellowship Community (845-356-8494), 241 Hungry Hollow Road, Chestnut Ridge. Organic fruits and vegetables sold Friday only, noon–5.

Nyack Farmers Market, the municipal parking lot at Main and Cedar streets, Nyack. Held May through November, every Thursday 8:30–2:30, rain or shine. This is a great place to stock up for the weekend. The market attracts farmers from throughout the region and offers an enormous variety of produce as well as specialty foods.

The Orchards at Concklin (845-354-0369), 2 South Mountain Road, Pomona. Open March through December. This farm has been in business since 1712. You can harvest your own apples and pumpkins in September and October, on weekends only, 10–5.

Schimpf Farms (845-623-2556), 13 Parrott Road, West Nyack, are open from March through Christmas Eve. They have a roadside market from April (flowers and shrubs) through October (pumpkins). In July there are fruits and vegetables, and at Christmastime they sell trees and decorations.

Van Houten Farms (845-735-4689), 68 Sickletown Road, Pearl River, is open March through December, with fruits, vegetables, and holiday greenery.

FISHING The state parks allow fishing, but you will have to check with them for their individual regulations and restrictions. Fishing is also allowed in the Ramapo River, which has a long trout season. Route 17 has parking areas, and the waters north of Ramapo are considered good fishing spots. On Route 202 near Suffern watch for the Mahwah River and the parking areas along its bank. Minisceongo Creek has good fishing from the Rosman Bridge upstream to the Palisades Mountain Parkway Bridge.

GOLF **Blue Hill Golf Course** (845-735-2094), 285 Blue Hill Road, Pearl River. Open weekdays 7 AM–dusk; weekends 6:30 AM–dusk. Operated by the town of Orangetown, this pleasant course boasts 27 holes. A good choice for beginners.

Philip J. Rotella Memorial Golf Course (845-354-1616), 100 Thiells Mount Ivy Road, Thiells. Open weekdays 7 AM–7 PM; weekends 6 AM–7 PM. Named for a former Haverstraw town supervisor, this challenging 18-hole championship golf course underwent a $3 million renovation in recent years. Duffers will enjoy a view of the Hudson River from one of the tees. Owned and operated by the town of Haverstraw.

Rockland Lake Champion Golf Course (845-268-7275), 100 Route 9W, Congers. Open weekdays 7 AM–dusk; weekends and holidays 6 AM–dusk. There are actually two golf courses at this state park, including an 18-hole par-3 course and an 18-hole full-size course. It is advised to call 10 days in advance to reserve weekend tee times.

Spook Rock Golf Course (845-357-6466), 233 Spook Rock Road, Suffern. Open weekdays 7 AM–dusk; weekends 6 AM–dusk. This 18-hole championship course was built in 1969; it is owned and operated by the town of Ramapo.

Tappan Golf Center (845-359-0642), 116 Route 303, Tappan. Open year-round, daily 6 AM–11 PM, this 18-hole miniature golf course is a great place to go with the kids.

HIKING AND WALKING Almost every park has hiking trails that wind through the woods or over mountains. Some unusual trails, set up to commemorate the American Revolution, also provide ways to get to know local history. The 1777 Trail, the 1777E Trail, and the 1777W Trail—known collectively as the **Bicentennial Trails**—are all less than 3 miles in length. Located in Bear Mountain and Harriman state parks, the trails are accessed from Route 9W, 1 mile north of Tomkins Cove. Look for the diamond-shaped white blazes with red numbers. This is also the starting area for the **Timp-Torne Trail,** a 10-mile hike that offers spectacular views down the Hudson River all the way to New York City. The trail ends at the Bear Mountain Lodge.

The shorter **Anthony Wayne Trail**—a 3-mile loop marked with white blazes—can be found along Seven Lakes Drive in Bear Mountain State Park, near the traffic circle. Another popular trail is the **Pine Meadow Trail,** which begins at the Reeve Meadow Visitors Center on Seven Lakes Drive. If you want to climb Bear Mountain, take the **Major Welch Trail** from the Bear Mountain Inn (see *Lodging*).

Buttermilk Falls Park, in Nyack, has trails from the parking lot to the falls themselves, lovely in early spring.

Kennedy Dells Park, Main Street, 1 mile north of New City (watch for signs), was once part of film producer Adolph Zukor's estate. Along with hiking trails, there is also a trail for people with disabilities.

Dutch Garden, at the County Office Building, New Hempstead Road, New City, is a 3-acre historic site with gardens and paths.

Shorter walks may be taken in **Betsy Ross Park,** Tappan; **Tackamack North** and **Tackamack South parks,** Clausland Mountain Road, Blauvelt; and along the **Erie Trail,** which runs from Sparkill to Grandview along abandoned railroad tracks. **Mount Ivy,** off Route 202, Pomona, is a rails-to-trails park, with hiking along the old tracks and a wetlands and nature study center.

✷ Green Space

Bear Mountain State Park (845-786-2701). Take the Bear Mountain exit off the Palisades Parkway or Routes 6 and 9W. Open daily, year-round. Parking fee. Part of the vast Palisades Interstate Parks System, Bear Mountain shares almost 54,000 acres with its neighbor, **Harriman State Park.** Noted on maps since the mid-18th century, Bear Mountain has been known as Bear Hill, Bread Tray, and

Bare Mountain (presumably because of a bald peak). Once the site of Revolutionary War forts Clinton and Montgomery, the area the park now covers was slated to become the home of Sing Sing Prison until public outcry and political pressure persuaded the state to change its plans early in the 20th century. Since then a parkway system has made the park accessible to the hundreds of thousands who visit each year, and several lakes add to the park's outdoor appeal. Visitors to the park will find a four-season outdoor wonderland featuring a wide program of activities and special events, including swimming, fishing, miniature golf, hiking, boating, sledding, and cross-country skiing. At the **Trailside Museum, Nature Trail, and Zoo,** located next to the Bear Mountain Inn (watch for signs; also see *Lodging*), exhibits and programs describe the Native American, military, and natural history of the area. (There are even mastodon remains!) Open year-round, daily 10–4:30. Donation requested. Across the field from the Bear Mountain Inn, a beautiful **carousel** has been built, housed in a stone-and-timber Adirondack-style building. Children may climb aboard carved animals native to the Hudson Valley—raccoons, bears, deer, eagles, fox, river otters, and bobcats—for an old-fashioned ride on this full-size merry-go-round.

The self-guided trail is the oldest continuously run trail in the country. The short trail also features a unique zoo with wildlife in natural settings, including a beaver lodge (which has been cut away for easy viewing), a reptile house, and trees, shrubs, and plants with identification tags. On into the park, visitors may want to bike or drive along the scenic interpark roads or rent a paddle- or rowboat at one of the lakes. (Canoes are subject to an inspection.) Three lakes—Welch, Sebago, and Tiorati—have swimming, picnicking, and other recreational areas, and special events are scheduled throughout the year at the Bear Mountain Inn and in the park. In the past there have been winter holiday fairs, orienteering meets, craft and ethnic festivals, professional ski-jumping competitions, even stargazing nights.

Harriman State Park, with rock formations dating back 1 billion years, has also become a center for geology buffs. For many years geological researchers neglected the New York region, but that has changed, thanks in large part to the efforts of Dr. Alexander Gates, who discovered garnets in the park dating back more than 2 million years. Gates and his research team have done geological mapping at Harriman, which is pretty much as it was 12,000 years ago when the last glacier retreated.

Hook Mountain State Park and **Nyack Beach Park** (845-268-3020). To reach Hook Mountain State Park, take North Broadway, in Nyack, east to the end; follow signs. To reach Nyack Beach Park, take Route 9W from Broadway. Both parks are open daily dawn to dusk; free. Hook Mountain was once referred to by the Dutch as *Verdrietige* (tedious) Hook because the winds could change rapidly and leave a boat adrift in the river. The area was also a favorite campground of Native Americans because of its wealth of oysters. For modern visitors the park provides a place to picnic, hike, bike, and enjoy scenic views of the Hudson. A hawk watch is held every spring and fall, and the park is said to be haunted by the ghost of the Guardian of the Mountain, a Native American medicine man who appears during the full moon each September and chants at the ancient harvest festival. Nyack Beach is open for hiking, kayaking, picnicking, and fishing; the views of the river are outstanding.

Piermont Marsh and **Tallman Mountain State Park** (845-359-0544), Rockland Road, off Route 9W, in Sparkill, near Piermont, north of Palisades Interstate Parkway, exit 4. Piermont Marsh can be reached through Tallman State Park by following the bike path or from the Erie Pier in the village of Piermont. Admission fee. This nature preserve covers more than 1,000 acres of tidal marsh, mountain, and river and is considered one of the most important fish-breeding areas along the Hudson. Wildflowers, such as the spectacular rose mallow, abound in portions of the marsh, and this is a prime bird-watching locale in all seasons. The area along the marsh is a marvelous place to view the river, and a hike up the mountain offers a spectacular panorama for photographers. Tallman State Park is a wonderful place to spend a summer day—along with its natural wonders, the park has complete recreational facilities, including bike paths, an 18-hole miniature-golf course, tennis courts, and hiking trails. Even some human-made ponds have become home for many varieties of reptiles and amphibians; ironically, the ponds were to have been part of a tank storage area for a large oil company earlier in the 20th century. Today, especially in spring, the ponds hum with the sounds of frogs, and the woods come alive with birdcalls.

Rockland Lake State Park (845-268-3020), Route 9W, Rockland Lake exit, Congers. Open year-round, daily 8–dusk. Use fee. Another jewel in the crown of the Palisades Interstate Parks System, this popular recreation area is located at the base of Hook Mountain. The lake was once the site of an ice farm, which provided a harvest of pure, clear ice for nearly a century before the advent of modern refrigeration. The park is a wonderful place to explore—in addition to hiking you can enjoy swimming, jogging, fishing, biking, boating, and golf. Rowboats are available to rent by the hour. During the winter, go ice skating on the lake or cross-country skiing and sledding on some of the challenging hills. At the nature center you will discover live animals and exhibits, special-events programs throughout the summer, and guided tours along the wetlands walkway (it's about 3.25 miles around the lake). Just outside the center, marked nature trails run along a boardwalk and contain Braille interpretation stops for the blind and visually impaired. Wildflowers and birds are particularly vibrant during the spring, but there are wonders to discover here any time of year.

✷ Lodging

Bear Mountain Inn (845-786-2731), 55 Hessian Drive, Bear Mountain 10911. ($$$) There are 64 guest rooms and 15 suites in this majestic landmark hotel that reopened in 2012 after extensive renovations. All rooms have 32-inch cable TV, high-speed Internet access, and kitchenette with microwave and refrigerator. Rustic elegance is the style here, and an array of recreational activities on the premises will delight visitors year-round, including swimming (in the outdoor pool), hiking, cross-country skiing, and ice skating on the lovely outdoor rink. There are lovely walking paths around the hotel, and guests may enjoy a short stroll in addition to longer day hikes. The inn is a terrific place for families who want to explore attractions in both Rockland and Orange counties. There is a fine gift shop in the hotel, and pets are welcome.

Best Western Nyack on Hudson (845-358-8100), 26 Route 59, Nyack 10960. ($$) There are 80 rooms and a family restaurant, open 7 AM–11 PM, at this establishment. A good choice for those traveling with children, it is located only 1 mile from the Palisades Center Mall and within walking distance to Nyack's attractions.

Bricktown Inn (845-429-8447), 112 Hudson Avenue, Haverstraw 10927. ($$) This renovated brick Colonial home built in the mid-1800s features a mansard roof, striking mahogany staircase, plaster moldings, and high ceilings. All four guest rooms include private baths and air-conditioning, and are decorated with antiques and family heirlooms. A separate parlor has a TV, VCR, and Wi-Fi access. The parlor is designed for conversation and the comfort of guests, and includes a baby grand piano. The Garden Room is a great place to read, relax, or watch a movie from the DVD/VCR collection. Guests get excellent value for the money here.

Crowne Plaza Hotel & Conference Center (845-357-4800), 3 Executive Boulevard, Suffern 10901. ($$$) There are 350 beautifully decorated guest rooms and suites in this renovated hotel. A three-story atrium includes a lovely waterfall surrounded by a koi pond, a full-service restaurant, and a fitness center. All rooms feature a 42-inch flat-screen TV and Internet access. All the expected amenities of a luxury hotel are offered here.

Hilton Pearl River (845-735-9000), 500 Veterans Memorial Highway, Pearl River 10965. ($$$) The 150 rooms in this luxury hotel are furnished in French country style, and the structure itself resembles a chateâu in rural France. Guests may enjoy an indoor pool, whirlpool, sauna, and fitness center. There is also a full-service restaurant on the premises. All rooms are furnished with wide-screen TVs and have Internet access. This is a nice choice for a romantic getaway.

Holiday Inn of Orangeburg (845-359-7000), 329 Route 303, Orangeburg 10962. ($$) Close to Piermont and Nyack, the Holiday Inn's 170 guest rooms have all the standard amenities. A nice feature is the outdoor pool; also here is a fitness room. Open year-round.

RiverView Bed & Breakfast (347-744-9322; 845-353-0778), Piermont Avenue, Piermont. ($$$) A charming Dutch Colonial home, circa 1835, furnished in an eclectic blend of antiques, with a large cozy living room, dining room, and parlor with upright piano, offers two guest rooms with private baths overlooking the Hudson River. A third room is available for families willing to share a bathroom. A full breakfast is served between 8 and 10 AM. (A lovely brick house with three guest rooms is also available through the same owner.) Both establishments are open year-round; there is a two-night minimum stay required.

Stony Point Conference Center (845-786-5674), 17 Crickettown Road, Stony Point 10980. ($) Once a privately owned estate, this spiritual retreat center offers a variety of lodging options and welcomes independent travelers. There are two houses on the property, with several bedrooms that share baths as well as rooms with private facilities. The accommodations here are simple and adequate. While there are no fancy extras, the staff is exceedingly helpful and gracious. Guests may enjoy a full breakfast (included in the reasonable rates).

Super 8 Motel of Nyack (845-353-3880), 47 Route 59 East, Nyack 10960. ($$) There are 43 spacious rooms, with king-size beds in many of the singles. Nice features are the restaurant next door—and that you are near the center of Nyack.

✷ Where to Eat

DINING OUT **Alain's Bistro** (845-535-3315), 9 Ingalls Street, Nyack. ($$$) Open for lunch Monday through Friday noon–4; dinner Monday through Saturday 5:30–10:30; Sunday brunch and dinner noon–9:30. When you enter this cozy bistro, you will feel far from its strip mall location. The cuisine is authentic French Alsatian, with such offerings as French onion soup, country pâté, steak frites, duck leg confit, braised short ribs, and pan-seared diver scallops. Desserts include apple tart, crème brûlée, and sorbet. Not recommended for children.

Antoine McGuire's Oyster & Ale House (845-429-4121), 19 Main Street, Haverstraw. ($$) Open for lunch Friday through Sunday noon–3; dinner daily, except Tuesday, 4–10. This restaurant offers an interesting fusion of classic Irish pub fare and French bistro-style dining. The Oyster & Ale bar has exposed brick walls, fireplace, and vintage decor, making it a cozy spot to relax for drinks. Diners may enjoy excellent steamers, mussels, and, of course, oysters. For landlubbers the offerings include hanger steak, pork chops, duck, and veal. Prices are moderate, and children are welcome.

Babe's (845-429-8647), 73 East Railroad Avenue, West Haverstraw. ($$) Open daily for lunch noon–3; dinner 5–10. This establishment welcomes diners with a pink and green neon sign that dates back to 1928, when it was Tony's Luncheonette. The new owners took over in 2000 and returned it to its speakeasy period looks. The menu offers traditional favorites, including salads, burgers, and ribs, with an array of hearty fish dishes as well as meat, pasta, and chicken entrées. Everything is prepared to order, and diners won't walk away hungry. Good value for the money here.

Banchetto Feast (845-624-3070), 75 W Route 59, Nanuet. ($$) Open daily 11–11. An informal Italian restaurant located in the Nanuet Mall, Banchetto's menu includes pasta, chicken, veal, and seafood dishes, all expertly prepared. There are several daily lunch and dinner (Monday through Thursday) specials. The spaghetti with white clam sauce is particularly good. Some diners will be pleasantly surprised to discover whole-wheat pasta may be substituted for the usual variety. Children welcome.

Bombay Grill Indian Cuisine (845-323-4049), 261 South Little Tor Road, New City. ($$) Open Tuesday through Sunday for lunch 11:30–3; dinner 5–9:30. The lunch buffet here has an enthusiastic local following, and the price is extremely reasonable. The tandoori chicken and chicken tikka masala are both flavorful and are prepared with the right amount of spiciness. There are several curry dishes offered, as well as both butter and garlic naan. Vegetarians will be pleased to discover a number of options.

Café Portofino (845-359-7300), 587 Piermont Avenue, Piermont. ($$) Open daily for dinner 5–10. Regional Italian cooking served in a warm, friendly atmosphere by the chef-owner. The daily specials include veal, chicken, fish, and seafood dishes. Save room for dessert; all are homemade.

Civile's Venice on the Hudson (845-429-3891), 16 Front Street, Haverstraw. ($$) Open Memorial Day through Labor Day, daily noon–10; closed Monday and Tuesday during the rest of the year. Restaurant is located at the foot of the Hudson River, with exceptional views. The menu features contemporary Italian cuisine, such as *pasta e fagioli* and *zuppa di pesce*. An extensive wine list is also offered. During the summer months, enjoy dining in their open-air tented terrace.

Confetti Ristorante & Vinoteca (845-365-1911), 200 Ash Street, Piermont. ($$) Open daily noon–10; Friday and Saturday until 11; Sunday until 9. Just steps away from the Piermont waterfront, this restaurant specializes in authentic Italian dishes created the way they are prepared in Italy. Branzino (sea bass), saltimbocca, and filet mignon are specialties of the house. The chef-owner, Arturo Lepore, recommends the chicken country style, a mélange of homemade sausage, potatoes, and an array of vegetables. On the lighter side, a variety of salads, pizzas, and paninis are offered. The breads, pastas, and desserts are all homemade on the premises, and a three-course lunch special is available daily. Children welcome.

Cornetta's Restaurant and Marina (845-359-0410), 641 River Road, Piermont. ($) Open daily noon–10. Closed Monday and Tuesday December through March. Italian family restaurant specializing in steaks and seafood. The lobster and crab legs are recommended by the chef.

Fireside Steak Pub (845-429-0484), 84 North Liberty Drive, Stony Point. ($$) Open daily 11:30–10; Friday and Saturday until 11. The fare here is simple and straightforward, and steaks, of course, are the house specialty. Prices are exceedingly reasonable, and diners will enjoy a nice view of the Hudson River. Children welcome.

Freelance Café and Wine Bar (845-365-3250), 506 Piermont Avenue, Piermont. ($$) Open daily, except Monday, for lunch noon–3; dinner from 5:30; Sunday brunch noon–3. Right next to Xavier's, this informal eatery offers specialties like coconut shrimp in a sharp mustard sauce, grilled chicken salad, and tiramisu.

Giulio's (845-359-3657), 154 Washington Street, Tappan. ($$) Open for lunch Monday through Friday 11:30–2:30; dinner Monday through Friday 5–10, Saturday until 11; Sunday brunch 11:30–2, dinner 5–9. Fine Northern Italian cuisine is served in this 100-year-old Victorian house. There is a romantic candlelit setting at dinner and a strolling entertainer weekday evenings. Sample the Valdostana vitello (veal stuffed with prosciutto and cheese in a champagne sauce) or the scampi Giulio (jumbo shrimp sautéed with fresh mushrooms). Children are welcome. Reservations suggested for dinner.

Il Fresco (845-398-0200), 15 Kings Highway, Orangeburg. ($$) Open for lunch Monday through Friday 11:30–2:30; dinner daily 5–10; Sunday 3–9. Located in a restored 1728 farmhouse with several fireplaces and quaint rooms, this restaurant is a neighborhood favorite and offers a romantic ambience. They feature imaginative Italian cuisine, with the emphasis on fresh local ingredients. Typical menu entrées include veal chop, steak pizzaiola, and Chilean sea bass. There is an excellent wine cellar, and the martini list is impressive. Not recommended for children.

Il Portico (845-365-2100), 89 Main Street, Tappan. ($$) Open Monday through Friday for lunch noon–3; dinner daily 5–10. There are different fish specials every day at this cozy spot featuring Northern Italian cuisine. The most popular dishes are the veal D'Vinci (with prosciutto and mozzarella) and the linguine à la Genovese (with pesto). The tiramisu and ricotta cheesecake are made fresh on the premises. Children are welcome.

La Cascada (845-429-0347), 35 Main Street, Haverstraw. ($) Open daily for lunch and dinner 10 AM–11 PM. If you have a hankering for authentic Ecuadorian cuisine, this is the place to go. Everything is well prepared, whether you order steak or chicken with rice, beans, and salad, or any of the pork dishes. There are approximately 40 seats here, and children are always welcome.

Lanterna Tuscan Bistro (845-353-8361), 3 South Broadway, Nyack. ($$) Open daily for lunch 11–3:30; dinner 4:30–10. Chef-owner Rossano Giannini specializes in terrifically imaginative dishes from his native town of Lucca in Tuscany, so don't expect the usual Italian restaurant menu selections. The cheese basket is literally a basket made of cheese filled with fresh mixed green salad and topped with prosciutto. Calamari is served with endive, radicchio, tomato, and a touch of pesto. The seafood over homemade pasta is first-rate; do try the ostrich, rabbit, wild boar, or venison in season. The atmosphere is casual; children are welcome.

Marcello's Ristorante (845-357-9108), 21 Lafayette Avenue, Suffern. ($$) Open for lunch Monday through Friday noon–2; dinner daily 5–9:30. The chef-owner, Marcello, travels to Italy twice each year and brings back new ideas for the continually changing menu. Every dish at this elegant spot is cooked to order, and all pastas are homemade. The seafood ravioli and veal chop with sage are just a couple of the superb house specialties.

Old '76 House (845-359-5476), 110 Main Street, Tappan. ($$) Open daily for lunch at 11:30; dinner at 5. Sunday brunch buffet 11–3. Located in a restored 1753 sandstone-and-brick house, this restaurant boasts beamed ceilings, fireplaces surrounded by Dutch tiles, and a real colonial atmosphere. (Legend says British major John André was imprisoned here during the Revolution.) The food is American and Continental, and entrées include veal Antoinette, steaks, and seafood selections.

Restaurant X & Bully Boy Bar (845-268-6555), 117 South Route 303, Congers. ($$) Open for lunch Tuesday through Friday noon–2:30; dinner Tuesday through Thursday 5:30–10; Friday and Saturday until 11; Sunday brunch 1–4:30; dinner 5–8. This charming country restaurant with lush landscaping and pond has four dining rooms, each with its own distinctive atmosphere. The modern American cuisine with an international flair includes dinner entrées like Pacific ahi tuna, classic beef Wellington, and prosciutto-wrapped Alaskan halibut, to name just a few of the dishes. A lovely place to celebrate a special occasion.

The River Club (845-358-0220), 11 Burd Street, Nyack. ($$) Open Wednesday through Saturday for lunch noon–3; dinner 5–10; Sunday brunch 11–3; dinner 5–9. Waterfront restaurant with outdoor dining, featuring seafood, ribs, chicken, and steak. A great place to go for drinks anytime. Children are welcome.

Sho Chiku Sushi (845-362-6031), 14 Thiells Mount Ivy Road, Pomona. ($$) Open daily noon–10; lunch buffet Sunday through Friday noon–3; dinner buffet Monday 5–10. This Japanese restaurant has been in business for over 20 years, and their sushi is renowned by local residents.

Sidewalk Bistro (845-680-6460), 482 Piermont Avenue, Piermont. ($$) Open daily for lunch and dinner noon–10. This charming French bistro, with a lovely outdoor café and elegant dining rooms and bar, offers up classic favorites like brochette Provençale (shrimp, scallops, polenta, grilled asparagus, and fennel), bouillabaisse Marseillaise, and mussels in white wine, as well as *pizzettes* (very thin crust individual pizzas). Their burgers are 10 ounces of Kobe beef, for those who prefer American fare. Desserts are superb. The wine list is on the pricey side, however.

Slattery's The Landing (845-398-1943), 5 Roundhouse Road, Piermont. ($$) Open daily 10 AM–11 PM; Friday and Saturday until 2 AM; Sunday brunch 11–3. Enjoy dining along the banks of the Hudson River at this popular spot renowned for steaks and seafood. The brunch is sumptuous and runs the gamut from omelets to oysters.

THERE IS LIVE MUSIC ALMOST EVERY NIGHT IN SEASON AT THE TURNING POINT.
Joanne Michaels

Thai House (845-358-9100), 12 Park Street, Nyack. ($$) Open for lunch Friday through Sunday 11:30–2:30; dinner served daily 5:30–10. Enjoy beautifully presented Thai dishes whether you are eating in the restaurant or getting take-out. The vegetables here are always cooked perfectly—al dente. Those who like Thai food should not pass up this gem. Reasonable prices and good service.

The Turning Point (845-359-1089; www.turningpointcafe.com), 468 Piermont Avenue, Piermont. ($$) Open for light fare during musical performances, which are often every night in the spring, summer, and fall months. This venue has been a hangout for creative people for decades, and it is still a popular local spot. There are over a dozen herbal teas and more than 20 kinds of beer listed on the menu. Check the continually changing evening schedule by visiting the website.

Two Henrys (845-735-9000), 500 Veterans Memorial Drive, Pearl River. ($$) Open daily for breakfast 7–11:30; lunch 11:30–3; dinner 5–10. Within the Pearl River Hilton, this elegant restaurant has a strong local following. The dining room overlooks a golf course, and the relaxing view further enhances the gracious cuisine. Continental and American entrées, served with homemade bread, include mushrooms filled with crabmeat and spinach, and broiled tuna on eggplant. Don't skip their luscious desserts (try the rich chocolate peanut butter pie). Reservations suggested for dinner.

Two Spear Street (845-353-7733), 2 Spear Street, Nyack. ($$) Open for dinner Wednesday through Saturday 5–10; Sunday brunch 11–4; dinner 4–9. This family-owned and family-operated restaurant is delightful. The cuisine is New American with a touch of Grandmother's cooking, and it is served in an intimate atmosphere. Entrées range from baked macaroni and cheese and rib eye steak to veal cordon bleu and whole roasted red snapper. Not recommended for children.

Union Restaurant & Bar Latino (845-429-4354), 22–24 New Main Street, Haverstraw. ($$) Open Tuesday through Saturday for lunch noon–3; dinner 5:30–10, until 11 Friday and Saturday; Sunday noon–9. Enjoy American cuisine with a Latin flair prepared by chef-owners who previously worked at **Xavier's** and **Freelance Café,** two of the county's finest restaurants. The atmosphere is inviting, with elaborate tin ceilings, rear skylight, dark wood, and romantic lighting. The menu features Cuban-inspired dishes such as Tilapia al Sarten, a panko-encrusted fillet served over a spinach and white bean ragout, as well as tuna ceviche with fresh mango, cilantro, and coconut milk. I enjoyed an excellent meal here; however, the service can occasionally be slow on crowded weekend nights.

Velo Wine Bar & Bistro (845-353-7667), 12 North Broadway, Nyack. ($$) Open Tuesday through Saturday 5–10. Enjoy New American cuisine with a French and Italian accent. Some favorites include goat cheese tartelet, tuna tartare, chianti risotto with black truffle, chicken on a bed of broccoli rabe, and salmon fillet over beet-infused couscous, as well as an excellent selection of wines by the glass and the bottle. The pizza is excellent as well if you want a lighter meal. A trip to Nyack should include a stop here.

Wasabi (845-358-7977), 110 Main Street, Nyack. ($$) Open Monday through Friday for lunch noon–2:30; dinner 5–10; Saturday 5–11; Sunday 4–9. You can enjoy fine sushi, sashimi, tempura, negimaki, teriyaki, and vegetarian dishes at this charming restaurant with elegantly simple Japanese decor. Everything is fresh and made to order before your eyes.

Xavier's at Piermont (845-359-7007), 506 Piermont Avenue, Piermont. ($$$) Open for dinner Wednesday through Sunday at 6; for lunch Friday and Sunday noon–2. An intimate, elegant spot, this is a perfect place for people who enjoy fine dining. The imaginative menu featuring Continental cuisine has included roast pigeon with truffle sauce and fettuccine with fennel sausage and white grapes. For dessert, there is maple walnut soufflé, a house specialty. Not recommended for children.

EATING OUT **Agnello's** (845-639-5373), 170 North Main Street, New City. ($) Open Monday through Saturday 11:30–10; Sunday 4–9. This is an excellent pizza restaurant specializing in brick-oven pizza "you can't refuse," as the owner describes his fare. There are no slices here, and everything is made to order from the freshest ingredients. Dozens of choices will delight pizza lovers, and there are whole-wheat and gluten-free options. The atmosphere is classy, so don't expect a hole-in-the-wall joint! Children are welcome.

The Art Café of Nyack (845-353-4230), 65 South Broadway, Nyack. ($) Open daily 7 AM–9 PM. This vegetarian café specializes in Mediterranean cuisine with a French accent and serves breakfast and lunch all day. There is always an omelet selection, and the soup of the day is a popular choice with local residents: It is made fresh daily, but *borekas* (phyllo dough stuffed with Bulgarian cheese) is a house specialty. The hummus is quite good, and there is always a cheese plate, to accompany the bagels, muffins, and croissants. Their excellent coffee draws local residents who stop by daily for their morning drinks.

Bella Rose Café (845-429-9400), 11 New Main Street, Haverstraw. ($) Open Monday 11–9, Tuesday through Saturday 8 AM–9 PM; Sunday 8–4. There is something here for everyone, anytime. It is a café, coffeehouse, and Italian restaurant rolled into one. The original brick walls, tin ceilings, and wood floors in a restored building make for a cozy atmosphere. There is always interesting artwork on display as well. You can opt for their signature lasagna, adult mac and cheese, meatballs, and grilled polenta or simply order a beverage brewed from locally roasted coffee beans. Whatever you order, you can sit around all day and enjoy the relaxed, inviting ambience. Many dishes are made from Italian family recipes passed down for generations. Children are welcome.

Blu Fig New City (845-708-5686), 191 South Main Street; **Blu Fig Stony Point** (845-786-7809), 32 South Liberty Drive. ($) Open daily at both locations 11–10. This eatery/coffeehouse features brick-oven pizzas, pasta dishes, salads, ciabatta sandwiches, small plates, and Mediterranean entrées. Everything here is prepared to order, and children are welcome.

Bunbury's Coffee Shop (845-398-9715), 460 Piermont Avenue, Piermont. ($) Open Monday through Friday 6:30–6; Saturday and Sunday 7–6. The early morning crowd in town grabs coffee along with muffins and croissants here. The coffee, array of teas, and baked goods are excellent. An inviting, cozy atmosphere prevails, if you decide to stay and read the newspaper.

Deli Central (845-786-3601), 65 South Liberty Drive (Route 9W), Stony Point. ($) Open daily 4:30 AM–6 PM. This is the place to stop for overstuffed sandwiches (there is a huge variety), fresh deli salads, and "boo boos" (tortillas bursting with several kinds of meats, whatever you like, made to order) if you are planning a picnic at Bear Mountain or Harriman State Park. Breakfasts are hearty as well. They are known for their generous servings and decent quality, and the deli is a mainstay for locals.

Didier Dumas (845-353-2031), 163 Main Street, Nyack. ($) Open daily 7 AM–8 PM. You will feel transported to France when tasting the wonderful croissants, brioches, fresh fruit tarts, layered mousse cakes, and superb café au lait and cappuccino here. After walking around Nyack, this is the perfect stop to relax and refresh!

El Bandito (845-425-6622), 196 Route 59, Spring Valley. ($) Open daily 11 AM–midnight. Strolling guitar players add to the fun atmosphere at this colorful Mexican eatery, where the portions are generous and the margaritas are first-rate.

Gilligan's on the Hudson (845-942-3966), 10 Grassy Point Road, Stony Point. ($$) Open for dinner Tuesday through Thursday 4–9; Friday and Saturday noon–10; Sunday noon–8:30. This is a clam bar and grill with an informal atmosphere and view of the Hudson River. The extensive menu features oysters, clams, mussels, calamari, shrimp, and lobster. The lobster over linguine is a popular dish, and all the seafood is superfresh. Make sure to check out the daily specials. Children will feel comfortable here.

Hogan's Family Diner (845-429-9603), 56 South Liberty Drive (Route

9W), Stony Point. ($) Open daily 6 AM–10 PM; Friday and Saturday until 11 PM. The food here is a cut above the usual diner fare. They always have several specials available, and portions are large. It's a favorite place among local residents, and some of the popular entrées are prime rib, eggplant parmigiana, pot roast, and lamb chops. Breakfasts are also hearty, and you will find this diner bustling in the early morning hours.

Hudson House (845-353-1355), 134 Main Street, Nyack. ($$) Open for dinner Tuesday through Thursday 5:30–10, Friday and Saturday until 11, and Sunday 5–9. Brunch is served on Saturday and Sunday 11:30–3:30. Located across the street from the Helen Hayes Performing Arts Center, this building was originally a firehouse in the 19th century and later became the Nyack Village Hall. The chef, a Culinary Institute graduate, features contemporary American cuisine served with an imaginative flair.

Khan's Mongolian Garden (845-359-8004), 588 Route 303, Blauvelt. ($) Open daily, except Sunday, for lunch, 11:30–2; dinner 5–9:30. Just off the NYS Thruway exit 12, this is one of the better Mongolian barbecue restaurants I have tried. Choose your own ingredients and sauces, and watch while the chef creates a delectable meal before your eyes. The buffet includes appetizers, soup, barbecue, and dessert. The all-inclusive price is exceedingly reasonable. Don't miss this if you are traveling with children.

La Bamba (845-365-1859), 627 Main Street, Sparkill. ($) Open daily 10:30–9:30. This restaurant offers home-cooked Mexican specialties prepared by the owners of the adjoining grocery. The enchiladas, tacos, and fajitas are delicious, and the price is right. Children of all ages will enjoy this informal eatery.

Latin Star Restaurant (845-429-1113), 39 Broadway, Haverstraw. ($) Open daily 6 AM–10 PM. The menu is quite extensive in this dinerlike establishment, serving Spanish specialties for breakfast, lunch, and dinner.

Little Bake Shop (845-268-5511), 491 Kings Highway, Valley Cottage. ($) Open Tuesday through Sunday 7:30–5 (closed for lunch from noon to 1). This bakery offers an array of classics—cookies, muffins, pies, and cupcakes for the kids, as well as gluten-free products.

The Mountain House (845-359-9191), 333 Route 340, Sparkill. ($) Open daily for lunch and dinner noon–10. While the fare is basic Italian American—burgers, salads, and pastas—the specialty of the house is the thin-crust pizza. A perfect place to go with young children.

Mt. Ivy Café (845-354-4746), 14 Thiells Mount Ivy Road, Pomona. ($$) Open for lunch Monday through Friday 11–3; dinner daily 3–9:30. Enjoy casual dining featuring traditional American fare at this family restaurant. Specialties of the house include rack of lamb, chicken, fresh fish, and seared tuna. Note that Monday through Thursday from 3 to 6 there are dinner specials that are an excellent value.

Nyack Main Essentials (845-512-8692), 145 Main Street, Nyack. ($) Open Monday through Saturday 10–9; Sunday 11–6. If you are interested in having a healthy meal that doesn't compromise on taste, this reasonably priced eatery specializing in Caribbean vegan cuisine is the place to go. There are several salads, kebabs, wraps, freshly squeezed juices, and smoothies; everything is prepared to order.

Potato Republic Café (845-634-8544), 28 North Main Street, New City. ($) Open daily for lunch and dinner 11:30–9. This eatery is a real find, next to Dunkin' Donuts, in a small strip mall. It offers soups, salads, falafel, and wraps; everything is homemade and prepared to order. Their European-style fresh-cut french fries are excellent. An oasis of fresh, healthful offerings in a sea of fast food!

Strawtown Café (845-358-3705), 11 Strawtown Road, West Nyack. ($) Open Monday through Saturday 6–3. The Clarksville Inn in West Nyack dates back to 1840 and was a hub of the community for over a century. Behind the inn, located in an old-fashioned corner cottage, is this café, opened in 2011 in what was once a blacksmith shop. They offer tasty omelets, pancakes, French toast, sandwiches, burgers, and wraps. Patrons can enjoy breakfast or lunch outdoors on a lovely deck in the warm weather months. Children will be comfortable here.

Tacos Marianita (845-942-1295), 10 West Street, Haverstraw. ($) Open daily 11:30–10. If you want authentic tacos, fajitas, enchiladas, or burritos that taste exactly like those to be found in Mexico, this is the place to go. If you crave those traditional Mexican favorites, don't miss this spot.

Temptations (845-353-3355), 80½ Main Street, Nyack. ($) Open Sunday through Thursday 11:30–10; Friday and Saturday until midnight. The shop is open late on summer evenings. Those with a sweet tooth won't want to miss this café. There are scores of dessert selections in addition to a wide variety of ice creams, frozen yogurts, cappuccinos, and exotic coffees. The light menu features soups, quiches, salads, and sandwiches.

True Food (845-480-5710), 166 Main Street, Nyack. ($) Open daily 8–8. Those who enjoy organic homemade food will appreciate this eatery. They offer dishes like yucca lasagna, fish tacos, and veggie burgers, as well as fresh baked goods, smoothies, juices, coffee, and chai or ginger tea. Everything is freshly prepared and tasty. Children are welcome.

Veggie Heaven (845-499-2289), 195 South Main Street, New City. ($) Open daily for lunch 11:30–3; dinner 3–9:30. If you have never experienced vegan Chinese American cuisine, this is the place to go; they have an enthusiastic local following. There are faux fish, chicken, beef, and shrimp dishes. I recommend the hot and sour soup, cold noodles, and General Tso's Chicken. There is a large and imaginative menu that goes way beyond tofu! Children will never know they are eating vegan cuisine.

✷ Entertainment

Levity Live Comedy Club (845-353-5400; www.levitylive.com), 4210 Palisades Center Drive, Space A-401, West Nyack. This club opened in 2012 and features some of the heaviest hitters in stand-up, including performers from *Saturday Night Live.* Check the website to see what is scheduled.

Nyack Village Theatre (845-826-2639; www.nyackvillagetheatre.com), 94 Main Street, Nyack. This community hub features a potpourri of entertainment, including films, music, poetry, and drama. There are intriguing performances year-round, and it is best to check the website to find out what's happening.

Penguin Rep (845-786-2873; www.penguinrep.org), 7 Crickettown Road, Stony Point. In 1977 an empty 100-year-old barn in Stony Point became the home of Rockland's first year-round nonprofit professional theater. There are 108 seats in 12 rows, all with a great view of the stage. Founder/artistic director Joe Brancato and executive director Andrew Horn have originated over 100 fine productions. The *New York Times* called Penguin Rep "the gutsiest little theater." The theater offers high-quality material and first-class productions.

Rivertown Film Society (845-353-2568; www.rivertownfilm.org), 58 Depew Avenue, Nyack. This is the place to go for first-rate independent films, including documentaries that are rarely offered in commercial theaters at the mall. Nyack is lucky to have this venue. Check the website for a schedule.

Rockland Center for the Arts (845-358-0877; www.rocklandartcenter.org), 27 South Greenbush Road, West Nyack.Open Monday through Friday 9–5; Saturday and Sunday 10–4. Known as ROCA by locals, this nonprofit cultural organization has sponsored exhibits, theater, summer camp, and extensive classes and workshops in a school for the arts (including painting, sculpture, crafts, and fashion) since 1947. Travelers will enjoy strolling through the Emerson Gallery and Gallery One, as well as the Catherine Konner Sculpture Park.

✷ Selective Shopping

In Nyack

Nyack has many shops that are worth a visit, and an entire day can be spent strolling the shopping district and enjoying the antiques and artwork on view. Most shops are open daily except Monday, but call ahead if you are planning to visit. The following establishments are just some of the highlights of the area, but there are many more offering great shopping.

Hickory, Dickory Dock (845-358-7474), 43 South Broadway, has clocks that tick, clocks that tock—hundreds of selections, so pity the poor mouse!

ML Gifts & Accessories (845-358-1293), 75 South Broadway. An eclectic collection of contemporary clothing, jewelry, footwear, and gift items in a range of prices. Make sure to stop in while walking around the village.

Nyack Tobacco Company (845-358-9300), 140 Main Street. For the cigar aficionado, this is the place. One of the most extensive selections outside Manhattan.

The Original Christopher's Antiques (845-358-9574), 71 South Broadway, is a fine gift shop with all kinds of unique items, including antiques and dried flowers.

The Palisades Center (845-348-1000), 1000 Palisades Center Drive, West Nyack. This 3-million-square-foot, four-level shopping mall offers more than 250 shops under one roof. In addition, there are 25 eateries and restaurants, an NHL-size ice-skating rink, a 68-foot Ferris wheel, a 21-screen movie complex, and an IMAX theater. Located off exit 12 of the NYS Thruway, at the junction of Routes 303 and 59, the mall is open Monday through Saturday 10–9:30, Sunday 11–7.

Squash Blossom (845-353-0550), 49 Burd Street, offers Native American jewelry and crafts.

In Piermont

Piermont is smaller than Nyack, yet both are ideal for shopping excursions. Piermont is best experienced by wandering down Piermont Avenue as well as around the waterfront. There are several interesting boutiques, specialty stores, art galleries, and restaurants. The village **farmers' market** is held from June through December, every Sunday 9:30–3, rain or shine. Visitors will usually find plenty of parking.

✷ Special Events

Throughout the course of the year, various local organizations sponsor concerts, parades, art shows, street fairs, and walking tours. It is impossible to list them all. Some of my favorite annual events in Nyack include the **Knickerbocker Ice Festival** in January, the **Springfest** street fair in April, the **Septemberfest** street fair, the **Hawk Watch** at Hook Mountain in September, and the **Halloween Parade** in October. The **farmers' market** is held from May through November, on Thursday, rain or shine. If you are planning a trip to Rockland County, check www.rockland.org for a complete list of special events.

Orange County

2

Orange County Tourism

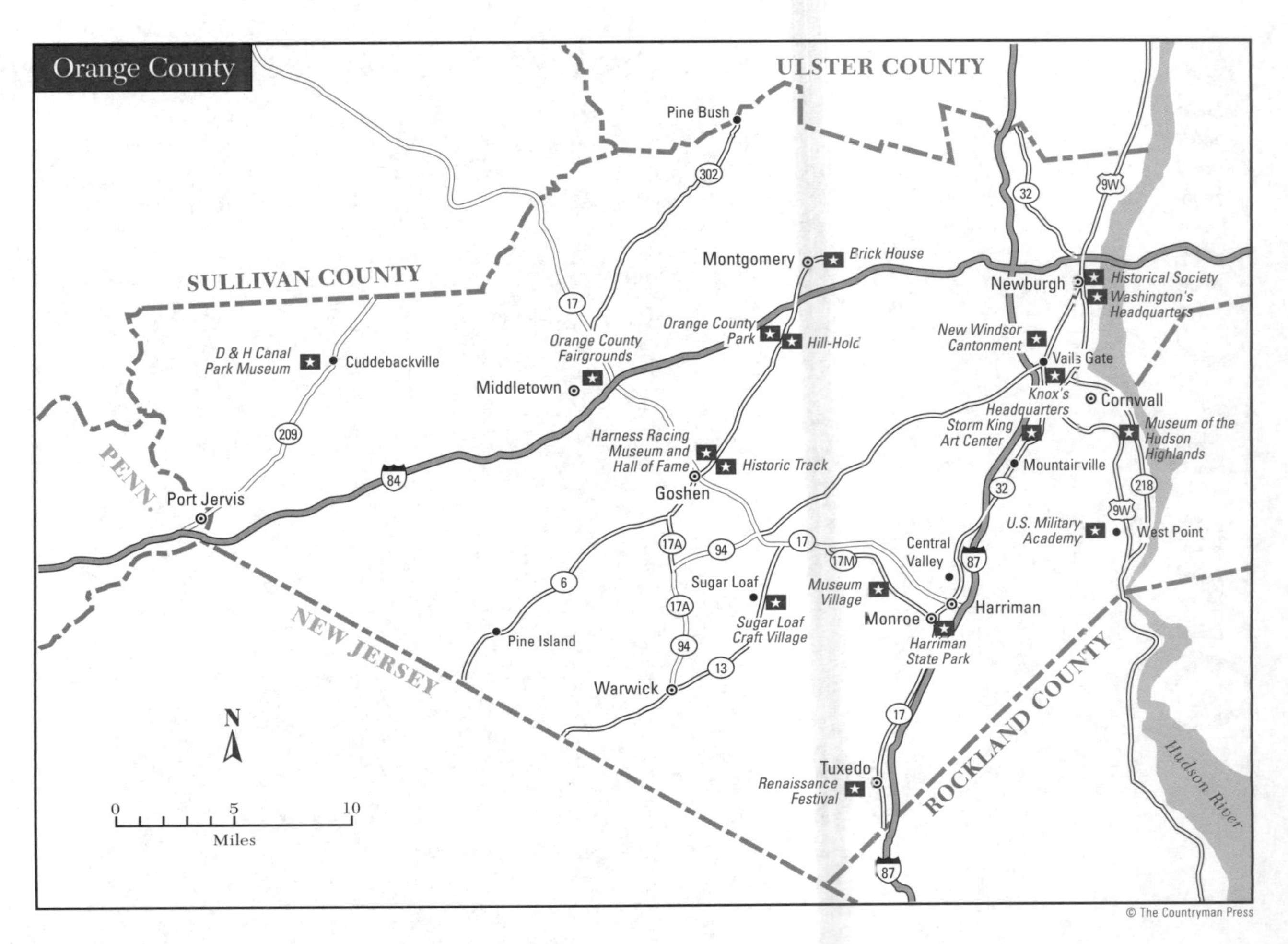

Orange County
ULSTER COUNTY
SULLIVAN COUNTY
ROCKLAND COUNTY
NEW JERSEY
PENN.
Hudson River
Pine Bush
Montgomery
Brick House
Newburgh
Historical Society
Washington's Headquarters
New Windsor Cantonment
Vails Gate
Knox's Headquarters
Cornwall
Museum of the Hudson Highlands
Storm King Art Center
Mountainville
U.S. Military Academy
West Point
Orange County Park
Hill-Hold
Orange County Fairgrounds
Middletown
D & H Canal Park Museum
Cuddebackville
Port Jervis
Harness Racing Museum and Hall of Fame
Historic Track
Goshen
Central Valley
Museum Village
Harriman
Monroe
Harriman State Park
Sugar Loaf
Sugar Loaf Craft Village
Pine Island
Warwick
Tuxedo
Renaissance Festival
N
0 5 10
Miles
9W 32 302 17 209 84 218 87 17A 94 6 17M 13
© The Countryman Press

ORANGE COUNTY

Visitors are reminded in every village and every park in Orange County that this is a place that cherishes its history. Museums, restorations, and historic exhibits are everywhere, from the Native American displays in the Goshen Courthouse to the collection of military equipment at West Point. You can imagine the life of a Revolutionary War soldier as he waited out the bitter winters in a wooden hut or watch as a costumed group of interpreters reenacts a battle that helped turn the tide of the American Revolution.

Orange County is also a place where the agricultural heritage of New York is still strong, a place where vegetable farming is a way of life for families and has been for generations. Stop at a farm and take home some just-picked peaches, or join in the fun at the Onion Festival. The Black Dirt area is a unique farming district where some of the best of New York's produce is grown, and a drive through the region in early summer gives new meaning to the word *bountiful.*

GUIDANCE **Orange County Tourism** (845-615-3860; 1-800-762-8687), 124 Main Street, Goshen 10924; www.orangetourism.org.

Palisades Parkway Tourist Information Center (845-786-5003), between exits 16 and 17 on the Palisades Interstate Parkway. This center offers trail and road maps, hiking and travel information, including NYS fishing licenses. Open April through October, daily 8–6; November through March, daily 8–5.

GETTING THERE *By car:* Orange County is accessible from exits 16 (Harriman) and 17 (Newburgh) off I-87; the New York State (NYS) Thruway, coming from the north or south; as well as from I-84 coming from points east and west. Route 17, which joins the Thruway at Suffern, is another route that goes into the county.

By bus: **Adirondack Trailways** (1-800-858-8555) runs buses from Kingston and Poughkeepsie to Newburgh. **New Jersey Transit** (973-275-5555; 1-800-772-2287) runs buses to Greenwood Lake and Warwick and trains to Harriman, Middletown, and Port Jervis. **Short Line/Coach USA** (1-800-631-8405) runs day trips and extended weekend trips stopping at several Orange County towns.

By train: **Metro North** (1-800-638-7646) stops in Beacon going to and from Grand Central Station in Manhattan. An inexpensive bus shuttle service across the Hudson from Newburgh connects with the trains.

By air: **Stewart International Airport** (845-564-7200), 1130 First Street, New Windsor, services major cities throughout the eastern United States.

MEDICAL EMERGENCY Orange Regional Medical Center (845-333-1000), 707 East Main Street, Middletown.

St. Anthony Community Hospital (845-986-2276), 15 Maple Avenue, Warwick.

St. Luke's Cornwall Hospital (845-561-4400), 70 Dubois Street, Newburgh; (845-534-7711), 19 Laurel Avenue, Cornwall.

* To See

Harness Racing Museum and Hall of Fame (845-294-6330/7542; www.harnessmuseum.com), 240 Main Street, Goshen. Open year-round, daily 10–5; closed Christmas, Thanksgiving, and New Year's Day. Admission fee. Messenger and Hambletonian, pacers, trotters, and standardbreds—all call to mind the speed and grace to be found on a trotting track, and the history and color of the sport can be discovered at this unique museum established in 1951. Trotters and pacers (trotters move their right front and left rear legs at the same time; pacers move both legs on one side at the same time) have long been a part of American history. Such notable figures as George Washington, Abraham Lincoln, and Ulysses S. Grant spent time breeding and racing these swift horses. At the Harness Racing Museum and Hall of Fame, the history of the sport can be traced through dioramas, prints, exhibits, and statues displayed throughout the former Good Time Stables building. Galleries contain permanent displays of Currier and Ives prints, famous racing silks, and the amazing Hall of the Immortals, where dozens of small, lifelike statues recall the greatest participants (human and four-legged) in the sport. Restored

HARNESS RACING MUSEUM AND HALL OF FAME

Orange County Tourism

Orange County Tourism

HISTORIC TRACK

stalls have full-size replicas of horses and their equipment, while you can see the sulkies and sleighs the horses once pulled (it wasn't unheard of to drive a horse many miles, then race it, then drive it home to the farm). There is even a room that reproduces the interior of the clubhouse from the nearby Historic Track. The room is so well maintained that you expect to hear the rustle of programs and the voices of members discussing the best bet of the day. There are films and shows in the auditorium, changing gallery exhibits, and the world's only 3-D harness racing simulator that makes you feel you are the driver in a race (you can even feel the wind blowing through your hair!).

Historic Track (845-294-5333; www.goshenhistorictrack.com), 44 Park Place, Goshen. Open year-round, daily 10–5. Located directly behind the Harness Racing Museum and Hall of Fame. The only sports facility in the country that is a National Historic Landmark, the Historic Track has been hosting meets since the 1830s. Although the Grand Circuit races visit here only once a year, the track is used as a training facility, so you may be able to see pacers, trotters, and a local blacksmith at work, no matter when you visit. The track is such a local institution that some of the private boxes have been passed down in families for generations.

Hudson Highlands Nature Museum (845-534-5506; www.hhnaturemuseum.org), P.O. Box 451, Cornwall 12518. There are two locations: The Wildlife Education Center (25 Boulevard, Cornwall-on-Hudson) is open year-round from Friday through Sunday noon–4; and the Quest Visitors Center (174 Angola Road, Cornwall) at the Outdoor Discovery Center is open May through October, Saturday and Sunday 10–4. There are programs for children at both sites. The Wildlife Education Center has a "Meet the Animals" program every Saturday and Sunday at 2:30. Admission fee. To get to the Wildlife Education Center, take Route 9W to the Angola Road exit. At the rotary in Cornwall, take the first right onto Hasbrouck Avenue and go to the end. Follow the signs. The Outdoor Discovery Center is on

Route 9W south, just after the Angola Road exit. The Wildlife Education Center is an excellent site to visit with children who love animals and want to learn more about their lives and habitats. The changing exhibits in the center are geared to children's interests. The Hall of Animals has an indoor mini zoo that houses small animals native to the Hudson Valley. Several amphibians, reptiles, small mammals, and birds crawl, creep, and, in the case of Edgar Allan Crow, talk. Outside the site, there are well-marked, easy trails to follow. At the Outdoor Discovery Center, families will enjoy hiking trails with a guidebook. Through riddles, hands-on activities, illustrations, and field notes, visitors will learn about nature in an interactive way that includes "hidden messages." There are four Quest trails that cover woodlands, meadows, and wetlands with ponds and streams. The museum is also known for summer camp and weekend programs for families. Teachers will like the environmental education classes offered to school groups. Strollers can navigate the Wildlife Education Center and some of the trails at the Outdoor Discovery Center.

Motorcyclepedia (845-569-9065; www.motorcyclepediamuseums.com), 250 Lake Street, Newburgh. Open year-round, Friday and Saturday 10–5; Sunday 11–5. Admission fee. Gerald Doering and his son, Edward, opened this motorcycle museum in 2011, featuring 400 bikes along with vintage photographs, posters, and lots of memorabilia. Several exhibit rooms include early American motorcycles dating back to 1865, as well as chopper bikes and Indian motorcycles built between 1902 and 1953. There is a military section as well as several Harley-Davidson models. A re-creation of the Captain America chopper from the film *Easy Rider* is also in one of the galleries. The Wall of Death, an exciting live demonstration given approximately every six months, always on a Saturday, requires reservations for any of the four shows given on that day. Those who desire a guided tour of the museum can make arrangements by calling in advance. Even those who aren't motorcycle aficionados will find this an interesting place to visit!

Museum Village (845-782-8247; www.museumvillage.org), 1010 Route 17M, Monroe. Open July and August, Tuesday through Friday 10–4; Saturday and Sunday 11–5. Closed Monday. During April, May, June, September, October, and November, check the website for hours, as they vary with the season. Special events are held throughout the year; call for a schedule. Admission fee. The daily life of preindustrial America has been preserved and re-created at this fascinating museum comprised of buildings and equipment moved to the site from other parts of the Hudson Valley. Set up like a small crossroads village, the museum is considered to have one of the largest sites devoted to the folk arts of everyday America. More than 20 buildings house crafts, equipment, and agricultural displays. At the blacksmith's shop, artisans hammer and pound hot metal into a door latch or horseshoe. In the newspaper office the master printer and the printer's devil (apprentice) are composing the weekly newspaper, and in the potter's workshop butter churns and mugs take shape on the wheel. Costumed guides answer questions; photos, prints, and tools trace the history of Orange County. The museum is a favorite place for children, and special events, offered throughout the season, have included a circus, a mineral show, America's birthday, and more. For a fun time set even further back in history, visit the mastodon, the most complete skeleton of this 11,000-year-old animal in New York State. Every Labor Day weekend there is a Civil War encampment, the largest in the Northeast, and it includes battles, camping demonstrations, and drills.

Orange County Tourism

MOTORCYCLEPEDIA

Storm King Art Center (845-534-3115; www.stormkingartcenter.org), Mountainville (street address for GPS: 1 Museum Road, New Windsor). Take the NYS Thruway to exit 16; the center is off Route 32 north, on Old Pleasant Hill Road—watch for signs. Open April 1 through November 15; indoor galleries open mid-May 11:30–5:30. Admission fee. Call regarding special events. There are classical concerts, garden talks, and family activities throughout the season. This 500-acre park and museum has one of the world's largest displays of outdoor sculpture. The permanent collection contains dozens of works by several contemporary artists, including Isamu Noguchi, Louise Nevelson, Alexander Calder, David Smith, and Mark di Suvero. The surrounding landscape is lovely, with a backdrop of Schunnemunk Mountain. This is truly one of the most impressive stops in the region and shouldn't be missed. (Trams and elevators now make the grounds handicapped accessible.)

HISTORIC HOMES Brick House (845-457-4921; www.orangecountynyparks.com), 850 Route 17K, Montgomery. Open mid-May to early October, Saturday and Sunday 10–4:30 (September and October by appointment only). Admission fee. A treasure trove of early American furniture and decorative arts owned by the same family since 1768. Now run by the county, the house—a red Georgian mansion constructed with bricks imported from England—is considered one of the finest private homes built between New York City and Albany in the 18th century. It was a meeting site for colonial officers during the Revolution, and many of the original furnishings are still intact. Pieces include a very rare 17th-century chest from Connecticut, fine crystal, Lafayette china (produced to honor the French

Orange County Tourism

BUDDHA SCULPTURE AT THE STORM KING ART CENTER

hero), chairs that may have belonged to the Washingtons, and an Eli Terry shelf clock. Brick House is also the site of a large autumn antiques show.

David Crawford House Museum (845-561-2585; www.newburghhistorical society.com), 189 Montgomery Street, Newburgh. Open April through October, Sunday 1–4, or by appointment. Admission fee. Maintained and run by the Historical Society of Newburgh Bay and the Highlands, Crawford House, a neoclassical structure, was built in 1830. There are changing exhibits in the gallery. Visitors will enjoy the spectacular river views and the collection of pint-size Hudson River sloop and ship models.

Gomez Mill House (845-236-3126; www.gomez.org), 11 Mill House Road, Marlboro. Open mid-April through mid-November, Wednesday through Sunday 10–4, with tours at 10:15, 11:30, and 1:45. Admission fee. The oldest surviving Jewish residence in the United States, and the oldest house in Orange County, this was the home of Lewis Moses Gomez, who arrived in America in 1703 and became a prosperous businessman. He built a stone trading post north of Newburgh, the site of the house, in 1714. In addition to the home, visitors will see the icehouse, root cellar, and restored mill and dam. Continuously inhabited for 290 years, the Gomez house has been a fur trading post and a home to merchants, farmers, and craftsmen.

Hill-Hold (845-291-2404; www.hillholdandbrickhouse.org), 211 Route 416, Campbell Hall. Open mid-May through October, Wednesday through Sunday 10–4. Admission fee. Once a section of a 30,000-acre estate, the land Hill-Hold stands on was presented to William Bull, an English stonemason, as a wedding present in the early 18th century. His son, Thomas Bull, built the home. Fortunately for lovers of 18th-century architecture, later family members donated the house and most of its furnishings to the county. The large Georgian mansion is graced by elegant wood and stonework, with barrel-backed cupboards, paneling, and deep-silled windows.

Rooms are furnished with many original Chippendale, Queen Anne, and Empire pieces. Two kitchens are still extant in the house: one in the basement and a newer one, added in 1800, in a separate stone wing. Like most manor houses of the era, Hill-Hold was also the center of a thriving farm. Surrounding the farmhouse are the original outbuildings, including the granary, barn, summer kitchen, wagon house, smokehouse, and, of course, the privy. On the working farm, sheep, cows, chickens, and geese are tended. Children will enjoy the farm animals, and flower lovers should spend some time in the summer gardens. Also on the site is the Goosetown School, a one-room schoolhouse still used for educational programs on daily life in the 19th century.

HISTORIC SITES **Clove Furnace** (845-351-4696), 21 Clove Furnace Drive, Arden. Open year-round, Monday through Friday 9–11 and 1–4, weekends by appointment. Free. Although not a very active site, this is an unusual one: a small museum devoted to the history of iron making in rural New York. The restored hot-blast furnace dates from 1854 and was used to produce artillery pieces during the Civil War. Exhibits outline the story of iron making and mining, and there are displays related to Orange County history (some include rare Parrott artillery pieces). An enlightening stop for those interested in the commercial development of what was once a major industry in America.

Constitution Island and the Warner House (845-446-8676; www.constitution island.org). Take Route 9W to West Point, enter the U.S. Military Academy gate, and take the first right past the Hotel Thayer. The dock and a large parking lot are at the end of the street. Tours are offered mid-June through late September, Wednesday and Thursday at 1 and 2 only. Call for reservations—only 40 people per tour. There are occasionally weekend tours and special events that begin in

DAVID CRAWFORD HOUSE MUSEUM

Orange County Tourism

Cold Spring. Buses for Constitution Island leave from the south end of the Cold Spring Metro North train station every 10 minutes from 10 to 3. Check the website to confirm schedule. Admission fee. To visit this Hudson River island, take the boat from West Point to Constitution Island. There you will find a 17-room Victorian mansion, home to the Warner family from 1836 to 1915. The daughters, Anna and Susan, grew up on the island and were best known for their writing; Anna penned many hymns, including "Jesus Loves Me," and Susan's *Wide Wide World* was a best-seller. After their father lost his fortune, the sisters stayed on in their home, living frugally and teaching Sunday school courses to West Point cadets, who never forgot the two spinsters. Their home is now a museum filled with their original possessions. Also on the island are the remains of **Fort Constitution,** a Revolutionary War–era fort, and the **Anna B. Warner Memorial Garden,** which is particularly lovely in late June. The surrounding Hudson is glorious anytime. If you visit the West Point cemetery, look for the sisters' graves; they were buried near their beloved home.

Knox's Headquarters (845-561-5498; www.nysparks.com), 289 Forge Hill Road, Route 94, Vails Gate. Open Memorial Day through Labor Day, Wednesday through Saturday 10–4:30, Sunday 1–4:30; grounds open daily. Admission fee. For several periods during the Revolution, the Ellison family's stone house served as headquarters for the colonial officers in the area. Generals Henry Knox, Horatio Gates, and Nathanael Greene were only a few of the men who met in the house and planned campaigns in the gracious rooms. Today it is furnished with military camp beds and folding desks such as those that displaced the Ellisons' fine 18th-century furniture. There are also two short hiking trails here that are perfect for those traveling with children.

New Windsor Cantonment (845-561-1765; www.nysparks.com), 374 Temple Hill Road, off Routes 32 and 300, Vails Gate. Open April through October, Monday through Saturday 10–5; Sunday 1–5. Admission fee. Washington's troops waited out the last months of the Revolutionary War here in anticipation of an announced cessation of hostilities. More than 10,000 soldiers, officers, cooks, and blacksmiths, along with their wives and other camp followers, constructed the snug log cabins, outbuildings, and a meeting hall, and here Washington quelled a mutiny of his troops, who resented Congress's slowness with wages and pensions. After the war, the buildings were auctioned off for the lumber, and the land remained unused until the state acquired 70 acres and began restoration of the site.

A visit to the cantonment today provides a look into the everyday life of Revolutionary soldiers. Displays depict the difficulties faced by both the troops and their leaders. The Purple Heart, which Washington presented to several soldiers, has its own Hall of Honor. A walkway leads from the orientation center to the rebuilt parade grounds and buildings. Costumed guides go about their business blacksmithing, drilling, cooking, and even entertaining (a fife player may be on hand). There are also demonstrations of 18th-century medical procedures. Although many of the buildings have been reconstructed from sketches that remain from the era, one is original. It had been carted away to become an addition to a local house, and there it remained for a century and a half, until its importance was realized, and it was returned to the site. Just across the road, on the west side of Route 300, are a small museum and re-created campground that illustrate the lives of the enlisted men during the war.

United States Military Academy (visitors center 845-938-2638; www.usma.edu), located off Route 9W, just north of Bear Mountain State Park; follow the signs. The visitors center is open 9–4:45 daily, except Thanksgiving, Christmas, and New Year's Day. The post is open year-round except major holidays; the museum opens daily at 10:30, except Christmas and New Year's Day. Admission is free, but there is a charge for a bus tour of the post. (Since September 11, 2001, visitors are no longer permitted to travel as freely within the academy, although at press time the grounds were open 9–2 to those with photo identification. To make arrangements for an organized tour, call 845-446-4724, West Point Tours, a private company.) Situated on the bluffs overlooking the Hudson River, this is where the nation's army officers have been trained since 1802; where Benedict Arnold attempted to bring the British to power; where such distinguished cadets as Robert E. Lee, Ulysses S. Grant, and Douglas MacArthur once marched; and where undistinguished cadets like James Whistler and Edgar Allan Poe discovered their other talents. Tradition is important at West Point, and tradition is what you will find here, from the Long Gray Line of cadets to the quiet cemetery and imposing stone barracks.

It is very difficult to see all of West Point in one visit—there are statues, museums, chapels, and points of interest everywhere you turn. But even if you can't stay overnight, use your time well, and make your first stop the visitors center on Main Street near the Thayer Gate entrance. Maps, schedules of events, and a display and movie about the cadets' lives at the Point are available at the center, where you can also pick up the USMA bus tour, which leaves every 20 minutes

WEST POINT PARADE, UNITED STATES MILITARY ACADEMY

Orange County Tourism

and lasts nearly an hour in the summer season. (The frequency of the tours changes seasonally.)

A must-see is the **West Point Museum** (845-938-3590), which is in Olmstead Hall. This is the oldest military museum in the country, and its holdings are among the largest in the world. Dioramas, permanent and changing exhibits, and thousands of artifacts are found throughout vast galleries, each with its own theme: the history of war, American warfare, weapons, the history of West Point. Visitors may see anything from a Stone Age hunting ax to the equipment used in Vietnam. Because the museum has so many collections, displays are changed frequently. Outside on the post itself, Trophy Point recalls the dead of the Civil War; there is also a 150-ton chain that was used to close off the Hudson River to British ships during the American Revolution. Although the attempt was unsuccessful, the chain represents the ingenuity that made America the victor. To the rear of the memorial is the Plain, the drilling area once used by Baron von Steuben to train and parade troops. It is still used on Saturday for full-dress parades by the cadets.

The **Cadet Chapel** contains stained-glass windows, the largest church organ in the world, and an overpowering sense of the men and women who have worshipped there. Another restored section of the Point is Fort Putnam, which was used as a fortification in the Revolutionary War and offers exhibits on the lives of Revolutionary soldiers and a show about the battles fought in the area. It also offers a panoramic view of the surrounding mountains. (Currently, the only way for travelers to see the chapel is with an organized tour, due to increased security within the academy.)

West Point is famous for its football games, played at Michie Stadium; tickets almost always have to be purchased in advance. In addition to football, there are basketball, hockey, and lacrosse games. Call the box office for a complete schedule (845-446-4996) or check www.goarmysports.com.

Concerts are given throughout the summer at various sites on the post; most are free and include the West Point Military Band. The concerts alone are well worth the trip. **Eisenhower Hall Theatre,** on the grounds of West Point, has shows that range from musical revivals and classic country to dramatic theater and just plain classics; call 845-938-4159 for schedules and ticket information or check www.ikehall.com.

Just south of the academy is a Revolutionary War site, **Fort Montgomery Historic Site** (845-446-2134, ext. 226), which offers magnificent views of the Hudson River, interpretive signs describing the "turning-point" battle that occurred here centuries ago, and a pedestrian suspension bridge permitting access to nearby Fort Clinton at the Bear Mountain Zoo. This is a wonderful destination for history buffs; the site is maintained by the Palisades Interstate Park Commission.

Washington's Headquarters (845-562-1195; www.nysparks.state.ny.us/sites), 84 Liberty Street, Newburgh. Take Route 17 from the NYS Thruway to downtown Newburgh; watch for signs. Open Monday and Wednesday through Saturday 10–5; Sunday 1–5. Call or check the website for the schedule of special celebrations. Admission fee. If Jonathan Hasbrouck's stone mansion set on a bluff overlooking the Hudson River could speak, it would say that Martha and George slept here. In fact, the end of the American Revolution was announced on the grounds. Construction began in 1750 but was not finished until 1782, when Washington's troops

Orange County Tourism

WASHINGTON'S HEADQUARTERS

added a gunpowder laboratory, a barracks, a privy, and a larger kitchen. Washington remained here for nearly a year and a half, waiting for the British to leave New York under the terms of surrender. The house and grounds were acquired by the government in 1848, and on opening day, July 4, 1850, Washington's Headquarters became America's first National Historic Site.

In the adjacent museum, opened in 1910, is an exhibit called "First in the Nation," which highlights the site's history of more than 150 years. The galleries were completely renovated and reopened in 2012 with several new exhibits of artifacts from the museum's permanent collection.

The story of the Revolution truly comes alive inside Hasbrouck House, where Washington is seen as a man who endured problems, boredom, and loss of the privacy that was so dear to him. (The house was owned by Tryntje Hasbrouck, a widow, who received notice of her eviction with a "sullen silence"—or so history records.) Visitors are guided through the eight rooms in which Washington and his staff lived and worked. The dining room where George and Martha ate their meals still contains the original jambless Dutch fireplace, open on three sides. The plain bedrooms and offices are sparsely furnished, and a field bed with its tentlike covering speaks clearly of the winter cold, while bedrooms show that not everyone was fortunate enough to have a room. The grounds are well kept and offer wide views up and down the Hudson. Special events are held throughout the year and include kite-flying days, Martha Washington's birthday celebration, and, of course, George Washington's birthday festivities.

SCENIC DRIVES The term *scenic drive* in Orange County is almost redundant; there are so many well-maintained roads where the pace is unhurried and the views are lovely that just about any drive around the county is certain to please. Even the Thruway softens up a bit as it moves through the Harriman area—

drivers will see deer at twilight and apple blossoms in the spring. Route 9W is an attractive road, but the section known as Old Storm King Highway, between West Point and Cornwall, is spectacular.

For a lovely country drive past lakes and trees, start at Harriman and take Route 6 east across Bear Mountain State Park to the Bear Mountain Bridge; from there 9W north offers vibrant Hudson River views on its way through West Point, Cornwall, and into Newburgh. Once in Newburgh, look for Route 32 around Cronomer Hill Park, a breathtaking sight in summer and fall.

Another noted scenic highway in Orange County is Hawk's Nest Drive, Route 92, near Sparrow Bush. The road runs along the Delaware River for a short distance, but you can then follow Route 209 north to the Delaware & Hudson Canal Park (see *Green Space*).

A different type of view is found along Route 17A, which cuts through the rich **Black Dirt Farming Region** around Pine Island. Kane Road near 17A in Warwick goes up Mount Peter between Warwick and Greenwood Lake, offering great views of the valley. This area is a major skyway for migrating hawks. If you follow Route 6 from Goshen to Pine Island, you will travel through one of the largest onion producing areas in the country. More than 14,000 acres of vegetable farms, with several farm stands along the way, the Black Dirt region was formed from a glacial lake more than 12,000 years ago. The area was once called the drowned lands before it was drained to create the farmland it is today.

WINERIES, BREWERIES, AND DISTILLERIES The following wineries in Orange County are open to visitors, but you might want to call ahead for operating hours, since they change depending on the season. Several special events are listed on www.shawangunkwinetrail.com.

Applewood Winery (845-988-9292), 82 Four Corners Road, Warwick. Open March through December, Friday, Saturday, and Sunday 11–5. This small operation produces fruit wines, grape wines, and cider, including three Naked Flock ciders: One is fermented with champagne and flavored with local honey, the pumpkin cider is spiced with cloves, and the draft has a fruity flavor. The winery is a nice place to stop in the autumn, when old-fashioned, Dutch-style doughnuts are served, and you can pick your own apples and pears in the orchard. Enjoy live music and light fare at the café every weekend from March through November.

Baldwin Vineyards (845-744-2226), 176 Hardenburgh Road, Pine Bush. Open July through October, daily 11–5; Thursday through Sunday in April, May, June, November, and December. Closed January through March.

Brimstone Hill Vineyard (845-744-2231), 61 Brimstone Hill Road, Pine Bush, is open Friday through Monday 11:30–5:30, with expanded hours in the summer and fall seasons. They offer a nice selection of wines.

Brotherhood Winery (845-496-9101), 100 Brotherhood Plaza Drive (off Route 94), Washingtonville, is open April through December, daily 11–5; January through March, Friday, Saturday, and Sunday 11–5. America's oldest winery offers visitors a tour of the wine production facility and the cellars. There is a fee, but a free tasting is included. Visitors can stroll around the grounds and enjoy the special events, including concerts and shows during the summer.

Orange County Tourism

BROTHERHOOD WINERY

Clearview Vineyard (845-651-2838), 35 Clearview Lane, Warwick. Open April through December, Saturday and Sunday noon–5. Ten varieties of red and white wines are featured here, and eight are produced from their organically grown grapes. While this is a small operation, it is one of very few Hudson Valley wineries growing organic fruit on their property.

Demarest Hill Winery and Distillery (845-986-4723), Grand Street, 81 Pine Island Turnpike, Warwick, is open year-round, daily 11–6. The wine here is made in the Italian tradition. Offerings include over 50 different products, including peach and cherry brandy.

Newburgh Brewing Company (845-569-BEER), 88 Colden Street, Newburgh. Open year-round, Friday 4–11, Saturday 1–10, and Sunday 1–8. This craft beer company is located in the former Newburgh Paper Box Factory across the street from Washington's Headquarters. The owner brings six years of experience working at the Brooklyn Brewery to this new enterprise, and the beers have been praised in industry publications. The Brown Ale is a favorite of mine. There's live music on occasion, so call and check to see what is happening before you go.

Palaia Vineyards (845-928-5384), 20 Sweet Clover Road, Highland Mills. Open June through December, daily noon–6; January through May, Friday, Saturday, and Sunday noon–6. A relative newcomer to the county's wineries, Palaia opened in 2006. Although they have only 10 acres of grapes, Jan and Joe Palaggi offer over 20 different red and white wines for tasting—something to please just about anyone.

Warwick Valley Winery and Distillery (845-258-4858), 114 Little York Road, Warwick, is open year-round, daily 11–6. Enjoy award-winning wines and ciders made from both pears (once called *perry*) and apples. They were the first to make brandy in New York State. There is a lovely vineyard, and visitors can pick their own apples and pears in season at the winery's 65-acre Friendship Farm. There is a bakery/café on the premises serving light lunch on weekends.

✱ To Do

BALLOONING AND HELICOPTER TOURS **Above the Clouds** (845-692-2556), P.O. Box 4816, Middletown 10941, open May through October, offers two one-hour flights daily (one at sunrise and the other two hours before sunset) from Randall Airport (100 Airport Road, New Hampton). Advance reservations are a must. The price is approximately $250 per person. This is an unusual, dramatic way to see the Hudson Valley's rolling hills, forests, and farmlands. Fully insured; certified pilot.

Enchanted Balloon Rides (845-649-9654), 577 Ridgebury Road, Slate Hill, is open year round and offers flights by advance reservation. FAA-certified commercial pilots; fully insured.

Fantasy Balloon Flights (845-856-7103), 2 Evergreen Lane, Port Jervis, offers half-hour rides, departing from Randall Airport (100 Airport Road, New Hampton), May through October; advance reservations necessary. FAA-certified commercial pilots; fully insured. All flights include champagne and a flight certificate. Groups accommodated.

Independent Helicopters (845-527-7808; www.independenthelicopters.com), Stewart Airport, 1035 First Street, New Windsor, is open year-round by appointment for both 30-minute and one-hour sightseeing flights in two- and four-seat planes. Check the website for detailed information about the planes and pilots. Prices range $150–500 depending on the length of the flight and number of passengers.

BOAT CRUISES One of the best ways to see the Hudson is from the river itself. As far back as the early days of European settlement in the region, the river catered to tourists in addition to being a major trade route. Today, a few companies offer travelers a relaxing way to take in the scenery while cruising.

Hudson Highlands Cruises (845-534-SAIL/7245; www.hudsonhighlandscruises.com), P.O. Box 355, Cornwall-on-Hudson 12520, has daily cruises aboard the *Commander* (on the National Register of Historic Places), leaving from Peekskill, Haverstraw Marina, and West Point. Sightseeing cruises are offered on weekdays, and it is best to check the website for complete schedule information.

Hudson River Adventures (845-220-2120; www.prideofthehudson.com), 26 Front Street, Newburgh, offers cruises—call for complete schedule—from May through October, Wednesday through Sunday, on the *Pride of the Hudson*, departing from Newburgh Landing (just off Route 9W near the junction of Route 84). Or from the NYS Thruway, take exit 17 and follow 17K east, which becomes Broadway; at the end of Broadway, turn left onto Colden Street and follow to the bottom of the hill. Newburgh Landing is on the opposite side of the train trestle. Bannerman's Castle, which rises from the north side of Pollepel Island like a medieval fantasy, is one of the most intriguing sights on the Hudson. Travelers can discover the mystery and history of the castle with the 40-minute narration as the tour boat approaches the island. Castle enthusiasts will love this cruise but should opt for a two-hour special guided walking tour of the island via water taxi (a 35-

Orange County Tourism

PRIDE OF THE HUDSON, HUDSON RIVER ADVENTURES

seat boat, the *Pollepel*). On this visit to Bannerman Island, visitors have a chance to walk along trails and see the castle itself up close along with the unique vegetation on the island. A Bannerman Castle Trust guide takes visitors, wearing hardhats, on a tour that has been closed to the public for decades. This island tour is truly spectacular, and any visitor to the Hudson Valley during the six months when it is possible to visit Bannerman Island should definitely make plans to go. As word spreads, this tour will become increasingly popular, so do call ahead and make reservations since the water taxi has limited seating. These more extensive tours are are available May through October on Saturday and Sunday; in July and August, on Friday as well. Snack bar.

The *River Rose* (845-562-1067; www.riverrosecruises.com), Newburgh Landing, Newburgh. This two-deck Mississippi-style paddleboat plies the Hudson May through October, Friday through Sunday, rain or shine. It's particularly nice during foliage season, with magnificent views of Breakneck Ridge and Storm King Mountain. Snack bar. Call for complete schedule and special-events excursions.

The Newburgh Waterfront is a wonderful place to visit, even if you aren't interested in embarking on a cruise. The paved walkway to the river offers spectacular views of Bannerman Island, Storm King Mountain, Mount

BANNERMAN'S CASTLE

Dutchess County Tourism

Orange County Tourism

THE *RIVER ROSE*

Beacon, and the Newburgh Bay. Stroll past several shops, and enjoy a drink alfresco in the warm-weather months at one of the area's restaurants. The **Yellow Bird Gallery,** 19 Front Street, is well worth a stop on your waterfront walk. However, it is open only when the Downing Film Center is open. The 10,000 square feet of gallery space feature 20th- and 21st-century painting and sculpture, and exhibits change frequently. **The Downing Film Center** (845-561-3686; www.downingfilmcenter.com), 19 Front Street, occupies 1,200 square feet of the lower level of the gallery, with a 55-seat theater that features independent, foreign, and classic films. About half the seats are recliners that rock (available at no extra charge, but arrive early to get one!). Patrons are permitted to take food and drinks inside the theater and sit at small tables while enjoying the film. Reservations are encouraged here, particularly on weekends. During weekday morning and evening rush hours a ferry goes across the river to the Beacon train station; it's a nice round-trip excursion if you don't have time for a sightseeing trip! (From the NYS Thruway, take I-84 east to exit 10, just before the Newburgh-Beacon Bridge. Make a right off the exit and a left at the next light. Follow to the waterfront.)

CANOEING AND KAYAKING The Delaware River may not have the same cachet as the Colorado, but it can offer a beautiful day of canoeing or kayaking. Most canoe and kayak rentals are in the western part of the county; the trips may range from drifting idylls to challenging whitewater in the spring. **Silver Canoe Rentals** (845-856-7055; 1-800-724-8342), 37 South Maple Drive, Port Jervis, also rents kayaks and rafts. Transport and pickup are included in their rates, and they are open April through September, daily 8–7. **Wild and Scenic River Tours and Rentals** (845-557-8783; 1-800-836-0366), 167 Route 97, Barryville; **Lander's**

River Trips (1-800-252-3925), 5961 Route 97, Narrowsburg; and **Kittatinny Canoes** (1-800-FLOAT-KC), 3854 Route 97, Barryville, all rent canoes, kayaks, and equipment. They will help you organize a safe, successful outing, particularly if you are a first-timer. Some of these outfitters offer guide services. For safety reasons, call and ask about river conditions before you go. (Because Orange and Sullivan counties overlap in relation to the Delaware River, check the listings in the Sullivan County chapter, as well.)

Mountain Valley Guides (845-661-1923), 2 Idlewild Avenue, Cornwall-on-Hudson, organizes Hudson River kayaking trips out of Cornwall, Hastings, and Rye for paddlers of all abilities. They supply the necessary equipment for these excursions that include two-hour children-only trips (ages 9–14), family outings and sunset paddles.

Storm King Adventure Tours (845-534-7800), 178 Hudson Street, Cornwall-on-Hudson, is the place to go for a three- or four-hour trip through Moodna Marsh or an excursion to Bannerman Island. They can tailor an outing on the Hudson River to your liking and supply all necessary equipment. If you would like to combine kayaking and hiking, they specialize in both here and will organize an excellent adventure incorporating a full day of the two activities.

FARM STANDS AND PICK-YOUR-OWN FARMS Few people know that Velveeta cheese was created at a factory on Mill Pond Parkway in Monroe in 1917. Because so much of Orange County is agricultural (the Black Dirt area produces half of the onions grown in New York State), you will find dozens of farm stands here. Some specialize in one particular fruit or vegetable while others offer a wide variety, but everything is as fresh as it gets. Try to plan a trip to the Orange County Onion Festival if you are visiting in September (see *Special Events* at the end of this chapter).

The Pine Island area offers several top-drawer farm stands and pick-your-own farms. **W. Rogowski Farm** (845-258-4574), 329 Glenwood Road, is a renowned second-generation certified, naturally grown farm with Cheryl Rogowski now at the helm. In season they have dozens of varieties of crops (several for pick-your-own), as well as a wonderful gift shop/farm store chock-full of tempting treats and fantastic produce. Open May through Labor Day, daily 9–6; rest of the year Friday through Sunday 9–5. Mid-November to Christmas, weekdays 10–5 and weekends 10–8.

One of my favorite stops is **Scheuermann Farms** (845-258-4221), 73 Little York Road, off County Road 1, open May through October, a fifth-generation family farm offering top-quality flowers, fruits, and vegetables grown on the premises.

Applewood Orchards (845-986-1684), 82 Four Corners Road, Warwick, is open in September and October. They operate a roadside stand with vegetables but specialize in several varieties of pick-your-own apples and pumpkins. There are free wagon rides, puppet shows, an animal petting area, and a nature walk. A great place to take the kids.

Blooming Hill Organic Farm (845-782-7310), 1251 Route 208, Blooming Grove. Open April through December, Saturday and Sunday 11–5; January through March, Saturday 10–2. This is a wonderful place, located along the banks of the Wallkill River. There are dozens of organically grown fruits and vegetables for sale as well as a small café serving breakfast and lunch items. Bakery on the premises.

Edgwick Farm (845-401-2301; www.edgwickfarm.com), 348 Angola Road, Cornwall. This microdairy and creamery makes farmstead cheese from their own pastured goats. It's a fascinating operation, and owners Talitha and Dan Jones welcome guests year-round. While the farm is open to the public, make sure to call first before heading out there. Check the website for special events.

Overlook Farm Market (845-562-5780), 663 Route 9W, Newburgh, sells local apples, peaches, nectarines, pumpkins, and a variety of home-baked pies, cakes, and cookies. Pick your own apples and enjoy a picnic lunch on the grounds from September through mid-October, daily 11–5:30. **Krisco Farms** (845-294-7784), Purgatory Road (off the Sarah Wells Trail) in Campbell Hall, is a dairy farm and offers some unusual delights: chocolate milk, fresh eggs, yogurt, and ice cream in their farm store. Christmas trees may be cut at **Fox Ridge Christmas Tree Farm** (845-986-3771), Fox Hill Road, Warwick; **Maples Farm** (845-344-0330), 749 Route 17M, Middletown (their shop includes homemade fudge, baked goods, and crafts); and **Pine View Farm** (845-564-4111), 575 Jackson Avenue, New Windsor. (Here you can cut your own balsam, Canaan, and Fraser fir, and blue, white, and Norway spruce. There are candy canes, coloring books, and live animals for the children. Open December weekends 9–4.)

Farmers' markets also bloom in Orange County. The selection is often unique. The **Goshen Farmers' Market** (845-294-7741) is held in Village Square, 33 Park Place, May through October, every Friday 10–5. **Late Bloomer Farm & Market** (845-742-8705), 31 Route 207, Campbell Hall, is open May through December daily, 10–6; January through April, Friday through Sunday 10–5. This family-owned and family-operated market offers cheeses, eggs, grass-fed beef, pastured chicken, baked goods, and more. The **Middletown Farmers' Market** (845-343-8075) sets up late June through October, Saturday 8–1, at the municipal lot on James and Depot streets. The **Warwick Farmers' Market** (845-987-9990) is held late May through October, Sunday 9–2, at the South Street parking lot.

GOLF **Central Valley Golf Club** (845-928-6924), 206 Smith Clove Road, Central Valley, was built in 1922 and is still owned and operated by the same family. An 18-hole challenging course set against the Ramapo Mountains, Central Valley is open from mid-March through November, daily dawn to dusk.

Mansion Ridge Golf Club (845-782-7888), 1292 Orange Turnpike, Monroe, is New York's only Jack Nicklaus Signature Design course open to the public. At one time a 220-acre estate, this 6,889-yard championship course features stunning rock formations and great scenery. The stone-barn clubhouse has a pro shop and restaurant. Open April through November, daily dawn to dusk.

Scenic Farms Golf Course (845-258-4455), 525 Glenwood Road, Pine Island. Open April through November, weekdays 7 AM–8 PM, weekends 6:30 AM–10 PM. This professionally designed nine-hole executive golf course is excellent for beginners and challenging for advanced golfers. There is a driving range as well as practice putting and chipping greens.

Stony Ford Golf Course (845-457-4949), 550 Route 416, Hamptonburgh. Located in Thomas Bull Memorial Park, just south of Montgomery, this 18-hole course is open March through November, daily dawn to dusk.

Wallkill Golf Club (845-361-1022), 40 Sands Road, Middletown; exit 119 off Route 17 West. Open April 1–November, this 18-hole championship course is fairly challenging. Driving range and restaurant on premises.

West Point Golf Course (845-938-2435), Routes 218 and 9W, on the outskirts of the USMA, West Point. Founded in 1948, this hilly, challenging course has a practice green with pitching and chipping areas. The course is open April through November; calling three days in advance for a tee time is suggested.

HIKING Trails range from easy to advanced and offer views of river, woodlands, and meadows. The first section of the **Appalachian Trail** was founded at Bear Mountain in 1923, and a portion of it offers spectacular views of Greenwood Lake as it weaves through the southwest section of the county; call the Palisades Interstate Parks Commission (845-786-5003) for maps and specific trail information.

For those hiking the Appalachian Trail, there are four bunks available at a hostel in Unionville from late April through early November. To make reservations, call 845-726-3956.

Black Rock Forest, Route 9W, north of West Point in Cornwall, has marked and unmarked trails that vary in length; decent hiking skill is required. Trail maps are available in a parking lot on the southbound lane of Route 9W.

The **Heritage Trail** (845-469-9459) is a converted railbed of the Erie Railroad. One can walk or bike this scenic route, which passes through Chester, Goshen, and Monroe. All three towns have entrances to the trail, and most of the 19-mile trail is paved. Handicapped accessible.

THE HERITAGE TRAIL IS GREAT FOR HIKING AND BIKING.

Orange County Tourism

The **Highlands Trail** is a rather rugged 35-mile trail that starts in Cornwall-on-Hudson, traverses the scenic highlands, continues over Schunnemunk Mountain, through Black Rock Forest, to the top of Storm King Mountain.

Two parks have trails of varying difficulty: **Schunnemunk,** Route 32 in Highland Mills, has six marked trails, the longest of which is 8 miles; **Winding Hills Park,** Route 17K, Montgomery, has trails, a place to picnic, and a nature study area.

Sterling Forest State Park (845-351-5907), 115 Old Forge Road, Tuxedo, has the 8-mile **Sterling Ridge Trail,** the 3-mile **Allis Trail,** the 4-mile **Indian Hill Loop,** 7 miles of the Appalachian Trail, and 10 miles of the Highlands Trail. The information center is located at the south end of Sterling Lake.

Stewart State Forest (845-256-3076), in the town of New Windsor, has semi-paved areas for walking, running, mountain biking, and horseback riding. There are three areas along Route 207, between Drury Lane and Route 208, to pull off the highway and access the trailheads.

HORSEBACK RIDING **Clove Acres Riding Academy** (845-496-8655), 299 Mountain Lodge Road, Monroe, specializes in English riding. The family atmosphere makes this place ideal for the youngest riders.

Gardnertown Farms (845-564-6658), 822 Gardnertown Farm Road, Newburgh. There is no trail riding here, but there are indoor and outdoor facilities, polo lessons, and tournaments. Riding by appointment only.

Ivy Rock Farms (845-534-0365), 99 Purdys Lane, New Windsor. This 85-acre facility is open daily year-round for lessons, and there is an indoor arena here as well. They offer something called "trail lessons" and will take you out on some of their hundreds of miles of trails if you are competent to handle the ride. This is a good choice for those who haven't been riding in some time and would like to learn something in addition to going out on a trail.

Juckas Stables (845-361-1429), 1204 Route 302, Pine Bush (located in Bullville). This establishment has been in business for more than 40 years. There are lovely trails, and both English and Western riding are offered. Friendly, informal atmosphere.

My Saddle Brook Farm (845-778-3420), 163 Berea Road, Walden. This riding facility offers both indoor and outdoor arenas and access to miles of trails; they are open daily year-round. Both English and Western riding lessons are offered to adults and children, either privately or in a group. There is also a summer camp.

SWIMMING **Arrow Park** (845-783-2044), 1061 Orange Turnpike, Monroe. Admission fee. This pristine private lake and picnic grounds has rowboat rentals as well as lots of shade for those who can't take the sun. There are food vendors, as well as hiking paths, volleyball courts, and basketball courts. This is a great place for a family outing.

Bear Mountain State Park Pool and **Harriman State Park Beaches** (845-786-2701), Route 9W, Bear Mountain. Open from mid-June through Labor Day. Admission fee. These swim areas will be particularly appealing to those traveling with young children. It is best to call ahead for the schedule.

Redwood Tennis and Swim Club (845-343-9478), 620 Van Burenville Road, Middletown. Open daily, June through Labor Day weekend. Admission fee. The pool is huge and is located in a 9-acre recreation area with picnic tables and outdoor and indoor clay tennis courts.

Thomas P. Morahan Beach (845-986-1124), Windermere Avenue, Greenwood Lake. Admission fee. There is lake swimming with lifeguards here on Greenwood Lake (Memorial Day weekend through late June, weekends only 11–7; late June through Labor Day, daily 11–7). There are picnic areas and volleyball courts as well.

✷ Winter Sports

ICE SKATING **Bear Mountain State Park** (845-786-2701), 55 Hessian Drive (off Route 9W), Bear Mountain. This outdoor rink offers public sessions of an hour and a half from mid-October to early March. There is admission, but kids under five skate free. Rentals available.

Ice Time Sports Complex (845-567-0005), 21 Lakeside Road, Newburgh, exit 6 off I-84 at Route 17K. Two Olympic-size indoor ice rinks offer public skating and figure-skating sessions. This is a great place for family fun. Lessons, rentals, and skating camp in July and August. Lockers, snack bar, pro shop, spacious seating area for spectators.

SKIING **Mount Peter** (845-986-4940), 40 Ski Lane (at junction of Route 17A and Old Mount Peter Road), Warwick, has a vertical drop of 400 feet, two double chairlifts, and eight downhill slopes for skiing and snowboarding. Open daily in season, but it's a good idea to call for hours.

Tuxedo Ridge (845-351-1122), 581 Route 17A West, Tuxedo, is open mid-December through mid-March, with night skiing weekdays until 9 and until 10 on Friday and Saturday. Vertical drop of 450 feet, four double chairlifts, and six slopes will delight both skiers and snowboarders. Snowmaking, rentals, and restaurant (open year-round).

✷ Green Space

Delaware & Hudson Canal Park/Neversink Valley Museum of History and Innovation (845-754-8870), 26 Hoag Road, Cuddebackville (just off Route 209, about 10 miles south of Wurtsboro). The park is open year-round, with special events scheduled in the warmer months. The museum is open April through October, Friday through Sunday noon–4, and by appointment. Admission fee. This 300-acre park, a registered National Historic Landmark, recalls an era when coal, lumber, and other goods were moved from Pennsylvania to New York by a combination of water, mules, and backbreaking labor. Huge barges were often run as family businesses, with the crew consisting of parents and children. And there wasn't much room for profit, since the barges moved at a leisurely 3 miles per hour. The park sponsors seasonal events that evoke life in old-time New York State. Demonstrations have included ice cutting, story evenings, nature walks, and even a silent-film festival (the park was once used by D. W. Griffith). The museum has exhibits about the canal and its people and is located in a restored blacksmith's house near the aqueduct; other buildings include a lockkeeper's house, a canal store, and a full-size replica of a canal barge.

Indian Hill/Southfields Furnace (845-473-4440), Orange Turnpike, Tuxedo. (From exit 16, NYS Thruway, take Route 17 south. Make a right on County Route

19, also known as Orange Turnpike. After approximately 1 mile, the entrance is on the right.) The fascinating ruins of a 19th-century iron furnace can be seen at this 500-acre park. The trails include a 4-mile loop traversing hardwood forest and rock outcroppings. Panoramic views of the Ramapo River Valley and Harriman State Park.

Moodna Creek Marsh (845-473-4440), Plum Point Lane, New Windsor. (Take Route 9W to Plum Point Lane, which is north of the intersection of Routes 9W and 94.) You can travel by canoe or kayak on the Hudson River from this state-owned, 60-acre Kowawese Unique Area, managed by the NYS Department of Environmental Conservation. You may see the historic homestead of one of George Washington's lieutenants, the Squire Nicoll house, which dates from 1735 (not open to visitors). There are wonderful views of Bannerman's Castle on Pollepel Island, Mount Beacon, and Storm King Mountain. Also see **Bear Mountain** and **Harriman state parks** under *Green Space* ("Rockland County") and **Storm King Art Center** under *To See* in this chapter.

✷ Lodging

Bed & breakfasts have proliferated throughout Orange County in recent years. In fact, there is now an Orange County B&B Association, which may be accessed through the Internet at www.new-york-inns.com. The following selections for overnight accommodations around the county are particularly charming or special in some way:

Anthony Dobbins Stagecoach Inn (845-294-5526), 268 Main Street, Goshen 10924. ($$) A former stagecoach stop, this inn is located in the middle of a country town, a few minutes' walk from shopping, dining, and the racetrack and museum. Four rooms, all with private bath; rates include a full breakfast. Open year-round.

Ashford Cottage (845-258-7167), 25 Oakland Avenue, Warwick 10990. ($$) There are three charming rooms, all with private baths, in this stone cottage, and the center of Warwick, with its plentiful restaurants and boutiques, is within walking distance. The owners prepare a fantastic full breakfast, and you may choose the most convenient time to be served. In the summer guests may enjoy the outdoor pool, and a media room with a large-screen TV offers the latest DVDs. This is a wonderful choice for a cozy romantic getaway; not a good choice for those traveling with children. Open year-round.

Caldwell House Bed & Breakfast (845-496-2954), 25 Orrs Mills Road, Salisbury Mills 12577. ($$$) If you want a truly deluxe B&B experience, try this establishment, a renovated home that dates from 1803. There are four rooms, all with private bath, TV, and VCR; one has a Jacuzzi. All rooms are decorated with antiques; the four-poster beds have handmade linens.

Cider Mill Inn (845-258-3044), 207 Glenwood Road, Pine Island 10969. ($$) There are three rooms here, all with private bath, in a meticulously restored 1865 Victorian farmhouse, formerly a working dairy farm and apple orchard, hence the name. The romantic lodgings offer down comforters, spa robes, and hot tub in addition to a full gourmet breakfast. Children over the age of 12 are welcome here. Open year-round.

Cromwell Manor Inn (845-534-7136), 174 Angola Road, Cornwall 12518. ($$$) This renovated inn, a historic country estate dating from 1820, is situated on 7 acres of woodland and gardens near West Point and Stewart Airport. The 13 rooms and suites (all with private bath) are beautifully decorated with period antiques. Many rooms have a working fireplace and Jacuzzi, and all are air-conditioned. A full breakfast is served in the country dining room or on the veranda. Step back in time without sacrificing modern amenities. This inn is only a 10-minute drive from West Point and a few miles from Storm King Art Center (see *To See*). The lovely village of Cornwall, with its charming shops and variety of restaurants, is down the road. Jones Farm Country Store (see *Selective Shopping*) is next door to the inn. Open year-round.

Glenmere Mansion (845-469-1900), 634 Pine Hill Road, Chester 10918. ($$$) This premier luxury hotel has 18 guest rooms and two restaurants on a 150-acre estate, the former home of a Gilded Age millionaire. Guests will feel transported to a beautiful Italian villa complete with lush gardens and gorgeous views at every turn. Open year-round.

Goldsmith Denniston House (845-562-8076), 227 Montgomery Street, Newburgh 12550. ($$) This Federal-style house was built circa 1820 for a local attorney. In the 1880s a bay window and marble fireplaces were added. The current owners, the Billmans, opened the house as a bed & breakfast in 2004. Mrs. Billman actually grew up in the house. They decorated each of the four bedrooms in a style reminiscent of a former owner. From Federal to Victorian, each air-conditioned room has a queen-size bed and private bath; three have fireplaces. Behind the house is a spacious patio where breakfast is served in warm weather. Open year-round.

Hambletonian House (845-469-6425), 19 High Street, Chester 10918. ($$) This elegant Victorian home, built in 1850, is situated on a hill surrounded by trees and gardens. The period furnishings will transport guests back in time to an era when the pace was slower. A full breakfast is served on the porch (in season) or in the dining room. There are two air-conditioned rooms, each with a private bath.

Hilton Garden Inn (845-567-9500), 15 Crosswoods Court, Newburgh 12550. ($$) There are 119 rooms and suites here, and the hotel is within a few minutes' drive of Stewart Airport. There is an indoor heated swimming pool, whirlpool, and fitness center, as well as a full-service restaurant on the premises.

Inn at Stony Creek (845-986-3660), 34 Spanktown Road, Warwick 10990. ($$) Enjoy a historic 1860 Greek Revival farmhouse that overlooks scenic meadows and a stream. The five rooms, with private baths, include TV, VCR, and computer lines. There is afternoon or evening tea served by the fireplace and a full breakfast. This is one of the most delightful accommodations in the Warwick area.

Meadowlark Farm (845-651-4286), 180 Union Corners Road, Warwick 10990. ($$) Enjoy staying in a farmhouse built in 1865. The three air-conditioned rooms all have private baths. In the summer months a full breakfast is served with fresh produce from the lovely garden. Living room with fireplace. No children. Open year-round.

Peach Grove Inn (845-986-7411), 1572 Route 17A, Warwick 10990. ($$) This restored 1850 Greek Revival home overlooks a 200-acre farm. There are six large rooms, all with private baths. The full breakfast features delicious home-baked breads and cakes. A great place to slow down and get away from everything! Open year-round.

Pine Bush House (845-744-3641), 215 Maple Avenue, Pine Bush 12566. ($$) Housed in a Victorian home built in 1904, this elegant B&B takes visitors back to another era. There are four bedrooms and one suite, some with steam showers or Jacuzzi, and all with private baths, fireplaces, flat-screen TVs, and high-speed wireless Internet access. A short walk takes guests to the center of Pine Bush. Not recommended for children. Open February through December.

Shadow Mountain Farm Bed & Breakfast (845-522-1892), 528 Angola Road, Cornwall 12518. ($$) This private two-story country cottage has all the modern conveniences. There are also great views, and a cozy sitting room with a porch on the first floor. Angola Road is beautiful, and Jones Farm Country Store (see *Selective Shopping*) and the Hudson Highlands Nature Museum (see *To See*) are located nearby. Open year-round.

Silent Farm (845-294-0846), 35 Axworthy Lane, Goshen 10924. ($$) This is the place for horse lovers. The four rooms and one suite overlook an 85-acre horse farm. Breakfast is served by the dining room fireplace or on the deck in the warm-weather months. Horseback riding (and lessons) are available. Open year-round.

Sleepy Valley Inn (845-986-7829), 117 Sleepy Valley Road, Warwick 10990. ($$) There are four rooms located in a large carriage house on 8 parklike acres surrounded by forest. All rooms are furnished with antiques and have private baths and Jacuzzis; three have fireplaces. A full breakfast is served to all guests. A wonderful spot for those who treasure privacy.

Storm King Lodge (845-534-9421), 100 Pleasant Hill Road, Mountainville 10953. ($$) This spacious and comfortable country lodge—the converted carriage house of a former estate—has views of Storm King Mountain, and it's only minutes away from Storm King Art Center (see *To See*) and close to West Point. The setting is just beautiful, with colorful gardens, a grand outdoor pool, and stunning mountain views. The six guest rooms all have private baths; a few have a fireplace. A wonderful two-bedroom cottage on the property is the perfect choice for families. The cozy ambience reflects the warmth of the family that operates the lodge. Gay and Hal Janks have been in the area for years and won't steer you wrong with their suggestions. Open year-round.

Sugar Loaf Village Bed & Breakfast (845-469-2717), 16 Pine Hill Road, Sugar Loaf 10981. ($$) This renovated house, more than 100 years old, features two antiques-filled guest rooms, each with its own bathroom complete with jet tub. A nice mix of the old and new and a great place to relax after shopping in Sugar Loaf. A country breakfast is served in the bird- and rose-filled garden. In winter the breakfast table is lit by candles and a cozy fire. Open year-round.

Thayer Hotel (845-446-4731), U.S. Military Academy, West Point 10996. ($$$) The Thayer Hotel reflects a long-gone time of grandeur, with many guest rooms overlooking one of the most scenic parts of the Hudson River: the Hudson Highlands. There are 148 renovated rooms here. Breakfast is not included in the room rate; the dining room serves on the terrace, which offers an exquisite panoramic view of the Hudson Valley. The hotel is within minutes of the military academy's points of interest. Open year-round; reservations are required, especially on special-events weekends at the academy. Make sure to ask about the many special package rates available throughout the year; they are exceedingly reasonable. They are known for their Sunday Champagne Brunch in their dining room, with spectacular views of the Hudson River.

Victorian River View (845-446-5479), 30 Scott's Circle, Fort Montgomery 10922. ($$) There are five rooms with shared baths in this 1888 Victorian home overlooking the Hudson River and Bear Mountain Bridge. The rooms are chock-full of bric-a-brac, and all the rooms have air-conditioning, TV, and VCR. Continental breakfast is included.

Warwickshire Bed & Breakfast (845-988-1946), 12 Linden Place, Warwick 10990. ($$) This bed & breakfast, located in a stately Tudor-style home, is within walking distance of shops and restaurants in the village. The house was built in 1893 and features intricate exterior stonework done by European stonemasons. The three guest rooms all have private baths, and one room has a king-size bed and separate sitting room. A home-cooked breakfast is served, and special dietary requirements will be accommodated. Open year-round.

Warwick Valley Bed & Breakfast (845-987-7255), 24 Maple Avenue, Warwick 10990. ($$) All four rooms have private baths in this 1900 Colonial Revival home, decorated with antiques and country furniture. The living room has a fireplace, and in season a full breakfast is served to guests on the covered porch. Open year-round.

Waterstone Inn (845-477-3535), 62 Sterling Road, Greenwood Lake 10925. ($$) Located on lovely Greenwood Lake, where guests can arrive dockside, there are five renovated guest rooms, all named after steamships and famous local citizens. In 2008 the Mulcahy family, residents of the town for four decades, took over the former Lynch's Lakeside Inn. All rooms have private baths, air-conditioning, and TV, and most have Jacuzzis. Beautiful lake and mountain views are delightful in all rooms. Inquire about reduced midweek rates. Open year-round.

Wildflower Cottage (845-258-1233), 93 Walling Road, Warwick 10990. ($$) This charming cottage provides a romantic getaway, complete with full bathroom, kitchenette, color TV, and queen-size bed. Depending upon the season, enjoy a crackling fire in the fireplace or stay cool with central air-conditioning after a swim in the lovely pool. A continental breakfast of freshly baked muffins, juice, and coffee or tea will be delivered to your door. Open year-round.

* Where to Eat

DINING OUT

In Cornwall and Newburgh Area (Eastern Orange County)

Canterbury Brook Inn (845-534-9658), 331 Main Street, Cornwall. ($$) Open for dinner Tuesday through Saturday 5–9. Hans and Kim Baumann offer up a touch of Switzerland in Cornwall. Fine Continental cuisine may be enjoyed while overlooking Canterbury Brook, or dining fireside in the cooler months. Specialties of the house include roast duckling, veal langoustine, classic Wiener schnitzel, pasta with *fruits de mer,* New York sirloin steak, filet mignon, and an array of fresh-fish specials. The desserts are truly spectacular, and cappuccino and espresso are available.

Captain Jake's Newburgh (845-565-3939), 40 Front Street, Newburgh. ($$$) Open daily 11:30–9; until 10 on

Friday and Saturday. This is the place to go for seafood. The raw clams and oysters are quite good here. My favorite is the lobster fettuccine. In the warm weather months it's delightful to dine al fresco as the Hudson River views are spectacular. Note that service can be slow on busy weekends.

Cena 2000 (845-561-7676), 50 Front Street, Newburgh. ($$) Open daily for lunch noon–3; dinner 5–10 (until 11 Friday and Saturday, until 9 Sunday). Northern Italian, Tuscan cuisine is featured here; there is fresh fish, pasta, seafood, filet mignon, veal chop, and grilled shrimp for entrées. Desserts include homemade gelatos, tiramisu, and Italian pastries. Hudson River waterfront dining May through October. Reservations recommended. Not too child friendly, but kids are accommodated.

Il Cenacolo (845-564-4494), 228 South Plank Road, Newburgh. ($$$) Open for lunch Wednesday through Friday and Monday noon–2:30; dinner daily at 5, Friday and Saturday at 6, Sunday at 4. Fine food from northern Italy is the byword at this excellent restaurant, based on an Italian supper room. Select from buffalo-milk mozzarella with roasted red peppers, spinach gnocchi with venison sauce, tuna steak in garlic and olive oil, and many types of pasta. Save room for the homemade desserts and excellent espresso. Not recommended for children; reservations required.

Lake View House (845-566-7100), 205 Lakeside Road, Newburgh. ($$) Open daily for dinner, except Tuesday, from 5; lunch served weekdays, except Tuesday, 11:30–2:30. Watch the sun set over Orange Lake while dining at a restaurant in operation since 1899. The chef-owner specializes in traditional American fare. Hearty soups, salads, and sandwiches are served for lunch.

Machu Picchu Peruvian Restaurant (845-562-6478), 301 Broadway, Newburgh. ($) Open daily, except Tuesday, 10–10 (until midnight Friday and Saturday). After traveling to Machu Picchu in 1984 and finding it one of the most amazing places on the planet, I was intrigued by the name of this restaurant. I wasn't disappointed. There are breakfast specialties here—the tacu tacu (eggs cooked with fresh garlic, diced tomatoes, onions, rice, and beans) is quite tasty, as well as hearty soups and fish stews that are a meal in themselves for lunch. The entrées, served with rice and beans, include chicken, lamb, steak, and seafood. Children welcome.

Mama Theresa's (845-561-6262), 374 Windsor Highway, New Windsor. ($) Open Monday through Saturday 11–10; Sunday noon–9. This is the place to go for first-rate Italian home cooking. Everything is made fresh on the premises—pasta, calzones, stromboli, and more. Whether you want pizza, pasta, veal, chicken, or seafood, it will be excellent. *Mangia!*

Painter's Tavern (845-534-2109), 266 Hudson Street, Cornwall-on-Hudson. ($$) Open for lunch and dinner Monday through Saturday 11:30–10; Sunday brunch 10:30–3, dinner 3–9. Perfect for any meal. There are nightly dinner specials, along with creative variations on burgers, sandwiches, and salads. The sun-dried tomatoes with cream pasta sauce is an excellent selection, and there are dozens of imported and domestic beers, bottled and on tap. Children welcome.

Riverbank Bar and Grill (845-534-3046), 3 River Avenue, Cornwall-on-Hudson. ($$) Open for dinner Tuesday through Sunday 5:30–10. Housed in a former bank, this restaurant's ambience is definitely unusual. The vault is now used to store wine. They offer an eclectic mix of French, Asian, and Italian dishes, including thin-crust pizza, tapas, pasta dishes, steamed mussels, and an array of salads. There is a nice variety of wines by the glass, craft beers, and martinis.

River Grill (845-561-9444), 40 Front Street, Newburgh. ($$) Open daily for lunch Monday through Saturday 11:30–3; dinner 5–9, till 10 Friday and Saturday; Sunday noon–9. Mark Mallia, the chef-owner, offers an array of seafood, steaks, chops, rack of lamb, and a nice selection of pastas. The River Grill Calamari is lightly coated in their own special blend of seasoned flour and served with two sauces: a spicy fra diavolo and chive horseradish. Enjoy the wonderful river view from the bar and most parts of the restaurant.

Schlesinger's Steak House (845-561-1762), 475 Temple Hill Road, New Windsor. ($$) Open for lunch and dinner Monday through Friday 11:30–9; Saturday 4:30–10; Sunday 3–9. Savor corn-fed Iowa beef, hand-cut and aged on the premises. The restaurant is located in the historic Brewster House (circa 1762), which dates from the Revolutionary War, when it was used as officers' quarters. In addition to steaks, the menu offers seafood, barbecued ribs, chicken, and pasta dishes. Children's menu.

Torches (845-568-0100), 120 Front Street (Newburgh Waterfront), Newburgh. ($$) This enormous restaurant has huge windows that offer river views. A 5,700-gallon fish tank filled with colorful tropical fish, plus clamshell lampshades, add to the nautical decor. There is an extensive raw bar, and a large mahogany bar where I have enjoyed the tricolor nachos with roasted corn jalapeño salsa and Vermont cheddar in the relaxing atmosphere. The soups, salads, sandwiches, steaks, and seafood are decent, but just about everyone goes here for the river views.

Yobo (845-564-3848), 1297 Route 300, Newburgh. ($$) Open daily for lunch and dinner 11–10. Serving Asian cuisine since 1980, this restaurant has a waterfall inside its walls, and the sound of the running water is relaxing and reminiscent of the Far East. One of my favorite dishes here is the Thai firecracker seafood, with a blend of hot-and-sweet-flavored sauce mixing scallions, cilantro, and peppers with seafood, served over a bed of vermicelli noodles. There are wonderful soups here as well as sushi and Korean and Indonesian favorites. Children welcome.

In Montgomery and Goshen (Central Orange County)

Back Yard Bistro (845-457-9901), 1118 Route 17K, Montgomery. ($$) Open for lunch Tuesday through Friday 11–2; dinner Tuesday through Saturday 5–9 (10 on weekends). Located a half mile west of Route 208 on Route 17K, this gourmet eatery is owned by husband and wife Jerry and Susan Crocker, who are graduates of the Culinary Institute of America. New American cuisine is served in a small, intimate dining room looking out on a lovely courtyard. Local seasonal ingredients are used in an array of imaginative dishes. The wine list is reasonably priced. Don't skip dessert (the crème brûlée was quite a treat).

Bistro Lilly (845-294-2810), 134 West Main Street, Goshen. ($$) Open for lunch Tuesday through Friday 11:30–2:30; dinner Tuesday through Saturday 5–9. The eclectic American cuisine includes wraps, sandwiches, and burgers for lunch, with the emphasis on fresh seasonal ingredients. Dinner entrées include steak and fresh fish; don't skip the first-rate homemade desserts.

Bull's Head Inn (845-496-6758), 120 Sarah Wells Trail, Campbell Hall. ($$) Open for dinner Wednesday through Sunday 4–10. Enjoy fine dining in a colonial atmosphere with many unusual American specialties. If you love garlic, make sure to order the baked garlic appetizer. Popular entrée selections include shrimp with four cheeses, filet mignon with peppercorn sauce, 22-ounce rib eye steak, paella, and crackling pork shank. The peanut butter cheesecake is delicious for dessert.

Camillo's at the Crossroads (845-457-5482), 2215 Route 208, Montgomery. ($$) Open for dinner Tuesday through Sunday 5–9; until 10 Friday and Saturday. American regional cuisine is offered at this spacious restaurant, housed in a convenient location "at the crossroads" of State Route 208 and I-84. The pan-roasted organic chicken and portobello mushroom in port wine sauce are popular entrées. The pastas are excellent; my favorite is the rigatoni Bolognese. Desserts are classic and include selections like apple crisp and chocolate mousse. Children's menu.

Catherine's (845-294-8707), 153 West Main Street, Goshen. ($$) Open for lunch Tuesday through Friday 11:30–2:30; dinner Tuesday through Saturday 5:30–9. Contemporary American cuisine here includes a variety of pasta and seafood specialties served in a comfortable country setting. Portions are generous. The restaurant is housed in a historic building that dates from 1869.

88 Charles Street (845-457-9850), 88 Charles Street, Montgomery. ($$) Open for lunch Monday through Friday 11:30–4; dinner 5–10, Saturday till 11; Sunday 2–10. The outstanding Northern Italian cuisine here features veal, chicken, pasta, seafood, and steaks. Large portions, reasonable prices, romantic atmosphere.

Glenmere Mansion (845-469-1900), 634 Pine Hill Road, Chester. ($$$) This luxury hotel (see *Lodging*) features two restaurants. The gourmet **Supper Room** is open for dinner Thursday through Saturday 6–10; Sunday brunch 10–2. They offer fresh fish, steaks, veal, duck, and many more seasonal specials. The less formal **Frogs End Tavern** ($$) serves lunch and dinner daily, and the fare here ranges from sandwiches, salads, and burgers to unusual light fare like their renowned fig and blue cheese pizza. The ambience here is that of an Italian villa.

Il Tesoro (845-294-8373), 6 North Church Street, Goshen. ($$) Open for lunch Monday through Friday noon–3; dinner 5–9, Friday and Saturday until 10, Sunday 4–8. Enjoy Northern Italian fare in an ambience reminiscent of a Tuscan villa. The veal scaloppine topped with grilled eggplant, mozzarella cheese, and prosciutto is first-rate. Braised rabbit with spicy chili sauce is a house specialty. Desserts are delicious and are prepared fresh daily by the pastry chef–owner.

Magoya (845-469-7874), 41 Brookside Avenue, Chester. ($$$) Open daily 11:30–10. This is the place to go for excellent fresh sushi in casual surroundings. They offer a wide selection of rolls as well as sashimi and various combinations of both. There are teriyaki dishes for diners who prefer cooked entrées.

Wildfire Grill (845-457-3770), 74 Clinton Street, Montgomery. ($$) Open Wednesday through Monday for lunch 11:30–3; dinner 5–10. This cozy spot has an open kitchen, and Black Angus meats are one of the specialties of the house. The lamb is first-rate, and on occasion you will find ostrich and buffalo on the menu. For lunch there are wraps, pizzas, burgers, and homemade fries. The chef was formerly a pastry chef, so make sure you try one of the signature desserts. I enjoy the filo-wrapped crème brûlée topped with fresh berries and the flourless chocolate espresso torte. Children's menu.

Zona Rosa (845-778-6696), 39 Main Street (Route 52), Walden. ($) Open for dinner Monday through Thursday 4–10; lunch and dinner Friday and Saturday noon–11; Sunday noon–9. The Mexican food here is quite good—as are the prices. There is a nice selection of entrées, including chicken and beef burritos, chimichangas, and enchiladas. The salsa and cheese quesadillas are quite good, and the sangria is made with decent wine from Spain. Children welcome.

In Central Valley and Warwick (South-Central Orange County)

Chateau Hathorn (845-986-6099), 33 Hathorn Road, Warwick. ($$) Open for dinner Wednesday through Saturday 5–9, Sunday 3–7. Enjoy Continental cuisine with a French touch in a restored mansion dating from the 1700s. The menu changes seasonally, but the rack of lamb and châteaubriand are specialties of the house. For dessert try the coupe Denmark: melted Toblerone chocolate served over homemade vanilla ice cream and topped with fresh whipped cream.

Coquito's (845-544-2790), 31 Forester Avenue, Warwick. ($$) Open Tuesday through Sunday for lunch 11–3; dinner 3–9. This eatery specializes in upscale Puerto Rican cooking. The empanadas, seafood stew (lobster, scallops, and shrimp), and flan were excellent when I dined there. On Friday night there is live jazz, and Saturday night features Latin bands. If you are in the Warwick area on a weekend, this is definitely a place to dine.

Crystal Inn (845-258-4232), 12 Amity Road, Warwick. ($$) Open for dinner Tuesday through Sunday 5–9; Friday and Saturday until 10. The contemporary American cuisine here, served in a casual atmosphere, is first-rate. The emphasis is on fresh, organic ingredients. Although there is a large menu, fish lovers will enjoy the wide-ranging choices including snapper, salmon, sea bass, and scallops. All desserts are homemade on the premises. Tasting menu available. Children welcome.

Gasho of Japan (845-928-2277), 365 Route 32, Central Valley. ($$) Open daily, except Sunday, for lunch at noon; dinner at 2:30. This authentic, graceful, 400-year-old farmhouse was dismantled in Japan, shipped to its present site, and reassembled. Gasho features hibachi-style fare: As you sit at heated steel-topped tables, Tokyo-trained chefs dazzle both eye and palate, preparing filet mignon with hibachi snow crab, prime beef, and lobster tail before your very eyes. Shrimp, scallops, and eel are other specialties, and all dinners include soup, salad, vegetables, rice, and tea. After dinner, take a stroll through the Japanese gardens. Children welcome.

Iron Forge Inn (845-986-3411), Iron Forge Road, Bellvale. ($$) Open for dinner Thursday through Saturday 5–9; Sunday 3–8. At the foot of Mount Peter, this historic inn is located on the site of a forge in a Revolutionary-era home dating from 1760. For the past half century it has been known for fine country dining. There are five intimate dining rooms with a warm colonial ambience; the adjoining Tap Room has a lovely bar and fireplace. Contemporary American cuisine that varies seasonally is the fare here. One winter menu included braised short rib of beef, duck breast, five onion and escarole lasagna, and organic salmon; all are prepared creatively. If you prefer light fare, the Tap Room has a pub menu with quesadillas, burgers, wings, and grilled chicken sandwiches. Children welcome.

Landmark Inn (845-986-5444), 526 Route 94 North, Warwick. ($$) Open for dinner Tuesday through Saturday 5–9:30; Sunday 3:30–8. Enjoy contemporary American cuisine in a historic house that dates from 1779. Choose from a wide variety of dishes, including steaks, seafood, chicken, and veal. Make sure to save room for the phenomenal desserts.

In Middletown (Western Orange County)

Blue Finn Grill & Sushi (845-342-5542), 157 Dolson Avenue, Middletown. ($$) Open for lunch Monday through Friday 11:30–2:30; dinner 4:30–9, until 10 Saturday; Sunday 4–9. American cuisine with an Asian accent; steaks, seafood, and sushi are the mainstays. Ginger-crusted salmon and soy-marinated sizzling steak are only a couple of the house specialties. The sushi bar will delight those seeking Japanese fare. Children's menu.

John's Harvest Inn (845-343-6630), 629 North Street, Middletown. ($$) Open for dinner Wednesday through Saturday from 5:30, Sunday 3–8. The Continental cuisine here is very good, and the portions are hearty. The fresh seafood and veal dishes are specialties of the house. There are more than 100 clocks decorating the walls in this cozy inn, which is popular with local residents.

Nina (845-344-6800), 27 West Main Street, Middletown. ($$) Open for lunch Monday through Saturday 11:30–2:30; dinner 5–9, until 10 on weekends. Sunday brunch 10:30–2; dinner 5–8. Eclectic American cuisine with a large menu including steak, seafood, lamb, chicken, and veal entrées. Their shrimp asparagus risotto is renowned. For lunch I especially love the Tuscan summer sandwich (grilled chicken with sun-dried tomato basil pesto and mozzarella cheese on focaccia bread).

The Park (845-342-6634), 339 Route 211, Middletown. ($$) Open daily 11:30–9; until 10 on Friday and Saturday. Enjoy international and American fare that combines the influence of French, Italian, Caribbean, Mediterranean, and Asian cuisines. The large, open dining room with 18-foot ceilings is adjoined by a spacious bar/lounge where evening entertainment is offered on weekends. For an appetizer, make sure to order the Hana spring roll (stuffed with bok choy, tofu, chicken, and bacon, and topped with a balsamic vinegar and passion fruit dressing). The filet mignon au poivre with crabmeat-stuffed shrimp scampi is the house version of surf and turf. A separate sushi bar serves up excellent Japanese favorites.

Saffron Fine Indian Cuisine (845-344-0005), 130 Dolson Avenue, Middletown. ($$) Open daily for lunch buffet 11:30–2:30; dinner 5–10. This is the only Indian/Pakistani restaurant in Orange County, and it's serving up excellent cuisine at moderate prices with classy decor (despite the fact it's in a strip mall). The lunch buffet is a bargain and offers a huge selection of Indian dishes. Definitely a great addition to the Middletown dining scene. Children are always welcome.

Something Sweet (845-343-2233), 17 North Street, Middletown. ($) Open Monday 9–4; Tuesday through Thursday 8–8; Friday and Saturday 8 AM–10:30 PM; Sunday closed. Imaginative creations include Israeli couscous on a bed of baby arugula with grilled shrimp, and baked four-cheese farfalle pasta, and there are sumptuous desserts. In addition to the traditional selections, there is a chocolate-raspberry parfait and hazelnut-praline mousse to choose from. A reason to go to downtown Middletown!

EATING OUT

In Newburgh and Cornwall

Café Fiesta (845-928-2151), 547 Route 32, Highland Mills. ($$) Open daily 11–9; Friday and Saturday until 10. This informal Mexican family restaurant with colorful decor offers a wide-ranging menu, including American fare. In addition to tacos, burritos, chimichangas, and quesadillas, there are vegetarian selections, low-fat dishes, and daily specials. Everything here is made from scratch. Portions are generous, and prices are reasonable. If you're hungry at lunchtime, try the grande burrito, a giant flour tortilla stuffed with "the works"!

Café Pitti (845-565-1444), 40 Front Street, Newburgh. ($$) Open daily for lunch and dinner 11:30–10. This is a wonderful place to go in warm weather to sit outside on the terrace by the waterfront and watch the boats go by on the Hudson. The interior is casual, a place to enjoy salads, personal thin-crust pizza, and paninis. For dessert there is gelato, cappuccino cake, and sorbet. Children welcome.

Commodore's (845-561-3900), 482 Broadway, Newburgh. ($) Open daily 10–6; closed Sunday during the summer. Located in an old-fashioned ice-cream parlor, Commodore's has been in business and run by the same family since 1935. They are famous for their handmade chocolates and candies. There are the usual delicious classics like marzipan and truffles, as well as Swedish fudge and almond bark. In late November call to find out when they start handmade candy cane demonstrations, which are held on weekends noon–4.

Cosimo's on Union (845-567-1556), 1217 Route 300, Newburgh. ($) Open daily 11:30–10 for lunch and dinner.

THERE ARE A NUMBER OF RESTAURANTS ON THE NEWBURGH WATERFRONT.

Orange County Tourism

The specialty here is the brick-oven-baked personal-size pizza. There are dozens of toppings. Also available is a large selection of pasta dishes. The restaurant is very close to Stewart Airport and the NYS Thruway (exit 17). If you are traveling with children, this is a good choice.

Hudson Street Café (845-534-2450), 237 Hudson Street, Cornwall-on-Hudson. ($) Open Monday through Wednesday 6–3; Thursday through Saturday 6 AM–9 PM (dinner served on these nights only); Sunday 6:30–2. This is the kind of place I love: They offer locally grown and fresh organic food at affordable prices. The breakfast and lunch selections—soups, salads, omelets, wraps, and sandwiches—include imaginative variations on standard fare. The offerings are consistently excellent, which is why this eatery is popular with local residents, families, and travelers. I haven't had dinner here yet but intend to soon!

Johnny D's (845-567-1600), 909 Union Avenue, New Windsor. ($) Located just off the NYS Thruway (exit 17), and open 24 hours a day, seven days a week. Salad lovers will be delighted with their extensive menu of "Glorious Salads." My favorite is the Mexicobb Salad, but there are nearly 20 to choose from, as well as more than a dozen types of enticing burgers. This is a diner with an imaginative flair, so expect the ordinary made somewhat extraordinary.

Pamela's on the Hudson (845-562-4505), One Park Place, Newburgh. ($$) Open Thursday through Sunday 3–9; until 10 Friday and Saturday; closed Monday through Wednesday. One of the best views of the Hudson River and the Newburgh-Beacon Bridge is from the dining room here. The romantic atmosphere, with soft candlelight and antiques throughout, creates an ideal spot to relax. The menu features fresh local produce and varies seasonally. An extensive light fare menu, with items like burgers, salads, an imaginative array of tapas, and wings, is always available. Finding this restaurant is a little tricky, so do call for directions.

Prima Pizza (845-534-7003; 1-800-22-NY-PIE), 252 Main Street, Cornwall. ($) Open Monday through Thursday 11–9; Friday and Saturday 11–10; Sunday noon–9. A family restaurant for many years, Prima Pizza's owner, Anthony Scalise, regularly airmails brick-oven-cooked pizzas to places as far away as California. (He was asked to send pizza to the troops in the Middle East during Operation Desert Storm.) The finest blends of mozzarella cheese and fresh dough are made daily. All sauces and meatballs are cooked on the premises, and cholesterol-free oil is used with everything served here. My favorite slice is the fresh basil and tomato. "Sweep the Kitchen," as the name implies, has everything on it. There are calzones, subs, salads, and an array of pasta dishes for those who prefer other Italian specialties.

Wherehouse (845-561-7240), 119 Liberty Street, Newburgh. ($) Open daily 11–11; Sunday until 7. This is the place for terrific comfort food—great ribs, pulled pork, and juicy burgers—as well as several vegetarian selections, including an array of salads, and homemade desserts. The Wherehouse Nachos are renowned in Newburgh. The eatery is located just a couple of blocks away from the waterfront. Children welcome.

Woody's (845-534-1111), 30 Quaker Avenue, Cornwall. ($) Open daily 11:30–8:30. Those who fantasize about fast food burgers that are actually healthy will appreciate Woody's natural beef. They serve locally raised, grass fed/grain-finished beef burgers, hormone-free chicken, local Pine Island onions, and Pennsylvania mushrooms. Milk shakes and malts are made with Jane's ice cream and milk from Hudson Valley dairies. Fries are cooked in trans fat–free canola oil. Located in a restored 1910 building, Woody's atmosphere is casual, with an open kitchen. This is a great place to go when traveling with young children, and the prices are exceedingly reasonable.

In Central Orange County

Elsie's Luncheonette (845-294-5765), 130 West Main Street, Goshen. ($) Open daily 6–2. This old-fashioned eatery specializes in comfort food. For breakfast, the waffles, pancakes, and omelets are good choices. Lunch offerings include fresh meat loaf or turkey and mashed potatoes, and a choice of homemade soups. There are several sandwich and burger choices as well. The kids will love it.

Goshen Gourmet Café (845-294-2800), 14 West Main Street, Goshen. ($) Open Monday through Friday 6–5; Saturday until 3; Sunday 7–2. This delightful spacious gourmet bakery/delicatessen specializes in soups, salads, wraps, and sandwiches. However, the decadent desserts are not to be passed up. My favorite is the chocolate mousse cup. Mouthwatering pastries, cookies, brownies, and cakes make choices difficult here! The sunny dining room is a nice place to enjoy one of their fresh breakfast or lunch creations.

Hacienda Restaurant (845-294-9795), 1753 Route 17M, Goshen. ($) Open daily 11–10 for lunch and dinner. This establishment is owned and operated by the chef, who turns out authentic Mexican fare—tacos, burritos, enchiladas—served in a casual atmosphere. The restaurant is housed in a restored Victorian mansion with a lovely fireplace. Children are welcome.

Vinum Café (845-496-9001), 84 Brotherhood Plaza Drive, Washingtonville. ($) Open Wednesday through Sunday noon–9. Enjoy a cheese platter and glass of wine or dessert and a cappuccino outdoors on the patio at the Brotherhood Winery (see *To See—Wineries*). The café offers a full menu for dinner, but it is a wonderful spot to stop and relax after wine tasting.

In Sugar Loaf & Warwick

The Barnsider Tavern (845-469-9810), 1372 Kings Highway, Sugar Loaf. ($$) Open Tuesday through Sunday from 11. This tavern has a beautiful taproom with handwrought beams, country decor, and a glassed-in patio with a view of the Sugar Loaf Crafts Village (see *Selective Shopping*). A fire is always crackling on the hearth in winter, and the menu of burgers, quiche, and other fine café foods makes this a nice stop for lunch. Children welcome.

Bellvale Farms Creamery (845-988-1818), 385 Route 17A (at intersection of Route 17A and Kain Road, Mount Peter), Warwick. ($) This family farm produces and sells its own ice cream. Open for ice cream April through October, daily noon–9; the main dairy barn is open June through October, Sunday at 12:30, for tours, when visitors may see baby calves being fed and cows getting milked. There are also Holstein cows, a fresh-vegetable stand open during the summer, pick-your-own pumpkins, and hayrides in the fall. This is a great stop for those traveling with children. Closed in the winter months.

Conscious Fork (845-988-KALE), 20 McEwen Street, Warwick. ($) Open year-round, daily 11–7. This farm-to-table vegan juice bar and market serves up smoothies and an array of juice specials. Their Whole Bowl special involves patrons in choosing grains, proteins, and vegetables topped with sauces to create their own delicious salads. The chef, Jamie Manza, worked at Blue Hill at Stone Barns, and the offerings are first-rate.

Jean Claude's Bakery & Dessert Café (845-986-8900), 25 Elm Street, Warwick. ($) Open Wednesday through Saturday 8–6; Sunday 8–3. Those who love fine pastries, brioche, fruit tarts, petits fours, baba au rhum, cream puffs, and handmade truffles should be sure to stop at this fantastic bakery.

La Petite Cuisine (845-988-0988), 20 Railroad Avenue, Warwick. ($$) Open Tuesday through Saturday 10–4; Sunday 9–4. Closed Monday. This French-style café is a real find for breakfast or lunch, and it specializes in soups, large salads, and sweet and savory crêpes of all kinds. The croissants and Lavazza coffee are prized among local residents. For breakfast the baked egg casserole (filled with fresh veggies or ham) is a wonderful variation on the usual omelet offerings. At lunchtime, I enjoy the mixed fresh greens accompanied by Gorgonzola cheese and sliced pears and topped with toasted pecans.

In Western Orange County

Jack's Irish Pub at Caitlin Gardens (845-355-3555), 2865 Route 6, Slate Hill. ($$) Open Wednesday through Sunday for lunch noon–3; dinner 5–9. This is a comfortable place to unwind and enjoy drinks and light fare at the large mahogany bar.

Pleasant Stone Farm (845-343-4040), 130 Dolson Avenue, Middletown. ($) Open Monday through Friday noon–4. This organic café and juice bar offers up some wonderfully fresh lunch and snack items, including soups, salads, paninis, and traditional sandwiches. All kinds of juices are available as well. A true oasis in Middletown. Children welcome.

Something Sweet (845-343-2233), 17 North Street, Middletown. ($) Open Monday 8–4; Tuesday through Thursday 8–8; Friday 8 AM–10:30 PM; Saturday 10 AM–10:30 PM. Closed Sunday. Everything here is freshly prepared, and there is something to suit just about every taste. The lunch fare includes soups, salads, baked Brie, bruschetta, salmon salad, and hummus, to name just some of the offerings. For dessert there are muffins, scones, turnovers, and cookies of all kinds. The dinner menu changes seasonally and is reasonably priced. Children are welcome.

* Entertainment

Eisenhower Hall Theatre (845-938-4159; www.eisenhowerhall.com), U.S. Military Academy, West Point. This is the second largest theater in the country (Radio City Music Hall is the biggest), and it offers a variety of entertainment, including Broadway touring companies, comedy, and pop, rock, and classical music. Also a venue for ballet and opera.

Jesters Comedy Club (845-345-1039; www.jesterscomedyclubny.com), 109 Brookside Avenue, Chester. This club showcases fine comedic talent from all over the metropolitan region—and beyond. The shows are on Friday and Saturday nights, and there are dinner packages offered as well. Check the website for an up-to-date schedule.

Lycian Centre (845-469-2287; www.lyciancentre.com), 1351 Kings Highway, Sugar Loaf. Opened in 1993, this 668-seat theater offers nearly 40 shows every year, many by its own Kings Theatre Company. They also showcase professional dance, musicals, and children's entertainment.

The Paramount Theatre (845-346-4195; www.bigscreenclassics.com), 17 South Street, Middletown. This venue offers music, dance, theater, and children's performances year-round. Check their website for a current schedule.

Railroad Playhouse (845-565-3791; www.rrplayhouse.org), 27 South Water Street, Newburgh. This unusual noteworthy theater is open year-round and showcases award-winning emerging new playwrights. The offerings range from comedy to drama, and a detailed schedule of performances is listed on their website.

Ritz Theater (845-784-1199; www.ritztheaternewburgh.org), 107 Broadway, Newburgh. There is an eclectic mix of entertainment being presented in this beautifully renovated theater—folk music, performance artists of all kinds, and children's programs. Do check the website to see a complete schedule.

✷ Selective Shopping

ANTIQUES The love of history found across Orange County extends to a love of antiques and collectibles, and many shops cater to the connoisseur. Some of my favorites are the following places:

Arnell's Gift Center & Fine Antiques (845-477-8747), 88 Windermere Avenue, Greenwood Lake. Open Monday through Saturday 10–5. Two floors of antique furniture are here, along with a large quantity of glass and silver.

Country Heritage Antiques Center (845-800-8955), 112 Maple Avenue (Route 302), Pine Bush. Open Thursday through Sunday 11–5:30 or by appointment. Furniture of all types is the specialty here. There is a good-size collection of armoires, cupboards, desks, bookcases, china closets, dressers, beds, tables, and chairs.

A number of antiques and novelty stores have clustered in the historic village of **Montgomery** in recent years, making it a great stop for those wanting to take a short break from traveling. It is a wonderful place to stroll or browse, whether you are traveling north or south. Make sure to stop in at the **Clinton Shops** (845-457-5392), 84 Clinton Street, where there are several shops open year-round with a variety of items.

Orange County Antique Fair & Flea Market (845-282-4055; www.ocfleamarkets.com), 100 Carpenter Avenue, Middletown. Open April through November, Saturday and Sunday 8–5. The Orange County fairgrounds are a wonderful venue for this large marketplace filled with antiques, furniture, china, and all kinds of treasures. There is free parking and free admission; this fair will delight bargain hunters and browsers alike.

Tuxedo Antiques Center (845-351-4466), 538 Route 17, Tuxedo. Open Thursday through Monday 11:30–5. There are several dealers under one roof, and the center is located 1 mile north of the village of Tuxedo.

ART GALLERIES Ann Street Gallery (845-784-1146), 104 Ann Street, Newburgh. Open Monday through Thursday 9–5; Friday and Saturday 11–5. Closed Sunday. This nonprofit gallery specializes in contemporary art and shows both emerging and established artists. The focus here is on cross-cultural and intergenerational subjects.

Art House (845-610-3930), 1397 Kings Highway, Sugar Loaf. Open Thursday through Saturday 11–5; Sunday noon–5. This spacious cooperative gallery shows high-quality oils, watercolors, sculpture, and handcrafted jewelry and photographs. There are a number of workshops and special events as well.

Exposures Gallery (845-469-9382), 1357 Kings Highway, Sugar Loaf. Open Thursday through Sunday 11–5. Hudson Valley landscape photographer Nick Zungoli displays his photographs of the region as well as those of his travels throughout the world. He has been photographing the region for over 30 years, and his work is stunning.

Wallkill River School & Gallery (845-457-2787), 232 Ward Street, Montgomery. Open Monday through Saturday 9–6. The gallery here features exhibits of local plein air artists throughout the year. The school describes itself as a fusion of plein air painting and environmental activism. If you are in the area, the gallery is definitely worth a visit.

AUCTIONS Auctions are usually held on a regular basis, whether once a month or once a week. Estate sales may provide the antiquer or junker with everything from Persian rugs to eccentric collectibles. The best way to locate what's going on where is to check the classified listings in a local newspaper. Flea markets are another treat springing up on warm weekends; look for markets that jumble together new and old rather than just offering overstock and discontinued items. Most auctions and markets will not accept out-of-state checks; they will accept credit cards (most of the time), cash, and traveler's checks.

Mark Vail Auction Services (845-744-2120; www.markvailauction.com), 188 Kelly Avenue, Pine Bush, has antiques and estate auctions approximately twice a month. Call or check the website for dates.

Old Red Barn Auctions (845-754-7122; www.oldredbarnauction.com), 35 Route 211, Cuddebackville, has weekend auctions the first Saturday of the month.

Pine Bush Auction (845-457-4404; www.pinebushauction.com), 157 Ward Street, Montgomery, holds auctions every other Tuesday year-round. Call or check the website for a schedule.

CRAFTS **Clearwaters Distinctive Gifts & Jones Farm Country Store** (845-534-4445), 190 Angola Road, Cornwall. Open every day year round, weekdays 8–6, weekends until 5. Since 1914 this fifth-generation family farm has served the Hudson Valley with homegrown produce, fresh eggs, maple syrup, honey, preserves, coffees, and many gourmet items. Grandma Phoebe's kitchen features homemade baked goods, cream and butter fudge, and wonderful apple cider doughnuts. Children are always welcome to visit the animals and enjoy the observation beehive. The second floor of the store is an enormous gift shop with books, china, novelty items, and wonderful handcrafted goods. This store makes an interesting stop in Cornwall, a lovely village with a number of fine shops and restaurants.

Sugar Loaf Crafts Village (www.sugarloafny.com). Take exit 16 off the NYS Thruway to Route 17, and go west for 8 miles to exit 127; follow the signs. Open year-round, Tuesday through Sunday 11–5. Named for the local mountain that is shaped the way sugar was during colonial times, Sugar Loaf—with its bare crest—has been the subject of unusual speculation. Originally the mountain was a Native American burial ground, and over the years various relics and bones have been uncovered there. Once a bustling stagecoach and river stop, the area lost its prominence when the railroads bypassed it in the mid-19th century. But over the last 30 years, Sugar Loaf has regained its spirit. Home to dozens of craftspeople who live and work in many of the buildings along Kings Highway and Woods Road, the village is a terrific place to find a special gift or add to a collection. Visitors will find handcrafted stained glass, pottery, paintings, photography, and jewelry. As befits an art colony, there are crafts fairs and art shows throughout the year, as well as a fall festival and holiday caroling. The village is charming; an excellent place to spend an afternoon talking to a number of artists at work in their studios. Visitors will do lots of walking; parking is at either end of the village in well-marked lots.

FACTORY OUTLETS If you ever tire of taking in the beauty of Orange County, there is always shopping to enjoy—and plenty of it. Factory outlets have come a long way from the dingy shops of the past, and a stop at **Woodbury Common** (845-928-4000), 498 Red Apple Court (off Route 32), Central Valley (open daily year-round, except major holidays), will prove this. There are more than 200 shops in this colonial-style mall, selling everything from shoes, clothing, sweaters, and watches to toys, wallets, crystal, and stockings. The mall sponsors special events throughout the year, and there is a large food court.

Gillinder Glass (845-856-5375), 39–55 Erie Street, Port Jervis. Open Monday through Friday 9:30–5:30; Saturday 9:30–4; Sunday noon–4. Call ahead for tour times and group information. This site offers visitors a rare chance to watch glass being heated, molded, shaped, and cooled into fine collectibles. The factory, which has an on-site shop, has a viewing area, and the furnaces glow as the craftspeople use the same techniques employed a century ago. After a tour, stop by the **Tri-States Monument** (at the junction of the Neversink and Delaware rivers, Laurel Grove Cemetery). Just under the I-84 bridge is a rock on which you

SUGAR LOAF CRAFTS VILLAGE

Orange County Tourism

Orange County Tourism

WOODBURY COMMON

can stand in three states (New York, Pennsylvania, and New Jersey) at once; it also notes the boundary between New York and New Jersey.

TWG Fabric Outlet (845-343-3423), 115 Wisner Avenue, Middletown, specializes in decorative fabrics and is an exclusive importer of 60-inch lace. They are open Monday through Thursday 9:30–6; Friday 9:30–1; Sunday 11–4. Closed Saturday.

✷ Special Events

March: **Hudson Valley Restaurant Week** (845-561-2022; www.hudsonvalleyrestaurantweek.com). This event takes place at several restaurants throughout the region. Celebrate the culinary riches of the valley by enjoying three-course prix-fixe lunches and dinners for two weeks, Sunday through Friday. Beverages, tax, and gratuity are additional. Register by calling or going to the website.

April: **Brigade of the American Revolution Spring Encampment** (845-561-1765), New Windsor Cantonment, 374 Temple Hill Road, Vails Gate (see *To See—Historic Sites*). The last encampment of the Continental Army is reenacted. This event is usually scheduled for a weekend in mid-April on both Saturday and Sunday between 10 and 4. Call or check the website for exact date and schedule of events at the site. Admission fee.

Earth Day at Rogowski Farm (845-258-4574), 327 Glenwood Road, Pine Island. Celebrate the environment at the open house on the farm. There are tours, chef demonstrations with the crops, and vendors of all kinds. Free and open to all, 10–4 (usually the third Saturday of April).

July–August: **Orange County Fair** (845-343-4826; www.orangecountyfair.com), 239 Wisner Avenue (fairgrounds), Middletown. Dates are usually mid-July to early August; gates open at noon. Admission fee. One of the oldest county fairs in New York State, this one started as an agricultural display between 1818 and 1825.

Local interest did not really begin to build until 1841, however, when the New York State Agricultural Society entered the picture. From then on the fair was a hit. The 1841 extravaganza featured horses, cows, pigs, farm exhibits, and races; a visit to the fair today will turn up top-name entertainment, scores of food booths, thrill-a-minute rides, and some unique events such as pig racing, where swift-footed swine dash for the purse: a cookie. Native American shows, stock-car racing, and petting zoos are also on-site, along with the finest local produce and livestock and even an old-fashioned tent circus.

July–September: **New York Renaissance Faire** (845-351-5171, after June 1; www.renfair.com), 600 Route 17A, Sterling Forest, Tuxedo Park; watch for signs. Open late July through mid-September, weekends only. Call for exact dates and hours. Admission fee. Knights and ladies, sorcerers and their apprentices, fools and varlets, bumpkins and wantons all gather on the glorious grounds of Sterling Forest to re-create the lusty days of a merry olde English fair. The festival runs for eight consecutive weekends and presents a colorful, noisy look at a misty period of time somewhere between King Arthur and Shakespeare. Falconers show off the skills of their birds, opera and Shakespeare are presented at the Globe Theatre, Maid Marian flirts with Robin Hood, ladies dance beneath a maypole, and the extensive rose gardens are open for strolling. Craftspeople display and sell their wares (many belong to the Society for Creative Anachronism and stock things like chain-mail shirts), and the aromas of "steak on a stake," mead, and cheese pie flavor the air. There are jugglers, knife throwers, mud fights, and a living chess game in which the "pieces" wander the gardens to their squares. The actors play their roles throughout the entire festival, so authenticity combines with the personal touch. Kids adore the noise and action, and there is enough to see and do for everyone.

September: **Barn Dance** (845-258-4574), Rogowski Farm, 327 Glenwood Road, Pine Island. A wonderful child-friendly event with live music, barbecue, and an evening of old-fashioned family fun; the farm is also a great place to enjoy a picnic dinner. **Orange County Onion Festival** (845-651-4266) is held annually, rain or shine, on the Sunday of Labor Day weekend at the Pavilion in Pine Island. Admission fee. There is always live music, which often includes Jimmy Sturr and his orchestra.

Sullivan County

3

FisherMears Associates

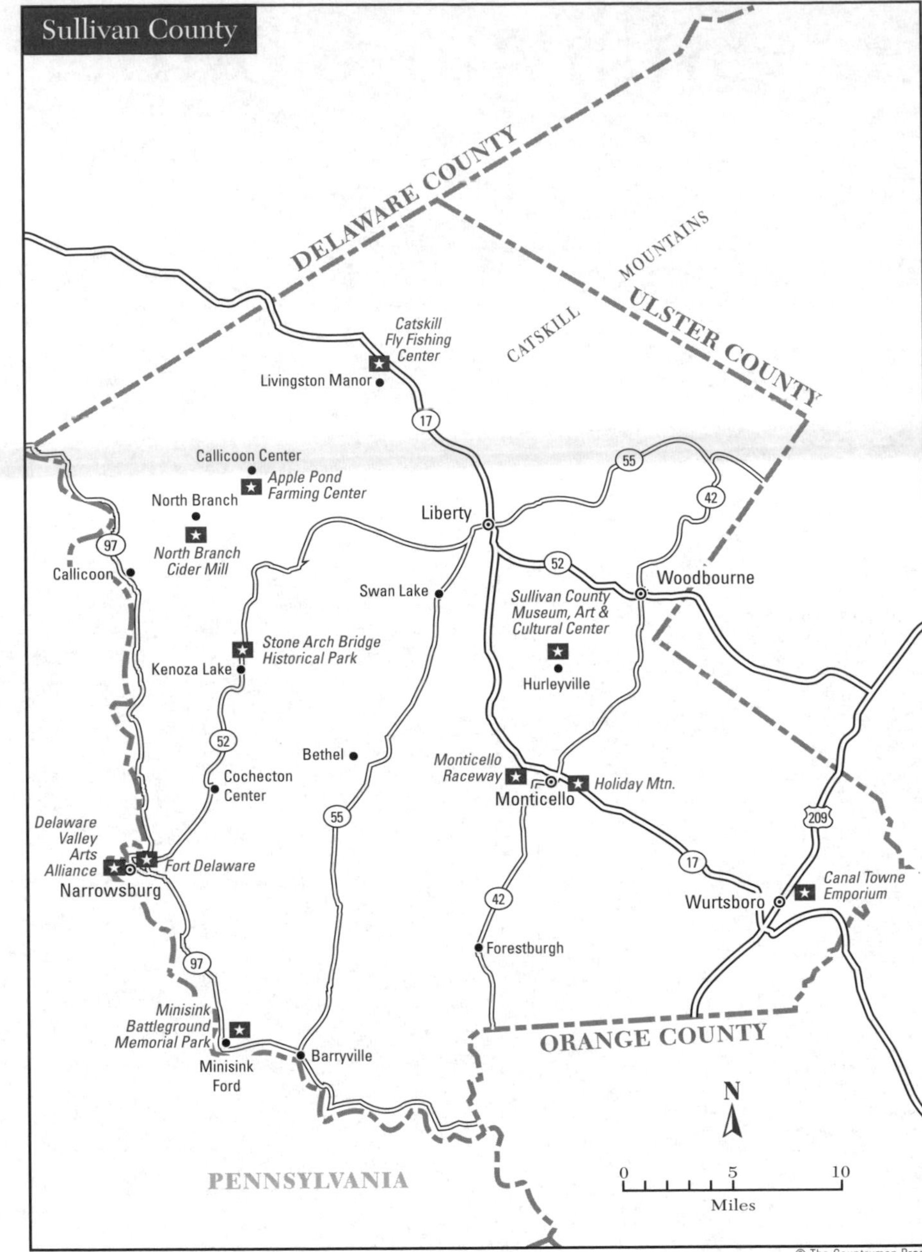
Sullivan County
DELAWARE COUNTY
CATSKILL
MOUNTAINS
ULSTER COUNTY
Catskill Fly Fishing Center
Livingston Manor
17
Callicoon Center
Apple Pond Farming Center
North Branch
North Branch Cider Mill
Liberty
55
42
52
Woodbourne
97
Callicoon
Swan Lake
Sullivan County Museum, Art & Cultural Center
Hurleyville
Stone Arch Bridge Historical Park
Kenoza Lake
52
Bethel
Cochecton Center
Monticello Raceway
Holiday Mtn.
Monticello
209
Delaware Valley Arts Alliance
Fort Delaware
Narrowsburg
55
17
42
Canal Towne Emporium
Wurtsboro
Forestburgh
97
Minisink Battleground Memorial Park
Minisink Ford
Barryville
ORANGE COUNTY
N
PENNSYLVANIA
0
5
10
Miles

SULLIVAN COUNTY

Only 90 miles northwest of New York City lies Sullivan County: 1,000 square miles of outdoor treasures. The Delaware River snakes along the county border and down into Pennsylvania, where the rugged, untamed countryside is home to bald eagles. To the north, visitors will discover the charm of tranquil, silvery lakes, lush forests, and narrow valleys where tiny villages nestle alongside bubbling streams. Sullivan also offers some of the world's best trout fishing, and on opening day of the season—rain or snow—rods and flies are taken from basements and garages across the county in pursuit of the annual dream of catching "the big one." Only a small percentage of the county is considered agricultural, but there are dairy and pick-your-own farms as well as abundant orchards. A drive through Sullivan County is a reminder that not too long ago this area was the frontier, a place where bears, bobcats, and the mysterious panther haunted the uneasy sleep of woodsmen and pioneers.

GUIDANCE **Sullivan County Visitors Association** (845-747-4449; 1-800-882-CATS), County Government Center, 100 Sullivan Avenue, Ferndale 12734; www.scva.net.

Liberty Chamber of Commerce (845-292-9797), P.O. Box 147, Liberty 12754; www.libertychamber.org.

Roscoe Chamber of Commerce, P.O. Box 443, Roscoe 12776; www.roscoeny.com.

Wurtsboro Board of Trade, P.O. Box 907, Wurtsboro 12790; www.wurtsboro.org.

GETTING THERE *By car:* Sullivan County is accessible from Route 17 (future Route 86) and Route 209. You can pick up Route 17 at NYS Thruway exit 16 (Harriman).

By bus: **Rolling V Transportation Services** (845-434-0511; 1-800-999-6593), 5008 Main Street, South Fallsburg, provides bus and limo services for the local area as well as long distance. **Short Line/Coach USA** (1-800-631-8405; www.shortlinebus.com), 45 Sturgis Road, Monticello, offers frequent express service from the Port Authority Bus Terminal in Manhattan as well as other parts of the metropolitan area.

By air: **Stewart International Airport** (845-564-2100), 1035 First Street, New Windsor, has service to major East Coast cities daily. Charter service and private

FisherMears Associates

DELAWARE RIVER

aircraft can be accommodated at **Sullivan County International Airport** (845-583-6600), 57 Route 183A, White Lake, and **Wurtsboro Airport** (845-888-2791), 50 Barone Road, Wurtsboro.

MEDICAL EMERGENCY **Catskill Regional Medical Center** (845-794-3300), 68 Harris Bushville Road, Harris, or **Grover Hermann Division** (845-887-5530), 8881 Route 97, Callicoon.

✷ To See

Bethel Woods Center for the Arts (1-866-781-2922; www.bethelwoodscenter.org), 200 Hurd Road, Bethel. Open Memorial Day weekend through Labor Day, daily 10–7, with extended hours on concert days; the rest of the year, Thursday through Sunday 10–5. Check the website for performance schedule. The actual **Woodstock Festival Site,** now part of Bethel Woods Center for the Arts, is on Hurd Road, in Bethel, not in Woodstock (Ulster County), more than 50 miles away. This is where it happened: three days of peace, mud, and rock 'n' roll, where 400,000 gathered in August 1969. This state-of-the-art performance venue (including an interpretive center/museum) opened in 2006 and features jazz, classical, and country music, as well as pop and rock. There are 4,800 seats under a pavilion and lawn space for up to 12,000; the 6,348-square-foot stage is twice the size of Radio City Music Hall. Bethel and the surrounding countryside is beautiful, a good place for a leisurely drive, a walk, or a picnic. The self-guided tour of the museum is a must-see for anyone who lived through the 1960s, as well as those who are interested in the decade. The museum is beautifully designed for wandering and is filled with displays, videos, and audiovisual experiences, as well as a 21-minute film, *Woodstock: The Music*. The high-definition images and surround sound in this captivating film capture the highlights of the 1969 festival. Additionally, the performing artists of the concert reflect on these inspiring and emotional experiences four decades ago.

Catskill Fly-Fishing Center and Museum (845-439-4810; www.cffcm.net), 1031 Old Route 17, Livingston Manor. Open April through October, daily 10–4; November through March, Monday through Saturday 10–4. Admission fee. Dry fly-fishing enthusiasts will certainly find a lot to do in Sullivan County, where they will discover some of the best trout streams in the nation. Visitors should not miss this museum, located on 53 acres along Willowemoc Creek. There is a changing exhibit of fly-fishing equipment (such as rods, reels, and flies), memorabilia, a library, and a hall of fame; it also presents the story of Lee Wulff, a streamside legend, who brought elegance and science to the fly-fishing art. Special appearances by well-known anglers and craftspeople take place during the summer season, and there are special events, including workshops, seminars, and just-plain-fun get-togethers.

The Eagle Institute (845-557-6162; www.eagleinstitute.org), P.O. Box 182, Barryville 12719. Open January through March, weekends only. Sullivan County attracts more bald eagles than anywhere else on the East Coast, drawn by the open waters and virgin forests. Every winter more than a hundred eagles migrate here from Canada, and in the spring they return north. The county now has an information clearinghouse for migratory and breeding eagle data, and it is open to the public. On-site interpretive programs are offered on weekends during the winter months, when the eagles are migrating. The birds are sure to intrigue just about

BETHEL WOODS CENTER FOR THE ARTS

FisherMears Associates

everyone, but children who have learned about eagles in school will particularly enjoy this stop. There are workshops, slide presentations, and guided eagle watches to habitat areas. Call ahead for schedule information; this is one of the few Sullivan County attractions where winter is high season.

Sullivan County Museum, Art and Cultural Center (845-434-8044; www.schs.org), 265 Main Street, Hurleyville. Open year-round, except January, Tuesday through Saturday 10–4:30; Sunday 1–4:30. An array of changing exhibits complements the permanent ones that relate the history of the region. One focuses on Frederick Albert Cook, an early-20th-century explorer who, in addition to being a physician and anthropologist, was the first American to travel to both the North and South Poles. The website lists a variety of special events at the museum year-round. They are one of the few places in the area that offer several fun activities during the winter months.

HISTORIC SITES **Apple Pond Farm and Renewable Energy Education Center** (845-482-4764; www.applepondfarm.com), 80 Hahn Road, Callicoon Center (call ahead for detailed directions). Open year-round, daily by appointment. Admission fee. Today most farms are run with advanced technology as older agricultural methods and theories are slowly being lost in an avalanche of computer information. But there are still many farmers who cherish the old ways and believe that if the land is worked well, it will yield a bountiful harvest. At Apple Pond, an educational center and working farm, visitors can judge for themselves the merits of organic farming practices, wind turbines, renewable energy sources, and sustainable agricultural practices. Visitors can enjoy one of several different tours, including Farming with Kids, Solar Sundays, and Alotta Ricotta, a cheese-making tour. The farm is stocked with sheep, draft horses, milking goats, and free-range chickens. Special activites like renewable-energy workshops, spinning, and cheese-making demonstrations and classes are held throughout the year, but most activities require reservations. The website has a list of special events, which are held throughout the spring, summer, and fall months. The gift shop offers items made with farm products, including honey and maple syrup. There is a pet-friendly three-bedroom guesthouse at the farm that is available for rental year-round, and visitors can participate in farm activities. Don't expect a quaint little restoration here, and do expect to get some mud on your shoes!

Fort Delaware Museum of Colonial History (845-252-6660), 6615 Route 97, Narrowsburg. Open Memorial Day weekend; weekends in June; late June until Labor Day, Friday through Monday 10–5. Admission fee. Much attention is paid to the people who settled the main cities of New York, but those who decided to take on the wilderness are often forgotten. At the Fort Delaware Museum, the daily life of the backwoods settler is explored through exhibits, crafts demonstrations, and tours. The fort is a reconstruction of the original frontier settlement of Cushetunk on the Delaware River, with its stockades and stout log homes, which offered the only protection from Native Americans and, later, English troops. The fort consists of a small settlement entirely surrounded by high log walls, or stockades. During the tour, visitors see the blockhouses (where arms and ammunition were stored), settlers' cabins, a meetinghouse, a blacksmith shop, a candle shed, a loom shed, and more. Outside the fort walls you'll find a small garden planted with crops typical of the era. Costumed guides and staff members demonstrate skills and crafts from the period, including candle making, blacksmithing, and even weaponry. Special events are scheduled throughout the season, so your visit may include a show by Revolutionary War soldiers, weavers, or cooks. There is an excellent gift shop here, so make sure to stop and check it out.

Minisink Battleground Memorial Park (www.minisink.org), Route 168, Minisink Ford. Open May through October, daily dawn to dusk. Free. One of the unusual and forgotten Revolutionary War battlegrounds in the region, this site offers visitors a chance to walk along trails that tell stories of both nature and combat. In July 1779 the area's most important historic battle took place when a group of American rebels were defeated by Mohawks in a massacre that took almost 50 lives. In an eerie postscript, the bones of the dead were not gathered and buried until more than 40 years after the battle because the area was wilderness, and not many people visited.

Today the 56-acre park has three walking trails from which to explore its history and the surrounding natural setting. The blazed trails have descriptive markers that tell the story of the area, and written trail guides can be picked up at the interpretive center. The **Battleground Trail** depicts the tactics and strategy of a woodland skirmish and includes stops at Sentinel Rock, where the lone American defender was killed; Hospital Rock, where a rebel doctor lost his life while tending to his wounded charges; and Indian Rock, which legend says was set up to commemorate the dead. The **Woodland Trail** meanders through wetland, dense foliage, and a variety of ferns. The park map points out the trail's flora and describes some of the animal life you may encounter, such as foxes, wood frogs, raccoons, and maybe even a bald eagle. On the **Old Quarry/Rockshelter Trail,** discover the logging, quarrying, and Native American histories of this section through trail markers. You may also want to plan a visit to the battleground in time for the small memorial service held each July 22, the anniversary of the fight, to honor those who fell here.

Roebling's Suspension Bridge. Look for the historical marker opposite the entrance to the Minisink Battleground. Built by the designer of the Brooklyn Bridge, this crossing on the Delaware River is the oldest of its kind still standing. The aqueduct was constructed because canal boats and logging rafts kept crashing into one another on the river; the aqueduct would actually carry the canal boats over the river itself. The aqueduct was turned into a bridge crossing in the late 19th century, and today it still carries traffic across to Pennsylvania.

SCENIC DRIVES Sullivan County has more than 1,000 square miles of countryside, so just about any drive through the county will take you past exquisite views that change with the seasons: The earliest blush of spring may be enjoyed by driving along any back road, or even on the Quickway (Route 17); summer is lush and lazy anywhere you turn; fall splashes the meadows and forests with color; and winter here is strikingly beautiful. Sullivan County offers detailed theme driving tours in their county literature (call 1-800-882-CATS for a copy). The following trips are my own favorites.

If you want to travel the southernmost section of Sullivan County and see some spectacular river and mountain scenery, start your tour in Monticello. From there head south on Route 42 to Sackett Lake Road (you will go through a town called Squirrel Corners), and keep going south to Forestburgh Road, where you will make a right. This is the reservoir area of **Mongaup Falls,** a good spot to sight bald eagles. At Route 97 head west along the snaking river drive known as **Hawk's Nest,** with its views of New York and Pennsylvania; you will pass Minisink Battleground Park and Roebling's Suspension Bridge (see *Historic Sites*). Head north on Route 52 to Liberty, where you can pick up Route 17 back to Monticello.

A second drive, which will take you past some of the few remaining **covered bridges** in the county, begins at Livingston Manor (exit 96 off Route 17). Turn onto Old Route 17 from the Vantran covered bridge, built in 1860 and one of the few existing bridges constructed in the lattice-truss and queen-post styles. Go back to Livingston Manor and follow the signs east from town along DeBruce Road to Willowemoc, which has a covered bridge that was built in 1860 in Livingston Manor, then cut in half and moved to its present site in 1913. From Willowemoc, take Pole Road to West Branch Road, which leads into Claryville. The Halls Mills covered bridge, built in 1912, is on Claryville Road over the Neversink River. Head south from Claryville to Route 55, then west back to Liberty.

Another sight worth making time to see is **Tomasco Falls,** often called the Niagara of Sullivan County. These spectacular waterworks are a refreshing sight on a hot spring or summer's day but are particularly dramatic after heavy rains. To get

FisherMears Associates

FisherMears Associates

there, take Route 209 to Kerhonkson. Turn onto County Route 55, and follow to Mountaindale. The falls are visible from this road.

Other roads that offer outstanding views include State Routes 209, 55, and 55A. Route 17 is the major north–south road through Sullivan County and provides access to most of the region's scenic areas and byways.

WINERIES AND DISTILLERIES **BashaKill Vineyards** (845-888-5858), 1131 South Road, Wurtsboro. Open year-round, Saturday noon–6; Memorial Day weekend through September, Sunday noon–6. This is Sullivan County's first commercial winery, and they offer both white and red wines. There is no charge for sampling four different wines.

Catskill Distilling Company (845-583-3141), 2037 Route 17B, Bethel. Open year-round, Friday 2–8; Saturday noon–8; Sunday noon–7. The owner, Monte Sachs, a veterinarian as well as a distiller, is often on hand to take visitors on a tour of the facility, where he created Peace Vodka in the same town where the 1969 Woodstock Festival took place. Artisan distilled spirits from New York State–grown products include bourbon, grappa, and gin as well. There is a beautiful bar rescued from the 1939 World's Fair in New York City. Make sure to have a meal at the Dancing Cat Saloon (see *Dining Out*), on the premises, where the food is first-rate.

Eminence Road Farm Winery (845-887-6282), 3734 Eminence Road, Long Eddy. Open year-round, Saturday 10–6; by chance or by appointment at other times. The red and white wines created here are naturally fermented and are unrefined and unfiltered. There are several wines to choose from: riesling, pinot noir, cabernet franc, and cabernet sauvignon, to name just some available for tasting and purchase.

✷ To Do

BICYCLING Liberty Bike Trail (1-800-516-0422, ext. 3; www.libertybiketrail.org), intersection of Chestnut and West streets, Liberty. Open year-round. Free. This 2.62-mile rustic trail, excellent for biking or walking, was formerly part of the O & W Rail Line. It is a great choice for families with young children. There are benches along the way where bikers can stop and rest.

Rails-To-Trails (845-434-7447), Greenfield Road, Woodridge. Open year-round. Free. This rail trail leads west and east of the village. No motorized vehicles are permitted on the trail, and it is open for walking, biking, and cross-country skiing.

Walnut Mountain Park (845-292-7690; www.townofliberty.org), 73 Walnut Mountain Road, Liberty. Open May through September, daily 8–dusk. This 265-acre public park has miles of hiking and biking trails.

CANOEING, KAYAKING, AND RAFTING Canoeists, kayakers, and rafters enjoy the Delaware River's rapids and eddies from spring to fall. Both the Upper Delaware (from Hancock to Port Jervis) and the main section of the river (from Port Jervis to the Chesapeake) are used for recreation, although there are sections that are particularly good for novices and the less adventurous. As with any other water sport, a few guidelines and suggestions will make your trip comfortable and safe. Most rental agencies require that you know how to swim and that flotation gear be worn by anyone in a canoe or raft—it may look harmless, but the Delaware can reach depths of 15 feet. For your own comfort, take along sunscreen, lightweight sneakers, extra clothing, snacks, and a hat. If you go early in the season, the water may be higher and colder than if you go in late July or the month of August. The following companies rent equipment, and some offer a return trip to your starting point. Although you don't need to make a reservation, on busy summer and holiday weekends it may pay to call before you go. Rates are often lower midweek.

Cedar Rapids Kayak and Canoe Outfitters (845-557-6158), 3799 Route 97 (at Cedar Rapids Campgrounds), Barryville, has double and single kayaks, canoes, rafts, and tubes for rent; there is also a nice riverside restaurant where you can have refreshments and watch the fun.

Kittatinny Canoes (1-800-FLOAT-KC), 3854 Route 97, north of Barryville, is one of the oldest (more than 60 years) operating canoe-rental companies, and it also has rafts, tubes, and kayaks. They offer camping and special discounts.

The **Kittatinny Zip Line,** open May through October, is 3,000 feet long and extends from the mountaintop overlooking the Delaware River Valley down to the valley floor. After a raft or canoe trip, this is an exciting way to end the day!

Lander's River Trips (1-800-836-0366; 1-800-252-3925), 5961 Route 97, Narrowsburg, has campgrounds for guests in addition to full river equipment (canoes, tubes, kayaks, and rafts) for rent.

The following companies also rent equipment: **Jerry's Three River Canoe Corporation** (845-557-6078), Pond Eddy; **Silver Canoe Rentals** (845-856-7055; 1-800-724-8342), Pond Eddy; **Whitewater Willie's Raft and Canoe Rentals** (1-800-233-7238), Pond Eddy; **Indian Head Canoes** (845-557-8777; 1-800-874-BOAT), Barryville.

FARM STANDS AND PICK-YOUR-OWN Nothing tastes like fruits and vegetables that still have the blush of the sun and the mist of the morning on them. Harvesting begins in Sullivan County in late spring with asparagus and berries and ends in late fall with pumpkins and apples (although some stands stock local eggs, maple syrup, and honey year-round). Hours vary with the season and type of harvest, and not all stands are open daily, so it is suggested that you call before you make a special trip. There are also lots of small, family-run farm stands that carry only one or two items and are open for only a few weeks a year; keep an eye out for these, too. They often have unusual selections or heirloom varieties. Whether you pick the produce yourself or buy from a roadside stand, the selection and quality in Sullivan County are excellent.

Many area farmers attend the **Sullivan County Area Farmers Market** (845-292-6180), with locations in five towns: In Bethel on Hurd Road, the market is held mid-August to early October, Sunday 11–3:30. In Callicoon Creek Park in Callicoon, the market is held mid-May through early November, Sunday 11–2. In Liberty (Darbee Lane) the market is held mid-May through mid-October, Friday 3–6. In Jeffersonville's west village parking lot, the market is held mid-May through early October, Thursday 2–6. In Roscoe the market is held mid-May through October, Sunday 11–2.

Butterfly Botanicals (845-733-7713), 363 Petticoat Lane, Bloomingburg. Open mid-May through mid-October, Sunday through Thursday 9–5, Friday and Saturday 9–7. There are live butterfly exhibits here and a hands-on educational environment that will particularly delight the kids. There are also perennials and annuals for sale in the greenhouse.

Diehl Farm (845-887-4935), 614 Gabel Road, Callicoon, is a well-stocked stand with a full range of local crops, from apples to eggs and dairy products. Call for hours.

Knaub's Farm (845-252-3781), 1168 County Route 23, Narrowsburg, is a roadside farm stand selling seasonal produce, eggs, pies, cakes, Christmas trees, cider, and candy apples. Open Memorial Day through Christmas Eve, weekends and holidays, Saturday 9:30–7, Sunday 10–4.

Neversink Farm (845-985-2519), Claryville Road, Claryville. Open year-round, Thursday through Sunday 9–5. This certified organic farm produces first-rate vegetables and fruits for sale throughout the year. In August and September you can pick your own raspberries. There is a farmhouse with four bedrooms for rent on the premises; it is ideal for a farm vacation. The kids will enjoy the animals here as well.

Peaceful Breeze Farm & Alpacas (845-794-1111), 3301 State Highway 42, Monticello. Open May through October, daily 10–5. There are approximately 20 alpacas and crias (baby alpacas) born every year from spring through fall. There is also an organic garden with fresh eggs for sale. The kids will see what raw fiber looks like as well as several finished products made from the fiber. Tours of the farm last about an hour, and picnics are permitted on the grounds.

River Brook Farm (845-932-7952), 18 C. Meyer Road, Cochecton, will provide heirloom potatoes along with beans, carrots, garlic, and lots of other greenery. Open July through November, Saturday 10–2.

Rosehaven Alpacas (845-953-2506), 540 County Route 164, Callicoon. Open weekends by appointment year-round. This alpaca farm has 100 alpacas for visitors to pet and enjoy.

Sonoma Falls Cider Mill & Country Market (845-439-4949), 140 Old Liberty Road, Morsston. Open year-round, daily 9–5. There is a seven-tier waterfall here, with hiking trails, fishing (for fee per pound), and apple cider pressing, with snow tubing and ice skating in the winter months. During maple syrup season, this is a great place to go to see the tapping of the trees. The store offers local produce, gifts, and ice cream. There is also a café on the premises that serves breakfast and lunch (see *Eating Out*).**Vita's Farm & Garden Market** (845-482-5776), 4789 State Route 52, Jeffersonville, is open May through October, daily 9–6; then weekends only through December. Flowering annuals, potted plants of all kinds, and gifts, crafts, and local produce are sold here—as well as baked goods.

Eggs are extra special at **Kaplan's Egg Farm** (845-434-4519), 715 Glen Wild Road, Woodridge. Open year-round, daily 8–4.

Some farms also offer visitors the chance to select and cut their own Christmas trees; you can bring your own saw or rent one for the day. Dress warmly, bring rope to tie the tree to the car, and have a nice holiday. But remember, call ahead for directions, hours, and prices: **Pine Farm Christmas Trees** (845-482-4149), Youngsville; **Trees of the Woods** (845-482-4528), Callicoon Center.

FISHING Sullivan County is an angler's paradise. The famed Willowemoc and Beaverkill streams produce prize-winning trout each year in addition to being recognized as the cradle of American fly-fishing. The Delaware River offers its rich bounty to the patient angler, as do Mongaup Creek and Russell Brook. Then there are the icy lakes of the county, with such entrancing names as Kiamesha, Kenoza, Swan, and Waneta. There are hundreds of fine fishing areas in Sullivan County and too little space to do them all justice. The following general information, however, will assist you in finding the perfect spot to enjoy a rocky stream, a sunny sky, and, just maybe, a record catch!

The county's streams and rivers are famed for their brook, brown, and rainbow trout, but bass, pickerel, walleye, and shad are also plentiful. All streams on state land are open to the public; other streams often have public fishing rights through state easements, which are indicated by signs. New York State requires fishing licenses for anyone over 16, as well as special reservoir permits (call 1-866-933-2257 or go to www.dec.ny.gov/permits for information regarding permits). Lake fishing is also popular in Sullivan, but there are separate use fees charged, and some lakes are privately owned by hotels or resorts, so check on the site before you fish.

The Beaverkill is one of the best known trout streams in the world and may be reached from Roscoe, Livingston Manor, Lew Beach, Beaverkill, and Rockland. Fly-fishing tackle may be purchased in Roscoe at the **Beaverkill Angler** (607-498-5194), Stewart Avenue. Make sure to stop in at **Roscoe Little Store** (607-498-5553), 59 Stewart Avenue, Roscoe, the oldest sporting goods and variety store in the county. In addition to licenses, tackle, live bait, and clothing, they carry all kinds of specialty items, toys, and gifts. The store is fun to explore and is open year-round, daily 9–5:30. Or call **White Cloud's Beaverkill Fly-Fishing School** (607-498-4611) in Roscoe: This private school offers students a chance to learn casting, fly tying, and moving-water fishing techniques. You can schedule lessons to meet your needs. **Baxter House River Outfitters & Guide Service** (607-290-4022), 2012 Old Route 17, Roscoe, is a fly-fishing guide service and is open daily April through November. **The Wulff School of Fly-Fishing** (845-439-5020), Box 948, Livingston Manor, is located in the beautiful upper Beaverkill Valley, set on 100 acres. The school has a building designed to meet teaching requirements. In addition to fly-fishing, you can learn wading, streamcraft, and obstacle casting. If you have extra time, enjoy fishing in the Delaware River's main stem and its east and west branches, as well as the no-kill stretches of the Beaverkill and Willowemoc rivers.

Willowemoc Creek is found between Roscoe and Livingston Manor, along Old Route 17. Mongaup Creek runs from Livingston Manor to Mongaup Pond. The Neversink River is at Claryville on County Routes 19 and 15, and you can pick up the Delaware River at East Branch on Route 17. Among the lakes are Kenoza Lake (Route 52, Kenoza Lake Village), Swington Bridge Lake (Route 17B, Mongaup Valley), Swan Lake (Route 55, between Liberty and Kauneonga Lake), White Lake (junction of Routes 17B and 55), Waneta Lake (County Route 151 in Deckertown), Cable Lake (Route 17 northwest of Roscoe, end of Russel Brook), and Kiamesha Lake (Route 42, Kiamesha).

The **Beaverkill Trout Hatchery** (845-439-4947), 8 Alder Creek Road, Livingston Manor, is a fish hatchery that will give you a tour if you call in advance. They are open April through September, Saturday and Sunday 8–5 for fish and pay pond on the premises. They also sell fresh and smoked trout.

The **Catskill State Fish Hatchery** (845-439-4328) in DeBruce is a great place to take young children. Open weekdays 8:30–4; weekends 8:30–noon.

FISHING IN ROSCOE

FisherMears Associates

The Eldred Preserve Resort (845-557-8316), Route 55, between Barryville and White Lake, has three stocked trout ponds and two bass lakes. There are some restrictions on fishing for nonguests, so call ahead. Trout fishing is allowed (no license required), and bass fishing with boat rental reservation only (license required).

GOLF The beauty of Sullivan County's farm country carries over to its golf courses. Many resorts have outstanding courses that are open to the public. Well-known championship courses at Grossinger's, Kutsher's, Villa Roma, and Lochmore coexist here with family-friendly nine-hole courses like Lake View. It is best to call ahead to confirm hours and check if reservations are needed for a tee time.

Grossinger Country Club (845-292-9000), 26 Route 52 East, Liberty, has 27 holes of golf, a driving range and putting greens, and full facilities. Rated four and a half stars by *Golf Digest*. Call for schedule.

Kutsher's Resort (845-794-6000; 1-800-431-1273), 1 Kutsher Road, Monticello, has an 18-hole championship golf course designed by William F. Mitchell. Lessons, pro shop, carts, clubhouse, and driving range. Open mid-April through mid-November, daily 8–sunset.

Swan Lake Golf and Country Club (845-292-0323), 38 Eagle Drive, Swan Lake, is an 18-hole PGA-rated course nestled high in the Catskills. Open April through November, daily 7–6.

Tennanah Lake Golf & Tennis Club (607-498-5000), 100 Fairway View Drive, Roscoe, is open April through October, daily 7 AM–9:30 PM. An 18-hole par-72 course, practice facility, driving range, and pro shop. They offer club rentals and lessons for novices.

Villa Roma Resort (845-887-4880; 1-800-533-6767), 356 Villa Roma Road, Callicoon, has an 18-hole course, a putting green, and full facilities. Open April through mid-November. Call for hours.

Public courses include **Sullivan County Golf and Country Club** (845-292-9584), 2514 Route 52, Liberty; **Tarry Brae** (845-434-2620), 387 Pleasant Valley Road, South Fallsburg; and the **Lochmore Golf Course** (845-434-1257), 586 Loch Sheldrake/Hurleyville Road, Loch Sheldrake, with its par-71, 18-hole course.

HARNESS RACING **Monticello Casino and Raceway** (845-794-4100; www.monticellocasinoandraceway.com), 204 Route 17B, Monticello. Open year-round, Monday through Thursday 10 AM–2 AM; until 4 AM Friday through Sunday. There are over 1,000 slot machines here, as well as electronic table games including roulette. There is also live entertainment, live harness racing, and simulcasting of thoroughbred and harness races. There are two restaurants on the premises. Check the website for the entertainment schedule.

HORSEBACK RIDING **Bridle Hill Farm** (845-482-3993), 190 Hemmer Road, Jeffersonville. Open year-round, daily 7 AM–9 PM. There is an indoor arena here, as well as lessons for all ages from beginner through advanced. There are miles of trails here, and great care is taken to match every rider with the right horse for his/her ability. Lessons and trail rides are combined, and the owners make a special effort to give young riders a great experience.

Oak Ridge Farm (845-482-4686), 222 Hessinger-Lare Road, Youngsville. Open year-round, daily 8–7. This working horse farm offers lessons, boarding, and training on 105 scenic acres. There are indoor and outdoor arenas. Most of the horses are Rocky Mountain horses and are well suited for the older, more experienced rider.

Rolling Stone Ranch (845-583-1100), 282 West Shore Road, Bethel. Open Saturday and Sunday year-round; daily late June through Labor Day. There are indoor and outdoor riding arenas here and trail riding for students who take lessons.

SOARING **Wurtsboro Airport** (845-888-2791), 50 Barone Road, Wurtsboro. Open daily, weather permitting. Established in 1927, this airport is home to the oldest soaring site in the country. Soaring is done in sailplanes, motorless craft that are towed into the air and released. The pilot then sails the plane on the air currents—sometimes for hours—before gliding in for a landing. A 20-minute demonstration flight with a certified pilot can be arranged; if you enjoy the sport and want to learn how to do it, flight instruction is available.

✷ Winter Sports

CROSS-COUNTRY SKIING There are so many places to cross-country ski in Sullivan County that you would have to spend several winters here to try all the trails. Many local parks allow skiing for free, but often the trails are not groomed, and there are no nearby rentals. At the large resorts some trails are open for a fee to day visitors, but if you are uncertain of a hotel's policy, it is suggested that you call ahead; policies may also change from year to year.

DeBruce Country Inn on the Willowemoc (845-439-3900), 982 DeBruce Road, DeBruce, has miles of cross-country trails, unmapped and unmarked within the Catskill Park. It is located near Mongaup State Park.

Kutsher's Resort (845-794-6000), 1 Kutsher Road (Route 17, exit 105B), Monticello, has both cross-country and downhill skiing but only for guests of the hotel.

Try the 160-acre **Town of Thompson Park** (845-796-3606), Old Liberty Road, 1.5 miles past the Monticello Post Office; the 110-acre **Hanofee Park** (845-292-7690), on Sunset Lake Road, off Route 52 east, in Liberty, where you will find approximately 3 miles of ungroomed trails; and 265-acre **Walnut Mountain Park** (845-292-7690), Liberty, with ungroomed trails. You will need to bring your own equipment here; there are no services.

DOWNHILL SKIING While downhill skiing in Sullivan County does not revolve around large resorts like Hunter or Windham, it does have a few centers that offer lots of fun for travelers of all ages. (See also *Cross-Country Skiing*.)

Holiday Mountain Ski Area (845-796-3161), 99 Holiday Mountain Road, Monticello (exit 107 off Route 17 at Bridgeville), has both day and night skiing, 15 slopes, 100 percent snowmaking, and a vertical drop of 400 feet. The longest run is 3,500 feet, and both beginners and advanced skiers will enjoy the slopes here; cross-country skiing is allowed, and so is snowboarding. A ski shop, snack bar, and parking are available. Open mid-December through mid-March, Tuesday through Thursday 3–9; Friday noon–9; Saturday and Sunday 9–9. Closed Monday.

Villa Roma Resort & Conference Center (845-887-4880), 356 Villa Roma Road, Callicoon. There are four slopes, a double chairlift and T-bar, snowboarding, rentals, lessons, night skiing, and a snow tube run for those who prefer not to schuss down the slopes. The resort also has snowmaking capability and is open to the public, not just guests of the hotel.

ICE FISHING Every winter ice-fishing contests are held, including an ongoing event at the **Eldred Preserve** (845-557-8316), depending on ice conditions.

✷ Green Space

Basha Kill Wildlife Management Area (845-764-0743), Haven and South roads, Wurtsboro. Open year-round, daily dawn to dusk. Free. A tranquil wildlife wetland habitat and recreation area where visitors can fish, boat, bird-watch, and hike. The Basha Kill is a famous stream in the history of Sullivan County, renowned for decades as teeming with fish. The area is managed by the Department of Environmental Conservation, and it is often overlooked; it's located just south of Wurtsboro.

Lake Superior State Park, Duggan Road, between Routes 17B and 55, Bethel. Open year-round; beach area open Memorial Day weekend through Labor Day, daily 9–dusk. Admission fee. This state park offers swimming, boating, boat rentals, fishing, and picnic facilities. The beach is a perfect stop for families traveling with children.

Stone Arch Bridge Historical Park (845-807-0261), Route 52, Kenoza Lake. Open year-round. Free. This three-arched stone bridge, which spans Callicoon Creek, is the only remaining one of its kind in this country. Built in 1872 by two German stonemasons, the bridge was constructed from hand-cut local stone and is

STONE ARCH BRIDGE HISTORICAL PARK

FisherMears Associates

supported without an outer framework. Replacing an earlier wooden span that finally collapsed from the constant weight of wagonloads of lumber, the Stone Arch Bridge gained fame not only for its graceful design and unusual construction but also for a bizarre murder that took place on or near it in 1892. A local farmer, believing that his brother-in-law had put a hex on him, convinced his son that only the brother-in-law's death could lift the curse. So the young man carried out the murder and dumped the body into the river. The case drew enormous publicity because of the witchcraft angle, and there have even been reports of a ghost appearing on the bridge. Today, visitors fish from the banks, picnic on shore, or just walk through the 9-acre landscaped park and along the nature trails. Children will enjoy the small play area.

* Lodging

Sullivan County is probably best known for the Catskills resorts that flourished there for nearly a century. While some of the hotels, like Kutsher's, still welcome guests, others, like the Concord, have shut their doors. But the region has a wide variety of bungalows, resort hotels, bed & breakfasts, and inns offering inexpensive to luxury accommodations. Be certain to call before you go; the resorts can be booked well in advance of the summer months and winter holidays.

Bradstan Country Hotel (845-583-4114), 1561 Route 17B, White Lake 12786. ($$) This unique bed & breakfast features three cottages and five comfortable suites, all with private baths, overlooking beautiful White Lake. A gourmet breakfast is served, and special diets can be accommodated. Open May through October.

DeBruce Country Inn on the Willowemoc (845-439-3900), 982 DeBruce Road, off Route 17 (exit 96), DeBruce 12758. ($$) This inn, which dates from the turn of the 19th century, is located within the Catskill Forest Preserve and on the banks of Willowemoc Creek. The 14 guest rooms all have private baths. There is a sauna, exercise room, and outdoor pool. The Dry Fly lounge is the perfect place to unwind at the end of the day. Room rates include a full breakfast and choice of dinner at the restaurant on the premises. Prices are exceedingly reasonable. A perfect retreat for bird-watching, fly-fishing, hiking, and outdoor recreation. Art and craft gallery on the premises. Open year-round.

Ecce Bed & Breakfast (845-557-8562), 19 Silverfish Road, Barryville 12719. ($$$) Ecce (pronounced et CHAY) means "behold" in Latin, an apt name for this beautifully renovated mountain house perched on a bluff overlooking the Delaware River. Guests will enjoy panoramic views of the Pennsylvania mountains on a 60-acre wooded property. The five elegantly appointed rooms, most with Jacuzzi baths, have all the modern amenities, including TV, refrigerator, DVD player, and Internet access. A wood-burning fireplace in the living room creates a warm, inviting atmosphere. This is a great place to relax or romance in a magnificent setting. There is a network of hiking trails on the property that guests will enjoy exploring. Open year-round.

Farmer's Little House (845-436-7980), 418 Heiden Road, Thompsonville 12784. ($$) This 64-acre secluded property offers several wooded walking trails as well as a pristine river: a great place to truly escape. Inside, the charming country house has a fireplace and baby grand piano. There are six rooms and one suite, all with private baths. A full breakfast is served. Open April through October.

Golden Guernsey (845-932-7994), 31 Mitchell Pond East, Cochecton 12726. ($$) There are two renovated rooms in a spacious barn located in a beautiful pastoral setting across from a dairy farm with golden Guernsey cows. Both rooms have private baths. Full breakfast complete with eggs from the free-range chickens on the property. Open year-round.

The Guest House (845-439-4000), 408 DeBruce Road, Livingston Manor 12758. ($$) The "guest house" consists of six cottages along the banks of the Willowemoc Creek, and all are distinctive in their ambience and decor. Guests will enjoy being surrounded by nature, and the locale will delight those who fly-fish. Open year-round.

Horse & Hounds (908-309-2799), 385 Hurd Road, Bethel 12720. ($$$) The luxurious accommodations here are within walking distance of the Bethel Center for the Arts. The three rooms are furnished in European hunt-style decor, with antiques and a large fireplace, and offer lovely views. The lakefront property is ideal for those who enjoy boating, fishing, and swimming. There is a gourmet continental breakfast and afternoon high tea. Children may stay by advance arrangement only. Open year-round.

The Inn at Lake Joseph (845-791-9506), 162 St. Joseph's Road (County Road 108, off Route 42), Forestburgh 12777. ($$$) A 19th-century Victorian mountain retreat nestled in the Catskills and surrounded by acres of forest, this inn was built by a prosperous businessman who then sold the house to the Roman Catholic Church, which used it as a retreat for Cardinals Hayes and Spellman. A private spring-fed lake offers swimming, boating, and fishing. There are two tennis courts, as well. This is a secluded spot where every detail is attended to, one of the county's best inns. The mansion has 16 guest rooms, all with fireplaces and canopied beds. The carriage house is perfect for families, with its own library, TV, and stereo. Fitness center and outdoor pool. Open year-round.

Jeffersonian Bed & Breakfast (845-482-5947), 4858 Route 52 (Main Street), Jeffersonville 12748. ($$) The seven renovated guest rooms have an eclectic mix of furnishings, making for a cozy atmosphere. Three rooms have private baths; four share two baths. The house dates back to 1922 and had once belonged to a local doctor. Conveniently located in town. Open year-round.

Lanza's Country Inn (845-439-5070), 839 Shandelee Road, Livingston Manor 12758. ($$) This family-owned and family-operated inn is housed in a building with a pub and restaurant. Each one of the nine guest rooms is different—all are furnished with period pieces and have private baths; some have canopied beds. The full breakfast includes homemade breads, juice, and coffee. A lake is nearby for swimming, fishing, and boating, and there are cross-country ski trails. Children welcome. Open year-round.

Lazy Pond Bed & Breakfast (845-292-3362), 79 Old Loomis Road, Liberty 12754. ($$) Although this B&B is only 1.5 miles from town, a stay here makes you feel as though you are transported back in time. This three-story Victorian houses 27 rooms, all with private baths, and all have queen-size beds. Enjoy breakfast in the West Wing on a wraparound porch that overlooks a beautiful pond. Open year-round.

The Lodge at Rock Hill (845-796-3100; 1-866-RH-LODGE), 283 Rock

Hill Drive, Rock Hill 12775. ($$) The hotel offers 70 renovated, beautifully appointed rooms and suites (some with Jacuzzis) on 55 acres with hiking and mountain biking, and cross-country skiing in the winter. Fitness center, cable TV, air-conditioning. Children welcome. Open year-round.

Old North Branch Inn (845-482-5925), 869 North Branch–Hortonville Road, North Branch 12766. ($$) Designer and owner Victoria Lesser has beautifully restored this 1860s inn, complete with juice bar/café on the main floor (the baked goods are fantastic here). All four rooms have private baths, and children over the age of 12 are welcome. Open May through December. A delightful place!

Reynolds House Inn (607-498-4422), 1934 Old Route 17, Roscoe 12776. ($$) Built in 1902 as a tourist home, this is the county's oldest operational bed & breakfast. The three-story Victorian offers fly-fishing, hiking, golfing, and fine restaurants nearby. The seven decorative guest rooms have private baths, cable TV, and air-conditioning. The elegant Rockefeller Suite, where John D. Rockefeller was a frequent guest in the 1920s, has a king-size bed and a claw-foot tub. A full breakfast is served in the parlor in winter or on the wraparound porch, weather permitting. Open April through mid-December.

Rolling River Café, Gallery and Inn (845-747-4123), 25 Cooley Road, Parksville. ($$) Inn open year-round. Café open May through September, Thursday through Sunday; October through December, Friday through Sunday. The inn here is a separate house with four charming rooms and two baths that accommodates seven guests comfortably. There is a full kitchen, washer/dryer, and a grill and picnic table where riverside barbecues may be enjoyed in the summer months. Children welcome.

Roscoe Motel (607-498-5220), Old Route 17, Roscoe 12776. ($) Located near some of the most famous fishing waters in the country, this is a funky motel that is inexpensive and provides the necessary amenities. A great place to stay if you are traveling with young children. Open year-round.

Samba Inn (845-482-5900), 4893 Main Street, Jeffersonville 12748. ($$) There are two efficiencies on the Callicoon Creek behind Samba Café. The owners of the restaurant renovated this lovely guesthouse, a perfect place for families to stay while traveling through the county. The village of Jeffersonville is just steps away. Your hosts, Andrea and Tim Corcoran, are friendly and aim to please. Open year-round, and children and pets are welcome.

Spring House Commons (845-557-8189), 3461 Route 97, Barryville 12719. ($$) There are three B&B rooms (two with shared bath and one with private bath), as well as three apartment-style rooms with kitchenettes. Located on Route 97, this clean, comfortable lodging option is open year-round.

Stone Wall Acres (845-482-4930), 142 Eagin Road, Youngsville 12791. ($$) There is one carriage house here, furnished in original antiques—the perfect spot for those seeking a secluded getaway. You will feel transported to England, being surrounded by a country garden on 6 private acres. The carriage house has a living room/dining room, loft bedroom, and fireplace. Breakfast may be served there, in the main-house dining room, or poolside on the patio, depending on your preference. Open year-round.

Sunrise House B&B (845-482-3778; 1-800-SUN-KATS), 193 North Branch

Road, Jeffersonville 12748. ($$) This restored farmhouse on 45 acres with wonderful views has four guest rooms with private baths, air-conditioning, and cable TV. The Retreat, the newest addition, is a lovely cottage separate from the main house. Enjoy the heated in-ground pool from May through October. The B&B is open April through October.

Sunshine Cottage and Pottery Bed & Breakfast (845-932-8873; 1-800-941-2251), 109 Stoney Road, Lake Huntington 12752. ($) Set on 14 acres of mountain pastures with lovely views, this restored farmhouse offers excellent value for the money. Two upstairs guest rooms share a bath; a downstairs room has a private bath. Ask about the Country Suite, a true romantic escape, with a whirlpool bathtub for two. Outside the main house is Sunset Cottage, with its own fireplace and private patio with hot tub. Enjoy a hearty breakfast with home-baked muffins and coffee cake. Open year-round.

Tennanah Lake Golf & Tennis Club (607-498-5502), 100 Fairway View Drive, Roscoe 12776. ($$) There are 24 rooms with private balconies (one is completely handicapped accessible) and all the amenities. The emphasis is on golf and tennis packages, but visitors can enjoy swimming in the lovely heated outdoor pool or relaxing by the lake. A restaurant and coffee shop are on the premises. A good place to stay if you are traveling with older children. Open April through October.

Villa Roma (845-887-4880; 1-800-533-6767), 356 Villa Roma Road, Callicoon 12723. ($$) Completely rebuilt and redesigned in 2008 after being destroyed by fire in 2006, this full-service resort with approximately 400 rooms and suites offers all the amenities: a full-service spa and fitness center, 18-hole championship golf course, indoor and outdoor tennis, five swimming pools, and cross-country skiing during the winter months. Inquire about the midweek specials throughout the year, as well as various special summer packages: They make this resort a good deal, especially for families. Kids will enjoy the outdoor water playground. There is also a dance club, 150-seat café, and 30-person Jacuzzi. Italian cuisine is served in the Clubhouse Restaurant, the main dining room on the premises. Open year-round. Children welcome.

* Where to Eat

Sullivan, although not a large county, has few major roads and is time-consuming to navigate. Restaurants in the *Dining Out* section are grouped according to location in the county: southeast, southwest, northwest, and northeast.

DINING OUT

In Southeastern Sullivan (Monticello, Rock Hill)

Bernie's Holiday Restaurant (845-796-3333), Route 17, Rock Hill. ($$) Open Tuesday through Sunday noon–10 for lunch and dinner. One of the largest restaurants in Sullivan County and also one of the best. The specialties here are steaks, seafood, and Asian American cuisine. The sushi bar is popular as well. Children welcome.

Buona Fortuna (845-796-4110), 46 Forestburgh Road, Monticello. ($$) Open Tuesday through Saturday noon–10 for lunch and dinner. Closed Sunday and Monday. Enjoy Northern Italian cuisine prepared to order by the chef-owner. Children welcome.

Mr. Willy's Restaurant (845-794-0888), 3695 Route 42, Monticello. ($$)

Open Tuesday through Saturday 5–10 for dinner; call for winter hours. American cuisine is the fare at this family restaurant with a rustic country atmosphere. The specialty of the house is prime rib. Another popular entrée is the shrimp splendora (seafood over pasta in a basil tomato cream sauce). There are always a few daily specials. The kids will love the peanut butter pie for dessert. Children's menu.

The Old Homestead Steakhouse (845-794-8973), 472 Bridgeville Road, Monticello. ($$) Open April through December, Wednesday through Sunday 4:30–10 for dinner. Hours change seasonally. This is the place to go for surf and turf. The large 24-ounce sirloin steak is a specialty of the house. You can also try steamed or stuffed lobster and grilled salmon or swordfish, along with a large menu featuring an array of steak dishes.

In Southwestern Sullivan (Barryville, Eldred, Kauneonga Lake, Narrowsburg, White Lake)

Baker's Tap Room (845-557-8558), 184 Barryville Yulan Road, Barryville. ($$) Open for dinner Wednesday through Sunday 5–9; until 10 on Friday and Saturday. The fare here is mostly American favorites, consistently well prepared. The welcoming casual atmosphere draws a mix of local residents, second-home owners, and hunters. The entrées range from thin-crust pizzas, burgers, and Caesar salad to steak tenderloin sandwiches, crabcakes, and their renowned lobster bisque. There is often live music on Friday and Saturday evenings.

Dancing Cat Saloon at the Catskill Distilling Company (845-583-3141), 2037 Route 17B, Bethel. ($$) Open for dinner Wednesday through Friday 5–10; Saturday noon–midnight; Sunday noon–8. This is one of my favorite informal places to dine in Sullivan County. They have an enormous menu that includes burgers, wings, chili, salads, and pizza, as well as hanger steak, ribs, meat loaf, and blackened tilapia. Their handcrafted spirits, like Peace Vodka, are a terrific accompaniment to the meal. Of course, there is a wide selection of cocktails and distilled spirits. The live music on Friday and Saturday nights is usually excellent. The atmosphere is casual, and the prices are extremely reasonable.

Eldred Preserve (845-557-8316), 1040 Route 55, Eldred. ($$) Open Wednesday through Saturday 5–9 for dinner. The dining rooms here overlook three stream-fed ponds—stocked with rainbow, brown, brook, and golden trout—as well as 2,000 acres of unspoiled forest. Needless to say, the specialty is trout from the preserve's ponds. The fish is served many ways, including smoked, and all baking is done on the premises. There is also a 25-room motel, and two private lakes are open for boating and fishing (see *To Do—Fishing*). Guests can enjoy the tennis courts and outdoor pool in warm weather. Children welcome.

Fat Lady Café (845-583-7133), 13 County Highway 141, Kauneonga Lake. ($$) Open Wednesday through Monday for lunch noon–3; dinner 6–9. Closed during February and March. Enjoy sitting at the edge of the lake with beautiful sunsets while dining on a combination of American and international favorites. Inside, the atmosphere is reminiscent of a SoHo bistro. There are freshly baked pastries and pies for dessert.

The Front Porch Café & Martini Lounge (845-583-4838), 1577 Route 17B, White Lake. ($$) Open April through January, Wednesday through Sunday 11:30–9 for lunch and dinner. Dine outdoors, weather permitting, and enjoy an eclectic menu featuring world fusion cuisine combining Asian, Italian, and American favorites. Chicken bouillabaisse, shrimp pad thai, and marinated tuna carpaccio are a few popular entrées here. Desserts, all baked on the premises, range from chocolate mousse and chocolate brownie torte to mango cheesecake and pumpkin banana tart. Art deco martini bar and lounge overlooking White Lake.

Gerard's River Grill (845-252-6562; www.gerardsrivergrill.com), 251 Bridge Street, Narrowsburg. ($$) Open for dinner Wednesday and Thursday 5–9, Friday and Saturday until 10; Sunday brunch 11–3, dinner 3–8. The restaurant is located only 16 miles from the Bethel Woods Center for the Arts. Narrowsburg is a wonderful village on the Delaware River to explore before enjoying a repast here. Diners will be pleased with American favorites like burgers, steak, seafood, salads, and pasta dishes. The place is popular with local residents. Children welcome.

Korean Arts Village (845-583-1010), 2572 Route 17B, Bethel. ($$) Open May through October, daily 11–10. Enjoy authentic traditional Korean cuisine, an unusual find in Sullivan County. As you approach the restaurant, there are carved wooden totem poles, a row of kimchi vessels, tepees, and then the building appears. Children welcome.

Luzon Station (845-583-4200), 3 Horseshoe Lake Road, Kauneonga Lake. ($$). Open Thursday through Saturday 5–10. This is a cozy, funky bar/restaurant with casual waterfront dining named after the whistle stop on the O & W railroad that passed through Hurleyville. The menu includes burgers, steaks, chicken, shrimp, and pasta; don't expect gourmet dining, but rather comfort food with decent-size portions. Live music most nights. Children welcome.

Michele's Lakeside 55 (845-583-4400), 3575 Route 55, Kauneonga Lake. ($$) Open April through October, daily noon–10. Enjoy lakeside dining at a restaurant where you will find steak, fresh seafood, and sushi under one roof. The desserts are excellent. Everything here is prepared to order, and it's an especially delightful place to have lunch or an early dinner.

The Millbrook Inn (845-856-7778), 1774 Route 97, Pond Eddy. ($$) Open for dinner Friday and Saturday 5–9:30; Sunday noon–8. The fine German cuisine here includes delicious homemade sauerkraut, along with Wiener schnitzel and sauerbraten. Other specialties of the house include French onion soup and an excellent black bean burger popular with vegetarians. Children welcome.

Tre Alberi (845-557-6104), 3402 Route 97, Barryville. ($$) Open for dinner Thursday through Monday 5–10; reservations suggested. This restaurant serves some of the best Northern Italian cuisine to be found in the Catskills. There are different pasta, fish, and poultry specials each day, and all are prepared to order. The desserts are made on the premises, and the chef-owner oversees their preparation. A worthwhile stop for those who appreciate fine dining.

In Northwestern Sullivan (Callicoon, Jeffersonville, Livingston Manor, Roscoe)

Matthew's on Main (845-887-5636), 19 Lower Main Street, Cochecton. ($$) Open daily for lunch 11–5; dinner 5–9, until 10 Friday and Saturday. It's hard to miss the bright-red building with green-and-tan trim that houses this chef-owned family restaurant, featuring upscale fare at reasonable prices. This beautifully renovated building dates from 1865, and outdoor dining may be enjoyed on the deck day and night in warm weather. You can order lunch all night; the light-fare menu is always available. The cuisine is international—fresh fish, smoked duck, prime rib, and sesame-crusted salmon are just some of the tasty entrées. Desserts include fruit sorbets, cakes, and pies, all made from scratch on the premises. This casual, comfortable spot also has a full bar with beautiful tin ceilings. Children welcome.

Michelangelo's Restaurant (845-482-3900), 4900 Route 52 (Main Street), Jeffersonville. ($$) Open Monday through Saturday 11–9. The Southern Italian cooking here features Neapolitan specialties, including the chef's favorites—eggplant parmigiana and eggplant rollotini. All sauces are fresh and homemade. I enjoyed the linguine Michelangelo: pasta topped with arugula, jumbo shrimp, a few cherry peppers, and a light tomato sauce. Desserts include cannoli, tiramisu, and sorbet . . . if you have room.

The 1906 House (845-887-1906), Main Street, Callicoon. ($$) Open daily 5–9 for dinner; call for winter hours. Enjoy both traditional favorites and nouvelle cuisine specialties prepared by a Culinary Institute–trained chef. The Black Angus beef is popular, and so are the game dishes, which include venison, quail, and rabbit. All soups and desserts are made on the premises. Entertainment on weekends. Reservations suggested.

Raimondo's (607-498-4702), 3 Stewart Avenue, Roscoe. ($$) Open daily 11–10 for lunch and dinner. This old-fashioned Italian restaurant offers everything from the basics (pizza and pasta) to more elaborate dishes. A couple of house specialties are linguine with crabmeat, and veal with wild mushrooms and asparagus topped with provolone cheese. There are cannolis and an array of cakes for dessert. A popular dining spot among local residents.

Riverside Café (607-498-5305), 16624 Route 17, Roscoe. ($$) Open for dinner May through October, Monday through Saturday 5–9:30; Sunday noon–9:30. Enjoy a meal overlooking the Beaverkill stream while dining in this cozy restaurant. The basic American cuisine includes hearty selections like grilled pork tenderloin, rack of lamb, baked stuffed brook trout, steak, and lobster. All breads and desserts are baked fresh daily. The apple pie, berry cobbler, and bread pudding with brandy sauce are only a few of the tempting dessert selections.

Rockland House (607-498-4240), 159 Rockland Road (Route 206), Roscoe. ($$) Open for dinner April through January, daily 5–9; until 10 on Friday and Saturday. Call for winter hours. You will see the sign on Route 206 before you approach this long-established restaurant: EAT HERE OR WE'LL BOTH STARVE. The specialties of the house are prime rib and a 10-ounce lobster tail. The salad bar has more than 30 items to choose from, and the homemade soups and breads are delicious. The spacious dining room with cathedral ceilings has long been a gathering place for local residents who have been patronizing this landmark steakhouse for decades. Children's menu.

Samba Café (845-482-5900), 4893 Main Street, Jeffersonville. ($$) Open for lunch Tuesday through Saturday 11–4; for dinner Thursday through Saturday from 5. Enjoy tasty comfort food infused with Latin flavors. Andrea Corcoran, a graduate of the French Culinary Institute, creates some of the best empanadas you will find anywhere. I loved the Brazilian-style fish stew; the roast beef with tomato salsa and potatoes was also excellent. The lunch specials and dinners are exceedingly reasonable. Children will love the soups here!

Ted's Restaurant (845-482-4242), 4896 Route 52, Jeffersonville. ($$) Open year-round, daily 7 AM–9 PM. Turkish, Mediterranean, and American cuisine meld here. Try the mixed grill, which combines lamb, chicken, and gyro items; the shrimp kebab is excellent, as well. The Turkish appetizers are a nice way to sample a variety of new tastes. For the less adventurous, there is the Gusburger, a half-pound bacon cheeseburger on a hard roll with fries (one of the most popular dishes here). Children's menu.

In Northeastern Sullivan (Hurleyville, Liberty)

Frankie & Johnny's/Nardi's (845-434-8051), 205 Main Street, Hurleyville. ($) Open year-round, daily 11:30–10. This reasonable Italian American restaurant, known locally for large portions, specializes in steak, seafood, pasta, and pizza. It's a great spot for lunch or dinner if you're traveling with children.

Piccolo Paese (845-292-7210), 271 Route 52, Liberty. ($$) Open for lunch Tuesday through Friday noon–3; dinner served daily 4:30–10. This elegant yet moderately priced Northern Italian restaurant features fresh homemade pasta, seafood, chicken, veal, and imaginative appetizers. The chef-owner creates terrific daily specials that I highly recommend.

EATING OUT **Benji & Jakes** (845-583-4031), 5 Horseshoe Lake Road, Kauneonga Lake. ($) Open for lunch Thursday through Sunday noon–4; dinner Wednesday through Sunday 5–9. The brick oven pizza is the specialty of the house at this place, right on the lake. The atmosphere is delightful, especially in the warm weather when one can dine alfresco. Try the beer-battered jalapeño onion rings served with marinara sauce or the dessert slice (banana flambé, chopped strawberries, goat cheese, ice cream, and chocolate shavings), for a change from the more conventional selections. Although nothing is quite ordinary here when it comes to pizza. My favorite was the aubergine (fire roasted eggplant sauce, Formaggio's mozzarella, sun-dried tomatoes, and Parmesan cheese). You can create your own pizza from an array of wonderful farm-fresh items. *Mangia!*

Blue Horizon Diner (845-796-2210), 4445 Route 42 North, Monticello. ($) Open daily 7 AM–midnight. While you can order all the usual diner fare here (burgers, sandwiches, pasta, and salads), they are known for sautéed dishes (shrimp and scallop scampi) as well as steaks and lobsters. There is almost always an early-bird special.

Brother Bruno Pizza & Restaurant (845-791-4600), 4050 Thompson Square, Monticello. ($) Open daily 11:30–10. This Italian American restaurant specializes in pizza and calzones as well as the standard favorites: lasagna, manicotti, and an array of other pasta dishes. Children welcome.

Catskill Harvest Gourmet Market & Garden Center (845-292-3838), 2758 Route 52, Liberty. ($$) Open Monday through Friday 9–7; Saturday and Sunday 9–5. A combination of organic farm market and gourmet grocery, Catskill Harvest also has a garden center, bookstore, and eatery on the premises. They sell high-quality, locally grown produce, meats, cheeses, breads, pastries, soaps, pottery, and more. The kitchen offers seasonal treats including soups, sandwiches, and chili, along with muffins, pies, and cookies for dessert. A first-class country store, this is a terrific place to shop as well as stop for a bite to eat. Children welcome.

Chocolate Mousse Café & Bakery (845-557-3611), 3461 Route 97, Barryville. ($) Open April through October, daily 8–4. Located in the historic Spring House Commons, this is a great place to enjoy homemade fare (soups, salads, and sandwiches for lunch, or pancakes, waffles, and omelets for breakfast) that is both healthy and delicious. And, of course, they are renowned for their chocolate mousse cake! In the warm weather, there is outdoor dining along the Delaware River. Children welcome.

Coffee Creation (845-252-6688), 25 Main Street, Narrowsburg. ($) Open daily 7–5:30; until 7 on Saturday and Sunday. Extended hours during the summer season. Enjoy hearty breakfast sandwiches, bagels, pastries, and hot oatmeal (breakfast is served all day here). For lunch there are soups, salads, and wraps, mostly from locally grown ingredients. There's a casual atmosphere, Wi-Fi, couches to lounge on, and tables available on the outdoor patio in the warm weather months. This eatery is truly a hub of the town!

The Corner (845-557-3321), 577 Route 55, Eldred. ($) Open daily 11–8. This combination ice cream–souvenir shop offers 16 flavors of Perry's and Edy's ice cream, as well as milk shakes, sundaes, and root beer floats. There are eight types of paninis, if you are interested in nonsweet sustenance. The kids will enjoy a stop here.

Flour Power Bakery (917-747-6895), 87 DeBruce Road, Livingston Manor. ($) Open year-round, Saturday 9–4; Sunday 9–2 (bakery is open until 6 both days). The ingredients used in the baked goods here are organic, and everything is superb. Whether you prefer sweet or savory items, you won't be disappointed. There is a huge menu including quiche, potpies, soups, tarts, rugelach, muffins, Danish, and cookies, to name just some of the offerings. Coffee and an array of teas may be ordered to accompany whatever treats you choose. Children welcome.

Floyd & Bobo's Bakery and Snack Palace (845-292-6200), 98 North Main Street, Liberty. ($) Open Tuesday through Saturday 7–5; Sunday 8–1. The comfort food here is tasty and fresh, and the owners aim to please. Whether you want a muffin or egg sandwich for breakfast, or chicken salad or panini for lunch, it will be well prepared. The atmosphere is relaxed and casual. Children welcome.

Java Grande (845-557-6110), 585 Route 55, Eldred. ($) Open March through December, Monday through Friday 7–4; Saturday 8–4; Sunday 8–3. This cozy Internet café serves freshly ground premium brewed coffee, lattes, cappuccinos, breakfast wraps, sandwiches, paninis, and much more. It's a nice place to stop for a drink and snack after spending time fishing or hiking.

Java Love Coffee Roasting Company (845-583-4082), 10 Horseshoe Lake Road, Kauneonga Lake. ($) Open year-round, Thursday through Monday 8–5; Friday and Saturday until 7. This is the place to go for excellent coffee in the Bethel area.

Lanza's Country Inn (845-439-5070), 839 Shandelee Road, Livingston Manor. ($$) Open April through mid-December, Tuesday through Sunday 5–10 for dinner. You can enjoy a variety of beef, seafood, pasta, and vegetarian dishes in the greenhouse dining room; pizza and "pub grub" (light fare) are available at the bar.

Liberty Diner & Restaurant (845-292-8973), 30 Sullivan Avenue,

Liberty. ($) Open daily 24 hours. You will find the standard diner fare here in this combination diner/restaurant with two large dining rooms. A local oasis.

River Market (845-557-FOOD), 3385 State Route 97, Barryville. ($) Open year-round, daily 7 AM–9 PM. This delightful deli has outdoor seating, and everything is homemade. If you are planning to picnic along the Delaware River, stock up here first, or perhaps eat on the premises. Whether you are looking for bagels with bacon and eggs for breakfast, or paninis with pulled pork or fresh turkey, this is the place to stop. Their veggie circle sub and "mambo Italiano" are unusual finds. They actually offer two types of coleslaw—creamy or vinaigrette. The pickiest eaters will find something to delight them here. I love their harvest chicken salad and macaroni salad.

Rolling River Café (845-747-4123), 25 Cooley Road, Parksville. ($) Open year-round, Wednesday through Sunday noon–8; until 10 Friday and Saturday. Closed Wednesday in winter months. This delightful café features hearty international favorites made from local organic ingredients. There is an art gallery on the premises and outdoor dining in warm weather. Live music on weekends.

Roscoe Diner (607-498-4405), 1908 Old Route 17, Roscoe. ($) Open daily 7 AM–11 PM. This Greek diner is a local mainstay, and their spanakopita, pastitsio, and moussaka are first-rate. In addition to the usual diner fare, there is a variety of broiled fish, wraps, burgers, and homemade soups. All baking is done on the premises, and the desserts are wonderful. The chocolate Bavarian cheesecake is huge—and delicious!

Sonoma Falls Cider Mill (845-439-4949), 140 Old Liberty Road, Morsston. ($) Open March through December, daily 9–5 (later in the summer months). This is a busy place and a great spot for a picnic. There is a seven-tier waterfall, hiking trails, a country store, and freshly pressed apple cider (you can watch the process on weekend afternoons). The store offers jams, jellies, and maple syrup along with fresh produce and local meats. Breakfast and lunch items are available. The kids will love it here.

Yulan Country Store (845-557-0425), 218 Airport Road, Yulan. ($) Open year-round, Monday through Saturday 6–6; Sunday until 2. This is a deli with all the usual offerings. What makes it special is the owner, Hank, who is renowned for his sausage, egg, and cheese breakfast sandwich. The doughnuts here are first-rate if you want something sweet.

✷ Entertainment

ARTS Sullivan County has a long tradition of supporting the arts, and the cultural programs and shows offered throughout the region are quite good. The **Delaware Arts Center** (845-252-7576; www.artsalliancesite.org) is headquartered in the historic Arlington Hotel in Narrowsburg, 37 Main Street, which is on the National Register of Historic Places. Its gallery is open year-round for exhibits and special events, so call for a schedule. This is also the home of the **Delaware Valley Arts Alliance,** the arts council for Sullivan County.

The **Catskill Art Society** (845-436-4227; www.catskillartsociety.org), 48 Main Street, Livingston Manor, sponsors art, studio, and architectural tours; workshops; and more. Call or check the website for locations and schedules of events throughout the county.

The Sullivan County Museum, Art and Cultural Center (845-434-8044; www.schs.org), 265 Main Street, Hurleyville, is open year-round, except January, Tuesday through Saturday 10–4:30; Sunday 1–4:30. Local historical material is on display, as well as the work of local artists. (See also *To See.*)

PERFORMING ARTS Bethel Woods Center for the Arts (1-866-781-2922; www.bethelwoodscenter.org), 200 Hurd Road, Bethel, is a major tourist attraction in Sullivan County from late May through Labor Day, when top entertainment is offered in a beautiful outdoor venue. (See *To See.*)

At **NACL Theatre** (845-557-0694), 110 Highland Lake Road, Highland Lake, NACL stands for North American Cultural Laboratory, a group that has been offering community theatrical productions year-round in Sullivan County since 1997. Call for a schedule.

A summer-stock theater housed in a century-old barn can only mean fun, and that's what you'll have when you attend a performance at the **Forestburgh Playhouse** (845-794-1194; www.fbplayhouse.org), 39 Forestburgh Road, Forestburgh. Drama, comedies, and musicals are all on the bill, and you can enjoy postshow cabaret and cocktails in the adjoining tavern. They are open from late June through Labor Day, closed Monday, but it is best to call for the summer schedule.

Sullivan County Community College (845-434-5750, ext. 4472), 112 College Road, Loch Sheldrake, has dance, theater, and musicals as part of its series, along with holiday offerings and family shows, in the Seelig Theater on campus.

The **Delaware Valley Opera** (845-252-3136; www.delawarevalleyopera.org) is headquartered at 170 Main Street in Narrowsburg. Two operas, one in July and one in August, are presented each year at the **Tusten Theatre,** 210 Bridge Street, where you will also find a variety of live music concerts, including jazz, classical, and bluegrass. A few dramatic productions

FORESTBURGH PLAYHOUSE

FisherMears Associates

are scheduled during the summer months. The theater is also home to the **Delaware Valley Chamber Orchestra.**

✷ Selective Shopping

There are some delightful specialty shops to be discovered while browsing the streets of Sullivan County's quaint villages, such as Narrowsburg, Roscoe, and Wurtsboro. There are 10 fine artisans on the **Sullivan County Pottery Trail.** Those travelers interested in meeting these craftspeople and visiting their studios to see how pots, plates, bowls, vases, and more are created should definitely follow this special itinerary. To obtain a "trail map," contact the Sullivan County Visitors Association (see *Guidance*) or Jill Wiener at earthgirlpottery@aol.com.

If you are in Wurtsboro, make sure to stop in to the **Canal Towne Emporium** (845-888-2100; www.canaltowne.com), 107 Sullivan Street, at the intersection of Sullivan and Hudson streets. Open year-round, daily 10–5. Free. Originally opened in 1845 as a dry-goods establishment near the Delaware and Hudson Canal and now restored to its turn-of-the-20th-century charm, this country store has received awards for historic preservation. The fixtures, furnishings, and equipment are all antiques and include the first electric coffee mill ever used in the store, along with advertising prints, tins, and jars. Today the emporium sells fine furniture, handcrafted items, and decorative accessories as well as books. Try the penny candy or the pickles!

Catskill Mountain Sugar House (845-985-7815), 227 Glade Hill Road, Grahamsville. Open year-round, but call first. This is the place to buy all kinds of maple products (candy, syrup, and sugar) and honey at reasonable prices. During the month of March,

SULLIVAN COUNTY POTTERY TRAIL

FisherMears Associates

take a tour of the sugarhouse and see how the syrup is produced.

Cutting Garden (845-482-3333), 4055 Route 52, Youngsville. Open Memorial Day weekend through Columbus Day, Friday through Monday 10–6; fall and winter open weekends and by chance. This is a place to pick your own flowers and vegetables in season, but they also sell vintage furniture, kitchenware, collectibles, and work by local artisans. Fair-trade products and gifts are also available.

Global Home (845-482-3652), 4929 Main Street, Jeffersonville. Open year-round, Thursday through Monday 11–5. You will find both exotic and modern furniture here, as well as gifts from the far corners of the globe (hence the name). Lighting fixtures, rugs, dishware, clothing, toys, jewelry, and candles are among the items for sale. It's a great place to browse!

Justus Asthalter Maple Syrup (845-292-8569), 865 Aden Road, Parksville. Open March and April, daily 10–5; during the rest of the year, call first. Tour the sugarhouse and discover how maple syrup is made in the Catskills. They sell maple syrup, maple candy, and several other treats here. Children will love this place.

River Gallery (845-252-3238), 8 Main Street, Narrowsburg. Open year-round, daily 11–5, Friday until 7, and Saturday until 8. This terrific gallery features an eclectic mix of Asian and American antiques in addition to local Delaware Valley School artists in changing exhibits throughout the seasons. There are also interesting gifts as well as a frame shop. Owners Tony and Barry are welcoming to those from out of the area and are knowledgeable about art and antiques.

ANTIQUES The search for treasures in the county can take you to a dusty little shop on a side road or into full-fledged auction barns where the prices are steep and the sales are fast. Many antiques shops are open all year, but some serve only the vacation crowds; call before you go to avoid disappointment. There are dozens of shops throughout the county, and the following is only a sampling.

The Antique Palace Emporium (845-292-2270), 300 Chestnut Street, Liberty, has more than two floors of restored furniture and original collectibles.

Antiques Center of Callicoon (845-887-5918), 26 Upper Main Street, Callicoon. Open May through September, Thursday through Saturday and Monday 11–4; Sunday 11–3. September through December, Saturday only, 11–4. There are over three floors of antique furniture, primitives, lamps, clothing, art deco items, and artwork displayed in a restored 19th-century building.

Callicoon Flea Market (845-887-5411), 43 Lower Main Street, Callicoon, has everything from furniture to

FisherMears Associates

collectible pottery, along with reproduction furniture and decorative items.

Ferndale Antiques Marketplace (845-292-8701), 52 Ferndale Road, Ferndale. Open July through Labor Day, daily 10–5. Call for hours at other times of the year. There are several dealers under one roof here, with vintage costume jewelry, furniture, lamps, and a wide array of pieces representing several periods and styles.

Fiddler's Flea Market (845-583-6375), 1080 Route 17B, Bethel. Open May through Labor Day, Saturday and Sunday 9–5. This outdoor country market offers flowers, plants, antiques, household items, and more. There are special events on holiday weekends, like the Old Time Fiddlers performing on the grounds.

In2Retro (845-583-3126), 1163 Route 17B, Mongaup Valley. Open Memorial Day weekend through June 30 and mid-September through October, Friday through Sunday 11–5:30; July through Labor Day, daily 11–5:30. They carry quality art deco, midcentury, and modern furniture, lighting, mirrors, glass, porcelain, ceramics, and decorative items. There is also costume jewelry, clothing, handbags, and other fashion accessories. For bargain items there is a backyard "tent sale"; make sure to check out what's for sale there as well.

Memories (845-292-4270), Route 17 between exits 98 and 97 (watch for signs), near Ferndale, has a large general line and has long been a popular stop with vacationers.

If you are in Liberty, there are some other antiques shops to visit: **Kraus Farm Antiques & Vintage** (845-295-9278), 110 Mill Street, is open Memorial Day to Labor Day, daily 9–5; January through May, Friday through Sunday 9–5. They have oak, mahogany, pine, and walnut furniture, as well as china, artwork, crystal, glassware, and pottery. **Town & Country Antiques** (845-292-1363), 1 North Main Street, is open September through June, Thursday through Sunday 10–5; July and August, daily 10–5. This multidealer shop in the heart of the downtown historic district is housed in a wonderful building dating from the late 1800s. A sign for Gold Medal flour was discovered and restored on the north side of the building. Wander around and find loads of interesting items here. **Treasure Box Antiques** (845-292-8585/6566), 342 Chestnut Street (Route 52 West), is open all year with hours varying, so call ahead. There are fine porcelains, glass, linens, dolls, and ephemera here, as well as stained glass. Do check out this shop on your travels through Liberty.

✷ Special Events

January: **Annual Ice Carnival** (845-292-5100), Rotary Park, Livingston Manor. Ice sculpture competition, children's skating races, demonstration with nationally ranked ice skaters. Held 11–2. **Weekend Eagle Watching** (845-557-6162). Guided eagle viewing excursions by van and bus on weekends 10–4. Volunteers are posted at popular sites. On February weekends also.

April: **Opening Day of Trout Season** (845-439-4810), Catskill Fly-Fishing Center and Museum, 1031 Old Route 17, Livingston Manor. Join other anglers at the museum for a traditional cup of hot soup on the first day of fishing, April 1, 10–4. **Annual Easter Egg Hunt** (845-887-5155), Delaware Community Center, Main Street, Callicoon. This is a fun event for anyone with young children. It begins at 11 AM sharp.

June: **Morningside Classic: Bass Season Opens** (845-436-5418); call for location. Always on the third Saturday in June. **Tractor Parade** (845-887-4444), Creamery Road, Callicoon. Both old and new tractors ride down Main Street and are available for inspection after the noon parade.

July: **Annual July 4th Celebration** (845-292-9797), Main Street, Liberty. Enjoy a street fair, music, food, an antique car show, and a parade at noon. Festivities run 10–4. **Callicoon Canoe Regatta** (845-887-5640), Delaware River, Callicoon. This canoe race follows the river for 7 miles from Hankins to Callicoon and is followed by music, food, and festivities at the Delaware Community Center on Creamery Road. **Riverfest** (845-252-7576), Main Street, Narrowsburg. Held 10–5. This environmental festival features art, crafts, and live music. Posters by area artists are auctioned as well. **Weekend Chamber Music for All Time Summer Festival** (845-932-8527), Lake Huntington. Outdoor venues are mostly in Jeffersonville and run for a 10-day period in mid-July. Check www.wcmconcerts.org for complete schedule.

August: **Shandelee Music Festival** (845-439-3277; www.shandelee.org), J. Young Road, Livingston Manor. This annual concert series features internationally acclaimed classical solo and chamber concert artists who perform in an outdoor pavilion.

September: **Annual Day to be Gay in the Catskills** (845-295-8721), Delaware Community Center, Creamery Road, Callicoon. Music, food, vendors of all kinds; a benefit for the Day to be Gay Foundation.

December: **Liberty Bell Drop** (845-292-2394), Liberty Museum & Arts Center, 46 South Main Street, Liberty. Enjoy refreshments and live music while waiting for the bell to drop at midnight on New Year's Eve.

Ulster County

Ulster County Tourism

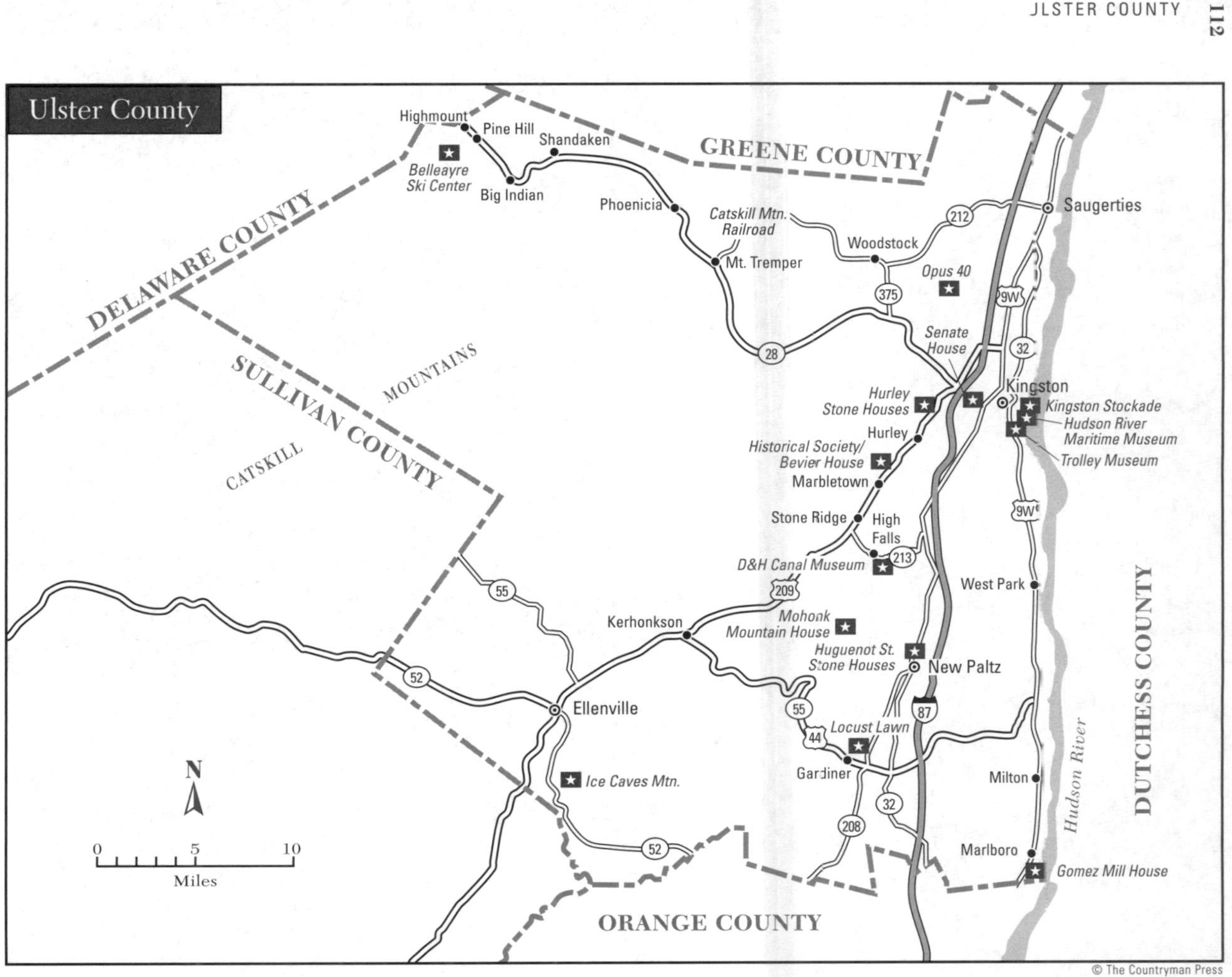
Ulster County
GREENE COUNTY
DELAWARE COUNTY
SULLIVAN COUNTY
CATSKILL
MOUNTAINS
ORANGE COUNTY
DUTCHESS COUNTY
Hudson River
Highmount
Pine Hill
Shandaken
Belleayre
Ski Center
Big Indian
Phoenicia
Catskill Mtn.
Railroad
Mt. Tremper
Woodstock
Opus 40
Saugerties
Senate
House
Kingston
Kingston Stockade
Hudson River
Maritime Museum
Trolley Museum
Hurley
Stone Houses
Hurley
Historical Society/
Bevier House
Marbletown
Stone Ridge
High
Falls
D&H Canal Museum
West Park
Kerhonkson
Mohonk
Mountain House
Huguenot St.
Stone Houses
New Paltz
Ellenville
Locust Lawn
Gardiner
Ice Caves Mtn.
Milton
Marlboro
Gomez Mill House
212
375
9W
28
32
213
209
55
52
87
44
32
208
N
0
5
10
Miles
© The Countryman Press

ULSTER COUNTY

Both the Dutch and the English settled in Ulster County, drawn by the lush farmlands along the Hudson. Snug, well-built homes were constructed of stone, brick, and wood; many still stand and are open to the public. Ulster County was not always blessed with peace and prosperity, however; it was the scene of conflict during the American Revolution, when the city of Kingston was burned by the British and spies were hanged in the outlying orchards. But the area rebuilt itself through the years, and today Ulster is a study in contrasts. Businesses have settled alongside farms, and artist colonies thrive among boutiques. Dutch names of towns and lanes recall the past, while a thriving community of second-home owners, immigrants, and vacationers has brought different cultures to the region.

Ulster is mountainous, flat, river lined, and forested by turns, and the outdoors offers excellent fishing, skiing, and hiking. There's enough here to keep visitors busy for another century or so! The region is easy to travel, with several major roads and enough byways to please every traveler. Bring a camera when you visit, because the seasonal changes in Ulster are dramatic, with spring giving way to summer overnight and winter making guest appearances as late as April.

GUIDANCE **Ulster County Tourism** (845-340-3566; 1-800-342-5826), 20 Broadway, Kingston 12401; www.ulstertourism.info.

Ulster County Chamber of Commerce (845-338-5100), 214 Fair Street, Kingston 12401; www.ulsterchamber.org.

GETTING THERE *By car:* Ulster County is accessible from the New York State Thruway exits 18, 19, and 20, and in the southern section of the county from Routes 17 and 9W.

By bus: **Adirondack/Pine Hill Trailways** (845-331-0744; 1-800-858-8555; www.trailwaysny.com), 400 Washington Avenue, Kingston, offers frequent daily service between the Port Authority in Manhattan and New Paltz, Kingston, Woodstock, and Phoenicia, as well as points north and west.

By train: **Amtrak** (1-800-872-7245; www.amtrak.com) operates trains between Manhattan and Rhinecliff, which is a 10-minute drive over the Kingston-Rhinecliff Bridge to Ulster County. **Metro North Railroad—the Hudson Line** (1-800-METRO-INFO; www.mta.info/mnr) operates train service from Grand Central Station to Poughkeepsie. There are usually trains every two hours, and more frequently at rush hours. There are reduced fares during off-peak hours. Ulster County runs bus service to and from the train station in Poughkeepsie to Kingston and points in between. For a complete bus schedule, call **Ulster County Area Transit, UCAT** (845-340-3333), 1 Danny Circle, Kingston.

By air: **Albany International Airport** (518-242-2200; www.albanyairport.com), 737 Albany Shaker Road, Loudonville, is the closest major airport to the northern part of the county. **River Aviation, Inc.** (845-336-8400), 1161 Flatbush Road, Kingston, operates Kingston Airport, located near the Kingston-Rhinecliff Bridge. **Stewart International Airport** (845-564-7200/2100; www.stewartintlairport.com), 1035 First Street, New Windsor, is the closest major airport to the southern part of the county.

MEDICAL EMERGENCY It is now possible to dial 911 anywhere in the county for emergency assistance.

Benedictine Hospital (845-338-2500), 105 St. Mary's Avenue, Kingston.

Ellenville Regional Hospital (845-647-6400), 10 Healthy Way, Ellenville.

Emergency One Urgent Care and Diagnostic Center (845-338-5600), 40 Hurley Avenue, Kingston.

First Care Walk-In Medical Center (845-691-3627), 222 Route 299, Highland. For the treatment of minor emergencies, illnesses, and injuries. Open daily 9–5.

Kingston Hospital (845-331-3131), 396 Broadway, Kingston.

✷ Villages

There are several beautiful villages in Ulster County. My three favorite places that are great for walking and self-guided tours are Hurley, Saugerties, and Woodstock, located near exits 19 and 20 off the NYS Thruway.

Hurley. Take Route 209 south to Hurley and follow signs. Every second Saturday in July, for one day only, the historic stone houses here are open to the public; it's called **Hurley Stone House Day.** Admission is charged for the house tours. The village of Hurley was established in 1651 by Dutch and Huguenot settlers who built wooden homes along the Esopus Creek. After a short war with the Esopus Indians, which resulted in the burning of much of the settlement, the homes were replaced with stone structures, 25 of which are still standing. Hurley was a hotbed of activity during the Revolution, serving as the state capital when Kingston was burned, a resting place for troops, and a meeting place for

DUTCH REFORMED CHURCH AND SPY HOUSE, MAIN STREET HURLEY WALKING TOUR

Ulster County Tourism

spies. Later Hurley was a stop on the Underground Railroad, the escape route for slaves fleeing to Canada, as well as the home of abolitionist Sojourner Truth.

Visitors can still walk around the town and see the largest group of stone houses still in use in the country. Although the homes are open only one day each year, Hurley is worth a walk anytime, and many of the buildings have historic markers that tell something of their history and lore. Along Main Street look for the **Polly Crispell Cottage** (built in 1735), which was once used as a blacksmith shop. This house was also equipped with a "witch catcher"—a set of iron spikes set into the chimney, presumably to discourage witches (and birds) from flying in. The **Jan Van Deusen House** became the temporary seat of New York's government in 1777, and a secret room was used to store important documents. The outer door is set off by the work of an early Hurley blacksmith, and a date stone is visible. There is an antiques shop in the back of the house (see *Selective Shopping—Antiques*).

Also on Main Street: the **Dumond House,** which was to confine a convicted British spy before he was hanged from an apple tree across the road; the **Parsonage,** built in 1790; and the **Elmendorf House** (once the Half Moon Tavern), built in the late 1600s. A burial ground can be found between the Crispell and Elmendorf buildings. If you drive west on Main Street, follow the Hurley Avenue Extension, and you will see several more stone buildings.

A corn festival, held in mid-August, celebrates the local sweet-corn industry. Held on the grounds of the Hurley Reformed Church, the festival offers crafts and corn. Fresh ears of corn by the thousands are dished up with butter. There is also corn chowder, corn bread with honey, and entertainment.

Saugerties. Once a prosperous river town, a center of the bluestone and tanning industries, Saugerties has had its ups and downs over the past 200 years. During the 1830s, the town was well situated on the Hudson River so that bluestone could be floated down to Manhattan from the docks for use in city sidewalks and streets. Today travelers will be treated to a renaissance in Saugerties—just walk up and down Main Street and Partition Street and visit the bookstores, antiques shops, galleries, and interesting eateries. There is a strong commitment to revitalizing the community through civic projects and commercial ventures. Don't miss **Krause's Homemade Chocolates** (845-246-8377), 41 South Partition Street, a fourth-generation chocolatier—the owner makes 44 types of candies on location. The **Saugerties Lighthouse,** with its wonderful Hudson River views, is now a bed & breakfast (see *Lodging*). Saturday 9–2 there is a **farmers' market** (see *To Do—Farmers' Markets and Pick-Your-Own Farms*). The best way to see the town is to wander and enjoy!

Woodstock. The town of Woodstock has long attracted creative people. Home to farmers and quarrymen for two centuries, the hamlet saw new changes in the spring of 1902, when Ralph Radcliffe Whitehead, an Englishman schooled in the theories of John Ruskin, was searching for a place where an arts colony could be organized. With two friends as partners, Whitehead bought seven lush farms and formed a community called Byrdcliffe (a combination of his and his wife's names). Workshops for metalworkers, potters, and weavers were soon built, and over the years the colony has continued to attract artists and craftspeople. Today the **Byrdcliffe Arts Colony,** America's first utopian arts and crafts colony, situated on 300 wooded acres with 30 picturesque buildings and listed on the

National Register of Historic Places, is worth a short walking tour—brochures are available at the Woodstock Guild on Tinker Street. During the 1930s, folksingers discovered Woodstock; later the town became a haven for "beatniks," and then talents like Pete Seeger; Bob Dylan; Joan Baez; Peter, Paul, and Mary; and other musicians of the 1960s who discovered inspiration there. In 1969 an eponymous concert, actually held nearly 50 miles away on a farm in Bethel (Sullivan County), made Woodstock a legend in the world of rock music—and the world at large. (The promoters/organizers of the event lived in Woodstock, hence the name.) **The Woodstock Museum** (845-246-0600), 13 Charles Bach Road, Saugerties, is a good stop for those interested in "hipstory." There is a guided tour here, a film, and the heritage of Woodstock from the town's earliest days is documented. Open May through October, Saturday and Sunday 10–4. Admission fee.

Today the somewhat eccentric but never dull town is still a gathering place for talent of all types. The surrounding mountains, and the shadow of Overlook Mountain, create a dramatic backdrop for local galleries and shops. Woodstock's main thoroughfare is Mill Hill Road, which becomes Tinker Street (according to legend, a tinker's wagon sank into the spring mud here). Just about all the shops and galleries in town can be reached by an easy walk, so enjoy a leisurely exploration. Of special interest are **Jean Turmo, H. Houst & Son, Chez Grand'mere,** and the **Center for Photography,** all on Tinker Street. (See *Selective Shopping—Art Galleries* for an art tour of the town.) **Mower's Saturday/Sunday Market** (845-679-6744), Maple Lane, in the center of town, has been a tradition in Woodstock since 1977. A large flea market offering antiques, crafts, collectibles, and an array of eclectic offerings, Mower's is a must for weekend shoppers in the village. Open mid-May through November, weekends 9–5; July through Labor Day, also open Wednesday 1–8 in conjunction with the Woodstock Farm Festival. There are parking lots on Rock City Road or Tannery Brook Road. There is also a municipal lot near the town offices; watch for signs. Off Tinker Street, across the street from the old firehouse, is Comeau Drive, where you will find the **Woodstock Historical Society Museum** (845-679-2256), which will be of interest to history buffs. They have displays with artifacts and old photographs of the town's past. The museum is open June through October, Saturday and Sunday 1–4. **The Colony Café** (845-679-5342), in the historic Colony Arts building, 22 Rock City Road, offers an eclectic mix of music nightly except Wednesday. Call for a schedule of events. The **River Rock Health Spa** (845-679-7800; www.riverrock.biz), 62 Ricks Road, just west of town toward Bearsville, is a great place to pamper yourself at the end of a day of sightseeing. They are open year-round, but do call in advance for an appointment to schedule a facial, massage, peel, or wrap. A variety of packages is available, and you can find one that suits you by visiting their website. And don't forget to take a drive up Rock City Road to the **Tibetan Buddhist Monastery** (see *To See*) before leaving town. And if you get tired, sit on the village green and watch the colorful parade of people go by. (Kids will love **Woodstock Wonderworks,** an amazing playground designed by the town's kids themselves and built in 1989 by the parents, youngsters, and townspeople under the guidance of an award-winning company. So if you are traveling with children, check out this play area at Woodstock Elementary School on Route 375.)

✷ To See

Century House Historical Society & A. J. Snyder Estate (845-658-9900; www.centuryhouse.org), 668 Route 213, Rosendale (watch for signs). Tours from May through Labor Day on Sunday 1–4 and by appointment. Admission fee. This estate sits directly across from the Delaware & Hudson Canal. The house is open for tours, and the carriage house, with its fine collection of more than 20 antique sleighs and carriages—some dating from the 1820s—is a must-see. Phaetons, wagons, and cutters are all here and in beautiful condition. There are also the ruins of old cement kilns on the property, the canal slip, and the Widow Jane Mine, a cave often used for special events, including concerts and plays.

The Emerson Country Store (845-688-5800; www.emersonresort.com), 5340 Route 28, Mount Tremper. Open year-round, daily 10–5; extended hours in summer season. The Emerson Resort and Spa is one of the county's premier family destinations for fine lodging and dining, shopping, and family entertainment. This is it: **Kaleidoworld,** home of the *Guinness Book of World Records*–certified world's largest kaleidoscope. Visitors actually walk into the 60-foot-high, silo-shaped room, where they experience a color and sound show unlike any other. Then step into the shops; one of them offers one of the largest selections of kaleidoscopes in the country. The other boutiques feature regional books, cashmere items, antiques, furniture, and unique gifts for the home. The Lodge at the Emerson Resort, a fantasy of what everyone thinks a mountain getaway should look like (see *Lodging*), is next door if you decide to stay overnight. A must-see for families traveling in western Ulster County.

THE WORLD'S LARGEST KALEIDOSCOPE, EMERSON COUNTRY STORE

Ulster County Tourism

Delaware & Hudson Canal Historical Society & Museum (845-687-9311; www.canalmuseum.org), 23 Mohonk Road, High Falls. Open May through October, Saturday and Sunday 11–5. Admission fee. This museum is dedicated to the history and lore of the great Delaware & Hudson Canal. Built in the early 19th century, the canal was used to ship coal from the mines in Pennsylvania to the factories of New York; later cement was shipped south to be used for bridges and skyscrapers. The canal's designer was also responsible for the Erie Canal, and the locks, basins, and dams were engineering wonders of their era. In the museum, visitors will find a miniature setup of the canal and its workings, offering a sense of what life was like on the canal boats used for the six-day trips. While you are at the museum, take the self-guided tour of the locks (located across the road); along the tour you will see examples of stonework, snubbing posts, weirs, locks, and loading slips.

Empire State Railway Museum (845-688-7501; www.esrm.com), Ulster & Delaware Railroad Station, 70 Lower High Street, Phoenicia. Open Memorial Day weekend through October, weekends and holidays 11–4. Donation. This small museum offers excellent exhibits about railroads and life in the Catskill Mountains. Past shows have included photographs and artifacts related to the building of the reservoirs, tourism history, and railroads in the Catskills. The volunteer guides all love trains and their history, and they make the tour fun for all.

Fred J. Johnston Museum (845-339-0720), 63 Main Street, Kingston. Open May through October, Saturday and Sunday 1–4. Admission fee. For the lover of American decorative history and fine antiques, a stop here is mandatory. This extraordinary collection was assembled by Johnston, a dealer and friend of Henry du Pont, who compared Johnston's furniture and decorative items to those found in du Pont's own museum, Winterthur. The house was built around 1812 for a prominent local attorney who counted Washington Irving and Martin Van Buren among his friends and guests. Visitors today will enjoy the fine 18th- and 19th-century examples of furniture, porcelain, and needlework that fill the house, including examples by local cabinetmakers and artists like John Vanderlyn.

Hudson River Maritime Museum (845-338-0071; www.hrmm.org), 50 Rondout Landing (at the foot of Broadway), Kingston. Open May through October, Friday through Monday 11–4. Admission fee. This museum is dedicated to preserving the maritime heritage of the Hudson River. For almost 200 years the Hudson was a major water highway between New York City and Albany. One of the ports of call along the way was the Rondout Landing in Kingston, once a bustling area of boatyards and rigging lofts that echoed with steam whistles and brass ships' bells. But when shipping on the Hudson fell into decline, so did the fortunes of the Rondout. Then in 1980 the museum was opened and has since restored several riverside buildings and historic vessels; visitors can now see a working part of the Hudson's legacy. An exhibit hall features shows on marine history. Outside there is an ever-changing display of river vessels, including the 1899 steam tug *Mathilda* and the cruise boat *Indy 7.* Visitors to the landing have also included the presidential yacht *Sequoia* and the sailing ships *Clearwater* and *Woody Guthrie.* Special weekend festivals are held throughout the year, including a Harvest Festival in October and sailing regattas and gatherings of antique wooden boats.

Klyne Esopus Museum (845-338-8109; www.klyneesopusmuseum.org), 764 Broadway (Route 9W), Ulster Park. Open June through mid-October, Friday

Ulster County Tourism

RONDOUT LANDING

through Monday 1–4. Free. This museum is located in a Dutch country church built in 1827 and features exhibits concerning the culture, business, and history of the town of Esopus. Check the website for the schedule of free Saturday speakers; topics include subjects like the stone houses of the area and tugboats on the Hudson.

Overlook Observatory (845-679-0785), 141 Silver Hollow Road, Willow; approximately 7 miles west of the village of Woodstock, off Route 212. Hours by appointment; fee charged for classes. Both home and scientific workshop to nationally known astronomer Bob Berman, the observatory offers visitors a guided tour of the night sky, with all its mysteries, quirks, wonders, and outstanding instruments for viewing the heavens. Bob is a knowledgeable and enthusiastic guide as well as the author of popular astronomy books that have been featured in national media.

O & W Napanoch Train Station Museum (845-647-7400; www.nyow.org), Institution Road, Napanoch. Open March through December, the first and second Sunday of every month 10–2. Free. The Ontario & Western Railway began operations in 1902 transporting supplies like coal—as well as prisoners—to the New York State Correctional Facility in Napanoch. The station is still located on prison property. Exhibits, artifacts, and memorabilia explain the history of this O & W station as well as its relationship to the D&H Canal and the region itself. There is a biography of James C. Atkins, the stationmaster for 50 years, that will be of interest to railroad buffs. The station is on the New York State and National Registers of Historic Places.

Samuel Dorsky Museum of Art (845-257-3844; www.newpaltz.edu/museum), SUNY New Paltz, 75 South Manheim Boulevard, New Paltz. Open year-round, Wednesday through Sunday 11–5. Closed Monday, Tuesday, and holidays.

Donation. Opened in 2002, this is the only art museum between Manhattan and Albany on the west side of the Hudson River. There are six galleries with a total of more than 9,000 square feet of space. Enjoy changing exhibits of contemporary art, which complement exhibits from the museum's permanent collection that spans more than 4,000 years. (The focus includes American and European works on paper, regional paintings, prints, sculpture, photographs, and metalwork.) There is an emphasis here on the cultural heritage of the Hudson Valley and Catskill Mountains as well as diverse world cultures.

Tibetan Buddhist Monastery (845-679-5906; www.kagyu.org), 335 Meads Mountain Road, Woodstock. At the village green, turn onto Rock City Road, which becomes Meads Mountain Road; follow up the mountain for 2.6 miles to the top. Group tours are offered by appointment. Free monastery tours for individuals leave the bookstore Saturday and Sunday 1:30–3. Karma Triyana Dharmachakra Monastery is situated high above Woodstock and is worth a trip any time of year. Founded in 1978, the monastery combines traditional Tibetan architecture and design with Western construction. The monastery has undergone a significant expansion in recent years and is worthy of a drive up the mountain by all weekend visitors to Woodstock.The main shrine room is 2,400 square feet and features one of the largest statues of Buddha in North America, while smaller shrines are decorated with traditional art. Be sure to see the gift shop, with its wide assortment of imported items from the Himalayas in addition to books. A nice change of pace from the crowded streets of Woodstock on weekend afternoons!

FOR FAMILIES Catskill Animal Sanctuary (845-336-8447; www.casanctuary.org), 316 Old Stage Road, Saugerties. Open April through October, Saturday 10–4; Sunday noon–2 for special free program. Admission. Tours are available every hour on the hour along with educational programming at the visitors center. This sanctuary is located on 110 acres of land dedicated as a haven for abused and abandoned farm animals. Stories of the rescue and rehabilitation of these animals as well as their friendly "personalities" will endear them to all who visit. The kids will be particularly delighted to see horses, cows, pigs, and goats in a bucolic atmosphere; it's a place where they will enjoy nature, make friends, and learn new things. There are hayrides, children's activities, and workshops and speakers on a variety of issues. Since 2001 this sanctuary has provided refuge for more than 1,000 needy animals and has placed them in loving local homes. A wonderful stop for families traveling with youngsters. The sanctuary now has its own inn, the Homestead, with three rooms and one apartment, for those who would like to extend their visit.

CATSKILL ANIMAL SANCTUARY
Ulster County Tourism

Ulster County Tourism

CATSKILL MOUNTAIN RAILROAD

Catskill Mountain Railroad (845-688-7400; www.catskillmtrailroad.com), 5408 Route 28, Phoenicia. Open Memorial Day weekend through Labor Day weekend, weekends and holidays only 11–5; September and October, weekends only noon–4; trains leave every hour on the hour. Admission fee, but children under the age of four ride for free. This 6-mile round-trip from Mount Pleasant to Phoenicia takes about 45 minutes. The train stops at the Empire State Railway Museum on High Street in Phoenicia (see *To See*), where riders will enjoy a guided tour. In November and December on Saturday and Sunday, there is a Kingston Shuttle train that travels through the city. Check the website for a schedule. This is a wonderfully relaxing way to take in the countryside if you are traveling with children; besides, just about everyone loves train rides.

Forsyth Nature Center (845-339-3053; www.forsythnaturecenter.org), 167 Lucas Avenue, Kingston. Open September through April, Monday through Friday 7–5, weekends and holidays 9–1; May through August, Monday through Friday 7–7, weekends and holidays 9–5. Free. There are nine species of mammals in this small zoo, which includes llamas, deer, bulls, pygmy goats, and sheep. An aviary on the premises is filled with a variety of birds. There is a large playground in the park, and the two activities make a nice outing for those with young children. A number of special programs are offered here year-round, including bird walks, estuary studies, story hour, and arts and crafts sessions; call in advance for details.

Skate Time 209 (845-626-7971; www.skatetime209.com), 5164 Route 209, Accord. Open year-round, Thursday through Monday 1:30–9:30; call or go to the website to check times of sessions. This indoor skate park and roller rink offers "wheelie" fun for kids—and parents. Skate and helmet rentals are available; no skateboard rentals. A great place for families to visit on weekends during the winter months.

Trolley Museum (845-331-3399; www.tmny.org), 89 East Strand, Kingston; follow Broadway south where it ends, turn left, and watch for signs. Open Memorial Day weekend through Columbus Day, weekends and holidays noon–5. Admission fee. Housed in an old trolley shed along the Rondout. For anyone who remembers the ring of a trolley bell or the rolling ride of a self-propelled car, this museum offers displays—and lots of nostalgia. Visitors may also enjoy a short ride on a restored trolley car.

Woodstock Farm Animal Sanctuary (845-679-5955; www.woodstocksanctuary .org), Van Wagner Road, Willow (8 miles west of the village of Woodstock, off Route 212). Open April through October, Saturday and Sunday 11–4 or by appointment. A nonprofit organization that cares for and rehabilitates neglected and discarded farm animals. They take in cows, pigs, chickens, turkeys, sheep, and goats. Most have been rescued from abusive situations or have escaped the slaughterhouse. A nice outing for families visiting the Woodstock area. The guesthouse, a renovated farmhouse with four bedrooms, opened in 2012 and offers visitors the opportunity to stay overnight and enjoy a vegan breakfast in the morning.

HISTORIC HOMES Bevier House and Ulster County Historical Society (845-338-5614; www.ulstercountyhs.org), 2682 Route 209, Marbletown (6 miles south of Kingston on the right side of Route 209). Open May through October, Thursday through Sunday 1–5. Admission fee. Built in the late 1680s, this stone house now serves as headquarters of the county historical society, and it is a treasure trove of odd collections and memorabilia. The house was once a single-story Dutch farmhouse, and much of the present structure was added during the last three centuries. Throughout the house you will see fine Hudson Valley Dutch and Victorian furniture in addition to the tool and kitchenware collections, ceramic

TROLLEY MUSEUM

Ulster County Tourism

Ulster County Tourism

BEVIER HOUSE AND ULSTER COUNTY HISTORICAL SOCIETY

pottery from an early factory in Poughkeepsie, portraits, and decorative accessories. The Bevier House is not a formal museum and has a great old-fashioned feel about it. Check the website for a schedule of special events, including a harvest fair, holiday candlelight tour, local history lectures, and craft workshops.

Gomez Mill House (845-236-3126; www.gomez.org), 11 Mill House Road, Marlboro. Open April through October, Wednesday through Sunday 10–4, with tours at 10, 11:30, 1, and 2:30. You must take a tour to see the inside of the museum and home. Open off-season by appointment. Admission fee. (*Note:* This site lies in both Orange and Ulster counties, which is why there are entries in both sections of this book.) Visitors will see the oldest surviving Jewish homestead in North America here, as well as a unique cultural landmark. Built in 1714 as a sawmill and trading post, the site was named after the Gomez family, who supplied traders roving the upstate New York wilderness. Later owners were farmers, boatmen, members of the Continental Army, writers, and painters; Dard Hunter (who owned the place from 1913 to 1919) was a paper mill owner whose mill is still in working condition (you can buy handmade paper in the gift shop). The site has also served as a home, inn, and school, and the buildings reflect the many personalities of those who have lived and worked here.

Huguenot Street Stone Houses (845-255-1660; www.huguenotstreet.org), 18 Brodhead Avenue, off Route 32 in New Paltz. The area is open year-round; open weekends only in May, November, and December. Tours are offered June through October, Thursday through Monday 10:30–5. Admission fee. The tours last one and a half hours, but those with younger children may choose to leave after an hour; the last half hour delves into more detailed history about the stone houses.

In 1677 a group of 12 Huguenot men purchased almost 40,000 acres of land from the Esopus Indians and began the settlement that was referred to as "die Pfalz," after an area in the Rhineland Palatinate. By 1692 their original dwellings were being replaced by stone houses, several of which still stand today as a result of the efforts of the Huguenot Historical Society. A trip to New Paltz offers a unique chance to see what life was like three centuries ago in upper-middle-class homes. The walking tour begins at the Dubois Fort on Huguenot Street, near the gift

BEVIER HOUSE AND ULSTER COUNTY HISTORICAL SOCIETY

Ulster County Tourism

Ulster County Tourism

STONE HOUSE, HUGUENOT STREET

shop. All the buildings are owned by the society, and many still have their original furnishings. At the Abraham Hasbrouck house (1721), the dark rooms include a cellar-kitchen, which was the heart of village social life, and a built-in Dutch bed. Other houses of the period include the Bevier-Elting House, distinguished by a long well sweep and covered walk for the convenience of the ladies; the **Freer House,** with its mow door, which made it easier to move provisions into the attic; and the **Dubois Fort,** reputed to be haunted by a headless lady. Possibly the most interesting house is the **Jean Hasbrouck House** (1678), which once served as a store and tavern. Downstairs is a bar as well as a jambless fireplace with its curtain-like decorations; upstairs is a massive brick chimney, the only one of its type in the United States. Several other buildings are also open to the public, including the reconstructed **French Church,** the Federal-style **LeFevre House,** and the **Deyo House,** a remodeled 17th-century home. Special programs are offered at this site year-round; check the website for a complete schedule.

DUBOIS FORT

Ulster County Tourism

The **Huguenot Path** is a self-guided walking tour through the Harcourt Nature Sanctuary spanning Huguenot Street and the Wallkill River trail; ask in the gift shop for a brochure to assist in guiding you along the way.

Hurley Patentee Manor (845-331-5414), 464 Old Route 209, Hurley. Open July 4th weekend through Labor Day, but call first since visits are by appointment only. Admission fee. This National Historic Landmark is a combination of a Dutch cottage, built in 1696, and a 1745 Georgian manor house. The manor was the center of the Hurley Patent, a 96,000-acre land grant that included the land between Woodstock and New Paltz but that today has been reduced to the 5 acres surrounding the house. The house is privately owned and has been restored to its original condition. The owners display many fine antiques from the 17th to the 19th centuries. The basement has one of the few indoor animal pens still in existence and is also the display area for Hurley Patentee Lighting, a company that crafts handwrought reproduction lighting fixtures and is still operating today.

Locust Lawn and **Terwilliger House** (845-454-4500), Route 32, outside Gardiner. Open May through October, by appointment only. Admission fee. These two sites are within minutes of each other and are administered by the Locust Grove Estate in Poughkeepsie. **Locust Lawn,** a Federal-period house, was designed by a Newburgh architect and built in 1814 for Col. Josiah Hasbrouck, a Revolutionary War veteran. The elegant white mansion has a magnificent three-story central hall and still houses a fine collection of 18th- and 19th-century furniture and decorative arts, as well as several portraits by the American folk painter Ammi Phillips. Since Locust Lawn remained in the Hasbrouck family until the 1950s, when it was donated to the society, many of the original furnishings remain. Also on the site are outbuildings typical of a farm of that era, and visitors can see the carriage house, smokehouse, and slaughterhouse. One rare artifact found here is the great oxcart that was used to transport supplies to the beleaguered army at Valley Forge.

Down the road from Locust Lawn stands the **Terwilliger House,** built in 1738 and left almost untouched over the last 250 years. This is a fine example of the architectural style used by the Dutch and French Huguenot settlers in the Hudson Valley. Built of stone, with a center hall and great fireplace, the house has been furnished in the style of the era. Both Locust Lawn and Terwilliger House are open by appointment only for groups of 10 or more. Call 845-454-4500, ext. 211 to schedule a group tour.

Matthewis Persen House (845-340-3040), 74 John Street, Kingston. Open Memorial Day weekend through Labor Day, Tuesday through Saturday 10–2; September to Thanksgiving, Saturday 10–2. Free. This house is named after its longest resident, Matthewis Person (1739–1819), and some parts of the structure date back to 1661. The house was burnt twice over the centuries and has been home to doctors, tailors, grocers, druggists, and innkeepers. There are four landmark buildings on each corner of John and Crown streets, and it is the only intersection in the country with 18th-century stone houses on all four corners. The house was purchased by Ulster County in 1914. Restoration began in 1999, and artifacts discovered in the process are on display in the house today. It was opened to the public in the spring of 2011.

HISTORIC SITES **Kingston Heritage Area Visitors Centers** (845-331-7517; 1-800-331-1518), 20 Broadway and 308 Clinton Avenue, Kingston. Open year-round, Monday through Friday 9–5; May through October, also open Saturday and Sunday 11–5. Free. New York State has designated Urban Cultural Parks as the interpreters of urban settings of particularly historic interest; Kingston is known for

Ulster County Tourism

VOLUNTEER FIREMEN'S HALL AND MUSEUM

its importance in the history of transportation. The center is located in the Stockade area (once surrounded by walls of tree trunks 13 feet high) and offers orientation displays that cover Kingston from 17th-century Dutch settlement to the present. Directions for self-guided walking tours are available, and guided tours may be arranged by appointment. While uptown, you may also want to stop by the **Volunteer Firemen's Hall and Museum** (845-338-1247), 265 Fair Street, open May through October, Friday and Saturday 10–4. The museum is in an old firehouse where antique fire apparatus, memorabilia, and period furniture are on display.

The Broadway location, on the Rondout, offers permanent exhibits on Kingston's history and architecture and offers brochures, maps, and a calendar of events for travelers.

Mohonk Mountain House (845-255-1000; www.mohonk.com), 1000 Mountain Rest Road, New Paltz (6 miles west of New Paltz). Take Route 299 west over the Wallkill River, turn right at the Mohonk sign, and then bear left and follow the road to the gate. Open year-round; call ahead or check the website for full-service spa appointments, ice skating, cross-country skiing, and hiking information and special-events weekends. Admission fee. When Alfred and Albert Smiley built this resort in 1869, they were determined to preserve the surrounding environment and offer gracious accommodations to visitors from the city. Guests here could hike the nearby Shawangunks, take a carriage ride around the manicured grounds, or enjoy the carefully tended flower gardens. There was a lake for ice skating as well as croquet lawns. The hotel itself was furnished with the best of the Victorian era: acres of polished oak paneling and floors, hidden conversation nooks, and homey, overstuffed furniture. Mohonk has endured the last century with timeless grace, and today visitors will find many things unchanged. The resort is still dedicated to preserving the natural world, and the gardens have won awards for their beauty. Mohonk sits next to a trout-stocked lake that becomes the focus of special winter carnival weekends. A stone tower atop the mountain offers a six-state view on sunny days. Hikers, birders, horseback riders, and cross-country skiers will find Mohonk unequaled. Day visitors are welcome, but it takes more than a day to sample all of the surprises at Mohonk. Note that on holiday weekends the hotel is often closed to day visitors, so make sure to call in advance.

Old Dutch Church (845-338-6759; www.olddutchchurch.org), 272 Wall Street, Kingston. Open year-round, Monday through Friday 10–3; guided tours by appointment. Free. Organized in 1659, the Reformed Protestant Dutch Church of Kingston has served the people of the area continuously ever since. The present building was constructed in 1852; its bluestone exterior is in the Renaissance Revival style, and the windows were made in the Tiffany studios. Local tradition once held that the bell was cast from silver and copper items donated by the congregation. Inside you will see bronze statues as well as artifacts from the 1600s onward. Take time to walk through the churchyard and view the fine examples of early gravestone art (Governor DeWitt Clinton's gravesite is located here). In the spring thousands of yellow and red tulips planted in honor of the Netherlands line the church walks. In addition to wonderful Christmas concerts, there are musical performances by local artists on Thursday at 12:15 PM during the spring, summer, and fall. Call for a schedule of events; the church is a magnificent place to hear music any time of year.

Opus 40 and the **Quarryman's Museum** (845-246-3400; www.opus40.org), 50 Fite Road, Saugerties. Follow Route 212 west from Saugerties, make a left on Glasco Turnpike, and then follow signs to the end of Fite Road. Open Memorial Day weekend through Columbus Day, Friday through Sunday, holidays, and Monday 11:30–5. Admission fee. In 1938 artist Harvey Fite's bluestone quarry outside Saugerties was merely the source of material for his sculpture. But as work on the individual pieces progressed, Fite realized that the terraces and steps he had

OPUS 40

Ulster County Tourism

created as a backdrop for the sculpture had themselves become the focus of his work. Naming the site Opus 40 because he believed it would take 40 years to complete, Fite set about creating a vast environmental work that would eventually contain 6 acres of steps, levels, fountains, pools, and paths. Each of the hundreds of thousands of bluestone pieces was hand-cut and fitted, and the 9-ton central monolith was lifted into place with a boom and winches. Today Opus 40 is open to the public as an environmental sculpture and concert site. Fite, who had studied theology and law and worked as an actor and teacher, also built a museum to house his collection of quarrymen's tools and artifacts. The museum offers a rare glimpse into a lost way of life.

Saugerties Lighthouse (845-247-0656; www.saugertieslighthouse.com), 168 Lighthouse Drive, Saugerties. From the center of Saugerties, follow Main Street to the end, heading north; make a right turn onto Mynderse Street, which becomes Lighthouse Drive—although there are no signs—and keep bearing to the left. The site is also accessible by boat from the Route 9W boat-launch area. Open Memorial Day weekend to Labor Day; tours given on weekends and holidays noon–3. Donation. Enjoy a walk through the Ruth Glunt Nature Preserve, and at low tide walk out to the historic lighthouse, which contains a museum with artifacts from the commercial heyday of the Saugerties waterfront. Overnight accommodations are available year-round (see *Lodging*), and a live-in lighthouse keeper resides on the premises. I spent a night here in the month of June, and it was truly a memorable experience!

Senate House State Historic Site (845-338-2786; www.nysparks.com), 296 Fair Street, Kingston. Open April through October, Wednesday through Saturday 10–5; Sunday and holiday Mondays 1–5. Group tours available by appointment year-round. Admission fee. When the New York State government was forced to leave New York City during the Revolution, it sought safety upstate. The house in which the committee met was built in the 17th century by a Dutch settler, Wessel Ten Broeck, and was partially burned by the British in 1777. After numerous additions and changes to the building, the house has been restored to reflect its part in history. Visitors can see several rooms, including the kitchen with its kitchenware and huge fireplace, and the meeting room in which the first state senate deliberated. The colonial gardens at this site are beautiful, especially in June, when the roses are in full bloom. A second Colonial Revival–style building on the site, added in 1927, houses a museum with historic displays and changing exhibits that reflect the story of Kingston. One room is given over to the works of John Vanderlyn, a Kingston native who was considered one of the finest painters in 19th-century America. The Italianate **Loughran House** (1873) is used for site offices. This historic site offers a variety of special events, including concerts, videos, and lectures throughout the year. Evening candlelight tours are given during the month of December.

SCENIC DRIVES Ulster County has hundreds of miles of well-maintained roads, coupled with some of the most spectacular views in the Hudson Valley. It doesn't matter if you travel in autumn, with all the riotous color, or in winter, with its icy beauty—Ulster will often surprise you with its striking scenery.

For a drive that offers history as well as scenic beauty, start at **Kingston** (exit 19 off the NYS Thruway) and go south along **Route 209.** This is one of the oldest roads in America: the Old Mine Road, which was a trading route between upstate New York and Pennsylvania in the 17th century. As you pass by Hurley, Marbletown, and Stone Ridge, you will see acres of fields planted with sweet corn, the area's largest agricultural crop, and you will see many farm stands in summer and autumn. The architectural styles of the homes range from Dutch stone to late Victorian. At Route 213 head east through High Falls, along the old Delaware & Hudson Canal. Stop in at the High Falls Food Co-op if you like natural foods, or just continue down the road that follows the canal into Rosendale. At Route 32 you can head south into New Paltz and explore the old stone houses; or head north back to Kingston.

For a second scenic route from **Kingston,** take **Route 9W** south along the Hudson River. At West Park you may want to follow the signs to Slabsides, once the writing retreat of naturalist John Burroughs; it's on your right across the railroad tracks (park at the bottom of the hill and walk up). Back on Route 9W, continue south and take Route 299 west through New Paltz, then follow Route 44/55 west for some of the finest views and overlook sites in the Shawangunks. At Route 209 head back north past old Dutch farms and stone houses to Kingston.

From Kingston you can also follow **Route 28** to Route 28A around the **Ashokan Reservoir,** a special treat in the autumn months. Follow the signs to the pump station, and walk around the fountain or have a picnic—it is a fairly uncrowded, undiscovered area, except on weekends. However, since New York City watches its watershed area very carefully, be wary of where you park, hike, or stop. The NO PARKING and NO STOPPING signs are serious; violators are usually fined.

For an unusual drive, take the **Hudson Valley Pottery Trail** to studios in Accord, High Falls, and Stone Ridge. A detailed map and list of craftspeople opening their

ASHOKAN RESERVOIR

Ulster County Tourism

studios to visitors is on www.potterytrail.com (see *Selective Shopping—Pottery & Ceramics*).

You can also take a **self-guided driving tour** through 300 years of European settlement in the Kingston area. Pick up information at the NYS Thruway (exit 19) tourism caboose (845-340-3766), just off the roundabout (Washington Avenue). They are open May through October, daily 10–4.

WINERIES, BREWERIES, AND DISTILLERIES The Hudson Valley has become an important center of wine production in New York, and visitors are welcome to stop at Ulster County's wineries. They range in size from tiny "boutique" wineries to full-size vineyards complete with restaurants, bottling plants, and cellars. Wherever you go, however, you will find people who love their work and are willing to share their expertise and wines with you. Some of the vintners offer formal guided tours; others just have a showroom and tasting area. You may want to call before you go—there are special events, concerts, and tours throughout the season, and hours may change when the harvest begins. Most of the sites are free, as are the tastings, but there may be admission charged to special events.

The **Shawangunk Wine Trail** (845-256-8456; www.gunkswine.com) is an 80-mile route that runs between the Shawangunk Mountains and the Hudson River. It wends its way through both Ulster and Orange counties, directing travelers to several wineries along the way. The trail is marked by signs along the roadways.

Adair Vineyards (845-255-1377), 52 Alhusen Road, New Paltz. Open June through October, daily 11–6; May, November, and December, Friday through Sunday 11–5. The vineyard has an old Dutch barn and offers tastings, tours (by calling ahead), and a picnic area. The picture-perfect Ulster County spot looks unchanged through the centuries. All wines here are made from estate-grown grapes.

Baldwin Vineyards (845-744-2226), 176 Hardenburgh Road, Pine Bush, is located on a 200-year-old estate where more than 40 acres of pastures, vineyards, and woodlands are open for strolling. Open July through October, Wednesday through Sunday noon–5; April through June and November and December, Thursday through Sunday 11:30–5. Their award-winning wines include chardonnay, merlot, Riesling, brut champagne, and a strawberry-flavored wine.

Benmarl Winery (845-236-4265), 156 Highland Avenue, off Route 9W, south of Marlboro (look for signs). Open April through December, daily noon–6; January through March, Friday through Sunday noon–5. Visitors may enjoy a tour, tasting, and a stop at the art gallery on the premises—the founder of the winery was an illustrator—at this scenic winery situated high on a hill overlooking the orchards, with magnificent views of the Hudson River and surrounding countryside. Special events include spring open house, summer concerts, and a grape-stomping festival in the fall.

Brimstone Hill Vineyard (845-744-2231), 61 Brimstone Hill Road, Pine Bush. Open May through October, daily 11:30–5:30; November through April, Saturday and Sunday only. French-style wines are the specialty here, especially dry reds and sweet whites.

Cereghino Smith Winery (845-334-8282), P.O. Box 193, Bloomington 12411. Open June through October by appointment only. This winery began in a New York City apartment in the late 1990s with traditional Italian blends inspired by the grandfather of the owner, Paula Cereghino. Paula and her husband, Fred Smith, now produce excellent red wines (try the lighter-bodied zinfandel Eaten by Bears) using New York State and Sangiovese grapes, as well as some California varieties. An interesting addition to the Ulster County group of wineries, it's small (300–400 cases per year), with an old-world approach, and makes five interesting blends. This one is definitely worth a stop for oenophiles.

El Paso Winery (845-331-8642), 742 Broadway (Route 9W), Ulster Park. Open April through December, Wednesday through Sunday 11–6. A variety of decent New York State wines are produced, bottled, and sold in this cozy barn, including a merlot and barn red (my favorite). The lovely shop on the premises has unusual gifts for the oenophile, as well as a nice selection of regional books. Make sure to check it out.

Glorie Farm Winery (845-236-3265), 40 Mountain Road, Marlboro. Open Memorial Day weekend through August and November through December, Saturday and Sunday noon–5; September and October, Saturday and Sunday noon–6. Housed in a 1913 barn on a fruit farm/vineyard near the top of Mount Zion, this winery came on the Ulster County winery scene in 2004. Most of the wine here is produced from estate-grown grapes and features Seyval blanc, Cayuga white, cabernet franc, and their own Red Monkey, as well as pear and apple wines. The tasting room has a fantastic view of the Hudson Valley.

Kedem Royal Winery (845-236-4281), 1519 Route 9W, Marlboro. Open year-round by appointment only, Sunday through Thursday 9–5. A short video explains the background of this unusual winery, which produces a variety of kosher wines.

Keegan Ales (845-331-BREW; www.keeganales.com), 20 St. James Street, Kingston. Open year-round for light fare and beer: Tuesday through Thursday 4–10; Friday and Saturday noon–midnight; Sunday 1–10. This microbrewery features several different beers: a golden ale, a pale ale, and a milk stout called Jo Mama's Milk: Brown sugar and Monkey Joe Roasting Company's coffee extract are added to the mix, creating an unusual flavor. Beer lovers will enjoy relaxing in the pub atmosphere. This is the only brewery in the Hudson Valley. There is often live music on weekends, so check the website for a schedule.

Magnanini Farm Winery (845-895-2767), 172 Strawridge Road, Wallkill. Open April through December, weekends only: Saturday 6–7 PM, Sunday noon–1, or by appointment. A restaurant on the premises serves Northern Italian fare by reservation only.

Robibero Family Vineyards (845-255-9463), 714 Albany Post Road, New Paltz. Open year-round, Thursday through Sunday 11–6. This is a small family-owned winery and a relatively new addition to Ulster County's vineyards, having opened in 2010 where Rivendell was located. Do try their Riesling!

Stoutridge Vineyard (845-236-7620), 10 Ann Kaley Lane, Marlboro. Open year-round, Friday through Sunday 11–6. This winery/distillery, built on the site of a historic farm, has had vineyards growing on the property since the early 19th century. Stephen Osborn and his wife, Kimberly Wagner, have restored the farmhouse and constructed a state-of-the-art winery using a gravity-feed design built on the original winery site. There is a 15,000-case annual capacity here, and they specialize in German-style whites from Riesling and pinot blanc varieties, as well as Northern Italian–style reds from Sangiovese, pinot noir, and Teroldego grapes.

There is also a distillery here, and the vodkas are derived from apples and pears grown on local Hudson Valley farms. Stoutridge is worth a visit to see sustainable practices employed in the winemaking process.

Whitecliff Vineyard and Winery (845-255-4613), 331 McKinstry Road, Gardiner. (Take Route 299 to County Route 7; McKinstry Road is off there.) Open year-round: June through October, daily 11:30–5:30; February through May, November, and December, Thursday through Monday 11:30–5:30; January, weekends only 11:30–5:30. This 75-acre farm grows chardonnay, merlot, cabernet franc, and pinot noir grapes. There are phenomenal views of the Shawangunks from the winery. Whitecliff has one of the largest vineyards in the region, and they are known for complex dry wines. Owners Yancey and Michael Migliore make their award-winning wines both from their own grapes and those of other New York State growers. Make sure to check out the gallery on the premises since there is always interesting work on display by an array of fine Hudson Valley artists.

Tuthilltown Spirits (845-633-8734), 14 Gristmill Lane, Gardiner. Open year-round for tours by appointment only. The retail store on the premises is open for tastings daily 9–4. The Tuthilltown gristmill is a landmark listed on the National Register of Historic Places. In 2001 the mill was converted to a distillery and now produces vodka, whiskey, and brandy using local fruit and grain. This is the only whiskey distillery in New York State and the first to open in the state since the Prohibition era.

✷ To Do

AIRPLANE RIDES, HANG GLIDING, AND SKYDIVING **Mountain Wings** (845-647-3377), 77 Hang Glider Road (off State Route 209), Ellenville, features hang gliding, and paragliding instruction. Open year-round; call ahead.

Skydive the Ranch (845-255-4033; www.skydivetheranch.com), 45 Sandhill Road, Gardiner. Open year-round, weekdays at 9:30 AM, weekends and holidays at 8 AM. Call in advance to reserve a place in class. Skydiving instruction available; first-timers welcome. If you want to try something new, this may be the activity you've been imagining. All first jumps are in tandem—divers are attached to an instructor both in free fall and under a specially designed parachute built for two. There is nearly a minute of free fall and several minutes under the canopy of the chute. Those who jump must be at least 18 years old and under 225 pounds; dress comfortably and bring sneakers. Price (approximately $200) includes training, equipment, and the jump.

BICYCLING **Ashokan Reservoir,** off Route 28A, Shokan. Open year-round, daily dawn to dusk. A wonderful place to bicycle, walk, run, or rollerblade, this 1.25-mile stretch of pavement that runs along part of the Ashokan Reservoir is a must-see for visitors. There are breathtaking views of the mountains here, and the area is renowned as a place where eagles nest. If you are lucky, you may see one fly by or get a glimpse of an eagle perched in a tree. There is no vehicular traffic, and dogs are not permitted. A sign on Route 28A that indicates public parking is also the entrance to this special spot.

Hudson Valley Rail Trail (845-691-2066; www.hudsonvalleyrailtrail.net), 12 Church Street, Highland. Open daily dawn to dusk. This 4.2-mile nature trail extends from the Mid-Hudson Bridge through the town of Lloyd. There is a 2-mile paved portion of the trail. A great spot for family bicycle outings. This trail is part of a network of a thousand rail trails that cover 10,000 miles across America. Turnoffs along the way run to overlooks and down to the banks of the river—great places to get off your bicycle for a picnic and take in the scenery.

Minnewaska State Park Preserve (845-255-0752; www.lakeminnewaska.org), 5281 Route 44/55, New Paltz. Open year-round, daily from 9 AM (closing time is posted each day). Admission fee. This preserve is located atop the dramatic Shawangunk Mountain Ridge, more than 2,000 feet above sea level, and offers miles of trails and carriage roads for bicyclists of all abilities.

Mohonk Preserve (845-255-0919; www.mohonkpreserve.org), 3197 Route 44/55, Gardiner. Open daily from sunrise to sunset. Day-use fee for nonmembers. There are more than 100 miles of trails and carriage roads for use by bicyclists. Visitors center is open daily 9–5 and offers exhibits free of charge.

Shawangunk Rail Trail (845-895-2611; www.gorailtrail.org), 14 Central Avenue, Wallkill. This 3-mile section of unpaved rail trail with views of the Shawangunk Mountains provides easy access to the Wallkill River and village of Wallkill. A nice ride for mountain bikers.

Wallkill Valley Rail Trail (www.gorailtrail.org). Open daily dawn to dusk. This 12.2-mile linear park between the New Paltz–Rosendale and Gardiner-Shawangunk town lines was where a busy railroad line existed in the late 19th century, transporting produce and dairy products from Ulster County to New York City. It also served as a commuter railroad. In 1977 the railroad took its last freight run; in

WALLKILL VALLEY RAIL TRAIL

Ulster County Tourism

1983, all the ties and rails were removed, and community volunteers cleared the trail. The rail trail officially opened to the public for recreational use in 1993. Enjoy a walk, jog, or bike ride along this scenic trail, maintained and managed by volunteers. Motorized vehicles are prohibited, except for those used by handicapped people. A detailed brochure is available (see website).

The following Ulster County shops rent both mountain bikes and road bikes: **Bicycle Depot** (845-255-3859), 15 Main Street, New Paltz; **Accord Bicycle Service** (845-626-7214), 5770 Route 209, Kerhonkson; **Overlook Mountain Bikes** (845-679-2122), 93 Tinker Street, Woodstock.

BOAT CRUISES The Hudson runs the length of Ulster County, and visitors can select from several companies that cruise the river. Even if you don't know port from starboard, there are tours that take all the work—but none of the fun—out of a river trip. One warning: It can be very breezy and cool yet sunny out on the river; bring a hat, scarf, sweater, and sunscreen.

Hudson River Cruises (845-340-4700; 1-800-843-7472; www.hudsonrivercruises.com), Rondout Landing, Kingston. Open July and August, Tuesday through Sunday with cruises at 11:30 and 2:30, and Friday evenings at 8; May, June, September, and October 2:30 only. Two-hour cruises head south of Kingston for one hour toward the Hyde Park area, passing both the Kingston and Esopus Meadows lighthouses. Enjoy the roomy ship *Rip Van Winkle,* which features plenty of seating, restrooms, and a snack bar. Because the river tends to be less choppy than the ocean, the ride is smooth and pleasant. Music is provided Friday evenings.

Tours of the **Rondout Lighthouse** are offered through the Hudson River Cruises Water Taxi on *The Lark* from early July through mid-October, Saturday and Sun-

THE *RIP VAN WINKLE* BOUNDING HOME

Ulster County Tourism

Ulster County Tourism

A SCENIC PLACE TO KAYAK IS THE RONDOUT CREEK WHERE IT ENTERS THE HUDSON RIVER.

day at 2 PM. The tour gives visitors a glimpse into a way of life that was once typical of Hudson River lighthouse keepers and their families. (*Note:* Visitors are able to leave the boat and tour the lighthouse; this site is not handicapped accessible.)

Hudson River Water Taxi (845-340-4700), Rondout Landing, Kingston. May through October there are trips to the Rhinecliff dock. On Saturday and Sunday at 2 PM there are trips to the Rondout Lighthouse.

Hudson Sailing (845-687-2440; www.hudsonsailing.com), 1 Broadway, Kingston, offers excursions on the *Cirrus,* a Corsair F-28R, a modern sailing vessel operated by owner Dan Feldman, a U.S. Coast Guard–licensed captain. These memorable trips are by appointment only but are well worth making the arrangements.

North River Charters (845-750-6025; www.theteal.com), West Strand Park, Kingston. The *Teal,* a medium-size boat docked at Rondout Landing in Kingston, holds up to 75 guests. The boat is fitted with rich wood and brass, and the atmosphere aboard takes you back to a time of genteel river travel, yet there are all the modern amenities. Available for private excursions and corporate sightseeing charters. There are sightseeing cruises open to the public during the summer months; check the website for a schedule.

CANOEING AND KAYAKING **Atlantic Kayak Tours** (845-246-2187; www.atlantickayaktours.com), 320 West Saugerties Road, Saugerties. Open April through mid-November for kayak trips on the Hudson River, Esopus, and other local waterways, this outfitter will make an excursion fun; a particularly good choice for first-timers. There are over 40 different kayak tours offered.

City of Kingston Kayak Tours (845-331-1682, ext. 132; www.forsythnaturecenter.org), 467 Broadway, Kingston, offers guided nature-oriented kayak tours seasonally on the Hudson River and Rondout Creek. Sightings include bald eagles, osprey, turtles, and other birds and wildlife.

FARMERS' MARKETS AND PICK-YOUR-OWN FARMS Since the earliest colonists arrived, fruit farming has been important to Ulster County's economy. The first commercial orchard in the country was established here in 1820. At that time, Robert Pell of Esopus began growing Newton Pippin apples for export to England. Apples are still the leading fruit crop, with more than 8,000 acres planted and about 3 million bushels produced annually. Notice that many orchards are located on the sides or top of hills, which reduces the likelihood of crop losses due to late-spring frost.

Some Ulster County farms are still owned by the families that founded them; others have been cultivating the same site for centuries. The harvest season here stretches from early-summer strawberries to late-fall pumpkins and holiday greenery. Some farm stands offer freshly baked pies and cakes, while others have recipes for you to take home, along with food and other local goodies. Pick-your-own farms let you do the work as well as give you the choice of what you want in the basket. Most growers provide containers, but if you bring your own, the price is usually lower. However you decide to gather in the harvest, the following is just a sampling of places to try. Because weather conditions make it difficult to predict exact harvest dates, do call ahead for information about the crops available when you intend to go.

Farmers' Markets

The Kingston Farmers' Market (845-853-8512), Wall Street between North Front and John streets, in uptown, close to exit 19 off the NYS Thruway. Open May through November, Saturday 9–2. There is a winter market held in the Old Dutch Church on Wall Street on the first and third Saturdays of the month, December through April. You will find fruits and vegetables, fresh-cut flowers, cheeses, breads, smoked meats, organic chicken, meats and game, honey, pies, and more.

New Paltz Farmers' Market (845-255-5995), North Front Street and Church Street. Open late June through October, Sunday 10–3. Local produce, breads, soaps, flowers, mustard, and jellies.

Rosendale Farmers' Market (845-658-3467), 1055 Route 32, Rosendale Community Center parking lot, Rosendale. Open June through November, Sunday 9–2. There is live acoustic folk music along with traditional and organic vegetables, potted plants, apples, berries, flowers, cookies, pies, fresh breads, cheeses, wine, cider, honey, pickles, and maple syrup. Rain or shine. Call for winter market hours.

Saugerties Farmers' Market (845-246-9371), 119 Main Street, Saugerties. Open June through October, Saturday 9–1. Produce, fruit, flowers, breads, and more. There is often music here, as well.

Woodstock Farm Festival (www.woodstockfarmfestival.com), Maple Lane, off Tinker Street, Woodstock. Open June through October, Wednesday 3:30–7:30. Local produce, baked goods, honey, and more are sold here. Each weekly farmers' market has a theme (like Mushroom Day or Local Chef Challenge), and there is always live music at the nearby flea market. Delicious local take-out food vendors enable shoppers to stop and enjoy a picnic supper while strolling through town. This festive Wednesday "happening" is a wonderful way to experience Woodstock.

Pick-Your-Own & Farm Stands

The Apple Bin (845-339-7229), 810 Route 9W, Ulster Park. Open daily March through December. Many varieties of apples, vegetables, gourmet take-out items, great baked goods, and pick-your-own apples in October.

Barthels Farm Market (845-647-6941), 8057 Route 209, Ellenville. Open April through December, daily 8–6. They offer an array of vegetables at this bountiful stand.

Davenport Farms (845-687-0051), 3411 Route 209, Stone Ridge. Open daily March through December. An extensive selection of local produce, including raspberries, grapes, corn, apples, pumpkins, and melons. There is a second market off the Kingston roundabout, Washington Avenue Extension, which specializes in flowers and fresh produce. They are open 6:30 AM–7 PM and have beautiful hanging baskets, cider, and plants of all kinds.

Dressel Farms (845-255-0693), 271 Route 208, New Paltz. Open daily, except Sunday, June through October. You can pick your own strawberries, apples, and pumpkins here in season, surrounded by magnificent views of the Shawangunk Mountains.

Four Winds Farm (845-255-3088), 158 Marabac Road, Gardiner, has certified organic vegetables; grass-fed lamb and beef, poultry (including turkey), and pork; as well as eggs and herbs. Do call ahead for directions and to make sure someone will be there. This place is a real find; stock up if you are on the way home. **The Gippert Farm** (845-247-9479), 266 Churchland Road, Saugerties, is an organic farm that offers eggs, chicken, turkey, and, at times, lamb. Two other organic farms are the **Phillies Bridge Farm Project** (845-256-9108), 45 Phillies Bridge Road, and **Taliaferro Farms** (845-256-1592), 187 Plains Road, both located in New Paltz; they offer a variety of fresh produce in season.

Jenkins-Leuken Orchards (845-255-0999), 69 Yankee Folly Road, New Paltz. Open August through May, daily 9–6. Pick-your-own apples and pumpkins. They have a large variety of apples, including Macouns. Pears, peaches, tomatoes, and vegetables are available in season. Honey and cider are produced on the farm, as well.

Liberty View Farm (845-883-7004; www.libertyviewfarm.biz), 340 Crescent Avenue, Highland. Open May through October, this delightful farm, with spectacular views of the Shawangunks, is one of the best places in the Hudson Valley to pick apples. Absolutely no chemical pesticides are used on the crops, and their Cortlands are among the best I've ever tasted. The free-range chickens are beautiful to look at and are fed organically, as are the goats. Make sure to check out the 100-foot historic chicken coop and buy eggs before leaving the farm! The heirloom chickens produce fantastic tasting eggs. Owner Billiam van Roestenberg has a variety of seasonal festivals at the farm (often they include the work of local artists displayed throughout the fields). Check the website for a complete schedule of events as well as the complete background on this historic farm. Make sure to inquire about the Lease-an-Apple-Tree and Charter-a-Chicken programs.

Migliorelli Farm (845-757-3276), 5150 Route 28, Mount Tremper, offers a dazzling array of local produce. They are open May through November, and you will find them where Alyce & Roger's Fruit Stand was located.

One of my favorite places to pick strawberries, blueberries, and pumpkins in Ulster County is **Saunderskill Farms** (845-626-2676), 5100 Route 209, Accord.

Open April through December, daily, except Monday, 9–6. This beautiful family-owned and family-operated farm and store, named for the tributary of the Rondout Creek that flows through the farm, offers home-grown vegetables (excellent corn and tomatoes), fruits, flowering annuals, perennials, and herbs. The on-site bakery makes fine fruit pies, cookies, brownies, and cider doughnuts. There is local maple syrup, honey, and jams. In autumn children will enjoy the horse-drawn hayrides. There are special events throughout the year, including an antique tractor pull, a corn festival, and winter holiday festivities, so call ahead to see what's happening before you go. Originally granted to Hendrick Schoonmaker by Peter Stuyvesant in 1663, the family's original 300 acres have been continuously farmed since 1680, making Saunderskill Farms the second-oldest family farm in the country. (It now includes more than 800 acres.) The stone manor house, built in 1787, still stands on the property. Jack, Dan, Dave, and Kathy Schoonmaker are on the premises every day.

Stone Ridge Orchard (845-687-0447), 3012 Route 213, High Falls. Open from July through October, daily 9–6 for pick-your-own apples, pumpkins, and raspberries. They have more than a dozen varieties of apples here, and the orchard is surrounded by hundreds of acres of forest and farmland. There are hayrides for the kids, picnic benches, and fresh cider. The shop on the premises offers maple syrup, home-baked pies, and other treats. This spot is easy to find, right on Route 213 off Route 209, and it's a beautiful place to spend a couple of hours on an autumn afternoon.

Weed Orchards (845-236-2684), 43 Mount Zion Road, Marlboro. Open August through October, Monday through Friday 10–4; Saturday and Sunday 9–5. Located on one of the most picturesque spots in the county, this fourth-generation working farm is nestled at the base of the Marlboro Mountains. They offer pick-your-own peaches, pears, grapes, pumpkins, beans, squash, eggplant, and, last but not least, 14 varieties of apples. There is a lakeside picnic area, and the farm market/bakery sells cider, doughnuts, cookies, candy apples, sandwiches, and more. There is always something happening on the weekends for the kids, including a hay maze, hayrides, and a visit to the petting zoo.

Wilklow Orchards (845-691-2339), 341 Pancake Hollow Road, Highland. From exit 18 off the NYS Thruway, turn right on Route 299, go 2.3 miles, turn right on New Paltz Road, go about 1 mile, and make a right onto Pancake Hollow Road for another mile to the orchard. One of the oldest family-run pick-your-own farms, it's been in business for more than 100 years, open daily Labor Day through October for pick-your-own apples (there are 10 varieties here) and pumpkins. The stand sells home-grown vegetables and fruits, and cider. Kids will enjoy the farm animals on the premises.

Some local fruit farms that specialize in pick-your-own fruits and more include the following: **Kelder's Farm & U-Pick** (845-626-7137), 5575 Route 209, Kerhonkson, with berries and pumpkins, as well as a petting zoo and hayrides; open April through December, daily 10–6. **Mr. Apples Low-Spray Orchard** (845-687-9498/0005), 25 Orchard Street, High Falls, with several varieties of apples, pears, and cider. Open August through November, daily 10–6. **Minard Farms** (1-866-632-7753), 250 Hurds Road, Clintondale, with apples, cider, picnic areas, and hayrides. Weekends only September and October 10–5. **Tantillo's Farm Market** (845-255-6196), 730 Route 208, Gardiner, for picking cherries, apples, peas, peaches, tomatoes, and pumpkins. Open March through December, daily 9–6. Also in Gardiner is **Wright Farms** (845-255-5300), Route 208, for apple and cherry picking; they are open year-round, and the Wright family has been farming here for more than 100 years. Open daily 8–6. In Milton: **Locust Grove Farm** (845-795-5194), North Road, with berries, cherries, peaches, apples, plums, and pumpkins in season. **Prospect Hill Orchards** (845-795-2383), 40 Clark's Lane, with cherries, peaches, apples, pears, and pumpkins. Open in season, weekends only 9–4.

A couple of larger farm markets worth stopping at include **Adams Fairacre Farm** (845-336-6300), on Route 9W in Lake Katrine, and **Wallkill View Farm** (845-255-8050), on Route 299 just outside of New Paltz. The produce and baked goods here are first-rate. You can also pick your own pumpkins in season.

Maple Syrup Farms

The time for maple syrup tastings and tours is mid-February to mid-April. The following places will be glad to show you around and sell you their delicious syrup, maple cream, and honey. It's a good idea, however, to call before you go, since erratic weather often affects the season. **Arrowhead Farm** (845-626-7293), 5941 Route 209, Kerhonkson, has tours during the season. **Lyonsville Sugarhouse** (845-687-2518), 591 County Route 2, Accord, offers tours. **Oliverea Schoolhouse Maple Syrup** (845-254-5296), 609 Oliverea Road, Oliverea, is open year-round. **Sugar Brook Maple Farm** (845-626-3466), 351 Samsonville Road, Kerhonkson, has wonderful tours and is open year-round for sales.

Christmas Tree Farms

There are several places to cut a tree for the holidays in Ulster County. These are some places local residents enjoy visiting. Do call before going, however, to make sure they are open. **Hurds Christmas Tree Farm** (845-883-7825), Hurds Road, Clintondale, is open weekends in December, Saturday 9–4; Sunday noon–4. **Digrazia Tree Farm** (845-687-0449), 469 Pine Bush Road, Stone Ridge, is open daily in December, 10–dusk. **The East Mountain Tree Farm** (845-647-5548), 9 Mancuso Road, Napanoch, is open weekends 8:30–dusk, and during the week by appointment only. **Zeeh's Tree Farm** (845-331-4355), Barbarossa Lane, Kingston, is open weekends in December 9–4. **Applegate Farms** (845-246-9046), 83 Wilhelm Road, Saugerties, is open weekends in December 9–4.

FISHING Ulster County offers fishing enthusiasts a chance to try their luck in scores of streams, a reservoir, and the great Hudson River. The waters are well stocked with a variety of fish—trout, bass, pike, pickerel, and perch are just some of the more popular catches. Fishing areas are well marked, and New York State licenses are required, as are reservoir permits. Call the **Department of Environmental Conservation Department of Fisheries** (845-256-3161), New Paltz, for detailed information.

There are very few fishing guide services due to the fact that the Esopus Creek and other waterways are very accessible. Just about anyone can get to many terrific fishing spots in the county with ease. Some of the better-known fishing streams include the renowned Esopus Creek (access points along Route 28, west of Kingston), Rondout Creek (access points on Route 209, south of Kingston), Plattekill Creek (access near Route 32 in Saugerties), and the Sawkill Creek (access

Ulster County Tourism

FISHING IN THE ESOPUS CREEK

along Route 212 in Woodstock). Most of the main access points are indicated by brown and yellow state signs; many also have designated parking areas. If you are uncertain about the stream, ask; otherwise you may find yourself on the receiving end of a heavy fine. Holders of reservoir permits will want to try the Ashokan Reservoir (Route 28A, west of Kingston), with 40 miles of shoreline, and trout, walleye, and bass lurking beneath the surface. The Kingston City Reservoir requires a city permit for fishing, but it is worth the extra effort to obtain.

GOLF Ulster County golf courses can be by turns dramatic, relaxing, and colorful, and the areas that offer golf cater to a wide range of skills and interests. Hotel courses are usually open to the public, but it is recommended that you call in advance since they schedule special events and competitions.

In the Kingston and Saugerties Area

Alapaha Golf Links (845-331-2334), 180 Sawkill Road, Kingston. Open daily 7–dusk. Note that the hours vary with the season. This nine-hole course, par 30, is 1,800 yards long and a great place for novices. Driving range and putting green.

Green Acres Golf Club (845-331-2283), 250 Harwich Street, Kingston. Open daily 7–dark. This nine-hole, par-36 course is 2,774 yards long. A driving range is also here. A popular place with local residents.

Lazy Swan Golf & Country Club Village (845-247-0075), 1754 Old Kings Highway, Saugerties. Open 8–dark. There are nine holes and a par 35 at this 3,100-yard-long course. There is a clubhouse restaurant on the premises; pro shop and lessons are available. Award-winning architect Les Walker of Woodstock designed the seven-building village, which includes the clubhouse, restaurant, and a Pilates facility.

In the New Paltz Area

Apple Greens Golf Course (845-883-5500), 161 South Street, Highland. Open weekdays 7–dusk, weekends 6–dusk. This 18-hole course, par 71, is 6,500 yards in length, and there is a driving range, putting green, clubhouse restaurant, pro shop, and lessons as well as a twilight rate.

Mohonk Mountain House (845-256-2143), 1000 Mountain Rest Road, New Paltz. Open daily dawn to dusk. There are nine holes, par 35, at this scenic course. Driving range, putting green, and lessons available.

New Paltz Golf Course (845-255-8282), 215 Huguenot Street, New Paltz. Open March through November, daily dawn to dusk. There are nine holes at this par-36 course with all the amenities: driving range, putting green, restaurant, pro shop, lessons.

In Accord, Kerhonkson, and Ellenville

Honor's Haven Resort and Spa (845-210-3106), 1195 Arrowhead Road, Ellenville. Open daily 7–dusk. There is a nine-hole championship course here designed by Robert Trent Jones Sr. There is also a driving range and golf school.

Hudson Valley Resort (845-626-2972), 400 Granite Road, Kerhonkson. Open daily 7–6. This 18-hole, par-71, 6,700-yard course is beautiful; it is on the grounds of a full-service resort, and you will find all the amenities here: driving range, putting green, restaurants, hotel facilities, pro shop, lessons, golf school, group packages. Make sure to make a reservation to tee off in advance, especially on weekends.

Rondout Golf Club (845-626-2513), 10 Bank Street, Accord. Open daily 6 AM–7 PM. This 18-hole, par-72 course has a driving range, putting green, restaurant, pro shop, lessons, golf packages, and twilight rate.

Shawangunk Country Club (845-647-6090), 38 Country Club Road, Ellenville. Open March through November, daily 7–7. This nine-hole, par-34 course has a putting green and restaurant; pro shop and golf packages available.

Stone Dock Golf Course (845-687-7107), 112 Stone Dock Road, High Falls. Open daily 7–dusk. This nine-hole, par-36, 3,315-yard course is pleasant to play. There is a driving range and a restaurant on the premises. You can register for lessons if you desire at the pro shop. They also offer group packages and a twilight rate.

Turtle Creek Golf Course at the Garden Cathay (845-564-3220), 219 Plattekill Ardonia Road, Wallkill. Open daily 7–dusk. This nine-hole course has a tight design that will challenge even the most experienced golfers. There are sand traps, grass bunkers, and water hazards on five holes.

HIKING Ulster County has some of the best hiking in the Hudson Valley, with views that go on for miles and trails that range from an easy walk to a hard day's climb. The following suggestions for afternoon or day hikes provide magnificent vistas, but it is recommended that you use maps available locally to make your hike as much fun and as safe as possible. And remember to dress appropriately; Lyme disease is prevalent in many areas.

Belleayre Mountain (845-254-5600), Belleayre Mountain Road, Pine Hill, offers excellent hiking in the Catskill Forest Preserve. There are marked cross-country ski trails that provide a nice walk in the woods, and a hike to the summit of Belleayre reveals sweeping views of the mountains below. Elevations range from 600 to 4,200 feet, and much of the area is rugged, steep terrain. A more moderate walk is the hike to Pine Hill Lake, which is part of the state preserve. In the summer months you can stop for a swim there.

Black Creek Forest Preserve (845-473-4440), intersection of Route 9W and Winding Brook Acres Road, Esopus. This 130-acre forest preserve lies along a major Hudson River tributary. Walkers will cross a suspension footbridge over the Black Creek and pass through forest woodlands with vernal pools on the three hiking trails (a total of 2.5 miles) that have direct access to the Hudson River. This is a lovely place for a short hike; a good choice on a hot day, since it always seems a bit cooler here, with much of the trail area being shaded.

Esopus Meadows Point Preserve (845-454-7673), located 1 mile from the intersection of Route 9W and River Road, Port Ewen. There are 3,500 feet of Hudson River shoreline in this 100-acre site that offers great views of the Esopus Meadows Lighthouse, three trails, and an environmental center. The trails go through lovely woodlands and in some places along the river. This is a fine place to take a hike for an hour or two on gently sloping terrain.

Frost Valley YMCA (845-985-2291), 2000 Frost Valley Road, Claryville, has hundreds of acres to explore on several different trails. Stop in and get a map before you start out. (See *Winter Sports—Cross-Country Skiing* for directions.)

Hurley Rail Trail, Route 209, Hurley. You can see some of this 6-mile trail from Route 209. It connects High Falls and Hurley and passes through dense wood-

ESOPUS MEADOWS LIGHTHOUSE

Ulster County Tourism

lands. There is a parking lot off Route 209, approximately 1 mile south of Route 28, at the intersection of Route 209 and Russell Road.

Mohonk Mountain House (845-255-1000), 1000 Mountain Rest Road, New Paltz; **Mohonk Preserve** (845-255-0919), 3197 Route 44/55, Gardiner; and **Minnewaska State Park** (845-255-0752), 5281 Route 44/55, New Paltz. These three areas are for day use only and charge a fee. The Shawangunk trails found at these sites are excellent (see *Green Space*), although somewhat crowded on summer weekends. Mohonk Mountain House has 128 miles of paths and carriage roads to hike, and there are several first-rate spots for rock climbing in this area, as well.

Overlook Mountain, Meads Mountain Road, Woodstock, is a moderate walk up a graded roadbed. From Tinker Street at the village green, take Rock City Road to Meads Mountain Road, which leads straight to the trailhead, across from the Tibetan monastery on the right side of the road (see *To See*). The summit takes about an hour to reach, depending on how fast you travel the 2-mile ascent. You will pass the ruins of the Overlook Mountain House on the way up; a lookout tower and picnic tables are at the top. The view of the valley and river is incomparable.

Shaupeneak Ridge Cooperative Recreation Area (845-473-4440), Old Post Road, Esopus (a parking lot is located 0.2 mile from the intersection of Route 9W and Old Post Road). There are 3.5 miles of trails that wend their way through this 561-acre wildlife conservation area owned by Scenic Hudson. You will see wetlands and Louisa Pond, which was carved out by glaciers thousands of years ago. This is a good place to go for a hike of moderate difficulty that is easily accessible from a main road. This site is used for several environmental education programs.

Vernooy Kill Falls in Kerhonkson can be reached by taking Route 209 to Lower Cherrytown Road, then bearing right and continuing 5 miles to Upper Cherrytown Road. In another 3 miles you will see the parking lot on the right and the trailhead on the left. The trail is a little more than 3.5 miles up and back.

The Wallkill Valley Rail Trail, 12.2 miles of linear park, on a former railroad track, between New Paltz and Gardiner. Good places to pick up the trail: in the historic Huguenot Street area or downtown New Paltz (across the street from the parking lot at the Water Street Market is one easy access area). Since October 1993 this valuable community resource has attracted visitors from around the Hudson Valley and beyond (see *Bicycling*).

Wilson State Park (845-679-7020), 857 Wittenberg Road, Mount Tremper. Open year-round; Memorial Day weekend through Labor Day, daily 9–6; limited winter hours. This small park has a lovely lake that is ideal for canoes. The park is surrounded by mountains and is only a short distance from the center of Woodstock. It's a wonderful place to stop for those traveling with young children. There are places to picnic and walking trails on paths through the woods along the stream. Campsites are available for overnight stays, and there are cross-country ski trails in the winter (no services, however, and it's ski at your own risk).

HORSEBACK RIDING/HORSE SHOWS Ulster County offers only a small number of places for visitors to go horseback riding on a trail through the woods. It is best to contact hotels like the Mohonk Mountain House (see *Lodging*) if you enjoy this sport. The following are a few privately owned establishments that still provide this pastime:

Ulster County Tourism

VERNOOY KILL FALLS

Braden Brook (845-647-7556), 19 Mountaindale Road, Greenfield Park. Open year-round, daily 10–6. There are trail rides and pony rides here for all ages and abilities.

Coyote Ridge Stables (845-236-1136), 583 Lattintown Road, Marlboro. Open April through October. They offer trail rides, pony rides, and lessons here. Groups will be accommodated. Do call in advance for an appointment.

HITS-on-the-Hudson Horse Shows (845-246-8833; www.hitsshows.com), 454 Washington Avenue Extension, Saugerties. Open Memorial Day weekend through Labor Day, Wednesday through Sunday 8–5. Admission is charged on weekends only. Horse lovers will enjoy seeing a show at this nearly 300-acre facility. There are 10 permanent all-weather hunter, jumper, and equitation rings; two amphitheaters; and hundreds of stalls on the show grounds. There are dozens of retail shops and food concessions on the premises.

Mohonk Mountain House (845-255-1000), 1000 Mountain Rest Road, New Paltz. Open daily year-round. Enjoy the trails (and carriage rides) through 7,500 historic acres by advance reservation only. Those who are not guests of the hotel must purchase a day pass in addition to the charge for horseback riding.

Payne Farm (845-255-0177), 125 Dubois Road, New Paltz. Open year-round, daily 10–6. There are trail rides for all levels of ability, along with phenomenal views of the Shawangunk and Catskill mountains. Indoor and outdoor arenas.

KAYAKING If you have never gone kayaking, the **City of Kingston Parks and Recreation Department** (845-331-1682, ext. 7336) sponsors two-hour guided kayak tours from late May through early September that depart from Kingston

Point Park. The cost for these outings is approximately $30 and includes all equipment as well as an experienced guide. There are morning and sunset paddles, but it is best to call for the most up-to-date offerings.

There is an excellent place to contact if you want to rent a kayak and head out independently:

Kenco (845-340-0552), 1000 Hurley Mountain Road (off Route 28), Kingston. Open Monday through Saturday 9–7; Sunday 11–5. This excellent outdoor-equipment and apparel store rents kayaks by the day and weekend. If you don't have a rack on your car, they will supply straps and foam blocks so you can transport the kayak on the roof. And if you need any gear, they are sure to have it here. Advance reservations for kayaks on summer weekends are strongly suggested. (Kingston Paddle Pals produces an online newsletter, www.waterfrontalliance.org, with several suggestions on the best places to kayak in Ulster County. Do check it out if you're unfamiliar with the area.)

ROCK CLIMBING The Shawangunk mountain range in Ulster County is renowned nationally for rock climbing. Those who want to learn should contact an outfitter that specializes in instruction.

Alpine Endeavors (845-658-3094), Rosendale. Open year-round by appointment only. This is the place to go if you are considering professional instruction or a guided trip either rock or ice climbing.

Eastern Mountain Sports Climbing School (845-255-3280; 1-800-310-4504), 3124 Route 44/55, Gardiner.

High Angle Adventures (845-658-9811; 1-800-777-2546), 178 Hardenburgh Road, Ulster Park. Open for full-day instruction with some of the best climbers in the East.

HITS-ON-THE-HUDSON HORSE SHOWS IN SAUGERTIES

Ulster County Tourism

The Inner Wall (845-255-ROCK), 234 Main Street (Eckerd's Plaza), New Paltz. This indoor rock climbing gym is open year-round and provides a great place to practice—even in the pouring rain or a snowstorm.

Sundance Rappel Tower (845-688-5640), 64 Route 214, Phoenicia. Open year-round on weekends or by appointment. Here you can practice rope-descent technique and rappelling.

SWIMMING Many of the best places to swim in Ulster County are reservoirs; naturally, they strictly forbid swimming. In recent years, community swimming holes have been quietly fading away due to owners expecting privacy on their land and a fear (a realistic one) of being sued in the event of an accident. However, there are rivers and creeks with access in several places along main roads that are not on private property; they are pleasant places to stop and cool off on a hot day. While driving through the county, you will discover such places.

The following are some scenic places to swim; all have lifeguards, a beach, and picnic areas:

Belleayre Beach at Pine Hill Lake (845-254-5600/5202), Route 28, Pine Hill. Open daily mid-June through Labor Day. Admission fee. This lovely lake offers swimming, boating, and fishing, with a beach area, picnic pavilions, and snack bar. Bring your own canoe, or rent a kayak, pedal-, or rowboat. Run by the state; admission is by the car. Reasonable boat-rental rates. The beach is roped off into different sections; there is a diving section and an area for toddlers.

Kingston Point Beach (845-331-1682), Kingston Point Beach, Kingston. Take Broadway to the end, turn left, and follow East Strand (which becomes North Street) 1 mile to the park. The beach is open year-round, daily dawn to dusk. Free. Open mid-June through Labor Day for swimming. This small beach on the Hudson River is run by the city. There are no services here, and it isn't advisable to swim in the Hudson River even now, but it is still a beautiful spot to sunbathe and enjoy the river views. Kids will love the sandy beach and small playground as well as watching the sailboats pass by.

Minnewaska State Park (845-255-0752), 5281 Route 44/55, New Paltz. Admission fee. Open mid-June through Labor Day, daily 11:30–5 for swimming in Lake Awosting at the designated beach area only. This is a great place to be since there is also great hiking in the park; being high up in the Shawangunks, the weather is always a few degrees cooler than in town below.

Sojourner Truth Ulster Landing County Park (845-336-8484; 845-340-3300), 916 Ulster Landing Road (off Route 32), Kingston. Open Memorial Day weekend through Labor Day, daily 11–7. This county-owned and county-run park offers a small, quiet, sandy beach area just north of the Rhinecliff Bridge, with swimming in the Hudson River—although, as with Kingston Point Beach, swimming in the Hudson is still not advisable. Restrooms and picnic pavilion. This spot is less frequented by people since it is a little off the beaten track.

TUBING Very popular in the area, tubing isn't so much a sport as it is a leisurely pursuit. It doesn't take any special skills and can be done by just about anyone. All you do is rent a huge, black inner tube, put it in the water, and hop on for rides that last anywhere from one to three hours. Maneuvering can be done with your hands, and proper tubing attire consists of shorts and a T-shirt, or a bathing suit, with old sneakers. A life jacket is recommended for those who are not strong swimmers. Although most of the waters are not very deep, they are cold, and the currents can be swift. The tubing season runs from the first warm weather until the last—somewhere between late May and early September—but the best time to go is the dog days of August. You will have to leave a security deposit for the tubes, and rental does not include extras like life jackets or "tube seats," which keep you from bumping along the rocky bottom; some sites will arrange to transport you back after the trip.

Tubes and gear, including helmets, can be rented at **F&S Tube and Raft Rental** (845-688-7633), 29 Main Street, Phoenicia. **Town Tinker Tube Rental** (845-688-5553), 10 Bridge Street, Phoenicia, is the grandfather of tubing services, with a well-stocked headquarters, having been in business for many years.

✷ Winter Sports

CROSS-COUNTRY SKIING Ulster County is a good place for cross-country enthusiasts. When valleys, meadows, and fields receive a cover of snow, new trails are broken, and old ones are rediscovered.

Belleayre Mountain (845-254-5600; see *Downhill Skiing*), Belleayre Mountain Road, Pine Hill (off Route 28), has several marked, groomed trails that cover 5.5 miles; they follow the old Ulster and Delaware Turnpike, and even pass an old family cemetery. Some are mogul trails—for those who want a particularly challenging experience. Lessons are available, but call in advance to schedule; rentals are offered just across the road from the trails. There is no fee for skiing, and no charge for parking or use of the lodges on the premises.

Frost Valley YMCA (845-985-2291), 2000 Frost Valley Road, Claryville. Take Route 28 west to Oliverea (County Route 47). Go 15 miles, and you will see Frost Valley. Admission fee. There are 20 miles of groomed trails that wind in and out of lovely forest and alongside streams. The trails are color coded, and there is a warming hut. A small use fee is charged; call for lesson and rental information.

BELLEAYRE MOUNTAIN
Ulster County Tourism

Minnewaska State Park (845-255-0752), 5281 Route 44/55, New Paltz. Free. There are 150 miles of cross-country trails for every ability here, from novice to advanced.

Mohonk Mountain House and Mohonk Preserve (845-255-1000; 1-800-772-6646; preserve 845-255-0919), 1000 Mountain Rest Road, New Paltz; preserve: 3197 Route 44/55, Gardiner. Admission fee. The hotel offers 35 miles of carriage-road trails opening onto views of distant mountain ridges, glens, and valleys. Trails are color coded and mapped, and there is a use fee. Rentals and refreshment sites available. The preserve also has many miles of cross-country ski trails; a map is available at the visitors center.

Wilson State Park (845-256-3099), 859 Wittenberg Road, Mount Tremper. Free. Enjoy approximately 5 miles of color-coded trails that wind through woodland forest, wetlands, and along a lake. Great for beginners. No services; you must have your own equipment.

DOWNHILL SKIING Downhill skiing in Ulster County offers the best of all worlds: country surroundings and challenging slopes convenient to several cities, including Albany and New York.

Belleayre Mountain (845-254-5600; www.belleayre.com), Belleayre Mountain Road, Pine Hill (off Route 28), is the largest downhill ski area in Ulster County, with the longest ski trail in the Catskills (the Deer Trail, at 12,024 feet). Open mid-November through mid-April, daily 9–4. Owned by New York State, Belleayre has a top elevation of 3,429 feet, the highest base elevation in any Catskill ski area. It is the only ski area in the state with a natural division: The upper mountain is for intermediate and expert skiers; the lower mountain is for beginners and novices. There is plenty of free parking, and a courtesy shuttle runs throughout the parking area all day. At the upper mountain nearly 40 trails are serviced by snowmaking equipment. There are eight lifts: two quads as well as double and triple chairlifts. Runs range from novice and intermediate to extreme expert. For those who want even more of a challenge, there is a complete racing program for both adults and children. The ski school at Belleayre is outstanding, with patient, capable instructors who can teach the youngest beginner or help advanced experts polish their skills. Snowboards are allowed (with rentals, sales, and instruction available), and there is a terrain park and rail park. The Overlook Lodge (upper lodge) is a huge, welcoming log building with a fieldstone fireplace, bar, ski shop, cafeteria, lounge area, and outside deck. The Discovery Lodge (lower lodge) has a cafeteria and ski shop. Both offer restrooms and locker areas. Belleayre has great children's programs, including the KidsCamp, and minimal-cost untimed beginner lessons for both skiers and snowboarders. Beginners should check out the "Learn to Ski 1, 2, 3" program, which *Skiing* magazine called the best learn-to-ski program in the East. There are music festivals and other activities in summer and fall (see *Special Events*). Belleayre is very family and service oriented. The old-fashioned feeling about this ski center reminds me of the place I learned to ski in the early 1960s. It's a favorite of many local residents, offering good value for the money and a variety of package deals. I shouldn't neglect to mention that you get to ski for half price on your birthday.

Sawkill Family Ski Center (845-336-6977; www.sawkillski.com), 167 Hill Road, Kingston (located off Sawkill and Jockey Hill roads). Open from late December through mid-March on weekends and holidays only 10–4. This is the smallest ski area in the East, with one magic carpet lift and a snow tubing run with its own lift. There are three trails for skiing and snowboarding; they make lots of snow here and keep the area in great condition. This is an ideal place for families with young children. Inexpensive lift tickets. Snowboard and ski rentals available.

ICE SKATING **Kiwanis Ice Arena** (845-247-2590; www.kiwanisicearena.com), Washington Avenue Extension and Small World Way, Saugerties. Open daily late

August through March. Call for schedule. This enclosed ice-skating rink, while not heated, is a great place to skate any day approximately 10–6. There is a series of one-and-a-half-hour sessions, and the cost is minimal. Children under the age of five skate free. Skate rentals are available. There are restrooms and a snack bar.

Mohonk Mountain House Ice Rink (845-255-1000), 1000 Mountain Rest Road, New Paltz. Open November through March. Those who are not guests of the hotel may purchase a day pass as well as admission to the rink. The setting, in a Victorian open-air pavilion, is lovely. It's unusual to find an outdoor rink these days, and although pricey, this is a lovely venue.

* Green Space

Catskill Forest Preserve (845-256-3000). This state-owned and state-maintained land within the Catskill Park—300,000 acres of forests, lakes, springs, cliffs, teeming with birds and other wildlife—serves as a watershed, recreational area, and ecological reserve. There are seven mountainous areas, each with hiking trails ranging from easy to difficult (see *To Do—Hiking*).

Minnewaska State Park (845-255-0752), 5281 Route 44/55, New Paltz. Open daily 9–dusk most of the year. Hours change seasonally and are posted daily at the entrance. Located on the dramatic Shawangunk Mountain Ridge, this park offers spectacular mountain views, waterfalls, and meadows. Lake Minnewaska itself is surrounded by a network of woodland trails and carriageways that are excellent for hiking, horseback riding, and cross-country skiing. The paved carriageways make for fine biking. You can take a leisurely 2-mile walk around Lake Awosting, a nice way to get oriented in this large park. Swimming is permitted at the sandy beach area, and there is a lifeguard on duty. The lake is about a 3-mile walk from the entrance if you decide to hike in. Minnewaska is a day-use area only; no camping is

MINNEWASKA STATE PARK

Ulster County Tourism

permitted. There are several places to picnic, however, some with raised portable grills. Those who visit in November and December should be aware that hunting is permitted in certain outlying areas of the park.

The Mohonk Mountain House (845-255-1000), 1000 Mountain Rest Road, New Paltz. Open year-round, daily dawn to dusk. Admission fee. This 2,000-acre natural paradise surrounding the Mohonk Mountain House resort is filled with miles of hiking trails and carriage roads stretching out in all directions. The trails are ideal for cross-country skiing and walking. From the tower at Sky Top, the highest point along the trails (1,500 feet above sea level), you can see six states on a clear day (New York, New Jersey, Pennsylvania, Connecticut, Massachusetts, and Vermont). Sky Top was built in 1920 as a memorial to Albert Smiley, one of the founders of Mohonk Mountain House, which opened in 1870. The panoramic vistas from some of the trails here are some of the most scenic views in the Hudson Valley.

The Mohonk Preserve (845-255-0919), 3197 Route 44/55, Gardiner. (Not far from the junction of Routes 44/55 and 299: If you are traveling from New Paltz on Route 299, turn right and look for signs on the right about 1 mile up 44/55.) Visitors center is open daily 9–5; preserve is open from dawn to dusk. Day-use fee for nonmembers. There are more than 100 miles of trails and carriage roads to explore in this preserve, which consists of more than 3,000 acres. Pick up a map at the visitors center.

Sam's Point Preserve and Conservation Center (845-647-7989), 400 Sam's Point Road, Cragsmoor (off Route 52, near Ellenville). The preserve and conservation center are open year-round. The preserve is open April through October, daily 8–7 (until 5 the rest of the year); the conservation center is open Thursday through Monday 9–5. This 4,700-acre preserve in the northern Shawangunk Mountains—known to locals as "the Gunks"—is now owned by the Open Space Institute and

THE MOHONK PRESERVE

Ulster County Tourism

managed by The Nature Conservancy. You will find one of the best examples of ridgetop dwarf-pine barrens in the world here. The views are magnificent, and the hiking trails are excellent, leading to Sam's Point, Verkeerderkill Falls, the Ice Caves, and Indian Rock. This is an environmentally sensitive area, and it is important that visitors stay on the marked trails. To reduce potentially damaging impact to the trail area, particularly to the delicate mosses, hike in early spring when there is still a protective snowpack. Formed by glaciers, the point is a little less than 0.5 mile above sea level and offers a flat viewing area from which you can see five states on a clear day. There are safety walls, but you will feel suspended over the valley below; if you don't like heights, don't stop here. Sam's Point supposedly got its name from a trapper who, fleeing a Native American war party, jumped over the edge and landed safely in some trees. Nature trails lead to a dwarf-pine barren. Trails are well marked, and tours are self-guided with signs. A walk will take you past chasms and tunnels and around incredible balanced rocks. Explore at your own pace.

✷ Lodging

Many of the bed & breakfasts in Ulster County are tucked away down private roads or are off the beaten path and in private homes. They are sometimes difficult to contact since they may not always have a separate listing in the local telephone directory. The most up-to-date listings can be obtained by contacting the website www.hudsonvalleybandbs.com or calling 1-800-957-0126. The following list is not comprehensive but is what I consider the best places in their class. They are organized by area of the county.

Northeastern Ulster County (Kingston, Saugerties, Woodstock)

Carol's Woodstock Country Inn (845-679-9380), 185 Cooper Lake Road, Woodstock 12498. ($$) This quiet, elegant inn is located in the countryside outside the village of Woodstock, yet it is near enough that a short drive will bring you to all the cultural action the town is famous for. The inn—which once belonged to artist Jo Cantine, whose work is in the permanent collection of the Metropolitan Museum of Art—has been restored and is filled with antiques. There are charming nooks throughout the place to relax or dream in. Several of Cantine's paintings and some of her hand-painted furniture are displayed in the common room. Accommodations include five rooms, all with private bath, air-conditioning, and private deck or porch; there is a lovely heated in-ground pool with magnificent mountain views. Special midseason rates. Open year-round.

Catskill Rose (845-688-7100), 5355 Route 212, Mount Tremper 12457. ($$) The four comfortable rooms have king-size beds, private baths, air-conditioning, and cable TV. The restaurant on the premises offers dinner, with a wide variety of free-range meats and poultry, wild fish, and organic produce (see *Dining Out*). Located about 15 miles from the center of Woodstock in a woodsy setting, this is a nice choice for those who want to be away from it all. Open year-round.

Chateau and Tudor Rooms, Saugerties Bed & Breakfast (845-246-4058), 122 Burt Street, Saugerties 12477. ($$) This architectural treasure, an English Tudor estate, offers two luxurious, spacious rooms (both have private baths) with views of the Catskill Mountains and Esopus Creek. Guests may enjoy the beautiful gardens, sculpture park, reflecting pool, and pond on the property. Open year-round. Children and pets welcome.

The Courtyard by Marriott Kingston (845-382-2300; 1-800-321-2211), 1300 Ulster Avenue, Kingston 12401. ($$) Opened in 2006 across from the Hudson Valley Mall, this is an ideal place for those traveling on business. The 89 spacious, comfortable rooms offer high-speed Internet access, cable TV, coffeemakers, and easy access to the county's best shopping and major highways. A breakfast buffet is available every morning.

Dancing Angel Cottage (845-657-2222), 157 Glenford Wittenberg Road, Glenford 12433. ($$) This charming, sunny three-room luxury cottage provides a lovely romantic getaway. The panoramic views of the Ashokan Reservoir and Catskill Mountains are stunning, and the center of Woodstock is only a five-minute drive down the mountain. Relax on the wraparound deck in summer or cozy up to a fire in the cast-iron gas fireplace in winter. All the amenities are here—a king-size bed, large flat-screen TV, kitchenette, and propane grill on the deck. Open year-round.

Diamond Mills Hotel (845-247-0700), 25 South Partition Street, Saugerties 12477. ($$$) The 30 rooms in this luxury hotel, opened in 2011, all have private balconies overlooking the beautiful waterfalls of the Esopus Creek. There is a choice of double queen, king, or two king suites; the latter offer more space and a fireplace. Included in the amenities here are sumptuous towels and bathrobes, fine linens, flat-screen TV, gourmet minibar, and high speed Internet access. There is a restaurant on the premises, the Tavern (see *Dining Out*). Open year-round. Children welcome.

Emerson Resort and Spa (845-688-2828; 1-877-688-2828; www.emersonresort.com), 5340 Route 28, Mount Tremper 12457. ($$$) Located minutes away from Belleayre Mountain and the town of Woodstock, this luxurious establishment—with 25 individually and lavishly decorated suites—has an exotic feeling about it, combining both Asian and Indian design. The resort, which first opened in 2006, is set along Esopus Creek, and every suite has a view of the stream, a fireplace, and whirlpool tub. You will find a full-treatment spa, the largest spa in the Catskills, which offers facials, massages, body wraps, ayurvedic treatments, sauna, indoor pool, and fitness facilities. The Phoenix Restaurant is open daily for breakfast and Thursday through Saturday for dinner (see *Dining Out*), and if you catch a fish in the Esopus, the chef will be glad to prepare it for you. An additional part of the resort complex is **The Lodge,** opened in 1997, featuring contemporary Adirondack-style decor in 27 rooms. The spacious private suites here offer wet bar, refrigerator, and whirlpool bath, and all have air-conditioning, cable TV, telephones, and dataports for computers. Many rooms also have decks overlooking scenic Esopus Creek. These accommodations are great for families; children and pets are welcome. The resort offers a range of lodging options and is open year-round.

Enchanted Manor of Woodstock (845-679-9012), 23 Rowe Road, Woodstock 12498. ($$) There are five rooms, all with private baths (two have large whirlpool tubs), cable TV, many with fireplaces, on this 8-acre secluded property owned by hosts Claudia and Rolan. Nice features here include the heated outdoor pool, hot tub, and large pond with rowboat and canoe available to guests. There is an exercise room, and massages and Reiki treatments are offered as well. Open year-round.

Holiday Inn–Kingston (845-338-0400), 503 Washington Avenue, Kingston 12401. ($$) Conveniently located less than a half mile off NYS Thruway exit 19, this full-service hotel is only a short walk from the historic uptown area of Kingston. Woodstock, Rhinebeck, and Stone Ridge are just a short drive away. There are 212 rooms and 5 suites here, and the indoor garden courtyard has a large heated swimming pool, whirlpool, sauna, and game room—a great place to relax if the weather isn't ideal. There is a fitness center and restaurant on the premises as well. This is a particularly good choice if you are traveling with children since there is always something to keep them occupied; it also offers all the modern amenities, including high-speed Internet access.

The Inn at Tamayo (845-246-9371), 89 Partition Street, Saugerties 12477. ($) There are three cozy rooms with private baths here, as well as one three-room suite. The inn is located in the midst of the antiques shops and boutiques of the village. Saugerties is only a short drive from Woodstock, Kingston, and the major ski areas. Open year-round.

Kate's Lazy Meadow Motel (845-688-7200), 5191 Route 28, Mount Tremper 12457. ($$) Sleep creekside in a vintage Airstream trailer, enjoy listening to the rushing stream, and kick back under the stars in a hammock. This unusual motel (co-owned by Kate Pierson of the B-52s) is located on 9 acres along the scenic Esopus Creek. There are also 10 lovely efficiency units with high-speed Internet service, cable TV, and private baths. Open year-round.

Renwick Clifton House B&B (845-246-0552), 27 Barclay Street, Saugerties 12477 ($$$), is a beautifully renovated 1812 Southern-style mansion. Within these 6,000 square feet there are four rooms, all with private baths, views of the Hudson River, air-conditioning, cable TV, and Wi-Fi. Luxurious details include fresh-cut flowers and truffles upon arrival, and marble-tiled bathrooms. Guest rooms are named after the old steamships that plied the Hudson River. A four-course gourmet breakfast is served. Open year-round.

Onteora: The Mountain House (845-657-6233), 96 Piney Point Road, Boiceville 12412. ($$) Onteora has the most spectacular mountain views of any B&B in the Catskills. Located 1 mile off Route 28, it was the estate of Richard Hellmann, the mayonnaise mogul. There are five bedrooms, all with cathedral ceilings and private baths. There is a separate luxurious two-room cottage, each room with its own bath. Breakfasts are made to order, with requests taken the evening before. Children over the age of 12 are welcome. Open year-round.

Saugerties Lighthouse Bed & Breakfast (845-247-0656), 168 Lighthouse Drive, Saugerties 12477. ($$) Treat yourself to a unique, romantic experience: Sleep in a renovated lighthouse. Watch the boats pass by, and see the stars from the bedroom window. The lighthouse keeper will prepare a hearty breakfast in the morning. Two upstairs rooms share a bathroom downstairs. Travel light since it's a 10-minute walk from the parking area. Open year-round.

Twin Gables of Woodstock (845-679-9479), 73 Tinker Street, Woodstock 12498. ($$) The architecture and furnishings of the 1930s create a relaxed, easy ambience at this guesthouse; its service and hospitality have earned it a reputation for comfort and affordability. There are 10 guest rooms, and a living room and refrigerator are available to visitors. Twin Gables is only a short walk from restaurants, shopping, galleries, and entertainment. The New York bus line stops nearby, so it's a great spot for those traveling to Woodstock without a car. Rooms are all air-conditioned; four have private baths; six share three baths. Children over the age of 12 are welcome. Open year-round.

Twin Lakes (845-338-2400), 198 Walton Lane, Hurley 12443. ($$) There are 12 cabins and two efficiencies here. The honeymoon suites have heart-shaped Jacuzzi tubs. A wonderful venue for families, with boating, hiking, and trails on the property, as well as an outdoor pool and stocked fishing lake. The restaurant on the premises serves breakfast, lunch, and dinner in a lovely dining room with scenic views. Open year-round.

Wild Rose Inn Bed & Breakfast (845-679-8783), 66 Rock City Road, Woodstock 12498. ($$$) Enjoy an elegant Victorian ambience in the heart of town. The five rooms are all beautifully furnished with antiques, and all have air-conditioning, cable television, and whirlpool baths. A gourmet continental breakfast is served. Children are welcome, and a portacrib is available. Open year-round.

Woodstock Inn on the Millstream (845-679-8211), 38 Tannery Brook Road, Woodstock 12498. ($$) This is almost a motel—efficiency units are available—but it has its own special charm. It's set right on a brook, and there are 18 separate rooms here. The innkeeper gives you the option of enjoying an elaborate continental breakfast buffet waterside or in the sunroom. There is a porch for rocking, and a short walk brings you to the village green. All rooms are air-conditioned, with cable TV and wireless Internet access. Children are welcome. Open year-round.

Woodstock Mountain View Guest House (845-430-0582), 112 Wittenberg Road, Bearsville 12409. ($$) This charming two-story, 650-square-foot guesthouse with spectacular mountain views is completely private and available by the day, week, or month. In warm weather, enjoy breakfast on the stone patio overlooking a lovely pond on the property. Upstairs is a large bedroom with king-size bed and day bed, as well as a Japanese-style bathroom with a sunken tub/shower. Downstairs is a living room with hardwood floors and beamed ceiling, and a kitchenette. This is the perfect place for a cozy romantic getaway. The shops and restaurants in Woodstock are only a few miles away. Open year-round.

Southeastern Ulster County (New Paltz, Gardiner, Stone Ridge)

Audrey's Farmhouse Bed & Breakfast (845-895-3440), 2188 Brunswyck Road, Wallkill 12589. ($$) This pastoral spot offers visitors a relaxing getaway. There are five guest rooms (three with private bath, two share a bath), each with air-conditioning and magnificent mountain views. Guests can use the in-ground pool in the warm-weather months and enjoy an outdoor Jacuzzi and fireplace in the main room. A gourmet breakfast is served. Pets welcome. Open year-round.

Buttermilk Falls Inn & Spa (845-795-1310; 1-877-746-6772), 220 North Road, Milton 12547. ($$$) This renovated gem combines modern luxury with historic charm. The main house overlooks the Hudson, and all rooms have wonderful river views. A total of 19 elegant yet comfortable guest quarters all have a fireplace, private bath, cable TV, high-speed Internet access, and air-conditioning. Rooms are furnished with antiques, canopy beds, plush comforters, and exposed stone walls, all evoking the aura of a bygone era. Complete spa services are available but must be arranged in advance. Open year-round. Children accommodated, but only in some rooms.

Captain Schoonmaker's Bed & Breakfast (845-687-7946), 913 Route 213, High Falls 12440. ($$$) A fine spot for antiques lovers, this 18th-century house will make you feel as if you are stepping back into an earlier time. Schoonmaker's has been featured in many publications, and the hostess serves a five-course breakfast that should hold you until dinner. Five rooms have private bath. Open year-round.

Country and Farm Bed & Breakfast (845-626-4596), 71 Stonykill Road, Accord 12404. ($$) Beth and Tim are your hosts on a 20-acre horse farm. Enjoy the privacy of a lovely, spacious apartment stocked with fresh baked goods, juices, coffee, and organic teas. There is a swimming hole on the property and plenty of space to walk or cross-country ski, so there is lots to do here, depending upon the season. Conveniently located to fine restaurants and local attractions. Open year-round.

Creek Locks Bed & Breakfast (845-331-5889), 1046 Creek Locks Road, Rosendale 12472. ($$) There are three rooms with private baths in this renovated 1866 Gothic Revival farmhouse on 4 wooded acres along the Rondout Creek. There is hiking, canoeing, and fishing easily accessible from this location. It's a great choice for those who want to be on the water. Open year-round.

Deerfield (845-687-9807), 300 Vly Atwood Road, Stone Ridge 12484. ($) Once a boardinghouse, this turn-of-the-19th-century building has been renovated for modern overnight guests. The rooms are airy and light, and there is a nice mix of antiques and country throughout the inn. You will find more than 30 acres to explore, with shops and points of interest a short drive away. Guests can enjoy an in-ground pool, a Steinway piano, and a large gourmet breakfast. Four guest rooms have private baths. Open year-round.

1850 House & Tavern (845-658-7800), 435 Main Street, Rosendale 12472. ($$) This charming boutique 12-room hotel is housed in a structure built in 1850. In fact, the building has had eight previous incarnations as a hotel. Reopened in 2012, this is a great place to stay for those who want to be within steps of the shops and restaurants on Main Street, as well as those traveling the area without a car. The completely renovated rooms have private baths, fine linens, air-conditioning, flat-screen TVs, and wireless Internet access. Continental breakfast is served on the river-view porch in the warm weather months. The Tavern (see *Eating Out*) on the premises is a nice place to relax and enjoy drinks. No children under the age of 17. Open year-round.

Elm Rock Inn (845-687-4492), 4496 Route 209, Stone Ridge 12484. ($$) This renovated brick Colonial, originally a 1770 farmhouse, features five unique air-conditioned guest rooms, all with private bath. A full gourmet breakfast is served fireside in the dining room or on the outdoor patio. Enjoy afternoon tea in the spacious great room. The accommodations in the carriage house are both pet and child friendly. Rooms in the main house require children be age 12 or over. Open year-round.

Fox Hill Bed and Breakfast (845-691-8151), 55 South Chodikee Lake Road, Highland 12528. ($$) This B&B is located about 5 miles from exit 18 off the NYS Thruway. Wander through the woods, sit by the garden pool and feed the colorful koi, or just relax in your room. There are three suites, all with private bath, air-conditioning, TV, and VCR; one with a fireplace. There is a whirlpool spa, fitness center, and heated in-ground pool. Open year-round.

The Guesthouse at Holy Cross Monastery (845-384-6660), 1615 Route 9W, P.O. Box 99, West Park 12493. ($) This monastery has spectacular views of the Hudson River and provides a unique bed & breakfast experience. The reasonable cost at $80 per night (they ask for a two-night minimum stay on weekends) includes a room, and three meals served in a large dining room with the monks. On some weekends special educational programs are offered; you can call for a schedule of events. Open year-round.

Highland Manor Bed and Breakfast (845-691-9080), 2 Windsor Hills Road, Highland 12528. ($$) This recently built country inn features five rooms, all with private baths, plush feather beds, and central air-conditioning. Three rooms also have a fireplace and large Jacuzzi tub. Enjoy a different full gourmet breakfast each morning. Vegetarian or special diets will be accommodated. Open year-round.

Inn at Stone Ridge (845-687-0736), 3805 Route 209, Stone Ridge 12484. ($$$) For a romantic getaway, this gem should be at the top of your list. It's a fantastic place to go year-round but particularly so in spring, when the flowers around the stone swimming pool (one of the most beautiful pools I have ever swum in) are in bloom. The former Hasbrouck House is an 18th-century stone mansion set on 40 acres amid magnificent gardens. There are six beautifully renovated suites and a two-bedroom carriage house. Listed on the National Register of Historic Places, the inn is open all year.

Inn at Twaalfskill (845-691-3605), 144 Vineyard Avenue, Highland 12528. ($$) This spacious, renovated Victorian (built in 1902) was once the home of a local businessman and congressional representative. The name of the inn comes from the creek that runs in front of the property. All three guest rooms have private bath, central air-conditioning, TV, and wireless Internet access. A continental breakfast is served. Located just outside the village of Highland, the inn is open year-round. No children under the age of 12.

Minnewaska Lodge (845-255-1110), 3116 Route 44/55, Gardiner 12525. ($$$) This contemporary 26-room mountain lodge is nestled on 17 acres at the base of the spectacular Shawangunk Ridge. The lodge successfully combines the ambience of a bed & breakfast with the conveniences of a fine hotel. Half the rooms have private decks and mountain views. Guests may enjoy the fitness center on the premises as well as hiking in nearby Mohonk Preserve and Minnewaska State Park. A full buffet breakfast is included in the price. Children are welcome. Open year-round.

Mohonk Mountain House (845-255-1000), 1000 Mountain Rest Road, New Paltz 12561. ($$$) This National Historic Landmark is a mountaintop Victorian castle that stands in the heart of 22,000 unspoiled acres. Dazzling views are everywhere, and serene Mohonk Lake adds to the dramatic setting. Although the hotel offers a full-service spa, museum, golf, disc golf, boating, tennis, a stable, modern sports facilities, and wonderful hiking and mountain biking on 85 miles of trails and carriage roads, the place is still very much the way it was more than 100 years ago (it is still managed by the Smiley family, who founded the hotel). During the winter the trails become a cross-country skier's paradise; there's an ice rink in a Victorian open air pavilion and snowshoeing with equipment available for guests. The spa opened in 2005 and includes a solarium, stone fireplace, outdoor heated mineral pool, indoor heated swimming pool, and state-of-the-art fitness center. Yoga, Pilates, and aerobics classes may be booked by guests. Midweek packages are available, and special-events weekends are held throughout the year (see *To See—Historic Sites*). Activities are offered for children ages 2–12. Of the 251 rooms, more than 100 have working fireplaces and nearly 200 have a balcony; all have private bath. Rates include three meals a day; men must wear jackets for the evening meal. Open year-round.

Mountain Meadows Bed and Breakfast (845-255-6144), 542 Albany Post Road, New Paltz 12561. ($$) This lovely country home nestled in the foothills of the Catskills is a fine place for people who enjoy a casual atmosphere, lounging by an in-ground pool, relaxing by a fireplace, or playing a game in a recreation room. The spacious landscaped grounds offer croquet, badminton, and horseshoes. All four rooms have private bath, central air-conditioning, and a king- or queen-size bed. Located only 4.5 miles from the NYS Thruway exit 18. Open year-round.

River Hill Bed and Breakfast (845-795-5706), 64 Sands Avenue, Milton 12547. ($) Relax on the porch or stroll through the gardens as you unwind at this Victorian inn overlooking the Hudson River. The three guest rooms are furnished with antiques; only one has a private bath, and two have river views. A highlight of any stay here is the gourmet breakfast, with homemade jams, breads, and local maple syrup. Open year-round.

Rocking Horse Ranch (845-691-2927; 1-800-647-2624), 600 Route 44/55, Highland 12528. ($$) There are 120 rooms at this well-maintained ranch resort with full facilities and evening entertainment. Guests may enjoy boating on the lake, indoor/outdoor pools, waterslides, tennis, exercise room, and sauna. There is snow tubing and ice skating during the winter months. There are children's programs and babysitting available. A great family getaway any time of year.

The 1712 House (845-687-7167), 93 Mill Dam Road, Stone Ridge 12484. (Take Route 209 south toward Ellenville from NYS Thruway exit 19; about 10 miles along, just before the first traffic light you see, make a right onto Mill Dam Road. The house is down the hill, past the pond on the left.) ($$$) When the King of England and a local Native American chieftain granted the Hardenbergh family a tract of land that encompassed about 250 square miles, the 1712 House was part of their original farm. Built in the style of the 1700s, its features include custom-made colonial furniture (all crafted from trees cut on the land and all pieces replicas of 18th-century items). Set on 80 acres, this majestic bluestone-and-wood structure offers guests a 6-acre front lawn, winding streams, sprawling hills, mountains, and meadows—as well as all the modern amenities. The spacious living and dining rooms are complete with an enormous fireplace, wide-board floors, and beamed ceilings. The six bedroom suites each offer private bath with whirlpool or claw-foot bathtub, air-conditioning, telephone, cable TV, VCR, and high-speed Internet access. Each one has a beautiful view of the grounds, sitting chairs, and table and chairs for in-room dining. A full gourmet breakfast will be made to your order: Enjoy it on the deck, the bluestone patio, or in your room. A place to celebrate a special occasion. Not recommended for children. Open year-round.

Whispering Pines Bed & Breakfast (845-687-2419), 60 Cedar Hill Road, High Falls 12440. ($$) This secluded contemporary B&B has skylights and is surrounded by 50 acres of private woods. There are four plush bedrooms, all with private bath, two with Jacuzzis. A four-bedroom, three-bath guesthouse on the premises is available for rent as well. There is a large video library as well as a reading library. The huge outdoor deck has a Jacuzzi that may be used any time of year by guests. Open year-round.

Northwestern Ulster County (Big Indian, Highmount, Pine Hill)

Alpine Osteria Bed & Breakfast (845-254-9851), 32 Galli Curci Road, Highmount 12441 ($$). The seven rooms have private baths and are comfortable and cozy. There is a dining room, lounge, fireplace, and game room. For those who want to be within walking distance to Belleayre Mountain, this is a particularly good choice. An excellent full gourmet breakfast is served to guests by the owner-proprietor, who is a Culinary Institute of America graduate. Open year-round.

Barneche Vacation Rental (845-688-5822), 361 Route 214, Chichester 12416. ($) This one-room streamside cottage is decorated with local and vintage art, making for a cozy getaway. Private steps lead down to the stream and a refreshing swimming hole; there is also access to a large yard. A kitchenette with microwave is included, along with a queen-size bed and twin bed. Open year-round. Pets welcome.

Beaverkill Valley Inn (845-439-4844), 1532 Beaverkill Valley Road, Lew Beach 12753. ($$$) This National Historic Site, built in 1893 and restored in recent years by Laurance Rockefeller, offers a perfect retreat for those who love the outdoors. Located within the Catskill Forest Preserve, near hiking trails and some of the best fishing anywhere, the inn also has tennis courts and a lovely indoor pool. During the summer you can bike, hike, swim, and fish; in winter, cross-country ski—and swim. There are a total of 20 rooms, and all have private bath. Children welcome. Open year-round.

Birchcreek Retreat (845-254-5222), Birchcreek Road, Pine Hill 12465. ($$) Those who want to lose weight, detoxify their bodies, and restore their health can go on a supervised juice fast (if they wish) in conjunction with personal training in this secluded spot on 23 private acres. More than 100 years old, the estate combines the rustic and the refined for an informal yet elegant ambience. Every guest room has a private bath. Some of the activities include water aerobics in a heated outdoor pool, exercise classes, and long walks or hikes on the tranquil acreage surrounding the inn. Open year-round.

Copper Hood Retreat and Spa (845-688-2460), 7039 Route 28, Shandaken 12480. ($$) Tucked away alongside a well-known fishing stream, the Copper Hood is a full-service spa, offering one of the few Olympic-size indoor heated pools in the region. Jacuzzi, massage, and herbal wraps are part of the various spa packages, which include meals, lessons, and an array of treatments. There are hiking trails and fishing on the premises, as well. All 20 rooms have private bath. Open year-round.

Full Moon Resort (845-254-5117), Valley View Road, Big Indian 12410. ($$) This mountain resort and performance venue is dedicated to the celebration of nature, music, and the arts. The rustic accommodations are located on a 100-acre wonderland of fields and streams surrounded by the Catskills. Esopus Creek gently wends its way through the property, and a variety of affordable lodges and cottages are available, including accommodations in a turn-of-the-20th-century country inn with simple, charming guest rooms. The main building has a wraparound sunporch, library, outdoor pool, and dining room/café. Tent camping is permitted on the fields and meadows. A full breakfast is included. Music is always in the air, with concerts, dances, and acoustic shows in the smoke-free performance space with a full bar. Guests are encouraged to bring instruments of their own. Three state trailheads are located within 5 miles of the front door, as the resort is located in the Catskill Mountain Forest Preserve. Breakfasts and lunches are served in the café on weekends. Children welcome. Open year-round.

Phoenicia Belle (845-688-7226), 73 Main Street, Phoenicia 12464. ($) Situated right on Main Street in the village, this restored 1875 Victorian was once owned by a local doctor. Each room has a queen-size bed and is uniquely decorated. Two rooms have private baths, and two rooms share a bath. Very reasonably priced. Open year-round.

Southwestern Ulster County (Kerhonkson, Ellenville Area)

Honor's Haven Resort and Spa (845-210-1600), 1195 Arrowhead Road, Ellenville 12428. ($$) The setting here is truly magnificent. Situated on 250 acres with gorgeous mountain views, this 232-room full-service resort offers a championship golf course, indoor and outdoor pools, tennis, lake fishing and boating, sauna, fitness center, and spa. The meals here are decent and are included in the room rate. Open year-round. Children welcome.

✷ Where to Eat

DINING OUT

Northeastern Ulster County

Armadillo (845-339-1550), 97 Abeel Street, Kingston. ($$) Open for dinner Tuesday through Sunday 5–10. Tex-Mex Southwest cuisine from an enormous menu includes great ribs, fajitas, and chicken specialties; make sure you try the grilled tuna with lime marinade and wasabi mustard. Outdoor dining in the warm-weather months in a charming patio area. A nice touch: Crayons are provided so that you—or the kids—can draw on the paper tablecloths. Children's menu.

Bear Café (845-679-5555), 295 Tinker Street, Woodstock. ($$) Open daily, except Tuesday, for dinner from 5; Sunday brunch served 11–2:30. This is a French American bistro that serves a range of imaginative entrées, from grilled fish and chicken to steaks and unusual pasta dishes. The appetizers, salads, and daily specials are consistently excellent. There is a nice view of Sawkill Creek from the dining area. Be sure to make a reservation, especially on weekends and any evening during the summer; it's busy year-round.

Boitson's (845-339-2333), 47 North Front Street, Kingston. ($$) Open for dinner Wednesday through Monday 5–10. If you don't intend to have dinner, at least enjoy drinks at the bar here, which has an extensive selection of cocktails and an all–New York State beer list. This American bistro, with leather banquettes and tables placed close together, features comfort food like meat loaf, fried chicken, and burgers; there are also hanger steaks, seafood, a vegetarian option, and daily specials on the menu. Be forewarned: They get very busy on weekends, and service can be slow at times. Owner-hostess Maria Philippis is always at the restaurant making sure things run smoothly. During the warm-weather months, enjoy outdoor dining on the back patio, where one will get a different view of uptown Kingston. Maria named the restaurant for her former Brooklyn landlord who passed away in 2007 and left her the money to pursue her dream of opening a restaurant.

Catskill Rose (845-688-7100), 5355 Route 212, Mount Tremper. ($$$) Open for dinner Thursday through Sunday from 5 PM. Contemporary American cuisine imaginatively prepared featuring the freshest local ingredients, organic meats, and chicken. Hosts Peter and Rose change the menu to reflect what is in season. Somewhat off the beaten path, but definitely worth a detour.

Catskill Seasons Inn (845-688-2505), 178 Route 42, Shandaken. ($$) Open for dinner Thursday through Sunday 4–10. Elegant seating, with a menu that emphasizes fresh seafood, steaks, and game during hunting season. Chef Michael Cottrone studied at the French Culinary Institute in New York City and worked at Le Cirque and the Four Seasons before serving his fine creations in the Catskills. The taproom has a bar menu featuring casual fare that includes sandwiches, salads, wraps, and burgers.

Cucina (845-679-9800), 109 Mill Hill Road, Woodstock. ($$) Open for dinner daily 5–10; Saturday and Sunday brunch 11–3. *Cucina* means "kitchen" in Italian, and this one is headed up by Gianni Scappin, from the Culinary Institute's Caterina de Medici restaurant. The building has been completely renovated with a distinctly modern feel and offers up healthy comfort food with a nice range of prices on an interesting menu. There are exceedingly thin-crust pizzas (excellent, by the way), fresh vegetables, and fish; several imaginative pasta selections; and rib eye steak and crisp calamari. Children welcome.

Diamond Mills—The Tavern (845-247-0700), 25 South Partition Street, Saugerties. ($$$) Open for dinner daily 5–10; Sunday brunch 10:30–2:30. The atmosphere here is delightful, and one can enjoy a meal alfresco in the warm weather months or in a booth by the fireplace in the main dining room during the winter. The menu includes appetizers like lobster corn chowder and beef carpaccio, and entrées like cedar plank–roasted wild steelhead trout and beef burger. The emphasis is on fresh local ingredients, and the menu changes seasonally.

Emiliani Ristorante (845-246-6169), 147 Ulster Avenue, Saugerties. ($$) Open for dinner daily, except Wednesday, from 5. Some of the finest Northern Italian cuisine you will find anywhere in the Catskills is served in this informal yet elegant establishment. The pastas are made on the premises, and all dishes are made to order. Children welcome.

The Golden Ginza (845-339-8132), 24 Broadway, Kingston. ($$) Open for lunch Monday through Friday 11:30–3; dinner is served daily 3–10. Enjoy all types of Japanese cuisine, including tempura, teriyaki, sushi, and sashimi. Children will love watching the flames rising from the grill at the center of the table if you order hibachi dinners; they are prepared Benihana style. There is a sushi bar for those who enjoy this delicacy; everything is prepared fresh.

Hoffman House Restaurant (845-338-2626), 94 North Front Street, Kingston. ($$) Open for lunch Monday through Saturday 11:30–4:30; dinner served 4:30–9; until 10 Friday and Saturday. Closed Sunday. Hoffman House is located in the Stockade area, in a historic stone building that dates back to the early 18th century. Musket holes in the steps leading to the roof indicate its possible use as a fort or lookout. The restaurant, on the National Register of Historic Places, serves Continental cuisine, including steaks, burgers, pasta, and seafood. Diners may enjoy fireside tables in the winter months and a large open patio in the warm weather. It's also a great place to stop and just have drinks.

Indian Grill (845-334-8400), 579 Broadway, Kingston. ($) Open for lunch and dinner Tuesday through Sunday noon–9:30. Aficionados of Indian and Pakistani cuisine will not be disappointed here. Keep in mind that good food, not a fancy ambience, is what you will find in this small midtown-Kingston restaurant, which seats about 25 people. The lunch buffet, truly a bargain, is available every day. If you arrive at an off hour, as I did, management will bring fresh selections rather quickly to the buffet table. Do not skip the bread course; the naan here is quite good. If you order off the large menu, do notice there are nearly 20 vegetarian entrées and about a half dozen vegan choices.

Joshua's Restaurant (845-679-5533), 51 Tinker Street, Woodstock. ($$) Open daily, except Wednesday, for breakfast and lunch 11–5 (10–5 Saturday and Sunday); dinner 5–9 (until 10 Friday and Saturday). This family-owned and family-operated restaurant has been in Woodstock for decades. They are known for their enormous menu, featuring an array of international favorites as well as Middle Eastern and Greek specialties. Whether you prefer traditional favorites like steak, pasta, and chicken, or enjoy falafel, baba ghanoush, and Mediterranean salads, it's all here in the center of town! There is often music upstairs in the evenings as well.

Kyoto Sushi (845-339-1128), 337 Washington Avenue, Kingston. ($$) Open for lunch Monday through Saturday 11:30–2:45; dinner 4:30–9:30, Friday and Saturday until 10. Sunday dinner only 4–9. Enjoy the artistry of Chef Chun Chao Chen from Manhattan, now in uptown Kingston, and dine on meticulously prepared sushi and sashimi. For those who prefer cooked cuisine, there's chicken or beef teriyaki on the bill of fare. A must for sushi aficionados while visiting Ulster County.

Le Canard-Enchaine (845-339-2003), 276 Fair Street, Kingston. ($$) Open daily for lunch noon–4 and dinner from 4 on. Enjoy a classic French meal in a casual bistro atmosphere, a touch of Paris in Kingston. A variety of the freshest fish is available daily, or choose from four classic duck entrées. The freshly baked pastries are excellent, and so is the café au lait and cappuccino. A good choice for lunch—there is a fixed-price option daily, as well as one for dinner, Sunday through Thursday 4–7:30.

Little Bear Chinese Restaurant (845-679-8899), 295 Tinker Street, Woodstock. ($) Open daily for lunch and dinner noon–10:30. Sit along the Sawkill Creek in the warm-weather months and enjoy Chinese cuisine. They offer an array of vegetarian dishes here, as well as imaginative entrées that are quite different than the usual Chinese-restaurant fare. The setting is lovely, and the service is excellent; great for take-out, as well. Children welcome.

Mariner's Harbor (845-340-8051), 1 Broadway, Kingston. ($$) Open Tuesday through Saturday 11:30–10; Sunday noon–9. Live Maine lobster, Black Angus beef, and fresh seafood are the specialties of the house. Enjoy waterfront dining in the historic Rondout district of Kingston. Even if you aren't interested in eating a full meal, this is a wonderful place to relax with drinks and appetizers (try the fried calamari) while watching the boats pass by. Children are welcome.

New World Home Cooking (845-246-0900), 1411 Route 212, Saugerties. ($$) Open for dinner daily 5–11; lunch Monday through Friday noon–2:30, summer months only. Eating here is like taking a tour of America's finest and funkiest restaurants. The house specialties are Jamaican jerk chicken, Thai mussel stew, and black-sesame-seared salmon (my favorite). Try the phenomenal blackened string beans with rémoulade appetizer—it's wonderful. According to chef-owner Ric Orlando, the emphasis is on peasant flavors, and the colorful, casual ambience reflects the many cultures represented on New World's menu. This is a marvelous, lively, fun place to eat, and there is often live music after 9, so call ahead to see what's happening. Children welcome.

The Red Onion Restaurant & Bar (845-679-1223), 1654 Route 212, Saugerties. ($$) Open for dinner daily 5–9; Friday and Saturday until 10. This was one of the only places in Ulster County with a smoke-free bar long before it was required by law. The creative international bistro cuisine is first-rate, and so is the service. Enjoy such appetizers as spicy shrimp ragout with garlic chilies and lemon. Entrées include wild striped bass on herbed risotto with lobster mushrooms—although the shallot- and herb-marinated New Zealand lamb chops over mashed potatoes with black-olive sauce and grilled asparagus is my favorite. Desserts range from crème caramel with fresh berries to tricolor chocolate mousse, made with white, milk, and dark chocolate. An all-around wonderful place to dine. Children welcome.

Reginato Ristorante (845-336-6968), 34 Leggs Mill Road, Lake Katrine. ($$) Open for lunch Tuesday through Friday 11:30–2:30; dinner Tuesday through Saturday 4–10; Sunday 1–9. Enjoy homemade Northern Italian specialties in a relaxed atmosphere. Children are welcome.

Santa Fe Uptown (845-339-7777), 11 Main Street, Kingston. ($$) Open for lunch Friday 11–2:30; for dinner daily, except Sunday, 4:30–9:30. All the Mexican favorites are available here—tacos, burritos, fajitas, and quesadillas—along with imaginative dinner salads. My favorite is the warm goat cheese and roasted beet salad with toasted pepitas and candied mango over mixed organic greens with a mango vinaigrette dressing. There are several vegetarian entrées. Everything is well prepared and delicious.

Savona's Trattoria (845-339-6800), 11 Broadway, Kingston. ($$) Open for lunch and dinner daily noon–10; Friday and Saturday until 11. This welcome addition to the Rondout area of Kingston serves up basic Italian fare in generous portions. During warm weather, dine outdoors on the patio along lower Broadway while enjoying classical Italian favorites, including a variety of thin-crust pizza, pasta dishes, veal, chicken, seafood, and more. The wine list is quite respectable, and the trattoria is family friendly.

Ship to Shore Restaurant (845-334-8887), 15 West Strand, Kingston. ($$) Open daily for lunch 11–4; dinner 4–11. The specialties here are steaks and seafood. One of my favorite dinner entrées is the 16-ounce boneless New York sirloin with peppercorn butter. For lunch there's the salmon club or grilled portobello mushroom burger with roasted red peppers and fresh mozzarella. Take a walk after your meal along the Rondout. Not recommended for children.

Skytop Steak House & Brewing Company (845-340-4277), 237 Forest Hills Drive (off Route 28 and exit 19 off the NYS Thruway), Kingston. ($$) Open for lunch Thursday through Saturday noon–3; dinner Wednesday through Saturday 4–10; Sunday brunch 10–2; dinner 4–9. This American regional steakhouse is located in a wonderful spot affording spectacular views of the Shawangunks on a clear day. Six different beers are brewed on the premises and are available on tap. (Do try the sampler of six if you enjoy tasting beers.) The sliced porterhouse steak for two is one of the specialties of the house. Outdoor dining on the terrace is available during the warm-weather months.

Steel House Restaurant & Bar (845-338-7847), 100 Rondout Landing, Kingston. ($$) Open Memorial Day weekend through October, daily for lunch noon–4; dinner 4–9:30. Closed Monday through Wednesday November through late May. Enjoy American cuisine with an emphasis on steaks and seafood in this beautifully renovated historic factory building. Outdoor dining is available in the warm-weather months on a large deck overlooking Rondout Creek, and a covered awning protects against the rain. Make sure to try the fresh fried calamari and twin lobster tails, which are my favorite dishes here. The menu is varied and includes ribs, pasta, steaks, and fresh fish. Free boat docking for patrons who want to dock and dine.

Stella's (845-331-2210), 44 North Front Street, Kingston. ($) Open for dinner Monday 5–9; lunch and dinner served Tuesday through Sunday noon–10. For some of the best traditional Italian home cooking, including baked lasagna, eggplant parmigiana, or spaghetti and meatballs, this is the place to go. The casual atmosphere and good-size portions make this a local favorite. Stella's has been open for many years (there's a popular local bar next door owned by the same people), and they offer a child-friendly menu.

Tomo Sushi (845-247-2488), 7 Grand Union Plaza, Saugerties. ($$) Open daily for lunch 11:30–2:30, dinner 4:30–9:30, until 10:30 Friday and Saturday; Sunday 3–9:30. I've discovered a jewel of a culinary experience tucked away in an obscure shopping center. Surprisingly, this Japanese restaurant offers some of the best quality sushi to be found anywhere in the mid–Hudson Valley. Steaks and seafood are available, as well as sashimi, teriyaki, and tempura. Children welcome.

Violette (845-679-5300), 85 Mill Hill Road, Woodstock. ($$) Open for lunch Thursday through Tuesday noon–4:30; dinner 5–9:30; Sunday brunch noon–4:30. Diners will enjoy country French cuisine in a cozy atmosphere here. The taproom adjoining the restaurant is a great place to stop for a drink and enjoy bistro fare. The food here is consistently very good.

Southeastern Ulster County

A Tavola (845-255-1426), 46 Main Street, New Paltz. ($$$) Open Thursday through Monday 5:30–10:30. This fine restaurant melds the recipes of the

Italian countryside and the freshest Hudson Valley ingredients. The chef had two decades of experience in Manhattan restaurants before opening his own trattoria. There are imaginative pasta dishes as well as osso bucco, duck, and bronzino. Everything is prepared to perfection. And make sure not to skip the dolci!

Bywater Bistro (845-658-3210), 419 Main Street, Rosendale. ($$) Open for dinner Thursday through Tuesday 5:30–10, until 11 Friday and Saturday. Rosendale was known for its cement in the early 1900s, when the natural limestone deposits were discovered in town. The cement could harden underwater, which made it the best choice for landmarks like the Statue of Liberty and the Brooklyn Bridge. This establishment is housed in a former saloon and brothel that date back 150 years. The contemporary eclectic cuisine includes comfort foods like pan-roasted half chicken and pasta dishes, although the restaurant is known for its Japanese-inspired entrées. The menu changes seasonally, reflecting what's freshest year-round. There are enticing meat entrées in addition to vegetarian selections. Desserts include a flourless chocolate cake, sorbets, and gelato. Children welcome.

The Country Inn (845-657-8956), 1380 County Route 2, Krumville. (From Route 209, take Krumville Road/County Route 2 for 6 miles; restaurant is on the right.) ($$) Open for dinner Wednesday through Saturday 5–9; Sunday 3–9. The road twists and turns as you approach this rustic oasis in the woods of Ulster County, and it has been a renowned local spot for decades. There are still 350 types of beer available, with 10 on tap, but the food has undergone a transformation (the prices have not). To start, or as a snack, don't pass up the calamari with roasted red pepper sauce for dipping—it's some of the best I've ever had. I thoroughly enjoyed the duck, which was cooked to perfection and served over white beans accompanied by string beans. The steak is excellent and is served with irresistible homemade fries. An unusual dining experience with a unique ambience. Credit cards not accepted.

DePuy Canal House (845-687-7700), 1315 Route 213, High Falls. ($$$) Open for brunch and dinner late May through October, Saturday 10–10; Sunday 10–4. Open for special dinners by advance reservation for small groups; also open for special holiday meals throughout the year. Housed in an 18th-century stone house, formerly a tavern, with each dining room decorated differently, this restaurant is nationally renowned. Owner John Novi, a master of culinary innovation for over 40 years, is still in charge of the kitchen, creating wonderfully original dishes. Those interested in a memorable culinary experience will want to participate in one of the fine-dining experiences here. Not for children.

Global Palate (845-384-6590), 1746 Route 9W, West Park. ($$) Open for dinner Wednesday through Sunday 5–9, Friday and Saturday until 10; Sunday brunch 10–2. The motto here is "where local ingredients greet the world." This is one of my favorite restaurants in the county—consistently good, with healthful international gourmet creations that are truly first-rate. Chef Jessica Winchell uses hormone-free meats and local produce to turn out some phenomenal dishes influenced by global cuisine. The atmosphere is casual and relaxed; decent wine and beer list as well. This is one not to miss.

Henry's at Buttermilk Falls Inn (845-795-1500), 220 North Road, Milton. ($$$) Open for lunch Friday and Saturday 11:30–3; Sunday brunch 11–3; dinner Wednesday through Sunday 5–9:30. This farm to table restaurant at the Buttermilk Falls Inn (see *Lodging*) serves the freshest organic ingredients, many sourced from their own 40-acre organic farm in season. Diners will enjoy entrées like Hudson Valley Cattle Company strip steak with roasted butternut squash and garlic sautéed spinach, or pan-seared scallops sautéed with shiitake mushrooms and black truffle oil. Make sure to order dessert: Everything is superb, with great attention to detail.

Hidden Cellar (845-236-1477), 1441 Route 9W, Marlboro. ($$) Open for dinner Wednesday through Sunday 5–9:30. This restaurant may not look like much from the outside, but the interior is surprisingly cozy. The cuisine is a mix of classical and regional Italian favorites (a specialty of the chef-owner, Vincenzo Incorvaia) as well as new American fare. The prices are reasonable, and the portions are ample. There is a separate children's menu as well.

Ship Lantern Inn (845-795-5400), 1725 Route 9W, Milton. ($$) Open for lunch Thursday and Friday noon–2; dinner Tuesday through Saturday 5–10, Sunday 1–8. This charming restaurant has nautical decor and serves fine Continental cuisine. The food and service are consistently excellent. House specialties include fresh fish, mignonette of beef bordelaise, and saltimbocca Romana. Children are welcome.

Suruchi (845-255-2772), 5 Church Street, New Paltz. ($$) Open Wednesday through Friday 5–9; Saturday 2–10; Sunday 2–9. The Indian cuisine here is first-rate, and all dishes are prepared to order with carefully chosen ingredients. Diners will enjoy organic brown basmati rice, freshly made chickpeas, and homemade yogurt and cheese from antibiotic-free local milk. There is a nice menu with a choice of several beef and shrimp dishes, vegetarian entrées, and Tandoori chicken.

The Would Restaurant (845-691-9883), 120 North Road, Highland. ($$) Open for dinner Tuesday through Saturday 5–10. A former gin mill once known as the Applewood Bar, this informal restaurant is becoming renowned for its high-quality creative cooking. There is a mix of international and New American cuisine, with several unique touches. The menu includes grilled lamb chops on roasted walnut–mint pesto with Mediterranean vegetable compote. The pastry chef bakes focaccia and pesto bread as well as great desserts. Try the flaky apple pie spiced with cinnamon, or the raspberry-chocolate brûlée.

Tuthill House at the Mill Restaurant & Tavern (845-633-8734), 20 Gristmill Lane, Gardiner. ($$) Open daily for lunch 11:30–3:30; dinner 3:30–9. Closed Wednesday in the winter months. The homemade American cuisine here features prime steaks, grass-fed beef, seafood, and pasta dishes in a gristmill that dates back to 1788. Diners will enjoy the freshest Hudson Valley ingredients and creative fare served in a historic setting. Not recommended for children.

Northwestern Ulster County

Peekamoose Restaurant & Tap Room (845-254-6500), 8373 Route 28, Big Indian. ($$) Open for dinner Thursday through Monday 5–10 (hours vary seasonally). Chef Devin Mills and his wife, Marybeth, have created a consistently excellent establishment close to Belleayre. A graduate of Hyde Park's Culinary Institute, Devin worked for Waldy Malouf at the Hudson River Club, Le Bernardin, and the

Gramercy Park Tavern. Marybeth has managed several landmark restaurants in both Manhattan and Boston, and the excellent service and attention to detail are truly special. Together the Millses tastefully renovated the former Rudi's Big Indian Country Kitchen; Peekamoose specializes in American cuisine with the freshest seasonal ingredients. Everything here is prepared with care, from the chicken potpie to the wild striped bass with eggplant caviar and warm lemon vinaigrette. Do not skip dessert; the classic vanilla bean crème brûlée is my favorite. Peekamoose is a great place to stop for drinks and a small meal, too; the taproom is cozy, classy, and comfortable, just like the restaurant. They have a first-rate wine list. This is one of my favorite restaurants in Ulster County.

The Phoenix (845-688-2828), Emerson Resort and Spa, 5340 Route 28, Mount Tremper. ($$) Open for breakfast Monday through Friday 7–10 AM, Saturday and Sunday until noon; dinner Thursday through Saturday 4–10. Hours may vary seasonally, so call ahead. Enjoy American favorites infused with Asian and Indian influences.

Ricciardella's Restaurant (845-688-7800), 54 Main Street, Phoenicia. ($$) Open Wednesday through Saturday 5–10; Sunday 3:30–10. This restaurant offers diners standard Italian fare and decent seafood in an informal atmosphere at reasonable prices. Check out the early-bird specials. Live lobster tank. Children welcome.

Southwestern Ulster County

Aroma Thyme Bistro (845-647-3000), 165 Canal Street, Ellenville. ($$) Open for lunch Friday and Saturday noon–3; dinner daily, except Wednesday, from 5. There is something for everyone at this "certified green" restaurant! There are steaks, seafood, pizza, vegan, and gluten-free selections. And the wine and beer list is excellent; do check out the single-malt Scotch collection. Some of the diverse selections include Kobe beef meat loaf, sesame-crusted albacore tuna, tempeh chili, and grilled New York strip steak (certified organic). Live jazz on Thursday night and local bands on Saturday night. A boon to the village of Ellenville!

White Wolf Restaurant & Lounge (845-647-4200), 7400 Route 209, Napanoch. ($$) Open for dinner Tuesday through Saturday 4:30–11; Sunday 2–8. This is a place to stop for a drink when traveling on Route 209, if only to take in the opulent decor that includes the granite-top zigzag bar and deluxe dining rooms with mahogany and cherry woods, and etched glass with wolf motifs on the mirrors. The food is straightforward American fare with a good selection and ranges from bar fare to prime rib, chicken, ribs, and pastas. Children welcome.

EATING OUT

Northeastern Ulster County

The Alternative Baker (845-658-3355; 1-800-399-3589), 407 Main Street, Rosendale. ($) Open daily, except Tuesday and Wednesday, 7–7; Sunday and Monday until 5. Fans of this eatery, formerly on the Rondout in Kingston, will find wonderful choices here, including soups, sandwiches, flans, and quiches, as well as the superb organic baked goods. In addition to standard favorites like brownie fudge cake, there is focaccia, buttermilk scones, and muffins, all baked with quality ingredients. Several dairy-free, sugar-free, and wheat-free choices make this a place with something delicious for everyone. This is a great stop if you want to pick up a snack or pack a picnic lunch. There's lots of room to eat in the café, as well as plenty of parking. Children welcome.

Bistro To Go (845-340-9800), 948 Route 28, Kingston. ($). Open Monday through Thursday 9–7; Friday until 8; Saturday and Sunday 11–5. Richard and Mary Anne Erickson of Blue Mountain Bistro Catering Company have opened this wonderful gourmet take-out shop with a small restaurant on the premises. There are interesting paninis, sandwiches, and hearty soups, as well as dozens of wonderful salads (my favorites here). The house-roasted turkey with pesto mayo is a terrific sandwich. All ingredients are fresh, and many are organic. The Mediterranean treats change continually, and if you are planning a picnic lunch or supper, make sure to stock up here before heading into the Catskill Park. If you need to find a gift for a gourmet, you will find it here as well. And don't leave without sampling one of their marvelous desserts!

Bread Alone (845-679-2108), 22 Mill Hill Road, Woodstock; also 2015 Ulster Avenue, Kingston. ($) Open daily 7–5. Don't miss this bakery, renowned for its fantastic bread—Norwegian farm, mixed grain, Swiss peasant, Finnish sour rye, and others—all baked in a wood-fired oven. Have a cup of tea or coffee, and satisfy your craving for something sweet and rich from the array of tempting desserts so beautifully displayed. Their soups and chilis are quite good, served with your choice of bread or a roll.

Café Mezzaluna (845-246-5306), 626 Route 212, Saugerties. ($) Open daily, except Monday, for breakfast, lunch and dinner. Call for hours, which vary. A Latin bistro with an eclectic menu offering pizzas, egg dishes, homemade gelati, and paninis. There is always something happening in this lively eatery. The walls are covered with the work of local artists, and in the evening or at weekend brunch, there is often live music or a poetry reading. A cultural hub located just outside of the village of Saugerties; call to find out what is going on if you plan to stop in. The proprietress is full of surprises.

Cheese Louise! (845-853-8207), 940 Route 28, Kingston. ($) Open Tuesday through Saturday 11:30–7; until 9 on Friday; Sunday noon–5. Sit down at one of the tables here for a light lunch or take home some of the world's best cheeses. Also available for take-out are artisanal breads and grass-fed beef. The lunch specials include soups, sandwiches, and tasty salads. Everything here is of high quality and freshly prepared. Children welcome (they will love the grilled cheese!).

Coffee Beanery (845-336-8146), 1090 Morton Boulevard, Kingston. ($) Open daily 7 AM–9 PM. Hours vary slightly in the winter. This spacious, immaculate café has an array of desserts (pies, pastries, frozen drinks), coffees, teas, yogurt, ice cream (waffle-cone sundaes, parfaits, banana splits, hot-fudge brownies), bagels, and muffins. This is a mom-and-pop operation, and all baked goods are made on the premises. Children will love it.

Cub Market and Deli (845-679-65 69), 3203 Route 212, Bearsville. ($) Open year-round, daily 7–7; until 5 PM on Sunday. This is a great place to get a breakfast wrap, hot soup, club sandwich, or garden salad. Everything here is super fresh, and organic ingredients are used. The coffee is excellent, and the tea selections are extensive.

Dallas Hot Wieners (845-338-6094), 51 North Front Street and 490 Broadway (845-331-6311), Kingston. ($) Open Monday through Saturday 9–8. Since 1927 this establishment has been serving up their legendary hot dogs. Brothers-in-law Spyros Pappas and

John Tampasis have owned the eatery since the mid-1970s. There are also burgers, fries, tuna salad, eggs, and omelets. Of course, the secret sauce topping the hot dogs is sold by the pint if you want to take it home! The prices are exceedingly reasonable, and note that it is cash only.

Deising's Bakery & Coffee Shop (845-338-7503), 111 North Front Street, Kingston. ($) Open for breakfast, lunch, and dessert Monday through Saturday 6–4; Sunday until 1. Deising's has quality pastries, breads, and other baked items (try the napoleons and butter cookies). The coffee shop offers large, overstuffed sandwiches, fresh quiches, and hearty soups—all made fresh daily. Breakfast is a bargain. Children welcome.

Duo's (845-383-1198), 50 John Street, Kingston. ($) Open Monday through Friday 10–3:30; Saturday and Sunday 8:30–3:30; dinner Friday through Sunday 5:30–9:30. The imaginative fare here features seasonal local ingredients. Breakfasts are excellent, and there are always soups to accompany the array of sandwiches and salads. The service is friendly and efficient. Vegetarians will love the menu!

The Dutch Ale House (845-247-2337), 253 Main Street, Saugerties. ($) Open for lunch and dinner daily 11–9, until 10 on Friday and Saturday. Call before you go on Sunday since they are closed at certain times of the year. Hearty American favorites in a tavern atmosphere. Try the stuffed garlic cheeseburger, a specialty of the house, or the Pilgrim (thinly sliced turkey breast, homemade stuffing, and provolone sandwiched between two slices of fresh rye bread and grilled). The sandwiches, salads, soups, and chili are very good; the portions are generous; and the price is right. Along with carnivorous fare, there's veggie-bean chili, veggie burgers, and veggie pitas. There are 15 craft beers on tap and more available by the bottle.

Eddy's Restaurant (845-338-9793), 742 Broadway, Kingston. ($) Open Tuesday through Friday 5–4; Saturday 6–3; Sunday 6–1. Watch your breakfast prepared before you in this small, unpretentious restaurant at the upper tip of Broadway. The atmosphere—and prices—are something out of another era, and it's worth a stop. They cook their own turkey, roast beef, corned beef, and ham here: Those are the best sandwiches to order for lunch—they're fresh and delicious. Many local folks have no idea this place exists, which is what I like best about it! Kids are welcome.

The 1850 House Inn & Tavern (845-658-7800), 435 Main Street, Rosendale. ($) Open Wednesday through Sunday 4–10. Light fare and drinks are served in this beautifully renovated tavern. Diners will enjoy burgers, sandwiches, and salads. A delightful place to relax after strolling through Rosendale or hiking in the area.

Fred's Place Restaurant & Bar (845-383-3883), 11 Lohmaier Lane, Lake Katrine. ($) Open Wednesday through Sunday, 4 PM–closing. Comfort food with an Italian flair is served here, along with renowned desserts by Cynthia (Fred's wife). This is a popular place with local residents.

Gabriel's Café (845-331-7161), Wall Street, Kingston. ($) Open Monday through Friday 10–9; Saturday 9–9. Closed Sunday. This restaurant is in a new location as of 2013, and it's a lovely place to enjoy lunch or dinner. For lunch there are wraps, sandwiches, grilled chicken, salmon Caesar, hot soup, an array of fruit and vegetable juices, and plenty of selections for vegetarians. In the warm weather months

Bob Barrett

THE 1850 HOUSE INN & TAVERN IN ROSENDALE

enjoy outdoor dining in a courtyard. Miles Asian Market is also on the premises and features local food products and the work of local artists. (They are open Monday through Saturday 11–6.)

Gypsy Wolf Cantina (845-679-9563), 261 Tinker Street, Woodstock. ($) Open for dinner daily, except Monday, from 5. This is an authentic Mexican cantina with colorful decor and a festive atmosphere. The chips and salsa are first-rate, and the Gypsy Wolf platter includes a little of everything to put in your tortillas. Wonderful margaritas. Children welcome.

Hickory BBQ and Smokehouse (845-338-2424), 743 State Route 28, Kingston. ($) Open for lunch and dinner daily noon–9. This is the place to go for ribs, chicken, pulled pork, smoked beef, chili, buffalo wings, and all things barbecue. The informal atmosphere makes for a great place to take the kids. No one will leave here hungry!

Hudson Valley Dessert Company (845-246-1545), 264 Main Street, Saugerties. ($) Open daily 8–6. Lachmann's Bakery is no longer on Main Street, but this terrific replacement (opened in 2008) offers high-quality desserts (cakes, cookies, pies, muffins, biscotti, and more) as well as potpies and quiche. A clean, contemporary, pleasant place to stop for afternoon tea and a sweet snack while sitting at a table looking out on Main Street.

La Florentina (845-339-2455), 604 Ulster Avenue, Kingston. ($) Open weekdays 11:30–10; weekends 4–10. Excellent pizza, calzones, and other baked specialties. A traditional wood-fired oven is used. Even the cheeses are homemade, and there are outstanding dishes such as pizza with veal and broccoli (the dough is yeast-free). Great Sicilian (and other Italian) desserts, including cannoli, ices, and layer cake. Children welcome.

Lori's Creative Café (845-679-8400), 98 Mill Hill Road, Woodstock. ($)

Open Sunday through Friday 8–5:30; Saturday 9–3:30. Enjoy egg sandwiches, bagels, oatmeal, or burritos for breakfast. Lunch selections include turkey meat loaf sandwiches, tuna melt with tomato and avocado, Cobb salad, and an array of soups. All baked goods are made on the premises daily. The brownies and cookies are wonderful!

Love Bites Cafe (845-246-1795), 85 Partition Street, Saugerties. ($) Open Thursday through Tuesday 8:30–4:30. Breakfast is served all day in this small cozy eatery with an open kitchen. The organically produced foods are reasonably priced (as well as made to order) and include carrot-coconut French toast (served with maple syrup and citrus-vanilla butter), smoked chicken panini (with cheddar, roasted red peppers, avocado aoli, and greens on peasant bread), and roasted apple porridge (with steel-cut oats, roasted apple compote, and spiced cream or vegan pudding). Excellent coffee. Don't bring the kids here, please; it's simply too small a venue.

Maria's Bazaar (845-679-5434), 21 Mill Hill Road, Woodstock. ($) Open daily 6:30 AM–8 PM, Sunday until 7:30. Maria is well-known in town for her home-cooked Italian specialties; her renowned vegetarian lasagna is wonderful. A variety of salad creations, fresh pastas, homemade soups, and baked goods are to be found here; vegetarians will find many selections from which to choose. This is one of the few places in Woodstock where you can dine outdoors—they have a lovely, large open-air patio, and it's off the street. Children welcome.

Monkey Joe's Roasting Company & Coffee Bar (845-331-4598), 478 Broadway, Kingston. ($) Open Monday through Friday 6:30–6; Saturday 7:30–4. This delightful café is housed in the Hutton building (1906), formerly an oyster house. The original tin ceiling, tile floor, schoolhouse lights, wainscoting, and fireplace make this charming renovated space relatively unchanged for 100 years. It's a wonderful spot to enjoy organic coffee—espresso, cappuccino, latte, café au lait, caffe mocha, or a Monkey Frost (a flavored frozen drink). Other offerings are chai frost, iced chai, raspberry tea frost, and several types of tea (black, green, and herbal varieties). For those who prefer hot chocolate, theirs is first-rate; so is the chocolate egg cream. Baked goods include bagels, muffins, scones, cakes, cookies, and biscotti. Children are welcome.

Olive's Country Store/Café (845-657-8959), 3110 Route 28, Shokan. ($) Open daily 6 AM–9 PM. The store here has just about everything you will need for a country weekend. The café offers standard deli fare, freshly prepared daily, with a dining room removed from the bustle of the retail business. Fresh soups, salads, and coffee are served up all day and into the evening. Don't leave without checking out their local book and map section.

Oriole 9 (845-679-5783), 17 Tinker Street, Woodstock. ($$) Open for breakfast and lunch daily 8:30–4:30. Enjoy omelets, crêpes, hearty soups, salads, and excellent French toast served until the late afternoon in a lovely European café atmosphere (except on summer weekends, when the restaurant is exceedingly busy). The walls here display changing exhibits featuring the work of Woodstock artists. The restaurant uses natural and organic products when possible. Their apple pie (with freshly whipped cream) and coffee is the best in town.

Phoenicia Diner (845-688-9957), 5681 Route 28, Phoenicia. ($) Open Thursday through Monday 7–5. This terrific eatery opened in the autumn of 2012 and has quickly become a popular destination, with its soda fountain, Formica counters, and retro barstools. The owner, Michael Cioffi, uses local purveyors, including Bread Alone products, Java Love coffee, and free-range eggs, to name just some. French toast and waffles are served all day long, along with wonderful egg dishes. Comfort food is featured for lunch and includes corned beef hash, meat loaf, and several hearty soups. There are also plenty of fresh-squeezed juices, milk shakes, and vegetarian selections. Don't pass this by on Route 28 if you're hungry or thirsty!

Pine View Bakery (845-657-8925), 3374 Route 28, Shokan. ($) Open daily 6–3; until 4 on Saturday and Sunday. This breakfast-and-lunch eatery offers simple, straightforward food at amazingly reasonable prices. It's an old-fashioned place with a counter and six or seven tables at most. The place has a large loyal customer base, almost all locals. I enjoy having breakfast on the terrace during the summer and always order the egg sandwich on their fresh eight-grain bread, which is excellent. Children are welcome, but it's a small place, so they can't run around here without getting underfoot.

Sissy's Café (845-514-2336), 324 Wall Street, Kingston. ($) Open Monday through Friday 8–4; Saturday 8–3; Sunday 9–2. This is one of the best places in Kingston to get breakfast or lunch. The sandwiches, salads, and paninis are fresh, and the portions are generous. Their fakin' bacon tastes just like the real thing, and there are several selections for vegans and vegetarians. I had the Hot Bird Panini (turkey, bacon, avocado, red onion, and chipotle mayo with cheddar), which was tasty and satisfying.

Southwestern Grill (845-246-6222), 244 Main Street, Saugerties. ($) Open daily 11–10. This Main Street restaurant features Texas nachos, wings, guacamole, quesadillas, fajitas, tacos, burritos, burgers, chimichangas, and enchiladas. Everything is well prepared, and the prices are very reasonable. It's a terrific lunch stop, and there is French onion soup every day!

Stockade Tavern (845-514-2649), 313 Fair Street, Kingston. ($$) Open Wednesday 4 PM–midnight; Friday and Saturday 4 PM–2 AM. If you are in Kingston and have a hankering for excellent unusual cocktails served in cozy contemporary surroundings, head for this bar. There are a few high-back booths and a pressed tin ceiling, and the building has been completely renovated. The pretzels, pickled eggs, and other savory snacks accompanying the imaginative drinks here are particularly tasty. The bar is named for the Stockade District in Kingston, a part of uptown that dates back to the mid-17th century.

Sunfrost (845-679-6690), 217 Tinker Street, Woodstock. ($) Open daily 8–6. In addition to a market with first-rate fruits and vegetables and a gourmet take-out deli, there is an adjoining juice bar/eatery with patio dining in the warm weather months. They serve several varieties of smoothies, burritos, overstuffed sandwiches, salads, and paninis. Everything is fresh, and much of the produce is organic. This is a great stop for a quick healthful snack or lunch. Local Woodstockers come here regularly for breakfast and lunch. My favorite soup is their three-bean chili!

Szechuan King (845-246-7090), 261 Main Street, Saugerties. ($) Open daily 11 AM–10:30 PM. Whether you desire Hunan boneless duck, Love in the Stars (spicy beef and shrimp Szechuan style), or steamed Triple Delight (shrimp, chicken, and scallops with brown rice), this immaculate Chinese restaurant, a neighborhood mainstay, will prepare a meal to your taste. Combination plates, pupu platters, and special noodle soups available for lunch and dinner. The service is excellent, and the colorful ambience is delightful. Children welcome.

Yum Yum Noodle Bar (845-679-7992), 4 Rock City Road, Woodstock; and another location (845-338-1400), 275 Fair Street, Kingston. ($) Open daily 4:30–10 in Woodstock; Monday through Saturday 11:30–10 in Kingston. These two small noodle bars offer tasty, healthful fun dishes at inexpensive prices. The offerings range from pad thai, chicken satay, and curry coconut soup to miso broth with salmon and vegetables, marinated green beans, and pork with watermelon salad. There are vegan and vegetarian options, as well as beer, wine, and saki. The Woodstock location has only a few tables inside and a counter where you can watch everything being prepared. However, there is outdoor dining on the patio in summer.

Southeastern Ulster County

The Bakery (845-255-8840), 13A North Front Street, New Paltz. ($) Open daily 7–7. The bagels, rugelach, and butter cookies are first-rate at this place, popular with students and local residents. The outdoor café is surrounded by gardens and provides a pleasant ambience for those who want to relax and enjoy a treat from the coffee bar. Overstuffed sandwiches, salads, and intriguing pasta dishes are a few of the lunch options.

Café Mio (845-255-4949), 2356 Route 44/55, Gardiner. ($) Open daily, except Tuesday, 8:30–4:30. This is a great place to stop for a hearty breakfast before setting out on a hike in the Shawangunks. They have a smoked salmon and dill omelet that is wonderful. Other choices include tofu scramble, organic yogurt with granola, and baked apple French toast. For lunch there are shrimp po'boy sandwiches along with more conventional choices, or you can design your own burger. The seared ahi tuna wrap with avocado, tomato, wasabi, and greens is my favorite. Cappuccino and lattes are available, and a wide variety of teas are served as well. If you don't have time to relax and eat, they will prepare whatever you like to go. Children welcome.

Cohen's Bakery (845-647-7620), 89 Center Street, Ellenville. ($) Open Monday through Saturday 6:30–6; Sunday until 5. Although this isn't a place where you can sit down and have a bite, it should be a stop for anyone passing through Ellenville. Since 1920 the Cohens have been a mainstay of the village. Their famous raisin pumpernickel is superb, and so are the other offerings, including rye bread, bagels, cakes, pies, muffins, and pastries.

The Egg's Nest (845-687-7255), 1300 Route 213, High Falls. ($) Open daily 11:30–10. Located in a former parsonage, this cozy restaurant with funky, fun decor has homemade soups, great sandwiches, and chili, and they're known for crispy-crusted praeseux, a pizzalike creation that's delicious. The place is an original, and it's worth a stop for lunch, early dinner, or an afternoon snack. The nachos are wonderful; the prices are great. Children welcome.

Gaby's Cafe (845-210-1040), 150 Canal Street, Ellenville. ($) You will find international favorites (with the emphasis on Mexican comfort food) in this informal, delightful café. The fajitas, quesadillas, and tableside guacamole are first-rate. There are also

Italian dinners, chicken Caesar salad, wraps, and more. The portions are generous, and the prices are reasonable. Children welcome.

Gadaleto's Seafood Market & Restaurant (845-255-1717), 246 Main Street, Cherry Hill Shopping Center, New Paltz. ($$) Restaurant is open Wednesday through Sunday 11:30–9. Enjoy fresh fish, shrimp, clams, crabs, or lobster in this informal eatery. A great place to get take-out, as well. Children welcome.

Gilded Otter Restaurant & Brewery (845-256-1700), 3 Main Street, New Paltz. ($$) Open daily noon–10:30. The dining room and pub here overlook the Wallkill River and offer views of the Shawangunks, as well. This is a place beer lovers should not miss; do try some of brewmaster Darren Currier's award-winning creations.

Harvest Café (845-255-4205), 10 Main Street, Water Street Market, New Paltz. ($$) Open daily 11–9. Organic American and vegetarian cuisine with imaginative specialties, including a salmon BLT with herb mayonnaise on a fresh-baked roll, Asian soba-noodle salad with soy ginger vinaigrette, and a barbecued pork burrito with chive sour cream and carrot slaw. Outdoor patio dining in the warm-weather months. Children welcome.

HopHeads Craft Beer Market & Tasting Bar (845-687-4750), 2303 Lucas Turnpike, High Falls ($) Open Tuesday through Friday 11–11; Saturday and Sunday noon–closing. The taps are constantly changing, but the specialties remain the same—American and Belgian beers paired with light Hudson Valley fare. Enjoy local cheeses and charcuterie, a Mediterranean salad, or vegetarian ploughman's lunch while tasting a half dozen different craft beers. The ambience is informal and relaxed.

Karma Road (845-255-1099), 11 Main Street, New Paltz. ($) Open daily 8–8. The fresh, organic ingredients here change with the season, and this is truly an oasis for those seeking healthy, fresh fast food to take out or eat at one of the few tables in the restaurant. The juices, smoothies, soups, and sandwiches are excellent. The deli case is filled with goodies that include roasted chickpea and tempeh paella, sautéed greens, Thai rolls with peanut-chili sauce, and karma pesto pasta (they use brown rice pasta). If you love health food well prepared and with a variety of dishes to choose from, this is the place to go in New Paltz.

The Last Bite (845-687-7779), 103 Main Street, High Falls. ($) Open Monday through Friday 7–6; Saturday and Sunday 9–6. An informal eatery serving soups, paninis, sandwiches, salads, quiches, and salads. This is the place to go to pick up the local paper and have a coffee or smoothie with a homemade pastry.

Main Course (845-255-2600), 175 Main Street, New Paltz. ($) Open for lunch and dinner daily, except Monday, 11:30–9. Fresh, delicious spa cuisine, featuring contemporary American dishes with grilled fish specials, homemade pasta, and imaginative salad creations (you can make your own entrée by choosing two, three, or four different salads). Casual and relaxing, with healthful—and tasty—choices.

Mariner's-on-the-Hudson (845-691-4711), 46 River Road, Highland. ($$) Open daily from 11:30 AM for lunch and dinner. Closed Tuesday November through March. This is the place to go to enjoy drinks and snacks or a waterfront meal right by the Mid-Hudson Bridge. The outdoor deck seats 200, and you can watch the boats pass by as you enjoy steamed clams, calamari, mussels, or the Mariner's renowned lobsters (served steamed, broiled, or stuffed). Children welcome.

Pure City (845-744-8888), 100 Main Street, Pine Bush. ($) Open Tuesday through Saturday 11–10; Friday and Saturday until 11. Closed Sunday and Monday. This vegan Chinese restaurant provides an interesting variation on traditional Asian cuisine, with offerings like barbecued veggie ribs, sesame Spanish roll, and steamed mushrooms. In addition, the menu includes veggie burgers, salads, noodle dishes, and intriguing desserts (like green tea ice cream and tofu cheesecake). They do a big take-out business here, and there are about 10 tables for eating in. Children are welcome.

Raccoon Saloon (845-236-7872), 1330 Route 9W, Marlboro. ($$) Lunch served daily 11:30–4; dinner daily 5–9. Some of the best burgers in the region, along with excellent fries, chicken, ribs, soups, and salads, have been prepared here for decades. This renowned local eatery, a popular casual stop for lunch or dinner, also has a cozy bar with great views. Children are welcome.

Rosendale Café (845-658-9048), 434 Main Street, Rosendale. ($) Open daily 11–10. This vegetarian restaurant offers a variety of soups, salads, sandwiches, and pasta dishes. Try the Fakin' Bacon FLT. The nachos and burritos are also tasty. Their meatless black-bean chili over brown rice is excellent. Organic coffees and homemade desserts. There's music on most weekend evenings, and it's usually quality entertainment.

The Tavern at the 1850 House (845-658-7800), 435 Main Street, Rosendale. ($$) Open daily noon–9; Saturday and Sunday brunch 10–2. ($$) Main Street in Rosendale is fun to explore any time of year. When you are ready to stop and relax, this is a terrific place to enjoy drinks and light fare including burgers, sandwiches, soups, and salads in a delightful country atmosphere. The beautifully renovated 1850 House (see *Lodging*) is upstairs.

36 Main Street Restaurant & Wine Bar (845-255-3636), 36 Main Street, New Paltz. ($) Open daily for dinner at 5; Sunday brunch noon–3. This interesting addition to the New Paltz dining scene features contemporary American fusion cuisine in a relaxed atmosphere. The menu changes with the seasons and includes some terrifically imaginative touches. There are smoked mashed potatoes that accompany the organic breast of chicken stuffed with oven-dried tomatoes and house-made mozzarella. The filet mignon is accompanied by lobster home fries (fries sautéed in lobster-infused oil). A fun place to hang out and snack as well as enjoy a meal!

Twisted Foods (845-658-9121), 446 Main Street, Rosendale. ($) Open daily 7:30–4:30. This is the home of a pretzel roll factory/eatery chock-full of fantastic snacks. The breakfast sandwiches on pretzel rolls with bacon, eggs, and cheese are memorable. Fresh chicken salad with avocado on a pretzel croissant is my favorite choice for lunch. This is a great place to take out food for a picnic on Joppenbergh Mountain, only a short walk away!

The Village Tea Room (845-255-3434), 10 Plattekill Avenue, New Paltz. ($) Open Tuesday through Sunday 8 AM–9 PM. Enjoy home-baked muffins, scones, and other treats, and light lunches and country suppers here, with an emphasis on fresh local products. All the eggs used are organic, and so is the oatmeal. The Murray's Natural Chicken and roasted pepper sandwich with cilantro almond relish on seven-grain health bread is delicious. The tearoom is located in a 200-year-old building with exposed hand-hewn beams that give the feeling of being in a colonial tavern. Afternoon tea is available all day and into the evening (it includes a selection of sandwiches, a scone served with fresh jam and clotted cream, a plate of cookies, and a pot of tea). There is outdoor dining in warm weather. Children are welcome; in fact, a children's tea is offered here with kids' tastes considered!

Yanni Restaurant & Café (845-256-0988), 51 Main Street, New Paltz. ($) Open for lunch and dinner Thursday through Monday 11:30–10; for dinner Tuesday and Wednesday 5–10. Enjoy Greek specialties (gyros, Greek salad, souvlaki sandwich, spinach pie, and kebabs) and American favorites (chicken parmigiana sandwich, eight types of burgers, salads) in an informal atmosphere. Everything here is fresh and prepared to order. Great vegetarian specialties (falafel, veggie platter, wraps). Prices, too, are great. Children welcome.

Northwestern Ulster County

Brio's (845-688-5370), 68 Main Street, Phoenicia. ($) Open daily 7 AM–10 PM. This luncheonette is a good place to stop for an overstuffed sandwich, hearty chili, or a snack. The breakfasts are terrific, and 10 kinds of pancakes are served. A popular place with local residents. Kids will love the spaghetti and meatballs.

Fruition Chocolate (845-657-6717), 3091 Route 28, Shokan. ($$) Open Friday through Sunday noon–6. Chocoholics take note: This handcrafted bean to bar chocolate workshop, owned and operated by Bryan Graham, is open to the public. The chocolate here is made from fair-trade organically grown cocoa beans, and it's first-rate. If you have a craving for chocolate, make sure to stop here and indulge!

Sweet Sue's (845-688-7852), 49 Main Street, Phoenicia. ($) Open daily 8–3. This is a great breakfast-and-lunch place, with more than a dozen types of spectacular pancakes (including fruited oatmeal) and French toast (including walnut crunch). Everything, from muffins to soups and all desserts, is homemade here. A casual café with an outstanding reputation. Get there early on weekend mornings; there's usually a line out the door. Great for children.

Winchell's Pizza (845-657-3352), Reservoir Road and Route 28, Shokan. ($) Open daily 11:30–9:30. Hearty soups, barbecue, and unusually tempting pizzas with a thick crust; enjoy creamy homemade ice cream for dessert. This is a great stop for people traveling with children.

✷ Entertainment

PERFORMING ARTS Backstage Studio Productions (845-338-8700; www.bspinfo.net), 323 Wall Street, Kingston. This is the center of an arts-and-entertainment complex with 75,000 square feet of space, a 2,000-seat concert hall, dance studio, and art gallery with changing exhibits. Open year-round, daily 10–6. Check the website for a complete schedule of events.

Bearsville Theater (845-679-4406; www.bearsvilletheater.com), 291 Tinker Street, Woodstock. Open Monday through Friday noon–5. There are nationally renowned musicians who perform here throughout the year. For updated concert and events listings, check the website.

Belleayre Music Festival (845-254-5600; 1-800-942-6904; www.belleayremusic.org), Belleayre Ski Center, Belleayre Mountain Road, Pine Hill. Admission fee. Since 1992 this fantastic outdoor music festival has attracted outstanding performers to its mountaintop setting. The likes of such diverse talents as Ray Charles,

Emmylou Harris, Lyle Lovett, Wynton Marsalis, and the Temptations have entertained thousands, and the festival continues to grow with each passing season. There are seats under a tent as well as lawn seating at reduced prices, and the evening concerts offer cool summer's night entertainment. Get there early if you intend to sit on the lawn. There is plenty of parking, and the events are always well organized. The music festival is truly where the mountains meet the stars!

Colony Café (845-679-8639; www.colonycafewoodstock.com), 22 Rock City Road, Woodstock. Open year-round; café open Wednesday through Sunday from 6 PM on. This is one of the few places in Woodstock to hear live music. The unusual building with its intimate setting is a great place to go to see local talent as well as renowned performers. Check the website for an up-to-date schedule.

CounterPoint Music and Arts Festival, Saugerties. At press time, plans were moving along for this multiday music festival. Michael Lang, the organizer of the 1969 Woodstock Festival in Bethel as well as the 25th-anniversary concert held in Saugerties on the Winston Farm property, has been working with the property's owners to bring music back to the site.

Kleinert/James Arts Center of the Woodstock Guild (845-679-2079; www.woodstockguild.org), 34 Tinker Street, Woodstock, offers a series of musical performances year-round. Call or check the website for a schedule.

Levon Helm's Rambles (845-679-2744; www.levonhelm.com), Levon Helm Studios, 160 Plochmann Lane, Woodstock. Although legendary musician Helm passed away in 2012, the barn on his property is still open for occasional weekend performances, usually held once a month. Woodstock is home to several well-known rock musicians who enjoy performing in this unusual venue, at one time Helm's recording studio. The shows used to begin around midnight, but these days it's usually around 8 PM. Check the website for a complete schedule. The spirit of Levon and 1960s Woodstock lives on here!

Live at the Falcon (845-236-7970; www.liveatthefalcon.com), 1348 Route 9W, Marlboro. Open year-round, with performances Thursday through Sunday nights, usually beginning around 10 PM; Sunday jazz brunch 10–2. This bustling live-music venue offers a potpourri of world-class blues and jazz performers. There are even occasional children's programs on Sunday mornings.

Maverick Concerts (845-679-8217; www.maverickconcerts.org), 120 Maverick Road, Woodstock (just off Route 375), features chamber-music concerts on weekends, usually in the afternoon at 4 during July and August. Admission fee. Founded in 1916 by author Hervey White, the Maverick Concerts were to be a blend of the best that chamber music and the natural world had to offer. White wanted to encourage other "maverick" artists, and he attracted some of the premier string and wind players of the time to this glass-and-wood concert hall. The small building seats only 400, but many people enjoy hearing the concerts from the surrounding hillside—a setting that was White's idea of perfection. The concerts are known as the oldest chamber-music series in the country, and they are still attracting the best groups in the world, among them the Tokyo, Shanghai, Miami, and Emerson string quartets. They also offer free children's concerts on Saturday mornings in July and August at 11. Check website for a complete schedule of events.

Mount Tremper Arts (845-688-9893; www.mounttremperarts.org), 647 South Plank Road, Mount Tremper. Mid-July through August. This world-class performance and visual arts venue is housed in a post-and-beam studio between Woodstock and Phoenicia. There are dance, opera, and music performances during the summer months, as well as art and photography exhibits. Check the website for a schedule of events.

Phoenicia International Festival of the Voice (845-688-1344; www.phoeniciavoicefest.org), Parish Field, Ursula Drive, Phoenicia, features world-class performances. From opera to gospel, world music to Broadway favorites, this venue celebrates the human voice in all its multifaceted glory. The summer season is when performances are held outdoors. Check the website for the schedule.

Ulster Performing Arts Center (845-331-1613; www.upac.org), 601 Broadway, Kingston, is on the National Register of Historic Places. The renovated Broadway Theatre is the largest arts showcase in the county, offering a variety of theater productions and concert performances year-round. Call or check the website for a schedule.

Unison Arts and Learning Center (845-255-1559; www.unisonarts.org), 68 Mountain Rest Road, New Paltz, is a multiarts center with performances of jazz, folk, world music, and dance. There are also poetry readings, children's theater, workshops, and monthly art gallery exhibits. Outdoor sculpture garden. Open year-round, Monday through Friday 10–5. Call and get on their mailing list—the quarterly catalog is large and includes something of interest to just about everyone.

Woodstock Film Festival (845-679-4265; www.woodstockfilmfestival.com), at various venues throughout the town, as well as Rhinebeck and Rosendale. Separate admission is charged at each film or seminar. Screenings are offered in different venues throughout Woodstock and surrounding communities. Since 2000 the five-day (Wednesday through Sunday) program, featuring more than 100 films—along with celebrity-led seminars, workshops, parties, and an awards ceremony—has grown in stature in the film industry. Book early to secure tickets. The festival is held in September or October, but it varies from year to year. Tim Robbins, Ethan Hawke, Benjamin Bratt, Aidan Quinn, Marcia Gay Harden, Patricia Clarkson, Woody Harrelson, and Lily Taylor are some of the featured speakers whose films were screened here before release. Do check the website, which is continually updated; tickets are available online.

Woodstock Playhouse (845-679-6900; www.woodstockplayhouse.org), 103 Mill Hill Road, Woodstock, is a year-round performing arts venue featuring a variety of events in music and theater. Children's performances are also offered from Memorial Day weekend through Labor Day at 11 AM. There is a lovely art gallery on the premises.

THEATER **Bird-On-A-Cliff Theatre Company** (845-247-4007; www.birdonacliff.org) produces a Shakespeare festival on the grounds of the Comeau property (by the town offices) in Woodstock every July and August, Friday through Sunday. They also feature dramatic productions. This is a wonderful place to enjoy a picnic dinner and take in some theater at the right price ($5 suggested donation per person). Performances begin at 5 PM; call or check the website for a schedule.

Coach House Players (845-331-2476; www.coachhouseplayers.org), 12 Augusta Street, Kingston. This community theater group performs four times a year in its venue, an original coach house. Call or check the website for a schedule.

Community Playback Theatre (845-691-4118; www.playbackcentre.org), Boughton Place, 150 Kisor Road, Highland. An improvisational theater company that weaves the stories told by audience members into scenes that are then "played back" on the spot. For a complete schedule of performances, check the website.

New Paltz Summer Repertory Theater (845-257-3880; www.newpaltz.edu/artsnews), SUNY New Paltz, 75 South Manheim Boulevard, New Paltz. Several plays are presented each summer in theaters on the campus. The repertory theater has presented a variety of productions for more than 35 years. Past seasons have included *Proof* by David Auburn and *Talley's Folly* by Lanford Wilson. Call for current schedule. SUNY also hosts the renowned **Piano Summer at New Paltz Festival-Institute** (845-257-3860; www.newpaltz.edu/piano) under the aegis of internationally acclaimed pianist Vladimir Feltsman; there are master classes (some may be audited by the public) as well as concerts during the month of July. Call or check the website for a complete schedule.

Performing Arts of Woodstock (845-679-7900; www.performingartsofwoodstock.org), Woodstock Town Hall, 76 Tinker Street, Woodstock. For over 40 years this company has been offering high-quality new and classic theater productions in the community. There are usually three plays presented each year. The presentations are well done, and the price is exceedingly reasonable. Check the website for dates and times of performances.

Shadowland Theatre (845-647-5511; www.shadowlandtheatre.org), 157 Canal Street, Ellenville. This is the county's only professional nonprofit theater company, featuring a five-play main-stage season from May through September. Offerings include contemporary dramas, comedies, classics, and new plays. The theater first opened on July 3, 1920, as an art deco movie and vaudeville house. Substantial renovations have rebuilt the interior, retaining the charm of the past and creating a tiered 148-seat intimate venue for theater. All seats are within 25 feet of the stage. Call or check the website for a complete schedule.

Shandaken Theatrical Society (845-688-2279; www.stsplayhouse.com), 10 Church Street, Phoenicia, is a community-theater organization that produces a musical in the spring, a drama or comedy in the fall, and a summer production. There are several films shown here as well. Check the website for a complete schedule.

✷ Selective Shopping

Ulster County has a number of interesting villages filled with boutiques, galleries, bookshops, and stores that sell everything from teapots and handblown glass to soaps and chocolates. *Note:* Make sure in the city of Kingston, the village of New Paltz, and the village of Saugerties you pay careful attention to the parking meters. The meter attendants in Kingston and New Paltz are particularly strict; I have received parking tickets in these towns despite the fact I put all the available change I had on hand in the meter. If you are only moments late, count on receiving a minimum of a $20 ticket. This does not make for a relaxing shopping experience, hence many locals frequent area malls. The following stores are my favorite places to shop in the county, and all offer plenty of free parking!

Barneche (845-688-5822), 361 Route 214, Chichester, just north of Phoenicia on the road to Hunter, is open Saturday and Sunday 10–5 or by chance. It's a lovely store by the Stony Clove stream filled with an eclectic array of exquisite clothing with fantastic colors and textures, literally wearable works of art, designed by owner Stephanie Barnes; home furnishings; handcrafted jewelry; scarves; pillows; antiques; books; dolls; lampshades; and fine art. It is worth a special trip. It's located in a century-old barn, and you can sit on the porch here with tea or coffee and thoroughly relax. **Basia Designs** (845-901-5293), 2019 Glasco Turnpike, Woodstock, a hidden gem, offers European-style couture, original designs by Basia, all hand-knitted (not loomed or machine knit). The stunning sweaters here were formerly sold at Bergdorf's and Bloomingdale's, as well as in Manhattan boutiques on Madison Avenue. Open Saturday and Sunday 11–5. **Bop to Tottom** (845-338-8100), 299 Wall Street, Kingston, is open Monday through Thursday 10–5:30; Saturday 10–5. (They're closed Sunday for rest and play!) Karen Clark Adin, one of the people responsible for the amazing renaissance in uptown, owns this fantastic bazaar. It's filled with the latest fashions in handbags, scarves, jewelry, an array of novelty items, and gifts, all at incredibly reasonable prices. The name of the store is hard to forget. When shopping here, you will find something you love but didn't know you were looking for. At **Crafts People** (845-331-3859), 262 Spillway Road, West Hurley, open Friday through Monday 10:30–6, there are three buildings on this country property chock-full of the work of over 500 contemporary craftspeople. There is jewelry, hand-blown glass, pottery, candles, clothing, clocks, wooden items, and more. It's easy to find the perfect gift for just about anyone here—including yourself! **Dry Goods** (845-247-3889), 129 Partition Street, Saugerties, is open daily, except Monday, noon–6, with extended hours in the warm weather months. There are marvelous original gifts here, as well as a large assortment of decorative wrapping paper, cards, novelty items, and regional books. Karyn Pavich has a talent for finding wonderfully unique items for this delightful store that opened in 2012. Steve Heller's **Fabulous Furniture** (845-657-6317), Route 28, Boiceville, near Bread Alone bakery, open Wednesday through Sunday 10–5, has been in business since 1973. All the imaginative creations (sculpture, furniture, gifts, and cards) are handcrafted on the premises. They do their own logging here, seeking out trees too large and misshapen to be used by other businesses. The quality hardwoods (black walnut, butternut, black cherry, and spalted maple) are inlaid with a variety of interesting designs. You will be interested to see several pieces of fascinating metal sculpture here, and Steve is a car freak—1950s Cadillacs are his favorites. Take a walk around outside as well as inside this entertaining emporium. **Fiber Flame** (845-679-6132), 1776 Route 212, Saugerties, open Tuesday through Sunday 10–5, is a make-your-own mixed-media art space where everyone is an artist. It is a great place for both adults and children to be creative. Whether you enjoy painting your own pottery, making collages, beading, or any array of fun endeavors, you are welcome to walk in and do your own thing. In addition, there are parties, after-school classes, and other activities by special arrangement. It's a wonderful stop for après-ski activities as well! **Karmabee** (845-443-3358), 73A Broadway, Kingston, offers an eclectic selection of unique handmade items by Hudson Valley artists and designers. A fine addition to the shops in the Rondout area of Kingston, this shop will delight aficionados of locally made merchandise. They are open Tuesday through Saturday noon–6. **Reader's Quarry** (845-679-5227), 97 Tinker Street, Woodstock, is open January through May, Friday and Saturday 11–5; June through December, Friday through Monday 11–5. This specialty bookshop features used books on the arts, literature, natural history, travel, philosophy, religion, history, and more. It is a wonderful place to browse when visiting Woodstock. **Scandinavian Grace** (845-657-2759), 2866 Route 28, Shokan, open Thursday through Monday 11–6, is a fantastic fun store with approximately 5,000 square feet of space. It's filled with furniture, rugs, glassware, and dozens of items for the kitchen and bedroom—all made in Denmark, Norway, and Sweden. There are Marimekko pillows and kitchen towels at reasonable prices, as well as soaps, gourmet food items, and even shoes. Owner Fredrik Larsson will be glad to answer any questions you may have about the merchandise. A lovely café serves gourmet coffees, teas, pastries, and, of course, Scandinavian cookies. The shop is truly an oasis not to be missed by travelers heading east or west on Route 28. You will see the colorful flags of all the Scandinavian countries prominently displayed outside as you approach the store. **The Tender Land Home** (845-688-7213), 64 Main Street, Phoenicia, is open daily, except Wednesday, 10–6; Saturday until 8. The fine furniture and tasteful home accessories here make it one of the best places in the county to find an unusual gift. High-quality merchandise at reasonable prices. **Morne Imports** (845-688-7738), 52 Main Street, Phoenicia, is open every day 7:30–6:30. This is the place to go for fishing, camping, hiking, and hunting gear, as well as great gift items, newspapers, and magazines. They have an excellent selection of regional books about the Catskills. The store is also the bus stop in town with service to New York City. **Green Cottage** (845-687-4810), 1204 State Route 213, High Falls, open daily, except Tuesday, 10–5, is both a florist and gift shop. There are a number of unusual items if you are looking for something special (jewelry, scarves, bags, and beautiful accessories). Also in High Falls, **High Falls Mercantile** (845-687-4200), 113 Main Street, is open Sunday and Monday 10–5; Wednesday through Saturday 10–6; closed Tuesday. This shop offers an eclectic sophisticated mix of unique fine home furnishings including tables, chairs, artwork, pillows, glassware, rugs, and much more. The wares here are high quality and beautifully designed. **Hurley Country Store** (845-338-4843), 2 Wamsley Place, next to the Hurley Town Hall, is one of the most eclectic shops you will find anywhere, with a variety of unusual toys, regional books, model trains, gourmet foods, and much more. **Jean Turmo Ltd.** (845-679-7491), 11 Tinker Street, Woodstock, is open daily 11–6, and the store has something for everyone. It's housed in a lavender building in the center of town, across from the village green. Jean and Rebecca will create your own shampoo and moisturizer depending upon what fragrance you select from the numerous choices. They carry all kinds of fine soaps and creams for both men and women, as well as all kinds of teas, teapots, cards, books, nightlights, handbags, and the best selection of sexy reading glasses you will find anywhere. This is a wonderful inviting place to browse, and the owners aim to please. A couple of doors away from Jean Turmo Ltd. on Tinker Street is **H. Houst & Son,** one of the best old-fashioned hardware stores you will find anywhere; it's chock-full of basic necessities but also has books, magazines, and gifts. And make sure to go across the street to **Clouds** (845-679-8155), 1 Mill Hill Road, to see top-of-the-line American crafts, including porcelain, glassware, woodwork, and jewelry. **Lucky Chocolates** (845-246-7337), 115 Partition Street, Saugerties, offers a fine selection of excellent dark and milk chocolate, as well as some of the best hot chocolate you will have anywhere! **Fed On Lights** (845-246-8444), 34 Market Street, Saugerties. Open Thursday through Monday, noon–5:30. This is an amazing shop, and the two floors here are worth browsing for anyone passing through Saugerties. It is packed with 19th- and 20th-century lamps and plumbing fixtures, claw-foot tubs, marble-top sinks, and all kinds of items you might have given up finding.

Don't forget to visit the **Water Street Market** (www.waterstreetmarket.com), a village within the village of New Paltz with more than 30 shops, cafés, and galleries. **Handmade and More,** at 6 North Front Street in New Paltz, is a fantastic gift shop featuring the work of local craftspeople, clothing, jewelry, glass, and toys; it should also be on your itinerary. And wonderful eateries abound, so that when you tire of shopping, you can relax and imbibe! (see *Eating Out*).

ANTIQUES Ever since the 17th century, people in Ulster County have been accumulating things, which now turn up as valuable antiques. But even if you don't collect rare furniture, you can enjoy hunting down that special

WATER STREET MARKET

Ulster County Tourism

collectible vase or colorful quilt. Auctions are listed in the local newspapers, and yard sales pop up every weekend during the spring and summer. There are numerous antiques shops throughout the county, but the following places include several centers that offer many dealers under one roof and give browsers a wide selection. And since no listing of a center's stock is ever comprehensive, visitors will never know what treasures they may find while exploring on their own.

Craftsmen's Gallery (845-688-2100), 48 Route 214, Phoenicia, has mission and mission-style collectibles and antiques. In nearby Shandaken, the **Blue Barn** (845-688-2161), 7053 Route 28, is a good place to stop for a variety of furniture items and decorative accessories.

In High Falls, **Barking Dog Antiques** (845-687-4834), 7 Second Avenue and Firehouse Road, is a fun place to browse, and it is open year-round. In Pine Bush, the **Country Heritage Antique Center** (845-744-3792), Route 302, has furniture and country collectibles. Open Saturday and Sunday 11–5:30.

In the New Paltz area, make sure to check out the **Water Street Antiques Center** (845-255-1403), 10 Main Street, at the Water Street Market, and **Jenkinstown Antiques** (845-255-4876), 520 Route 32, open weekends or by appointment only. Both have interesting selections of furniture and collectibles.

Hi Ho Home Market (845-255-1123), 132 Main Street, Gardiner, is a multilevel house with 15 themed rooms that are continually changing their offerings of both new and vintage home decor. One room is devoted to vintage Christmas ornaments. The shop combines old and new treasures, and owner Heidi Hill-Haddard is a delightful presence who will help you find whatever you are looking for. Open Monday and Wednesday 10–5; Thursday until 7:30; Friday and Saturday until 6; Sunday 11–5. Closed Tuesday.

Van Deusen House Antiques (845-331-8852), 59 Main Street, Hurley, has a nice selection of furniture and collectibles. **Skillypot Antique Center** (845-338-6779), 41 Broadway, Kingston, is a co-op of 25 dealers who offer lamps, furniture, glassware, and collectibles. Open April through December, daily 11–5. The **Saugerties Antiques Center** (845-246-8234/3227), 220 Main Street, is located in the antiques district of town. They are a co-op and are open year-round, daily 10–5. Check out the many other smaller shops in Saugerties on both Main and Partition streets.

If you are interested in attending an auction, **JMW Auction Service** (845-339-4133; www.jmwauction.com), 148 Aaron Court, Kingston, specializes in fast-paced, fun sales. Check the website for a schedule of auctions.

ART GALLERIES Anyone interested in the arts should leave a couple of hours free (in the afternoon since most are closed in the morning) to drive to the following galleries and points of interest in Kingston and Woodstock; both towns are filled with wonderful paintings, photography, and sculpture in an array of places, some off the beaten path. The **Art Society of Kingston** coordinates the **First Saturday Art Openings** at galleries throughout the city on the first Saturday of the month. Check the website www.askforarts.org for a full schedule of events. The Art Trolley runs 5–9 PM to take visitors to different venues throughout the city.

On North Front Street in the uptown section of the city is **A.S.K. Gallery** (the Art Society of Kingston) (845-338-0331; www.askforarts.org), 97 Broadway, which features the work of local artists; it is open Tuesday through Saturday 1–6 or by appointment. **The Wright Gallery** (845-331-8217), 50 North Front Street, is open Monday through Saturday noon–5:30.

In the Rondout area of the city, make sure to call the **Donskoj & Company Gallery** (845-338-8473), 93 Broadway, which is open by appointment only and features artists from throughout the Hudson Valley. A couple of doors down is the **Jane Bloodgood-Abrams Studio** (845-331-3755), 89 Broadway, open Friday through Sunday 1–4 (longer hours in the summer months), which exhibits local artists in a range of mediums. There is a nice backyard with tables for people to relax in warm weather.

Before you leave Kingston, stop in "midtown" at the **Gallery at R&F** (845-331-3112), 84 Ten Broeck Avenue, open Monday through Saturday 10–5, which offers an array of workshops, including one on pigment sticks, in addition to changing exhibits.

West of Kingston is the perpetual art colony of Woodstock. Don't miss the **Center for Photography at Woodstock** (845-679-9957), 59 Tinker Street, open year-round, Wednesday through Sunday noon–5, which offers a changing selection of photography exhibits throughout the year. Participants include some of the most innovative photographers in the world, both established and new. Past shows have focused on local scenes, the nude, and videos. There are workshops, lectures, a library, and archives here. The **Woodstock Guild & Byrdcliffe Arts Colony** (845-679-2079), 34 Tinker Street, is open year-round, Friday through Sunday 10–5. There are art exhibits, concerts, readings, and classes. A few doors away is the **Woodstock Artists' Association** (845-679-2940), 28 Tinker Street, open year-round, Thursday through Monday noon–5, which offers a variety of work by local artists as well as being a museum representing artists of the original Woodstock Art Colony of the past. **Woodstock Framing Gallery** (845-679-6003), 31 Mill Hill Road, is open daily, except Wednesday, 11–5. The emphasis in this beautiful gallery, owned by Sneha Kapadia, is on contemporary art, and the majority of exhibitors are Hudson Valley artists. Nationally renowned painter Richard Segalman, whose work is in several museums as well as galleries in New York City; Santa Fe, New Mexico; and Naples, Florida, shows his work in this gallery.

Diagonally across the street is the **Fletcher Gallery** (845-679-4411), 40 Mill Hill Road, with its focus on 20th-century American artists. The work of Peter Max, among others, has been shown here. Open Thursday through Sunday noon–5 and by appointment.

The **BMG Gallerie** (845-679-0027), 12 Tannery Brook Road, offers hand-painted photographs and changing shows by guest artists. Open May through February, Friday through Monday 11–6. Another interesting gallery is the **Evolve Design Gallery** (845-679-9979), 88 Mill Hill Road, featuring original art, modern sculpture, fine woodworking, and home furnishings from American and Finnish designers. Open Friday through Monday 11–6 and by appointment.

If you travel west out of the village of Woodstock toward Bearsville and make a right, staying on Route 212 when the road forks, you will come to the **Elena Zang Gallery** (845-679-5432), 3671

Route 212, Shady, just 4 miles outside of town. Open year-round, daily 11–5, this on-site pottery features handmade porcelain and stoneware along with contemporary painting and the sculpture of many internationally known artists, including Mary Frank, Joan Snyder, and Judy Pfaff. There is an outdoor sculpture show year-round in a beautiful garden setting. Visitors may walk around the grounds and enjoy the stream that runs through the property. Children are welcome.

A little farther along on Route 212 on the right is Harmati Lane; at this junction is the **Genesis Gallery** (845-679-4542), 26 Harmati Lane. The gallery, open May through December, daily noon–5 or by appointment, features exotic creations inspired by the Middle East. Paintings and prints of the Holy Land, silver miniatures, Yemenite and Bedouin jewelry, replicas of ancient pottery, and ceramic dolls may be found here. Marble, stone, and steel sculptures are displayed along a path that encircles a pond. Visitors can take this walk and enjoy art in the outdoors. It is best to call before going.

If you continue west on Route 212, you will come to the **James Cox Gallery** (845-679-7608), 4666 Route 212, Willow, which is open year-round, Tuesday through Sunday 10–5. Cox is a veteran art dealer who relocated to Woodstock from Manhattan in 1990, and his gallery has changing exhibits of painting and sculpture in a beautiful garden setting. His wife, Mary Anna Goetz, exhibits her lovely paintings here, as well.

Farther south it's worth stopping in at the **Mark Gruber Gallery** (845-255-1241), 17 New Paltz Plaza, New Paltz, close to the NYS Thruway exit 18, which specializes in Hudson Valley artists (primarily painters and photographers), with exhibits changing every six weeks. They are open Monday 11–5:30; Tuesday through Saturday 10–5:30. **The Women's Studio Workshop** (845-658-9133), 722 Binnewater Road, Rosendale, is open to the public, but call before you go, this is a working studio space. Changing exhibits year-round feature artists from throughout the world. **The Arts Upstairs** (845-688-2142; www.artupstairs.com), 60 Main Street, Phoenicia, is open Friday 3–6, Saturday 10–6, and Sunday 10–4. This cooperative gallery features a new themed show every month of the year. Their openings are held regularly on the third Saturday of every month, and there is always a potluck buffet open to the public. A visit here is a great way to get to see the work of some Hudson Valley artists.

POTTERY & CERAMICS Ulster County is home to the studios of several nationally renowned potters. For those travelers interested in visiting the artists' studios, 10 potteries are open to the public. They are located in High Falls, Stone Ridge, Accord, West Park, Bloomington, and West Hurley. The website www.potterytrail.com contains detailed directions and visuals of the work; or you can call Ulster County Tourism for the *Hudson Valley Pottery Trail* brochure (1-800-331-1518). A detailed map is included, along with the hours that each studio is open.

✷ Special Events

February through March: Maple tours take place in late winter when the sap begins to run. There is absolutely nothing to match the fragrance of steamy maple syrup. At **Arrowhead Maple Syrup Farm** (845-626-7293), 5941 Route 209, Kerhonkson, tours are offered daily noon–5, but call before you go. **Lyonsville Sugarhouse and Farm** (845-687-2518), 591 County

Route 2, Accord, also offers tours, but call ahead for the schedule in season. **St. Patrick's Day Parade** (845-331-7517; 1-800-331-1518), Broadway, Kingston. Numerous bands and floats celebrate the wearing of the green with this annual colorful celebration.

May: **Annual Women's Health & Fitness Expo** (845-802-7025), Tech City (300 Enterprise Drive), Kingston. Admission fee. This mobile health expo is designed for women and their families, and has been held on the first Saturday in May since 2000. Meet local, regional, and national health experts and learn how to live a healthier lifestyle. Free health screenings, seminars, and consultations. Dr. Debra Karnasiewicz, founder and director of the Women's Health and Fitness Foundation and Expo, organizes this wonderful event, which has grown in size and stature. **Annual Wing Fling** (845-338-5100), Cantine Field, Washington Avenue, Saugerties. Sunday noon–5. Hosted by the Ulster County Regional Chamber of Commerce, at this festival you can try the best wings in the area. There is live music and children's entertainment at this festive event held in mid-May. **Minnewaska Mountain Bike Festival** (845-255-0752), 5281 Minnewaska State Park, Route 44/55, New Paltz. This annual event offers group rides for all levels of ability on the park's miles of carriageways. There are also clinics for trailside bike maintenance and repair, as well as for custom bike and helmet fitting. Several local food vendors participate in the festivities.

Memorial Day Weekend (and Labor Day Weekend): **Woodstock/New Paltz Art and Crafts Fair** (845-679-8087), Ulster County Fairgrounds, 249 Libertyville Road, New Paltz (follow Route 299 to the turnoff and signs). Shows are held Saturday and Sunday

ST. PATRICK'S DAY PARADE IN KINGSTON

Ulster County Tourism

Bob Barrett

MARK HAMM OF CHESTER P. BASIL'S DISPLAYS HIS WOODEN SPOONS AT THE WOODSTOCK/NEW PALTZ ART AND CRAFTS FAIR.

10–6; Monday 10–4. Admission fee. This huge fair offers more than just booths of crafts; some of the region's finest artisans are on hand each year to exhibit their works. The craftspeople demonstrate their skills, which include quilting, scrimshaw, weaving, etching, pottery, and broom making. There is a children's center with art projects for young fairgoers; face painting is a popular activity. Furniture and architectural crafts, regionally produced foods, entertainment, wine, and dozens of food vendors are all there. The large tents will shield you from the sun, but dress appropriately for the weather—it can get very hot, both inside and outside the tents (and if it rains, make sure to wear heavy shoes . . . it does get muddy).

June: **Independence Day Celebration in Kingston** (845-331-7517), Rondout waterfront. They always celebrate the weekend *before* July 4th in Kingston. Enjoy music, food, games, and fireworks after sunset.

July: **July 4th Celebrations** (SUNY New Paltz campus, 845-255-0604) offer music, food, and festivities starting at 5, and fireworks begin at dusk. In Saugerties (Cantine Field, 945-246-3090) there is a parade at 11 AM and bands and vendors during the day. The fireworks begin at 9 PM. Free. On **Hurley Stone House Day** (845-338-2283; 845-331-4121), visit eight of America's oldest private homes (and a cemetery) that date from the 17th and 18th centuries in this National Historic Landmark Dutch village on the second Saturday in July. There are costumed guides, a 1777 militia encampment, and colonial demonstrations. For those interested in history, this is a fascinating outing.

July through Labor Day: **Belleayre Music Festival** (845-254-5600; www.belleayremusic.org), 181 Galli

Curci Road, Highmount. July through Labor Day weekend, world-class performers come to this gorgeous mountain setting. The music festival has been going on now for over 20 years. Check the website for a complete schedule of entertainment.

August: **County Fair** (845-255-1380), Ulster County Fairgrounds, 249 Libertyville Road, New Paltz. Admission fee. This annual country fair is a bargain since one-price admission includes all entertainment, shows, parking, exhibits, and the midway. If you have a bunch of kids with you, it's a great place to go the first weekend of the month. **Annual Artists' Soapbox Derby** (845-331-7517), Rondout waterfront, Kingston. Free. The carlike creations that ride down lower Broadway in the Rondout area are something to behold. If you are in town at this time, make sure to see this event. **Wild Blueberry & Huckleberry Festival** (845-647-4620), Ellenville. A street fair celebration of the Shawangunk Mountains, with folk music, barbecue, all-blueberry bake sale, pie-judging contest, crafts, and exhibits. Free. **Hurley Corn Festival** (845-338-1661), Hurley Reformed Church, Hurley. The festival usually takes place on the second Saturday in August, 10–4. Small admission; children under 12 free. There are colonial craft demonstrations, corn chowder, sweet corn, live music, antiques, vendors, and a quilt raffle at this celebration of the corn harvest. Kids will enjoy the day here. **Saugerties Artists Studio Tour** (845-246-7493; www.saugertiesarttour.com), at independent studios throughout Saugerties; Saturday and Sunday 10–5. This event, usually held on a weekend in mid-August, showcases the work of painters, sculptors, potters, furniture makers, and more. Individuals and small groups are welcome to tour studios and meet the artists. The website provides a map and directions.

September: **Hooley on the Hudson** (845-331-2750), T R Gallo Memorial Park on the Rondout, Kingston. 11:30–9. This Irish festival sponsored by the Ancient Order of Hibernians in Ulster County usually takes place each year on Sunday of Labor Day weekend. Free. There is Celtic music, Irish step dancing, pipes and drums, crafts, and food vendors. Fun for the entire family. **Headless Horseman Hayrides** (845-339-2666), Route 9W, Ulster Park (last two weekends in September and every Friday, Saturday, and Sunday in October). Admission fee. There are spectacular illusions, special effects, acres of thrills and chills, and a cast of more than 100 performers to entertain you on this 35-minute hayride. Children will love this experience. **Hudson Valley Garlic Festival** (845-246-3090), Cantine Field, Saugerties, last weekend of the month. Admission fee. Visitors won't have to use a map to find this festival; the nutty fragrance of garlic attracts tens of thousands to this weekend celebration, where garlic-flavored foods—from pizza to ice cream—await the connoisseur. Craftspeople and entertainment enliven the daily activities, and there are dozens of garlic vendors and culinary information on hand. An unusual and fun weekend, regardless of how much garlic means to you! **Jennie Bell Pie Festival** (845-626-7137), Kelder's Farm, 5755 Route 209, Kerhonkson, noon–dusk on the last Saturday of September. There's a pie baking contest, talent show, art and craft vendors, silent auction, children's activities, corn maze, hayrides, car show, and fireworks at dusk. This is a fun event that has something to please everyone in the family. **Taste of New Paltz** (845-255-0243), Ulster County Fairgrounds, New Paltz. Admission;

children under 12 free. Held on a Sunday in mid-September, 11–5, rain or shine, this Hudson Valley festival of food and fun has been a town tradition since 1991. Local restaurants, caterers, and farmers' markets offer tastes of their finest cuisine for $1–3. The wineries, breweries, and food purveyors also have booths. Local artists, businesses, and musicians all contribute to this celebratory harvest gathering.

October: **Reenactment of the Burning of Kingston** (845-331-7517). In 1777 the British invaded and burned the city of Kingston. Now the city reenacts the battle, complete with British and American troops and period music, crafts, food, and entertainment, including a colonial dance. The battle takes place the first weekend in October, but call for specific times and events. **Belleayre Mountain Fall Festival and Concerts** (845-254-5600), Belleayre Mountain Road, Pine Hill. Open 10–5. Free (there is a charge for the ski lift). Held Saturday and Sunday of Columbus Day weekend, this festival attracts thousands of leaf-peeping visitors. The fun goes on all day and includes bands, crafts, entertainment, German food, beer, chicken barbecue, and ski equipment sales. The festival is well run, and the site offers magnificent views of the mountains. Wear appropriate clothing, and get there early; the festival goes on rain or shine. (Keep in mind that the weather at Belleayre is always much cooler than you may expect, due to the high elevation.) **Mum Festival** (845-246-2809), Seamon Park, Route 9W, just south of the village of Saugerties. Open dawn to dusk. The park is free; admission fee to festival. For the entire month of October, Seamon Park is one big chrysanthemum celebration. Thousands of mums bloom throughout the 17-acre park at this time, and the display of yellow-, lavender-, and rust-

REENACTMENT OF THE BURNING OF KINGSTON

Ulster County Tourism

colored flowers in shaped beds is breathtaking. The actual festival is usually held the first Sunday in October, with music, entertainment, and a parade.

November: **Greek Festival** (845-331-3522), St. George Greek Orthodox Church, 294 Greenkill Avenue, Kingston. Free. Enjoy all the Greek culinary specialties here, along with a holiday boutique. Held the weekend before Thanksgiving, Friday 5–10, Saturday 10–10, and Sunday 11–8. **International Pickle Festival** (845-658-9649), Community Center, 1055 Route 32, Rosendale. Small admission fee. This unusual, fun festival is held the Sunday before Thanksgiving. There are dozens of food booths with wares from Germany, Romania, and Japan, as well as throughout the United States. Enjoy free samples, listen to live music, and discover great holiday gifts. You can enter your pickled goods in the contests. There is even a pickle toss and pickle juice drinking contest. Kids of all ages will love this one. **Family of New Paltz Turkey Trot** (845-255-1403), Water Street Market, 10 Main Street, New Paltz. Held on the morning of Thanksgiving Day, this town tradition features a 5K run/walk through New Paltz beginning at the Water Street Market. The event raises money to provide food for area residents during the holidays and gives participants a healthy way to start the holiday season.

December: **Garden Club Tea** (845-647-5530), Terwilliger House Museum, Ellenville. Enjoy afternoon tea accompanied by homemade delicacies at this Queen Anne Victorian home decorated with seasonal greens and garlands. Held the first Saturday in December, 1–3. **Wreath Fineries at 12 Wineries** (845-255-2494). Follow the Shawangunk Wine Trail and receive a handmade grapevine wreath at the first winery on the itinerary. At each of the 12 wineries, receive an ornament to decorate your wreath, along with tastings of special holiday wines and foods. One ticket admission price admits you to all 12 wineries. Oenophiles will not want to miss this seasonal event. **Frozendale** (845-546-5358), Main Street, Rosendale. This annual December tradition celebrates the coming of winter with programs and events held both indoors and out. There is hot chocolate, live music, gifts for sale, and open houses at the art galleries. The event is usually held the first weekend in December. **Open House Woodstock** (845-679-6234), Tinker Street, Woodstock. Held on the first Friday in December 5–9. The shops stay open late and offer treats including cookies and hot cider to holiday shoppers. Windows are decorated beautifully, and there is a festive air throughout the town. **Holiday in the Village of Saugerties** (845-246-0553), throughout Saugerties. There are horse-drawn wagon rides, Santa delights the kids at the historic Kiersted House, and carolers sing on Main Street. Merchants remain open late with free refreshments for shoppers. The festivities are usually the first Saturday in December.

Delaware County 5

Delaware County Chamber of Commerce (www.greatwesterncatskills.org)

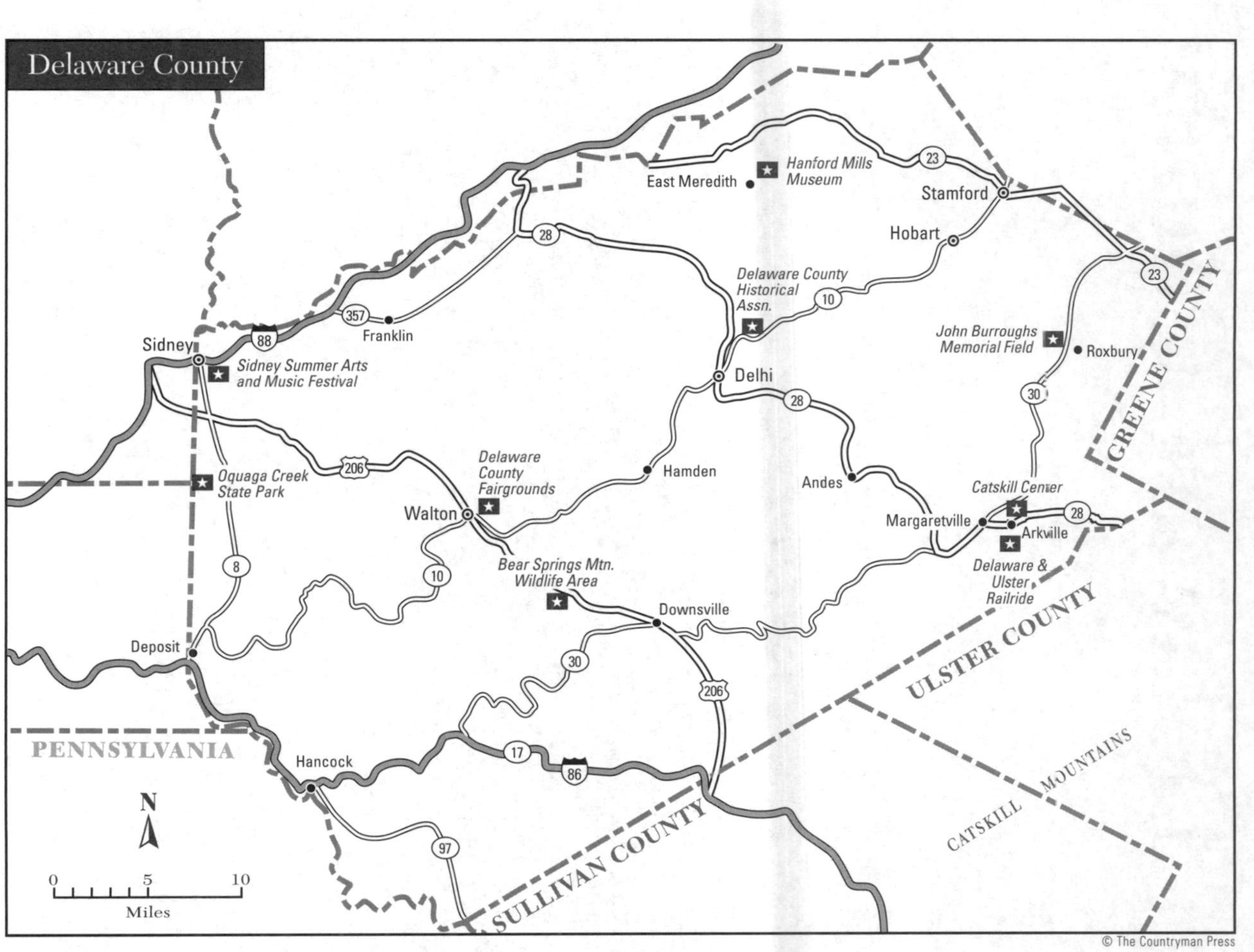
Delaware County
Sidney
Sidney Summer Arts and Music Festival
88
357
Franklin
28
East Meredith
Hanford Mills Museum
23
Stamford
Hobart
Delaware County Historical Assn.
10
Delhi
John Burroughs Memorial Field
Roxbury
30
GREENE COUNTY
Oquaga Creek State Park
206
Delaware County Fairgrounds
Walton
Hamden
Andes
Catskill Center
Margaretville
Arkville
Delaware & Ulster Railride
8
10
Bear Springs Mtn. Wildlife Area
Downsville
Deposit
30
206
ULSTER COUNTY
PENNSYLVANIA
Hancock
17
86
97
SULLIVAN COUNTY
CATSKILL MOUNTAINS
N
0 5 10
Miles
© The Countryman Press

DELAWARE COUNTY

One of the largest counties in New York (about the size of Rhode Island), Delaware County is a region of rolling meadows, curious cows, and small villages that look as if they were plucked from a 19th-century picture book. More than 64,000 acres are state owned and have been proclaimed "forever wild." This foresight has resulted in an area that is a paradise for anglers, canoeists, kayakers, hikers, bikers, walkers, and those who just enjoy rural charm and an old-fashioned way of life coupled with modern convenience and an easy drive.

Much of the charm of Delaware County comes from the strong influence of the 19th century, which turns up in local architecture and community get-togethers. Towns throughout the county are filled with homes and commercial buildings of Federal, Queen Anne, Greek Revival, Italianate, and other styles; drive along the back roads, and you will find dairy farms and mountain views nearly unchanged for more than a century. From winter pancake breakfasts to holiday open houses, from county fairs to summer auctions, the region brings back a sense of community celebration that has been lost in much of modern life.

GUIDANCE **Delaware County Chamber of Commerce** (607-746-2281; 1-866-775-4425), 5½ Main Street, Delhi 13753; www.delawarecounty.org, www.delawarecountytoday.com.

GETTING THERE *By car:* Delaware County is most easily reached by taking the New York State (NYS) Thruway, exit 19 at Kingston, to Route 28 west (toward Pine Hill), and following Route 28 into the county. Route 30 intersects with Route 28 in Margaretville.

By bus: **Adirondack Trailways** (1-800-858-8555; www.trailwaysny.com) operates daily bus service from New York City to several towns in Delaware County. Call for information on tours and charters, as well as schedules and fares if you are traveling on your own.

MEDICAL EMERGENCY Be aware that public telephones are scarce in the county, and cellular service may be limited. In the event of an emergency, call 911 or the **Delaware County Sheriff** (607-746-2336).

Delaware Valley Hospital has three family health centers in the county that have 24-hour emergency care: **Walton** (607-865-2100), 1 Titus Place; **Downsville** (607-363-2517), 15205 Route 30; **Roscoe** (607-498-4800), 1982 East Main Street.

Margaretville Hospital (845-586-2631), 42084 Route 28, Margaretville.

O'Connor Hospital (607-746-0300), 460 Andes Road, Delhi.

✱ To See

Andes (www.andesnewyork.com). This delightful village is filled with fine eateries, antiques shops, art galleries, gift emporiums, and wonderful architecture. Sidewalks were built in 2007, making walking through town a pleasure, especially during the winter months and mud season! The best way to explore the village is by walking. The town got its name due to its surrounding hills, including Mount Pisgah, the highest point in Delaware County at 3,400 feet. Originally called Tempersville due to its location along the Tremperskill Stream, it was a milling and lumbering outpost first settled in the late 18th century and became a town in 1819. The hamlet is certainly worth a day trip; it is listed on both the State and National Registers of Historic Places.

Franklin Walking Tour. Main Street in historic Franklin is only 1 mile long, but it is filled with buildings of architectural interest. The town was first settled in 1784 and was named after the eldest son of Benjamin Franklin, who owned land in the area. The Delaware Literary Institute, the cultural center of the village, was a school that opened in 1835 in town. Architectural styles range from early Federal and Greek Revival to Gothic Revival and Italianate. Some buildings of note are the Franklin Central School, Chapel Hall, St. Paul's Episcopal Church, and several homes along Main Street, as well as Center Street. The Ouleout Valley Cemetery, at the northeastern edge of the village, is where James McCall, founder of *McCalls* magazine, and Rev. Willard Parsons, founder of the Fresh Air Fund, are buried. In 1983 the entire village was placed on the National Register of Historic Places.

Gideon Frisbee Homestead at the Delaware County Historical Association (607-746-3849; www.dcha-ny.org), 46549 Route 10, 2 miles north of Delhi. Open May through October, Tuesday through Sunday 11–4. Admission fee. A fascinating site comprised of historic buildings that have been donated, purchased, or just rescued from neglect, where visitors can get a taste of life in rural America during the 19th century. The main building houses a library and exhibit hall, where changing displays of farm tools, household goods, folk art, and crafts are offered each season. Additional interpretive exhibits focus on different aspects of farm life in several of the other buildings. The Gideon Frisbee House, a 1797 example of Federal architecture, once served as a tavern, county meeting room, post office, and the private home of a local judge. The interior has been restored to reflect the changes in life from pioneer days to the period just before World War I. Decorative arts and furniture collections include Belter chairs, woven rugs, souvenir glassware, and a chair that tradition holds was used at the Constitutional Convention in Philadelphia. The Frisbee barn houses a collection of farm implements and a permanent exhibit titled "It's a Fine Growing Time," which guides the visitor through the joys and hard work of a farmer's year. Other buildings include the gunsmith's and blacksmith's shops, the schoolhouse (still in use for educational programs), a tollhouse, and even a family cemetery. Special events include an enchanted evening under the stars with live music in the summer.

Hanford Mills Museum (607-278-5744; www.hanfordmills.org), 73 County Route 12, East Meredith. Take Route 28 to the intersection of Routes 10 and 12 in East Meredith; follow the signs. Open May 15–October 15, Wednesday through Sunday 10–5. Admission fee. Once the industrial center of the surrounding farm country, the mill has today been restored to its clanking and chugging past. Flour, lumber, wooden goods (like butter tubs and porch posts), and electricity (courtesy of nearby Kortright Creek) were all produced at Hanford Mills, one of the few remaining industrial mills of the 19th century still in use. Visitors will see lathes, jigsaws, and other machines used to produce woodenware, along with the pulleys and belts that were once the staples of manufacturing. Inside the mill itself, a series of catwalks and walkways wind through the workrooms, where museum interpreters are hard at work; downstairs, the enormous metal reconstruction of the original wooden waterwheel is turned by the millpond waters. Throughout the site, water-generated electricity powers lightbulbs and machines, a reminder of the time when light didn't come with the simple flick of a switch. Also on the site is the Gray Barn, in which there are agricultural and farm equipment displays, a shingle mill, the millpond, and the mill store, where local crafts are sold. Hanford Mills hosts several special events each year, including blacksmithing workshops; Independence Day, complete with ice cream and speeches; and late winter's Ice Harvest Day (when the ice is cut and stored for the summer ice-cream social). There are several educational programs for children's groups visiting the museum. Check the website for information.

Hobart Book Village (607-538-9788; www.hobartbookvillage.com), Main Street, Hobart. There are five eclectic bookshops on the main street in town here—and **Bibliobarn** (607-538-1555), at 627 Roses Brook Road in nearby South Kortright. They are wonderful for browsing, particularly for those interested in rare and used books, and include a sizable collection of fiction, nonfiction, history, biography, mysteries, and children's books. **Mysteries and More,** 688 Main Street, is a great place for strollers to relax and enjoy a drink after walking around town. Don't miss **Adams Antiquarian Books** (607-538-9080), 608 Main Street. Make sure to check the website for special events that include a Winter Respite Lecture series, book signings, and art walks. This is a must-see for bibliophiles. I spent several delightful hours in this unusual, delightful village of books!

Hunting Tavern Museum (845-676-3775; www.andessociety.org), Main Street, Andes. Open Memorial Day weekend through Columbus Day weekend, Saturday 10–3. This beautifully restored building is filled with exhibits detailing local history, particularly the Anti-Rent Wars. Those interested in the county's past should not miss this small museum. There are some interesting programs here during the summer months. Previous workshops include soap making in today's kitchen and sketching using historical costumes and community scenes. A good place to begin a Saturday morning walking tour of Andes!

HISTORIC SITES **Covered Bridges** (www.coveredbridgesite.com). The county has three historic covered bridges, and visitors are welcome to enjoy them. The Downsville Covered Bridge (1854), Route 206, is in the center of the village. Other bridges include Fitches Bridge (1870), on Route 10, north of Delhi at the

Delaware County Historical Association, and Hamden Covered Bridge (1859), on Route 10, northwest of the village. Additionally, the Tappan (or Kittle) Bridge in Arkville is southeast of town off Dry Brook Road. A 43-foot-long, single-span bridge, the Tappan was built in 1906 as a king truss, but it was rebuilt in 1985 without the functional truss.

Delaware and Ulster Railride (845-586-DURR; www.durr.org), 43510 Route 28, Arkville. Open late May through mid-October: Thursday through Sunday in July and August, and Saturday and Sunday at other times of the season. Trains depart from Roxbury and Arkville depots. Entrance to the site and depot is free, but admission is charged for the ride. The Catskill Mountains were once a daily stop for tourist and milk trains from New York City, but when the service stopped in the 1960s, many believed the echo of a train whistle was gone forever from the valleys. The Railride has resurrected some of the favorite trains that rattled along the tracks, and there is no better way to sample the fun of old-time travel than to hop aboard any of the vintage propelled trains still at work. Or take some photos of the farms and homes; many tell a tale or two about train history. Special events, held throughout the summer and fall, include a costumed train robbery, a fiddler's get-together, Halloween ghost trains, foliage runs, and more. At the Arkville Depot you will find a gift shop, snack caboose, and restrooms on-site. Wheelchair accessible.

John Burroughs Homestead and Woodchuck Lodge Historic Site (607-326-3722; www.roxburyny.com), John Burroughs Memorial Road, Roxbury. Take Route 30 north through Roxbury and follow signs. Open June through September, weekends only 10–5, or by appointment year-round. Free. Although this is not an active site, the former writing studio and grave of nature writer John Burroughs is worth

DELAWARE AND ULSTER RAILRIDE

Delaware County Chamber of Commerce

a stop. A friend of Teddy Roosevelt, Henry Ford, and Thomas Edison, Burroughs is a respected American nature writer whose many essays spoke of Delaware County, the Catskills, and the Hudson Valley. Today his writing nook, Woodchuck Lodge, is maintained by his family (the site, although open on a limited basis, also can be viewed from the road). Just up the road is Memorial Field—which contains Boyhood Rock, where Burroughs spent many hours observing the natural world—and the Burroughs gravesite. This is a quiet spot with a breathtaking view of the Catskills, a lovely place to sit and enjoy the same scene that inspired a great author.

SCENIC DRIVES Delaware County offers the driver many lovely views and well-maintained main roads, but—as in any other rural area—some of the back roads can be tricky in bad weather, four-wheel drive or not. Snow and ice can make the steeper stretches of both paved and dirt roads treacherous. And once off state or county routes (town roads), there are often no signs with road names, and it's easy to get lost unless you have a county road map. Deer and other wildlife are also a problem, especially at night, so be aware and don't speed.

If you want to see dairy farms, cornfields, the county seat, and the Pepacton Reservoir, start in **Margaretville** and follow Route 28 to Delhi. The town square in Delhi was painted by Norman Rockwell about 50 years ago and appeared on the cover of the *Saturday Evening Post.* The town square still looks very much as it did back then, and the gazebo was recently restored. Pick up Route 10 and take it south to Walton; pick up Route 206 and go east to Downsville. Then take Route 30 back to Margaretville. The roads are well marked, and you will pass two covered bridges along the way, one near Hamden, the other outside of Downsville. This drive also takes you past farm stands (some on the honor system: Choose your produce, and put your money in a box), including Octagon Farms near Walton, where you will see an eight-sided house. Legend has it that the ghost of a young woman killed in a carriage accident roams the road at night. If you have the time, you can detour through Delhi and follow the signs west to Franklin on the Franklin Turnpike, a winding road that offers beautiful vistas in summer.

A second county drive follows part of the old turnpike, which was a major stagecoach route through the area. From Margaretville, follow Route 28 west to Andes and then to Delhi, then take Route 10 north to Stamford, make a right onto Route 23 and drive to Grand Gorge, and finally, turn right onto Route 30 and head south back to Margaretville. If you have a chance, stop in Stamford and look at some of the grand homes that made this village a popular turn-of-the-20th-century resort area and gave it the name Queen of the Catskills.

If you wish to drive up **Mount Utsayantha,** follow Route 23 east to Mountain Avenue; the twisty road is accessible in spring, summer, and fall, and the views are beautiful. Call the **Department of Environmental Conservation** in Stamford (607-652-7365) for more information about this drive or hike. The headwaters of the Delaware River East Branch rise alongside Route 30 between Grand Gorge and Roxbury, and the road back to Margaretville passes through farm country.

The Catskill (Susquehanna) Turnpike once ran from the village of Catskill in Greene County to the village of **Unadilla** on the Susquehanna River. In Delaware County, the turnpike is now followed by town roads from Stamford west to Franklin, then along Route 357 to Unadilla. Some of the original stone mileage markers for the turnpike can still be seen along this route. There are hilltop views for miles along the turnpike near where it crosses Route 28.

A lovely drive follows along the shores of the two reservoirs: Pepacton and Cannonsville. From **Margaretville** head southwest along Route 30, which follows the Pepacton Reservoir to Downsville; then go northwest to Walton on Route 206, and head southwest again along Route 10 to Deposit. There are a few crossings over the reservoirs, and both dams are in view.

✷ To Do

AUCTIONS It may seem that everything is auctioned off in Delaware County: Don't be surprised—it is. Cows, puppies, cabbages, eggs, Shaker chairs, Irish pewter, even antique coffins have all shown up in the hands of auctioneers. Auction lovers don't need to plan ahead; just pick up a copy of the local newspaper and look for a sale. (Local newspapers include the *Delaware County Times,* the *Mountain Eagle,* and the *Walton Reporter.*) Some auctions are weekly institutions, attended by locals and weekenders alike; others are specialty sales for real estate or farm equipment; and still others are one-time-only house sales, where the contents of a home can include some surprises.

Country auctions are fun, but there are some helpful tips to follow: Get there early, carefully examine the goods before the sale, and sign up for a card or paddle. Bring a chair for outdoor auctions, plus a hat or umbrella, depending on the weather. Most auctions advertise that they accept "cash or good checks"—but in the latter case, this can be tricky if you are from out of state or not known to the auctioneer; call ahead for information. Don't buy anything you can't carry, unless you plan to make shipping arrangements. And, finally, know what you're bidding on: Don't get stuck with the overstuffed armchair because you thought you were getting the Tiffany lamp.

McIntosh Auction Service (607-832-4829; www.mcintoshauction.com), 213 Fair Street, junction of Routes 28 and 30, Margaretville, has Saturday-night auctions at 6:30 year-round. There is plenty of parking here. Seats go fast, and auctioneer Chuck McIntosh keeps everyone happy with quick sales and good humor. Everything from furniture to blackberries to fine antiques is sold here. They also do many on-site auctions throughout the summer.

Roberts' Auction (845-586-6070; www.robertsauctiononline.com), 43311 Route 28, Arkville, has an auction every Saturday night at 6 year-round. You will find everything here from fine antiques to a better grade of junk. Auctioneer Ed Roberts Jr. keeps the sale moving, and you will never be bored. The crowd is often a lively mix of locals and visitors; there are restrooms and a snack bar. Get there early since many seats are reserved, and the others go fast.

BICYCLING Delaware County offers a range of terrain that will appeal to downhill racers as well as those seeking a scenic tour by bike. For those seeking on-road routes, the **Delaware County Chamber of Commerce** has developed a series of bike tours that range in length from 15 to 100 miles and are graded according to terrain. The tours are posted on their website, or you can request a printed version (see *Guidance*).

Delaware County Chamber of Commerce (www.greatwesterncatskills.org)

For **off-road trips,** there is the **Catskill Scenic Trail** (607-652-2281; www.durr.org), a 19-mile Rails-to-Trails corridor. The CST can be accessed at various points, and there are designated parking areas: One is at the historic Stamford Depot at the intersection of Railroad Avenue and South Street in the village of Stamford. There is also a parking lot north of Route 10, just east of the village of Bloomville. The CST is marked with octagonal signs that show the distance to the trailhead in the direction you are facing. There is only a 400-foot change in elevation over the entire 19 miles. Stamford is the peak, and it is downhill in both directions from that point, so I suggest you begin the tour there!

Bike Plattekill Mountain Resort (607-326-3500; 1-800-NEED-2-SKI; www.plattekill.com), 469 Plattekill Mountain Road, Roxbury. Open April through November on weekends and holidays, July through Labor Day on Friday, weekends, and holidays. Admission fee. This outstanding mountain bike area offers equipment rentals, a chairlift ride to the summit, and more than 60 miles of trails. Beginners shouldn't be wary of trying mountain biking here since a package deal provides a bike, lift ticket, helmet, and one-hour lesson with a guide; riders can then enjoy the exercise all day. There are also guided road tours available, including a historical biking tour of the village of Roxbury.

Arkville Bikeville Hikeville Snowville (845-586-5637), 43358 Route 28, Arkville. Open July and August, daily 10–5; call ahead during the rest of the year. Mountain bikers in the county should be aware of the bicycle shop owned by Joe Moskowitz and Pauline Liu, his wife. The place is housed in a 19th-century converted red barn. Whether you need to rent, buy, or have a repair done, this is the place to go for bikes, snowshoes, and skis.

Delaware County Chamber of Commerce (www.greatwesterncatskills.org)

CANOEING & KAYAKING The East and West branches of the Delaware River as well as the Susquehanna offer spectacular opportunities for canoeists and kayakers. Some of the best canoeing in the county may be found along the western border near Pennsylvania. A word of caution: As with all water sports, don't attempt to canoe or kayak unless you are familiar with the rivers. Both the Delaware and Susquehanna can be treacherous, especially in spring or after a heavy rain. Your best bet is to use one of the canoe outfitting services, which will provide the right equipment, maps, and even a shuttle service.

Al's Sport Store (607-363-7740), 6964 River Road, Downsville, is a clearinghouse for canoe, kayak, and fishing information. They rent equipment and have tours in season.

Catskill Outfitters (1-800-631-0105), Delaware and North streets, Walton, can supply kayaks, canoes, and tubes—everything you need for an outing. Open daily 10–4.

Peaceful Valley Campsite (607-363-2211), 485 Banker Road, Downsville, offers limited outfitting services. You will find canoe rentals by the day, week, or month here.

Car-top boat launches are permitted at **Big Pond,** Andes (607-652-2654); **Little Pond,** Little Pond Campground (845-439-5480); **Trout Pond and Mud Pond,** Cherry Ridge Wild Forest, Colchester (607-652-2654); **Huggins Lake,** Middle Mountain Wild Forest (607-652-2654); and **Bear Spring Mountain Public Campground,** 512 East Trout Brook Road, Downsville (607-865-6989).

FARM STANDS When the harvest begins in early summer with strawberries and flowers, farm stands begin to blossom along the roadsides, as well. In Delaware County there are many farm stands where you can pick out the produce, bag it, and leave the money for the owner. Other stands are a bit more formal, but they all stock the best local fruits, vegetables, maple syrup, and honey. Days and hours of operation vary widely with the season and the stock, and some crops, including strawberries, seem to disappear after only a few days, so the best way to find local produce is to watch for roadside stands or stop and ask at the nearest town. This is also savvy farm country; in the past few years, county agriculture has "grown" to include such specialty crops as blue potatoes and garlic, which often turn up in Manhattan's trendiest restaurants.

The largest and best produce market in the county is the **Pakatakan Farmers' Market** (845-586-3326), at the Round Barn, Route 30, Halcottsville (north of Margaretville). Open May through October, Saturday 9–3. Vendors offer everything from fresh trout, organic produce, and bouquets of wildflowers to fine crafts and home-baked pies. Selections change with the seasons, and there is plenty of food to sample, so have a light breakfast or lunch!

Other county farmers' markets include **Andes Farmers' Market,** 72 Main Street, Andes, open Memorial Day weekend through Columbus Day weekend, Saturday 10–2; **Delhi Farmers' Market,** Courthouse Square, Main Street, Delhi, open June through September, Wednesday 9–1:30; **Koo Koose Farmers' Market,** 171 Second Street, Deposit, open June through October, Saturday 9–1.

Betty Acres Farm Stand (607-746-9581) is located at 21529 Route 28 in Delhi and is open May through October, daily 9–6. (Hours vary the rest of the year.) They offer farm-raised organic vegetables and meats, as well as local cheeses, jams, honey, and maple syrup. There are also farm tours by appointment.

The Brovetto Dairy and Cheese House (607-278-6622), 1677 Route 29, Jefferson, has a farm store that is open daily 11–4. Learn about the cheese-making process here; do make sure to visit the cave, which has 600 wheels of cheese! Visitors will have a chance to taste a variety of cheeses in the farm store.

Byebrook Farm (607-538-9796), 7531 Route 18, Bloomville. Open daily year-round. This 45-cow dairy of Holsteins has been in the same family for eight generations. They make raw milk Gouda that is aged a minimum of 60 days. The bottled raw milk, Gouda cheese, and free-range eggs are for sale at the farm stand.

Honey lovers may want to check out **Ballard's Honey** (607-326-7100), 53996 Route 30, Roxbury, which stocks honey from its hives. Make sure to call first.

Because the tree-tapping season is so changeable, maple syrup lovers should call the **Delaware County Chamber of Commerce** (607-746-2281) for up-to-date information on farms that offer sap-season tours; the chamber also publishes a farm-bounty map.

Hillhaven Farms (607-652-2274), 2 Hobart Road, Stamford (corner of Routes 23 and 10), is open May through December and has blueberries as well as a variety of local fruits and vegetables. This is a great place to find handcrafted wreaths and trees for Christmas.

Maple Shade Farm (607-746-8866), 2066 County Highway 18, Delhi. Open mid-September through early November, Saturday and Sunday 10–5. Explore the barn, pick a pumpkin, make a scarecrow, see the farm animals, or enjoy the corn maze and wagon rides in autumn at this 200-acre historic family farm. Open for group and school tours by appointment.

Octagon Farm Market (607-865-7416), 34055 State Highway 10, Walton, sells its own fruits and vegetables along with lots of other local offerings. Open July through October, daily 10–5.

Stone & Thistle Farm and Kortright Creek Creamery, 1211 Kelso Road, East Meredith, is open year-round, daily 9–6, and farm tours are available Memorial Day weekend through Columbus Day on weekends or by appointment. Visitors can tour the farm, pet the animals, and milk a goat, as well as enjoy free tastings of grass-fed meat or milk. The specialty here is organic beef, pork, lamb, goat, chicken, turkey, rabbit, and eggs. Kids will love this farm. They serve a prix-fixe dinner by reservation only, June through mid-November, on Saturday night at Fable (a lovely modern restaurant within their 1860 Greek Revival farmhouse). The repast features products from the farm as well as New York State wines and beers. Only 24 diners may be accommodated, communal-style, at two large tables; seating is at 7 PM, preceded by a half-hour farm tour (see *Dining Out*). For those who would like to spend a night on the farm, inquire about the one-bedroom suite with adjoining library that can accommodate a family.

Stony Creek Farm (607-865-7965), 1738 Freer Hollow Road, Walton. Open daily year-round. The Marsiglio family sells beef, pork, lamb, chicken, eggs, and vegetables in season. They adhere to rigorous free-range pasturing practices for all the animals and supplement their grazing diet with local organic grains. Farm tours are offered at 11 AM on Saturday.

FISHING Delaware County is home to the East and West branches of the Delaware River, the Susquehanna River, and Beaverkill Creek; it is served by the Cannonsville, Pepacton, and Schoharie reservoirs, making fishing a popular sport in this region. The Beaverkill is probably the most famous trout fishing stream in America, the birthplace of fly-fishing, so if you want to try the sport, this is one of the best places anywhere to start. New York State fishing licenses are required. They are easy to purchase in most towns; check with the town clerk or at the village offices. For reservoir fishing, special permits are required—call the **Department of Environmental Conservation** regional office (607-652-7366) for information on permits and maps. Stream fishing areas that are open to the public are indicated by brown and yellow wooden signs along the streams and rivers; most areas offer off-road parking, as well. Detailed maps are available where you purchase your fishing license and at town offices. Riverfront property may be posted off-limits as part of the New York City watershed, so the maps should be consulted; heavy fines could result from illegal fishing.

GOLF Golf enthusiasts will appreciate the courses in Delaware County, where the lush greens of summer and the blazing trees of autumn provide everyone—duffer and hacker alike—a lovely setting in which to play. Greens fees vary depending on the season and the length of the membership, so call for specific information.

Delhi College Golf Course (607-746-GOLF), 85 Scotch Mountain Road (off Route 28), Delhi, has a course that is used as a training area for students in the turf management program. It's a small gem—though it's a full 18 holes—and rarely overcrowded.

French Woods Golf & Country Club (607-637-1800), 17440 Route 97, East Newman Road, Hancock. This 18-hole, par-72 course is a challenging one in a beautiful country setting.

Hanah Mountain Resort & Country Club (845-586-2100), 576 Hubbell Hill Road, Margaretville, has an 18-hole course, practice greens, and a driving range. There is also a golf school and restaurant on the premises.

Hancock Golf Course (607-637-2480), Golf Course Road, Hancock, is a nine-hole, par-36 course that is a good choice for novices.

Hardwood Hills Golf Course (607-467-1031), 11160 Route 8, Masonville is a nine-hole, par-36 course.

Meadows Golf Center (845-586-4104), 42565 Route 28, Margaretville, has a nine-hole, par-27 course; miniature golf; lessons; night golf; and a driving range. Those who just want to practice their techniques should head here, where young golfers will enjoy themselves, as well.

Shephard Hills Golf Course (607-326-7121), Golf Course Road, Roxbury, has a hilly 18-hole course with beautiful views of the countryside.

Stamford Golf Club (607-652-7398), 163 Taylor Road (off Route 10), Stamford. Complete facilities, 18 holes, and a driving range.

HIKING A large part of Delaware County is part of the "forever wild" park system in New York State. A number of the existing hiking trails are for experienced hikers only, and some require overnight stays in simple trail huts; those who would like detailed trail information should contact the **Catskill Forest Preserve** regional office (607-652-7366), 65561 Route 10, Stamford. However, the preserve does contain more than 300 miles of trails that vary in length from a half mile to almost 100 miles, so even novice hikers will find something that they are comfortable taking on, whether for a day or an overnight.

The Catskill Center for Conservation and Development (845-586-2611; www.catskillcenter.org), Route 28, Arkville, has special events, including guided hikes, bird walks, and snowshoe excursions. Check website for a schedule and to find out about membership.

Catskill Outdoor Education Corps (607-746-4051), 4112 Route 28, Delhi, offers woods walks, educational excursions, and a nature preserve with marked trails. A good place to introduce children to hiking.

Catskill Scenic Trail (CST) (607-652-2821; www.catskillscenictrail.org), Railroad Avenue, Stamford (see *Bicycling*), has a marked 19-mile Rails-to-Trails area that offers a hard-packed surface and gentle grade perfect for hiking, biking, horseback riding, and cross-country skiing. An excellent choice for families with young children.

Oquaga Creek State Park (607-467-4160), 5995 Route 20, Masonville. Open year-round. There are 6.5 miles of marked hiking trails that will delight people of all abilities. The park is in three counties: Delaware, Broome, and Chenango.

Utsayantha Trail System (607-652-2821), Stamford. This marked trail system takes hikers through scenic mountaintops and serene valleys. From Stamford follow signs on Route 10 to Archibald Field. The trail begins there and is marked.

West Branch Preserve, County Road 26, Hamden. This 446-acre preserve features a 0.7-mile moderate trail and a strenuous 2-mile mountainside trail for experienced hikers.

CATSKILL SCENIC TRAIL

Delaware County Chamber of Commerce (www.greatwesterncatskills.org)

HORSEBACK RIDING There are miles of trails to ride on in Delaware County, as well as private stables where beginners can go on a guided ride or take lessons.

Bear Spring Mountain State Park (607-865-6989; 1-800-456-CAMP), East Trout Brook Road, Walton. This is the only campground in New York State specifically designed for use by horseback riders. Specially designed campsites accommodate horse trailers and provide horse lodging facilities. They have miles of trails here that will delight those who like to travel with their horses.

Broken Spoke Stables (607-538-9651), 874 Narrow Notch Road, Hobart. Open year-round. They offer trail rides here, as well as lessons in both English and Western riding. There is also a children's summer camp.

Catskill Scenic Trail (607-652-2821). The CST may be picked up in Bloomville, Stamford, Grand Gorge, or Hobart by those who are looking for wooded trails. There are 19 miles of gently graded trails here (see *Bicycling* and *Hiking*).

Circle A Stables (607-752-2520), 538 North Harpersfield Road, Jefferson. Open year-round. This 60-acre equine facility offers trail rides at reasonable prices, as well as lessons and summer camp.

For those seeking trail rides and riding lessons: **Sanfords Horse Farm** (845-586-2985), Margaretville, offers lessons only; **Stone Tavern Farm** (607-326-3600), 2080 Upper Meeker Hollow Road, Roxbury, offers trail rides, lessons, summer camp, and more; and **Broken Spoke Stables** (607-538-9651), 874 Narrow Notch Road, Hobart, offers trail rides. These establishments are usually open from May through October, so make sure to call before heading out.

Mountain Breeze Miniature Horse Farm (607-588-6208), Route 23, Grand Gorge, breeds little horses as well as the larger minis. The owners, Glenda and Earl Krom, offer a variety of horses for sale year-round. (The animals are handled regularly, which makes them friendly.) Stop by this lovely farm if you are considering a miniature horse as a potential pet. The kids will love petting the miniature donkeys and newborn horses.

The Night Pasture Horse Farm (607-588-6926), Route 23, 2 miles west of the center of Grand Gorge. This 56-acre horse farms boasts a large indoor arena, a tack room, lessons, and quality horses for sale at reasonable prices. The Horseplay Tack Shop (on the premises) offers the horse enthusiast everything from bridles and saddles to a variety of gifts. Both new and used equipment are also for sale. The Catskill Scenic Trail may be accessed from the parking area.

SKIING

Downhill

Ski Plattekill (1-800-NEED 2 SKI), Plattekill Mountain Road, Roxbury. Open December through March, Friday through Sunday and during the week on school holidays 9–4. There is a vertical drop of 1,100 feet, 35 trails, and 4 lifts, including the Northface Express double chairlift. They make snow here, and snowboarders are welcome. There is a snowtubing park, along with rentals, lessons, and a snack bar.

In 2012 there were several improvements made at the ski center. They opened the Snowkidding Children's Learning Center that caters to the youngest skiers. The Powder Puff Beginner's Trail, a popular run, was substantially widened, and the outdoor deck at the base lodge was expanded. The food service offerings now incorporate locally grown produce and meats.

Cross-Country

Catskill Outdoor Education Center (607-746-4112), Route 28, Delhi. There are marked trails here for cross-country skiing, and guided snowshoe walks for groups of six or more by advance reservation.

Kirkside Park (607-326-3722), Main Street, Roxbury. Free. This historic 11-acre treasure was formerly the estate of Helen Gould-Shepard, daughter of railroad magnate and Roxbury native son Jay Gould. Rich in natural beauty and history, and restored to its glorious splendor, Kirkside has rustic Adirondack-style bridges, graceful paths along the East Branch of the Delaware River, and lush plantings to admire in the warm-weather months. During the winter, however, this is a wonderful place to cross-country ski. A good bet for those with young children. A variety of special events are held here year-round (see *Special Events*).

Ski Plattekill Mountain Resort (607-326-3500), 469 Plattekill Mountain Road, Roxbury. There are more than 12 miles of cross-country ski trails (beginner to advanced); open to the public for a fee. Maps of the trails are provided. Lessons and guided snowshoe tours available by reservation.

* Lodging

Bed & breakfasts provide a special way to stay in Delaware County, and most are moderately priced; some offer package rates or special discounts during the midweek period. Make reservations since many book up over holiday weekends and when there are special events. For further information contact the **Delaware County B&B Association** at www.bnblodgings.com. Since Delaware County is the second-largest county in New York State, all entries are listed by village for your convenience.

Andes

The Andes Hotel (845-676-4408), 110 Main Street, Andes 13731. ($) Located in the center of the charming village of Andes, this hotel, tavern, and restaurant (see *Dining Out*) is a community gathering place that combines rustic country warmth and elegance. There is usually live music at the hotel/restaurant on weekend evenings during the summer months. This is a jewel of a place and a real bargain! All 10 rooms were completely renovated in 2008. Each of the rooms has two full-size beds, a private bath, and cable TV. Guests are within walking distance to shops, eateries, and other points of interest. Open year-round.

Arkville, Fleischmanns, Halcottsville, Margaretville

Hanah Mountain Resort & Country Club (845-586-2100), 576 West Hubbell Hill Road, Margaretville

Delaware County Chamber of Commerce (www.greatwesterncatskills.org)

12455. ($$$) A renovation has expanded this inn into a full-service resort and conference center. There is a championship 18-hole golf course (see *To Do—Golf*), health club, indoor swimming pool, fishing stream, and restaurant. (Golfers may want to note that a nationally recognized school is held at the inn every summer.) The lovely rooms have private bath and all the amenities one would expect at a fine hotel. Children welcome. Open year-round.

Margaretville Mountain Inn (845-586-3933), 1478 Margaretville Mountain Road, Margaretville 12455. ($$$) This restored 11-bedroom Victorian home was built as a boardinghouse and functioned as a working farm. It offers a spectacular view of the New Kingston Valley from the old-fashioned veranda. It's just a short drive from town. A full breakfast is served in an elegant dining room; outdoors on the veranda, if you like, in summer. Six rooms, all with private bath. There are limited facilities available for children and pets; call ahead for information. Open year-round.

Meadowood Inn (845-586-5199), 50 Hornbeck Street, Arkville 12406. ($$) This turn-of-the-20th-century Victorian operated as an inn 100 years ago. Located on an acre of land on a pastoral country road, it is within walking distance of the village of Margaretville. There are five spacious two-room suites, all with private bath (two are Jacuzzi tubs), cable TV, and furnished with antiques. One pet-friendly room, separate from the main part of the inn, has its own separate entrance. The country breakfast is usually served in the dining room, or outside on the wraparound porch in the warm-weather months. Open year-round. (Innkeeper Tanya Minteer runs a cozy place with excellent value for money. Rates include a kids ski-free, stay-free program as well as discounts on lift tickets and rentals at Belleayre Mountain, only a few minutes' drive from the Inn. Breakfast here is fantastic; the pancakes are the tastiest I've eaten in years!)

River Run (845-254-4884), 882 Main Street, Fleischmanns 12430. ($$) This restored 20-room house has a two-bedroom suite and eight guest rooms with either private or shared bath. The yard slopes down to the river, and guests can easily walk into the center of town. The unusual aspect of this inn is that it welcomes both children and pets (just give the innkeepers some notice about the four-footed family members). Breakfast is hearty and healthy, and the inn has lots of antiques, stained glass, and old-fashioned comfort to offer visitors. There is a labyrinth with a stone path in the backyard, at the foot of the garden, by the water—the owners created this for fun; I am told that it intrigues many guests.

Susan's Pleasant Pheasant Farm (607-326-4266), 1 Bragg Hollow Road on Lake Wawaka, Halcottsville 12438. ($$) This is a terrific place to go if you want to kayak or canoe when you wake up in the morning. There are four rooms, all with private baths. Open year-round.

Roxbury Motel (607-326-7200), 2258 Route 41, Roxbury 12474. ($$) Don't let the name fool you. Gregory Henderson and his partner, Joe Massa, don't run the usual motel. Every room here is unique. Each guest room is decorated differently—and imaginatively—some in bold colors and filled with interesting, yet tasteful, touches. The owners genuinely care about the comfort of guests and make sure they enjoy their stay. It is possible to choose from a variety of accommodations at a range of prices; some rooms have a king-size bed and flat-screen TV. A spa is available on the premises with hot tub, steam room, and sauna, for an additional charge. Open year-round.

Roxbury Village Inn (267-977-2116), 53856 Route 30, Roxbury 12474. ($$) There is a beautiful two-room suite in this historic Victorian home, with private bath, fireplace, and sleeping porch. Several other rooms are singles and are suited to a small-family stay. There is also a heated swimming pool, library, and living room. They don't serve a full breakfast but do offer coffee and cake in the morning. Open year-round.

Bovina Center

The Carriage House Inn (607-832-4209), 471 Jim Lane Road, Bovina Center 13740. ($) This family-friendly place surrounded by 150 acres of farmland is like having your own one- or two-bedroom apartment in the country (complete with spacious living room, full kitchen, and bedroom). If you are traveling with children or a pet, you will find any of the three units here ideal. In the summer, enjoy boating or fishing on the pond. During the winter, there are nearby trails for snowmobiling. Open year-round.

The Mountain Brook Inn (1-877-MYBROOK), 5333 County Route 6, Bovina Center 13740. ($$) When you walk across the brook to the inn, you will hear the brook and see the garden. This 36-acre miniparadise with an 18th-century stone bridge will be particularly appreciated by those who love seclusion. Eight suites, all with private bath, living room, and kitchen. It's like having your own place in the country, with acres of hiking trails and places to fish (there are two waterways on the property). Enjoy playing croquet, badminton, and horseshoes. Continental breakfast, custom made to your taste, arrives at your door at 8. A 15-minute drive to Margaretville, Andes, Delhi; 45 minutes to Cooperstown. Open year-round.

Delhi and Grand Gorge

The Colonial Motel (607-588-6122), 37283 Lower Main Street (a few hundred feet east of the junction of Routes 30 and 23), Grand Gorge 12434. ($) Calling this establishment a motel is really a misnomer. Several rooms are located in a large Victorian house adjacent to the motel. All have private bath. Reasonable prices; a good bet for those traveling with children. Many rooms have microwave ovens and refrigerators; some have small kitchens. Open year-round.

Fisk House Bed & Breakfast (607-832-4544), 116 Fisk Road, Delhi 13753. ($) Open year-round, this historically restored farmhouse with modern conveniences, as well as a heated swimming pool and antiques center on the premises, has five rooms, only two with a private bath. A good choice for families, the B&B is located on State Highway 28 between Andes and Delhi.

Harrison Center B&B (212-724-8782; 917-783-9324), 156 West Main Street, Stamford 12167. ($$) This majestic 17-room Victorian home built in 1898 overlooks the lake in Churchill Park. Located in the historic district of town, the Uplands Mansion is filled with antiques and has been completely restored. Guests have a choice of rooms with private bath or shared. Open year-round.

West Branch House Bed and Breakfast (607-746-3378), 28 Franklin Street, Delhi. ($$) This lovely mid-19th-century village house has been completely renovated and includes two beautiful rooms, each with its own bath, one with a whirlpool tub. The owners make a full breakfast using local, seasonal ingredients. A short walk from the B&B takes you into town, where there are a number of fine eateries.

Deposit

Dream Catcher Lodge (877-275-1165), 393 River Road, Deposit 13754. ($$) Built in 1854 and fully renovated in 2004, this lodge, decorated in Southwestern decor, has five rooms with two baths, as well as a lodge that sleeps eight people. There are also six cabins along the river. Rates are reasonable; furnishings are simple and comfortable. There is excellent fly-fishing in the area, as well as fine hiking and biking.

Scotts Family Resort at Oquaga Lake (607-467-3094), P.O. Box 47, Oquaga Lake, Deposit 13754. ($$) This family vacation resort on 1,100 acres offers evening entertainment (cabaret show) as well as an array of daytime activities, including golf, tennis, waterskiing, fishing, biking, and hiking. Three meals daily are included with the price of the room. Good value.

Downsville

Victoria Rose B&B (607-363-7838), 15146 Bridge Street, Downsville 13755. ($$) A lovely Queen Anne home, filled with antiques and country touches, where guests enjoy breakfast, tea, and evening snacks. Four rooms, each with private bath. Open year-round.

East Meredith

Harmony Hill Lodging and Retreat Center (607-278-6609), 694 McKee Hill Road, East Meredith 13757. ($$) Located on 70 secluded acres, yet less than 15 miles from fine restaurants in Delhi, the two yurts here provide a wonderfully different kind of getaway. Both are equipped with fine bathrooms, kitchens, and king-size beds, all in a circular structure reminiscent of a luxurious cabin in the woods. Harmony Hill is a special place with a natural stone labyrinth, a few miles of groomed nature trails in the surrounding woods, and phenomenal sunsets. Host Chris Rosenthal creates a first-class getaway at amazingly reasonable rates. There is also a cozy lodge available—a perfect getaway for a family or small group.

Hancock

Bird House Inn (917-655-5638), 167–169 East Front Street, Hancock 13783. ($$) The three guest suites here, each with private bath and full kitchen, provide an adventure in sustainable living. There is a geothermal heating system, Energy Star–rated appliances and fixtures, low-flow faucets, and Watersense toilets. The century-old wood floors and moldings have been restored along with the entire building. Furnished with salvaged treasures, this inn makes an interesting getaway.

Hancock House (607-637-7100), 137 East Front Street, Hancock 13783. ($$) There are 29 rooms and suites decorated in mission style in this terrific small hotel just a short walk away from the best trout fishing in America. The East and West branches of the Delaware River converge right here. The owners, Lynn and Russell Bass, are local residents and have renovated every room with care and attention to detail. This is definitely the best place to stay in the area. Open year-round.

Sidney

Keepers of the Flag B&B (607-563-2554), 474 Thorpe Road, Sidney 13838. ($$) Located conveniently off exit 9 of I-88. There are cozy accommodations here up the mountain, with a full breakfast, tranquility, and fabulous views. Two rooms share a bath, and both have satellite TV, wireless Internet access, and air-conditioning. A family suite with bath is also available.

Walton

D'Angelo's Bed & Breakfast (607-865-6285), 24 Griswold Street, Walton 13856. ($$) This Victorian is in the town of Walton, next to a park with a gazebo. There are three guest rooms: One has a private bath, and two share a bathroom. The rooms are air-conditioned for summer comfort; in the winter electric blankets are provided. Open year-round.

Octagon Motor Lodge (607-865-3190), 34350 Route 10, Walton 13856. ($) This motor lodge across the road from the Octagon Farm Market is operated by the same owner. For those who prefer motel lodgings with private bath, cable TV, air-conditioning, and Internet access, this is a good choice. Self-serve continental breakfast available every morning in the lobby. Open year-round.

Roaring Brook Inn (607-829-3509), 4486 County Route 14, Treadwell 13846. ($) This 1844 Greek Revival house was built in 1844 and has been owned since 2005 by Jean and Artie Swenson. There are only three rooms here, and they share a bathroom. No children are accommodated, and the inn is open March through December. Treadwell is a tiny village, with Barlow's General Store, the hub of the town, just across the street from the inn.

✷ Where to Eat

Casual is the word for Delaware County restaurants, where moderate prices are the rule, even at dinner. Hours and days of operation may vary with the seasons, so it is wise to call ahead if you are making a long trip. In general, reservations are not necessary, except on holiday weekends.

DINING OUT

Andes/Delhi

The Andes Hotel (845-676-4408), Main Street, Andes. ($$) Open for lunch and dinner daily 11:30–9; Sunday brunch served 10–4:30. Housed in a historic building, this bustling restaurant and tavern features mouthwatering American favorites at reasonable prices. The prime rib, steak au poivre, house-cut fries, twice-baked horseradish potato, and garlic spinach are some of my favorites from the imaginative menu. Children are welcome.

Cantina (845-676-4444), Route 28, Andes. ($) Open daily, except Tuesday, 11:30–9; Friday and Saturday until 10. Limited hours in winter months. Mexican and American favorites including burritos, tacos, and fajitas, as well as salads, burgers, ribs, and steaks, served in a casual atmosphere. The restaurant is in a former general store built in 1863. The bar offers excellent margaritas. Children's menu.

Midtown Grill (607-464-4023), 97c Main Street, Delhi. ($$) Open for dinner Tuesday through Saturday 5–9; closed Sunday and Monday. In addition to a large, reasonably priced wine and beer list that includes unusual selections like Stone Mill Beer, organic from California, the chef-owner here prepares all dishes to order. Many of the ingredients are sourced from local purveyors.

Signatures by Candlelight (607-746-4351), SUNY Delhi. ($) Open when college is in session, Friday nights only 5–7, second floor of Alumni Hall. The culinary students here offer a prix-fixe six-course meal (either American regional, international, or classical French, with wine pairings available). If you are in the area, the award-winning students here do a wonderful job, and the cuisine and service are quite good. The meal is a bargain at $30 per person (plus tax and gratuity).

Arkville, Margaretville, Fleischmanns

Inn Between (845-586-4265), Route 28, Margaretville. ($$) Open for dinner Wednesday through Friday 4–9:30; for breakfast, lunch, and dinner Saturday and Sunday 8 AM–9:30 PM. As the name implies, this is the inn between, offering a full spectrum of culinary possibilities. There is everything from fajitas, wraps, and burgers to Danish-crusted filet mignon, salmon Dijon, and rack of lamb. The chef worked for several years at LaGriglia in Windham (one of my favorite restaurants in the Catskills) and took over this establishment in 2002. Casual atmosphere. Children welcome.

La Cabana (845-254-4966), 966 Main Street, Fleischmanns. ($$) Open Monday through Friday 4–10; Saturday and Sunday noon–10. This is a delightful place to enjoy Mexican favorites, with specialties like mole poblano (a combination of four peppers and various fruits and spices over chicken) or carnitas Yucatan (pan-seared pork in orange sauce), as well as an array of burritos, tacos, and enchiladas. There are fresh soups daily and a full service bar separate from the dining room. Children welcome.

Maine Black Bear Restaurant (845-586-4004), Route 28, Arkville. ($$) Open for dinner late May through October, Thursday through Sunday 6–9. This is a fish shack like those in coastal Maine, only it's in the Catskills. There is a retail fish market here, as well as a restaurant with a rustic ambience. For nearly 30 years owner Bruce Beddoe has obtained the freshest salmon, lobster, swordfish, scallops, shrimp, and tuna every Thursday. Those who love seafood can dine alfresco on the outdoor deck. Make sure to arrive early since the place is small and fills up quickly! Children welcome.

The Square Restaurant (845-586-4884), Binnekill Square, Main Street, Margaretville. ($$) Open for dinner Thursday through Sunday 5–9. A casual, relaxing restaurant, the Square has windows and a dining deck overlooking a small stream. The food has a Swiss touch, and the veal dishes are particularly good. Venison is served in season, and there are excellent daily specials. Everything is prepared to order. Children are welcome.

Downsville

Old Schoolhouse Inn (607-363-7814), 28218 Route 206. ($$) Open Wednesday through Sunday for lunch 11:30–5, dinner 5–9. Sunday brunch 10–2 in the summer months. This restaurant is housed in a renovated schoolhouse that dates from 1903. In a Victorian-style dining room, hearty portions of standard American favorites are the mainstay. The lobster, prime rib, and seafood medley are the most popular entrées, and a shrimp and salad bar is included with all dinners. Desserts are homemade and are excellent. Thanks to a local taxidermist, a grizzly bear, a bison, and a deer decorate the bar.

East Meredith

Fable (607-278-5800), 1211 Kelso Road. ($$) Open for Sunday brunch and dinner Saturday by reservation only. Farm tour at 6:30; table seating at 7. The prix-fixe menu here features the farm's organic grass-fed meats, milk, yogurt, and produce. There is an intimate, relaxed atmosphere in a beautifully renovated open kitchen/dining room with two large tables; 12 people are seated at each one. The outdoor patio is used during the warm-weather months. An imaginative wine and beer list, primarily organic, features New

York State selections. Menus change seasonally and reflect what is raised at the farm: lambs, goats, cows, pigs, chickens, turkeys, and rabbits. The Kortright Creek Creamery on the premises produces excellent milk products, including yogurt. This unusual farm-to-table dining experience should not be missed if you are traveling to Delaware County!

Hamden

Lucky Dog Cafe (607-746-9345), 3596 Route 10. ($$). Open for lunch Tuesday through Sunday 11–3; store open Tuesday through Saturday 11–5. The Lucky Dog has enjoyed an excellent reputation in Hamden. The restaurant is known for its farm fresh salads, homemade soups, and hearty sandwiches, as well as comfort food entrées like meat loaf made from local grass-fed beef and several imaginative options. The emphasis is on seasonal ingredients from local purveyors. Don't skip the heavenly desserts! Children welcome.

Hancock

River Run Restaurant & Bar (607-467-5533), 150 Faulkner Road. ($$) Open mid-April through mid-October, Wednesday through Sunday 5–9. There is a Western atmosphere in the large dining room here, decorated with game animals from all over North America. The American cuisine includes steaks, seafood, pasta, and nightly specials. There is an 80-foot covered deck where diners can enjoy a meal alfresco and watch the sunset. The Trout Skellar Pub has an 1,800-square-foot cherrywood bar and serves food as well.

Teddy's Roadhouse Grille (607-637-2536), 21 Sands Creek Road. ($$) Open Friday 5–midnight; Saturday noon–midnight; Sunday 11–9. Enjoy indoor and outdoor dining with views of Sands Creek. Some of the specialties in this informal restaurant are oversized shredded pulled pork sandwich, rack of ribs, shell steak, grilled scallops, and asparagus quesadilla. Children welcome.

Roxbury

The Public Restaurant & Lounge (607-326-4026), 2318 County Highway 41. ($) Open for dinner Wednesday through Sunday 5–9. This trendy cocktail lounge offers Chocolate Godivas (Absolut with Godiva chocolate) and Flamingo Cosmos (with pomegranate juice), along with other tempting selections. The kitchen serves up thin-crust pizzas and quesadillas, as well as New York cheesecake for dessert.

South Kortright

Hidden Inn (607-538-9259), 10860 Route 18. ($) Open for dinner Tuesday through Saturday 5–9; Sunday noon–7. This quiet country inn in a pastoral setting features an international menu. The specialty of the house is prime rib, but you will also find that the lamb, duck, and seafood entrées are tasty.

Stamford

Gabrielle's (607-652-2535), 60 Main Street. ($$) Open daily 11:30–9; Friday and Saturday until 10. The American fare, served in a casual atmosphere, includes prime rib, strip steak, and seafood, as well as burgers, salads, and pizza. The adjoining tavern offers a separate menu as well as over 20 types of bottled and draft beers.

Mama Maria's Restaurant (607-652-2372), 26817 Route 23. ($) Open Tuesday through Sunday noon–10. Eat lunch or dinner at this authentic Southern Italian restaurant in a country setting that offers home-cooked (by Mama Maria!) lasagna and manicotti, as well as steaks, chops, fresh fish, and salads. A great place for the entire family.

Walton

Danny's Restaurant (607-865-7811), 14 Gardiner Place. ($) Open daily, except Sunday, 10:30–9; Friday and Saturday until 10. This is an informal Italian American eatery serving burgers, steaks, pizza, pasta, soups, and salads. Children welcome.

EATING OUT

Andes/Delhi

Blue Bee Café (607-746-8060), 114 Main Street, Delhi. ($) Open daily 10–5. This café, located within an excellent bookstore, is a welcome addition and will delight bibliophiles. They serve fresh coffee, tea, cappuccino, espresso, and cold drinks, along with paninis, salads, soups, croissants, and cookies. Everything is fresh and delicious.

Cross Roads Café (607-746-7007), 80 Main Street, Delhi. ($) Open Monday through Friday 7–5; Saturday 8–4; Sunday 9–3. Healthful, great-tasting fare is what you will enjoy here. Everything is made fresh on the premises: salads, desserts, breads, and an array of fruit smoothies. Vegetarian and vegan dishes are also noted on the menu. There is a coffee bar with gourmet coffees. Live music in the evenings.

Hogan's General Store and Restaurant (845-676-3470), 103 Main Street, Andes. ($) Open Friday through Sunday 5–9; Sunday brunch 10–4. This general store is renowned for its fantastic pizza and soft-serve ice cream. They also offer hot and cold subs, daily lunch specials like Philly cheesesteak, hearty soups, meat loaf, pot roast, and other comfort foods.

Tay Tea Bar (845-676-4997), 131 Main Street, Andes. ($) Open Friday through Sunday 10–6. This tearoom is located in a charming 1840s Greek Revival building with a spacious porch, two-story house, and lovely backyard. Enjoy artisanal teas, both hot and cold, along with vegetarian quiches, unusual salads, paninis, breads, pies, and brownies. Just about everything here is sourced locally; whatever you order will be fresh and tasty.

Woody's Country Kitchen (845-676-4500), 85 Main Street, Andes. ($) Open for breakfast and lunch daily 7–4; until 8 on Wednesday for dinner specials. Bacon and eggs, waffles, French toast, grilled chicken sandwiches, salad, and homemade cakes and pies. Soups are hearty here as well. Early dinners are a bargain.

Arkville/Roxbury

Arkville Bread & Breakfast (845-586-1122), 43285 Route 28, Arkville. ($) Open daily, except Tuesday, 7–2. This roadside restaurant is an ideal stop for a casual breakfast or lunch, and the food is hearty and tasty. A couple of my favorite breakfast items are the egg sandwiches and the stuffed French toast (with bananas, strawberries, and Nutella) made with their amazing bread.

Casey Joe's Coffeehouse (845-586-5637), 43311 State Highway 28, Arkville. ($) Open weekends after Labor Day; daily during the summer. Located in a large red barn along with Arkville Bikeville (see *To Do—Bicycling*), Casey Joe's offers coffee, tea, and pastries, as well as live music throughout the warm weather months. If you are passing through town, stop by to find out what's happening while you're there. An eclectic venue!

East Branch Café (845-326-7763), 53657 Route 30, Roxbury. ($) Open daily, except Tuesday, 7–2. This country casual restaurant serves omelets, muffins, bagels, breakfast burritos, and just about anything you might want in the morning. For lunch there are paninis, thin-crust pizzas, sandwiches, salads, burgers, and homemade soups. In the warm weather diners may enjoy a meal outdoors on the lovely patio.

Oakley's Place (845-586-3474), 44681 Route 28, Arkville. ($$) Open daily 11–11. This is a good choice for casual dining at moderate prices. They offer burgers, salads, and sandwiches. Children are welcome.

Bloomville

Table on Ten Café (607-643-6509), 52030 Main Street. ($) Open Wednesday through Friday 8–3; Saturday and Sunday 9–3; Friday and Saturday 6–9 (pizza nights). There are frittatas, granola, and egg wraps for breakfast, with an array of soups and sandwiches for lunch. The coffee and espresso drinks are excellent, but do try the house-made sodas, a delicious treat on a hot summer day. Friday- and Saturday-evening pizza nights feature wood-fired-oven pizza. This café is truly an interesting gathering place in Bloomville.

Bovina Center

Russell's Store (607-832-4242), 2099 County Route 6 (Main Street). ($) Open weekdays, except Tuesday, 7–6; Saturday and Sunday 9–4. Serving breakfast and lunch, either at the counter or tables, in this marvelous general store (see *Selective Shopping*). For breakfast there are first-rate pancakes and French toast; for lunch, enjoy wraps, soups, and overstuffed sandwiches.

Two Old Tarts Bakery and Cafe (607-832-4700), 1927 County Route 6. ($) Open Friday through Tuesday 9–3. Scott Finley and John Schulman offer a variety of freshly baked tarts, cakes, muffins, and croissants in this inviting bakery, located in a historic building. There are also tempting breakfast and lunch specials made from fresh local ingredients.

Downsville

Downsville Diner (607-363-7678), 18 Main Street. ($) Open daily 7–7. All the diner favorites are served here, along with daily specials and pizza. All baking is done on the premises, and there is even a full line of sugar-free desserts.

Hancock

Bluestone Grill (607-637-2600), 62 West Main Street. ($) Open for lunch seasonally; call for hours. Open for dinner daily 5–10; closed Sunday through Tuesday November through March. This contemporary, informal eatery, located in a renovated building, offers something for everyone. The hot chipotle hawg wings (buffalo wings with pork rather than chicken), steak nachos, and grilled Caesar salad with warm veal meatballs are some of the interesting offerings here. There are several pizzas and salads, and fun food choices.

The Maple Room (607-637-7100), Hancock House Hotel, 137 Front Street. ($$) Open or dinner daily 5–10. Entrées like duck à l'orange, chicken Gorgonzola, wild Alaskan salmon, and rib eye steak are served.

Margaretville

The Cheese Barrel (845-586-4666), 798 Main Street, Margaretville. ($) Open daily 7:30–5. An excellent selection of snacks and cheese is found in this shop, and the dishes are great for take-out and picnics. Try the homemade soups. There is a small, close dining area, so if you want quiet and privacy, this isn't the place to go.

The Flour Patch (845-586-1919), 75 Bridge Street, Margaretville. ($) Open Tuesday through Sunday 7–2. Here you will find the best made-from-scratch muffins in the Catskills—plain, simple, hearty—along with great bagels and sandwiches

Walton/Masonville

Candido's Old World Italian Restaurant (607-865-4873), 29 Gardiner Place, Walton. ($) Open daily, except Tuesday, 11:30–9. Joe and Millie Candido prepare fresh specialties daily using their homemade sauces made from Neapolitan family recipes. There is a complete lunch and dinner menu, as well as coal-brick-oven pizza. *Mangia!*

Crescent Wrench Café at the Masonville General Store (607-265-3808), 2095 Route 206, Masonville. ($) Open daily, except Wednesday, 8–6:30. This beautifully renovated building has been a general store since 1849. The emphasis in the store is on local and regional products as well as organic and natural food items. The café serves light fare—soups, cookies, croissants, tea, and coffee. If you're very hungry, go elsewhere, but if you want to relax and have a drink or snack, this is a delightful place to stop.

T.A.'s Place (607-865-7745), 249 Delaware Avenue, Walton. ($) Open daily for breakfast, lunch, and early supper 6 AM–7 PM. Old-fashioned American favorites like meat loaf and mashed potatoes, grilled pork chops, and marinated chicken breasts are the specialties here. Everything is homemade.

✱ Entertainment

Franklin Stage Company (607-829-3700; www.franklinstagecomany.org), Chapel Hall, 25 Institute Street, Franklin. Founded in 1996 and dedicated to the production of classic and new plays that unsettle, provoke, and entertain, this is one of the only free professional theaters in the country. The venue, Chapel Hall, is a majestic Greek Revival structure that dominates the town of Franklin. If you are in the area during the summer months, make an effort to see one of their fine productions that usually run from late June through mid-September.

Stamford is home to **Friends of Music** (www.friendsmusic.org), where lovers of classical music can hear concerts from May through December at the Frank W. Cyr Center on West Main Street.

The Historic Walton Theatre (607-865-6688; www.waltontheatre.org), Gardiner Place, Walton. In the historic district of Walton, this theater, built in 1914, now features live theater, first-run movies, hometown productions, and concerts. For a full schedule, go to their website.

The Open Eye Theater (845-586-1660; www.theopeneye.org), 200 Stoneridge Road, Margaretville. Enjoy new plays and classics, including Shakespeare, by the company that has been performing in town for more than 30 years. Productions run from May through Labor Day, but call for current schedule.

Roxbury Arts Group (607-326-7908; www.roxburyartsgroup.org), 5025 Vega Mountain Road, Roxbury. There is a full range of performances here—concerts, theater, film, and children's events—year-round at various venues. The best idea is to check the website for a full schedule and locations.

West Kortright Centre (607-278-5454; www.westkc.org), 49 West Kortright Church Road, West Kortright. Take Route 28 to East Meredith, then follow signs to the center, which is in West Kortright. Open Memorial Day weekend through October; performance schedules vary. Admission fee. Nestled in a hidden valley, the West Kortright Centre is housed in a charming white-clapboard 1850s church that was rescued from neglect by dedicated volunteers. Stained-glass windows and kerosene chandeliers glow in the twilight. The center offers unique performances throughout the summer, with concerts and special events for every taste, from bluegrass to zydeco, performance art to dance. Concerts are held both outdoors, in the green fields, and inside, where guests are seated in unique rounded pews; the lawn is often dotted with preconcert picnickers. The intimate setting makes all events a delight, and you may just bump into the evening's featured performer as he or she warms up in the churchyard.

✷ Selective Shopping

Delaware County has several unique gift and antiques shops. Villages like Andes, Bovina, Margaretville, and Walton are fun to walk through; there is a variety of stores; antiques emporiums abound; and the best way to see everything is to wander. Although you can find good shopping in just about every village, Arkville is home to a small flea market called **The Miracle Mile,** on Drybrook Road (off Route 28). It's held every Saturday and Sunday, mid-May through October, weather permitting, beginning at 8 AM and usually continuing until 5. There are approximately a dozen vendors of all kinds.

The following shops are just some of my favorites, but enjoy exploring on your own and discovering new places.

Andes Antiques & Art (845-676-3420), 173 Main Street, Andes. Open year-round, Thursday through Sunday 10–4. If you are looking for rare prints, old photographs, books, or jewels, both real and fake, stop in here. **Chace-Randall Gallery** (845-676-4901), 49 Main Street, Andes. Open May through Columbus Day, Thursday through Sunday 11–5; weekends only the rest of the year. This contemporary fine-art gallery features six annual shows, ranging from solo to group exhibits. The high caliber of the work includes internationally renowned artists in a variety of media and will interest just about everyone; however, art aficionados visiting Andes should definitely include a stop here. **Tay Home** (845-676-4997), 131 Main Street, Andes. Open May through December, Saturday and Sunday noon–5. This amazing teashop offers a range of handcrafted teas. The owner is a colorful character and loves to serve samples of her eclectic tea collection to visitors on weekends. If you are lucky, you will find the teas in select restaurants as you travel the county, as I did.

Paisley's Country Gallery (845-676-3533), 75 Main Street, Andes. Open Thursday through Sunday 10–5. Paisley's has an amazing collection of baskets from all over the world, fine rugs, and jewelry. All kinds of ordinary items and some extraordinary ones may be found at **Stewart's Department Store** (607-746-2254), 85 Main Street, Delhi.

Russell's Store (607-832-4242), 2099 County Route 6 (Main Street), Bovina Center, is a don't-miss experience; they still tie up packages with string from a dispenser, the old-fashioned way. There is delicious comfort food, groceries, gifts, local crafts, homemade baked goods, maple syrup, eggs, produce, and more. They are open weekdays, except Tuesday, 7–6; Saturday and Sunday 9–4.

Andes

Delaware Trading Post (845-676-3313), 62 Main Street, is an eclectic shop offering an array of books, gifts, and vintage items for both the home and garden. Open May through December, Saturday and Sunday 11–4. **Kabinett & Kammer** (845-676-4242), 7 Main Street, is a medical, botanical, and zoological design resource. It is packed with antiques and art, everything from vintage science charts and taxidermy to 19th-century furniture. Open year-round, Saturday and Sunday 10–6. **Sixty One Main Gallery** (845-676-4020), 61 Main Street, specializes in contemporary fine art and has shows of local artists that include paintings, sculpture, photographs, jewelry, fabric, and handmade furniture. Open April through December, Thursday through Sunday 10–5.

Bloomville

Turquoise Barn (607-538-1719), 8052 County Highway 18. Open June through December, Thursday through Sunday 11–5, and by appointment. This gem is chock-full of artwork in the gallery section. There is a variety of wood products, jewelry, and unusual gifts. If you are driving in the area, make sure to stop here.

Delhi

The Steinway Book Company (607-746-8060), 114 Main Street, a beautiful bookstore offering hundreds of used books, meticulously organized, as well as a nice selection of local titles. Book lovers will thoroughly enjoy a stop here. **Stephen's Antiques** (607-746-9942), 110 Main Street, has 5,000 square feet packed with furniture and a range of interesting items to peruse. This is a great place for browsing as well as shopping! Open year-round, Thursday through Monday 11–5. **Dee's Tiques & Train Shop** (607-746-6900), 1260 Peaks Brook Road, 0.33 mile off Route 10, is one of the region's most complete train stores, with accessories, paint, tools, books, Aladdin lamps, and parts. Open Wednesday through Sunday 10–5. **The Yarn Shop at Highland Springs Farm** (607-746-3316), 3.5 miles off Route 10, at 3428 Peakes Brook Road outside Delhi, features their own 100 percent merino wool and a unique collection of vintage buttons and fabrics.

Hancock/Deposit

Delaware Delicacies Smokehouse (607-637-4443), 420 Rhodes Road, Hancock, has all kinds of smoked delicacies—trout, salmon, turkey, Cornish hens, even shrimp—and they will be glad to mail them anywhere. The **Ultimate Fly-Fishing Store** (607-637-4296), 159 East Front Street, Hancock, will delight anglers, but I like looking around in there myself, and I am not into fishing at all. **Karcher's Country Kottage** (607-637-2555), 156 Leonard Street, and **City Mouse, Country Mouse** (607-637-2951), 67 Apex Road (Route 268), both in Hancock, both have a good selection of antiques and collectibles. But call first since both are open more or less by chance or by appointment. In Deposit, **Axtell Antiques** (607-467-2353), 1 River Street, specializes in early Americana. They have been in business since 1968 and are located in the oldest building in town, a historic brick structure that dates back to 1799. Hours of operation are Thursday through Saturday and Monday 10–4; Sunday noon–4.

Margaretville/Roxbury

On Margaretville's Main Street, in the **Commons,** which houses a number of specialty shops, you will find **Home Goods** (845-586-4177), one of the best kitchenware and specialty shops in the Catskills. The best way to see Margaretville is to take a leisurely walk along Main Street. There are several small shops, and the retail landscape is continually changing. In Roxbury, **Antiques at Rick's Barn** (607-326-7700), 50061 Route 30, is the place to find an enormous inventory of American and fine European furniture. For those interested, it's worth a special trip since there is a large inventory. Open year-round, Saturday and Sunday 10–5.

Masonville

Masonville General Store (607-265-3808), 2095 Route 206, is one of the most unusual general stores you will find anywhere. They carry a variety of distinctive items for the kitchen, pantry, bath, and home, as well as interesting greeting cards. The emphasis is on local products from the Catskills. Don't miss this if you are traveling through the area; it's also a nice place to stop for a drink (see *Eating Out*).

Walton

The Country Emporium, Ltd. (607-865-8440), 134 Delaware Street, will intrigue all kinds of shoppers with an interesting variety of gifts, gourmet food items, and clothing; it would be difficult to list everything carried in this wonderful place. **Full Circle Antiques** (607-865-5819), 147 and 164 Delaware Street, offers two stores, both multi-dealer locations, chock-full of furniture, glassware, old postcards, and vintage items. There are several hidden treasures here. Open year-round, daily 10–5. **Hidden Antiques** (607-510-4245), 6 Townsend Street, is a consortium of 10 antiques and collectibles dealers, and offers furniture, glassware, and an array of small items. Open Friday through Monday 10:30–7; extended hours during the summer months.

✷ Special Events

Since Delaware County is still a rural area, the special events here tend to take place during the "better-weather" months, from late spring through summer. For specific dates and times, contact the **Delaware County Chamber of Commerce** (607-746-2281; 1-866-775-4425) or visit their website, www.delawarecounty.org/calendar.

February: **Ice Harvest Festival at Hanford Mills** (607-278-5744; www.hanfordmills.org), 73 Route 12, East Meredith. The event is held on the first Saturday in February 10–4. Admission fee. Children will enjoy the hands-on ice-cutting activities, and adults will appreciate the vintage films about ice harvesting in days of yore. Walk out on the frozen millpond, weather permitting, and help cut the ice using vintage tools. The ice is then hauled by sled to a traditional ice-house. There are hot drinks and food on hand, horse-drawn sleigh rides, and ice-sculpting demonstrations. This is a wonderful winter activity, both fun and educational!

June: **Meredith Dairy Fest** (607-746-2006), Catskill Turnpike Road (7 miles north of Delhi; 12 miles south of Oneonta, just off Route 28), Meredith, is held for an entire weekend in the middle of the month, complete with exhibits, games, tractor pulls, music, crafts, hayrides, butter making, milk shakes, ice cream, and all things dairy.

July: The week of July Fourth ushers in the **Firemen's Field Days** at the village park in Margaretville, where a carnival, rides, entertainment, games of skill (and chance), and food concessions keep everyone busy. At the Andes Presbyterian Church, Route 28, Andes, the **Strawberry Festival** is celebrated each July Fourth weekend. July also brings the four-day **Lumberjack Festival,** Riverside Park, Deposit, which includes fireworks, an art show, antique cars, raft races on the Delaware River, a walking tour of historic homes, a carnival, and lots of food, along with demonstrations of lumberjack skills. The **Peaceful Valley Bluegrass Festival** (607-363-2211), Downsville, features some of the best in traditional music. Dozens of bands perform all weekend, and there are square dances, jam sessions, and food concessions. Held on a 500-acre farm, the festival is great for families or anyone who wants to bring along a banjo, guitar, or mandolin. There are overnight camping facilities, but spaces are limited, so call ahead. **Taste of the Catskills** (607-746-8866; www.tasteofthecatskills.com), 2066 Route 18, Delhi, is a free event, usually held at Maple Shade Farm; the dates are always the Saturday and Sunday of July 4th weekend 10–6. At this family-friendly event showcasing the summer crops, beer, and wine of the Catskills, attendees will experience the rich agricultural heritage of the region. A variety of vendors participate, including several local farmers and food purveyors. There's live music throughout the day and lots of children's activities, including hayrides.

August: The charming village of Franklin hosts **Old Franklin Day** on Main Street, with sales, open houses, displays, and special events. Call the Delaware County Chamber of Commerce for dates and times. **The Delaware County Fair,** at the fairgrounds off Route 10 in Walton (follow signs), runs the second week of August. Open daily 9 AM–10 PM. Admission fee. Part of the agricultural and social life of Delaware County for more than a century, this is one of the last of the truly agricultural county fairs in New York State. Each year hundreds of 4-H members gather to show off their prize goods, including sheep, pigs, cows, horses, and rabbits. The finest local produce is displayed and sold, and the handiwork building bursts with the colors of hundreds of quilts. The celebration begins on Main Street with a parade, and visitors will enjoy the show of the best livestock and the latest farm equipment, and agricultural news, demonstrations, and other "country stuff." Sample milk punch served by the Delaware Dairy Princess and her court; try your hand at games of skill and chance; let the kids have fun on the carousel. You may not bid on the livestock, but you will enjoy the demolition derby, tractor pulls, horse shows, and animal dress-up days. Don't worry about going hungry here. The pancake and pie tents, the sausage sandwiches, and the antique popcorn wagon—on the National Register of Historic Places—will take care of the greatest appetite. **Sidney Summer Arts and Music Festival,** downtown Sidney (exit 9 off I-88; near Routes 7 and 8). Free. Enjoy more than 15 bands, a craft fair, classic car cruise, children's carnival, games of chance, and more. This celebration is usually held the first Saturday of the month of August, but check with the Sidney Chamber of Commerce for exact date and time of events (www.sidneyonline.com/festival).

September: **Turn of the Century Day** "Vintage Baseball" in Kirkside Park, Roxbury, is celebrated on the Sunday of Labor Day weekend. Free admission. Roxbury turns the clock back to 1898 and offers the public all the pursuits of Victorian times. There is period dress, croquet, sack races, horseshoes, a barbershop quartet, chicken BBQ, and a pie social to enjoy. These are just some of the activities at this daylong event highlighting the renowned Roxbury Nine's last baseball game of the season. **Cauliflower Festival** (1-866-775-4425; www.cauliflowerfestival.com), village of Margaretville pavilion, Bridge Street, Margaretville. Free. This celebration is held the last Saturday in September 10–4, showcasing the farming, cooking, and culture of the Catskills, both past and present. There is a farmers' market, local artists and craftspeople, a history tent, traditional music, clogging, pony rides, cooking demos, and petting zoo. The tractor parade is usually at 11:30 AM, so plan to arrive early!

Delaware County Chamber of Commerce (www.greatwesterncatskills.org)

VINTAGE BASEBALL GAME AT TURN OF THE CENTURY DAY

October: **Taste of the Catskills** (607-746-8866; www.tasteofthecatskills.com), 2066 Route 18, Delhi. Free. This event is held at Maple Shade Farm in Delhi on the Saturday and Sunday of Columbus Day weekend, 10–6 each day. At this family-friendly event featuring the wonderful fall harvest crops, beer, and wine of the Catskills, and more, attendees will experience the rich agricultural heritage of the region. A variety of vendors participate, including several local farmers and food purveyors. There is live music throughout the day and lots of children's activities, including hayrides, a pumpkin patch, and corn maze.

Greene County 6

Greene County Economic Development

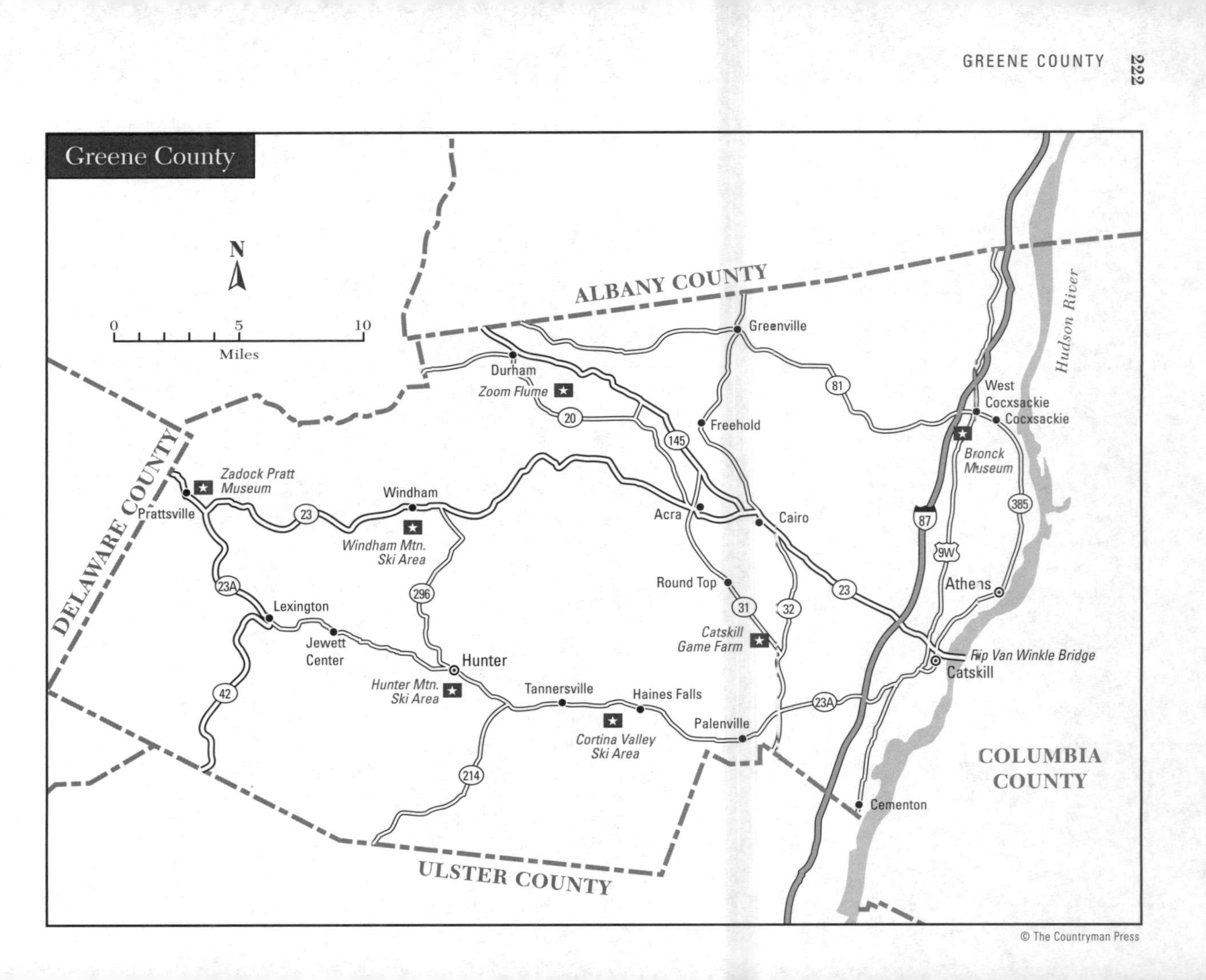
Greene County
N
0
5
10
Miles
ALBANY COUNTY
DELAWARE COUNTY
ULSTER COUNTY
COLUMBIA COUNTY
Hudson River
Greenville
Durham
Zoom Flume
Freehold
West Coxsackie
Coxsackie
Bronck Museum
Zadock Pratt Museum
Prattsville
Windham
Windham Mtn. Ski Area
Acra
Cairo
Round Top
Athens
Catskill Game Farm
Rip Van Winkle Bridge
Catskill
Lexington
Jewett Center
Hunter
Hunter Mtn. Ski Area
Tannersville
Haines Falls
Palenville
Cortina Valley Ski Area
Cementon
23
23A
42
296
214
20
145
81
31
32
87
9W
385
© The Countryman Press

GREENE COUNTY

Greene County offers the perfect outdoor experience any time of year. In winter dramatic, snow-filled gorges yield to gray and white fields, and cross-country skiers may come across bear tracks; others can fly down the slopes at Hunter or Ski Windham, which provide some of the best downhill skiing in the East. In spring bright wildflowers cling to wind-scraped rocks, and visitors to the county can watch (or join in) the Spring Rush, a running, biking, and canoeing competition. Each June a tour of homes, farms, and estates is held to benefit the county historical society. Summer celebrates its warmth with the gifts of icy brooks for tired feet and a flood of cultural festivals. This is a fine time of year to visit North and South lakes and Kaaterskill Falls. Autumn is a season to wonder at the colors that transform the hills and villages into paint pots full of orange and red—the magic that drew Rip Van Winkle to Catskill still enchants visitors today. Or stop by Thomas Cole's house, the place where the Hudson River School of landscape painting began. There are also hiking trails, museums, country auctions, breathtaking waterfalls, waterfront villages, festivals, and fine restaurants to enjoy.

GUIDANCE **Greene County Promotion Department** (518-943-3223, 1-800-355-CATS), 700 Route 23B, Leeds 12451; www.greatnortherncatskills.com.

GETTING THERE *By car:* Greene County is off exit 21 of the New York State (NYS) Thruway. Routes 23 and 23A run east–west across the county; Route 32 runs north–south. Almost all sites in this chapter can be accessed from these roads.

By bus: **Adirondack Trailways** (1-800-858-8555; www.trailwaysny.com) has daily bus service from Port Authority Terminal in New York City to Catskill, Palenville, Hunter, and Windham.

By train: There are frequent daily **Amtrak** trains between New York City and Hudson (8 miles from Catskill across the Rip Van Winkle Bridge). Call 1-800-872-7245 or check the website, www.amtrak.com, for information and schedules.

By air: **Albany International Airport** (518-242-2222; www.albanyairport.com) is approximately 35 miles north of the county.

MEDICAL EMERGENCY Greene County is a 911 community; dial 911 in the event of an emergency. The **Greene County Sheriff's office** (518-943-3300) and **New York State Police** (518-622-8600) may also be called directly.

Columbia Memorial Hospital (518-828-7601), 71 Prospect Avenue, Hudson (only 8 miles from Catskill, across the Rip Van Winkle Bridge).

✷ To See

Bronck Museum and Greene County Historical Society (518-731-6490; www.gchistory.org), 90 County Route 42, Coxsackie. Open Memorial Day through October 15, Wednesday through Friday noon–4; Saturday and holidays 10–4; Sunday 1–4. Admission fee. The **Vedder Memorial Library** (518-731-1033) is open Tuesday and Wednesday 10–4; Saturday 9–noon. Once home to nine generations of the Bronck family (which also gave its name to the Bronx), the museum's collection traces the history of the Upper Hudson Valley. Visitors should begin with the original structure, a 1663 stone house that contains an Indian lookout loft—from a time when settlers were not welcome. The house was remodeled in the late 18th century, when a wing was added, along with fine paneling and fireplaces. Displays include an impressive exhibit of local textiles, looms, and spinning wheels that chronicle the production of Bronck cloth and clothing. The 1738 brick house was connected to the stone house through the hyphen hall. This part of the family home is now used to display, among other things, a fine collection of paintings by 18th- and 19th-century artists, including Ammi Phillips, John Frederick Kensett, Nehemiah Partridge, Ezra Ames, Benjamin Stone, and Thomas Cole. Outside is a kitchen, a charming tiny house itself, set apart from the main house in the style of plantations. The displays here consist of furniture and kitchen tools. Farm buffs will enjoy the three barns that are found at the complex, each representing a different era. The Dutch barn, with its huge beams; the center-pole-supported, 13-sided Liberty Barn, once the storage area for the wheat harvest, now the oldest documented multisided barn in New York; and the Victorian horse barn (called the Antiquarium). Each offers the visitor a look at the tolls, carriages, and wagons of the day. A walk through the family and slave cemeteries will bring you even closer to the people who made the Bronck complex a working and living farm. The Bronck Museum sponsors a Greene County house tour each June (see *Special Events*), when a different area of the county offers a look into the region's many historic homes. Researchers into local history and genealogy will want to stop at the Vedder Memorial Library, with its extensive collections of Greene County and New York State history and records.

Cedar Grove (The Thomas Cole National Historic Site) (518-943-7465; www.thomascole.org), 218 Spring Street, Catskill. Open May through October, Thursday through Sunday 10–4. Groups by special appointment. Admission fee. The grounds are open at no charge daily 8–sunset. Thomas Cole, a painter, poet, and essayist, played a significant role in determining how America viewed its landscapes and vistas; his 19th-century paintings helped inspire the land conservation movement, and tourism became an industry as visitors trooped to the Catskills in search of the sites Cole depicted. His family home, Cedar Grove, is open to the public and presents an unusual look into the daily life of a Hudson River painter (in fact, Cole is credited with founding the Hudson River School of landscape art). The graceful Federal-style house and gardens still look off to the Catskill Mountains, and a locust tree that Cole mentioned in his writings remains outside the front entrance. Inside, interpretive exhibits introduce the visitor to Cole and his family, the Catskills region, artists such as Asher B. Durand and Frederic Church,

Greene County Economic Development

CEDAR GROVE (THE THOMAS COLE NATIONAL HISTORIC SITE) IN CATSKILL

and the Hudson River School. Several small oils and sketches by Cole are on display, along with family heirlooms, including his aeolian harp (a wind-powered musical instrument), sketching stool, paint box, and Bible; you'll also see leaves from his journal and his traveling trunk. Outside on the grounds, you can stop and see the family's Greek Revival privy (with a front door for family and a back door for servants) and Cole's "Old Studio," which once served as slave quarters. There are lectures and events scheduled throughout the summer, usually on Sunday afternoons, and visitors can take a short walk to the Cole family gravesite. The gift shop has an excellent selection of regional books. Make sure to stop in before leaving the site.

Hudson-Athens Lighthouse (518-828-5294; www.hudsonathenslighthouse.org). Built in 1874, this architectural gem visible from Riverfront Park in Athens was designed in the Second Empire style. If you are interested in taking a tour, they are held July through October, the second Saturday of the month, or by appointment. Make sure to check the website or call in advance.

Zadock Pratt Museum (Homestead) and Pratt's Rocks (518-299-3125; www.prattmuseum.com), Route 23, Prattsville. Open Memorial Day weekend through Columbus Day, Thursday through Monday 1–4. School and group tours may be arranged year-round by appointment. Born in 1790, genius businessman Zadock Pratt started out as a harness maker and soon went into the leather-tanning business. He became such a prominent community leader that the town of Prattsville was named in his honor. His tanning facilities were among the largest in the state, and he built many of Prattsville's homes for his workers (more than 90 percent still stand). In later years Pratt served in both the state and federal governments. Today his home is a museum that shows what life in New York was like in the 1850s.

Exhibits focus on the tanning industry as well as the story of Greene County, with rooms displaying period furniture and decorative arts. In a separate gallery the work of local artists is shown, and special events like the holiday decorating show are held. When your visit to the museum is completed, you can stop just outside Prattsville (on Route 23—there is a sign) at Pratt's Rocks, a memorial carved by an itinerant stonemason. Free and open year-round, the huge stone reliefs show Pratt's son, a favorite horse, and Pratt himself. A small picnic area overlooks Schoharie Creek, and there are great views from the summit.

FOR FAMILIES **Armstrong's Elk Farm** (518-622-8452), 936 Hervey Sunside Road, Cornwallville. Take the NYS Thruway to exit 21, pick up Route 23 west for 12 miles, and make a right on Hervey Sunside Road. Open year-round by appointment. Free. This is a fascinating educational detour for just about anyone. There are more than 40 Rocky Mountain elk in their own environment; spring is when the baby elk are born. Learn how the velvet antlers are harvested and used for a variety of drugs and natural remedies that prevent bone deterioration. The farm is also an excellent place for birdwatchers—you will see orioles, finches, bluebirds, and many more species. Les Armstrong, the owner, loves to enlighten visitors about his farm and the business of raising elk. He is an interesting character and makes this a special stop. The farm has "gone green," according to Les, and there is a huge wind turbine on the property; he will explain to visitors how this addition is saving money at the farm.

Bear Creek Landing Family Sport Complex (518-263-3839), 4393 Route 214, Hunter. Open year-round, Monday, Tuesday, and Thursday 4–10; Friday through Sunday noon–10; closed Wednesday. Call for winter hours, which vary. Admission fee for activities. There is a challenging sport-putting course featuring 18 holes of dramatic rock waterfalls, sand traps, and great views. There is a 400-yard golf driving range, and lessons are available in season. There is also horseback riding for riders of all skill levels. A trail guide takes you through beautiful trails through the mountains. There is a snowmobile track here, as well as tours through the woods on the vehicles. The restaurant and pub on the premises (see *Eating Out*) is a delightful place to relax and enjoy a drink or lunch. An oasis of activities—all under one roof!

Round Top Raptor Center (518-622-0118; www.roundtopraptorcenter.com), 733 Bald Hill Road, Round Top. Open Memorial Day weekend through Labor Day, Friday through Sunday 10–5. Admission fee. Falconing is one of the oldest sports known to man. Enjoy the sights and sounds of falcons and hawks presented by master falconer Gino Altimari. There are demonstrations of lure flying, one of the best ways to exercise falcons that doesn't require a large field, along with fascinating facts about these remarkable creatures.

Zoom Flume Water Park (518-239-4559; www.zoomflume.com), 20 Shady Glen Road, East Durham. Open daily Father's Day weekend (mid-June) through Labor Day, Monday through Friday 10–6; Saturday and Sunday until 7. Admission fee. This aquamusement park is set into the Shady Glen canyon, a natural formation of steep walls and running water, so the site itself is beautiful, even if you are going to observe rather than participate in the array of water activities. The Raging River Ride and Zoom Flume let you slosh and slide your way down the canyon; the Rip Tide Wave Pool is a recent addition to the park. There's an enormous activity pool with several slides of all sizes, a game area, and a Toddler Section for one- and two-year-olds. The Black Vortex Speed Slide takes three at a time through an exciting water adventure that older kids will love. There are nature trails, scenic overlooks, and waterfalls, and a restaurant with an observation deck for drying out in addition to a good-size outdoor food court and picnic area. A wonderfully unique and scenic water park that is sure to make everyone in the family happy.

SCENIC DRIVES Mountains, deep gorges, valleys, and waterfalls can all be seen during a leisurely drive through Greene County, and a tour can take all day or only a few hours, depending on the number of stops you want to make. Some of the roads are narrow and winding, though, so use the designated parking areas to take in scenic views. And be careful to check driving conditions if you take a ride in winter or early spring.

Some lovely parts of the county can be seen by taking Route 42 north over the **Deep Notch,** which is cool even on the hottest days. At Route 23A head east through Hunter, Haines Falls, and Palenville. Along the road you will see Hunter Mountain, breathtaking waterfalls, winding streams, and the **Amphitheatre,** a natural, bowl-shaped rock formation. Follow Route 23 into Catskill, where you can pick up the NYS Thruway at exit 21.

Another tour starts at the junction of Routes 23A and 23C; follow 23C east to **Jewett.** The large and elegant homes lining the roads and tucked into the hills were part of Onteora Park, a "cottage" colony where many wealthy families summered during the 19th century. The junction of Routes 25 and 23C shelters the **Old Stone Church,** in which there are some lovely murals. (The church is closed in winter.) At County Route 17 head south to Route 23A, where you can pick up the aforementioned scenic drive into Catskill.

To see some exceptional churches, begin on Route 23A in **Jewett Center.** Here you will see the **St. John the Baptist Ukrainian Church** and the **Grazhda,** which were constructed in the traditional style, using large beams and wooden pins instead of nails. The interior of the church is decorated with wood carvings and panels, and the education building has displays relating to Ukrainian history. Concerts and art shows are held in the Grazhda (518-263-3862). On Route 23A in Hunter you will find **Our Lady of the Snows,** one of the oldest Catholic churches in the Mountaintop region. Continue on Route 23A to Haines Falls, where you will find the **Grotto of Our Lady of the Mountain.** This shrine was constructed in the 1920s and recalls the miracle at Lourdes. The grotto is open to the public. Continue on 23A to Palenville, where the **Gloria Dei Episcopal Church** is open for tours on Saturday. Then take Route 23A to Route 32 north into Cairo, then Route 24 to South Cairo. There you will find the **Mahayana Buddhist Temple** (518-622-3619), a retreat complex complete with Chinese temple, dragon decorations, and fine artwork. The walkways are open to the public year-round. From South Cairo, you can take Route 23B east to the NYS Thruway.

WINERIES AND BREWERIES **Cave Mountain Brewing Company** (518-734-9222), 5359 Main Street, Windham. Open Saturday and Sunday noon–2 AM. This brewery/eatery is decorated with beer cans from around the world. In addition to the sampler of six beers they brew here, a variety of others are offered. The food is what would be expected at a brewpub—burgers, wings, sandwiches, and steaks—but it's all served on paper plates. The place is packed during ski season, and service is extremely slow at that time. Days and hours vary with the season.

Crossroads Brewing Company (518-945-BEER), 21 Second Street, Athens. Open Monday through Thursday 4–9; Friday 4–midnight; Saturday noon–midnight; Sunday 1–9. Located in the historic village of Athens, this brewery offers 10 of their own craft beers on tap, 6 New York State wines, and their own root beer. The beers are excellent. Enjoy live music on Saturday nights.

Windham Vineyard & Winery (518-734-5214), County Route 10, off Route 23, between Windham and Ashland. Open year-round, Saturday and Sunday noon–5; weekdays by appointment. Windham offers wine and handmade chocolate truffle tastings on weekends. Their 2005 Mount Zoar Estate white is made from 100 percent estate-grown grapes. There is also an un-oaked chardonnay. This is a wonderful place to stop after skiing. In-season, visitors can pick their own grapes.

✷ To Do

BICYCLING The **Tannersville Bike Path** (518-589-5850) runs from Clum Hill Road across from Cortina Valley, down around Tannersville Lake, to Bloomer Road. This path covers about 2 miles, and walkers, hikers, and cross-country skiers are all welcome to use it. The path is marked well and is easily found.

The **Twilight General Store** (518-589-6480), North Lake Road, Haines Falls, rents mountain bikes (see *Green Space*); they are located 2 miles from the entrance of North Lake.

Enthusiasts looking for an interesting way to spend a summer or autumn day may want to make tracks to **The Bike Shop at Windham Mountain Outfitters** (518-734-4700), 61 Route 296, Windham, where you can hire a guide—or purchase trail maps and rent a mountain bike to ride the trails on your own. They also have guided group mountain bike rides, and there are excursions for all abilities. Then head down the road to **Windham Mountain** (518-734-4300), Route 23, Windham, for a chairlift ride and views that are magnificent, a great way to begin an autumn bike tour. The mountain maintains a network of trails for bikers. (The lift operates July through October, weekends 11–3.)

BOAT CRUISES ***The Spirit of the Hudson*** (518-822-1014; www.hudsoncruises.com) departs from the waterfront in Athens and offers one-and-a-half-hour sightseeing cruises on the Hudson River from May through October, on Sunday afternoons. The company plans to link Hudson, Athens, Catskill, Coxsackie, and Saugerties, but call for a schedule. Brunch and dinner cruises depart from Hudson.

Sunny Sail Charters (518-210-3309; www.sunnysailcharters.com), Catskill Marina, 10 Greene Street, Catskill. This company provides private sailing cruises on the Hudson River for couples or small groups, by advance arrangement.

BOATING **North-South Lake State Park** (518-589-5058), County Route 18, Haines Falls. This is the place to go if you want to rent a canoe, kayak, or rowboat, and relax on a couple of the most beautiful lakes in the county.

Riverview Marine Services, Inc. (518-943-5311), 103 Main Street, Catskill, is a full-service marine facility with a store, motorboat service, and accessories. How-

Greene County Economic Development

HUDSON-ATHENS LIGHTHOUSE

ever, they do rent kayaks, canoes, and motorboats. If you are interested in motoring on the Hudson River, this is one of the only places that offers rentals.

FARM STANDS AND PICK-YOUR-OWN FARMS Greene County is filled with farm stands: big ones, little ones, and specialty stands that carry everything from maple syrup to mushrooms. The **Catskill Region Farmers' Market** (518-622-9820), at Catskill Point (end of Main Street), Catskill, is held June through October, every Saturday 9:30–1:30. A great place to see what farmers throughout the county are offering, this riverside market, on the bank of the Hudson River, usually has several different activities going on, in addition to the market (see *Entertainment*). For those who want to explore on their own, the following are some of my favorite places to discover the bounty of Greene County:

Black Horse Farms (518-943-9324), Route 9W, Athens, is open April through December, daily 9–6 and stocks everything from vegetables, herbs, eggs, plants, and pumpkins to maple products, flowers, Christmas trees, and honey.

Boehm Farm (518-731-6196), 233 County Route 26, Climax, is open mid-August to mid-December, daily 9–5. At this farm you can pick your own apples (several varieties are available) and peaches. They also sell sweet cider, plums, jams, and jellies.

Catskill Mountain Country Store (518-734-3387), Route 23 (Main Street), Windham. Open daily 9–6. This unique country market, bakery, café (see *Eating Out*), and gift shop specializes in organic produce in season, local maple syrup and honey, plants, Christmas trees, and even has a small petting zoo on the premises for the young ones. A terrific oasis for travelers and local residents alike.

Catskill Mountain Foundation Farm Market (518-263-4908), 7970 Main Street, Hunter. Open Friday through Sunday 10–4. An enormous array of seasonal produce, both organic and nonorganic.

Dines Farms (518-239-4206), 176 Dingman Road (off Route 81), Oak Hill. Open year-round, but call for directions. Buy natural and pasture-raised meats (including chicken, duck, pork, rabbit, chicken sausage, and lamb) directly from the farmer. No hormones or antibiotics are used on this farm.

Hull-O Farms (518-239-6950), 3739 County Route 20, Durham. Open year-round; call for hours. There is a corn maze, as well as pumpkins to be picked in season at this seventh-generation working dairy farm. Families can stay overnight in private guesthouses and have a chance to milk cows, feed baby calves, and collect eggs from the chickens. So if you like picking pumpkins, you might want to stay overnight and see what a working farm is all about (see *Lodging*). Great for families.

Maple Hill Farms (518-299-3604), 135 County Route 2, Lexington (9 miles west of Hunter), is open daily, but call first. They have maple cream, sugar, and syrup; pure honey; and farm-fresh preserves.

Pathfinder Farms (518-943-7096), 2433 Old Kings Road, Catskill. Do call before going to this farm, which features organically grown products: vegetables, fruit, beef, pork, chicken, herbs, and honey.

Schnare's Sunset Orchard (518-731-8846), 1008 Route 81, Climax. Open daily in September and October for apple picking. Call for hours.

Traphagen's Honey (518-263-4150), 8350 Main Street, Hunter, is open year-round, Friday through Monday 9–5, selling all kinds of honey and honey products, as well as maple products and gourmet foods.

FISHING Fishing in Greene County can mean a lazy day spent pondside or an exciting, nerve-ripping hour fighting a sturgeon in the Hudson. There are more than 58 streams that shelter wild trout here, as well as lakes, ponds, and, of course, the Hudson River. A state fishing license is required in Greene County, and town permits are also needed for the Potuck Reservoir in Catskill and the Medway Reservoir in Coxsackie. Permits and licenses can be obtained at many of the bait and tackle and sports shops across the county, as well as in town clerks' offices and the county clerk's office in Catskill. Seasons and limits vary with the species of fish; check with the **Department of Environmental Conservation** (845-256-3000) for specifics. In Greene County, public fishing areas are marked by yellow signs; parking spaces are available, although they're sometimes limited. If you want to catch one of the more than 150 species of fish that are found in the Hudson River—shad, perch, herring, and sturgeon among them—you may want to use the public boat ramps that can be found in Athens, Coxsackie, and Catskill. Route 23A will take you past Rip Van Winkle Lake in Tannersville, Schoharie Creek, and the Schoharie Reservoir, all of which are great fishing areas. Route 145 leads to Lower Catskill Creek, Upper Catskill Creek, and Ten Mile Creek, while Route 296 provides access to the Batavia Kill boat launch and the East Kill Trout Preserve. BASSmaster invitational fishing tournaments have been held in Greene County; information may be obtained by calling the **Greene County Promotion Department** (518-943-3223).

Fins and Grins (518-943-3407), 5571 Cauterskill Road, Catskill, offers fishing charters as well as scenic rides on the Hudson River. Capt. Bob Lewis even supplies all the equipment you will need for the excursion. **Hunter Mountain Expeditions and Sports Center** (518-263-4666), in Hunter, offers half- and full-day guided fly-fishing trips. **Reel Happy Charters** (518-622-8670), in Cairo, specializes in light tackle and fly-fishing for striped bass on the Hudson River.

GOLF The greens of Greene County require widely varying levels of skill, but no one who picks up a club will leave the region disappointed. The following establishments are open to the public. It is suggested that you call before you go to determine hours and available tee times.

Blackhead Mountain Lodge and Country Club (518-622-3157), 50 Crows Nest Road, Round Top, has an 18-hole, par-72 championship course that is quite challenging. There is a pro shop, lessons (home of Blackhead Golf Academy), restaurant, and bar on the premises.

Catskill Golf Club (518-943-0302), 27 Brooks Lane, Catskill, has an 18-hole, 6,382-yard course. There is a pro shop, club rentals, and restaurant, all in a beautiful country atmosphere.

Christman's Windham House Country Inn and Golf Resort (518-734-6990; 1-888-294-4053), 5742 Route 23, Windham, one of the oldest inns in the region, offers an 18-hole, 7,072-yard Mountain Course. With five sets of tees, this forest links layout is fun to play at any skill level. There is also a nine-hole Valley Course that will please walkers and beginners. Cart and club rentals, pro shop, snack bar, driving range. There is a Ben Sutton Golf School that offers lessons, and overnight packages are available for golfers (see *Lodging*).

Colonial Golf Club (518-589-5310), Route 23A, Tannersville, has a nine-hole course, par 35, 2,718 yards. There are carts, a pro shop, snack bar, club rentals, and lessons. A good place for novices. Gorgeous views.

Rainbow Golf Club (518-966-5343), 3822 Route 26, Greenville, offers an 18-hole, USGA-regulation championship course; driving range; carts; restaurant; bar; rentals; and golf packages in vacation apartments just off the course.

Rip Van Winkle Country Club (518-678-9779), 3200 Route 23A, Palenville, has a nine-hole Donald Ross–designed course with alternate tees, par 36, 3,120 yards. A restaurant and bar are on the premises. Nice for beginners.

Sunny Hill Resort & Golf Course (518-634-7642), 352 Sunny Hill Road, Greenville, has a challenging 18-hole, par-66 course that overlooks a beautiful lake; clubhouse with pro shop and snack bar. Gas and handcart rentals.

Thunderhart Golf Club (518-634-7816), 2740 County Route 67, Freehold, offers an 18-hole championship course, par 74, 6,863 yards; driving range and pavilion for outings. An informal atmosphere prevails here.

Windham Country Club (518-734-9910), 36 South Street (Route 296), Windham, has an 18-hole, par-71, 6,024-yard championship course; pro shop; lessons; and driving range. They were awarded three and a half stars by *Golf Digest* magazine within the last few years. Restaurant and bar on the premises.

HIKING Greene County provides some of the best hiking and views in the Catskill region. You don't have to be a seasoned hiker to enjoy a day walking on the clearly marked trails. The magnificent vistas have inspired Thomas Cole and other Hudson River painters.

Although the **Escarpment Trail** runs from Kaaterskill Creek on Route 23A to East Windham on Route 23 (24 miles in all), there are several short hikes along the path to Kaaterskill High Peak, North Point, and Mary's Glen. The trails in the North Lake area are renowned for their waterfalls and fantastic views of the entire Hudson Valley. **Kaaterskill Falls** and the **Catskill Mountain House** are particularly noteworthy sites. The easy-to-find entry point for these trails is at the junction of Route 23A and Kaaterskill Creek on the north side of the highway. These hikes are usually very popular on summer weekends, so you might want to go during the week to avoid the crowds. North Lake and decent campgrounds are nearby for those who want to take a swim or stay overnight.

For more experienced and adventurous hikers, there is the **Devil's Path,** named for its steepness and relative isolation. The path passes over much rugged terrain, particularly Indian Head Mountain, and includes the Hunter Mountain Trail and West Kill Mountain Range Trail. To reach the trailhead, turn south off Route 23A at the only light in Tannersville. Continue 1.5 miles to the road's intersection with Bloomer Road. Turn left, and after a short distance bear left onto Platte Clove Mountain Road. Stay on this road for 1 mile to Prediger Road, then go about 0.5 mile farther to find the trail. Each single mountain on the Devil's Path can be hiked in a day or less.

At 4,040 feet, **Hunter Mountain** is the second highest peak in the Catskills and is best hiked on the trail that starts on Spruceton Road. To get there, take Route 42 north from Lexington and go 4 miles to Spruceton Road. The trailhead and trail are well defined.

CATSKILL MOUNTAIN HOUSE SITE IN HAINES FALLS

Greene County Economic Development

Another pleasant day hike takes you to **Diamond Notch** and **West Kill Falls.** Located 5 miles north of Phoenicia, near Route 214, it is also easy to find. From Route 214, take Diamond Notch Road about 1 mile to a bridge, cross it, and park. The hike is about 4.5 miles and should take approximately three and a half to four hours.

The **Cohotate Preserve** (518-622-3620), Route 385, Athens, is a nature preserve with a self-guided tour on nature trails that run along the Hudson River. You can see the sign for the preserve on the right side of the highway if you are heading from Catskill toward Athens. This is an easy walk and is a good choice for those traveling with children.

The **Four Mile Point Preserve** in Coxsackie may be reached by taking Route 385; it is located 8 miles from the Rip Van Winkle Bridge. This 7.6-acre riverfront preserve offers picturesque shoreline vistas and a tranquil inland pond. There are nature trails, and it's a wonderful place to observe all kinds of birds.

The **Rams Horn–Livingston Sanctuary** in Catskill may be reached by following Route 9W south from the Rip Van Winkle Bridge for 2.5 miles. Make a left onto Grandview Avenue, and follow for 0.5 mile to a parking area. There are 480 acres of the Hudson's largest tidal swamp forest here, a breeding ground for American shad and bass, and more than 3 miles of trails. Following a 0.5-mile walk, you can canoe from the tidal marsh out to the Hudson River.

Shinglekill Falls, on the Catskills' eastern fringe, are only a few hundred feet from the road. From Cairo, head south, then west on County Route 24. After passing South Road, the falls are about 500 feet farther along on the right side. Shinglekill Grist Mill, a small store, once an old mill, provides access to the falls. For those who want to enjoy a few hours by a cool stream or are looking for an easy walk to a waterfall, this is the perfect spot.

HORSEBACK RIDING **Catskill Equestrian Center at Bailiwick Ranch** (518-678-5665), Castle Road (take Route 32 to Game Farm Road and follow signs to the ranch), Catskill. Open year-round, daily 10–6. In business for more than 40 years, Bailiwick offers riding for all ages and abilities. Scenic mountain trail rides are available for a half hour, as well as one or two hours; riders must be over the age of seven. For those who would like something more intensive, there are all-day mountain trips and overnight camping excursions. Children under the age of six will enjoy pony rides and the petting zoo. For those interested in lessons, both English and Western riding instruction are offered in the indoor and outdoor riding arenas.

Hidden Meadow Farm (518-928-0939), 352 Brown Road, Durham. Open year-round by appointment. If you are an experienced rider, you will enjoy going out on acres of private trails at this establishment. Owner Erika Rose gives lessons as well.

K&K Equestrian Center (518-966-4829), 5203 Route 67, East Durham. Open May through October. This establishment has been owned and operated by the Phillips family for more than 30 years. They offer guided scenic trail rides, pony rides, lessons, and overnight trips. Nice, informal atmosphere.

ZIP LINE AND CANOPY TOUR **Hunter Mountain Zipline Adventure** (518-263-4388; www.ziplinenewyork.com), Hunter Mountain, Route 23A, Hunter. Open

Greene County Economic Development

ZIP LINE IN HUNTER

year-round, rain or shine. Make sure to check the website for details on both cold- and warm-weather apparel requirements as well as age restrictions. Closed-toe shoes that can sustain high winds are necessary: no sandals. There are two experiences offered:

The Mid-Mountain Tour is family friendly and takes participants into the canopy with six zip lines, four rope bridges, nine aerial tree platforms, and a rappel. The longest zip line on this excursion is about 650 feet and nearly 60 feet aboveground. The tour lasts three hours and is the best option for first-timers.

The Skyrider Tour is the second-largest zip line in the world and is classed as an extreme activity. There are about 5 miles of zip lines, including five side-by-side racing zip lines, and one reachs a speed of 50 mph. This tour last about three hours and is recommended for those who have experience with this sport and enjoy a difficult challenge.

For those who decide the zip line adventure isn't for them, they can enjoy the **Hunter Mountain Skyride,** the longest and highest in the Catskills and the only six-passenger chairlift in the state. It takes you to a height of 3,200 feet and offers panoramic views. The skyride is open on weekends only, July through October, weather permitting.

✷ Winter Sports

CROSS-COUNTRY SKIING Greene County is home to some of the best cross-country skiing to be found in New York State. More than 1,000 acres of groomed and ungroomed trails snake their way through the county's forests and fields, and many of the areas are patrolled by Nordic Ski Patrol members.

Mountain Trails X-C Ski Center (518-589-5361; www.mtntrails.com), Route 23A, Tannersville, offers 20 miles of woodland trails that are groomed, track-set, and marked. After skiing, enjoy hot chocolate in the snack bar or the warming hut, which has a wonderfully welcome fireplace. Ski and snowshoe rentals; ski lessons available. Open on weekends and holiday weeks.

North-South Lake (518-357-2289), County Route 18, Haines Falls. There are no services, only open trails here on old carriage roads. The scenic overlooks are magnificent. Ski and snowshoe rentals are available at a nearby general store. A great place for more experienced cross-country skiers.

DOWNHILL SKIING Skiers from beginner to expert will enjoy excellent snow conditions, modern facilities, and some of the best skiing and most spectacular views anywhere in Greene County, which lies in New York's snowbelt. Here, sudden storms can dump several inches of powder in an hour, and the ski season usually lasts six months. In addition to their specialty offerings, the following slopes have rentals, child-care services, dining facilities, picnic areas, and ski shops:

Hunter Mountain (518-263-4223; 1-888-486-8376; www.huntermtn.com), Route 23A, Hunter. (From exit 21, NYS Thruway, the trip is approximately 24 miles, taking Route 23 east to Route 9W south, then 23A west; or 18 miles from exit 20, taking 32 north to 32A north to 23A west.) Open daily 8:30–4; Hunter West 9:30–3:30. Hunter Mountain's reputation as the snowmaking capital of the East is

Greene County Economic Development

well deserved. The three different mountains—Hunter One, Hunter West, and Hunter Mountain—offer skiers of all skill levels a chance to test themselves on more than 55 trails. Runs at Hunter can extend more than 2 miles, with a 3,200-foot summit elevation and vertical drops of 1,600 feet, and there are some extremely difficult areas, even for the expert. Hunter Mountain has New York State's first six-passenger high-speed detachable lift. The double, triple, and quadruple chairlifts (there are now 11 lifts) cut the lines down to size, but this is such a popular area that you should be prepared for crowds on holidays and weekends. There are special discounts during the week and no lift lines.

Hunter offers ski and snowboard lessons for all levels, and a wide variety of amateur and professional races are held during the season, including one for chefs, firemen, and nurses. There are two Terrain Parks for snowboarders with a 1,000-watt stereo system that blasts motivational music. Two slopes wide, the Terrain Park offers a dozen features and several rails for jibbing, jumping, and pumping action. (There are also snowshoeing and snowtubing areas, with nine 1,000-foot-long chutes.) Hunter also offers 100 percent snowmaking capability, so the season sometimes begins as early as November and lasts into April. There are complete facilities here, including a full-service hotel, the Kaatskill Mountain Club (see *Lodging*), restaurant (see *Dining Out*), art gallery, babysitting, cafeterias, demo center, a lodge, museum, a ski shop, and plenty of parking.

Hunter Mountain also offers zip lining. See *To Do—Zip Line and Canopy Tour.* If you want to see the slopes from a different perspective, this is a great way to do it!

Windham Mountain (518-734-4300; 1-800-SKI-WINDHAM), Clarence D. Lane Road, off Route 23, Windham. Open Monday through Friday 9–4, weekends and holidays 8–4; night skiing and snowboarding mid-December through early March, Friday through Sunday 4–8, depending on weather conditions. The hours for the Adventure Park (including the ice skating rink located there) are Friday 4–8; Saturday and holidays 10–8; Sunday 10–4. This is a wonderful place to ski in the Catskills; it has one of the nicest lounge areas—and bar—with a panoramic view of the mountain. The atmosphere here is friendly and relaxed. Diversity is a hallmark of Windham Mountain: It's a wonderful place for either a family excursion or a romantic escape. There are 49 trails on 269 skiable acres, and elevations of 1,600 feet at the base and 3,100 feet at the summit. Trail difficulty ranges from easy to expert, and the longest trail is more than 2 miles long. Windham Mountain Adventure Park near the mountain has several snowtubing lifts and dozens of tubes for sliding. Windham Mountain is renowned for the high quality of its private lessons and employs over 200 ski instructors. A conveyor lift on the beginner slope makes learning to ski and snowboard easier than ever. The Children's Learning Center offers fun for young nonskiers (or tired kids). Windham has won awards for its courtesy services, including valet parking and excellent dining facilities, along with a senior-skier development program and lessons in racing, freestyle skiing, and snowboarding. The area is well-known for its remarkable work with disabled skiers. For those who prefer ice skating to schussing down the slopes, there is a 60 foot by 120 foot ice rink lighted for night use, as well as a timber frame warming and rental center, within the Adventure Park. There are also kid snowmobiles and a 500-foot zip line in the park. Fees at the Adventure Park are charged by activity ($20 for snowtubing; $10 for ice skating, kid snowmobiles, and the zip line).

Mountain-bike lovers may wish to inquire about the autumn special events at Windham Mountain (see *To Do—Bicycling*).

✷ Green Space

Mountaintop Arboretum (518-589-3903; www.mtarboretum.org), 4 Maude Adams Road (off Route 23C), Tannersville. Free. Open year-round, but call about guided tours, offered by appointment. A nonprofit organization that features a living collection of both exotic and native trees and shrubs on a 193-acre site. Some are indigenous to the Catskills, others are not. Each season brings delights, from the flowering height of spring to the brightly colored autumn foliage. Many of the plants have identification markers, and there are workshops throughout the year. Horticulturalists and those who just want to know "What is that tree?" will enjoy this stop. This center serves as a botanical research facility and a place for educational programs on a variety of horticultural topics.

North Lake and South Lake (518-589-5058; 518-943-4030). Take Route 23A to County Route 18, Haines Falls. Open late May through early December, daily 9–dusk. Admission fee, with an extra charge for campsites. This recreational area offers breathtaking scenery and a multitude of activities. Visitors can swim in a mountain lake with a clean, sandy beach. Boat rentals and fishing are also available. An ideal spot for a family outing.

A short hike from the North Lake is Kaaterskill Falls, one of the highest falls on the East Coast and a popular subject for Hudson River School artists. The area also has a multiuse campground with hookups for recreational vehicles; it is advisable to make reservations early in the season since this is a popular site, and it gets busy on summer weekends.

A true oasis in the wilderness (selling soft drinks, toys, T shirts, and groceries) is the **Twilight General Store** (518-589-6480), North Lake Road, Haines Falls, on the left side of the road, 2 miles before you get to the entrance of the park. They stock all kinds of camping supplies (in case you forgot something) and rent mountain bikes (see *To Do—Bicycling*). The gift shop is also filled with dozens of regional history books and guides to the Catskill Mountains.

Point Lookout Mountain Inn Gardens (518-734-3381), Route 23, East Windham. Open Thursday through Monday year-round. Free. There are perennial and herb gardens on the mountainside next to this historic inn and restaurant (see both *Lodging* and *Dining Out*), and seating areas to enjoy. But it's the view that really counts: five states, 180 miles, and 270 degrees. Breathtaking all around.

✷ Lodging

Greene County is an extremely popular resort area, and there are hundreds of B&Bs, inns, motels, and campgrounds. Some of the establishments cater to lovers of Irish, Italian, or Scandinavian heritage; others offer a full range of camping facilities on lakes and rivers. The following list is only a quality sampling of what can be discovered throughout the county.

Catskill Area (Leeds, Round Top, Purling)

The Bavarian Manor Country Inn (518-622-3261), 866 Mountain Avenue, Purling 12470. ($) This historic Civil War–era inn has been operating for over a century. The third-generation-owned property offers 18 lovely rooms, all with private baths, cable TV, and air-conditioning; some have fireplaces. There is a restaurant/bar on the premises, and a full breakfast is served to all guests. Special off-season package rates are available. The inn offers plenty of old-world charm and is located on 100 acres of wooded property. There are plenty of trails for those who enjoy walking and hiking. Children and pets are welcome. Open year-round.

Caleb Street's Inn (518-943-0246), 251 Main Street, Catskill 12414. ($$) This beautiful, elegant home is filled with antiques and has a large veranda that overlooks the Catskill Marina. There are four rooms here: two share a bath, and two large suites have private baths. It's a nice place to stay for those who want to walk to shops and restaurants and prefer to stay in town. Open year-round.

Carl's Rip Van Winkle Motor Lodge (518-943-3303), 810 Route 23B, Leeds 12451. ($$) There are 27 log cabins and 14 motel rooms here. I recommend staying in one of the log cabins, which have been renovated and are charming. Facilities include an outdoor pool, air-conditioning, phones, and cable TV. There are hiking trails on the premises and fishing, as well. Open mid-April through November.

The Kaaterskill Inn (518-678-0026), 424 High Falls Extension, Catskill 12414. ($$) This 100-year-old farm, set on 32 acres with panoramic views of the Catskills, is now an inn with six private suites, each with a Jacuzzi, kitchenette, fine linens, stone fireplace, and wireless Internet access. Guests will enjoy the private hiking trail as well as access to the Katterskill Creek. The inn welcomes pets and is open year-round.

Tumblin' Falls House (518-622-3981), 44 Falls View Lane, Cairo 12413. ($$) There are four guest rooms, and most have gorgeous views. The Falls View Suite makes for an especially romantic experience. You can wander the gardens and trails, or relax listening to the sound of "tumblin'" water on the multilevel deck (with spa) overlooking Shinglekill Falls (see *To Do—Hiking*). Open year-round.

Winter Clove Inn (518-622-3267), 557 Winter Clove Road, Round Top 12473. ($$) Located on 400 acres adjoining the Catskill Forest Preserve, this inn opened in 1830 and is still run by the same family. There are swimming pools, tennis courts, a golf course, cross-country skiing, hayrides in autumn, and even a bowling alley on the premises. All baked goods are homemade, and many of the recipes have been passed down in the family for generations. Children are welcome. All meals are included in the rates, unless special arrangements are made in advance. The 51 rooms all have private baths. Open year-round.

Coxsackie

Coxsackie Guest House (518-731-2145), 1 Mansion Street, Coxsackie 12051. ($) There are four rooms, all with private baths, in this guesthouse in the village. For those travelers who want to stay in town with simple, clean, inexpensive accommodations, this is a great choice. There are flat-screen TVs, and the rooms are tastefully decorated with artwork and antiques. While they don't serve breakfast, there is a diner within walking distance. Open year-round.

Greenville

Greenville Arms 1889 Inn (518-966-5219), 11135 Route 32, Greenville 12083. ($$$) Special care is taken to provide a quiet retreat for guests at this gem of a Queen Anne Victorian home, built by William Vanderbilt in the late 19th century. Each room is decorated with antiques, and the 7 acres of lush lawns and gardens are a riot of color each spring and summer. Old-fashioned country cooking is served at the full breakfast. There are 16 rooms in three buildings, all with private bath. Some have private porches, fireplaces, and double Jacuzzis. There is a 50-foot outdoor pool. Older children are welcome. Pets welcome. Open year-round.

Hunter Area (Palenville, Tannersville)

Clark House Bed & Breakfast (518-678-5649), 3292 Route 23A, Palenville 12463. ($$) This turn-of-the-20th-century Victorian guesthouse offers five rooms, all with private bath, as well as his and hers bathrobes. Guest rooms are decorated in a range of styles: The Lodge has a woodburning stove; the Sea Room, a gas fireplace; and the French Quarter Room offers a canopy bed and claw-foot bathtub. The Asian Room is simple yet chic, with antique furnishings, and the American Room has stunning mountain views. This establishment is open to guests year-round—and so is their 10-person hot tub!

Deer Mountain Inn (518-589-6268), 790 County Route 25, Tannersville 12485. ($$) This gracious, elegant turn-of-the-20th-century country estate has seven beautiful guest rooms. All have private bath and TV; some have working fireplaces and sitting areas. Fine restaurant on the premises (see *Dining Out*). Open year-round.

Fairlawn Inn (518-263-5025), 7872 Main Street, Hunter 12442. ($$) This inn is the epitome of Victorian charm, from the three-story corner turret and wraparound porches to the elaborately designed wallpapered ceilings and cozy brass beds. A stunning grand staircase and antiques-filled lobby are only a preview for the inn's several large common rooms, which provide a variety of settings for quiet contemplation or socializing. Each of the nine bedrooms has a queen-size bed and private bath. A breakfast feast here may include a spinach quiche or stuffed French toast. Special midweek rates. Open year-round.

Kaatskill Mountain Club (518-263-5580), Hunter Mountain, Hunter 12442. ($$) This lovely slopeside resort opened in 2005 with 109 guest rooms, Van Winkle's Restaurant (see *Dining Out*), an outdoor heated pool, fitness center, and spa. Each guest unit has a full kitchen, gas fireplace, private terrace, cathedral ceilings, and windows that offer scenic views of the surrounding mountains. All have cable TV, central air-conditioning, and Internet access. The convenience of being able to ski in and ski out during the winter months makes this an ideal place for skiers to stay overnight, so do check the variety of package deals available. A great place for families. Open year-round.

Hunter Mountain Hotel and Spa (518-263-4919; 1-800-232-2772), 48 Clover Road (off Route 214), Hunter 12442. ($$) This 15-acre resort at the base of Hunter Mountain is an informal, somewhat rustic retreat with all the amenities of a full-service spa. Located in the midst of the Catskill Forest Preserve, the spa provides a fitness room, sauna, indoor and outdoor swimming pools, tennis courts, and basketball and volleyball courts. Daily exercise options include aerobics, yoga, hiking, tai chi, dance, and water activities. The daily price is reasonable and includes three diet meals (vegan and vegetarian meals available) as well as use of all facilities. Some packages include a free massage. Open year-round.

Scribner Hollow Lodge (518-263-4211), 13 Scribner Hollow Road (off Route 23A), Hunter 12442. ($$) For people who enjoy a full-service lodge; the main building offers 37 private rooms, and town houses can also be rented. Every room is different, and the lodge has a sauna, a whirlpool, and an unusual grotto swimming pool. The Prospect Restaurant (see *Dining Out*) is on the premises. Children welcome. Open year-round.

Washington Irving Inn (518-589-5560), Route 23A, Hunter 12442. ($$) Set back off the road, this old-world Victorian bed & breakfast may have 15 rooms, but every one has its own distinctive charm. The beautifully renovated building, more than a century old and listed on the National Register of Historic Places, is covered in cedar siding that blends nicely with the lush landscape. All rooms have renovated baths, a few with Jacuzzis, and many have fireplaces. There is also an outdoor swimming pool. Owner Stefania Jozic combines country hospitality and European elegance: Guests will feel at ease from the moment they arrive. A unique feature here is the afternoon tea, served on weekends 2–5 (see *Eating Out*)—I had not tasted freshly made scones, pastries, and canapés like this since visiting tearooms in Vienna. This is the perfect way to spend a Sunday afternoon if the weather is too hot or too cold; the tearoom offers a relaxing, romantic ambience. Children are welcome; a good choice for a family reunion. Open year-round.

The Waterfall House (845-246-6666), 370 Malden Turnpike, Palenville 12463. ($$) This lovely country house, with a gorgeous waterfall in the backyard, has two bedrooms and two baths (ideal for two to six people, especially families). It is fully furnished and is a wonderful country retreat that may be rented by the night or the week, by advance reservation only. Children are welcome, and so are well-behaved dogs. Open year-round.

Windham Area (Durham, East Windham)

Albergo Allegria Bed & Breakfast (518-734-5560), 43 Route 296, Windham 12496. ($$$) Step up on the wicker-furnished porch here, and feel the grace and beauty of days gone by. The Victorian theme is continued throughout this bed & breakfast with antique furnishings and period wallpaper and decorations. A full breakfast of fresh fruit, home-baked muffins, croissants, omelets, and local honey and jams is served daily. In summer enjoy breakfast on the porch. The main lounge, with its overstuffed couches and fireplace, and the library are especially warm and inviting. There are 14 rooms, and 7 suites with Jacuzzis. Several fine restaurants are within walking distance of this B&B, which is open year-round.

Country Suite Bed & Breakfast (518-734-4079), 11365 Route 23, Windham 12496. ($$) This restored farmhouse is only minutes from skiing, shopping, and festivals, and guests will enjoy the country furnishings and antiques. There are five rooms, each with private bath. Reservations suggested. Open year-round.

Christman's Windham House Country Inn and Golf Resort (518-734-4230), 5742 Route 23, Windham 12496. ($$) There are 49 rooms, all with private bath, at this beautifully located inn, with two golf courses, an outdoor heated pool, fishing, tennis courts, hiking, a library, and a restaurant. Children welcome. Open year-round, except for the months of April and November.

Danske Hus (518-734-6335), 361 South Street, Windham 12496. ($$) Walk to the slopes at Windham from your room (there are five here, all with private bath, air-conditioning, and cable TV). The large, comfortable living room has a cozy fireplace and piano. Outside, a large deck offers panoramic views of the mountains. Breakfast is served in an heirloom-filled dining room. Your hosts provide an afternoon snack after skiing or hiking. Children and dogs welcome. Open year-round.

Hull-O Farms (518-239-6950), 3739 County Route 20, Durham 12422. ($) For those traveling with children, this is a homespun experience that will be long remembered. You can live the country life on this 300-acre working dairy farm that has been in the same family for seven generations. Milk a cow, collect chicken eggs, feed pigs and calves, fish, or go on a nature walk. The hands-on experience is unusual and fun for everyone. Hayrides and barbecues. Extremely comfortable guesthouses (there are three), with home-cooked meals served in the homestead. Rates include breakfast and dinner. Children under 2 are free; ages 2–12 less than half price. There is a two-night minimum stay. Open May through October.

Point Lookout Mountain Inn (518-734-3381), Route 23, East Windham 12439. ($$) This full-service inn has a spectacular 180-mile panoramic view of five states. The 14 guest rooms, all with private bath and cable TV, are housed in a building adjoining the Victorian Rose Restaurant (see *Dining Out*). Other facilities include game room, gardens, decks, and fireplace. Continental breakfast included. Open year-round.

The Thompson House (518-734-4510), 19 Route 296, Windham 12496. ($$) Since 1880 the Thompson family has provided gracious hospitality and a vacation destination with spectacular views for guests in the lovely Catskills. There is a golf course across the street, a large heated outdoor swimming pool, and a variety of entertainment every day. An exercise room and a recreation room (with video games and a Ping-Pong table) are on the premises, making this an ideal getaway for families. Check out the special package rates that include breakfast and dinner daily. Rooms without air-conditioning are available at reduced rates. Children under the age of four stay free. Open year-round, except for the months of November and April.

Winwood the Mountain Inn (518-734-3000), 5220 Route 23, Windham 12496. ($$) Take the NYS Thruway to exit 21, and then pick up Route 23 west; it's 25 miles to the hotel. Only 0.5 mile from Windham Mountain, and the ski center's own hotel, this establishment combines a country setting with comfortable rooms and spectacular mountain views. It is ideal for families, with a dining room, tennis court, indoor recreation center, and outdoor pool on the premises. It combines the convenience of a hotel with the warmth of a country inn. The 47 rooms range from standard doubles to deluxe suites and have TV, telephone, and private bath. Rock'n Mexicana (see *Dining Out*) is on the premises, and the food here is first-rate. Ask about the Kids-Stay-Free policy for children under the age of 12 staying in parents' room. Open year-round.

✷ Where to Eat

DINING OUT The Basement Bistro (518-634-2338), 776 County Route 45, Earlton. ($$) Open for dinner Wednesday through Sunday 5–9. Reservations required. This unique restaurant gives diners the opportunity to try everything offered. There is a prix-fixe menu made up of a dozen courses that change daily, depending on seasonal produce available. Located on a pastoral country road in the basement of a house hand-built by the chef-owner, who lives with his family upstairs, the restaurant seats only 26. The kitchen specializes in a healthful, imaginative style of cooking that uses purees and infused oils instead of butter and cream. Adventurous diners shouldn't pass up this restaurant. The chef-owner makes his own aged cheeses and prosciutto, and grows much of the produce used in the restaurant. In fact, since 1989 when the restaurant opened, almost all the fruits and vegetables on the menu have been organically grown.

Bavarian Manor (518-622-3261), 866 Mountain Road, Purling. ($$) Open for dinner Thursday through Saturday 5–9; Sunday 1–9. Located in a historic building that has been operating as an inn and/or restaurant since 1865, the manor's specialties are sauerbraten, Wiener schnitzel, spaetzle, dumplings, and bratwurst. Those who don't care for German cuisine will find fresh seafood entrées and hand-cut steaks on the menu. The German beer on draft is excellent, and diners may enjoy marvelous black forest cake and apple strudel for dessert. Children are welcome.

Bistro Brie & Bordeaux (518-734-4911), 5386 State Route 23, Windham. ($$) Open for dinner Thursday through Sunday 5–9. This French-country restaurant, owned and operated by a native-born French chef, offers wonderful prix-fixe dinners for $19.95 per person on select evenings; call for details. This is an amazing deal since the cuisine is absolutely first-rate—it is one of my favorite restaurants in the Catskills. Dine alfresco in the warm weather months. Children welcome.

Brandywine (518-734-3838), Route 23, Windham. ($$) Open for dinner daily from 5; Saturday and Sunday noon–11. An excellent informal dining spot; the Italian specialties here are superb. Try the rich fettuccine Alfredo, the shrimp Brandywine, or the chicken Scarpariello. Desserts include fantastic cheesecake. There is a bright greenhouse room for dining and cozy booths in the main area. Children are welcome.

Cameo's Restaurant (518-945-2375), 7 Second Street, Athens. ($$) Open for dinner Wednesday through Sunday 5–9. This casual, moderately priced Italian restaurant serves up a wide variety of pasta, veal, chicken, and shrimp entrées. There is also a children's menu.

Chalet Fondue (518-734-4650), South Street, Windham. ($$) Open for dinner daily from 4, Sunday from 2. The Swiss, Austrian, and German dishes are excellent, and the atmosphere is elegant yet relaxed. The specialties include veal entrées and a full line of fondues. They make a wonderful salad with excellent honey-lemon dressing. Children are welcome.

Chateau Belleview (518-589-5525), 6589 Route 23A, Tannersville. ($$) Open for dinner Thursday through Sunday 5–10. Fine Continental cuisine and spectacular mountain views are found here, along with candlelight and fine service. Not recommended for children.

Deer Mountain Inn (518-589-6268), 790 County Road 25, Tannersville. ($$) Open daily, except Tuesday, for dinner from 6. Enjoy eclectic international cuisine in a romantic, quiet atmosphere where steaks, seafood, duck, and lamb (a specialty of the house) are quite popular with diners. There are also seven rooms in the adjoining inn, all with private bath (see *Lodging*). Not recommended for children.

Dionysos Italian Restaurant (518-945-3225), 11 North Water Street, Athens. ($$) Open for dinner Wednesday through Saturday 5–10; Sunday brunch buffet 11:30–2, dinner 3–8. Limited hours in the fall and winter months. Southern Italian cuisine is the specialty here, with a wide variety of intriguing pasta entrées. There are steaks, pork chops, and seafood for those who prefer American dishes. Some tables have a lovely view of the Hudson River, and there is a large stone fireplace. Children are accommodated with smaller portions of any dish on the menu. In the warm weather, enjoy drinks on the outdoor patio.

Fernwood Restaurant and Bistro (518-678-9332), Malden Avenue, Palenville. ($$) Open for dinner Wednesday through Sunday at 5. Standard American favorites are the specialty here. Try the steak, ribs, or seafood. All entrées are served with vegetable and pasta; the pasta dishes include a house salad. There are always a variety of intriguing specials. Both Caesar and spinach salads are prepared tableside. The bistro, renowned for its full bar, particularly the margaritas, features live music on weekends. Fernwood has been in business for over 40 years, and the cuisine is consistently excellent.

La Conca D'Oro (518-943-3549), 440 Main Street, Catskill. ($$) Open Wednesday, Thursday, and Friday for lunch 11:30–3 and dinner daily, except Tuesday, 5–10; open Saturday 3–10 and Sunday 2–9. The name means "the golden bay," and this unpretentious Italian restaurant serves fine food at exceedingly reasonable prices. The veal entrées, chicken dishes, and homemade mozzarella are house specialties. For dessert, there are excellent cannoli. Children are welcome.

Messina's Italian Restaurant (518-734-4499), 5658 State Route 23, Windham. ($$) Open daily, except Tuesday, for dinner from 4:30. Ed Messina worked at La Griglia for many years; he's now the proprietor of his own restaurant. A graduate of the Culinary Institute of America, his elegant restaurant serves excellent Northern Italian cuisine, featuring some of the best fresh seafood around. House specialties include osso buco Milanese, roast duck, all kinds of fresh fish entrées, and pasta (made on the premises). Children welcome. Reservations suggested.

Millrock Restaurant (518-734-9719), 5398 Main Street, Windham. ($$) Open year-round, Thursday through Monday 5–10 for dinner. This Italian American family restaurant features an open kitchen and wood-burning oven that turns out an array of gourmet pizzas. A specialty of the house is seafood, and I enjoy the Seafood Lovers for Two entrée: a mix of mussels, clams, calamari, and shrimp topped with a zesty red sauce over pasta. Most desserts are homemade on the premises, and all are first-rate. Try the cannoli, crème brûlée, imported sorbets, or pumpkin cheesecake. Children are welcome.

The Prospect Restaurant (518-263-4211; 1-800-395-4683), 13 Scribner Hollow Road (off Route 23A), Hunter. ($$$) Open for dinner Friday through Sunday from 5; breakfast served Saturday and Sunday from 8. Dinner served during the week from Thanksgiving through the end of ski season. Call for hours. Enjoy breathtaking views of Hunter Mountain and the Catskills from just about every table in the dining room. The fusion of American regional and New York State dishes include tantalizing choices like wild game mixed grill with acorn juniper sauce, apple-braised free-range chicken, and chocolate tartlet with ripe pears for dessert. There are several wine dinners throughout the year featuring some of California's most elegant varietals, as well as other wines that complement the regionally inspired cuisine.

Reds Restaurant (518-731-8151), 12005 Route 9W, West Coxsackie. ($$) Open for lunch and dinner Tuesday through Saturday 11:30–9. Open since 1944, Reds is synonymous with fresh fish and seafood, although you can get just about anything here for lunch or dinner. The service is efficient and friendly; it's a down-home, family restaurant that aims to please. Children welcome.

Rock'n Mexicana (518-734-4055), 5220 Route 23, Windham. ($$) Open for dinner daily from 5 PM on. During the spring and summer months, the restaurant is often closed on Monday and Tuesday, so do call ahead if you intend to dine there during that time of the year. Just minutes from the slopes, this restaurant offers a relaxed, cozy atmosphere with an open-hearth fireplace and reasonable prices. There are all the Mexican favorites—burritos, quesadillas, tacos—as well as burgers, salads, and sandwiches. There is a nice selection of beer and wine. The margaritas are particularly good. This is the perfect place for après-ski in winter as well as informal summer dining.

Ruby's Hotel (518-634-7790), 3689 Route 67, Freehold 12431 ($$$) Open for dinner Friday and Saturday 6–10. Housed in a renovated 19th-century hotel converted into a terrific restaurant, Ruby's serves seasonal American fare with a French accent. Entrées include salmon, rib eye steak, and seafood, served in a cozy bistro atmosphere. There's an art deco bar here, as well as a gallery featuring the work of local artists on the second floor. Chef Ana Sporer serves up fresh, simple flavorful dishes; do not pass up the dessert course. Many of the vegetables and herbs are grown in the giant garden behind the restaurant. Open year-round. (There are also two guest rooms above the restaurant, both with private baths.)

Tatiana's Italian Restaurant (518-943-1528), 601 Main Street, Catskill. ($$) Open for dinner Tuesday through Saturday 5–9:30; Sunday 3–8. Enjoy dining on the deck overlooking Catskill Creek in warm-weather months. Thomas Cole used to come here to paint; he loved the views. All types of Italian cuisine are served; one of the house specialties is *zuppa di pesce.* Do try the eggplant Tatiana (spinach, ricotta, kalamata olives, and mozzarella cheese) or the veal and crab Adelaide (sautéed veal stuffed with crabmeat served in a lobster tarragon sauce). For dessert, there is tiramisu made fresh by the owner. Children's menu.

Van Winkle's at the Kaatskill Mountain Club (518-263-5580), Hunter Mountain, Hunter. ($$) Open daily for breakfast 8–11; lunch noon–3:30; dinner 5–10. Hours may vary slightly after ski season ends. Enjoy the open-kitchen bistro-style atmosphere here, featuring regional American cuisine. The Mediterranean pizzas and imaginative salad and sandwich creations are offered for lunch. Dinner entrées include steaks, seafood, pasta, and chicken. Children are welcome.

Vesuvio (518-734-3663), Goshen Road, Hensonville. ($$) Open daily at 4:30. The warm atmosphere and provincial charm make this Italian restaurant a popular stop. Candlelight makes dining elegant, and the specialties include veal and fish, along with outstanding desserts like tortoni and spumoni. Children are welcome.

Victorian Rose Restaurant at Point Lookout Inn (518-734-3381), Route 23, East Windham. ($$) Open for lunch Thursday through Monday noon–4; for dinner Saturday 4–10; Sunday 10–10. Hours vary depending on the season, so call first. Eat here on a clear day, and you can see five states from your dining booth. The chef-owner prepares a variety of American and Continental favorites including steaks, seafood, and pasta dishes. There are tempting seasonal creations like fresh salmon baked in white wine, olive oil, garlic, and lemon, topped with fresh tomato salsa; or try the blackened Black Angus strip steak seared in spicy seasonings topped with citrus butter. For lunch there are sandwiches, salads, and wraps. Children are welcome; casual family atmosphere and fine dining are combined. Overnight accommodations available (14 rooms with private bath; see *Lodging*).

Village Bistro (518-589-5855), 6033 Main Street, Tannersville. ($$) Open for dinner daily, except Wednesday, 5–9:30. There is lots of fine wood and an elegant bar at this renovated eatery, featuring a variety of international favorites. Lunches range from first-rate gyros, burgers, and paninis (grilled chicken, sausage and peppers, and several other options) to corned beef Reuben and shepherd's pie. For dinner make sure to order rack of lamb or the bistro tournedos (filet mignon grilled with French brandy demi-glace)—both are excellent. The extensive menu changes with the seasons. The chef, Edward Lanzinger, is from Europe, and his partner, Shake Kertoyan, has been known for two decades as the gyro lady of Hunter Mountain for the tasty ethnic foods she has sold at the summer festivals. Streamside outdoor dining in warm-weather months.

EATING OUT **Bear Creek Restaurant** (518-263-3839), 4394 Route 214, Hunter. ($) Open daily for lunch and dinner during the summer months from noon; during the winter, open Monday, Tuesday, and Thursday 4–10, Friday through Sunday noon–10. Enjoy hearty soups, sandwiches, burgers, and fries here while overlooking the array of activities. (See *To See—For Families.*) Wine and beer available.

Bell's Café (518-943-4070), 387 Main Street, Catskill. ($) Open for lunch Saturday 11–4; Sunday 9–3. Dinner served Wednesday through Saturday 5–10. Limited days and hours in the winter months. This wonderful bistro serves an array of international dishes with imaginative daily specials. Although it's housed in a historic building with the original tin ceiling (it's more than 100 years old), the atmosphere is reminiscent of a French café. The panini offerings at lunch run the gamut from roast pork to fresh mozzarella and pesto, and they are made with whole-grain bread. There are a number of eclectic salads, as well. Dinner entrées include seared salmon on coconut spinach, fresh tuna, lamb, and homemade pasta. Children welcome.

Beth's Café (518-299-3478), 14548 Route 23, Prattsville. ($) Open daily for breakfast and lunch 5 AM–2 PM. This is an old-fashioned, small-town eatery offering the basics–eggs, waffles, and French toast in the morning, and salads, sandwiches, and burgers in the afternoon. If you are there on Wednesday for lunch, try the stuffed pizza; there is a choice of cheese, meat, or vegetable stuffing. Everything here is made on the premises, including the soups and baked goods. Bring the kids.

Catskill Chocolate Café (518-943-2122), 1 Brandows Alley, Catskill. ($) Open Monday through Thursday 8–7; Friday 8 AM–9 PM; Saturday 9–9; Sunday 10–6. This dessert café is the place to go when you have a hankering for something sweet and a caffeinated beverage to go with it. The handmade chocolates here are all coated and decorated by hand. Fillings are made from scratch with no preservatives. There are peanut butter cups, caramels, nut clusters, and turtles, as well as cookies, napoleons, cannolis, and cupcakes. The certified organic coffee is sourced from Albany, and a variety of Harney's Teas are also offered.

Catskill Mountain Country Store & Restaurant (518-734-3387), 5510 Route 23, Windham. ($) Open Monday, Thursday, and Friday 9–3; Saturday 8–4; Sunday 8–3 (the store itself is open until 6 PM daily). This charming country store/café has a bakery, small petting zoo, and an array of produce and gourmet items on the premises. Enjoy fantastic muffins, breads, pastries, pancakes, omelets, wraps, hearty soups, and all kinds of wonderful treats. My favorite here is the chocolate-cherry French toast. The kids will love this bustling eatery, and if they get impatient waiting for the food to arrive, you can always walk around and visit the animals.

Catskill Mountain Foundation Farm Market and Café (518-263-4908), Hunter Village Square, Main Street, Hunter. ($) Open Thursday through Monday 10–5. Limited hours during winter months. The café serves an array of tasty salads, sandwiches, paninis, and wraps made with fresh local ingredients in season. The baked goods are delicious as well, so don't skip dessert.

Circle W General Store (518-678-3250), 3328 Route 23A, Palenville. ($) Open daily 8–4. This beautifully restored general store is a wonderful place for breakfast or lunch—or to pick up gourmet picnic fare. A few of the sandwich choices include fresh turkey BLT, roast beef with smoked Gouda and caramelized onions, or prosciutto with goat cheese and figs. There are also hearty soups, quiche, and fresh coffee to savor. Organic and local products like fine chocolate, maple syrup, cereals, and jams abound. There is also an impressive selection of regional books. If you are heading up to Hunter on Route 23A, make sure not to miss this gem. You will find something to buy even if you aren't in the mood to shop!

Daly's Coffee Bar (203-979-1224), 5410 Route 23, Windham. ($) Open daily 7–7; extended hours in summer and ski season. This coffee bar serves up cappuccino, espresso, café au lait, hot chocolate, chai, cider, smoothies, frappes, and more. There are brownies, scones, cakes, and cookies, and soups and chili for those who want more solid fare. The atmosphere is laid-back and casual, so enjoy the mountain views and relax. This is the perfect place to stop after a day of skiing.

Frank Guido's Port of Call (518-943-5088), 7 Main Street, Catskill. ($$) Open for dinner Monday 4–10; for lunch and dinner Tuesday through Sunday 11:30–10. Located on the Hudson River, this is a great spot to enjoy drinks outdoors in warm weather. For those who choose to arrive by boat, there is free dockage at the restaurant's marina. Basic American fare is served here, including steaks, seafood, pasta, and burgers.

Last Chance Antiques and Cheese Café (518-589-6424), Main Street,

Tannersville. ($) Open daily 11–9, but hours vary in the spring and fall, when they are open on weekends only. This retail gourmet store, antiques shop, and café all in one offers up some of the best homemade soups you will find in the county. There are cheeses, chocolates, quiche, huge sandwiches, and salads that make this a wonderful place to go for a meal or take-out. Children welcome. A new addition adjoining the Last Chance is **The Tavern,** a bar/nightclub where there is often live music on Friday and Saturday nights, and food is served until midnight.

MAMBO! Mission Style Burritos (518-731-2012), 18 Hope Plaza, West Coxsackie. ($) Opened in 2012, this has become a Mexican culinary hot spot in the northern Catskills. There is only space to seat 12 people, but the most expensive items on the menu are $8. The mainstays here are tacos and burritos, and diners can personalize their wraps. There are also several choices for vegans and vegetarians. Make sure to try the grapefruit guacamole! Children welcome.

Pancho Villa's Mexican Restaurant (518-589-5134), 6037 Main Street, Tannersville. ($) Open for lunch and dinner Friday through Sunday noon–10; Sunday until 9. Monday, Wednesday, and Thursday for dinner only 4–10. Closed Tuesday and for two weeks in mid-April. Mexican favorites including burritos, tacos, quesadillas, enchiladas, and tamales served in a festive yet informal atmosphere. Children welcome.

Washington Irving Inn (518-589-5560), 6629 Route 23A, Hunter. ($) Open for breakfast Saturday and Sunday 8–10, for afternoon tea 2–5. A fantastic full breakfast is served here, complete with homemade breads, pastries, and croissants. Diners can enjoy buttermilk pancakes topped with locally produced maple syrup, fluffy French toast, or sizzling bacon and eggs prepared to your taste. Chef-owner Stefania Jozic has restored the mansion housing the restaurant to its turn-of-the-20th-century splendor. The dining room is filled with fine silver and china collected from antiques shops throughout the Catskills. An eclectic mix of china fits in nicely with the Victorian motif. The large variety of teas is sure to please every taste, and the mélange of treats that accompanies the soothing beverage will provide sustenance for a relaxing afternoon repast with an old friend or a new lover.

✷ Entertainment

Altamura Center for Arts and Culture (518-622-0070; www.altocanto.org), 404 Winter Clove Road, Round Top. Open Memorial Day weekend through Labor Day. The charismatic founder of this philanthropic center offers amazing theater (including Shakespeare), opera, jazz, concerts, and a variety of cultural events during the summertime in Round Top. Carmela Bucceri Altamura, a former child musical prodigy, also organizes a voice competition. Check the website for a schedule of events.

The Catskill Mountain Foundation (518-263-4908; www.catskillmtn.org), Route 23A (7950 Main Street), Hunter. This nonprofit organization has revitalized the town of Hunter. Stop in at the film and performing arts center, bookstore, and gallery on Main Street and pick up a current schedule of events that include classical, folk, and jazz concerts; dance performances; a film series; art exhibits; poetry readings; festivals (see *Special Events*); and more. This is the center to find out what is happening culturally in the mountaintop region.

It's a good idea to check their website if you're planning a visit and want to include some cultural events.

Doctorow Center for the Arts (518-263-2063; www.catskillmtn.org), Main Street, Hunter. This performance center has a theater that seats 160 as well as three film auditoriums. In addition to showcasing films, it is a venue for children's theater, puppet shows, and musical performances.

Dutchman's Landing (518-943-3830), Catskill Point, Main Street, Catskill. This area once served as a boat landing for Hudson River craft, and today visitors can enjoy spectacular views of the river and eastern shore. You will find a farmers' market and crafts market weekends from summer through fall, displays of the river and cultural history of the Catskills, travel information, a picnic and dining area, and entertainment. A great place to start a tour of Greene County, and one of the easiest access areas to the Hudson River for nonboaters who just want to enjoy the area.

Greene Room Players (518-589-6297; www.greeneroomplayers.org), P.O. Box 535, Hunter 12442. This theater group has been presenting professional musicals, revues, children's shows, comedies, and drama for more than 10 years now. The performances are given year-round. There are play readings, stand-up comedy, cabaret, and musical events at the Dancing Bear Theater in the village.

Hi-Way Drive-In (518-731-8672), 10769 Route 9W, Coxsackie. Open March through mid-October, daily 6 PM–midnight. Located between Catskill and Coxsackie, this drive-in has good quality sound and shows first-run films. It's a fun way to watch a movie in the warm weather months, especially if you have kids. There are four screens here with four different options. The snack bar offers popcorn, hot dogs, and other expected treats.

Steven E. Greenstein Piano Collection (518-263-2036), 7971 Main Street, Hunter. Open Memorial Day through Labor Day, Friday and Saturday noon–4 or by appointment. This one-of-a-kind collection of historic pianos and musical artifacts showcases early and modern keyboard instruments, tuning tools, piano shawls, and much more. A visit here offers unique insight into the development of pianos in Europe and America over the past four centuries. For those interested, make sure to also see the Pleshakov Piano Museum in Hudson (see *To See* in "Columbia County").

Windham Chamber Music Festival (518-734-3868; www.windhammusic.com), 740 County Route 32C, Windham. The former Presbyterian church on Main Street in Windham (built in 1826) is the perfect venue for this series of chamber music performances; the acoustics are superb. The directors of this festival, Robert Manno and Magdalena Golczewski, were both musicians with the Metropolitan Opera for many years. Manno is also a composer and has written more than 30 chamber works. The festival features top-notch soloists (including a variety of musicians and opera singers), and the ticket prices are exceedingly reasonable. Performances take place May through September; call or check the website for a schedule.

✷ Selective Shopping

Greene County's towns and villages have some terrific gift shops. The following are some of my favorite places to find unusual items for the home and garden, as well as the kids.

Catskill Mountain Country Store (518-734-3387), 5510 Route 23, Windham. Open Monday through Friday

9–6; Saturday and Sunday 8–6. In addition to the eatery (see *Eating Out*) and looking zoo at this busy hub in town, the gift shop here sells candy, toys, maple syrup, and other local products. There are mugs, metal art, wooden signs, bear wood sculptures, and all kinds of handmade art.

Mahalo (518-943-7467), 397 Main Street, Catskill. Open Monday through Saturday 10–6; Memorial Day weekend through Columbus Day, also Sunday noon–5. This warm inviting shop is chock-full of eclectic giftware, including home decor, handbags, candles, regional books, and more. The emphasis is on handmade items created by local craftspeople and artists.

Village Square Bookstore & Gallery (518-263-2050), 7950 Main Street, Hunter. Open Thursday through Monday 10–5; Saturday until 6. This bookstore is located in a spacious, well-lighted building that is wonderful for browsing. Their Catskill books and children's sections are among the best you will find anywhere. On the opposite side of the building is an art gallery featuring the work of local artisans and includes glassware, jewelry, paintings, and more.

ANTIQUES Greene County offers the antiques lover everything from the funky to the fabulous, although with a small range of shops, auctions, and flea markets. Some establishments are open year-round, but most tend to have limited hours in the off-season, so call before you go.

American Gothic Antiques (518-263-4836), Route 23A, Hunter, stocks a wonderful array of antique lamps and accessories, as well as many other items. They are open by appointment only.

The Coxsackie Antique Center (518-731-8888), 12400 Route 9W, New Baltimore, is open daily 10–8, with wares ranging from glass and lamps to books and postcards.

Kings of Old Antiques (518-734-5768), 5316 Route 23 (Main Street), Windham. Open Thursday through Monday 10–5. There are two floors of collectibles here filled with old farm signs, postcards, vinyl records, and more. There are also the original signs from the Catskill Game Farm. A fun place to browse.

ART GALLERIES Greene County has a wealth of artists and art galleries, but many places are open only by chance or by appointment. For further information on their offerings, contact the **Greene County Council on the Arts** (518-943-3400), 398 Main Street, Catskill. The council also operates two crafts galleries that represent regional artists, so ask for a calendar of exhibits and events or go to their website (www.greenearts.org).

Sugar Maples Center for Arts and Education (518-263-4104), 29 Big Hollow Road, Maplecrest. This community resource, owned and operated by the Catskill Mountain Foundation, offers a variety of classes in fine arts, crafts, ceramics, jewelry, natural agriculture farming, painting, sculpture, and woodworking. There are arts programs for young people in renovated facilities. Check the website for full schedule (www.catskillmtn.org/sugarmaples).

Two of my own favorite galleries in Greene County: **Stanley Maltzman's Four Corners Art Gallery** (518-634-7386), 3392 Gayhead Road, Freehold. Stanley is a nationally renowned, award-winning artist who works in the Hudson River Valley tradition. He has drawings, pastels, watercolors, and lithographs for sale at his studio, but call in advance for an appointment. The other is **Windham Fine Arts** (518-734-6850), 5380 Main Street, Windham. This traditional fine-arts gallery has exhibits of local and regional artists that change every month. Open Friday through Monday and holidays noon–5.

✷ Special Events

From spring through autumn, fairs and festivals abound throughout Greene County. **Greene County Promotion Department** (1-800-355-CATS; www.greatnortherncatskills.com) can supply you with a complete calendar of special events to coincide with your stay there. The following are just some of my favorite celebrations held annually in the county.

April: **Tap New York Craft Beer & Food Festival** (518-263-4223), Hunter Mountain, Route 23A, Hunter. Admission fee. The festival is usually held the last weekend in April, Saturday 1–5; Sunday noon–4. No one under the age of 21 will be admitted. Fine beers produced by over 30 of New York State's craft breweries may be sampled here, along with all kinds of food. The event is a huge draw and gets extremely crowded as the afternoon progresses. To avoid long lines for tasting, make sure to arrive early.

May: **East Durham Annual Irish Music Festival** (518-634-2286/2319), Michael J. Quill Irish Cultural & Sports Centre, 2119 Route 145, East Durham. Enjoy two days of Ireland in America with musical entertainment and activities for all ages.

May through September: **Cat'n Around Catskill** (518-043-0989), Main Street, Catskill. Free. This summer-long celebration showcases the talent of local artisans who create imaginative fiberglass cat sculptures displayed throughout Main Street. In the fall these cats are auctioned off at a town fund-raiser, with a percentage of the proceeds going to the artist and the remainder to the town. Make sure to walk up and down Main Street (on both sides of the street) to see dozens of these amazing creations.

June: **Annual Bavarian Summerfest** (518-622-9584), Riedlbauer's Resort, 43 Ravine Drive, Round Top. This annual festival has been taking place since 1992 and is usually held the third weekend in June (both Saturday and Sunday noon–10). Enjoy Bavarian bands and German American food and drink. **Greene County Historical Society Tour of Homes** (518-756-8805; 518-731-6490). The location changes every year, so call ahead. Picnic lunches are offered for sale, and tickets usually cost about $20. It's a wonderful opportunity to visit a dozen or so historic homes and support the county historical society.

July: **Independence Day Parade & Fireworks** (518-734-3852), Windham. There is a parade through town at 7 in the evening ending at Windham Mountain followed by an outdoor barbecue and fireworks at sunset. **Music in the Park and 4th of July Fireworks** (518-943-0989), Dutchmen's Landing, Main Street, Catskill. There is live music sponsored by the Village of Catskill and fireworks following the outdoor concert at sunset. **Grey Fox Bluegrass Festival** (1-888-946-8495; www.greyfoxbluegrass.com), Walsh Farm, 141 County Route 22, Oak Hill. This four-day outdoor music festival features award-winning bluegrass and acoustic music with performances on four stages. There are food and craft vendors as well as music workshops. On-site camping available, as well as day tickets. The festival begins at noon on a Wednesday in mid-July and runs through the weekend. Check the website for current information. **Greene**

County Youth Fair (518-313-9333; www.greenecountyyouthfair.com), Cairo. Thursday through Sunday; hours vary. Kids will love this fair that is full of competitions, live animals, rides, food vendors, and more. **Athens Street Festival** (518-945-1551), Riverfront Park, Athens. This daylong festival (10 AM–11 PM) on the Hudson River includes vendors, food, and entertainment. A great family outing.

August: **International Celtic Festival** (1-888-486-8376), Hunter Ski Bowl, Route 23A, Hunter. Admission fee. This celebration of Celtic spirit transforms Hunter Mountain into the Emerald Isle. The weekend is filled with caber tosses, border collie sheepherding demonstrations, entertainment, food, crafts, and a pipe and band competition.

September: **Catskill Mountain Thunder Motorcycle Festival** (518-634-2541), Blackthorne Resort, 348 Sunside Road, East Durham. Admission fee. This shindig lasts from 9 AM until the wee hours of the morning. All bike brands are welcome at the vendor expo. There are fireworks, an antique bicycle exhibit, fashion show, parade, and rodeo games. **Leeds Irish Festival** (518-943-3736), Leeds Festival Fair Grounds, Route 23B, Leeds. Enjoy Irish music and dancing with bands from Ireland. For those who enjoy Irish traditional music.

October: **Oktoberfest** (1-888-486-8376), Hunter Mountain, Route 23A, Hunter. The mountains are magnificent in autumn and provide a colorful backdrop for musical entertainment from Germany, craftspeople selling their wares, hayrides, and an array of children's activities. It all takes place at Hunter Mountain.

7 Albany

Courtesy of the Albany County Convention & Visitors Bureau; albany.org

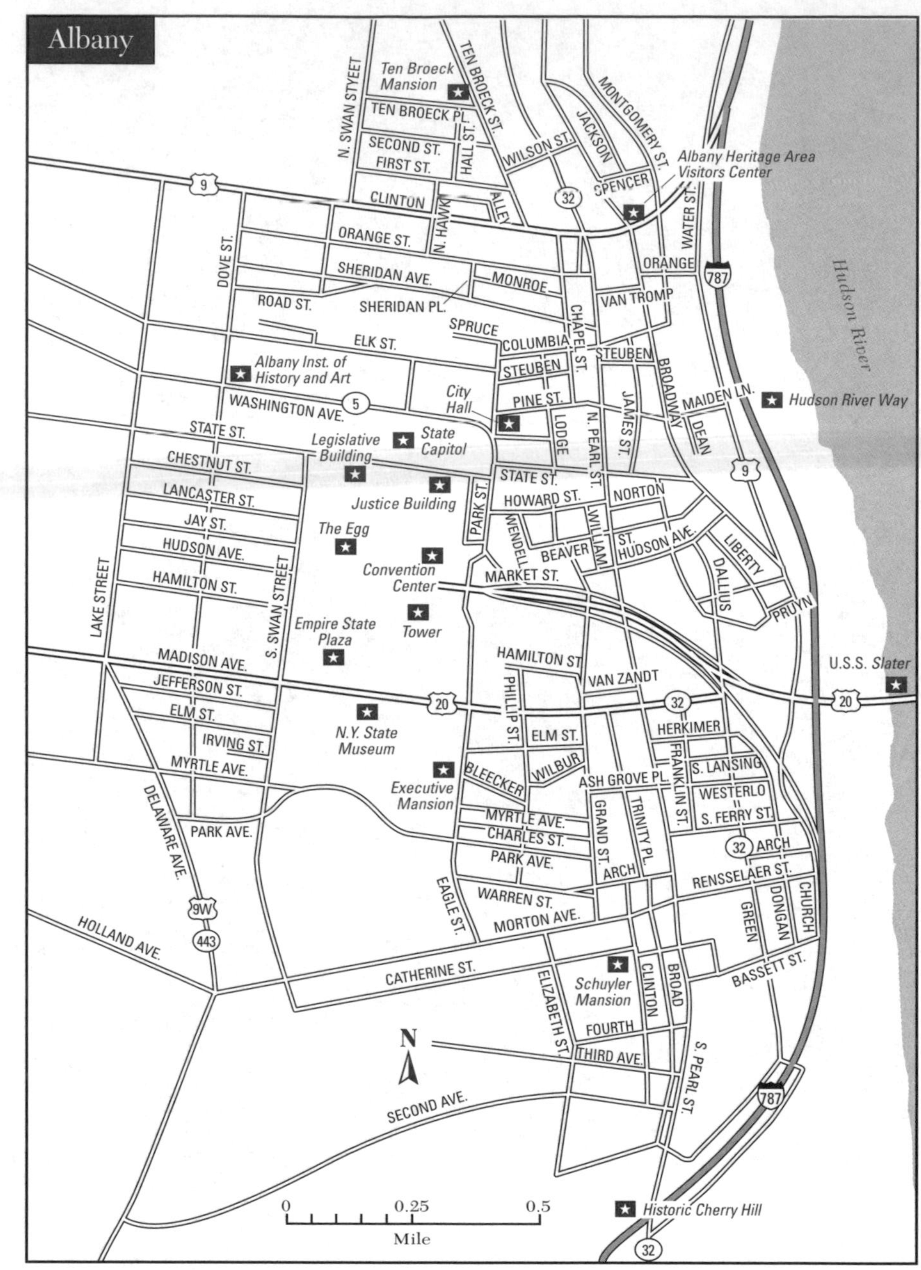
Albany
Ten Broeck Mansion
Albany Heritage Area Visitors Center
Hudson River
Albany Inst. of History and Art
City Hall
Hudson River Way
Legislative Building
State Capitol
Justice Building
The Egg
Convention Center
Empire State Plaza
Tower
U.S.S. Slater
N.Y. State Museum
Executive Mansion
Schuyler Mansion
Historic Cherry Hill
N
0
0.25
0.5
Mile
N. SWAN STYEET
TEN BROECK ST.
TEN BROECK PL.
SECOND ST.
FIRST ST.
HALL ST.
WILSON ST.
JACKSON
MONTGOMERY ST.
SPENCER
WATER ST.
CLINTON
N. HAWK
ALLEY
ORANGE ST.
ORANGE
DOVE ST.
SHERIDAN AVE.
MONROE
VAN TROMP
ROAD ST.
SHERIDAN PL.
SPRUCE
ELK ST.
COLUMBIA
CHAPEL ST.
STEUBEN
BROADWAY
MAIDEN LN.
WASHINGTON AVE.
PINE ST.
LODGE
N. PEARL ST.
JAMES ST.
DEAN
STATE ST.
CHESTNUT ST.
LANCASTER ST.
PARK ST.
HOWARD ST.
NORTON
JAY ST.
WENDELL
WILLIAM
HUDSON AVE.
BEAVER
ST.
LIBERTY
HAMILTON ST.
S. SWAN STREET
MARKET ST.
DALLIUS
PRUYN
LAKE STREET
MADISON AVE.
HAMILTON ST
VAN ZANDT
JEFFERSON ST.
PHILLIP ST.
ELM ST.
HERKIMER
IRVING ST.
FRANKLIN ST.
S. LANSING
MYRTLE AVE.
BLEECKER
WILBUR
ASH GROVE PL.
WESTERLO
DELAWARE AVE.
GRAND ST.
TRINITY PL.
S. FERRY ST.
PARK AVE.
CHARLES ST.
ARCH
RENSSELAER ST.
EAGLE ST.
WARREN ST.
GREEN
DONGAN
CHURCH
HOLLAND AVE.
MORTON AVE.
CATHERINE ST.
ELIZABETH ST.
BROAD
BASSETT ST.
FOURTH
THIRD AVE.
S. PEARL ST.
SECOND AVE.
9
32
787
5
20
9W
443

ALBANY

Albany is the oldest chartered city in the United States. It is also the second oldest continually inhabited settlement in the country. Long before Albany received its city charter, granted July 22, 1686, by Governor Thomas Duggan, the settlement was an important river stop and trading center. After Henry Hudson visited the region in 1609, Albany's fertile valleys and abundant game attracted Dutch settlers. Albany was to become a city of tremendous contrast—stagecoaches and steamboats, muddy roads and medical colleges, farmers and politicians. But through a combination of pride, pluck, and foresight, Albany has made the best of it all. A visit to the city today can focus on many things—history, politics, art, architecture—and can be made at any time of year. Spring brings the blossoming of thousands of tulips, pools of color that reflect Albany's Dutch origins. The Pinksterfest, a weekend celebration in May, welcomes the warm weather in the Dutch tradition, and the city parks come alive with fairs and shows. In summer the great Empire State Plaza becomes a unique combination of outdoor park, art gallery, and seat of government, and autumn turns out to be a perfect time to explore the city on foot and discover the tiny side streets that still remain from three centuries ago. Winter ushers in Victorian greenery displays, snow festivals, and the lighting of the state Christmas tree. Whatever the season, be prepared to discover an area where the past and future coexist.

GUIDANCE **Albany County Convention and Visitors Bureau** (518-434-1217), 25 Quackenbush Square, Albany 12207; www.albany.org.

GETTING THERE *By car:* The city is located off exits 23 and 24 of I-87 (NYS Thruway); watch for signs.

By bus: **Adirondack Trailways** (1-800-858-8555; www.trailwaysny.com) runs several buses daily to the city of Albany from the Port Authority Bus Terminal in Manhattan.

By train: **Amtrak** (518-462-5763; 1-800-872-7245; www.amtrak.com) service is available to 525 East Street in Rensselaer, just across the river from Albany. Trains leave from Penn Station in Manhattan.

By air: **Albany International Airport** (518-242-2222; www.albanyairport.com), 737 Albany Shaker Road, is located at exit 4 off the Northway (take the NYS

Thruway to exit 24; pick up the Northway there at exit 1N just after passing through the tollbooth).

MEDICAL EMERGENCY **Albany Medical Center** (518-262-3125), 43 New Scotland Avenue.

Albany Memorial Hospital (518-471-3221), 600 Northern Boulevard.

St. Peter's Hospital (518-525-1550), 315 South Manning Boulevard.

Urgent Care Center (518-783-3110), Capital Region Health Park, 711 Troy-Schenectady Road, Latham. Open Monday through Friday 5 PM–midnight; Saturday and Sunday 10–8. This facility sees patients in the evening hours or weekends.

✷ To See

Albany Heritage Area Visitors Center and Henry Hudson Planetarium (518-434-0405; 1-800-258-3582; www.albany.org), 25 Quackenbush Square. Open daily 10–4. Free. This site offers guests a series of changing exhibits, interactive displays that highlight history and culture in the capital city and provide an overview of the region. The planetarium features star shows on the third Saturday of the month at 11 for young children and at 1 for older children and adults; A permanent exhibit highlighting Albany's role in the Underground Railroad is open to the public at the visitors center. It is the only permanent exhibit in the capital and offers a glimpse into local and state connections to the Underground Railroad.

AERIAL VIEW OF THE CITY OF ALBANY

Courtesy of the Albany County Convention & Visitors Bureau; albany.org

If you are interested in seeing downtown Albany on foot, download a free **walking tour** to an MP3 player or smartphone for a personally guided tour. Go to www.albany.org for instructions. There are two versions of the walking tour from which to choose. The full-length version takes in the Empire State Plaza, the capitol, and the surrounding neighborhood. The shorter route leads to the steps of the capitol and returns to the visitors center. There is also a printed brochure available that takes walkers through four centuries of Albany history by way of its buildings and streets. The tour begins at the visitors center where an exhibit features highlights from the city's past.

The Albany Institute of History and Art (518-463-4478; www.albanyinstitute.org), 125 Washington Avenue. Admission fee. Open year-round, Wednesday through Saturday 10–5; Sunday noon–5. Founded in 1791, this exceptional museum is one of the oldest in the country, and it is still providing visitors with a chance to see varied, changing exhibits that focus on the Hudson Valley's cultural history. The building is a graceful collection of individual galleries and sweeping staircases, and there is even a small display area in the entrance hall. The institute's collections include fine European porcelain and glass; Dutch furniture, paintings, and decorative arts from the early settlement period in Albany; pewter and silver produced by local smiths in the 18th century; and breathtaking examples of the Hudson River School of painting. The Dutch Room offers an interesting look into early Albany family life. Be sure to see the Egyptian Room on the lower level, where human and animal mummies rest along with some of their prized belongings. Changing exhibits are featured throughout the year.

THE ALBANY INSTITUTE OF HISTORY AND ART

Courtesy of the Albany County Convention & Visitors Bureau; albany.org

Albany Pine Bush Discovery Center (518-456-0655), 195 New Karner Road, Albany. Free. Open year-round, Tuesday through Friday 9–4; Saturday, Sunday, and holiday Mondays 10–4. Constructed in 1987, the building was once a local bank. New York State acquired the facility and added solar panels, a composting toilet system, native landscape restoration, a discovery trail, and various exhibits. There are several hands-on activities for children here, but the center is dedicated to educating everyone about the natural and cultural history of the Albany pine bush. The center received a LEED gold rating, making it one of the nation's most advanced in design, construction, and operation of high-performance green buildings.

The Albany Trolley (518-462-3825; www.albanyaquaducks.com), Visitors Center, 25 Quackenbush Square. Open daily June through Labor Day. Reservations recommended. Free parking. This is a great way to see the historic sites of the city during the summer months and to get oriented upon arrival. A narrated tour tells the story of the city and the legends behind several stately landmarks and important attractions. All tours begin with a film, *Albany: A Cultural Crossroads.*

Irish American Heritage Museum (518-427-1916; www.irishamericanheritage museum.org), 370 Broadway, Albany. Open year-round, Wednesday through Saturday 11–4; Sunday noon–4. Tours may be arranged at other times by appointment. Admission fee. The many exhibits here reveal the impact of Irish heritage in America. There are also videos, lectures, educational programs, and special events throughout the season, so check the website for a schedule.

New York State Museum (518-474-5877; www.nysm.nysed.gov), Madison Avenue, Empire State Plaza. To reach the Plaza, take exit 23 off the NYS Thruway. Pick up I-787, and get off at the Empire State Plaza exit. Open year-round, except national holidays, Monday through Saturday 9:30–5. Free. Today it anchors one end of the Empire State Plaza, but the museum has been a part of the state's history since 1836, making it one of the oldest state museums in the country. It is not, however, a dusty old repository with outdated displays of rocks and unidentified bones. This museum is alive with multimedia presentations that allow visitors to experience everything from a thunderstorm to a Lower East Side pushcart alley of the 1920s. The permanent exhibits include "Adirondack Wilderness," which explores the natural history of that region; "New York Metropolis," which focuses on New York City and the surrounding counties (here you will find a Duke Ellington–era A train and a set from *Sesame Street*); and displays that focus on Native American life and the ice age in the Empire State. A moving September 11th exhibit was installed in 2002. Another relatively recent addition is the second-floor exhibit that has a huge carousel and an old-fashioned soda fountain, depicting life in an era long past. Changing exhibits may feature folk art, dinosaurs, giant insects, or contemporary art and fine crafts, and shows are given in the museum's theater. Special events are scheduled all year; you may get to enjoy a Victorian holiday in December.

U.S.S. *Slater* Destroyer Escort-766 (518-431-1943; www.ussslater.org), the Snowdock at Broadway and Quay, at the foot of Madison Avenue. Exit 3B off I-787 South. Open April through November, Wednesday through Sunday 10–4. Admission fee. Step back in time aboard the last Destroyer Escort warship still in World War II battle configuration. See how the crew lived and carried out its mission of antisubmarine warfare. Armament, combat-information and radio rooms, pilot house, galley, mess, officers' quarters, and crew's sleeping area are authentically restored. Military-history buffs will enjoy this stop.

HISTORIC HOMES **Historic Cherry Hill** (518-434-4791; www.historiccherry hill.org), 523½ South Pearl Street. Open April through December; call for times of tours, which are on the hour but change seasonally. Admission fee. Built in 1787 by Philip Van Rensselaer to replace what was called the Old Mansion, this Georgian house was the centerpiece of a 900-acre farm. Cherry Hill remained in the family for five generations, until 1963, and provides the visitor with a rare picture of the growth and care of a home over 176 years. The farm has, of course, disappeared under Albany streets, and the view across the road is now of oil tanks instead of orchards, but the house itself still offers a sense of grace and elegance. A visit begins in the basement orientation center, where a wall chart untangles the complicated series of marriages and relationships that kept Cherry Hill in the family. Upstairs, many of the 31 rooms have not been restored to match one particular period but contain the designs, belongings, and personal touches of their inhabitants. The collections found here are irreplaceable as a record of America's social history. There are more than 150 chairs, more than 30 tables, and thousands (20,000 at last count) of decorative objects, which include 18th-century paintings, 19th-century Oriental export ware, and even 20th-century clothing. Although the house was modernized over the years, things such as heating ducts and plumbing are carefully hidden away. Cherry Hill is a special place, chock-full of New York history and spirit. A holiday tour is usually offered in December; call to check the exact dates.

Schuyler Mansion (518-434-0834; www.nysparks.com), 32 Catherine Street. Open year-round for tours by appointment only. Admission fee. Once home to Philip Schuyler, a general in the Revolutionary War, the Schuyler Mansion was completed in 1764 on a rolling plot of land known as the Dutch Church Pasture. Schuyler was an important figure during the war, and many well-known statesmen, including Washington, Franklin, and the defeated English general John Burgoyne, visited the mansion over the years. During the war, Schuyler's daughter married Alexander Hamilton here, and a kidnap attempt was later made against her by the Tories; a gash on the wooden banister is said to have been made by a kidnapper's tomahawk. The house did not remain in the family after Schuyler's death but passed through a succession of owners before being purchased by New York State in 1912. Although numerous changes have been made to the exterior of the house over the years, including the removal of all the outbuildings, visitors can still see many examples of 18th-century furniture, glassware, pottery, and art as well as Schuyler family possessions.

Ten Broeck Mansion (518-436-9826; www.historic-albany.org), 9 Ten Broeck Place. Open year-round, daily 10–4 for tours, by appointment only. Admission fee. Home of the Albany County Historical Association, this Federal mansion was built in 1798 for Gen. Abraham Ten Broeck, who was a member of the Continental Congress and fought in the nearby battle of Saratoga. Once called Arbor Hill, the house now offers a look at the lifestyle of Albany's upper class during the last two centuries. Exhibits include period furniture and decorative items, and the house also contains a wine cellar, which when rediscovered during renovations was found to have a valuable collection of very aged wines!

HISTORIC SITES **Executive Mansion** (518-473-7521), 138 Eagle Street. One-hour tours are offered Thursday 10–2, on the hour, but call at least two weeks in advance for reservations during the busy summer and autumn months. Closed during the months of July and August. This mansion is tucked down a side street just around the block from the Empire State Plaza. Built in 1850 as a private home, it now serves as the governor's residence. The tour covers the public rooms, which are filled with art from the 18th through the 20th centuries.

Courtesy of the Albany County Convention & Visitors Bureau; albany.org

TEN BROECK MANSION

State Capitol (518-474-2418; www.ogs.ny.gov), located at the State Street end of the Empire State Plaza. Open for tours year-round, Monday through Friday at 10 AM, noon, 2, and 3. Tours leave from the Empire State Plaza visitors center on the concourse of the Plaza. This fairy-tale building, with its red towers and hundreds of arched windows, is one of the few state capitols not topped by a dome. Construction, completed in 1899, took more than 30 years and cost the then-unheard-of sum of $25 million. This is where the state senate and assembly meet, and where you will find the governor's offices once used by Theodore Roosevelt, Nelson Rockefeller, and Franklin D. Roosevelt. Throughout the building are thousands of fine stone carvings, a tradition that can be traced back to the great churches of the Middle Ages. Many were caricatures of famous politicians and writers; others were of the families and relatives of the artisans; still others were self-portraits of the stone carvers themselves. But the most compelling carvings are the ones that form the **Million Dollar Staircase,** which took years to complete and is the best known of all the capitol's embellishments. Another unusual architectural feature is the senate fireplaces: The huge chimneys did not draw well, so the fireplaces' original function was abandoned in favor of using them as private "discussion nooks." And if you enjoy military history, don't miss the small military museum here; it traces the history of the state militia and National Guard. Flower lovers should make a special point of visiting the Capitol Park in spring, when thousands of tulips blaze into red and yellow bloom.

WALKING TOURS There is so much to see in this historic city that a walk down just about any street will give you a glimpse into Albany's colorful past.

The **Hudson River Way** opened for all to enjoy on August 10, 2002, extending from Broadway at Maiden Lane, over I-787, to the **Corning Riverfront Park** and amphitheater (see *Green Space*). This magnificent pedestrian walkway was designed to connect downtown Albany to the shores of the historic Hudson River, and also to tell the story of Albany through a series of paintings depicting historical artifacts. Created by mural principal artist Jan Marie Spanard and her talented crew, the paintings adorn the two staircase landings and the 30 lampposts that line both sides of the bridge. The story begins hundreds of millions of years ago when Albany was at the bottom of a prehistoric sea. As you progress over the bridge, the story continues through time and includes the early Dutch merchants and other scenes of historic importance. There are two large murals on the landings that divide the three flights of the grand staircase. The paintings are done in a permanent liquid stone paint called "keim" that will not fade, peel, or change for decades. Although this isn't a tour for people with young children, I recommend a walk over the pedestrian bridge for visitors who can walk stairs and don't mind the river breezes (beware that they can be quite brisk in the cool-weather months).

The following are not specific city tours, but rather suggestions for starting points on an Albany exploration:

An example of a 19th-century row-house community, the **Pastures Historic District** is bounded roughly by Morton and Second avenues and Elizabeth and Pearl streets. Here you will also find the Schuyler Mansion (see *Historic Homes*) as well as many impressive private homes. The **Mansion Historic District,** bounded by Eagle, Dongan, Hamilton, and Ferry streets, is a kaleidoscope of building styles, Italianate, Federal, and Greek Revival being only a few. Although the area became run-down earlier in the 20th century, people have been rediscovering the richness of the district, and there is a sense of renewal here. The **Center Square–Hudson**

STATE CAPITOL

Courtesy of the Albany County Convention & Visitors Bureau; albany.org

Park Historic District, bounded by South Swan Street, Madison Avenue, South Lake Street, and Spring Street, is the largest historic district. Its centerpiece is **Washington Park,** a 90-acre area that once served as parade grounds and cemetery. Throughout the park you will find statues, lovely flower beds, and a lake (see *Green Space*). The district itself has scores of restored houses and commercial buildings.

For a schedule of walking tours of **Underground Railroad sites** in the downtown area, call 518-432-4432. There are some fascinating ones, and they are located throughout the city.

✷ To Do

BICYCLING The Mohawk Hudson Bikeway (1-800-258-3582). This 41-mile bike path is one of the area's most popular recreational features, traveling along the Hudson and Mohawk rivers and connecting the areas of Albany, Schenectady, and Troy. For those who prefer other means of travel, rollerblading is also permitted here. To access the bikeway, head to the **Corning Preserve,** along the west bank of the Hudson River. (Take exit 23 off the NYS Thruway and pick up I-787 north to exit 4. Follow the signs for Colonie Street.) The bikeway also includes the **Colonie Riverfront Bike-Hike Trail** (518-783-2760), a 5.5-mile trail that runs along the Mohawk River; the **Niskayuna Riverfront Bike-Hike Trail** (518-372-2519), a 7-mile paved path built on an old railroad bed along the Mohawk River; and the **Rotterdam Riverfront Hike-Bike Trail** (518-386-2225), a 7-mile paved path.

CENTER SQUARE–HUDSON PARK HISTORIC DISTRICT
Courtesy of the Albany County Convention & Visitors Bureau; albany.org

BOAT CRUISES Dutch Apple Cruises, Inc. (518-463-0220; www.dutchapplecruises.com), 141 Broadway. River tours daily, April through October; there are two-hour sightseeing cruises or three-hour dinner cruises available on a tour boat that holds 145 people. Reasonable prices; discounts for children and seniors.

FARM MARKETS Empire State Plaza Farmers' Market (518-457-7076), Empire State Plaza. Open July through October, Wednesday and Friday 11–2. Approximately 20 vendors gather on the Plaza to sell fruits, vegetables, baked goods, honey, maple syrup, and other local produce in season. During the winter months the market moves indoors to the concourse of the Plaza and is open on Wednesday 11–2.

Goold Orchards (518-732-7317), 1297 Brookview Station Road, Castleton. Head across the Route 9 and 20 Bridge into Rensselaer County and down Route 9 (follow the GOOLD ORCHARDS signs) for pick-your-own apples and raspberries in September. The farm store and bakery offer homemade cider doughnuts and fresh-pressed cider, and an array of fruit pies and cookies, all made fresh on the premises. The bakery is open Labor Day through November. The store is open year-round for apples and cider. The Brookview Station Winery produces five white wines, including seyval blanc, a blush, and four reds (the merlot and meritage are quite good). Their Whistle Stop White won an award for the best Hudson River region wine in 2007. The semidry pear and peach wines are interesting additions to their wine list. This winery is definitely worth a detour.

Lansing's Farm Market (518-464-0889), 204 Lishakill Road, Colonie. Open daily 9–6. (Take NYS Thruway to exit 24, then pick up Route 5 west to Lishakill Road.) Pick your own strawberries here in June. Other goodies on sale in the market include tomatoes, corn, peppers, squash, and all other fruits and vegetables grown on the Lansing farm in season. This eighth-generation family farm was founded in 1788, and their doughnuts, breads, and homemade pies are first-rate.

Shaker Shed Farm Market & Greenhouse (518-869-3662), 945 Watervliet Shaker Road, Colonie. (Take the NYS Thruway to exit 24; pick up the Northway to exit 4, make a left off the exit and another left onto Albany-Shaker Road—staying to the left. You will pass the airport. At the stop sign, make a left. The market is over the hill on the left side of the road.) Open Easter through Christmas, daily 9–6. Pick your own tomatoes here in late August. The market offers home-grown produce, crafts, candles, and fresh pies. Enjoy a drink and dessert in the café. During the spring months there are plants galore; at Christmas, a nice selection of wreaths and trees.

GOLF **Capital Hills at Albany** (518-438-2208), 65 O'Neil Road, Albany. This 18-hole, par-71 public course, owned by the city of Albany, is the only place to golf in the capital. For walkers who accompany golfers to this course, there is a 2.6-mile trail that wends its way through wooded areas. Open mid-March to mid-November, weather permitting. Call in advance for tee time. Restaurant, full bar, driving range.

Mill Road Acres (518-785-4653), 30 Mill Road, Latham. This 18-hole, par-58 public course is open April through October. There is equipment rental and senior discounts. Restaurant and snack bar on the premises.

Town of Colonie Golf Course (518-374-4181), 418 Consaul Road, Colonie. This 36-hole, par-72 course is open April through October. Call two days ahead to ensure a tee time if you are a resident of Colonie; otherwise, there are no reservations. There is equipment rental and a driving range. Restaurant, full bar, snack bar on the premises.

ICE SKATING Albany County Hockey Training Facility (518-452-7396; www.albanycounty.com), Albany-Shaker Road, Albany. Open year-round, except the months of May and June, for both figure skating and hockey. There are public sessions for figure skating. Snack bar on premises.

Empire State Plaza (518-474-8860), Outdoor Plaza, Albany. Outdoor skating in the winter months, weather permitting.

Swinburne Rink and Recreation Center (518-438-2406), Clinton Avenue below Manning Boulevard, Albany. Outdoor skating rink, but call before you go for time of sessions; keep in mind that the schedule is weather-dependent here.

SPECTATOR SPORTS Albany Devils (528-487-2000; www.albanydevils.com), American Hockey League–New Jersey Devils affiliate, Times Union Center, 51 South Pearl Street, Albany. The season runs from October through April for hockey, and the website lists a complete schedule.

Siena Saints Basketball (518-487-2000; www.sienasaints.com), Division 1 College Basketball, Times Union Center, 51 South Pearl Street, Albany. Check the website for a schedule of games.

✷ Green Space

Corning Riverfront Park (1-800-258-3582). This section of the Corning Preserve lies along the west bank of the Hudson River. (To get there, take exit 23 off the NYS Thruway; pick up I-787, and get off at exit 4. Follow signs for Colonie Street.) This is a delightful park where strollers will enjoy walking along the river. Rollerskaters and bikers can pick up the Mohawk Hudson Bikeway here and enjoy miles of paths (see *To Do—Bicycling*).

Governor Nelson A. Rockefeller Empire State Plaza (518-473-0559; 1-877-659-4ESP) is located off exit 23 of the NYS Thruway (go through the tollbooth to I-787 and take the Empire State Plaza exit) and bounded by Swan, Madison, State, and Eagle streets. Open daily year-round. Free. Popularly called the Plaza, this is really a government complex that includes office buildings, a convention center, a performing arts center known as **The Egg** (see *Entertainment*), a concourse, and the state museum (see *To See*). Built at a cost of more than $2 billion and finished in 1978, the Plaza has fulfilled then-governor Nelson Rockefeller's dream of a government center that would draw visitors and allow them to feel in touch with their state government. Tours of the Plaza are offered several times a day, but you may enjoy walking it yourself. The esplanade area is wonderful to explore, with tranquil reflecting pools, plantings, modern sculpture by such artists as David Smith, and even a play area known as the Children's Place. An environmental sculpture called *The Labyrinth* offers benches to the weary. Lining the interior halls of the concourse are fine examples of modern art on permanent display—the largest publicly owned and displayed art collection in the country, and they are all the work of New York artists. More than 92 sculptures, tapestries, paintings, and constructions are displayed, among them works by such artists as Calder, Nevelson, Frankenthaler, and Noguchi.

A series of **12 memorial statues and sculptures** provides an interesting walking tour through the Plaza. In addition to the New York State Vietnam Veterans

Courtesy of the Albany County Convention & Visitors Bureau; albany.org

MODERN ART AT EMPIRE STATE PLAZA

Memorial, there are memorials honoring fallen firefighters, George Washington after Houdon, Gen. Philip Henry Sheridan, police officers, women war veterans, those from New York State who fought in World War II and the Korean War, Dr. Martin Luther King Jr., children who died at the hands of abusers, parole officers who were killed in the line of duty, and crime victims.

For an above-the-clouds view of the entire mall, take the elevator to the 42nd floor of the **Corning Tower Observation Deck** at Empire State Plaza. Open Monday through Friday, except holidays, 10–4. *Note:* For security purposes, anyone over the age of 16 must present photo ID before being allowed to enter the elevator. From the observation deck, one can see a magnificent 270-degree view looking southeast toward the Taconics and Berkshires, west to the Catskills, and northeast toward the Adirondacks. A great stop on a clear day.

Outside, near the wide stairway to the New York State Museum, special events are held throughout the summer, among them an Independence Day celebration, concerts, ethnic celebrations, a Blues Fest, and the Empire State Plaza Farmers' Market (see *To Do—Farm Markets*). First Night Albany, a citywide New Year's Eve celebration, may be enjoyed at the Plaza, as well. Children who like to walk will enjoy the activities on the mall.

Washington Park (518-434-2032), State and Willett streets, Madison and Lake avenues. This 90-acre park in the center of Albany is the site of several interesting and enjoyable special events throughout the year (see *Special Events*).

✷ Lodging

The Albany area is filled with dozens of motels and hotels, but very few inns and bed & breakfasts; most are located outside the city itself. The lodging selection here emphasizes establishments within the city proper, as well as some of the better alternatives that are conveniently located near the capital's major attractions.

Albany Hilton (518-462-6611; 1-800-227-6963), 40 Lodge Street, Albany 12210. ($$$) Located in the heart of downtown near the capitol and Empire State Plaza, this luxury hotel has 384 guest rooms and 18 suites. You will find an exercise room, indoor heated pool, and whirlpool. Complimentary airport transportation is provided. There is a gift shop and car-rental facilities on-site. The hotel has two restaurants: **Webster's Corner** serves breakfast daily and has an excellent, reasonably priced lunch buffet Monday through Friday 11:30–2. **Kelsey's** is open for both lunch and dinner. Complimentary airport transportation and free parking are provided; a gift shop, auto-rental facilities, and an airline office are on-site.

Albany Mansion Hill Inn (518-465-2038), 115 Phillip Street, Albany 12202. ($$) This bed & breakfast is within walking distance of the state capitol and the downtown business district. Winner of a preservation award, the inn has eight rooms, each with private bath. Choose from a wide variety of dishes on the breakfast menu. Children welcome. This is one of the few inns in the city that is pet friendly. Restaurant on the premises. Open year-round.

Albany Marriott Hotel (518-458-8444; 1-800-443-8952), 189 Wolf Road, Albany 12205. ($$$) This hotel is near four major shopping malls, a 5-minute drive from the airport, and less than 20 minutes from downtown. Each of the 359 rooms in this luxury hotel is equipped with cable TV (including HBO) and other modern amenities. There are indoor and outdoor pools, sauna, whirlpool, and exercise rooms. There is a restaurant on-site. Open year-round.

Angel's Bed & Breakfast (518-426-4104), 96 Madison Avenue, Albany 12202. ($$) A historic urban inn built in the early 19th century; a great place to stay for those who want to be within walking distance of downtown Albany's major museums and restaurants. Governor Joseph Yates rented the house in 1822 and hosted several prominent people here. Each of the three small, cozy guest rooms has a private bath and is located on the second floor. There is a café on the first floor, and the innkeeper lives on the third floor. Open year-round.

Courtyard by Marriott (518-482-8800; 1-800-321-2211), 168 Wolf Road, Albany 12205. ($$$) Enjoy swimming in the indoor pool at this 80-room hotel with all the amenities, including a restaurant, exercise room, and free transportation to the airport.

The Desmond Hotel & Conference Center (518-869-8100; 1-800-448-3500), 660 Albany Shaker Road, Albany 12211. ($$$) The best features of an inn and a hotel are combined at the Desmond, with its period reproduction furniture, paintings, handsome wood paneling, and courtyards that bloom with flowers and plants all year. All rooms have custom-made furniture, and guests can use the heated pool, a health club, exercise rooms, and a billiard room. The Scrimshaw Restaurant in the hotel has fine food. Open year-round.

Hampton Inn & Suites (518-432-7000), 25 Chapel Street, Albany 12210. ($$$) This hotel, in the center of the city, is a class act. There are 121 lavishly appointed guest rooms, 35 suites with microwaves and refrigerators, and 8 whirlpool suites. In addition to all the modern amenities, there is an exercise room with sauna and steam room, wireless Internet access throughout the hotel, and complimentary hot breakfast. Open year-round.

Holiday Inn (518-458-7250; 1-800-HOLIDAY), 205 Wolf Road, Albany 12205. ($$$) There are more than 300 rooms in this luxurious hotel, with both indoor and outdoor pools, exercise room, and restaurant on the premises. Open year-round.

Holiday Inn Express (518-434-4111), 300 Broadway, Albany 12207. ($$) This economy motel with 135 rooms has an exercise room, indoor pool, sauna, and steam room, and it's not far from several of the city's attractions. Open year-round.

Hotel Indigo (518-869-9100), 254 Old Wolf Road, Latham 12110. ($$) There are 107 guest rooms here, and the decor has been selected for its calming affect. The unique design and serenity here are a little different from the usual chain hotels. Guests will enjoy plush bedding, spa-style bathrooms, hard-surface flooring, and large murals on the walls. There is a restaurant, the Blu Stone Bistro, and a Starbucks on the premises. Open year-round.

The Inn on South Lake Bed & Breakfast (518-438-7646), 145 South Lake Avenue, Albany 12208. ($) This cozy bed & breakfast is housed in an 1890s Victorian home that combines mission-style influences with modern amenities. It is within easy walking distance of the capitol and Empire State Plaza. The main floor features a library, fireplace, wood-beamed ceilings, and leaded glass doors. The five guest rooms are on the second floor; three have private baths, and two share a bathroom. Guests may enjoy the enclosed front and rear porches as well as a backyard. Continental breakfast is served. Parking is available in the rear of the inn. Air-conditioning, laundry facilities, Internet access, and a lounge with cable TV. Open year-round.

Morgan State House (518-427-6063; 1-888-427-6063), 393 State Street, Albany 12210. ($$$) This luxury inn on Washington Park offers 16 rooms, all with private bath; 6 are located in the 19th-century main house, and 10 are in the condominium suites that date from the early 20th century. Full breakfast served on weekends only. Children over the age of 16 only. Open year-round.

Quality Inn & Suites (518-785-5891; 1-800-830-5205), 611 Troy-Schenectady Road, Latham 12110. ($$) There are 132 rooms in this moderately priced establishment, where you will find an outdoor pool and exercise room. Close to the airport. Open year-round.

74 State Hotel (518-434-7410; www.74state.com), 74 State Street, Albany 12207. ($$$) There are 74 guest rooms and suites with all the amenities (marble-top vanities, Wi-Fi, and HD-TV in all rooms) in this upscale sophisticated lodging option with first-class restaurant, Marché, on the premises (see *Dining Out*). A Clarion Collection Hotel, they offer special packages at reduced prices throughout the year; check the website for information.

State Street Mansion Bed & Breakfast (518-462-6780; 1-800-673-5750), 281 State Street, Albany 12210. ($$) This B&B is located in the center of the city's Center Square Historic District, only one block away from the capitol and the Empire State Plaza. One of the oldest B&Bs in Albany, in business for 25 years, it offers easy access to cultural activities, entertainment, and dining, making it a popular stop with businesspeople. The brownstone dates from 1889; the seven rooms all have private bath. A continental breakfast is served. Parking is available and included in the room charge.

Travelodge (518-459-5670), 42 Wolf Road, Albany 12205. ($) There are approximately 100 rooms in this budget motel, which offers exercise facilities and a continental breakfast. Open year-round.

✷ Where to Eat

Albany offers a wealth of restaurants to choose from, and they offer a range of culinary traditions—from fusion cuisine to Indonesian—for both the adventurous and the less daring diner alike. The following establishments were selected for their particularly good quality food or interesting offerings and atmosphere; they provide only a hint of the culinary treasures in the capital city.

DINING OUT **Angelo's 677 Prime** (518-427-7463), 677 Broadway. ($$$) Open for lunch Monday through Friday 11:30–2; dinner Monday through Saturday 5:30–10. Closed Sunday. Live music Wednesday through Saturday 9:30–midnight (no cover charge). Enjoy fine dining at this New York City–style steakhouse, where you can choose from eight different types of aged, hand-cut steaks. There are several tempting fish and seafood entrées as well, including seared ahi tuna. Glass-enclosed wine lockers display the extensive wine list. Desserts are made fresh daily at the restaurant bakery. The crème brûlée and homemade ice creams are first-rate. For the carnivorous, this restaurant is a must.

Athos Restaurant (518-608-6400), 1814 Western Avenue. ($$) Open Monday through Saturday 4–10; Sunday 3–9. The classic Greek cuisine here is a rarity in the capital. The wide spectrum of offerings includes lamb, veal, wild rabbit, pastitsio, and moussaka, as well as several fish entrées. I recommend the fixed price dinner that includes three courses for $22.95. Everything here is prepared with attention to detail.

The Barnsider (518-869-2448), 480 Sand Creek Road. Located just off Wolf Road. ($$) Open for dinner Monday through Saturday 5–10; Sunday 4–9. The specialties here are the hand-cut steaks and fresh seafood, which include entrées like prime rib of beef and baked stuffed shrimp. Light fare is also available, and there is a full bar. Children are welcome.

Bongiorno's (518-462-9176), 23 Dove Street. ($$) Open for lunch Monday through Friday 11:30–2; for dinner 5–9; Thursday through Saturday 5–10. The seafood and veal dishes are superb at this excellent Italian restaurant. The clams marinara, seafood fra diavolo, and veal Francese are a few of my favorites. There are always lunch specials during the week. *Mangia,* and feel like you escaped to Italy for a repast!

Brown Derby (518-463-1945), 22 Clinton Avenue. ($$) Open for lunch and dinner daily noon–10. A renovated Salvation Army building is now a fine-dining establishment that pays homage to a landmark from the golden era of Hollywood, the Brown Derby. The restaurant is not shaped like a giant brown bowler hat, however! There are 130 seats here, and American and international favorites are served up in a fun atmosphere.

Café Capriccio (518-465-0439), 49 Grand Street. ($$) Open for dinner daily 5:30–10; Friday and Saturday until 11. Dine leisurely on Northern Italian cuisine with a Mediterranean accent in this Albany institution that has been serving patrons for more than 25 years. Vintage posters decorate the wood-paneled walls, and the intimate booths take you back to the 1950s. For an appetizer, make sure to order the eggplant with four cheeses (Gorgonzola, grated mozzarella, smoked Gruyère, and pecorino romano), which can be a meal in itself. The calamari sautéed in its black ink and served over pasta is delicious. Do save room for the freshly made desserts, which include tiramisu, gelato, sorbet, flourless chocolate cake, and bananas Foster.

Caffè Italia (518-459-8029), 662 Central Avenue. ($$$) Open for dinner daily 5–10. This family-run Italian restaurant is a popular spot with members of the state legislature (a dish or two are even named after lawmakers). Everything is prepared to order, and the veal and pasta specialties are worth the trip. Reservations required. Not recommended for children.

Creo (518-482-8000), 1475 Western Avenue, Stuyvesant Plaza. ($$) Open for lunch and dinner Monday through Saturday 11:30–10; Sunday 10–9. They serve an eclectic mix of American cuisine with Asian and Mediterranean touches here. Some of the imaginative dishes include ahi tacos, buttermilk fried oysters, lobster and avocado tart, and wood-fired eggplant. The menu is intriguing, and adventurous eaters who enjoy fine dining will love this restaurant and the lovely ambience. *Creo* means "I create" in Latin, and the chef (formerly of McGuire's) lives up to the name!

DeJohn's Restaurant & Pub (518-465-5275), 288 Lark Street. ($$) Open for dinner Monday through Thursday 4–midnight; Friday through Sunday 11:30 AM–midnight. This comfortable neighborhood restaurant has simple fare (burgers, pizza, and sandwiches) as well as pasta, steaks, and fresh fish. There are two dining rooms to choose from, depending on your mood; one is informal. Children welcome.

dp An American Brasserie (518-436-3737), 25 Chapel Street. ($$) Open Monday through Friday 11:30–11; Thursday through Saturday 5:30–midnight. Located in the Hampton Inn & Suites (see *Lodging*), this restaurant offers intriguing choices for every taste. Enjoy such diverse treats as Asian glazed Pacific salmon, grilled strip steak, softshell crab sandwich, lobster ravioli, pork pot stickers (with assorted dipping sauces), and Black & Bleu salad (sliced sirloin over mixed greens topped with crumbled blue cheese). The warm mahogany, massive windows, and luscious earth tones throughout are a fitting setting for the inventive cuisine, which combines traditional favorites and Chef Yono's signature Indonesian touches. Children's menu.

Elda's On Lark (518-449-3532), 207 Lark Street. ($$) Open for dinner Monday through Saturday 4–11; late-night menu 11 PM–2 AM; closed Sunday. Their Northern Italian cuisine with a French twist is first-rate. All the breads and pastas are made fresh daily on the premises. The beef carpaccio with arugula and fresh romano cheese is a specialty of the house; so is the swordfish carpaccio served with capers. For an entrée, there is steak, veal, pork, chicken—the "a little of everything," according to owner, Elda. But the best choice here is the pasta. I recommend the *panvaroti* (pasta stuffed with lobster, ricotta, and fresh herbs) or the homemade ravioli. Another house specialty is lamb chops with sage. The chocolate cake and sorbets are imported from Italy. Fine food in a romantic, candlelit Victorian atmosphere . . . at a reasonable price.

El Mariachi (518-432-7580), 289 Hamilton Street; also (518-465-2568) 144 Washington Avenue. ($) Open Monday through Friday 11–10; Saturday and Sunday 1–10. Authentic homestyle Mexican and Spanish regional dishes, including paella. There is a full bar with more than 45 fine tequilas to make those margaritas special. For those like me, who prefer the homemade sangria, they offer both white and red. Enjoy lunch specials during the week; they're good value for the money.

Franklin's Tower (518-431-1920), 414 Broadway. ($$$) Open for lunch and dinner Monday through Friday 11:30–9; dinner only Saturday 5–10. Closed Sunday. Named for the lyrics from a Grateful Dead song, this renovated restaurant is housed in a historic building. The downstairs has mahogany booths, an art deco bar, tile floors, and a romantic atmosphere. Upstairs in the red-walled dining room there is a sense of history. Babe Ruth spent time here, since this floor was once a meeting room for the Albany Baseball Club. Mayor Erastus Corning and other politicians also frequented a former restaurant incarnation. There is often live music; it's a nice place to have drinks and light fare. Entrées include standard American favorites with international touches. The roasted red pepper swordfish au poivre, pork tenderloin, and chicken marsala are just a few of the dinner selections. Not recommended for children.

Jack's Oyster House (518-465-8854), 42 State Street. ($$) Open for dinner daily 5–10. This is Albany's oldest restaurant, and for over 80 years it has been run by the same family. The steak and seafood are traditions, and the specialties are consistently good. Reservations suggested. Children are welcome.

Justin's (518-436-7008), 301 Lark Street. ($$) Open daily for lunch 11:30–2:30; dinner served from 5; late-night menu available until 1 AM. Saturday and Sunday brunch 11–4. Located in Albany's answer to Greenwich Village, part of this restaurant dates from the 1700s, and there has been a tavern or inn on this site ever since. All soups are made fresh every day. The New American cuisine varies with the seasons and can best be described as eclectic. It ranges from Jamaican jerk chicken with jasmine ginger rice and black beans to pomegranate-glazed duck breast. The meat loaf with macaroni and cheese is popular comfort food year-round. There are always daily specials, and the café menu has unusually enticing gourmet sandwiches. There is live jazz on Sunday. Reservations suggested. Not appropriate for children.

La Perla Restaurant (518-674-3774), 3016 Route 43, Averill Park. ($$) Open for dinner daily, except Tuesday, 4–10; Sunday 2–10. The Italian/Continental cuisine here features steaks, seafood, veal, chicken, and more; in fact, there are close to 100 items on the menu, not including the daily specials (which may be a game dish like wild boar or buffalo). There are two dining rooms; one is informal, where pizza and pasta are the mainstays and children will be more comfortable. Although located outside of the city at the Gregory House Inn, this is a popular dining spot with local residents.

La Serre Restaurant (518-463-6056), 14 Green Street. ($$$) Open for lunch Monday through Friday 11:30–2; dinner served Monday through Saturday from 5. This elegant Continental restaurant is housed in a historic building complete with bright awnings and window boxes full of flowers. The service is superb, and specialties include an award-winning onion soup, bouillabaisse Marseillaise, loin of veal with béarnaise sauce, and steak au poivre. Sumptuous desserts are made fresh daily.

Lombardo's (518-462-9180), 121 Madison Avenue. ($$$) Open for lunch Monday through Friday 11–4; dinner 4–11; Saturday dinner only 3–11. Closed Sunday. An Albany mainstay since 1919, this restaurant, with black-and-white tiled floors, murals on the walls, and a bar with old-world charm, serves fine Italian American fare. There is a large menu including mouthwatering pasta dishes, veal, chicken, beef, and seafood. The clientele is a mix of politicians, businesspeople, and tourists.

Marché at 74 State (518-434-7410), 74 State Street. ($$$) Open Monday through Friday for breakfast 7–10; lunch 11–3; and dinner 6–10. Open Saturday for dinner only 6–10. Open Saturday and Sunday for brunch 7–3. A first-rate establishment located in the 74 State Hotel (see *Lodging*), the restaurant features imaginative American cuisine. Chef Brian Molino was the sous-chef at Craft, the trendy eatery in New York City, brainchild of Tom Colicchio, best known as the head judge on the TV show *Top Chef*. This is definitely worth a visit.

McGuire's (518-463-2100), 353 State Street, near Lark Street, close to the capitol. ($$$) Open Monday through Saturday 5–10. Housed in a restored, historic structure that was once an ice-cream parlor, this intimate, elegant establishment, which seats about 60, features fine Continental cuisine. Chef Andrew Plummer's Delmonico steak attracts a loyal following. For those interested in surf, the lobster risotto appetizer and red snapper are favorites of mine. The sea bass, which combines Caribbean and Japanese flavors, is one of several fish entrées. And save room for the beautifully presented, imaginative desserts. The service is often excellent. Advance reservations are recommended here, even during the week. Valet parking. Not recommended for children.

Mezza Notte Ristorante (518-689-4433), 2026 Western Avenue. ($$) Open Tuesday through Saturday 5–10. Closed Sunday and Monday. This classic Northern Italian restaurant has fine food, a decent wine list, and excellent service. Everything is well prepared, and diners won't be disappointed, whether ordering pasta, calamari, veal, chicken, or seafood. Don't skip dessert here; the tiramisu is wonderful.

My Linh (518-465-8899), 272 Delaware Avenue. ($$) Open for dinner Thursday through Sunday 5–10. Albany's first Vietnamese restaurant, it opened in 1993 and is still popular among local residents. Dinner is served in a casual, comfortable atmosphere. One of my favorite dishes is the shrimp summer rolls. The crispy pan-fried boneless duck is tender and served perfectly. And the crêpes filled with chicken or sliced beef sauté in a spicy curry sauce are quite good. Vegetarians will have an array of items to choose from, like grilled tofu topped with spicy bean curd sauce. Children welcome.

New World Bistro & Bar (518-694-0520), 300 Delaware Avenue. ($$) Open for dinner daily 5–9:30; Friday and Saturday until 11; Sunday brunch 11–3. A fun place to dine, New World has its own unique style of "global neighborhood cuisine," including lustily spiced dishes of the American melting pot. Chef Ric Orlando garnered national attention when he appeared on the Food Channel show *Chopped* in 2011. He operates another restaurant, New World Home Cooking, in Saugerties (see *Dining Out* in "Ulster County") and divides his time between the two places. This restaurant serves many of the same popular dishes—Cajun pan-blackened string beans, Jamaican jerk chicken, and purple haze shrimp—but also has a terrific bistro bar menu that includes choices like yeast-free pizzas, burgers, and pot roast sandwich. It's a great place to stop before heading to the nearby Spectrum Theater (see *Entertainment*). There are gluten-free and vegan menus, as well as a children's menu. Many local ingredients are used in the kitchen here, and the menu changes seasonally to reflect what's freshest.

Provence (518-689-7777), 1475 Western Avenue, Stuyvesant Plaza. ($$) Open daily 11:30–10; Friday and Saturday until 10:30; Sunday brunch 10:30–2; dinner 2–8:30. This lovely French bistro will transport you back to the south of France. A few specialties of the house are duck and steak frites, bouillabaisse, and mussels in white wine. There is even a Kobe burger with foie gras ($26.50). It's also a great place to have an interesting salad or sandwich for lunch. Enjoy patio dining outdoors from May through October. Not recommended for children.

Real Seafood Company (518-458-2068), 195 Wolf Road, Colonie. ($$) Open Monday through Thursday 11 AM–10 PM; Friday and Saturday 3–11; Sunday 3–9:30. This popular seafood emporium has an impressive raw bar. The menu features such entrées as char-grilled Block Island swordfish, tuna medallions in white wine and herbs, and a blue-plate combination special of the day that changes seasonally. Children welcome.

Scrimshaw (518-452-5801), The Desmond Hotel, 660 Albany-Shaker Road. ($$$) Open for dinner Tuesday through Saturday 5:30–10. Enjoy steaks and seafood delicately prepared in an elegant atmosphere. The restaurant is renowned as one of the best places for fish in the capital. Enjoy oysters Rockefeller, cedar planked salmon, and a wide variety of "surf" selections. Turf lovers will enjoy veal Oscar, filet mignon, and rack of lamb. Not recommended for children.

Sitar (518-456-6670), 1929 Central Avenue. ($$) Open Tuesday through Friday for lunch buffet 11:30–2; dinner 5–10. Sunday lunch noon–3 and dinner 5–9. Indian specialties are prepared to your taste, among them tandoori or curry dishes, chicken, and vegetarian entrées. This is one of the best Indian restaurants in the Hudson Valley; it's reasonably priced, as well. Children are welcome.

Taste (518-694-3322), 45 Beaver Street. ($$$) Open for lunch Tuesday through Friday 11:30–4; dinner Tuesday through Saturday 5–10. Closed Sunday and Monday. Enjoy fine contemporary dining with an emphasis on healthy choices. For lunch there are selections that include Kobe meat loaf sandwich, turkey burger, grilled chicken salad, and salmon Reuben. Dinner features rack of lamb, fish kebab, and filet mignon. Not recommended for children.

Van's Vietnamese Restaurant (518-436-1868), 307 Central Avenue. ($$) Open for lunch Tuesday through Sunday 11–2; dinner 4–10. Closed Monday. Chef-owner Hung Van Nguyen serves some of the best spring rolls you will find anywhere in this spacious, cheerful restaurant. The whole crispy duck is my favorite entrée, but there are many tempting Vietnamese specialties from which to choose. Children are welcome.

Victory Café (518-463-9113), 10 Sheridan Avenue. ($$) Open Monday through Friday 11:30–10; Friday until 11; Saturday 5–10. Closed Sunday. This casual dining spot is excellent for lunch or an informal dinner. The fresh turkey sandwiches, gourmet pizzas, and build-your-own burger options are tasty choices for lunch. My favorite here is the seafood mac and cheese; it's loaded with shrimp and scallops. Grilled New York strip steak is popular with meat lovers. Children welcome.

Yono's (518-436-7747), 25 Chapel Street. ($$$) Open for dinner Monday through Saturday from 5:30 on. Live jazz on Friday and Saturday evenings. An intriguing blend of French technique and Indonesian influence is found here, along with Continental specialties. Excellent steaks, chicken, and vegetarian selections coexist on the eclectic menu with Far Eastern specialties. Relocated in 2006 to the Hampton Inn & Suites (see *Lodging*), Yono's now has the rich warm atmosphere of an elegant bi-level dining room highlighted by bronzed mirrors, a marble fireplace, and a magnificent crystal chandelier. Extensive wine list. Reservations are strongly suggested; this is one of the most popular restaurants in the city.

EATING OUT Albany Pump Station & C.H. Evans Brewing Company (518-447-9000), 19 Quackenbush Square. ($) Open Monday through Thursday 11:30–10, until 11 Friday and Saturday; Sunday noon–8. This downtown city brewpub offers a wide variety of American favorites. The menu includes everything from meat loaf, burgers, and calamari to mango salmon, dinner salads, and overstuffed sandwiches. There is a full bar, and the place is a popular spot for the younger crowd to grab drinks and a light dinner after the workday. Not recommended for children.

Beff's (518-482-BEFF), 95 Everett Road. ($) Open Monday through Friday 11–11; Saturday and Sunday noon–11. Beff is an acronym for Big Ed Fat Field, a high school nickname of the owner. They opened in 1991 and soon became known for their half-pound burgers, buffalo wings, pizza, Irish nachos, and Reubens. There are also soups, salads, sandwiches, and wraps, as well as several beers from which to choose. The kids will love it here.

Bombers Burrito Bar (518-463-9636), 258 Lark Street. ($) Open for lunch and dinner daily 11 AM–1 AM. This colorful eatery serves up all the standard Mexican favorites—and more! In addition to their fantastic burritos (12-inch tortillas filled with beef, chicken, vegetables, black beans, or whatever else you desire), there is barbecued tofu (yes!), pork, and chicken, as well as vegetarian chicken nuggets. A variety of vegan dishes and salads are also available. The kids will love this place, and you'll love the prices!

Daily Grind (518-427-0464), 204 Lark Street. ($) Open daily 7 AM–8 PM. There is more than coffee here; upstairs is a retail store specializing in fresh-roasted coffee beans, while downstairs a European-style café offers an eclectic variety of light fare (soups, sandwiches, wraps, desserts, biscotti, cookies). There is a decent selection of teas for those who don't indulge in coffee in the daily grind!

Debbie's Kitchen (518-463-3829), 456 Madison Avenue. ($) Open Monday through Friday 10–6; Saturday 11–4. This is the downtown Albany place to go for homemade soups and sandwiches with a creative flair. The chef weaves a touch of color and crunch into the ordinary. The smoked turkey-breast sandwich with garlic mayo, sliced pears, sunflower seeds, roasted onions, and cheddar cheese is a wonderful variation on the usual turkey sandwich. Vegetarian combos and fresh salads are available, and a wide variety of freshly baked cakes and cookies are difficult to pass up for dessert. The chocolate brownies are some of the best in the city. Children are welcome.

El Loco Café (518-436-1855), 465 Madison Avenue. ($) Open for lunch and dinner Wednesday through Saturday noon–10; Sunday dinner only 4–9:30. This lively café specializes in Tex-Mex fare and is located in a restored 19th-century building. El Loco is well known for its chili (the heat is up to you) and its large selection of Mexican beer. Even after all the chili and beer you can down, the desserts are still tempting. Children are welcome.

Graney's Stout (518-427-8688), 904 Broadway. ($) Open daily 11:30–10; Friday and Saturday until 1 AM. This spacious Irish pub in the city's warehouse district features Irish nachos, shepherd's pie, bangers and mash, wings, burgers, and pizza. The bar is huge and offers a great selection of beers, as well as 16 on tap, including Guinness, Harp, O'Hara's, and many more. It gets very crowded on weekends.

Honest Weight Food Co-op Cafe (518-482-2667), 484 Central Avenue. ($) Open Monday through Friday 7 AM–9 PM; Saturday and Sunday 8–8. The organic café at this large, fully stocked food co-op has a hot bar filled with an array of offerings, including falafel, noodle dishes, pastas, and soups. There are also sandwiches and salads. You don't have to be a member of the co-op to shop here. Their cheese section is enormous, and free samples are always given away. The bulk food section offers great value for the money, but that can't be said about the organic frozen meats—they are way overpriced. This is a good place to stop for a quick nutritious lunch. There are plenty of vegan and gluten-free options, as well as a coffee bar.

Mamoun's Restaurant (518-434-3901), 206 Washington Avenue. ($) Open daily 11:30–10. In addition to the vegetarian fare at this Middle Eastern restaurant, there is a variety of chicken and lamb dishes. Try the shish kebab—it's a house specialty. The food is prepared to order and will appeal to everyone. Mamoun's is a family-run business; once when I arrived with a friend, the restaurant was closed. However, someone came to the door, invited us in, and within minutes, we were seated and ordering a meal.

Peaches Café (518-482-3677), 1475 Western Avenue. ($) Open Monday through Thursday 8 AM–9:30 PM, Friday and Saturday until 10 PM; Sunday 8–8. Enjoy breakfast all day, every day, in a relaxing atmosphere; Belgian waffles and specialty omelets are what they are known for here. At lunchtime, the soups, salads, sandwiches, and wonderful wraps are the perfect antidote to the hectic pace of shopping. Children welcome.

Wine Bar & Bistro (518-463-2881), 200 Lark Street. ($) Open daily 5–midnight. This cozy intimate wine bar in the Albany downtown area offers 70 wines by the glass and five beers on tap. When you enter the grottolike space, with three fireplaces and low light, there is a relaxing romantic ambience. Tapas, appetizers, and light dinners are the fare at this French bistro. During warm weather, enjoy dining on the outdoor patio on Lark Street, where there is always a lively scene. No reservations are accepted. Not recommended for children.

✷ Entertainment

Albany Civic Theater (518-462-1297; www.albanycivictheater.org), 235 Second Avenue. Admission fee. Musicals and dramas are offered throughout the year. There is also a playwright's showcase, an annual spring event, that is offered free of charge.

Albany Symphony Orchestra (518-465-4755; www.albanysymphony.com), 19 Clinton Avenue. Admission fee. The season runs from September through May, and performances are given at the renovated Palace Theatre in Albany and the acoustically renowned Troy Savings Bank Music Hall across the Hudson River in the city of Troy. There is a varied mix of concerts, as well as a series of children's musical performances. Every May the American Music Festival delights local residents and visitors alike. Call for schedule.

Capital Repertory Theatre (518-462-4531; 518-445-SHOW; www.capitalrep.org), 111 North Pearl Street. Admission fee. Theater lovers will enjoy the year-round performances here; Capital Rep has been offering first-rate entertainment for nearly 30 years. The company employs professional equity actors and designers from New York City. There are usually six productions over the course of the year; they include musicals, comedies, dramas, and family-oriented productions. Several student matinees are also offered in conjunction with the educational department.

The Comedy Works (518-275-6897; www.comedyworks.com), 200 Wolf Road, in the Best Western Hotel. The nightclub here features comedians from all over the country at 9 PM on Friday and Saturday. Check the website for a full schedule.

eba Dance Theatre (518-465-9916; www.eba-arts.org), 351 Hudson Avenue. Once known as electronic body arts, this company offers dance performances throughout the year. The emphasis is on modern dance, but there is an Arts in Education program that takes a variety of works into the city schools. Call for schedule.

The Egg (518-473-1061; www.theegg.org), Empire State Plaza. This marvelous venue includes year-round ballet, modern dance, theater, rock concerts, and other musical performances, even storytellers and monologists. Visitors may enjoy a virtual cornucopia of entertainment here. Check the website for a complete schedule.

Palace Performing Arts Center (518-465-3334; www.palacealbany.com), 19 Clinton Avenue. The Palace Theatre, a cultural entertainment facility in the heart of the capital, first opened in 1931. Today it offers a diverse calendar year-round filled with popular musical acts, cultural events, and classic movies.

Spectrum Theater (518-449-8995), 290 Delaware Avenue. There are eight theaters at this locally owned, independent movie theater, which is committed to showing the best first-run independent and foreign films. Check the website to see what is being offered when you intend to go. It's rare to find this kind of theater anywhere these days; the owner installed 216 photovoltaic solar panels on the roof in 2011 to conserve energy!

Times Union Center (518-487-2000; www.timesunioncenteralbany.com), 51 South Pearl Street. (Take NYS Thruway to exit 23. Pick up I-787 north and go to the downtown Albany exit—Routes 9 and 20 West. At the light, make a left onto Broadway, and go under the bridge. At the next light, make a left, and then at the following light make a right onto Madison

Courtesy of the Albany County Convention & Visitors Bureau; albany.org

PALACE PERFORMING ARTS CENTER

Avenue. Go two more lights and make a right onto South Pearl Street. Follow signs into arena.) This sports and entertainment complex is home to two athletic teams (see *To Do—Spectator Sports*); it's also where you can see a range of entertainment: from Cher, *Stars on Ice,* and Yanni to Bon Jovi, Nelli, and Sesame Street. There are car and motorcycle shows, regional basketball playoffs, and more.

✱ Selective Shopping

Lark Street in Albany is known as "the village in the city." There are over 30 restaurants, two dozen shops, and several fine-art venues on this one street. The best way to experience this area is to walk up and down the street and wander into the boutiques and galleries. Throughout the year there are various festivals on Lark Street, so make sure to check www.larkstreet.org to see what is happening when you plan to visit. The Albany area is known for its excellent shopping, and the majority of shops may be found in the city's malls. The following three shopping districts are all different in style and provide enough variety for just about any visitor.

Colonie Center (518-459-9020; www.shopatcoloniecenter.com), 131 Colonie Center, Wolf Road and Central Avenue, Albany. (Take the NYS Thruway to exit 24, go through the tollbooth, and head to exit 1N—the Northway. Get off at exit 2, Wolf Road.) Macy's and Sears are the anchor stores in this huge mall, which is filled with shops as varied as the Christmas Tree Shop and Victoria's Secret. The mall is also surrounded by stores: across the street are Bed, Bath & Beyond and Barnes & Noble.

Crossgates Mall (518-869-9565; www.shopcrossgatesmall.com), 1 Crossgates Mall Road, Albany. (Take NYS

Thruway to exit 24; go to the farthest right tollbooth. Make a right onto Western Avenue. Crossgates Mall Road is less than a mile ahead on the right.) This enormous mall has 180 stores, as well as an 18-theater (stadium seating) and a 12-theater cineplex.

Stuyvesant Plaza (518-482-8986; www.stuyvesantplaza.com), Western Avenue and Fuller Road, Albany. (Take the NYS Thruway to exit 24. Go south on Route 87, the Northway, to Western Avenue. Make a left turn. Approximately 1,500 feet ahead of you, on the left, is Stuyvesant Plaza. Look for sign.) What I like best about this shopping area is that the upscale stores are not enclosed in a mall; the setup is rather old-fashioned, and you must walk outdoors along a sidewalk from store to store. However, the shops (and restaurants) are first-rate and include the Book House, one of the best independent bookstores you will find anywhere. Unless it's raining, I'd head here first—especially if you are looking for something a little different.

✷ Special Events

Seasonal events abound in the capital city and enhance any vacation stay. So if you are planning a trip to Albany, call 1-800-258-3582 for a complete listing, or check out www.albany.org for what's happening when you will be there.

February: **New York in Bloom** (518-474-5877; www.nysm.nysed.gov), New York State Museum, Empire State Plaza, is the capital's "flower show," a terrific outing for the entire family—and the perfect antidote to the winter blues.

March: **The Capital District Garden & Flower Show** (518-356-6410), deemed one of the top 100 events in America by a national tour organization, is held across the Hudson River at Hudson Valley Community College

TIMES UNION CENTER

Courtesy of the Albany County Convention & Visitors Bureau; albany.org

in Troy. Learn more about the art of gardening with vendors, workshops, lectures, floral designers, and more.

May: The **Annual Tulip Festival,** also known as Pinksterfest (518-434-2032), is usually held the second weekend in May and includes outdoor crafts and food fairs in Washington Park, entertainment, the crowning of the Tulip Queen, scrubbing down State Street, and a dance. The celebrations are colorful and peopled with costumed performers—and, of course, more than 100,000 tulips. **Mother's Day Art & Craft Show** (518-786-1529), Empire State Plaza, North Concourse, Albany. Free. This annual juried show is a nice place to go on Mother's Day weekend. It's held on both Saturday and Sunday 10–6.

June: **Art on Lark** (518-434-3861; www.lark.org), held on Lark Street in the city, is a fantastic display of painting, sculpture, jewelry, and more. There are food vendors from local restaurants as well as live music. Artists and the public have a chance to mingle at this festive spring event. The **Father's Day Concert** (518-434-2032), an annual tradition in Riverfront Park, makes for a wonderful outing with Dad.

July: **Cross State Bicycle Tour** (518-434-1583) is a 400-mile bicycle tour from Buffalo to Albany along the historic Erie Canal. Half the ride is off-road, on the traffic-free Canalway Trail; the rest is on rural roads. The tour draws participants from many states, and it takes eight days. Sponsored and organized by Parks and Trails New York, the tour usually begins the first Monday after July 4th. **Summer Craft Fair** (518-456-7890), Shaker Heritage Society, Shaker Meeting House, Albany Shaker Road. Several vendors exhibit their wares, offering the crafts and herb traditions of this fascinating group. **Fabulous 4th on the Plaza** (518-473-0559), Empire State Plaza, Albany. Free. Price Chopper sponsors this dazzling display of fireworks at sundown. There are also food vendors, crafts, and live music. It's a great place to enjoy the holiday festivities.

August: **Latin Fest** (518-434-2032), Washington Park, offers the best in

CONCERT IN RIVERFRONT PARK, ALBANY

Courtesy of the Albany County Convention & Visitors Bureau; albany.org

Latin music, food, and crafts. Children's rides will delight the young ones and make this a festive family outing. **Hudson Valley Pedal** (518-434-1583), sponsored by Parks and Trails New York, is a 200-mile tour on back roads from Albany to Manhattan.

September: **JazzFest** (518-434-2032) is held in downtown Albany in Riverfront Park. Right by the water, listen to jazz in the Riverfront Amphitheater. **LARKfest** (518-434-3861), held on Lark Street in the city, is the capital's enormous end of summer open-air street festival. There are four stages showcasing live music and entertainment, a family activity area, and a variety of vendors selling crafts and food from local restaurants. **Capital District Scottish Games** (518-785-0507), Altamont Fairgrounds, 129 Grand Street, Altamont. Admission fee. Held every year on Saturday and Sunday of Labor Day weekend, this Celtic festival of culture and arts features pipe bands, Highland dancing, athletic events, Celtic folk music, and sheepdog exhibitions, to name just some of the attractions.

October: **Goold Apple Festival & Craft Show** (518-732-7317), Goold Orchards, 1297 Brookview Station Road, Castleton-on-Hudson. Free. This celebration of the arts, crafts, and agriculture of the capital region is held on Saturday and Sunday of Columbus Day weekend, 9–5. There are several activities for children, and it's a great family-friendly event. **The Capital District Apple Festival & Craft Fair** (518-786-1529), Altamont Fairgrounds, 129 Grand Street, Altamont, offers the wares of over 100 of the finest craftspeople and artisans; there are quilts on display, wine lectures, children's activities, and more. It is held the weekend after Columbus Day, both Saturday and Sunday 10–5.

November: **Capital Holiday Lights in the Park** (518-258-3582), Washington Park, is a dazzling drive-through holiday light display with more than 40 illuminated scenes and characters. At the end, there are surprises and holiday treats in the park's Lakehouse. Thanksgiving through January 5. Admission fee. **Pride of New York Harvest Festival** (518-474-0538), Empire State Plaza, Albany. Free. This is the place to purchase fine quality food, wine, and beer from New York State growers and producers. The event is held at the Plaza both Saturday and Sunday 10–5. Call for exact date. The **Harvest Maple Festival** (518-474-0538), Empire State Plaza, Albany, is usually held the second Saturday of the month 9–5. Free. The event celebrates New York State's maple syrup, and the festivities get under way early with a pancake breakfast, as well as lunch featuring a full array of maple products.

December: **Holiday Tree Lighting & Fireworks Festival** (518-473-0559), Empire State Plaza, Albany. Free. A spectacular fireworks display is part of the festivities as the official New York State holiday tree is lit, ushering in the holiday season. Kids will be thrilled to watch this celebration. The **Annual Holiday House Tour** (518-465-0876), throughout Albany's historic neighborhoods. Admission fee. There are usually a dozen private homes beautifully decorated for the holidays that participate in welcoming visitors. Call for details. **Winter WonderLARK** (518-434-3861), Lark Street, Albany. Free. Usually held on the second Saturday in December, this festival includes a Santa Speedo Spring, family-friendly activities, a holiday market, and winter window display contest.

Saratoga Springs and Environs

8

Saratoga Springs Chamber of Commerce

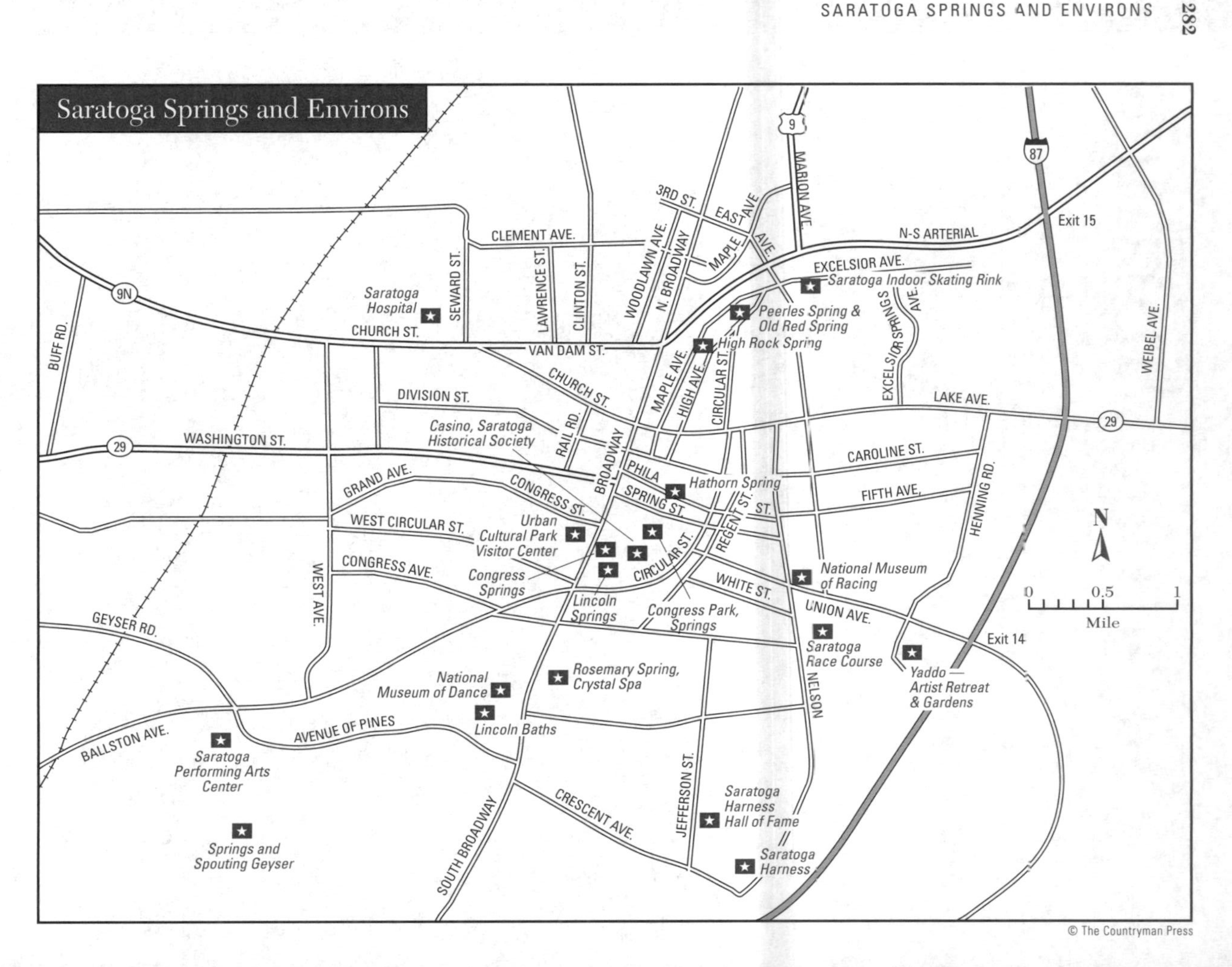
Saratoga Springs and Environs
MARION AVE.
3RD ST.
EAST AVE.
MAPLE AVE.
N-S ARTERIAL
Exit 15
EXCELSIOR AVE.
Saratoga Indoor Skating Rink
Peerles Spring & Old Red Spring
High Rock Spring
EXCELSIOR SPRINGS AVE.
WEIBEL AVE.
CLEMENT AVE.
WOODLAWN AVE.
N. BROADWAY
LAWRENCE ST.
CLINTON ST.
SEWARD ST.
Saratoga Hospital
CHURCH ST.
VAN DAM ST.
BUFF RD.
CHURCH ST.
DIVISION ST.
MAPLE AVE.
HIGH AVE.
CIRCULAR ST.
LAKE AVE.
Casino, Saratoga Historical Society
RAIL RD.
BROADWAY
WASHINGTON ST.
CAROLINE ST.
PHILA
Hathorn Spring
GRAND AVE.
CONGRESS ST.
SPRING ST.
REGENT ST.
ST.
FIFTH AVE.
HENNING RD.
WEST CIRCULAR ST.
Urban Cultural Park Visitor Center
CIRCULAR ST.
CONGRESS AVE.
Congress Springs
WHITE ST.
National Museum of Racing
N
0 0.5 1
Mile
WEST AVE.
Lincoln Springs
Congress Park, Springs
UNION AVE.
GEYSER RD.
Saratoga Race Course
Exit 14
Yaddo — Artist Retreat & Gardens
National Museum of Dance
Rosemary Spring, Crystal Spa
NELSON
Lincoln Baths
AVENUE OF PINES
BALLSTON AVE.
Saratoga Performing Arts Center
JEFFERSON ST.
CRESCENT AVE.
Saratoga Harness Hall of Fame
Saratoga Harness
Springs and Spouting Geyser
SOUTH BROADWAY
© The Countryman Press

SARATOGA SPRINGS AND ENVIRONS

It is nearly impossible to describe Saratoga Springs—*elegant, gracious, exciting, mysterious,* and *eccentric* are only some of the words that come to mind. Since the 18th century, when natural medicinal springs were discovered in the region, Saratoga Springs has played host to visitors from around the world. There are 15 outstanding public golf courses in the area. Parks and nature preserves abound for hiking and biking. Ice skate in July at the indoor rink. Fish the Kayderosseras Creek, a Class A trout stream, or try out Saratoga Lake, often referred to as the Bass Capital of the World. The museums and specialty boutiques are excellent; when you tire of exploring, the springs and spas will revive you. Classical music and dance enthusiasts can enjoy a picnic dinner while great orchestral selections and ballets are performed under the stars. Lovers of Victorian architecture can stroll down a side street or two, where they will spot grand old mansions and exquisite gardens. With all of this, Saratoga Springs also offers the best thoroughbred horse racing in the world. Each July and August this quiet place pulses with the color, crowds, and excitement of the famed Saratoga Race Course, where the best jockeys and horses vie for enormous winnings and fame. In addition, there are horse auctions and polo matches, and the public is invited to just about every event. You can spend a month in Saratoga Springs and still not experience all it has to offer. The only thing you must not do is miss it!

GUIDANCE **Saratoga County Chamber of Commerce** (518-584-3255; 1-800-526-8970), 28 Clinton Street, Saratoga Springs 12866; www.saratoga.org.

Saratoga Springs Heritage Area Visitor Center (518-587-3241), 297 Broadway (Drink Hall), across the street from Congress Park, is open Memorial Day weekend to mid-November, Monday through Saturday 9–5, Sunday 10–3; closed on Sunday mid-November through late May. This well-located information center is a good place for summer visitors to find out what's going on in town upon arrival.

GETTING THERE *By car:* Saratoga Springs (approximately 200 miles from New York City and Boston and 30 miles from Albany) is located north of Albany on I-87 (the Northway), exits 13N through 15.

By bus: **Adirondack Trailways** (518-583-7490; 1-800-858-8555; www.trailways ny.com), 135 South Broadway, Saratoga Springs, provides service to Albany, Boston, and New York City, as well as other destinations.

By air: **Albany International Airport** (518-242-2222; www.albanyairport.com) is less than a half-hour drive from Saratoga.

MEDICAL EMERGENCY **Saratoga Hospital** (518-587-3222), 211 Church Street, Saratoga Springs.

✷ To See

Children's Museum at Saratoga (518-584-5540; www.childrensmuseumatsaratoga .org), 69 Caroline Street. Open Labor Day through June, Tuesday through Saturday 9:30–4:30; Sunday noon–4:30; July through Labor Day also open on Monday. Admission fee. This unique museum offers children ages one to nine a chance to explore the world, from the local community to the international level. Interactive exhibits allow them to run a general store, make giant bubbles, and "freeze" their shadows. A tree house, fire truck, science section, movie theater, and two toddler areas are also popular with young visitors. Special events have included art workshops and magic shows. The museum is so centrally located that a visit can be combined with shopping or stops at the Canfield Casino Museum and park.

Congress Park, Broadway and Circular Street. Open daily from dawn to dusk. Part of the daily life of Saratoga Springs a century ago was "taking the waters," and Congress Park was a popular watering hole. The wealthy who came to Saratoga Springs each summer to escape the plagues and stink of the industrial cities would stay at the area's fine hotels and stroll along the park's pathways to various fountains (see *Springs & Spas*). Today the park has lovely plantings, places to sit and ponder the past, and some interesting decorative offerings. Daniel Chester

THE SPRINGS IN CONGRESS PARK

Saratoga Springs Chamber of Commerce

French's statue *The Spirit of Life* greets visitors near the entrance (he also created the renowned seated president's statue in the Lincoln Memorial), and two huge, lovely urns called "Day" and "Night" bloom with flowers each summer. Tucked in the back of the park is a small reflecting pool with the most popular of the park's denizens: a pair of Triton figurines that shoot out streams of water and are nicknamed Spit and Spat. Enjoy walking among the columns in the Italian Gardens. Both young and old visitors to the park will enjoy the antique carousel that operates from May through October, Friday through Sunday noon–6. Also located in the park is **Canfield Casino** (518-587-3550), which was once one of the most famous gambling establishments in the country. Today it is home to a museum and art gallery.

Saratoga Springs History Museum (518-584-6920; www.saratogahistory.org), 1 East Congress Street. Open year-round, Wednesday through Sunday 10–4. Admission fee. The museum maintains a lovely series of rooms that offer vignettes of life in Saratoga Springs during the Gilded Age of the late 19th century, when Lillian Russell, Diamond Jim Brady, and a host of others sparkled each night over the gaming tables. Downstairs in the museum's art gallery there are changing exhibits of works by local and regional artists. The museum also hosts crafts shows each summer and fall. (During the racing season, the casino becomes the site of one of the most glamorous society events in the old style: philanthropist Mary Lou Whitney's "fantasy" parties, where guests may enjoy visiting Oz or watching Cinderella arrive in a real pumpkin coach. Of course, this is not a public event, but if you are in the area, you can watch the Saratoga glitterati arrive. A one-of-a-kind event, really.)

National Bottle Museum (518-885-7589; www.nationalbottlemuseum.org), 76 Milton Avenue (Route 50), Ballston Spa (7 miles south of Saratoga Springs on Route 50). Donations appreciated. Open year-round: June through September, daily 10–4; October through May, Monday through Friday 10–4. This museum focuses on the history of the handmade bottle. Until 1903 bottles were handmade, not manufactured. The permanent collection consists of approximately 2,000 bottles, but there are also changing exhibits that borrow from collections throughout the nation. When I visited, there was an exhibit of blue-decorated stoneware bottles, a bottle-dating exhibit that explained how to recognize various marks made on the glass by hand tools, and a cross-section of a privy dig (many bottles are often found in old privies since during winter they had to be stored in a place where a hole had been dug in the ground).

Make sure to stop at the working glass studio across the street, owned by the museum; classes in glassblowing and workshops with internationally renowned guest artisans are offered. And every June the museum has a bottle show and sale, featuring antique-bottle dealers from throughout the East Coast (see *Special Events*).

National Museum of Dance (518-584-2225; www.dancemuseum.org), 99 South Broadway. Open March through November, Tuesday through Saturday 9–5. Admission fee. This is the only museum in the country dedicated to preserving the history and art of dance in America, and it does a good job. Changing exhibits feature costumes, artwork, personalities, and choreography of American dance. Videos help place various dances in their historical settings, and it is one of the few places where dance enthusiasts may get up close to the costumes and accessories of their favorite dance "characters." Special events include talks and films; call for a schedule of events.

National Museum of Racing and Hall of Fame (518-584-0400; 1-800-562-5394; www.racingmuseum.org), 191 Union Avenue. Open year-round, Monday through Saturday 10–4; Sunday noon–4. During racing season, daily 9–5. Closed holidays. Admission fee. This museum is one of the most modern sports exhibits in the world, and it is a must-see for anyone who ever enjoyed the sight of a racehorse blasting out of a starting gate. The film *Race America* is an introduction to the racetrack, and throughout the various galleries video and audio exhibits let visitors experience the sounds and sights of racing. Silks, fine paintings, furniture, and historic items all tell the story of the thoroughbred in America; the museum covers nearly 300 years of history. Special exhibits held in smaller galleries feature art and photography from contemporary artists. Even if you've never placed a bet in your life, the gift shop will immediately turn you into a horse fan. Make sure not to miss the steeplechase gallery dedicated to the sport, featuring several interactive exhibits.

Harness racing fans will want to visit the **Saratoga Harness Racing Museum and Hall of Fame** (518-587-4210), 352 Jefferson Street, which is located at the Saratoga Harness Raceway and offers memorabilia and artwork depicting the history of harness racing. Free.

New York State Military Museum and Veterans Research Center (518-581-5100; www.nysmm.org), 61 Lake Avenue. Open year-round, Tuesday through Saturday 10–4. (The research center is closed on Saturday; only the museum is open.) Admission fee. Some 10,000 military artifacts—weapons, artillery, flags, and more—from New York State's participation in military conflicts, dating from the War of 1812 to Desert Storm, are displayed in this armory, built in 1898. (Visitors will see the largest battle flag collection in the world, with more than 1,700; most of the flags are from the Civil War, but they range from the War of 1812 to the Gulf War.) The Veterans Research Center contains 2,000 volumes and 6,000 photographs (half of the photos are from the Civil War era). This is a great stop for Civil War buffs, particularly those interested in New York State involvement. Note that there are no federal records in the research center, just those from the state of New York.

Saratoga Automobile Museum (518-587-1935; www.saratogaautomuseum.com), Spa State Park. Open May through October, daily 10–5; November through April, Wednesday through Sunday 10–5. This museum is housed in a restored 1930s Saratoga Water Bottling Plant in the park. Dozens of classic cars are on display, including a 1928 sedan once owned by Charles Lindbergh and a 1931 Duesenberg Model J Roadster.

Tang Teaching Museum and Art Gallery (518-580-8080; www.tang.skidmore.edu), Skidmore College, 815 North Broadway. Open Tuesday through Sunday noon–5. Suggested donation. The two-story building that houses this relatively new museum (it opened in 2000) was designed by Antoine Predock. Paid for by a gift from the Chinese-born American businessman Oscar Tang, whose daughter and wife both graduated from Skidmore, the museum covers postwar art, giving preference to visual work with an aural component. In addition to fine art, the Tang has a few peripheral exhibits (films, performances) in progress and some intriguing auditory treats, including collaborative exhibits with Skidmore's science and history departments.

HISTORIC SITE **Saratoga National Historical Park** (518-664-9821; www.nps.gov/sara), 648 Route 32, Stillwater. Open year-round, daily 9–5; closed holidays. Park road for bikers open seasonally. The **Philip Schuyler House** is open daily Memorial Day weekend through Labor Day. Admission fee. The Battle of Saratoga turned the tide of the American Revolution, and history buffs will enjoy spending a day here. The British hoped to cut New York into sections with a three-pronged attack and destroy communications among the areas. At Saratoga the supposedly untrained, undisciplined American troops won the field, and history was changed. Your tour should begin at the battlefield visitors center, where dioramas, maps, and explanatory exhibits show how the battle was fought and won. Weapons, uniforms, and other items are on display, and because the battle was such a large one, it is necessary to read the material before you set out on the 10-mile self-guided driving tour. Markers at each stop explain what went on during the battle. At the Schuyler House, memorabilia of Gen. Philip Schuyler and his wife show what life was like for people who lived through the battle and the days after. There is even a monument on the field to a leg: Benedict Arnold was wounded in the leg during the battle and became a hero—until he later turned traitor. Special events, including military encampments, are held at the park throughout the year (call for a schedule). **Saratoga Monument** is a 155-foot obelisk commemorating the American victory in the Battles of Saratoga. Open late June through Labor Day, Wednesday through Sunday 9–5.

SPRINGS & SPAS Saratoga is famous for its springs, many of which are still open. A spring-tasting guide is available from the **Heritage Area Visitor Center**

SARATOGA NATIONAL HISTORICAL PARK

Saratoga Springs Chamber of Commerce

Saratoga Springs Chamber of Commerce

SARATOGA NATIONAL HISTORICAL PARK

opposite Congress Park (see *Guidance*). The center is only open in July and August, but it has small exhibits on the history of Saratoga Springs and its commerce. The springs in Saratoga each have their own chemical makeup and characteristics; there are explanatory signs at each spring and, usually, paper drinking cups. Just remember that too much of the spring water might not sit well with your digestive system; try no more than a sip or two to start. You can also find lots of bottled spring water at shops in Saratoga or at the spas.

Congress Park, on Broadway, houses Congress Spring, located underneath an elaborate pavilion. Its waters were some of the first to be bottled and sold commercially in the early 19th century. Also in the park, along the path, are the Columbian Spring, Congress 3, and, in the northeast corner, Freshwater Spring. Across from the park, on Spring Street, the Hathorn No. 1 Spring is a popular stop on a hot summer's day; it has a small seating area, and lovely plantings surround it.

The Crystal Spa (518-584-2556; www.thecrystalspa.com), 120 South Broadway (diagonally across from Saratoga Spa State Park), has been in business since 1988. Built on the same property where you will find the Rosemary Spring, the Crystal Spa has 15 rooms and 35 employees, marble floors, and modern amenities, and it offers a luxurious pampering experience. Here the serenity of the spa (no cell phones allowed) draws more than 25,000 people each year for mineral baths, saunas, and massages. There is even a moderately priced 64-unit motel (the Grand Union Motel—see *Lodging*) on the premises. Open year-round; it is advisable to book appointments four to six weeks in advance. At **High Rock Park** (go north on Broadway, make a right onto Lake Avenue, then a left onto High Avenue), you can sample water from Old Red, the Peerless, and the Governor springs. These were the original public springs of Saratoga Springs, and each one has its own distinctive taste; Old Red, so called because of its high iron content, was considered good for the complexion.

Saratoga Spa State Park (from the center of town, take Route 9 south to the Avenue of Pines, on the right, and follow that into the park; the site is well marked, and it isn't far from the highway) has springs and bathing facilities (see *Green Space*). Drinking springs throughout the park include Island Spouter (the only spouting geyser east of the Mississippi), Hayes Well (with an inhaling hole), Orenda Spring, Coesa, and Ferndale. A marked walking path leads to many of the springs—a lovely stroll on a summer afternoon. There is no charge for tasting the springs. **The Roosevelt Baths & Spa** (518-226-4790), 39 Roosevelt Drive, is just a 10-minute walk across the park from the Gideon Putnam Resort. The building housing the baths and spa was renovated and reopened in the summer of 2004; it was originally opened in 1935 as a bathhouse. The mineral springs like those here have been used for centuries as a health treatment. Today the spa offers a full menu of services including mineral baths and herbal mineral baths, as well as massages, facials, scrubs, body wraps, waxing, manicures, pedicures, and hair styling. This is the place to go when you want to treat yourself to a special relaxing experience and de-stress!

WALKING TOUR A walk through Saratoga Springs gives visitors a chance to see the great variety of architectural styles in vogue during the 19th and early 20th centuries, but it would be impossible to list all the houses that are worth looking at. A self-guided tour is usually available at the information booth near Congress Park or from the Saratoga Chamber of Commerce, 28 Clinton Street. Scores of homes offer a look at Italianate, Gothic Revival, Queen Anne, Romanesque, and

BROADWAY IN DOWNTOWN SARATOGA IS BUSTLING WITH ACTIVITY DURING RACING SEASON
Saratoga Springs Chamber of Commerce

other styles popular with the upper middle class and wealthy residents of the city. The **Batcheller Mansion,** corner of Whitney and West Circular, is a fantasy of French Renaissance and Eastern influence (see *Lodging*); the **Jumel Mansion,** 129 Circular Street, was the summer home of the infamous Madame Jumel, one-time wife of Aaron Burr; the **Adelphi Hotel,** on Broadway, recalls the hotels of the past, with tall columns and many arched windows. Several streets and areas you may want to enjoy for their architectural wealth include Broadway, Circular Street, Franklin Square, Clinton Street, Lake Avenue, and Union Avenue. All the homes are private, but their beauty can easily be appreciated from the sidewalk (or the window of a car if you are tired and prefer driving).

Saratoga's main thoroughfare is Broadway, which has won numerous awards for its main-street restoration. There are dozens of shops, galleries, and places of interest to check out—an Irish specialty store, rare-book shops, clothing boutiques, fine glass and porcelain, jewelry, and more—both fashionable and funky. Don't forget to wander the side streets just off Broadway (Phila, Spring, and Caroline), where many other surprises await the intrepid walker. One of my favorite bookstores anywhere is the **Lyrical Ballad** (518-584-8779), 7 Phila Street, just off Broadway, an enormous emporium housed in an old bank. You can wander through room after room (the old vaults and inner recesses of the building) and discover thousands of used and rare books, maps, and literary treasures that will surprise and delight. On a hot summer day, this is the perfect escape from the crowds and the sizzling sidewalks.

WINERIES AND BREWERIES **Olde Saratoga Brewing Company** (518-581-0492), 131 Excelsior Avenue. The tasting room here is open Monday through Friday 5–10; Saturday noon–10. Closed Sunday. This is the fourth-largest brewery in New York State, turning out 30 different kinds of beer in addition to root beer, which children will have an opportunity to sample. Tours are offered of the facility on Saturday by advance reservation. Olde Saratoga beer is served at several restaurants throughout the city.

Saratoga Winery (518-584-9463), 462 Route 29. Open Wednesday, Thursday, and Saturday noon–7; Friday noon–9; Sunday noon–5. Closed Monday and Tuesday. Located only 4 miles from downtown, this Adirondack-style tasting room and vineyard showcases several wines made largely from grapes of the Finger Lakes region. The offerings include Rieslings, chardonnay, merlot, and cabernet sauvignon. Their signature wine, Melomel, is made of grapes and honey fermented in Kentucky bourbon barrels with no additives whatsoever. Visitors may enjoy live music and barbecue dinners on Friday nights from 6 to 9.

Swedish Hill Winery (518-450-1200), 379 Broadway. Open year-round, Monday through Friday 11–6; Saturday 11–8; Sunday noon–6. Extended hours during the summer months. This tasting room, which opened in 2011, offers 19 award-winning Swedish Hill wines, including sparkling selections. The vineyard is located in the Finger Lakes, but visitors can enjoy tasting their wines here.

✷ To Do

BICYCLING **Blue Sky Bicycles** (518-583-0600), 71 Church Street, rents hybrid bicycles (for recreational touring and riding). Open April through September, daily 10–7; October through March, Monday through Saturday 10–5.

BOATING **Fish Creek Marina** (518-587-9788), 251 County Route 67, on Saratoga Lake. From town, take Route 29 east, and make a right on Staffords Bridge Road (about 2 miles out of town). Go another 1.5 miles over the bridge, and you'll see the marina. Open May through September, daily from noon on. Rent canoes, kayaks, and rowboats here; there's a pizzeria on the premises that serves up slices, pies, calzones, and cold drinks. Learn how to kayak and canoe from a certified instructor, but call in advance to arrange lessons. Large pavilion available for barbecues and campfires. The most dramatic sunset can be seen from this spot on the lake—people come from all over Saratoga to see it!

Point Breeze Marina (518-587-3397), 1459 Route 9P, on Saratoga Lake. Open April through November, daily 9–6. This is a place to rent just about anything you want: canoes, kayaks, rowboats, pontoon boats, speedboats, and fishing boats. They have it all.

Saratoga Boat Works (518-584-BOAT), on Saratoga Lake. Open most of the year, Tuesday through Saturday 9–5. At the north end of the lake, near the bridge, just past the racetrack, this full-service marina is a good place to rent power boats or pontoon boats. If you want to water-ski, this is where to rent the necessary equipment, as well.

FARM STANDS AND PICK-YOUR-OWN FARMS Among the many things Saratoga is famous for is melon; more specifically Hand melons, named after the family that first grew them. **The Hand Melon Farm** (518-692-2376) is located 13 miles east of Saratoga Springs on Route 29; the melons are usually ready to go from late July through mid-September. They are sweet and resemble cantaloupes; you will see signs for them at many farm stands. You can also pick your

Saratoga Springs Chamber of Commerce

own strawberries in June; raspberries may be picked in September. The farm stand is open May through September.

A great deal of excellent produce is raised on local farms, as well. At **Ariel's Vegetable Farm** (518-584-2189), 194 Northern Pines Road, Gansevoort, 5 miles north of Saratoga Springs, visitors can pick their own berries, buy fruit and vegetables off the stand, or take a tour of the farm. Open April through December, daily 9–6.

Bowman Orchards and Farm Store (518-371-2042), 141 Sugar Hill Road, Rexford, has pick-your-own berries and apples. Try the farm store's apple pie ice cream; they sell more than 20 varieties of fudge. Open June through October, Wednesday through Saturday 10–5; Sunday noon–5.

Riverview Orchards (518-371-2174), 660 Riverview Road, Rexford, has pick-your-own apples (September and October) and farm tours. They are open year-round, daily 9–5.

The **Saratoga Farmers' Market** (518-747-9492) is held at High Rock Park (take Broadway north to Grover Street and watch for signs) May through October, every Wednesday evening 3–6 and Saturday 9–1. You can also sample more of the famous local waters there. There is a winter market held November through April on Saturday 9–1, at Division Street Elementary School, 220 Division Street.

FISHING Head out to **Saratoga Lake** early in the morning, and stop at one of the marinas or bait and tackle shops you will see around the lake for information on the local fishing scene (see *Boating*).

GOLF **Eagle Crest Golf Club** (518-877-7082), 1004 Route 146A, Clifton Park. Open April through October, 6 AM–8 PM. The 18-hole, par-72 championship course is fairly open—a good bet for novices. Also on the premises: a driving range, par-3 course, miniature golf course, restaurant, and snack bar.

Pioneer Hills Golf Course (518-885-7000), 3230 Galway Road, Ballston Spa. Open mid-April through October, weather permitting. This 18-hole, par-70 championship course has a restaurant and bar on the premises. In the summer months, golfers will enjoy the large outdoor patio (canopy covered), a nice place to enjoy refreshments after playing.

Saratoga Lake Golf Club (518-581-6616), 35 Grace Moore Road. Open April through October, 6:30 AM–8:30 PM. This 18-hole, par-72 course was designed in what was once the middle of a forest. Although not a championship course, it is quite challenging. The course has shorter distances for each hole, but there are many elevation changes. Accuracy will help you do well here. There is a snack bar, a pleasant spot to enjoy a drink after golfing.

Saratoga Mini Golf (518-581-0852), 3071 Route 50, Wilton. Take the Northway to exit 15. Make a right off the exit; the course is three lights down on the right side of the road. Open mid-April through mid-October. This is great stop for families traveling with children; it's only a 5- to 10-minute ride from the downtown area. Enjoy after-game treats from the snack bar after your round of miniature golf.

Saratoga National Golf Club (518-583-GOLF), 458 Union Avenue. Next to Longfellow's restaurant. Open late April through mid-November, depending on the weather, daily 7 AM–sunset. This beautifully maintained 18-hole, par-72 championship golf course has 24 bridges and several wetland areas, and is reminiscent of courses in South Carolina. The club opened in 2001, and *Golf Digest* magazine rated it the fifth best new course in the country. Call to reserve a tee time over the phone with a credit card 30 days in advance during summer months or a week or two in advance at other times of the year.

Saratoga Spa Golf Course (518-584-2006), 60 Roosevelt Drive, Saratoga Spa State Park. Open April through October, weekdays 6 AM–dusk, weekends from 5 AM. This beautifully maintained 18-hole, par-72 championship course boasts that no two holes touch each other. The towering pine trees make the surroundings special, and the prices are exceedingly reasonable. There is also a driving range, restaurant, and complete facilities. The Victoria Pool is adjacent to the golf course (see *Swimming*). They will take reservations one week in advance if you call 518-584-2008 to reserve a tee time. This is the way to go, particularly in the summer months.

HORSEBACK RIDING Muddy Acres Farm (518-581-0264), 95 County Route 21, Greenfield Center. Open during the summer months daily, except Wednesday, 10–dusk; the rest of the year, Saturday and Sunday 10–dusk, weather permitting. They offer one-hour trail rides and one-hour pony rides at reasonable rates here. Wagon and sleigh rides are also available. For those who want Western riding lessons, there is a certified instructor on staff. No reservations are necessary.

Schauber Stables (518-399-2484), 428 Schauber Road, Ballston Spa. Open spring through autumn, weather permitting. They offer trail rides combined with a trail lesson lasting 45 minutes to one hour. The minimum age requirement is seven, and there is a weight limit of 220 pounds; the cost is $30. Mini trail rides are available for half price. Family Fun Tours include a tour of the facility as well as an opportunity to feed the horses, pony rides for the children, and a craft activity. The cost is $30 for up to two adults and two children; each additional person is $5. For further details about this program, or to make a reservation, call Karen at 518-281-0088.

HORSE RACING Saratoga Casino and Raceway (518-584-2110; 1-800-727-2990), 342 Jefferson Street. Open year-round, daily 9 AM–4 AM. Admission fee. Formerly a plain harness track, the raceway was often overshadowed by its sassier cousin, the Saratoga Race Course. But it has expanded to include gaming (slot machines, electronic table games, etc.) in a 55,000-square-foot facility and now offers lots of excitement around the clock. This is the first video gaming property to open in New York State. Visitors can also enjoy watching horses vie for purses on the world's fastest half-mile trotting and pacing track, which, unlike the "flats," is open year-round. (The backstretch area contains the only pool in the state located on the grounds of a racetrack and reserved solely for the use of horses.) There are two polo fields and an outdoor arena with more than 200 acres and 1,100 stalls for the equine patrons. Several restaurants are in a large food court. Special events include a Fourth of July fireworks display. In order to enter the casino, you must be 18 years of age.

Saratoga Race Course (518-584-6200 in season; 718-641-4700 out of season; www.nyra.com), 267 Union Avenue. Open for six weeks from late July through

Labor Day only; call for specific dates, which change each season. Closed Tuesday. Admission fee. The Saratoga racetrack is a hub of activity for a month and a half, and it is busy from early in the morning until the late afternoon. Rub shoulders with celebrities, rail birds, and just plain people; dress in jeans and T-shirts or elegant suits and hats; the choice is yours, and the ghost of Damon Runyon hovers over all. You can begin with Breakfast at Saratoga (7–9:30 AM; get there early; free admission), a popular way for people to enjoy the horses and jockeys close up. An announcer keeps things lively as the horses and their riders breeze by. Handicapping seminars—very useful for novice bettors—are held at the track and are announced at breakfast; the seminar times are also posted throughout the track. Breakfast is also served daily in the clubhouse dining room, in an outdoor tent, and buffet style in the box seats; outside, a continental breakfast is served near the clubhouse. Visitors can enjoy a tour of the backstretch area, as well, where the horses board during the racing season. The tour is escorted, and the area is viewed from an observation "train"; sign up for the tour early during breakfast.

The track opens to the racing crowd at 11 AM weekdays and 10:30 AM weekends. Although there is lots of parking and seating available, remember one thing: The crowds can be large, and the track is smaller than many modern racetracks. Get there early for good viewing. You can park in an official track lot or at a private lot. The latter cost more, but the former fill up quickly; again, get there early so at least you have a selection. Bring your own chair if possible, and remember that both restaurant food and snacks, though usually good, can be very expensive. You are allowed to bring coolers into the track. Both steeplechases and flat races are held throughout the season; check the daily racing forms to see exactly who is racing in what. Races begin (post time) at 1 PM weekdays, 12:30 PM weekends, rain or shine.

POLO You can't play polo unless you have your own string of ponies, but you can watch in season at Saratoga. The players come from all over the world and are the best in their sport. Matches are held July through Labor Day, Friday and Sunday at 5:30 PM. For hours and a complete schedule, call 518-584-8108 or check the website www.saratogapolo.com.

The events are held at Whitney Field, out Seward Street. To get to the polo grounds at Whitney Field, go north on Broadway, turn left onto Church Street, go about 0.5 mile, and make a right onto Seward Street. Go 1 mile to the railroad overpass and turn right; the polo field is on the left.

SCENIC RAILROAD RIDE **Saratoga and North Creek Railway** (1-877-726-7245; www.sncrr.com), 26 Station Lane. Open Memorial Day weekend through October, Thursday through Monday. There are three trips daily starting from North Creek to Saratoga. A nice excursion is to leave Saratoga for North Creek at 10 AM and arrive at 12:15 PM. There are several places to have lunch in North Creek, and the village is filled with interesting shops. A train leaves at 3:45 PM and arrives back in Saratoga at 6 PM. It is possible to return later at night, and those who go fishing or rafting may choose to do so, or perhaps stay overnight. Check the website for the up-to-date schedule.

SWIMMING **Saratoga Spa State Park** (518-584-2000), South Broadway. There are two pools in the park, and both are open to the public. The **Victoria Pool**

opens Memorial Day weekend and remains open until Labor Day, daily 10–6. Admission fee. There is a smaller pool here for young children in addition to the larger pool. The **Peerless Pool** is open from late June to Labor Day, also daily 10–6. Admission and parking fee. This Olympic-size pool is a great place to cool off after a day at the races or walking the streets of the city. If you have small children, however, the Victoria Pool is probably a better choice.

YMCA (518-583-9622), 262 Broadway. Indoor pool only. Open year-round; call for information on public swimming sessions, which change daily. There are family swim times, as well. The pool is 25 yards long and five lengths wide; temperature is usually around 84 degrees.

✷ Winter Sports

CROSS-COUNTRY SKIING **Saratoga Spa State Park** (518-584-2535). A network of marvelous groomed trails here should delight cross-country skiers of all abilities.

ICE SKATING **Saratoga Spa State Park** (518-584-2535), South Broadway. There is an outdoor rink here in season, weather permitting. Call for hours, which change depending on the weather. There is open adult hockey here.

Saratoga Springs Ice Rinks (518-583-3462), Weibel Avenue. There are two rinks here, and they accommodate both hockey and figure skating. Open year-round, except from mid-April to late June. Call for a schedule, which varies from week to week. Weibel rink is Olympic size, and the Vernon rink is smaller. Both offer public skates and family skate, open adult figure, and hockey sessions.

✷ Green Space

Bog Meadow Nature Trail (518-587-5554). Open year-round, daily dawn to dusk. Free. (From Broadway make a right onto Route 29 east. Go through the traffic light at Weibel Avenue; the trail entrance is about 500 feet farther on the right.) This 2-mile nature trail is ideal for people traveling with children. It's fairly flat and goes through the wetlands just outside town. You can run or walk in the warm-weather months and cross-country ski or snowshoe in the winter. Parking area.

Congress Park (518-587-3550). Open year-round. This is a lovely city park to stroll through, particularly after shopping on Broadway (see *To See—Springs & Spas*).

East Side Recreation Field (518-587-3550), 226 Lake Avenue. (Make a right turn on Lake Avenue and go about 1.5 miles. The field is on the right side, just after the East Avenue light.) Open year-round. This 20-acre park is free; it has an excellent skateboard park (open daily May through October—a small fee is charged for this activity only). There is also a spray fountain for small children, as well as tennis courts, playground, basketball courts, and a quarter-mile paved circular track that's great for rollerblading and running.

Saratoga Spa State Park (518-584-2535; www.saratogaspastatepark.org), 1 mile south of Saratoga Springs on Route 9. Open year-round. This park is free; there is a small charge for swimming and the bathhouses. This 2,000-acre park is a gem;

clean, wide open, full of activities to keep visitors busy—and located only minutes from Saratoga Springs. Listed on the National Register of Historic Places, the park is home to the Saratoga Performing Arts Center, known as SPAC (see *Entertainment*), and the Gideon Putnam hotel (see *Lodging*). Recreation opportunities abound in Spa Park: Two pools, tennis courts, streamside trails for walking, and two golf courses (reservations required) are open during the summer months; in the winter months, cross-country skiing and ice skating are available. Special film evenings, nature walks, tours, and other special events are held throughout the year (call for a schedule).

Yaddo (518-584-0746; www.yaddo.org), 312 Union Avenue (Route 9P). Open year-round, but the gardens are at their height from June through September. Free. The plantings here are superb, and visitors are welcome to walk among the paths and enjoy the fountains, roses, and peaceful seating areas. Yaddo, once a private home, is now an artists' retreat offering residencies to professional creative artists working in virtually all media and used by both the famous and the someday-to-be-famous; the site offers a respite from the August frenzy of racing and the society scene. *Note:* Mid-June through Labor Day, Saturday and Sunday at 11 AM (also Tuesday during racing season), a guided garden tour is given. A small fee is charged.

✱ Lodging

A note on lodging—and dining—in Saratoga Springs: The Spa City is a wonderful place to visit and spend a day or a week. As in many other resort areas, prices range from moderate to expensive. But during the "season"—late July through Labor Day, when thoroughbred racing is the main event—prices can go sky-high, and accommodations may be difficult to obtain (some places are booked solid as early as April). Restaurants can be crowded, expensive, and difficult to obtain reservations for—that is, unless you know someone. I'm not suggesting that you pass up the excitement that is Saratoga Springs during the summer—it's still a great time to visit—but be prepared to pay top price for lodging and dining out. I prefer to go in May and October, when the city is much calmer and the weather is still beautiful. If you are going to visit the area during the summer, you may want to consider staying in Albany (see "Albany"), which is about a half hour south. *Note:* All listings are in Saratoga Springs 12866 unless otherwise indicated. They are organized by type of accommodation: hotel, motel, or inn/bed & breakfast.

HOTELS Adelphi Hotel (518-587-4688), 365 Broadway. ($$$) This renovated grand Victorian hotel, originally constructed in 1877, is located in the heart of Saratoga, and it exudes elegance and charm, transporting visitors back to another era. There are 39 rooms, including 18 suites of varying sizes; two have private balconies. Every room is different, but all are elaborately decorated in the Victorian style, and most have queen-size beds. A Saratoga tradition is to air oneself on the balcony in the afternoon; if you want to do so, ask for a room facing Broadway, since those are the rooms with balconies. The peaceful courtyard within the hotel looks out on a beautiful old-fashioned swimming pool. The Grand Lobby, with its stenciled walls and ceilings, opens up into the Adelphi Café, a bar-café that is a popular local gathering spot (see *Eating Out*). The café serves desserts, light snacks, and drinks 3 PM–2 AM and is an oasis away from the bustle of Broadway just outside the hotel. A continental breakfast is served to guests (on the piazza, which overlooks Broadway, in the warm-weather months). Children are welcome. Open mid-May through mid-October.

Gideon Putnam Resort and Spa (518-584-3000; 1-800-732-1560), Saratoga Spa State Park. ($$$) This historic Georgian-style resort hotel is set in the 2,200-acre park, a few minutes' walk from the Saratoga Performing Arts Center (see *Entertainment*) and minutes away from the track and downtown Saratoga Springs. The resort is named after one of Saratoga's first settlers, Gideon Putnam, the founder of the hotel business in Saratoga. Born in Massachusetts in 1763, Putnam arrived in Saratoga with his wife in 1789 and set up a sawmill that became successful. He then invested in another business, the Putnam Tavern and Boarding House; a bathhouse followed later. Today referred to as the Jewel of Saratoga, the Gideon Putnam stands as a reminder of Saratoga's history. Don't forget to check out the murals by renowned artist James Reynolds in the dining room, depicting scenes from Saratoga society and the Adirondacks. Several celebrities have stayed at the hotel, including Robert Redford, in 1997, when he filmed *The Horse Whisperer.* A scene from the Dustin Hoffman film *Billy Bathgate* was shot in the hotel lobby in 1991. It's my favorite place to stay in the city, and it blends the ambience of the past with all the modern conveniences. In addition to 102 double rooms, 18 parlor and porch suites are available. The service is quite good, and guests may choose to have meals included in the rate. In fact, several packages are available, so inquire about them, particularly if you will be staying midweek or off-season. Children welcome. Open year-round.

Hampton Inn & Suites (518-584-2100), 25 Lake Avenue. ($$$) This 2008 addition to the hotel scene in Saratoga has 123 rooms in the heart of the downtown area. There is an indoor pool, fitness center, and Internet access. The hotel is conveniently located to Broadway. Children welcome.

The Inn at Saratoga (518-583-1890; 1-800-274-3573), 231 Broadway. ($$$) This establishment combines the modern comforts of a hotel and the charming touches of an inn. There are 42 rooms and suites, all decorated in Victorian style. A restaurant downstairs serves dinner nightly, and continental breakfast is served to all hotel guests. Children welcome. Open year-round.

Marriott Courtyard (518-226-0538; 1-866-4-COURTYD), 11 Excelsior Avenue. ($$$) Located within walking distance of shops and restaurants, this luxury hotel has 146 rooms and suites. There is an indoor pool, whirlpool, fitness center, and Internet access. A restaurant on the premises serves breakfast and lunch. Children welcome.

Residence Inn by Marriott (518-584-9600), 295 Excelsior Avenue. ($$) There are 102 spacious suites here, all with a fully equipped kitchen and separate areas for sleeping and relaxing. An extended-stay hotel with homelike surroundings, it is a good choice for families traveling with young children. There are all the modern amenities, including high-speed Internet access, indoor heated pool, and fitness room. Open year-round.

Saratoga Arms (518-584-1775), 497 Broadway. ($$) This concierge hotel, with 31 rooms, in the middle of the downtown area, is perfect for those who want to be within walking distance of shops, restaurants, and cultural activities. It is housed in a brick building that dates from 1870 and is filled with grand staircases, ornate moldings, and ceiling medallions. Every room is beautifully restored and custom decorated with period pieces and antiques; the rooms also have phones, TVs, and wireless Internet access. Some have working fireplaces. The antique wicker furniture on the wraparound porch overlooking Broadway is a great place to get comfortable and relax after sightseeing or attending the races. A full breakfast is served. There is also a fitness room and small spa on the premises. Children over the age of 12 welcome. Open year-round.

Saratoga Hilton (1-866-773-7070), 534 Broadway. ($$$) This full-service hotel in the heart of Saratoga's downtown is only a short walk from shops and restaurants. The 212 renovated guest rooms and 30 spacious suites are decorated in vibrant colors. Facilities include an indoor heated pool and fitness center with sauna. All rooms have cable TV, wireless Internet access, telephones, and air-conditioning. Open year-round.

MOTELS **Adirondack Inn** (518-584-3510), 230 West Avenue. ($$) Located on 3.5 acres, yet only five blocks from Broadway, this inn offers visitors either a private cottage or a standard motel room. All rooms, however, have cable TV and refrigerators. There is an outdoor pool, barbecue grill, and shuttle-bus service to the race course. A continental breakfast is served, but a three-day minimum stay is required in season. Children welcome. Open year-round.

Carriage House Inn (518-584-4220), 198 Broadway. ($$) There are 14 spacious Victorian- and Adirondack-style suites here, all with private bath. Some have canopy beds and a fireplace, others have a kitchenette and Jacuzzi tub. All have air-conditioning and TV. Guests will enjoy the atmosphere of an inn as well as the privacy and convenience of a hotel. Enjoy coffee or tea in the morning on the lovely porch during the warm-weather months. Open year-round.

Grand Union Motel (518-584-9000), 120 South Broadway. ($) There are 64 clean, quiet, well-maintained rooms at this reasonably priced motel, located between the race course and SPAC. There is an outdoor pool for swimming, and guests will enjoy taking the waters at the Rosemary Spring on the property (see *To See—Springs & Spas*). The Crystal Spa on the premises offers a variety of services: from mud and seaweed body wraps to scalp treatments, facials, and aromatherapy. Children welcome. Open year-round.

Saratoga Motel (518-584-0920), 440 Church Street. ($) Set on 5 acres, located only a few miles from downtown, this small motel has nine rooms, all with air-conditioning and refrigerators, two with kitchenettes. There is no breakfast served and there is no swimming pool, but the queen-size beds are comfortable. Good value.

Springs Motel (518-584-6336), 189 Broadway. ($) This clean, comfortable standard motel is a short walk from the race course and the state park. There are 28 rooms, all with air-conditioning, cable TV, and telephone. An outdoor pool here makes this a good place to stop if you are traveling with young children. Open year-round.

INNS/BED & BREAKFASTS

Batcheller Mansion (518-584-7012), 20 Circular Street. ($$$) Built in 1873 by George Sherman Batcheller, an attorney and judge, this magnificent structure is resplendent with beautiful gardens and architectural details that will delight history buffs. In fact, President Ulysses S. Grant slept here shortly after the house was built. They still host guests in the timeless tradition of grace and ease reminiscent of a century long gone. The nine graciously appointed rooms, four with fireplaces, offer a warm and inviting reprieve from the outside world. This is the perfect spot for a romantic getaway. The luxurious surroundings include a plush sitting room and a library where you can recline on one of the red-velvet sofas. The formal dining room breakfast offers a glorious start to the day, with freshly baked breads and pastries of your choice. No children. Open year-round.

Brunswick Bed & Breakfast (1-800-585-6751), 143 Union Avenue. ($) This is one of the oldest continuously operating lodging facilities in Saratoga Springs; they have been serving guests since 1886. There are 10 private rooms, 2 of them suites; all are centrally air-conditioned, with a good deal of variety—one room has a gas fireplace; two rooms have Jacuzzis; one suite has a kitchenette. All rooms have wireless Internet access, cable TV, and a VCR; a video library offers dozens of movie selections. If you are planning to stay for a week during the summer racing season, attractive discount rates are available here, which is unusual. The value for the money is excellent. Children welcome. Open year-round.

Chestnut Tree Inn (518-587-8681; 1-888-243-7688), 9 Whitney Place. ($$) Named after the last remaining chestnut tree in Saratoga Springs, this inn offers country ambience within walking distance of the racetrack and other points of interest. Continental breakfast is served on the Victorian porch in summer, and the inn is furnished with antiques. Seven rooms, all with private bath. Children welcome. Open May through November.

Circular Manor (518-583-6393), 120 Circular Street. ($$) This 6,000-square-foot Victorian home was built in 1903 by Newton Breeze, a well-known Saratoga architect at the turn of the 20th century. There are five beautifully decorated guest rooms, all with private bath, central air-conditioning, claw-foot tubs, and marble floors. This is a place where you will feel pampered yet comfortable. All the important details have been attended to here: There are beautiful duvets, cotton sheets, and luxurious Egyptian-cotton towels. The full gourmet breakfast (a few choices are available daily) features freshly baked breads, fruit, and wonderful egg creations. Enjoy relaxing on the huge wraparound porch in the heart of Saratoga's historic district, a quiet section of town surrounded by lovely Victorian homes yet only a few blocks away from the shops and restaurants. No children. Open year-round.

Geyser Lodge Bed & Breakfast (518-584-0389), 182 Ballston Avenue. ($) For those travelers on a limited budget, this is the place to go in Saratoga. A comfortable Queen Anne–style Victorian dating from 1896, this spacious, 16-room B&B was once referred to as a "cottage" by the wealthy New York City family who used it as a summer residence. Located near Skidmore College, this B&B offers four guest rooms, all with private bath and air-conditioning; some have TV and telephone. Full breakfast on weekends; continental during the week. In-ground pool in the backyard and wireless Internet access. Great value for the money. Children over the age of 12 welcome; their policy is flexible with younger ones, so be sure to inquire. Open year-round, except the month of January.

The Mansion (518-885-1607; 1-888-996-9977), 801 Route 29, Rock City Falls 12863. Located 7 miles west of town on Route 29. ($$$) This inn was built in 1866 as the summer home of a prominent industrialist, George West, across the street from his Excelsior Mill. (He also invented the folded paper bag and became known as the Paper Bag King!) The inn has had only six owners and is a dream come true for lovers of Victoriana. The mansion has been featured in several publications (in fact, a Chico's catalog was photographed here). Designed to suggest a Venetian villa, the building retains its original mirrored fireplaces and elaborate chandeliers. The rooms are comfortably furnished with Victorian antiques, and Mamie Eisenhower's piano is the striking centerpiece of the downstairs library. A full gourmet breakfast is served in the dining room from 8:30 to 10. Guests may use the parlor, the library, walk the grounds, or relax on the porch. This is truly a special spot, and it's worth traveling outside Saratoga Springs to stay here, particularly if you want a respite from the crowds during the summer racing season. The old mill and lovely waterfall across the street from the inn are perfect for taking a short stroll after breakfast. (I enjoyed running on a beautiful road that follows a stream on the grounds of a state fishing preserve, close to the B&B; ask the owners, and they will direct you.) All nine rooms have private bath, wireless Internet access, and individually controlled air-conditioning. Adults only. Open year-round, except the month of January.

Saratoga Farmstead Bed & Breakfast (518-587-2074), 41 Locust Grove Road. ($$) This bed & breakfast is 2 miles from downtown Saratoga Springs and is located in a restored 18th-century farmhouse. Guests may enjoy seven air-conditioned rooms, all with private bath, plus a large gourmet breakfast (many items in season come from the organic garden on the premises). This is a casual farm setting, a nice change from the rush of downtown in the summer. Bring your binoculars with you; there are a few acres of walking trails filled with wildflowers and birds of all kinds. Children welcome. Open year-round.

Saratoga Sleigh (518-584-4534), 203 Union Avenue. ($$) The location here is attractive to those who want to be near the action: This moderately priced B&B overlooks the race course. Housed in a historic 1887 Queen Anne Victorian, the B&B's four rooms, all with private bath, are filled with antiques. Each room is air-conditioned and has a TV. A full breakfast is served. Children must be over the age of 12. Open year-round.

Six Sisters Bed & Breakfast (518-583-1173), 149 Union Avenue. ($$) This charming establishment, named after the six sisters of one of the owners, is located on the flower-bedecked Union Avenue approach to the racetrack. At Six Sisters guests will enjoy a gourmet breakfast and their choice of four guest rooms or suites, all with private bath and air-conditioning. Only minutes from most of the goings-on in Saratoga Springs, this inn is a lovely place to enjoy a special weekend. Older children welcome. Open year-round.

Union Gables Bed & Breakfast (518-584-1558), 55 Union Avenue. ($$) This restored Queen Anne Victorian, circa 1901, is a family-owned and -occupied bed & breakfast. Each of the 10 guest rooms is exquisitely decorated to reflect the style of Old Saratoga. Every room has a modern bath, TV, telephone, wireless Internet access, and a small refrigerator. The establishment is conveniently located near the downtown area and only one block from the thoroughbred racetrack. Children and pets are welcome. Open year-round.

Westchester House Bed & Breakfast (518-587-7613; 1-800-581-7613), 102 Lincoln Avenue. ($$) Built in high Gothic style—complete with towers, crenellations, and oddments—this charming inn is a fairy tale come true. There are seven rooms, all with private bath, telephone, and wireless Internet access. The rooms offer luxury touches like ceiling fans, air-conditioning, and fresh flowers from the surrounding gardens in summer. Downtown Saratoga Springs is a few minutes' walk away, and guests can enjoy sitting on the porch while looking forward to the morning's breakfast of fruit salad, choice of cereal, home-baked goods, and fresh gourmet coffee. Older children only. Open May through October.

✷ Where to Eat

There is a wealth of wonderful restaurants in the Spa City. Some of the establishments listed are popular with both travelers and local residents. I have included my favorite places to eat in Saratoga Springs, whether you are seeking a leisurely gourmet dinner or a quick, informal lunch. All are top-notch. Please note that restaurants are located within the city limits unless otherwise indicated.

Due to the fact that life in Saratoga Springs changes so drastically during the summer racing season, some restaurants may cut back their hours in the winter months. If you are visiting during the months of January through March, especially on a Monday or Tuesday, do call ahead to make sure the restaurant of your choice is open. The days and hours of operation listed here are for *most* months of the year.

DINING OUT **Beekman Street Bistro** (518-581-1816), 62 Beekman

DINING AL FRESCO AT SARATOGA'S ADELPHI HOTEL ON BROADWAY

Saratoga Springs Chamber of Commerce

Street. ($$) Open for dinner Tuesday through Sunday 5–9. This bistro, located in Saratoga's art district, features changing exhibits of local artists on its walls. The oak floors are made from salvaged 19th-century barn boards. Warm colors and a cozy atmosphere make this a vibrant addition to the city's restaurant scene. The chef-owner prides himself on the fact that 85 percent of the menu items are from within 30 miles of the restaurant. Pork, lamb, and seasonal produce come from local farms. A popular winter entrée is the slow roasted pork shoulder with local potatoes. The homemade goat cheese and chervil ravioli is also a favorite dish. Desserts are all made from scratch and include maple crème brûlée and panna cotta with local honey and nuts. Children are welcome.

Capriccio Saratoga Restaurant/Café (518-587-9463), 26 Henry Street. ($$) Open for dinner daily from 5 PM. This first-rate Italian restaurant features Neapolitan cuisine, with phenomenal pizza and pasta prepared to perfection. The stuffed eggplant is excellent. Don't skip dessert: I recommend both the tiramisu and orange ricotta cheesecake.

Chianti Il Ristorante (518-580-0025), 18 Division Street. ($$$) Open for dinner daily 5:30–10. Savor new trends in Northern Italian cuisine in this upscale establishment with impeccable service. The chef suggests the capellini with lobster and prawns, or the penne pasta with cannellini beans and sausage. Some of the other entrées include stuffed quail, risotto with porcini and filetto al Gorgonzola, and salmon dishes (I sampled one of these, and it was superb). The portions are exceedingly generous, and there are more than 300 selections on the wine list. Make sure to leave room for dessert; the tiramisu and chocolate soufflé are excellent. Reservations are not taken here, so it is best to arrive before 6 or after 9 to avoid waiting. Not recommended for young children.

Duo Japanese Restaurant and Lounge (518-580-8881), 175 South Broadway. ($$) Open Monday through Thursday 11:30–10; Friday until 11; Saturday noon–11; Sunday 1–10. Bar is always open until 2 AM. Enjoy modern Japanese cuisine in a contemporary atmosphere. The sushi and sashimi are excellent. Lunch specials are offered daily and are quite reasonable. This is also a nice place to relax and have a couple of rolls and a pot of green tea—or sake—after shopping downtown. Not recommended for children.

Forno Bistro (518-581-2401), 541 Broadway. ($$) Open for dinner daily 5–10. The casual yet elegant ambience here is inviting and romantic. An enclosed terrace is a lovely place to dine in the warm weather. The Tuscan cuisine is "rustic Italian," and the imaginative pastas created by the chef-owner from Tuscany are superior. The wood-fired pizzas and calamari are excellent as well. Make sure to stop in here when you visit Saratoga.

Gideon Putnam Hotel/Putnam's Restaurant & Bar (518-584-3000), Saratoga Spa State Park. ($$) Open daily for breakfast 7–10:30; lunch and dinner served 11–8, until 9 on Friday and Saturday. Sunday brunch served 10:30–2. Set in the lovely Spa Park, this hotel restaurant is often packed in the evening before a concert or ballet. The cuisine here combines contemporary American favorites and classic Continental fare. The Sunday brunch is outstanding and well worth the wait (seatings every half hour between 10:30 and 2). Reservations are required for dinner. Children welcome.

Jacob and Anthony's American Grille (518-871-1600), 38 High Rock

Avenue. ($$) Open Monday through Thursday 11–9:30; Friday and Saturday until 10:30; Sunday 11–9. They serve up classic American favorites here—soups, salads, burgers, wraps, steaks and seafood—with interesting variations on the usual fare. There is an enormous menu with something for everyone. Children welcome.

Lake Ridge Restaurant (518-899-6000), 35 Burlington Avenue, Round Lake (exit 11 off the Northway). ($$) Open Tuesday through Saturday for lunch 11:30–2:30; dinner 5–9. Chef Scott Ringwood offers fine Continental dining at reasonable prices. The menu includes excellent steaks, seafood, and pasta. The pork rack and breast of duck are imaginatively prepared; they're my favorites. It's worth the drive south of the city. Children welcome.

Longfellow's Inn & Restaurant (518-587-0108), 500 Union Avenue. ($$$) Open for dinner Monday through Saturday 5–10; Sunday 4–9. Located in an old country estate dating from the late 1800s, this establishment prides itself on its warm, relaxing ambience. The restaurant is unusual in that it has a waterfall and pond *inside.* The American cuisine here includes several mesquite offerings. In addition to prime rib, rack of lamb, seafood, and pasta entrées, there are some rather imaginative creations. Try the bourbon-glazed salmon or pan-roasted garlic shrimp. There is something on the menu here to please every taste. Children are welcome.

Max London's (518-587-3535), 466 Broadway. ($$) Open for dinner daily 5–10; brunch served Friday through Sunday 11–3. Mrs. London's son, Max, has created a wonderful contemporary restaurant serving pizzas, pastas, and small plates of treats like Copper River salmon tartare or grilled quail salad. The "big plates" include grilled pork porterhouse chop and Painted Hills hanger steak. Don't skip dessert. In addition to the black bottom butterscotch budino with soft caramel I sampled (truly ambrosia-like), there is Chocolate Maximus with pistachio ice cream, along with a sizeable selection of after-dinner drinks.

One Caroline Street Bistro (518-587-2026), 1 Caroline Street. ($$) Open for dinner daily 5:30–10. This family-owned and family-operated bistro-style restaurant has live music nightly. The cuisine is an international mix featuring Cajun, Italian, and Asian dishes. The chef tells me that the jambalaya and filet mignon are among the most popular entrées—but adventurous diners won't want to miss the tasty Thai-style bouillabaisse.

Panza's on the Lake (518-584-6882), 510 Route 9P, Saratoga Lake. ($$) Open for lunch daily, except Tuesday and Saturday, noon–4; dinner Wednesday through Sunday 5–10. Solid Italian American cuisine with a Continental flair is what you can enjoy here, along with beautiful views of the lake. There is a full bar with an extensive wine list, and this is a nice place to just enjoy cocktails. Known for his veal dishes, the chef suggests the veal martone (with shrimp, artichoke hearts, and mushrooms). The shrimp sorentino (topped with eggplant, prosciutto, and fresh mozzarella) is another popular entrée. All desserts are homemade on the premises. Children welcome. Reservations suggested.

Prime at Saratoga National Golf Club (518-583-4653), 458 Union Avenue. ($$$) (Located off exit 14 of I-87; take Route 9P south 1 mile.) Open for lunch Monday through Saturday 11–4; dinner served daily 5:30–10; Sunday brunch 10–2. If you are a major carnivore and enjoy prime steak, this is the place to go. You will be paying handsomely for the meal, however. From USDA prime to steak au poivre as well as fish and seafood selections, the cuisine is excellent. The restaurant here is a satellite operation of Angelo's 677 Prime in Albany. There is a full-time pastry chef, so save room for the mouthwatering desserts. In the warm-weather months, dine alfresco on the lovely outdoor terrace. There is an extensive wine list here. Reservations suggested.

Siro's (518-584-4030), 168 Lincoln Avenue. ($$$) Open daily for dinner during racing season only (late July through Labor Day). Call for hours, which may vary. This is probably the most popular dinner spot with race-goers. Reservations are required, although the bar area is open and crowded. The food here is Continental, with steak and seafood the specialties. Recommended if you want to continue enjoying the horsey atmosphere—and the crowds—during the evening hours.

Siro's Trattoria at the Lodge (518-584-7988), 1 Nelson Avenue. ($$) Open Wednesday through Sunday from 6 PM on (daily during racing season). Siro's restaurant has been a mainstay in Saratoga for decades. Now diners may enjoy this offshoot of the restaurant closer to the track. There is even an outdoor lawn bar that serves drinks after the races end in the late afternoon. The cuisine is Mediterranean, with an emphasis on Italian offerings, steaks, and seafood. The two-story structure was built in the early 20th century and was once owned by philanthropist Harry Payne Whitney. Reservations are essential. (Note that Siro's also has a kiosk serving food at the racetrack.)

Sperry's (518-584-9618), 30 Caroline Street. ($$) Open for dinner daily 5–10; Saturday and Sunday brunch 11–2. This American bistro-style restaurant offers grilled seafood and steak specials, fresh pasta, and sautéed soft-shell crabs in season. The homemade pastries and desserts are first-rate: The crème caramel was featured in the *New York Times*. They butcher their own meats here, there is a pastry chef on the premises, and many of the herbs used in the warm-weather months are grown in their own garden. The bar is a favorite of jockeys and trainers. One of Saratoga's most reliable year-round gems. Reservations are recommended.

Sushi Thai Garden (518-580-0900), 44–46 Phila Street. ($$) Open daily for lunch 11–3; for dinner 5–10. Step off the busy streets of Saratoga Springs into the Far East for a taste of fine, exotic Thai cuisine. They make every dish to order here, with the freshest ingredients. Japanese entrées like chicken teriyaki are offered, as well as several vegetarian selections. The sushi bar is excellent. Children welcome.

Tiznow (518-226-0655), 84 Henry Street. ($$) Open for dinner Tuesday through Thursday 4–9; Friday and Saturday 3–10. A former machine shop has been transformed into a stylish bistro with black woodwork, brick walls, and jewel-colored votive candles. International cuisine highlighting French and Asian specialties is featured here, with such starters as pork pâté with pistachios or tuna and salmon tartare. For entrées there is lobster and crab ravioli or Burmese orange chicken. Latin music and dancing on many Friday and Saturday nights.

The Wine Bar (518-584-8777), 417 Broadway. ($$) Open for dinner Tuesday through Sunday 4–10. Live piano music on Friday and Saturday 7–10 during the summer months.

Oenophiles rejoice: There are nearly 50 different wines that may be ordered by the glass here. The eclectic American menu complements the large wine list with entrées like rack of lamb, panko-crusted ahi tuna, and Cuban spiced pork tenderloin. There is also a cheese sampler featuring both European and American offerings. Outdoor dining during the summer months. This is one of the few places that has a separate smoking lounge.

EATING OUT **Adelphi Café** (518-587-4688), 365 Broadway. ($$) Dessert, light snacks, and drinks are served from mid-May through mid-October, daily 3 PM–2 AM. The Victorian surroundings, which echo the old-time elegance of Saratoga Springs, should not be missed on a walk up Broadway—even if you don't have the time to enjoy a repast in this wonderfully unique café, stop in for a look around.

Caffè Lena (518-583-0022; www.caffelena.org), 47 Phila Street. ($$) Open Wednesday through Sunday, but hours change depending on the entertainment. Almost all major folk, jazz, and blues artists have appeared at this well-known coffeehouse and nightspot over the years. The food is secondary to the performances, although the coffee, including specialties like iced mocha java, is excellent. Thursday evenings are open-mike nights, and on Sunday afternoons there are occasionally special programs for children. This is worth a stop, no matter who is on the bill. Not recommended for children in the evening. Check the website for detailed information on the performance schedule.

Cantina (518-587-5577), 430 Broadway. ($) Open daily 11:30–9; Friday and Saturday until 10. The hearty Mexican cuisine with international influences is served in a festive casual atmosphere, with alfresco dining on the patio in the warm weather. Portions are generous, and the margaritas are first-rate. Children welcome.

Country Corner Café (518-583-7889), 25 Church Street. ($) Open Monday through Friday 6–2; Saturday and Sunday 7–3. One of the best breakfasts in town is served until closing time in this cozy café. Try the home-baked breads and muffins with preserves or the fresh fruit pancakes with maple syrup. The hearty soups and sandwiches make this a popular lunch spot with local residents.

Dango Fitzgerald's Irish Pub, Steakhouse & Sports Bar (518-587-2022), 38 Caroline Street. ($$) Open daily 11 AM–4 AM. All the basic pub fare may be found here—salads, sandwiches, burgers, wraps, steaks, seafood, and pizza. The Irish chowder is a house specialty.

Druthers Brewpub (518-306-5275), 381 Broadway. ($$) Open daily 11 AM–midnight. This brewpub, which opened in the summer of 2012, is one where you can actually have a conversation! The floors, tables, and bar were made from wood taken from an 1840s-era Columbia County barn. The brewmaster, George de Piro, from the Albany Pump Station, explains the name of the place comes from the saying, "given our druthers, we would brew beer." There are 12 different beers on tap. The menu offers something for everyone and features steaks, fish, ribs, burgers, pasta, sandwiches, chili, salads, and more.

Esperanto (518-587-4236), 6 Caroline Street. ($) Open for lunch and dinner Sunday and Monday 11 AM–10 PM; Tuesday and Wednesday until 2 AM; Thursday until 3 AM; Friday and Saturday until 4 AM. International cuisine, using the freshest ingredients for soups, salads, pizza, and sandwiches. Enjoy falafel, jambalaya, Mexican specialties, and a few imaginative daily specials, as well.

Gaffney's (518-587-7359), 16 Caroline Street. ($) Open daily for lunch 11:30–3; dinner 5–11. Also open for Sunday brunch 9:30–3. The menu is huge and offers a range of selections including steak, seafood, burgers, soups, omelets, and salads.

Hattie's (518-584-4790), 45 Phila Street. ($) Open for dinner 5–10 daily; Saturday and Sunday brunch 9–2. Since 1938 this is the place Saratogians have been going for Southern-style fried foods: chicken, fish, potatoes, and more. For lovers of the lost art of the deep fry, this is the place to go. Children are welcome.

The Local Pub & Teahouse (518-587-7256), 142 Grand Avenue. ($) Open Monday through Friday 11:30 AM–midnight; Saturday and Sunday brunch 9:30–3; dinner 3–midnght. There is decent basic are here—soups, salads, burgers, tea sandwiches, and the usual kind—and the prices are inexpensive. They are known for their fish-and-chips. It's a nice place to go for a break from shopping and enjoy afternoon tea. There is a separate tea menu, of course!

Maestro's at the Van Dam (518-580-0312), 353 Broadway. ($) Open daily for lunch 11:30–3; dinner 5–9:30. This delightful bistro located in a historic hotel, the former Rip Van Dam, serves regional American cuisine (on their beautiful stone terrace during the summer months). For lunch there are wraps, sandwiches, and salads. Dinner entrées include steaks, scallops, salmon, smoked chicken pasta, duck, and veal. Everything is first-rate here; it's a popular choice among local residents. The menu offers something to please every palate!

Mrs. London's (518-581-1652), 464 Broadway. ($$) Open daily 7–6. The homemade soups, sandwiches, and wraps are first-rate, and the baked goods are the best in the city. Don't miss this spot for an elegant lunch.

Nunzio's Pizza (518-584-3840), 119 Clinton Street. ($) Open daily 11–9; Friday and Saturday until 11. This place may not look like much from the exterior, but those who venture inside may be treated to wonderfully tasty gluten-free pizza as well as the usual Italian specialties. They also offer a few gluten-free entrées and rolls, so make sure to ask if you don't see them on the menu. It isn't easy to find an inexpensive pizzeria in Saratoga; this is also a great place to go when traveling with young children.

Old Bryan Inn (518-587-2990), 123 Maple Avenue. ($) Open daily at 11 AM for lunch and dinner; there's one menu all day long. This unpretentious country inn is a nice stop for hearty burgers and fries, fresh salads, grilled steaks, and pasta dishes. Try the hot spinach salad or deep-fried cheese sticks with an unusually delicious raspberry sauce. Children welcome.

The Parting Glass (518-583-1916), 40 Lake Avenue. ($) Open daily from 11 AM until the early-morning hours. An Irish pub–style restaurant. Try the Guinness and black bean soup served with home-baked bread for a hearty meal. There is entertainment on Friday and Saturday nights, and the place is a favorite with the racetrack crowd. Great fun if you enjoy pubs; there's a vast selection of beers and even a serious dart league on Tuesday nights. Not recommended for children.

PJ's Bar-B-Q S.A. (518-583-RIBS), Route 9 (South Broadway). ($) Open year-round, daily at 11 AM until closing; serving lunch and dinner. You will smell this restaurant before you see it, and the aroma will be irresistible to barbecue aficionados. There are huge barbecue pits behind the place, and they're smoking with racks of chicken, ribs, beef brisket, and pulled pork. Sides include homemade coleslaw, macaroni salad, barbecue beans, and corn on the cob. This is the home of the unique "wick" sandwich and old-fashioned custard ice cream. Also enjoy PJ's Loganberry fruit beverages, to accompany the thick smoky ribs and chicken. Spicy and satisfying for either take-out or eating at one of the outdoor picnic tables. There are hot dogs and burgers for those who don't or won't indulge. Children love the place.

The Putnam Market (518-587-FOOD), 435 Broadway. ($$) Open Monday through Saturday 9–7; Sunday 10–5. This gourmet eatery with an open deli and bakery specializes in take-out for picnics if you are heading to SPAC or the track. About a dozen tables are available if you choose to eat at the market, and it's a great place to stop for soup, a sandwich, or a salad while shopping on Broadway. The side dishes, like green beans and hazelnuts topped with a light lemon dressing, are what I enjoy here. I make a meal of a few of these fresh seasonal salad creations—in full view when you enter the store. Sandwiches include items like boneless free-range turkey breast with cheddar cheese and cranberry mayo, and the salmon en croûte is baked to perfection. Menus change seasonally. Save room for the wonderful brownies, cookies, and other dessert treats! Children can't run around here; space is tight.

Saratoga City Tavern (518-581-3230), 19–21 Caroline Street. ($$) Open daily 4 PM–4 AM. This is the only rooftop bar in the city, and it's a delightful place to have drinks, particularly in the warm-weather months. The building was renovated in 2002 and dates back to 1903. There's a mahogany bar and comfortable atmosphere.

Scallions (518-584-0192), 44 Lake Avenue. ($) Open daily 8:30 AM–9 PM. A gourmet eatery with a cheerful café atmosphere. Try the unique sandwich combinations, homemade soups, and specialty chicken and pasta dishes. Desserts are first-rate: The carrot cake is the best around. This is a great place to take out a meal for a picnic if you are heading to the Saratoga Performing Arts Center or the race course.

Shirley's Restaurant (518-584-4532), 74 West Avenue. ($) Open Tuesday through Saturday 6 AM–8 PM; Sunday 7–2. There are exceedingly reasonable prices here, and the service is efficient and friendly. There are the usual diner standards, daily dinner specials like roast turkey breast, and all kinds of overstuffed sandwiches. All pies are homemade on the premises. A great place to go if you are traveling with children.

✷ Entertainment

PERFORMING ARTS **Home Made Theater** (518-587-4427; www.homemadetheater.org), at the Spa Little Theater, Saratoga Spa State Park, 19 Roosevelt Drive. Open October through April. This theater is open during a calmer time of year in Saratoga Springs. Visitors may enjoy comedy, drama, or children's theater in this venue.

Opera Saratoga (518-584-6018; www.operasaratoga.org), at the Spa Little Theater, Saratoga Spa State Park, 19 Roosevelt Drive. Mid-June through mid-July. Three operas are performed in repertory every other night, and some are performed with their own orchestra. The tickets are sold through SPAC, and there are only 500 seats, so it is difficult to get tickets

Saratoga Springs Chamber of Commerce

DANCE PERFORMANCE AT SPAC

last minute. Opera lovers will enjoy the intimacy of this little theater.

Saratoga Film Forum (518-584-FILM; www.saratogafilmforum.org), Saratoga Arts Center Theatre, 320 Broadway. Admission fee. Films are shown on Thursday and Friday nights and Sunday afternoons. No reservations are taken; just show up a half hour before showtime.

Saratoga Performing Arts Center (518-587-3330; www.spac.org), Saratoga Spa State Park, Route 50. Open from May through early September; schedules, performances, and ticket prices vary. Each summer there are performances here by the New York City Ballet, plus top names in the concert circuit in jazz, rock, and folk visit SPAC, with matinee and evening shows. You can bring a picnic, select items from the gourmet food carts, or stop at one of the restaurants in town and arrange for an elegant take-along dinner. There is a covered, open-air seating area as well as lawn seats under the stars and plenty of parking. SPAC is but a few minutes' drive from the center of town, but beware: A popular concert can create traffic tie-ups and bottlenecks throughout the area, so plan to get there early. Lawn tickets can be purchased the night of most performances, but it's a good idea to call in advance and inquire about ticket availability.

VENUES PROVIDING MUSIC

There are several cafés and restaurants in town that offer wonderful blues, jazz, and dance bands. The schedules (days and hours) vary with the time of the year. If you are visiting and want to hear live music, give the following places a call.

Bailey's Café (518-583-6060), 37 Phila Street; **Caffè Lena** (518-583-0022), 47 Phila Street; **Gaffney's** (518-587-7359), 16 Caroline Street; **Horseshoe Inn Bar & Grill** (518-587-4909), 1 Gridley Street; **9 Maple Avenue** (518-583-CLUB); **One Caroline Street** (518-587-2026), 1 Caroline Street, has jazz and blues year-round; **The Parting Glass** (518-583-1916), 40 Lake Avenue, is a local haven for Irish music and folk; **Thirteen Vodka Bar & Lounge** (518-581-1316), 13 Caroline Street, has a full bar with 150 vodkas and features a DJ every weekend; and the **Wishing Well Restaurant** (518-584-7640), 745 Saratoga Road, Wilton, may be out of town a little way, but it offers excellent piano and jazz, and features local musicians. The food is excellent, too. Open for dinner daily, except Monday, 5–10.

✷ Special Events

The following events are held annually during the month listed. If you know you will be in Saratoga Springs at a particular time, do call to find out the exact dates of these fairs, festivals, and events. Attending any of them will enhance your stay in the city.

February: **Chowderfest** (518-587-3241) is a community festival that takes place the first weekend of the month. The public may sample chowders from 30 to 40 restaurants for $1 per taste and vote on the best one. There is even dog chowder! A fun event for the family, and it happens whether or not it snows.

May: **The Eastern New York Dressage and Combined Training Association** (www.enydcta.org) sponsors a dressage exhibition at the Saratoga

LAWN SEATING AT SPAC

Saratoga Springs Chamber of Commerce

Race Course and Equine Center, Union Avenue. Admission fee.

June: **National Bottle Museum Collectors Expo** (518-885-7589), Ballston Spa High School, 220 Ballston Avenue, Ballston Spa. Admission fee. Bottle collectors from around the country meet here to exhibit and sell their wares. For those who have any interest in old bottles, don't miss this weekend expo! (See *To See*.) **Saratoga Jazz Festival** (518-587-3330), SPAC, Saratoga Spa State Park, Route 50. Admission fee. From noon to midnight, this weekend festival attracts some of the biggest names in jazz from throughout the country. Bring a blanket and picnic; the lawn seats are the best way to experience this.

July: **Hats Off to Saratoga Music Festival** (518-584-3255), various venues in downtown Saratoga Springs. Enjoy an array of music, including jazz, bluegrass, classical, folk, country, Latin, Cajun, and Dixieland, during this weekend festival, Friday and Saturday nights 7–11. **Independence Day Celebration** (518-664-9821), Saratoga National Historical Park, 684 Route 32, Stillwater. Hear breaking news of American independence from the town crier. Kids will enjoy this afternoon celebration. At sunset, there are fireworks in Congress Park and the Equine Sports Center. **Saratoga County Fair** (518-885-9701), Saratoga County Fairgrounds, Ballston Spa. Admission fee. From 9 AM to midnight Tuesday through Sunday, enjoy exhibits, food, rides, shows, animals, and entertainment.

August: **Travers Festival Week** (518-584-3255). This weeklong celebration centers around the race course's midsummer derby, the Travers Stakes—the oldest stakes race. There are numerous events at various locations, so if you're in town, call for information.

September: **Battle of Saratoga Anniversary and Encampment** (518-664-9821), Saratoga National Battlefield Park. Admission fee. Enjoy a comedic portrayal of British general Burgoyne. Everyone is in period costumes. There's a festive atmosphere, yet it's also educational. A great place to take the kids. **Saratoga Wine and Food Festival** (518-587-3330), SPAC, Route 50. Admission fee. Hundreds of wine merchants and gourmet-food purveyors display their tempting wares at this annual event. Anyone interested in food and wine shouldn't miss it.

November: **Victorian Street Walk** (518-587-8635), Broadway and downtown area. Enjoy strolling musicians, street theater, horse-drawn trolley rides, and more. Santa is on hand, and most retail stores in town have an open house with refreshments.

December: **First Night Celebration** (518-584-8262), Broadway and downtown area. The purchase of a button gives you admission to a variety of music and other venues throughout the city, where you'll enjoy Christmas music, jazz, and carols, as well as dance and theater performances. The event on December 31 starts with a 5K race at 5:30 PM and ends at midnight with fireworks.

Columbia County

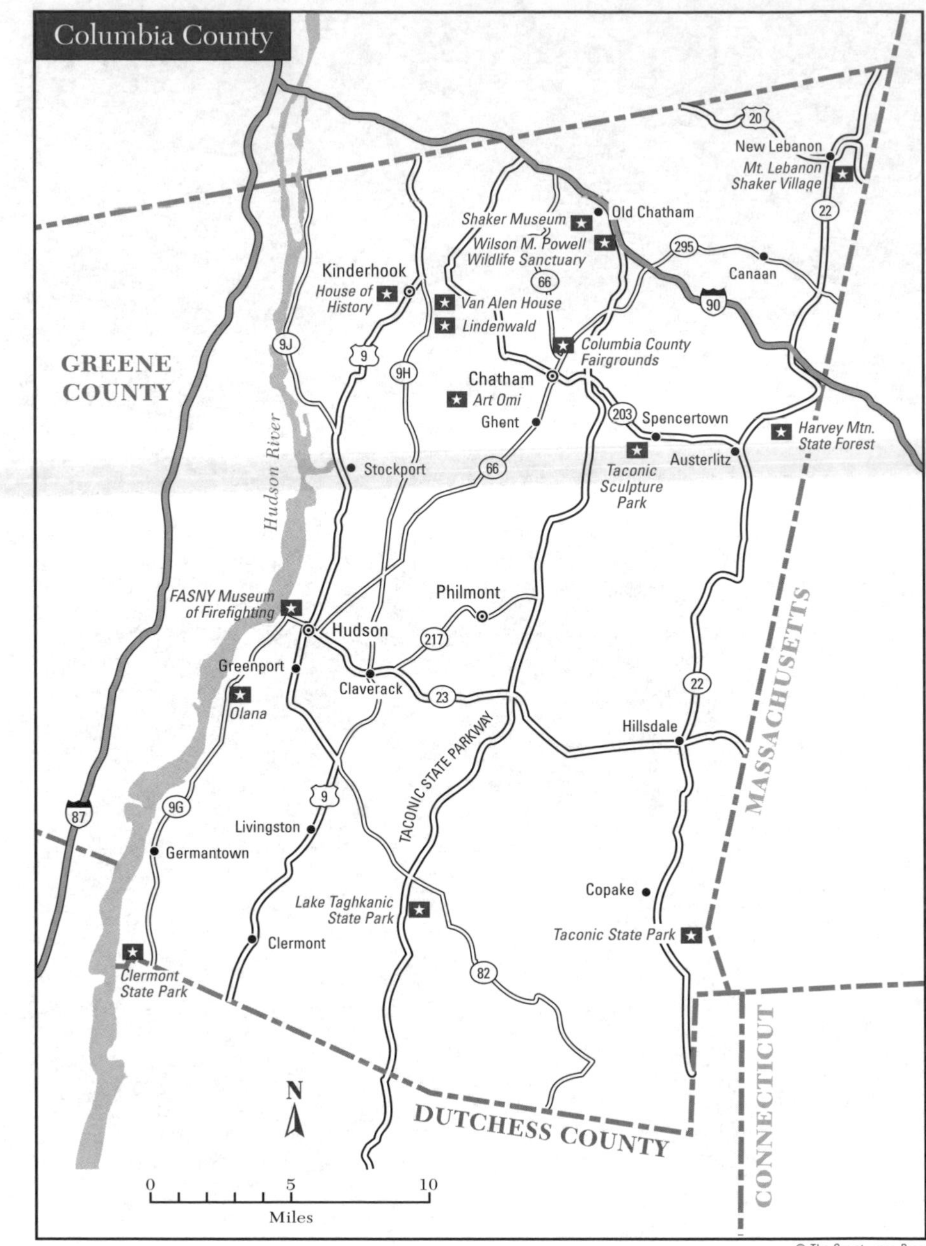
Columbia County
GREENE COUNTY
Hudson River
Kinderhook
House of History
Van Alen House
Lindenwald
Shaker Museum
Wilson M. Powell Wildlife Sanctuary
Old Chatham
New Lebanon
Mt. Lebanon Shaker Village
Canaan
Columbia County Fairgrounds
Chatham
Art Omi
Ghent
Spencertown
Austerlitz
Harvey Mtn. State Forest
Taconic Sculpture Park
Stockport
FASNY Museum of Firefighting
Hudson
Philmont
Greenport
Claverack
Olana
Hillsdale
TACONIC STATE PARKWAY
Livingston
Germantown
Copake
Lake Taghkanic State Park
Taconic State Park
Clermont
Clermont State Park
MASSACHUSETTS
CONNECTICUT
DUTCHESS COUNTY
20
22
295
66
90
9J
9
9H
203
217
23
87
9G
82
N
0
5
10
Miles

COLUMBIA COUNTY

First the home of the Native Americans who greeted Henry Hudson, Columbia County later attracted Dutch, German, and New England settlers with its river and fertile land. Whaling became a major industry, with the ships moving up the Hudson River and unloading their international cargo at Hudson in the 1830s. The city echoed with the noises of shipping, rope making, trading . . . and prostitution. Fine homes resembling the wood-and-brick extravaganzas of Maine and Massachusetts were built for men and women of substance and sophistication. The unusual is the rule here: a colorful museum filled with firemen's equipment and a library that was once an asylum for the mentally ill. The Shakers built settlements here and led their sober lives, which were also filled with song, dance, and fine craftsmanship. Across the county antiques glow in the windows of well-appointed shops, while the simplicity of Shaker furniture offers its own comment on life. Martin Van Buren lived in Columbia County (in fact, the term *OK* is thought to have originated from Van Buren's nickname, Old Kinderhook). Thoroughbred racehorses are bred, raised, and trained in Columbia County, and every Labor Day weekend the state's oldest county fair brings together folks of all ages in celebration of the harvest's best at the county fairgrounds in Chatham.

GUIDANCE **Columbia County Tourism** (518-828-3375; 1-800-724-1846), 401 State Street, Hudson 12534; www.columbiacountytourism.org.

Columbia County Council on the Arts (518-671-6213), 209 Warren Street, Hudson 12534; www.artscolumbia.org.

Columbia County Chamber of Commerce (518-828-4417), 1 North Front Street, Hudson 12534; www.columbiachamber-ny.com.

GETTING THERE *By car:* Columbia County can be reached from the Taconic State Parkway and by Routes 9, 9H, and 22, all of which run north–south; I-90 (the Mass Pike in Massachusetts) cuts east–west across the county.

By train: **Amtrak** (1-800-872-7245) runs regular service between Penn Station in New York City and Hudson (518-828-3379), 69 South Front Street.

By air: **Albany International Airport** (518-242-2200), 737 Albany Shaker Road (exit 4 on the Northway), is less than 30 miles from many parts of Columbia

County. **Columbia County Airport** (518-828-9461), 1142 Route 9H, West Ghent.

MEDICAL EMERGENCY Columbia Memorial Hospital (518-828-8500), 71 Prospect Avenue, Hudson.

✱ To See

Art Omi (518-392-4740; www.artomi.org), 59 Letter S Road, Ghent. From Hudson, take Route 9H north; make a right onto County Route 22, then left onto Letter S Road. They are located at the second driveway on the left. Open daily sunrise to sunset. Free. Founded in 1988 as public grounds for viewing contemporary sculpture—as part of the Art Omi International Arts Center—the park features more than 70 sculptures on view, with works by Liberman, Lipski, Pepper, Highstine, Knowlton, Venet, and others. There is a visitors center open May through October, Thursday through Sunday 11–5; Saturday and Sunday only the rest of the year. It is best to stop there upon arrival to find out what is being exhibited in the art gallery. Temporary exhibits change throughout the year and are made possible with the assistance of independent curators. This arts center is located on more than 150 acres, of which 90 are dedicated to the sculpture park that stretches through rolling fields, wooded knolls, and wetlands. Allow an hour to tour the entire park. There are free guided tours for groups of six or more people, but reservations must be made in advance. A great place to expose children to art and an unusual attraction!

Columbia County Museum (518-758-9265; www.cchsny.org), 5 Albany Avenue, Kinderhook. This museum, owned by the Columbia County Historical Society, which is also headquartered here, is open May through November, Monday through Friday 10–4; December through April, Monday, Wednesday, and Friday 10–4. Free. The exhibits here include paintings, textiles, and other items that tell the story of Columbia County. The county historical society also administers the **Luykas Van Alen House** and the **James Vanderpoel House** (see *Historic Homes*).

FASNY (Farmers' Association of the State of New York) American Museum of Firefighting (518-822-1875; 1-877-347-3687; www.fasnyfiremuseum.com), 117 Harry Howard Avenue, Hudson. Open year-round, daily 10–5, except national holidays. Admission fee. Take a step back in time to the glory days of firefighting at this fascinating museum, located next door to the **Firemen's Home.** You will discover the oldest and broadest collection of firefighting gear and memorabilia in the United States. Scores of horse-drawn and steam- and gas-powered pieces of equipment are on display, some dating from the 18th century. Greeting you as you enter the museum is a wooden statue of a volunteer fire chief dressed in patriotic red, white, and blue, complete with stars and golden trumpet. The museum is divided into five halls that house firefighting pumps, mobile apparatus, and engines, as well as paintings, clothing, banners, photographs, and other memorabilia. A Newsham engine, built in 1725, was used to quench flames in Manhattan houses and saw more than 150 years of use. A delicate silver parade carriage from Kingston, New York, is topped by the figure of a fireman holding a rescued baby. Throughout the museum you will see lots of gleaming brass, bright-red paint, and an oddity or two, like ornate firemen's parade trumpets, hand-grenade-style fire extinguishers, and brass fire markers that indicated which fire company had the right to fight a particular fire. There are even modern fire clothes that show the difference in firefighting techniques through the years. A September 11th memorial display filled with photographs lists the names of all the firefighters who lost their lives that day. The museum and gift shop consist of 50,000 square feet of memorabilia and exhibits that will be of interest to older children and just about anyone interested in the history of firefighting in New York State.

Pleshakov Piano Museum (518-263-3333; www.pleshakov.com), 337 Warren Street, Hudson. Open year-round by appointment only. Admission. This impressive collection of five pianos includes an 1826 Tischner, which was built for Russian royalty, and a Longman and Broderip built in London in 1789. There is also an 1863 Steinway concert grand, formerly the piano of the Vienna Philharmonic. Vladimir Pleshakov and Elena Winther began this collection of instruments, books, and historical recordings pertaining to classical music decades ago. Today the collection is open to the public to educate both students of music and visitors to the region.

Shaker Museum–Mount Lebanon (518-794-9100; www.shakermuseumand library.org), 202 Shaker Road, New Lebanon. Open July through Labor Day, weekends only 10–5; call for other times. Free. On the site of a former Shaker settlement is a walking tour through several buildings, including the stone dairy barn; it takes approximately one hour and is offered free of charge.

The museum and library, formerly located in Old Chatham, will be moved to Mount Lebanon over the course of the next few years. The journals, letters, and drawings are considered one of the foremost study collections of Shaker cultural materials in the United States.

In the late 18th century a group of English people immigrated to the colonies with the hope of being allowed to practice their communal religion. Called Shakers because they danced and moved during worship services, the group established settlements throughout their new country and became as well-known for their fine crafts and innovations as for their unusual celibate lifestyle. Industry, thrift, and simplicity were their bywords. In their workshops, chairs, seed packets, tin milk pails, and jams were made with equal skill and care, and today Shaker-made items are still valued for their beauty and grace. The Shakers are credited with inventing the circular saw and the revolving bake oven, although they rarely took out a patent, preferring that the world benefit from their work.

This site is worth a visit for those interested in Shaker history.

Taconic Sculpture Park and Gallery (518-392-5757; www.taconicnet/kanwit), Stever Hill Road, Spencertown. Open daily 10–5. Free. Roy Kanwit, a working sculptor, has 40 of his works exhibited on his grounds. His home/studio is an enormous stone castle–like structure. Here is a chance to witness the sunset through solar disks. The park attracts a few thousand visitors each year. Older children will love this stop.

FOR FAMILIES **Catamount Adventure Park** (518-325-3200; www.catamount trees.com), 3290 Route 23, Hillsdale. Open May through October, daily 9–5:30, weather permitting. After Labor Day until closing, Saturday and Sunday only. Admission fee. (The charge, $49 for adults and $29 for the youngest children, is

Columbia County Tourism (columbiacountytourism.org)

CATAMOUNT ADVENTURE PARK IN HILLSDALE

good for a three-hour stay; a discount is offered to those who arrive before 10 AM.) Note that children must be a minimum of seven years of age to be admitted. The 5-acre wooded setting near the base of the Catamount ski area is now an aerial forest challenge park with 150 platforms in trees connected by cable, wood, rope, and two 2,000-foot zip lines to form a series of bridges. The courses are designed from easy to expert and are designated with colors to denote the degree of difficulty. All participants must wear a harness attached to a lifeline at all times. There are no rides here, but the park provides a fun adventure that will long be remembered.

Mud Creek Environmental Learning Center (518-828-4386; www.ccswcd.org), Route 66, Ghent. The center, located behind the USDA building, is open year-round, daily 8–4:30, but the nature trail is open all the time to visitors. Free. The nature trail wends its way through wetlands with two loops—one is a mile long, and a shorter loop is about a half mile long. A number of kiosks along the way provide information about the flora and fauna on the trail. Special programs for groups are available by advance reservation; a full-time educator is on staff to assist visitors from schools and private groups. An interesting stop for families traveling with children between the ages of 3 and 12.

Old Chatham Sheepherding Company (518-794-7733; 1-888-SHEEP-60; www.blacksheepcheese.com), 99 Shaker Museum Road, Old Chatham. Visit this farm from October through February or June through September, and you can watch the ewes being milked. They produce several types of sheep's-milk cheeses and yogurt, and it is the largest sheep dairy farm in the country. The farm began in 1994 with a flock of 150 sheep, and there are now more than 1,200 East Friesian crossbred sheep grazing on 600 acres of rolling pastures. European methods are used to create new American original cheeses, which have won awards and been praised in many gourmet-food publications. There is a shop on the premises where visitors can purchase the cheeses and yogurt.

HISTORIC HOMES **Clermont State Historic Site** (518-537-4240; www.friendsofclermont.org), 400 Woods Road, Germantown. Open April through October, Wednesday through Sunday 11–5; weekends only November and December. Call for winter hours, which may vary depending on budgetary constraints. The grounds are open year-round from 8:30 AM until sunset. Admission fee. Standing on land that was awarded to the Livingston family in 1686, this Georgian mansion remained in the family for nearly three centuries. The family's illustrious history—Judge Robert Livingston wrote the letter of protest to King George just before the Revolutionary War, and Chancellor Robert R. Livingston helped draft the Declaration of Independence—is evident throughout the house. Although Clermont itself was burned by the British during the war, it was later rebuilt around the old walls and foundation. Alterations and additions were made into the late 19th century, so the house today reflects changes wrought by several generations. Clermont's 46 rooms are furnished with family heirlooms and fine examples of period furniture and decorative accessories. A crystal chandelier brought from France in 1802 hangs above the drawing room, where you will also find a French balloon clock made to commemorate the first hydrogen balloon in Paris in 1783. Family portraits decorate the hallways and help visitors sort out the confusing Livingston family tree, and there are exquisite examples of cabinetmaking throughout the mansion.

CLERMONT STATE HISTORIC SITE IN GERMANTOWN

Columbia County Tourism (columbiacountytourism.org)

But as lovely as Clermont is, the setting makes it more so. In fact, the first steamboat, the *Clermont,* made its way up the Hudson River here in August 1807. The views of the Catskill Mountains across the Hudson River are magnificent; the family purchased as much land as possible to preserve the setting. Tradition holds that the black locust trees flanking the house were planted by many generations of Livingstons. The roses in the Italian walled garden transform the month of June into an enchanting time. Several special events are held at Clermont, including a July Fourth celebration with costumed colonial soldiers, Legends by Candlelight at Halloween, and a Christmas open house that takes place every weekend in December. There is a small gift shop and visitors center, where you can see a short video that tells the story of the Livingston family. The house tour is not recommended for young children.

James Vanderpoel House (518-758-9265), Broad Street, Kinderhook. Open Memorial Day weekend through Labor Day, Thursday through Saturday 11–5; Sunday 1–5. Call for off-season hours. Admission fee. This site is also called the House of History, and indeed it does present some fine exhibits of life in Columbia County, especially the era when the area was a bustling industrial and whaling center. Built in 1819 for lawyer and politician James Vanderpoel, the Federal house is characterized by delicate ornamentation, including plasterwork ceilings, graceful mantelpieces, and a wide staircase that seems to float to the second floor. The work of several New York cabinetmakers—who created a blend of American pride and European style—is displayed throughout the rooms. A fine selection of paintings, including many by country artists, depicts Columbia County life.

Luykas Van Alen House (518-758-9265), Route 9H, Kinderhook. Open Memorial Day weekend through Labor Day, Thursday through Saturday 11–5; Sunday 1–5. Admission. After visiting Lindenwald, home of Martin Van Buren, you may want to stop at the Luykas Van Alen House, which is operated by the Columbia

LUYKAS VAN ALEN HOUSE IN KINDERHOOK

Columbia County Tourism (columbiacountytourism.org)

County Historical Society. This brick Dutch farmhouse of the early 18th century has been restored to reflect its heritage. The site contains the **Ichabod Crane School House**—a restored one-room schoolhouse open to the public and named after the character in Washington Irving's tale. In fact, Irving based Crane on a local schoolteacher who actually worked in this schoolhouse.

Martin Van Buren National Historic Site (518-758-9689; www.nps.gov/mava), 1013 Old Post Road (off Route 9H), Kinderhook. Open mid-May through October, daily 9–4. Admission fee. Known as **Lindenwald,** the house was the home and farm of Martin Van Buren, eighth president of the United States. Built in 1797 and renovated in 1849, the resulting structure is a blend of Federal, Italianate, and Victorian styles. Van Buren was born in Kinderhook (Dutch for "children's corner"), the son of a tavern keeper. He studied law and from Kinderhook embarked on a 30-year political career. At Lindenwald, visitors will see the house to which Van Buren returned to look back on three tumultuous decades of public service. Named after the linden trees on the property, the graceful building—complete with shutters, double chimneys, and arched windows—is today a National Historic Site; it was renovated in recent years to remove or lessen the impact of certain Victorian "improvements." The grounds offer an escape to the peace of rural 19th-century America, but it is inside that the renovations are more evident. A center stairway winds upward through the house, the hundreds of turned spindles so polished that they gleam. The old wallpaper was stripped and replaced with paper appropriate to the era, and furniture and decorative objects finally look as if they belong to the home. The house contains a fine collection of Van Buren memorabilia, and a visit is an excellent way to become acquainted with the president known as the Little Magician because of both his size and his political acumen.

Olana (518-828-0135; www.olana.org), 5720 Route 9G, 1 mile south of the Rip Van Winkle Bridge, Greenport. Open April through October, Wednesday through Sunday 10–5; November through March, Friday through Sunday 11–3. The house is viewed by guided tour only, and group size is limited; call to reserve tickets before you go. Admission fee. The grounds can be viewed from 8 AM to sunset without a guide at no charge or with a landscape guide for a minimal charge. Frederic Edwin Church was one of America's foremost artists, a painter who captured the grandeur and mystery of the nation in the 19th century. Church first gained acclaim for his vision of Niagara Falls, a painting that won a medal at the 1867 Paris International Exposition. In 1870 Church and his wife, Isabel, returned from their travels in the Middle East and Europe to their farm in Hudson and began the planning and building of the Persian fantasy that would become known as Olana. Hand-painted tiles on the roof and turrets of the 37-room mansion, situated 460 feet above the river, add touches of pink and green to the sky. Church called his style "personal Persia," and inside you will discover hand-carved, room-size screens; rich Persian rugs; delicate paintings; decorative pottery and china; and even a pair of gilded crane lamps that look as if they stepped out of an Egyptian wall painting. Olana is also rich in examples of Church's paintings, including *Autumn in North America* and *Sunset in Jamaica.* His studio is still set up as it was in his time. During the holiday season, the house is decorated with elaborate greenery, and Yuletide confections grace the tables. Visitors can hike year-round along the carriage paths and roadways that wind through the property or take in the Hudson River views; just across the river is Cedar Grove, Thomas Cole's home (see *To See* in "Greene County"), and the place where Church apprenticed as an artist. The 40-minute house tour is not recommended for young children. The visitors center contains an excellent museum shop and offers a short video about Frederic Church and the site. An extensive schedule of weekend art and nature programs is held at the Wagon House Education Center on the premises. An array of activities is featured, and many are oriented toward families. They are held from April through December on Saturday and Sunday afternoons. Check the website for a complete listing. There is a marvelous open house in December (see *Special Events*). Olana is one of my favorite places in the Hudson Valley; visit, and you will see why. It is truly a unique treasure.

Steepletop: House & Gardens of Edna St. Vincent Millay (518-392-3362; www.millay.org), 436 East Hll Road, Austerlitz. Open for tours of the house and garden Memorial Day weekend through mid-October, Friday through Monday 11–4. Admission fee. Only six people are permitted in each tour, so do call ahead to reserve space on weekends. The house and garden tours may be purchased separately; each takes approximately one hour. A tour of the farmhouse also includes the writing cabin and icehouse.

Edna St. Vincent Millay was a Pulitzer Prize–winning poet born in Maine in 1892. She lived in Manhattan in the 1920s and was in the forefront of the American literary movement. The line of poetry she is best known for is "my candle burns at both ends." In 1925 Millay and her husband purchased the 19th-century farmhouse at Steepletop, and it soon became a social gathering place for other writers and artists. Millay died in 1950, and her gravesite is on the property. There is a half-mile, narrow country road known as the Poetry Trail marked with a dozen of Millay's favorite nature poems. The trail ends at the family cemetery and is open year-round free of charge.

STEEPLETOP IN AUSTERLITZ

Columbia County Tourism (columbiacountytourism.org)

SCENIC DRIVES It is difficult to *avoid* taking a scenic drive in Columbia County—wherever you look, you can see rolling, bright-green meadows, misty ponds, and quiet villages that look the same as they did a century ago. You may find yourself on a bluff overlooking the Hudson River or in a city that recalls the glory of the whaling industry. The roads are well maintained, and you can't get lost for very long.

For a sampling of the county's charms, both Routes 9 and 9H will take you through Hudson, Kinderhook, and Valatie, with plenty of museums, shops, and historic sites to explore. Other routes worth a drive include north–south Route 7 and Route 22, in the eastern part of the county, and Route 82, which runs northwest from the county line at Ancram to near Hudson. Route 11 between Routes 23 and 27, in the town of Taghkanic, has actually received an award for its scenic beauty, having been declared a National Beauty Award Highway (you will see the sign marking this road when you pass by).

One marvelous driving tour through Stuyvesant offers a chance to see many old barns in varied styles, reflecting the agricultural heritage of the town. With more than 12,000 acres of tillable land bordering the Hudson River and Kinderhook Creek, the agricultural area of the town of Stuyvesant dates back centuries. You will see "historical roots" barns, with their distinct architectural features; "English roots" barns, which are rectangular in shape; the large square "Dutch roots" barns, with their H shape; and the "German roots" barns, which are rectangular, with doors on the long side and rooflines that are higher than the Dutch barns. Begin the tour in the town of Kinderhook south of the Martin Van Buren National Historic Site on Route 9H and bear to the right onto County Route 25. At the intersection of County Routes 25 and 25A, turn left. Proceed for about 2 miles to County Route 46, where you will see three silos across a field on the right. At the T junction with Route 9J, go right for about 0.5 mile to Sharptown Road. Turn right onto Sharptown, where you will see a barn practically in the road; this is a side-hill barn with a lower floor built into the hill, and it is now used as a woodworking shop. Farther along this road you will see the Gleason Farm barns.

WALKING TOUR—HUDSON The city of Hudson, located roughly between Routes 9 and 9G, is rich with the traditions and cultural heritage of its settlers: first the Dutch, then seafarers from Massachusetts and Rhode Island, and later, Quakers and whalers. Carefully designed in the 1780s as a shipping center, with straight streets and "gangway" alleys, ropewalks, wharves, and a warehouse, Hudson was the first city to receive a charter after the Declaration of Independence. Soon whaling and industry took over as the mainstays of the economy, and although Hudson has had its ups and downs since, the city is now in the full flower of a renaissance. On a walking tour of Hudson you will see dozens of architectural styles and hundreds of commercial buildings and homes that have been maintained or restored to their earlier glory. A walk around several main streets will reveal the architectural heritage of the area. Visitors to Hudson who enjoy antiques will discover some of the best antiques shopping on the East Coast. Many of the shops are located along Warren Street (see *Selective Shopping*) and range in selection from fine European and 18th-century American furniture, glassware, and fine arts to 1950s lamps, textiles, and ephemera. Many stores are open by chance or appointment, although Thursday through the weekend is a good bet for browsers.

Coming from the south, from Route 9G follow Warren Street west to Front Street (by the river), and park. At Front Street you will see the Parade, an 18th-century park that was kept open for use by the city's inhabitants. From the park, also called Promenade Hill Park, you will have a dazzling view of the Hudson River and the Catskill Mountains, plus the Hudson-Athens Lighthouse, built in 1874 and used to warn ships off the Hudson Middle Ground Flats. Inside the park you will find a statue of St. Winifred, donated to the city by a man who felt that Hudson needed a patron saint.

The easiest walk in Hudson is up Warren Street, the aforementioned antiques mecca. The architectural styles to be found here include Greek Revival, Federal, Queen Anne, and Victorian. At the **Curtiss House,** 32 Warren Street, look up at the widow's walk, which was built by the house's whaling owner in the 1830s to provide a sweeping view of the river. Some of the houses here sport "eyebrow" windows—narrow windows tucked under the eaves that are often at floor level within the houses. The house at 116 Warren Street is considered a rare remnant from the early 19th century and boasts an enclosed private garden.

The 1811 **Robert Jenkins House** (518-828-9764), 113 Warren Street, is open to the public in July and August, Saturday 1–3 or by appointment. The house serves as the headquarters of the local chapter of the Daughters of the American Revolution and was built by an early mayor of Hudson. The exhibits here offer a look at the city over the past two centuries and contain material on whaling and genealogy, paintings by Hudson River School artists, and other historic items.

At Warren and Fourth streets is the *Register Star* newspaper building, with its tiny park. Like many other of the buildings here, it has served several purposes: It was a dance hall, an opera house, a county jail, and an assembly hall. Head north on Fourth Street to State Street. The **Hudson Area Library Association,** 400 State Street, is an 1818 stone building guarded by stone lions. The structure has also served as an almshouse, an asylum for the mentally ill, a women's seminary, and a private home. If the building is open, stop in at the second-floor History Room, which has some local memorabilia, prints, and books. **Hudson City Books** (518-671-6020), 553 Warren Street, also has a nice selection of used and rare books. And don't miss the **Spotty Dog Books & Ale** (518-671-6006), 440 Warren Street, a wonderful bookstore as well as dessert/coffee/beer bar. It's located in a renovated historic firehouse that was in operation from 1890 to 2003, and the ceiling of the main room is original to the firehouse (see *Eating Out*).

Backtrack to Warren Street and spend some time looking at the fine 18th- and 19th-century buildings, many of which are undergoing restoration. Other walking areas with interesting architecture include Union Street, East and West Court streets—appropriately, by the courthouse—and East Allen Street.

WINERIES, DISTILLERIES, AND BREWERIES **Harvest Spirits** (518-253-5917), 3074 Route 9, Valatie. Open year-round, Saturday and Sunday noon–5. Located at Golden Harvest Farms (see *To Do—Farm Stands and Pick-Your-Own Farms*), this microdistillery creates alcoholic drinks from apples grown at the farm. The fruit is pressed, fermented, distilled, and bottled in the same place. The result is a wonderful vodka, applejack, and brandy, all available for tasting.

Columbia County Tourism (columbiacountytourism.org)
HARVEST SPIRITS IN VALATIE

Hudson-Chatham Winery (518-392-WINE), 1900 Route 66, Ghent, is Columbia County's first winery (opened in 2007), and it's conveniently located between Hudson and Chatham (watch for the sign). Open year-round, Friday through Sunday noon–6. Situated on the former Brisklea Farms Ayrshire Dairy, with views of the Berkshires and Catskills, the winery features of full selection of wines, regional cheeses, and local maple syrup. Their award-winning wines are made from New York State fruits; some are handcrafted classic, dry wines, and there are sweeter dessert wines as well. *Note:* For those who love beer, **Chatham Brewing Company** (518-697-0202), 30 Main Street in Chatham, the county's only microbrewery, offers three styles of unfiltered ale—porter, India pale ale, and amber. They are open for tours year-round on Saturday from 11 to 2.

Tousey Winery (518-567-5462), 1774 Route 9, Clermont. Open year-round, Friday noon–7; Saturday and Sunday noon–5. A relative newcomer to the Hudson Valley winery scene, they produce chardonnay, Riesling, pinot noir, cabernet franc, rosé, and cassis. The cassis is a blend of four grapes grown on the estate and sweetened with honey from their own hives, rather than sugar, giving it a distinctive flavor. Kimberly and Ben Peacock describe Tousey as "a drier winery," and their cabernet franc is not to be missed!

✷ To Do

AIRPLANE RIDES Columbia County Airport (518-828-9461), 1142 Route 9H, Ghent. Richmor Aviation provides scenic flights by special appointment; you can go for a half hour or by the hour.

BALLOON RIDES Russ Barber Hot Air Balloon Rides (518-828-3735), 73 County Route 25, Hudson. The flights here are approximately one hour long and cost $220 per person. However, the length of the flight is subject to weather conditions, fuel, and availability of landing sites. Call for an appointment.

BICYCLING Harlem Valley Rail Trail (518-789-9591; www.hvrt.org). This 12.2-mile paved bicycle/pedestrian path, built on the old railroad line that connected New York City, the Harlem Valley, and Chatham, has a few places

APPLEJACK BARRELS
Columbia County Tourism (columbiacountytourism.org)

where it can be accessed: In Ancram, off Route 22, at Undermountain Road; in Copake, take Valley View Road; and the Taconic State Park entrance (not to be confused with Lake Taghkanic State Park) near Depot Deli in Copake Falls (see *Hiking*).

For those who want to explore the countryside with an organized bike tour, **Great Freedom Adventures** (508-545-1864; www.greatfreedomadventures.com), headquartered in the nearby Berkshires, offers a few trips that might be of interest.

The following parks have excellent paved roadways for bicycling:

Lake Taghkanic State Park (518-851-3631), 1528 Route 82, Taghkanic.

Martin Van Buren Park (518-758-9689), Route 9H (across from the Van Buren home), Kinderhook. There are three trails here, and the longest will take about one hour to walk at a leisurely pace and a half hour to bike.

Taconic State Park (518-329-3993), Route 344, off Route 22, Copake Falls.

CANOEING AND KAYAKING Columbia County doesn't have an array of outfitters where visitors can rent canoes or kayaks. The state parks are the best places to rent a canoe or rowboat on a lake. However, if you have your own canoe or kayak, the following two spots are wonderful to explore.

Rogers Island (under the Rip Van Winkle Bridge). Row or paddle out to this paradise for bird-watching. There are eagles, waterfowl, and an amazing array of birds that inhabit this intriguing island, in the Hudson River between Greene and Columbia counties.

Stockport Flats, Station Road, Greenport. If you are traveling north on Route 9, look for Station Road, which is on the left, just after you cross the Columbiaville Bridge. This state land offers the perfect place to explore by canoe. There are 250

KAYAKING

Columbia County Tourism (columbiacountytourism.org)

acres here. I paddled a canoe here in the early 1990s and remember the waters of these flats being easy to navigate; a good place for beginners to practice.

There are a few places in the county where there is access to the Hudson River for boaters. The **boat launch in the city of Hudson** is located on Front Street, at the end of Warren Street. The **town of Germantown has a boat launch** on County Route 35A (Northern Boulevard), off Route 9G. In the **town of Stockport** off Station Road in Columbiaville, there is a small boat launch only, and use is recommended at high tide only.

FARM STANDS AND PICK-YOUR-OWN FARMS Not only are the lush, rolling farmlands of Columbia County a lovely place to visit, but you will find a remarkably large variety of farm stands and pick-your-own farms here, as well. Along with the traditional apple orchards and berry fields, discover the county's vineyards, melon patches, and cherry orchards, where the selection of the fruit is left up to you. If you go to a pick-your-own-farm, bring along a container, a hat to shade you from the sun, and a long-sleeved shirt to protect you from insect bites, sunburn, and scratches. The delightful thing about the smaller farm stands, which sprout as fast as corn in the summer, is that many of them carry unusual or hard-to-find varieties of corn, apples, and tomatoes.

In Ancram, make sure to stop at **Thompson-Finch Farm** (518-329-7578), 750 Wiltsie Bridge Road, open daily 9–5, if you love to pick your own strawberries, blueberries, or raspberries. Theirs are some of the best you will ever taste—all grown without synthetic fertilizers or pesticides on compost-fed soil. Make sure to call first and check that the berries are ripe for picking.

The **Berry Farm** (518-392-4609), 2309 Route 203, Chatham, is a haven for berry lovers, raising wonderful blueberries, strawberries, and raspberries. Call the farm to find out when the crops are ready to pick.

In Germantown, **Wintje Farms** (518-537-6072), Route 9G, lets you buy or pick apples, cherries, melons, berries, squash, plums, and more.

A truly special farm is found in Ghent, north of Hudson: **Loveapple Farm** (518-828-5048), 1421 Route 9H, open mid-June through November, lets you pick all kinds of fruit, and you can also buy pears, prunes, cherries, and more. The pies and doughnuts are wonderful, and they are all created at the bakery on the premises. The kids will enjoy the petting zoo, with llamas, goats, pigs, and lambs, as well as the small playground. Also available is lunch, featuring Mexican specialties, served under a tent.

Kinderhook is home to **Samascott Orchard** (518-758-7224), 5 Sunset Avenue (open June through November), which has more than a dozen pick-your-own harvests, including grapes, pears, plums, and strawberries, and just as many varieties of apples.

Near Claverack you will find **Philip Orchards** (518-851-6351), 270 Route 9H, with pick-your-own apples and pears; **Holmquest Farm** (518-851-9629), 516 Spook Rock Road (County Route 29), has fruits and vegetables; and **Bryant Farms** (518-821-6839), 5498 Route 9H, is strictly a roadside market but offers a huge selection of fruits, vegetables, and local products. (They also have an indoor flea market year-round on Saturday and Sunday 9–4.)

Columbia County Tourism (columbiacountytourism.org)

SAMASCOTT ORCHARD IN KINDERHOOK

The region around the city of Hudson is filled with seasonal farm stands, including **Taconic Orchards** (518-851-7477), 591 Route 82, where you can pick berries and buy everything else imaginable; **Klein's Kill Fruit Farm** (518-828-9542), Route 10, which has sweet and sour deep-red cherries mid-June through mid-July; and **Don Baker Farm** (518-828-5890), 183 Route 14 (follow signs), with more than seven varieties of apples, both standard and heritage.

Valatie is home to **Golden Harvest Farms** (518-758-7683), 3074 Route 9, with pick-your-own or already-picked apples and a large roadside stand, and **Yonder Farms** (518-758-7011), Route 9, with pick-your-own apples, blueberries, raspberries, and strawberries.

There are three farmers' markets in the area. The **Chatham Farmers' Market** (518-392-3353) is held at 15 Church Street (at the Chatham Real Food Market Co-op) from June through mid-October on Friday 4–7. The **Hudson Farmers' Market** (518-828-7217), North Sixth Street and Columbia Street, operates May through mid-November, Saturday 9–1. The **Kinderhook Farmers' Market** (518-758-1232) is held in the village square on Route 9 from June to mid-October, Saturday 8–noon. **Stuyvesant Farmers' Market** (518-758-6474) is held at 55 Riverview Street, by the railroad station, from May through September on the first Saturday of the month from 2 to 5.

FISHING The county is filled with deep lakes, clear streams, and stocked ponds and creeks. Keep in mind that a New York State fishing license is required for anyone over the age of 16 partaking of the sport.

The following creeks are stocked by the Department of Environmental Conservation:

Claverack Creek. At Roxbury Road, off Route 217, a bridge crosses the creek at Hess farm; there is access from the bridge. There is also access on Route 23 at

Red Mills, off the south side of the bridge only (not where the falls are); at the bridge on Webb Road (off County Route 29); and on County Route 29 halfway between Webb and Hiscox roads.

Kinderhook Creek. From the county line in New Lebanon at Adams Crossing Road to the county line at Route 20 behind the Lebanon Valley Speedway. Access can be obtained from Route 66 in the town of Chatham at Bachus Road. There is also access to the creek at the bridge in Malden Bridge.

Roeliff Jansen Creek. Access this area from County Route 2 between Elizaville and the Taconic State Parkway; at the junction of County Routes 2 and 19, at Turkey Hill Road; at Buckwheat Road (off Route 9 between County Routes 8 and 6, at the bridge known as Oars Bridge); or about 2 miles south of Hillsdale on Black Grocery Road, which is off Route 22.

There is also fishing at other places in the county, including **Lake Taghkanic State Park,** off Route 82, 3 miles south of the Taconic State Parkway exit. Here you will find year-round fishing for sport fish such as chain pickerel; largemouth, smallmouth, and rock bass; bluegill; pumpkinseed sunfish; yellow perch; brown bullhead; and the occasional cisco in deeper waters. **Taconic State Park,** Route 344 off Route 22, Copake Falls, has **Ore Pond,** where there is stocked trout and other fish native to ponds. **Oakdale Pond,** at Clinton Street and Glenwood Boulevard in Hudson, is stocked annually with trout, and it's a nice family fishing spot. **Queechy Lake,** at the intersection of Route 22 and County Route 30, Canaan, is heavily stocked with trout.

GOLF Copake Country Club (518-325-4338), 44 Golf Course Road, off County Route 11, Copake. Open March through November, daily 7–7. This 18-hole, par-72 course offers a range of facilities, including riding cart and pull cart rentals, pro shop, lessons, and seasonal memberships. Senior-citizen and group rates offered. There is a fine restaurant, **The Greens,** on the premises (see *Dining Out*).

Meadowgreens Golf Course (518-828-0663), 1238 Route 9H, Ghent. Open April through October. Call for hours. This nine-hole, par-36 course has both pull cart and riding cart rentals, lessons, and a pro shop. The restaurant/bar on the premises offers outdoor dining in the warm-weather months.

Undermountain Golf Course (518-329-4444), 274 Undermountain Road, off Route 22, Ancram. Open April through November, daily 7–7. This 18-hole, par-65 executive course offers club, pull cart, and riding cart rentals; pro shop; lessons; snack bar; practice green. Group rates available.

Winding Brook Country Club (518-758-9117), 9117 Route 203, Valatie.

FISHING IN KINDERHOOK CREEK
Columbia County Tourism (columbiacountytourism.org)

Open April through October, Tuesday through Sunday 8–7. This 18-hole, par-70 course is 6,400 yards long. There are lessons; pro shop; pull cart, riding cart, and club rentals; as well as group discounts. The restaurant on the premises opens at 11.

The following offers driving ranges, not full golf courses and facilities:

Farmer's Range (518-758-8101), 2878 Route 203, Valatie. Open March through October, daily sunrise to sunset. This 350-yard range also has a putting green; club rentals available.

HIKING Precautions should be taken when walking through wooded and grassy areas; Lyme disease is transmitted by deer ticks and is *extremely* prevalent in this county. Ticks, which are spread by wildlife, are found in grassy areas as well as in brush, shrubbery, and woodland habitats. Wear appropriate clothing, and be careful if you wander off marked trails for any reason.

Also note that raccoon rabies is present in this part of the state. Don't approach, feed, or touch any wild animals you see while walking. If an animal is behaving strangely, report this to a member of the park staff.

In an effort to reduce operating costs, trash receptacles have been removed from many day-use areas. Plastic disposal bags are available for the transport of trash from the park. Dispose of waste responsibly, which will keep user fees low.

The **Columbia Land Conservancy** (www.clctrust.org) maintains 2,000 acres in Columbia County, with 20 miles of trails open to the public for hiking and outdoor education. This private land trust manages several sites, and their website has a complete listing of these conservation areas. If you know when you will be visiting the county, check their website for a complete schedule of year-round free public programs, many of them designed for families visiting these preserves.

Beebe Hill State Forest (518-828-0236), County Route 5, Austerlitz. Open year-round. There is a nice network of trails here, and they're being expanded. Most are of moderate difficulty. In addition to use by hikers and bicyclists, horses and snowmobiles are permitted on the trails; however, no ATVs are allowed. A 6-mile trail now runs from the top of Beebe Hill to Harvey Mountain, with a lean-to along the way for overnight camping; otherwise, no facilities.

Borden's Pond Preserve (518-392-5252), 1628 Route 203, just outside the village of Chatham. Open year-round, daily dawn to dusk, this 62-acre preserve provides a nice change of pace after shopping or grabbing a bite to eat in town, and it is within walking distance of the main village streets. This is a fairly new area, with an old woodland millpond surrounded by forest land. There is a parking area if you choose to drive.

Drowned Lands Swamp Conservation Area (518-392-5252), 654 County Route 3, Ancram. Open year-round, daily dawn to dusk. This wetland, consisting of 110 acres, is one of the largest in southeastern New York. Home to bog turtles and several species of rare plants, it offers a 0.5-mile steep walk to the summit, Old Croken (an old English word meaning "crooked"; the path twists and turns). The views of the Taconic Hills and Catskill Mountains from this point, 800 feet above sea level, are wonderful; you can also see the entire Drowned Lands Swamp. There is a lower swamp trail that makes for an easier walk.

Greenport Conservation Area (518-392-5252). Located in Greenport at the corner of Daisy Hill Road and Joslen Boulevard, off Route 9. There is a parking area and information kiosk with interpretive brochures detailing the 3.5 miles of trails, which are marked (red, blue, and green). This is a great place for those want to take a short hike and are traveling with children; the trails wend their way through meadows, woodlands, and wetlands along the Hudson River. A hand-hewn cedar gazebo overlooking the Hudson is a great spot to rest and enjoy the view.

Harlem Valley Rail Trail (518-789-9591), Undermountain Road, off Route 22, Ancram; Valley View Road, Copake; Taconic State Park entrance near Depot Deli, Copake Falls. When completed, this paved bicycle/pedestrian path will stretch from Wassaic in Dutchess County to Chatham in Columbia County and run some 46 miles. It was built on the old railroad bed that connected New York City, the Harlem Valley, and Chatham. Trains stopped running on the Harlem Line north of Dover Plains in 1976. So far the State of New York has purchased 22 miles of land to build this linear park—about half of which lies in southern Columbia County—which is ideal for hiking, bicycling, and cross-country skiing. Those who travel the trail may see many species of birds, as well as deer, coyotes, foxes, hawks, turtles, and beavers (or at least their visible dams), to name just some of the wildlife that flourishes here. The trail passes through the hamlets of Amenia and Millerton in Dutchess County to Copake Falls, so hikers can explore these towns along the way.

Harvey Mountain State Forest (518-828-0236), East Hill Road, off Route 22, near I-90 B-3 exit, Austerlitz. Open year-round. Walk either the former logging road or hike through the woods on a marked trail (look for the red blazes) to the top of Harvey Mountain, with a spectacular view (and a picnic table) at the summit. It's about 1.5 miles long and not too difficult. A good choice for those with older children, but keep in mind that there are no facilities here.

Lake Taghkanic State Park (518-851-3631), 1528 Route 82, Taghkanic; direct access off Taconic State Parkway. Open year-round. Admission fee. This 1,569-acre park was donated to the state in 1929 by a descendant of the Livingston family. Find an extended series of hiking and fitness trails here; obtain a map when you enter the park. Overnight camping is available May through October. Facilities include a cabin and cottage area, two bathing beaches, picnic areas, boat rentals, playgrounds, and a ballfield. During the winter visitors can enjoy cross-country skiing, ice fishing, snowmobiling, and ice skating.

New Forge State Forest (518-828-0236), New Forge Road, off Route 82, Taghkanic. Open year-round. This state forest consists of 655 acres. A rather easy 2-mile hike on an old logging road goes through the park.

Pachaquack Preserve (518-758-9806), Elm Street, off Route 203, Valatie. This 43-acre preserve is operated by the town of Valatie, and it's a lovely place for a walk in any season. There are 2 miles of walking trails here, picnic tables, and a gazebo. This is relatively easy walking; the trails follow Kinderhook Creek, where there is excellent fishing. *Pachaquack* is a Native American word that means "cleared meadow and meeting place."

Taconic State Park (518-329-3993), Route 344, off Route 22, Copake Falls. Open year-round. Parking fee. A 25-mile network of hiking trails here range from very easy to quite difficult in this 5,000-acre park, one of the largest in the Hudson

Valley, spanning two counties (Dutchess and Columbia) and bordering Massachusetts and Connecticut. The park runs for 16 miles along the Taconic Ridge, offering spectacular views in many places. This is a good stop for families; there's a small nature center with a few displays, and camping areas are open May through October (however, there is winter camping here: Small cabins may be rented year-round). The historical section of the park includes the Copake Iron Works, which dates from 1845, when ironmaking was the main industry in town. For more than 60 years, iron ore, limestone, and hardwood were taken from local deposits with water power from Bash Bish Creek; 2,500 tons of blast iron, much of which was used for making car wheels, was taken out of the "park." In the 1920s the owner of the foundry sold the site to the state. The cabins that once housed laborers are now rented out as overnight lodging for park visitors.

Wilson M. Powell Wildlife Sanctuary, Hunt Club Road, off County Route 13, Old Chatham. Open year-round, daily dawn to dusk. This 130-acre sanctuary offers a variety of walks with lovely views of the mountains; some meander around a pond. A marked trail leads you on a 0.5-mile walk to the observation area called Dorson Rock. At the pond, one can observe waterfowl. This is also a good place to go cross-country skiing in the winter.

HORSEBACK RIDING **Western Riding Stables** (518-789-4848), 228 Sawchuk Road, Ancramdale. Open year-round, weather permitting. Riding is by appointment only. There are over 5,000 acres of trails here and horses for every age and ability. Additionally, there are lessons, pony rides, and sleigh rides in winter.

SWIMMING **Knickerbocker Lake** (518-758-9754), 23 Knickerbocker Lake Road (off Route 9), Valatie. Open late June to mid-August. This large lake, operated by the town of Kinderhook, has a nice beach, making it a popular place to swim, especially for those with young children. It is open to the public; $10 per car.

Lake Taghkanic State Park (518-851-3631), 1528 Route 82, Taghkanic. Open Memorial Day weekend through Labor Day. Parking fee. This 156-acre lake has two beaches. The west beach is larger, with boat rentals (rowboats and paddleboats) and volleyball courts; the east beach is good for people traveling with young children. Both beaches have snack-bar concession stands and restrooms.

Taconic State Park (518-329-3993), Route 344, off Route 22, Copake Falls. Open Memorial Day weekend through Labor Day. Free. This flooded iron ore mine/quarry with a dock allows swimmers to step into 8 feet of water. There is no beach here, and it is not recommended for people with small children. There is an adjacent small pond for kids with 2 feet of water; do come prepared, since there is no snack bar or services, just restrooms.

✷ Winter Sports

CROSS-COUNTRY SKIING Cross-country skiing in Columbia County is centered in the state parks, where well-marked trails are uncrowded—and free—and natural surroundings are breathtaking. You must bring your own equipment.

Clermont State Historic Site (518-537-4240), 400 Woods Road (off Route 9G), Germantown, offers skiing, as does **Taconic State Park** (518-329-3993), east of

Route 22 in Copake, and the **Harlem Valley Rail Trail,** Route 22, off Undermountain Road in Ancram.

Lake Taghkanic State Park (518-851-3631), 1528 Route 82 at Taconic Parkway, 11 miles south of Hudson, has skiing and ice skating.

Queechy Lake (518-367-2069), Queechy Lake Drive, Canaan, offers some of the best ice fishing in the county.

DOWNHILL SKIING **Catamount Ski Area** (518-325-3200; www.catamountski.com), 2962 Route 23, Hillsdale, straddles the borders of New York and Massachusetts. Open Monday through Friday 9–4; Saturday and Sunday 8:30–4; night skiing Wednesday through Saturday 3–9. It's a popular area with skiers of all ages and abilities, beginner to expert. First opened in 1939, Catamount is one of the oldest ski areas in the state. It is still privately owned and operated, and the atmosphere reflects a down-home warmth that is nice for young skiers and families. There are 32 slopes and seven lifts, as well as a terrain park for snowboarding, night skiing, lessons, and day care. Trail expansions and improvements include such popular runs as Sidewinder and Catapult (the steepest run in the Berkshires). Upper Promenade gives beginners a mile-long run, and more experienced skiers get a 2.5-mile route to the base lodge from the summit. Catamount offers 98 percent snowmaking, rentals, and even RV and camping facilities. In summer enjoy grass skiing and mountaincoasters—sort of bobsleds on tracks.

ICE FISHING Ice fishing is allowed at **Lake Taghkanic State Park** (518-851-3631), 1528 Route 82 at Taconic State Parkway, 11 miles south of Hudson, and at **Rudd Pond** (518-789-3059), 59 Rudd Pond Road, Millerton. Make sure to check if the ice is thick enough for ice fishing in these locations before setting out.

✷ Lodging

The following fine establishments welcome visitors and are my favorite places to stay in Columbia County, but if you need more information about bed & breakfasts, motels, and hotels in the region, contact the **Columbia County Lodging Association** (1-800-558-8218; www.columbiacountylodging.com), P.O. Box 795, New Lebanon 12125.

Chatham

The Chatham Bed & Breakfast (518-956-3296), 164 Hudson Avenue, Chatham 12037. ($) There are four beautiful rooms, all with private bath, within walking distance of shops and restaurants in the village. The hot gourmet breakfast is particularly noteworthy and includes treats like pecan ginger waffles or lemon soufflé pancakes. While guests will find wireless Internet service, air-conditioning, and self-service coffee and tea, there are no televisions in the rooms. Not recommended for children. Open year-round.

Spencertown Cottages (518-392-7449), 1909 County Route 9, Chatham 12037. ($$) Located just a couple of miles from the Taconic Parkway, these two charming cottages are ideally designed for family getaways. Each one is 1,500 square feet, with two bedrooms, a bathroom, kitchen, living room, and dining room. There is a minimum requirement of a three-night stay (cost ranges from $350 to $650 depending on the time of year). There are also weekly and monthly rates.

Wireless Internet service and cable TV on the premises; no pets permitted. Open year-round.

Hillsdale

Bell House Bed & Breakfast (518-325-3841), 9315 State Route 22, Hillsdale 12524. ($$) Named for the Bell family, who lived in this house for 140 years until 1970, this elegant 1830 two-story country inn has three rooms, all with private bath; each one is tastefully furnished with Early American antiques. A full gourmet breakfast is served outdoors in the summer months, when guests can also enjoy the lovely swimming pool. Children over the age of eight are welcome. Open year-round.

Honored Guest Bed & Breakfast (518-325-9100), 20 Hunt Road, Hillsdale 12529. ($$) Located 2 miles from the Catamount ski area, this 4,000-square-foot house (a Frank Lloyd Wright design built in 1910) is a delightful, comfortable establishment run by an innkeeper who loves her work. Originally the building was a guesthouse on the 68-acre estate of the architect who built St. Patrick's Cathedral. There are four guest rooms, all with private bath, and they are all on one floor of the three-story structure. A five-course gourmet breakfast is served, complete with home-baked muffins and an exotic fruit course; it includes nothing you would consider making yourself. A favorite offering of mine: the banana-pecan pancakes topped with fresh strawberry sauce. Afternoon tea is offered 4:30–6, with wonderful baked treats; during the winter guests gather around the lovely fireplace. Expect turndown service at night—complete with romantic lighting in the room and chocolates on your pillow. Children welcome with advance notice. Open year-round.

Inn at Green River (518-325-7248), 9 Nobletown Road, Hillsdale 12529. ($$) Set on an acre of lawn and gardens above a meadow where Cranse Creek flows into the Green River, this 1830 Federal house is a truly special place for a relaxing weekend. The Green River is a good spot to fish or cool off in the summer months. Tanglewood (in the Berkshires) is just 20 minutes away. A full breakfast is elegantly served in the dining room or on the screened-in porch. The lemon-ricotta pancakes and honey-spice French toast are house specialties. There are seven beautifully decorated rooms, all with private bath; four have gas fireplaces, and two have Jacuzzis. This is a great spot for an anniversary weekend or special occasion. Children over 12 only on weekends; the policy is flexible on weekday nights. Open year-round.

Hudson Area

Country Squire Bed & Breakfast (518-822-9229), 251 Allen Street, Hudson 12534. ($$) This restored 1900 Victorian home has many of its original details intact and decor that is sophisticated yet cozy. The five guest rooms offer private bathrooms (they're large, with wonderful claw-foot tubs), cable TV, air-conditioining, and wireless Internet access; parking is free. The delicious continental breakfast will keep you going all morning. Walk to the Amtrak train station. Children welcome. Open year-round.

Front Street Guesthouse (518-828-1635), 20 South Front Street, Hudson 12534. ($$) This lovely hotel includes 10 beautifully decorated rooms with pillow-top mattress, 500-thread-count sheets, wireless Internet service, a flat-screen TV, and air-conditioning. Fresh fruit and coffee are served in the morning. Half the rooms have private baths. The three large suites include kitchenettes. Mod Restaurant is located downstairs (see *Eating Out*). Open year-round.

Hudson Merchant House (518-828-9200), 10 South Front Street, Hudson 12534. ($$$) This boutique guesthouse offers sophisticated surroundings in a beautifully renovated building that dates back to the 1700s. There are four rooms, and the most spacious features luxury linens, hardwood floors, a king-size bed, and a grand bay window with views of the Hudson River and Catskill Mountains. The bathroom floors are tiled with Italian marble, and there is a soaking tub as well as a shower. Another room has a private balcony. Not recommended for children. Open year-round.

Inn at Ca'Mea (518-822-0005), 333 Warren Street, Hudson 12534. ($$) Located in a historic landmark 1800s Federal-style house, the inn has four beautifully renovated rooms, all with queen-size bed, air-conditioning, and cable TV; two have balconies overlooking the garden connecting the inn to the restaurant (see *Dining Out*). Guests will find fresh flowers in their room upon arrival. Fans of the fine cuisine here will appreciate this lovely oasis to spend the night. All guests receive a 20 percent discount on dinners here. Open year-round.

The Inn at Hudson (518-822-9322), 317 Allen Street, Hudson 12534. ($$) The architecturally elegant Morgan Jones House, built circa 1906, has been beautifully restored and is now a majestic inn. Four spacious rooms with separate baths each have a queen-size bed, cable TV, air-conditioning, and wireless Internet access. Two rooms share a bath and are available at a reduced rate. The inn is within walking distance to the city's shops and restaurants. Children and well-behaved dogs are welcome. Open year-round.

Mount Merino Manor (518-828-5583), 4317 Route 23, Hudson 12534. ($$$) This beautifully renovated and decorated historic home across from Olana was built by Frederic Church's physician. Guests may enjoy reading on the lovely wraparound porch or walking on the trails around the manor, which is situated on a 100-acre estate overlooking the Hudson River. Although presiding over an elegant Victorian mansion, innkeepers Rita and Patrick Birmingham make visitors feel completely relaxed. Many of the seven guest rooms have wonderful river views, and all have large, luxurious private bathrooms with whirlpool tubs and spa showers. Most rooms also have fireplaces and king-size beds. While guests will feel transported back in time to another era (yet with all the modern amenities), the manor is conveniently located only a few minutes away from the shops and restaurants in the city of Hudson. The perfect place to celebrate a special occasion. Children over the age of 10 welcome. Open year-round.

Union Street Guest House (518-828-0958), 349 Union Street, Hudson 12534. ($$) This meticulously restored 1830s Greek Revival establishment consists of a main house, bungalow, and town house, all featuring attractive private guest suites with a wide range of rates, depending on the season and length of stay. No breakfast is served here; however, there are several eateries within walking distance. Open year-round.

Vanderbilt House (518-672-9993), 161 Main Street, Philmont 12565. ($$) This historic 1860 hotel was completely renovated, reopening under new ownership in 2011, and now houses a restaurant as well (see *Dining Out*). There are eight charming guest rooms with private bath, air-conditioning, wireless Internet service, and cable TV. A one-bedroom suite with a full wall of windows overlooks Summit Lake and the surrounding woods. Open year-round.

Kinderhook/Stuyvesant Area

Angel Wing Hollow Bed & Breakfast (518-784-2989), 898 County Route 28, Niverville 12184. ($) This charming one-bedroom B&B is located in an 1888, fully restored Victorian farmhouse in the hamlet of Niverville (town of Kinderhook). The antiques-furnished room, with private bath, has a claw-foot tub in addition to a stall shower. A full country breakfast is served. The retired couple who own and operate this bed & breakfast have two cats and believe in angels! Open year-round.

Red Robin Song Guest House (518-794-0186), 94 Schoolhouse Road, West Lebanon 12195. ($) They are set on over 100 acres here, with several trails for hiking and snowshoeing. This is a good choice for those who like to be in the woods, yet close to the attractions of the Berkshires. There are three cozy rooms: one with private bath and two share a bath. A vegan breakfast is served with a variety of healthy choices like tofu scramble or banana French toast. Snacks are also provided in the afternoon. One room is pet friendly. Children welcome. Open year-round.

The Van Schaack House (518-758-6118), 20 Broad Street, Kinderhook 12106. ($$$) This Georgian-style historic house was built in 1785 and has had only six owners. In 1865 Victorian touches were added, including a slate mansard roof; the porches were built on in the early 20th century. This grand old mansion, decorated with antiques and fine paintings, was once the home of Peter Van Schaack, a prominent 18th-century attorney and close friend of John Jay. His sister married into the Roosevelt family. There are four guest rooms, all with private bath, air-conditioning, TV, VCR, and DVD player. You will find a plush bathrobe and bottle of Old Kinderhook water in your room. There is an extensive library for guest use, as well as a gym and computer room. One of the innkeepers graduated from the Culinary Institute, so the full gourmet breakfast includes freshly squeezed orange juice, terrific breads, and a different egg dish every day. No children. Open year round, but advance reservations are always required.

New Lebanon

Churchill House Bed & Breakfast (518-766-5852; 1-800-532-2702), 228 Churchill Road, New Lebanon 12125. ($$) This beautiful 1830 Greek Revival farmhouse with a wraparound porch is located on 18 acres on the edge of the Berkshires. A lovely stream flows through the property, and guests can enjoy a view of the Taconic Valley and Berkshire Hills. Three rooms and one suite, all with private bath, range in price, so inquire about the variety of accommodations, especially if you are traveling on a budget. There are special midweek and off-season rates, making this B&B great value for the money. Savor the hearty breakfast served in the dining room. Children over the age of six are welcome. Open year-round.

Shaker Meadows Bed & Breakfast (518-794-9385), 14209 Route 22, New Lebanon 12125. ($) This 1821 farmhouse, located on 50 scenic acres of meadows and hills, overlooks a pond. The centrally air-conditioned farmhouse has three large rooms (each with private bath) and three small bedrooms (each with private bath outside the room). This is an ideal place for a family reunion or large gathering of friends as the farmhouse sleeps 12. A second adjacent building has three guest suites; these rooms have phone, TV, VCR, full kitchen, air-conditioning, living room, and private deck. A dining room, separate from the farmhouse, is where guests are served a hearty full breakfast. During the summer months, make sure to get a pass to the private town beach on Queechy Lake; the innkeepers will provide towels and beach chairs. A minimum stay is never required. Children welcome. Open year-round.

Spencer House Bed & Breakfast (518-794-6500), 466 Route 20, New Lebanon 12125. ($$) Originally the home of Col. Allen Spencer, who served in the War of 1812, this classic Shaker-style structure is located in a pastoral country setting. You will find plenty of peace and quiet here yet still be conveniently located near a few excellent restaurants. The extended continental breakfast, between 8 and 11 AM, includes muffins, bagels, fruit, and cereal. The six rooms (four with private bath and queen-size bed; two share one bath) are cozy, comfortable, and nicely decorated. Children over the age of 12 are welcome. The bed & breakfast is located next door to Mario's restaurant (see *Dining Out*) and is owned by the same family. Open year-round.

✷ Where to Eat

DINING OUT **American Glory BBQ** (518-822-1234), 342 Warren Street, Hudson. ($$) Open daily 11 AM–midnight. Housed in a renovated firehouse, American Glory's specialties reflect barbecue styles from all areas of the country. There are also ribs, macaroni and cheese, grilled steaks, and fish, along with sides like cheesy fries, coleslaw, and corn bread. All smoking of the meats is done on the premises. The 30-foot bar serves a variety of craft beers, including their own. There is almost always live music on weekends.

Backwater Bar & Grille (518-781-0199), 42 Queechy Lake Road, Canaan. ($$) Open Monday through Thursday for lunch 11–4, dinner 4–10; Friday through Sunday breakfast 8–noon, lunch noon–4, dinner 4–11. This informal restaurant and cocktail lounge is a great place to enjoy year-round lakeside dining. The large menu features homemade soups, salads, sandwiches, and wraps for lunch. Dinner entrées include several steak and seafood choices, as well as pastas and vegetarian options. Children are welcome, and there is a separate menu for the kids.

Blue Plate (518-392-7711), Central Square, Chatham. ($$) Open for dinner Wednesday through Sunday from 5:30. This American bistro housed in a Victorian building serves a variety of pastas, steaks, seafood, and salads. Notice the antique copper bar downstairs and wonderful murals. This spot has earned a fine reputation with local residents, weekenders, and travelers.

Ca'Mea (518-822-0005), 333 Warren Street, Hudson. ($$) Open Tuesday through Sunday for lunch noon–3; dinner 5–10. Winter hours are slightly different. Enjoy Tuscan and Northern Italian specialties in casual elegance. Soft colors complement the mahogany ceilings, hardwood cherry floors, and granite bar. Try the paninis for lunch or one of the homemade pastas. The gnocchi and the calamari casserole (with fresh squid, capers, black olives, and fresh tomatoes) are popular dinner entrées. The buffalo mozzarella and gelato are just a couple of items on the menu that are imported from Italy. For dessert, there is homemade tiramisu. Outdoor dining in the summer in a charming courtyard garden that seats about 40. There is a lovely four-room inn adjacent to the restaurant connected by a courtyard (see *Lodging*).

Club Helsinki (518-828-4800), 405 Columbia Street, Hudson. ($$) Open for dinner daily, except Wednesday, 5–10. Their New American cuisine with a Southern accent adds another wonderful dimension to this eclectic entertainment venue in Hudson. The chef hails from Georgia and appreciates comfort food: His talent is making the familiar taste extraordinary. Some of the offerings include lowcountry shrimp and grits, Southern-style lump crabcakes, cast-iron-seared rib eye steak, and BBQ steelhead trout.

Crimson Sparrow (518-671-6565), 746 Warren Street, Hudson. ($$$) Open for lunch Wednesday through Saturday 11:30–2; dinner 5:30–10; Sunday brunch 11–3. This 2012 addition to the Hudson dining scene specializes in creative American cuisine. There are small and large plates, and fried green tomatoes, buckwheat waffles, fois gras, and sashimi are just some of the diverse offerings here. Drinks can be rather pricey, and service is uneven. It will be interesting to see how things progress as the restaurant settles into Hudson! The outdoor garden dining in the warm weather is delightful.

DA/BA (518-249-4631), 225 Warren Street, Hudson. ($$$) Open for dinner daily, except Sunday, 6–10. The name here comes from the first two letters of chef Daniel Nilsson's name and his mother's name; she helped finance the restaurant. The extraordinary menu in a sophisticated contemporary setting makes this a wonderful part of Hudson's fine-dining scene. The tables have lots of space between them, and there is piped-in jazz that sets the romantic mood. The appetizers (listed on the menu as "Essentials") include wild boar pâté, foie gras, and brûlée. The salads ("Roughage") are delicately prepared. The entrées ("Sustenance") include grilled filet mignon, rack of lamb, elk fillet (I opted for this, and it was excellent), vegetable risotto, and monkfish. The long mahogany bar is a busy place, especially on weekends, and divides the restaurant's two dining rooms. There are exceedingly reasonable prices for the bar menu items, which include beef burgers, a BLT, and several vegetarian options. Don't pass up the sweet potato fries . . . or the phenomenal desserts. The DA/BA Cheesecake is infused with white chocolate and forest berries, and is one of the best I've had in years.

Destino Cocina Mexicana (518-392-6663), 112 Hudson Avenue, Chatham. ($$) Open for dinner daily 5–9; Friday and Saturday until 9:30. This is the best authentic Mexican food in the county. The homemade chips and salsa are excellent, and there are about a dozen different types of margaritas as well as a good selection of beers. The large menu offers a range of burritos, fajitas, and enchiladas, but there are burgers and steaks along with several vegetarian options. The pozole, a traditional Mexican pork soup, is delicious. On weekday nights there are usually a variety of specials. Outdoor seating on the patio is available during the warm-weather months.

The Greens at Copake Country Club (518-325-0019), 44 Golf Course Road, Copake. ($$) Open April through October, daily 11–9 for lunch and dinner. Call for winter hours (November through March). Enjoy American cuisine—steaks, seafood, chicken, and pasta—while looking out over the beautifully manicured golf course. The porterhouse steak, saffron fettuccine with scallops, and Herondale Farm beef stew are just a few of the popular offerings here. There are also burgers, nachos, quesadillas, sandwiches, and salads for both lunch and dinner. There's an informal atmosphere here, and the children's menu offers a variety of selections.

Hillsdale House (518-325-7111), 2654 Route 23, Hillsdale. ($$) Open daily for lunch noon–3; dinner 5–10. They offer a full menu of American fare, including steaks, seafood, and pasta, but the best choices on the menu are the wood-fired pizzas and calzones. This is a great stop if you're traveling with children.

Jackson's Old Chatham House (518-794-7373), 646 Albany Turnpike, Old Chatham. ($$) Open daily 11:30–10 for lunch and dinner. Enjoy American cuisine in an informal atmosphere at this establishment, which has been in business for more than 60 years and owned by three generations of the same family. The steaks and prime rib are first-rate; there's also a good selection of seafood and pasta dishes. Children welcome.

Lipperas' at the Chatham House (518-392-6600), 29 Hudson Avenue, Chatham. ($$) Open daily for lunch 11:30–5; dinner 5 on. You can get lunch all day in the tavern. Sunday brunch 11–3; dinner 4–9. Closed Tuesday, September through May. The international cuisine here includes an array of freshly prepared, imaginative entrées, featuring filet mignon, prime rib, potato-encrusted salmon, fresh trout, linguine with seafood, and several vegetarian dishes. The menu changes seasonally and uses the freshest ingredients from local dairies and farmers. Save room for one of their homemade desserts: Key lime pie, chocolate fudge cake, strawberry shortcake, cannoli, flan, peanut-butter mousse, or coconut sorbet. Children welcome.

Mario's (518-794-9495), 458 Route 20/22, New Lebanon. ($$) Open Sunday, Monday, Wednesday, and Thursday 4–9; Friday and Saturday 4–10. Closed Tuesday. The Italian American cuisine here is excellent, and the prices are reasonable. There's linguine with white clam sauce, osso buco Milanese, veal parmigiana, tournedos of beef, and shrimp scampi. Desserts are all made on the premises and include fried ice cream, tiramisu, chocolate-raspberry mousse cake, and a variety of homemade gelatos. Children's portions are offered, and those with young children will feel comfortable here.

Mexican Radio (518-828-7770), 537 Warren Street, Hudson. ($$) Open daily for lunch and dinner 11:30–11. In case you are wondering, the song "Mexican Radio" by Wall of Voodoo was released in the early 1980s, and the owners love the song, which is about how rock 'n' roll radio got its start when it was banned in the United States. Hence the name here. . . . This brightly colored, upbeat, candlelit restaurant has a festive atmosphere, with dining rooms on two floors. Everything is made fresh daily, including the salsa. All drinks are made with fresh lime juice (there are dozens of tequilas for margarita lovers). Some might call their offerings Mexican comfort food: The burritos, enchiladas, and tacos have imaginative fillings. The Cajun burrito is a popular entrée—it's filled with shrimp and chorizo sausage. An array of hot sauces line the tables, there is a large number of vegetarian entrées, and the nachos are delicious. There are no refried beans or heavy brown sauces here. Children welcome.

The Pillars Restaurant (518-794-8007), 860 Route 20, New Lebanon. ($$) Open for dinner Wednesday through Saturday 5–9; Sunday 4–8; closed for the month of January. The American and Continental cuisine here is reliable and quite decent. The fillet of beef Charlemagne—beef tenderloin sautéed with onions and mushrooms and topped with Hollandaise sauce—is popular; another favorite is the fillet of sole baked with lobster butter and cream. I prefer the grilled sea bass marinated in miso and saki and served with a wasabi soy sauce. Desserts are homemade on the premises; do not pass up the dark chocolate sack filled with chocolate mousse. Children's menu.

PM Wine Bar (518-301-4398), 119 Warren Street, Hudson. ($$) Open Tuesday through Thursday 5–10; Friday and Saturday until midnight. A small, cozy local bar where there is a large selection of wines by the glass in a range of prices. The fare consists of all kinds of tempting tapas, like the sun-dried dates wrapped in bacon and filled with blue cheese. If wine isn't your thing, the martinis are excellent, and two kinds of absinthe are offered!

Red Dot Bar & Restaurant (518-828-3657), 321 Warren Street, Hudson. ($$) Open for dinner Wednesday through Monday 5–10; Saturday and Sunday brunch 11–3. Eclectic Continental cuisine is served in this bistro: There are burgers, steaks, pasta, duck, and roast chicken. Diners will be delighted to discover the standard favorites done imaginatively and well. It's in a former butcher shop, now completely renovated with a bright red door; the atmosphere is casual and relaxing. The low-key bar is a nice place to enjoy dinner. The French onion soup is excellent; the daily specials are wonderful. Not recommended for children.

Swiss Hütte (518-325-3333), Route 23, Hillsdale. ($$) Open for lunch Saturday noon–2, Sunday until 3; dinner Wednesday through Sunday 5:30–9. Hours vary slightly with the season. Overlooking the slopes at the Catamount ski area, the dining rooms here are wood paneled, and the three fireplaces make them warm and cozy. The Swiss chef-owner is both a master chef and a ski racer. The menu features French-Swiss dishes and excellent home-baked pastries.

Swoon (518-822-8938), 340 Warren Street, Hudson. ($$) Open for dinner daily, except Wednesday, 5–10; for lunch Saturday and Sunday 11:30–5. Enjoy a taste of SoHo in Hudson at reasonable prices. The finest, freshest ingredients are used in a menu that changes seasonally. The owners have a passion for fine wine, which is reflected in the wide variety of wines served by the glass. Imaginative menu featuring contemporary American cuisine; all desserts are made on the premises and are particularly noteworthy.

Vanderbilt House (518-672-9993), 161 Main Street, Philmont. ($$) Open for dinner Tuesday through Sunday 5:30–10; Sunday brunch 11–3. This 1860 hotel (see *Lodging*) was completely renovated by the new owner. It now includes a restaurant headed by a Culinary Institute chef and features American cuisine, with most ingredients sourced from local farmers. The fare is hearty and changes with the seasons. On a recent winter visit the choices included salmon, steak, roast duckling, and shepherd's pie. The restaurant/hotel is a wonderful addition to Philmont's Main Street.

Vico (518-828-6529), 136 Warren Street, Hudson. ($$) Open for lunch Saturday and Sunday noon–3; dinner Thursday through Monday 5–10. *Vico* means "village" in Italian, and this terrific dining spot offers contemporary Italian cuisine using products from local purveyors. (One of my favorite labels is Grazin' Angus grass-fed and grass-finished beef, which are the best I've ever eaten, and Vico offers their meats.) The pastas are homemade, with a range of imaginative creations—this is definitely not your usual Italian restaurant. Lunch offers wonderful paninis, salads, and pasta dishes. Nice wine list featuring Italian vino that complements the menu selections.

Wasabi Japanese Restaurant (518-822-1888), 807 Warren Street, Hudson. ($$) Open for lunch and dinner Monday through Saturday 11:30–9:30; Sunday 3–9:30. Set in contemporary Japanese simplicity, this restaurant offers sushi, sashimi, tempura, teriyaki, udon and soba noodles, and more. If you want to taste something particularly unusual, ask for the chef's special appetizer (this dish doesn't appear on the menu).

EATING OUT For those who enjoy grabbing something quick to eat, the **City of Hudson** now has several food trucks, most of them on Warren Street between Third and Fourth. You find them from April through October, and they are usually open 11–7. **Tortillaville** is my favorite, and they serve up phenomenally delicious Mexican treats. **Truck Pizza** serves first-rate wood-fired Neapolitan style pizza with a crispy crust and lots of cheese. **Winnie's Jerk Chicken & Fish** offers shrimp and curried goat, as well as jerk chicken and fish, and orders come with rice, beans, and steamed vegetables. (Note that Winnie's truck is located at 708 State Street.)

Baba Louie's (518-751-2155), 517 Warren Street, Hudson. ($) Open daily, except Wednesday, for lunch 11:30–3; dinner 4:30–9:30, until 10 Friday and Saturday. They create some of the best thin-crust pizza you will find anywhere, and the selections are incredibly imaginative. I love the one with roasted portobello mushrooms, garlic, tomatoes, and goat cheese. There is a vegetarian pizza with spelt (wheat-free) crust filled with an array of veggies and soy mozzarella cheese. The barbecued chicken pizza is one of the more ordinary choices. For those who aren't pizza aficionados, there are pasta specials and fresh salads for lunch and dinner. The soup du jour is always vegetarian based. I enjoy their veggie paninis or tuna and chicken salad for lunch, as well.

Bean's Place (518-758-2500), 3 Albany Avenue, Kinderhook. ($$) Open daily, except Tuesday, 8–2; Friday until 7. This is a fantastic small-town café with excellent omelets, homemade soups, salads, and baked goods, created from largely organic ingredients. The owner, Bonnie, aims to please, and her Bean's Salad is one of my favorite treats here—an enormous serving of fresh greens and veggies with their tasty house dressing. The coffee is first-rate, too. It's a small venue and tends to get crowded on weekends, but this eatery is definitely worth a stop if you're in the area.

Café Le Perche (518-822-1850), 230 Warren Street, Hudson. ($$) Open Tuesday through Thursday and Sunday 7 AM–8 PM; Friday and Saturday 7 AM–10 PM. Closed Monday. This popular café/bar/bakery turns out croissants, walnut sourdough loaves of bread, and pesto rolls that are absolutely amazing. Luckily, they can keep up with demand: The 17-ton wood-fired oven imported from France bakes 200 baguettes per hour. Owner Allan Chapin, inspired by the cuisine of the Le Perche region of France, is a great-great-grandson of Herman Melville; interestingly, he chose Hudson, once a whaling port, as the place to open his bakery. Make sure to sample a taste of France; it's a wonderful stop for refreshments after walking on Warren Street. My favorite treat here is the *pain au chocolat.* I've also thoroughly enjoyed the roasted vegetable grilled sandwich with roasted red peppers, zucchini, eggplant, and goat cheese.

The Cascades (518-822-9146), 407 Warren Street, Hudson. ($) Open daily, except Sunday, 8–4. This café/gourmet deli has just about every type of fresh bagel imaginable. It's a terrific stop for a simple, healthful breakfast or lunch and features homemade soups, salads, and sandwiches. The desserts are sumptuous (try the chocolate silk pie).

Chocolate Bar (518-821-1274), 4 Front Street, Hudson. ($$) Open Thursday through Sunday 11–5. Chocoholics rejoice! Owner Kim Bach offers a variety of drinking chocolates, pastries, tea, and coffee, as well as exotic chocolate bars from around the world. It's a tiny place but large enough to satisfy all those cravings.

Claverack Food Mart (518-851-9164), 6 Park Street (at the junction of Routes 9H and 23), Claverack. ($) Open daily 8–8, Sunday until 4. This is the place to go for enormous sandwiches (made with high-quality meats) and salads at reasonable prices. A good place to stop if you are planning a picnic and need basic take-out items. Excellent fresh roast beef sandwiches!

The Cottage Restaurant (518-392-4170), 1267 Route 295, East Chatham. ($) Open daily, except Tuesday, 9–9. Enjoy the peaceful country atmosphere and friendly service at this restaurant, where all soups, breads, and desserts are prepared fresh every day. Specials include meat loaf and mashed potatoes, and pastrami surprise (hot pastrami, mushrooms, and cheese on rye). A good place for children.

Earth Foods (518-822-1396), 523 Warren Street, Hudson. ($) Open daily, except Tuesday, 9–3; Friday through Sunday until 4. The hearty soups (their black bean is excellent), pasta, pizza, wraps, sandwiches, and imaginative salads make this a great place to stop for lunch after antiquing in the city. There's a counter, so if you're eating alone, it's a comfortable place to enjoy a meal. Children are welcome.

The Farmer's Wife (518-329-5431), 3 County Route 8, Ancramdale. ($) Open Monday through Saturday 7–5; Sunday 7–3. High-quality gourmet prepared foods and baked goods to eat in or take out are available in this cozy eatery next door to the local post office. It is truly an oasis in the midst of Columbia County's pastoral countryside.

Grazin' (518-822-9323), 717 Warren Street, Hudson. ($$) Open daily, except Wednesday, 11–8; Sunday 9–3. Dan Gibson, owner of Grazin' Angus farm in Ghent, now offers his grass-fed, hormone-free beef in this landmark diner. Traditional favorites are created from high-quality, locally sourced ingredients. In addition to all types of burgers, there is smoked pork sirloin, pulled short rib sandwich, steaks, and omelets. They even make their own soda!

Lick (518-828-7254), 253 Warren Street, Hudson. ($) Open May through Columbus Day, daily 1–9. If you have never tried exotic-flavored ice creams like lavender, prune, Armagnac, or Thai coconut chili, this small eatery is the place to splurge. My favorite treat is the made-to-order ice cream sandwich on a choice of oatmeal, chocolate chip, or ginger cookies with the flavor of your choice. The ice cream here isn't cheap, but it's a worthwhile indulgence. You won't be disappointed!

Local 111 (518-672-7801), 111 Main Street, Philmont. ($$) Open Wednesday through Sunday for breakfast 10–2; dinner 5–9. This former garage on

Main Street in town is now an eatery serving full breakfasts, organic egg sandwiches, and an array of freshly baked muffins, scones, and breads. At dinnertime, the eclectic American cuisine, using local ingredients, ranges from burgers and salads to grilled fish and steaks. This local hub is a welcome addition to the dining scene in this rural part of Columbia County.

Main Street Diner (518-758-1233), 3032 Main Street, Valatie. ($) Open daily 6 AM–9:30 PM; until 8 on Sunday. This is a great place to get a home-cooked turkey sandwich. Or if you prefer wraps, there are several to choose from. Breakfast here includes choices like waffles, pancakes, or homemade muffins baked on the premises. Dinner includes Italian American favorites like eggplant parmigiana, lasagna, and a variety of pasta dishes. There are also steaks and seafood. Children welcome.

Mod Restaurant (518-828-1880), 20 South Front Street, Hudson. ($$) Open for lunch and dinner Tuesday through Thursday 11–9; Friday and Saturday until 10. This is the place to find comfort food like meat loaf and macaroni and cheese prepared with a creative flair. Vegan, vegetarian, and gluten-free entrées are also available.

Old Chatham Country Store (518-794-6227), 639 Albany Turnpike Road, Old Chatham. ($) Open Tuesday through Thursday and Sunday 7–4; Friday and Saturday 7 AM–9 PM. Breakfast served 7–11; lunch 11–2; dinner Friday and Saturday 6–9. A landmark building houses this eatery owned by two Culinary Institute graduates, and the fine fare reflects their attention to detail. The homemade salsa and chips are the best I've had anywhere, and I always stock up when passing through the area. The soups, salads, sandwiches, and quesadillas are excellent. Local products are sold here, including cheeses, ice cream, maple syrup, and other gourmet items. Ice cream aficionados will be pleased to know they sell Jeni's Splendid Ice Cream from Columbus, Ohio, a rare treat in the Hudson Valley! An adjoining dining room to the deli area is a lovely place to enjoy breakfast, lunch, or dinner. Open year-round.

Olde Hudson (518-828-6923), 434 Warren Street, Hudson. ($) Open daily 11–6. The European gourmet cheeses here include Mirabo walnut (Germany), Urgelia (northwestern Spain), Flor di Capra (Sardinia, Italy), and Queso Azul (Basque region of Spain), to name just some of the treats that await visitors to this shop. There are meats and other provisions as well. This is a wonderful place to pick up items for that gourmet picnic in the Columbia County countryside.

Otto's Market (518-537-7200), 215 Main Street, Germantown. ($) Open Monday through Saturday 7–7; until 3 on Sunday. This delightful grocery/café has an amazing selection of products in a well-organized small space. It is also an ideal spot to have a tasty breakfast burrito or bagel with eggs and cheese. Their hearty soups and hot and cold sandwiches are first-rate, employing ingredients from local purveyors. Last, but not least, the prices are extremely reasonable! And you have a chance to browse through the Germantown Variety store across the street, which is a wonderful gem that opened in 2012.

Our Daily Bread (518-392-9852), 54 Main Street, Chatham. ($) Open Tuesday through Friday 7–6; Saturday 8–5; Sunday 8–4. Enjoy breakfast and lunch at this kosher and vegetarian restaurant, where soups, salads, sandwiches, and quiche are the mainstay. All breads, cookies, cakes, and pies are baked on the premises. Beer and wine available. Outdoor dining in the summer months. Children welcome.

Park Falafel & Pizza (518-828-5500), 11 North Seventh Street, Hudson. ($) Open Monday through Saturday 9:30–9; Sunday 11–9. This is the place to find healthful, tasty, inexpensive fare. All baking is done on the premises here, at Hudson's first kosher restaurant in 70 years. For breakfast there are omelets and hot oatmeal. Lunch offerings include homemade soups, salads, falafel, carrot salad, and pita sandwiches stuffed with fantastic fillings and fresh vegetables. This is a wonderful unusual addition to the Hudson dining scene.

Parlor Coffee & Teahouse (518-828-2210), 742 Warren Street, Hudson. ($) Open Monday through Saturday 7 AM–10 PM; Sunday 8 AM–9 PM. This coffeehouse is a wonderful place to relax after walking around the city of Hudson. They offer an array of coffee drinks, including lattes, cappuccino, espresso, and even regular coffee, in addition to a nice selection of organic teas. The pastries, cakes, and cookies are all baked fresh daily in Hudson.

The Spotty Dog Books & Ale (518-671-6006), 440 Warren Street, Hudson. ($) Open Monday through Thursday 11–6; Friday and Saturday 11–9; Sunday noon–4. This independent bookstore/lounge/café is housed in a renovated historic firehouse that dates from 1890. There are books for sale, and the bar/café serves several types of microbrewery beer as well as a variety of coffees, teas, and desserts.

Taghkanic Diner (518-851-7117), 1016 Route 82 (off the Taconic Parkway), West Taghkanic. ($) Open daily 7 AM–9 PM, Friday until 11 PM, Saturday and Sunday until 10 PM. This old-fashioned diner is a mainstay in this part of Columbia County; it has been in business since 1953. The breakfasts are excellent and inexpensive. My favorite meal here is the Taghkanic Club sandwich, which is difficult to consume in one sitting! If you are looking for good food and hearty portions at reasonable prices, this is a good place to go.

Tanzy's (518-828-5165), 223 Warren Street, Hudson. ($) Open Monday, Tuesday, and Thursday through Saturday 8–3; Sunday 8–noon; closed Wednesday. Enjoy breakfast, lunch, or afternoon tea in a delightful atmosphere. There are omelets, egg sandwiches, and cinnamon French toast for breakfast. Lunch offerings include turkey pesto melt (they roast their own turkey here), Angus burger, buffalo chicken salad with blue cheese dressing, and homemade soups. The hot fudge sundae is one of their signature desserts, so do indulge.

White Stone Café (518-392-7171), 2337 Route 66, Ghent. ($) Open Sunday and Monday 6 AM–3 PM; Tuesday through Thursday 6 AM–8 PM; Friday and Saturday 6 AM–9 PM. The international cuisine here combines American, Greek, Italian, and Mexican specialties. Enjoy pastas, steaks and chops, chicken, sandwiches, omelets, and hot open-faced sandwiches. The all-you-can-eat lunch buffet is served every day. This is a great place to stop if you're traveling with children.

Wunderbar & Bistro (518-828-0555), 744 Warren Street, Hudson. ($) Open for lunch and dinner daily 11:30 AM–2 AM. Lunch specials include entrées like grilled chicken breast over salad, meat loaf and mashed potatoes, linguine with sausage, and fish-and-chips. The dinner menu offers a range of comfort food including pork chops, pasta primavera, bratwurst, and burgers. This isn't the place to go if you're a vegetarian or seeking gourmet touches. Children welcome.

✷ Entertainment

Club Helsinki Hudson (518-828-4800; www.helsinkihudson.com), 405 Columbia Street, Hudson. There are two performance spaces here, a full-service restaurant (see *Dining Out*), gallery space, recording facilities, and office space. The calendar is packed with all kinds of entertainment, including musical and comedy acts as well as children's programs. The restaurant serves dinner daily, except Wednesday, 5–10. Check the website for the array of offerings here.

Crandell Theatre (518-392-3331; www.crandelltheatre.org), 48 Main Street, Chatham. This is one of the few remaining independently owned movie theaters showing first-run films. The single screen, lantern lights, and a balcony with wooden seats make the 1930s theater a landmark. Tickets are a bargain at $5—and a box of popcorn will set you back a whole $1.50.

Ghent Playhouse—Columbia Civic Players (518-392-6264; www.ghentplayhouse.org), 6 Town Hall Place, Ghent. The season runs from October to early June. Offerings range from drama to comedy and musicals. Past productions have included *Dracula, Private Lives,* and *H.M.S. Pinafore.*

Hudson Opera House (518-822-1438; www.hudsonoperahouse.org), 327 Warren Street, Hudson. Open year-round, daily noon–5. There is no opera here, but rather a cultural center for the city of Hudson, with lectures, performances, readings, and art exhibits. Stop in while you are strolling through Hudson and find out what's happening.

Mac-Haydn Theatre (518-392-9292; www.machaydntheatre.org), 1925 Route 203, Chatham, specializes in summer-stock musical productions. The intimate theater is the perfect venue for all-time favorites like *Oliver! Oklahoma! Fiddler on the Roof,* and other performances that will appeal to the entire family.

Spencertown Academy (518-392-3693; www.spencertown.org), 80 Route 203, Spencertown. Open April through December. Built in 1847 as a private school, it is now a cultural arts center where visitors will enjoy films, dance, theater, poetry, lectures, concerts, and a variety of other cultural events. The academy has a reputation as a leading area venue for great folk music and jazz. Groups of local, regional, and national renown entertain in an intimate setting year-round. The two galleries on the premises feature changing art and crafts exhibits. Check the website for a schedule.

Stageworks/Hudson (518-828-7843; www.stageworkshudson.org), 41 Cross Street (opposite Amtrak station), is the home of the only professional equity theater in Columbia County. There is a variety of theatrical performances here year-round. The focus of the dramas produced here is the work of playwrights who have a statement to make about the contemporary world. This is one of the best regional theaters in the Hudson Valley, with exciting productions May through November. Check the website for a complete schedule.

Tannery Pond Concerts (1-888-820-9441; www.tannerypondconcerts.org), off Route 20, New Lebanon. On weekends June through mid-September, chamber-music concerts are held in an original Shaker tannery on the campus of the Darrow School and Mount Lebanon Shaker Village. The 300-seat performance space is an unusual and interesting venue, and featured performers have included the Tokyo String Quartet, Susan Graham, Earl Wild, and the Emerson String Quartet.

The Theater Barn (518-794-8989; www.theaterbarn.com), Route 20, New Lebanon, a professional theater that is well worth a visit, offers the best of Broadway and off-Broadway in the country, July through September. The productions range from musicals to dramatic offerings. Check the website for current schedule. The plays are usually performed Thursday through Sunday, with matinees on Saturday and Sunday.

Time & Space Limited, TSL Warehouse (518-822-8448; www.timeandspace.org), 434 Columbia Street, Hudson. Open year-round; call for performance times. This is one of the most interesting venues to emerge anywhere in the Hudson Valley in recent years. Housed in a converted bakery with 8,800 square feet, it is now a performance space offering independent films with talks by filmmakers, opera, and theatrical and musical productions, as well as readings and open forums dealing with community issues. This interdisciplinary arts organization, run by two transplanted New Yorkers, was described in the *New York Times* as "making unusual statements in the area ever since they packed up their Manhattan theater company [in 1991] and handed back a $10,000 check to the politically charged National Endowment for the Arts." Make sure to get on the mailing list, and check out the event-filled calendar if you are going to be in Hudson. This is exactly the kind of independent, dynamic programming that is needed everywhere in America today.

✷ Selective Shopping

ANTIQUES When searching for antiques in Columbia County, expect to discover rare and lovely items at shops that are often as well stocked as many museums. You will see everything from unembellished Shaker rockers to ornate English sideboards, from fine examples of American folk art to the just plain odd. Quality antiques and shops are located throughout the county, but you may have to look around for bargains; many of the dealers here carry only the best, with prices to match. This is not to say that an English hunt table isn't worth several thousand dollars; just don't expect to find a Shaker table at a yard-sale price since many sellers have relocated from New York City and are savvy about their goods.

Shop hours vary widely and by season, so call before you go. Most shops are closed on Wednesday, some on Tuesday. Most are open Thursday through Monday 11–5. You can contact the Hudson Antique Dealers Association (518-822-6522; www.hudsonantiques.net) for more information.

In the city of Hudson, an antiques hub, Warren Street is a popular haunt, with dozens of shops located in a five-block area. Some have regular hours; others are open by appointment. The best way to enjoy Hudson antiquing is to spend a day wandering the streets and looking around. The following stores are just a small sample of what you will find in this vibrant city. Stop at **Arenskjold Antiques Art** (518-828-2800), 605 Warren Street, which has a nice blend of fine 18th- and 19th-century European antiques, paintings, and Danish Modern furniture. **Hudson House Antiques** (518-822-1226), 738 Warren Street; **Doyle Antiques** (518-828-3929), 711 Warren Street; and **Kendon Antiques** (518-822-8627), 508 Warren Street, will all be of interest to antiques buffs. **Rural Residence** (518-822-1061), 316 Warren Street, has wonderful unusual home furnishings and linens, as well as a great collection of coffee table books, larger than many bookstores'.

And after wandering through the antiques shops of Hudson, make sure to stop at **Vasilow's** (518-828-2717), 741 Columbia Street, for take-out truffles, chocolates, licorice, and dozens of kinds of candy, all made with natural ingredients by the Vasilow family since 1923. They are open Monday through Friday 10–6; until 5 on Saturday and 4 on Sunday. Or, if you are a tea drinker, don't miss **Vertigris** (518-828-3139), 135 Warren Street, where there is an enormous selection of teas from around the world, as well as cakes to sample while shopping. The shop is open Thursday through Monday 11–5:30.

In Austerlitz, visit **Sandy Klempner Antiques & Interiors** (518-781-4141), 2188 Route 295, open Friday through Sunday 10–5 or by chance; they have decorative, folk art, and country antiques, as well as one-of-a-kind furnishings. Chatham Center's **The White Goose** (518-766-3909), 317 Reed Road, is open March through November, daily 9–4, and has a wide variety of antiques and collectibles. **Pitkin Company Refinishers & Antiques** (518-392-3162), 14 River Street on Central Square in the village of Chatham, specializes in antique furniture of all kinds and from various periods. The shop is open Monday through Friday 8–5; Saturday 8–noon. Hillsdale's **Barn Antiques** (518-325-1357), 10394 Route 22, is open April through October, Friday through Sunday 11–5, and has a good collection of American country furniture, folk art, rugs, quilts, stoneware, and baskets from the 18th through the early 20th centuries. In Philmont, **Out of the Barn Antiques** (518-672-4506), 1063 Route 217, has a nice selection of collectibles and furniture; they are open throughout the summer, Saturday and Sunday 9–5, or by appointment. Feel free to call if you are in the area since someone is usually around to open the shop! In New Lebanon, stop at **Meissner's Auctions** (518-766-5002), 438 Route 20/22, which holds auctions year-round on Saturday starting at 5 PM. **Stair Galleries** (518-751-1000; www.stairgalleries.com), 549 Warren Street, Hudson, is an auction house specializing in estate sales of fine and decorative art, antiques, furniture, and decor. There are monthly auctions here, and it's best to check the website for the date and time. **Copake Auction** (518-329-1142; www.copakeauction.com), 266 Route 7A, Copake, handles Americana sales and conducts specialty auctions only; one features all types of antique bicycles. The auctions are usually held once every month (May through September) on a Saturday at 5 PM, but check the website or call for a schedule.

ART GALLERIES, BOOKSTORES & GIFT SHOPS It is impossible to list every gallery and interesting new shop that opens in the county, especially in Hudson, with its ever-changing, dynamic scene. These are some of my favorite places in the city—and county—at this writing, so do explore and discover much more on your own.

Basilica Hudson (212-594-0883; www.newartdealers.org), 110 South Front Street (near train station), Hudson. This historic structure is the headquarters for NADA Hudson (the New Arts Dealer Association); they sponsor art fairs in the city and showcase exhibits year-round featuring the work of emerging Hudson Valley artists. If you are walking around town, make sure to stop in and see what is happening. Check the website for special events and tours of the building.

The Bee's Knees (518-697-0888; www.thebeeskneeshudson.com), 302 Warren Street, Hudson, is chock-full of clothing, books, toys, natural baby products, and gifts for young children. They are open Monday and Wednesday through Saturday 11–5; Sunday noon–4. Closed Tuesday. Owner Amanda Hummel's shop is always bustling with activities: There are story hours as well as music and classes for kids in a room at the back of the shop. Check the website for a full schedule.

Carrie Haddad Gallery (518-828-1915), 622 Warren Street, Hudson, features prominent local artists in a bright, well-lit open space; exhibits change monthly. They are open daily 11–5.

Classic Country (518-392-2211), 2948 County Route 9, East Chatham, offers something for every taste, with furniture, kitchen items, regional books, and carefully chosen intriguing accessories. Owner Meg Stratton also operates a huge barn behind the store that is chock-full of all kinds of garden furniture and antiques. A must-stop if you're driving through East Chatham on your way to the Berkshires. Open Wednesday through Saturday 10–5.

The Fields Sculpture Park (518-392-7656), 59 Letter S Road, Ghent. (See Art Omi under *To See.*)

Germantown Variety (518-537-7400), 212 Main Street, Germantown, is open Monday through Saturday 9–6; Sunday until 3. Step into this fabulous new gift shop, which opened in 2012 across the street from the renowned Otto's Market, and take a journey back in time to the variety store of 100 years ago. Everything you can possibly need is under one roof—hardware, housewares, stationery, notions, toys, candy, books, and much more. *And* everything is made in the USA, virtually unheard of these days. You won't find anything here made in China! Owner Otto Leuschel has done a spectacular job of finding a fascinating array of merchandise.

Hudson City Books (518-671-6020), 553 Warren Street, Hudson, specializes in used and rare books. Bibliophiles shouldn't pass up this well-organized, excellent shop owned by ex-Westchester residents Karen and Neil Montone, who owned a bookstore in Scarsdale. They are open Thursday through Monday 11–5.

Make sure to stop at the **Hudson Valley Arts Center** (518-828-2661), 337 Warren Street, Hudson, open Friday through Monday 11–5, which features a nice selection of handcrafted items, including pottery, jewelry, and metalwork, as well as paintings, from local artists.

John Davis Gallery (518-828-5907), 362 Warren Street, Hudson, offers two floors of exhibit space, as well as a courtyard sculpture garden in the summer months. The gallery is open Thursday through Sunday 11–5.

Liliandloo (518-822-9492; www.liliandloo.com), 259 Warren Street, Hudson, specializes in home furnishings and accessories. The selection of items here is particularly interesting, and the prices are reasonable. Don't pass by this store on your wanderings up and down Warren Street without going in! Open daily 11–6.

Rodgers Book Barn (518-325-3610; www.rodgersbookbarn.com), 467 Rodman Road, Hillsdale, is one of the best used-book stores, with more than 50,000 volumes in a huge barn. Open year-round, Friday through Monday 11–5. Call for expanded summer hours (June through Labor Day).

Rural Residence (518-822-1061), 316 Warren Street, Hudson, is open daily 11–5; Friday and Saturday until 6.

Timothy Dunleavy, owner of this marvelous eclectic shop, has assembled an amazing array of housewares and accessories that are truly special in design. The shop also has one of the best collections of coffee table books in the Hudson Valley!

Taconic Sculpture Park and Gallery (518-392-5757), Stover Hill Road, Spencertown. (See *To See.*)

✷ Special Events

April: **The Sheep and Wool Festival** (518-537-4240), Clermont State Historic Site, 400 Woods Road, Germantown. This is a wonderful family-friendly event with sheep shearing, several craft and food vendors, and live music on the beautiful grounds of Clermont along the Hudson River. It's a great way to usher in spring.

May: **Annual Columbia Land Conservancy Country Barbecue** (518-392-5252), Clum and Patchen Farm, Livingston. This benefit festival is held rain or shine on Memorial Day, 4:30–8. Activities include a silent auction, music, an environmental education program, and lots of barbecued chicken and ribs!

July: **Old Fashioned Family 4th of July** (518-537-4240), Clermont State Historic Site, off Route 9G, Clermont. This is a celebration complete with fireworks, all kinds of drinks, food, and activities for the kids. Bring a picnic and enjoy the action by the Hudson, at one of the most beautiful spots along the river. **Falcon Ridge Folk Festival** (860-364-0366; 1-866-325-2744), 44 County Route 7D, North Hillsdale. This four-day festival of folk music and dance with more than 40 acts on four stages includes mainstage concerts, dancing, song swaps, crafts, workshops, ethnic food, and activities for the kids. Come for a day, or camp all weekend. Some of the people who have appeared include Arlo Guthrie, Holly Near, Tom Paxton, and Lucy Kaplansky. **Blueberry Festival** (518-392-0062), Old Austerlitz historic site, Route 22, Austerlitz, is held the last Saturday in July and includes 19th-century craft demonstrations, live music, a blueberry pancake breakfast, and more. **Open Studio Tour at Art Omi** (212-206-5684), 59 Letter S Road, Ghent, allows visitors to view the works of several artists in residence at this artists' colony. The tour is usually held every year in July.

September: **Columbia County Fair** (518-392-2121; www.columbiafair.com), County Fairgrounds, Routes 66 and 203, Chatham. Held Labor Day weekend. Admission fee. The oldest continuously held fair in the country, this one is still as lively as ever. A six-day celebration, it's less raucous and somewhat smaller than many other county fairs but just as much fun. Horses, sheep, cows, and other livestock are all displayed proudly by 4-H members, while prizewinning vegetables and fruits are shown off in the Grange buildings. Handmade quilts and needlecrafts make a colorful display. Sheep-to-shawl demonstrations and antique gas engines enliven the fairgrounds throughout the week; modern farm machinery has its place here also. But the fair is more than just exhibits—it's also entertainment in the best country tradition. Bluegrass bands, folksingers, and country-and-western stars entertain the crowds in the evening—and what would a county fair be without the midway games and fair food? Children will love this fair, with all the usual fun rides. **Art at Steepletop** (518-392-4144), 454 East Hill Road, Austerlitz, is the annual festival at the Edna St. Vincent Millay Colony featuring the work of former residents of Steepletop. It is held on a weekend in late September.

October: **Film Columbia** (518-392-1162), Crandell Theatre, Main Street, Chatham. This film festival is small but will interest film buffs. The Crandell Theatre is a landmark in the town and the county (see *Entertainment*). **Hudson-Chatham Arts Walk** (518-671-6213), Warren Street, Hudson, and throughout the village of Chatham. The galleries and antiques shops in both Hudson and Chatham are bustling with activity on Columbus Day weekend. Just walk up and down Warren Street in Hudson and wander around Chatham and enjoy. **Legends by Candlelight** (518-537-4240), Clermont State Historic Site, 1 Clermont Avenue (off County Route 6, off Route 9G), Germantown. This Halloween celebration is particularly fun for young people and combines history and legends with this enjoyable holiday.

December: **Olana Holiday Open House** (518-828-0135), Route 9G, just south of Hudson. The home of Frederic Church is decorated beautifully for the holiday season. This is a beautiful time to visit Olana and see what it must have been like when the Church family celebrated their traditional Christmas. **Winter Walk on Warren Street** (518-822-1438), Warren Street, Hudson. This lovely tradition is held on the first Saturday in December and begins the holiday shopping season. All the shops are decorated beautifully for the holidays, and most serve refreshments.

Dutchess County

10

Dutchess County Tourism

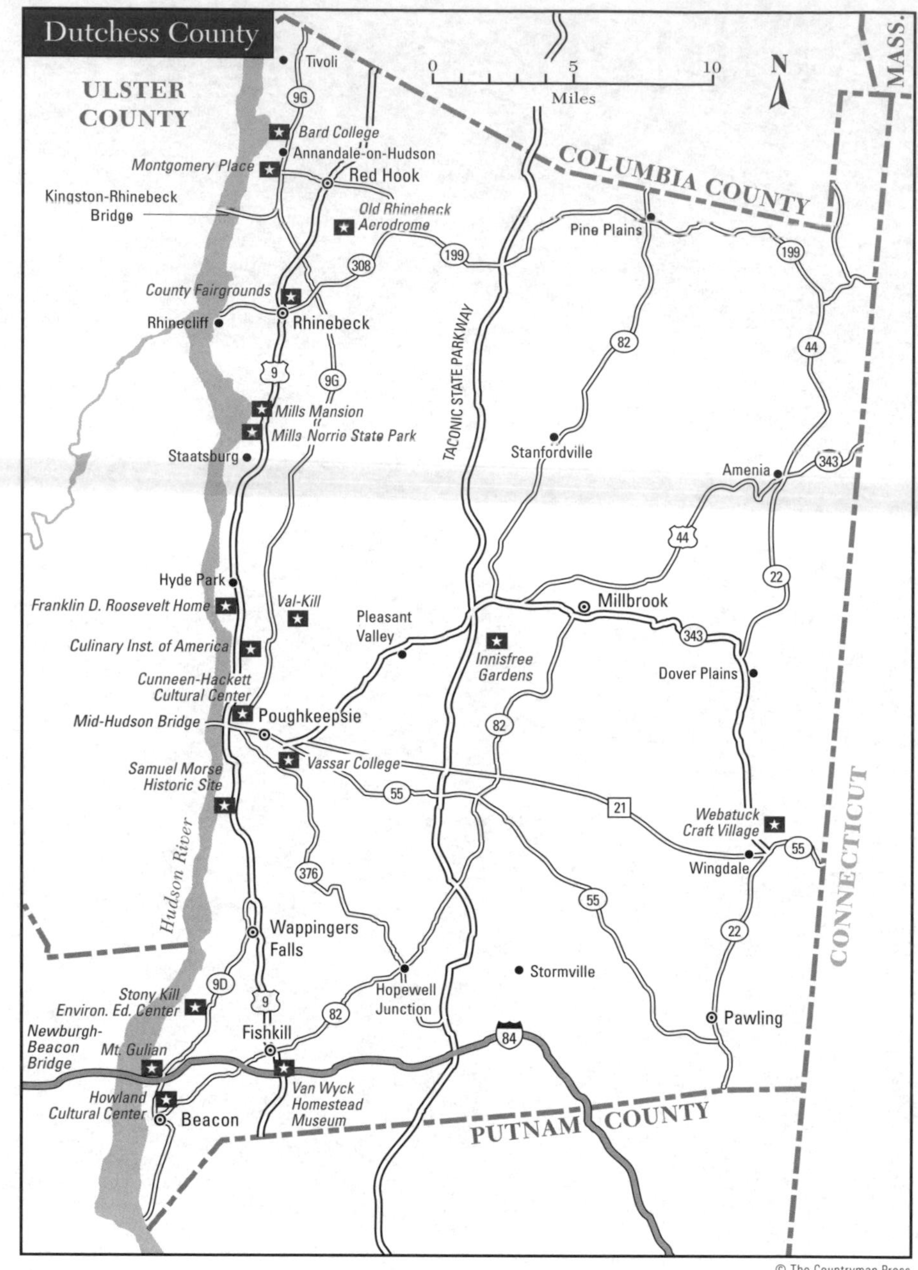
Dutchess County
ULSTER COUNTY
COLUMBIA COUNTY
MASS.
CONNECTICUT
PUTNAM COUNTY
0 5 10
Miles
N
Tivoli
Bard College
Annandale-on-Hudson
Montgomery Place
Red Hook
Kingston-Rhinebeck Bridge
Old Rhinebeck Aerodrome
Pine Plains
County Fairgrounds
Rhinecliff
Rhinebeck
TACONIC STATE PARKWAY
Mills Mansion
Mills Norrie State Park
Staatsburg
Stanfordville
Amenia
Hyde Park
Franklin D. Roosevelt Home
Val-Kill
Pleasant Valley
Millbrook
Culinary Inst. of America
Innisfree Gardens
Dover Plains
Cunneen-Hackett Cultural Center
Poughkeepsie
Mid-Hudson Bridge
Vassar College
Samuel Morse Historic Site
Webatuck Craft Village
Wingdale
Hudson River
Wappingers Falls
Stormville
Hopewell Junction
Stony Kill Environ. Ed. Center
Pawling
Newburgh-Beacon Bridge
Mt. Gulian
Fishkill
Howland Cultural Center
Beacon
Van Wyck Homestead Museum
9G
9
199
308
82
44
343
22
55
21
376
9D
84

DUTCHESS COUNTY

When Henry Hudson sailed up the river that bears his name, one of his crew described the region known today as Dutchess County as "as pleasant a land as one can tread upon." With an area of 800 square miles, Dutchess boasts more than 30 miles of Hudson River shoreline and thousands of acres of farms and fields. The generous forests, impressive mountains, and abundance of wildlife attracted the Dutch first, but the county was named for the Duchess of York and, later, Queen Mary of England. Powerful families controlled local industries like farming, lumbering, and mining, and built elegant stone and wood manors overlooking the river and mountains. Today much of the county's past is still visible in the grand homes perched over the Hudson, the gracious villages, and the historic restorations that dot the region. The Fisher Center for the Performing Arts at Bard College and Dia:Beacon arts museum draw thousands of visitors to Dutchess County.

GUIDANCE **Dutchess County Tourism Promotion Agency** (845-463-4000; 1-800-445-3131), 3 Neptune Road, Poughkeepsie 12601; www.dutchesstourism.com.

Dutchess County Regional Chamber of Commerce (845-296-0001, 845-454-1700). The south office is located at 2582 South Avenue, Wappingers Falls 12590; the north office is located at One Civic Center Plaza, Suite 400, Poughkeepsie 12601; www.dutchesscountyregionalchamber.org.

Rhinebeck Chamber of Commerce (845-876-4778), 23F East Market Street, Rhinebeck 12572; www.rhinebeckchamber.com.

GETTING THERE *By car:* Dutchess County can be reached via I-84, the Taconic State Parkway, or Route 9.

By bus: **Short Line/Coach USA** (201-529-3666; 1-800-631-8405; www.coachusa.com/shortline), 4 Leisure Lane, Mahway, NJ, has daily service to and from New York City, Long Island, and New Jersey to Dutchess County.

By train: **Amtrak** (1-800-872-7245; www.amtrak.com) has daily service to both Poughkeepsie and Rhinecliff from Penn Station in New York City. **Metro North** (212-532-4900; 1-800-METRO-INFO; www.mta.nyc.ny.us/mnr) offers daily service to Poughkeepsie and Beacon, as well as several other smaller towns in the county. The **Roosevelt Ride** (845-229-5320) is a free shuttle that runs daily, May through

October. The bus meets the 8:45 AM train from Grand Central in Poughkeepsie and returns travelers in time to make the 5:40 PM train back to New York City. The shuttle bus runs throughout the day between the Roosevelt Home, Vanderbilt Mansion, Valkill, and Top Cottage, and visitors may tour all four sites, or only one or two. This is a great way for those who live in the metropolitan area to enjoy several historic sites without having to drive. Reservations are strongly suggested, particularly on weekends.

By air: **Stewart International Airport** (845-564-7200), 1035 First Street, New Windsor. There is connecting service to and from the Hudson Valley throughout the country. **Dutchess County Airport** (845-463-6000), 263 New Hackensack Road, Wappingers Falls. **Sky Acres Airport** (845-677-5010), 30 Airway Drive, LaGrangeville.

MEDICAL EMERGENCY **Northern Dutchess Hospital** (845-876-3001; 1-877-729-2444), 6511 Springbrook Avenue, Rhinebeck.

St. Francis Hospital (845-483-5000), 241 North Road, Poughkeepsie.

Vassar Brothers Medical Center (845-454-8500), 45 Reade Place, Poughkeepsie.

✷ To See

The Beacon Institute for Rivers and Estuaries (845-838-1600; www.bire.org), 199 Main Street, Beacon. If you are in Beacon, make sure to include this stop on your itinerary. An evolving global center for research and education, it is dedicated to rivers, estuaries, and their connection to the world. Those traveling with children will find the activities and exhibits offered here of particular interest. The Center for Environmental Innovation and Education (CEIE) is the primary education facility at the institute, and it is equipped with surround-sound video conferencing and broadcasting capabilities. The building is used for seminars and cultural events, as well as a visitors center for Denning's Point, where there is public access to the Hudson River and a network of walking trails. The building has solar panels, composting toilets, and a "green roof" filled with plants that act as natural insulation. (Make sure to take a walk while you are here on one of the two short scenic trails. The Denning Point State Park trail offers wonderful views of the Hudson River and is an easy loop less than 2 miles in length. The Riverside Trail connects this area to the train station and is less than a mile walk.) In 2007 the institute and IBM (and later, Clarkson University) joined to create REON, the River and Estuary Observatory Network, the first technology-based monitoring and forecasting center for rivers and estuaries. There are other continually changing venues to explore as well. The website contains up-to-date information about the array of exciting exhibits and events taking place here, so it's a good idea to check in advance and discover what will be happening when you visit the city.

Crown Maple Syrup (845-877-0640; www.crownmaple.com), 47 McCourt Road, Dover Plains. Open year-round, Saturday and Sunday 11–5, with tours during maple season. Admission fee. This magnificent maple syrup processing business opened in 2012. It is located on 800 scenic acres filled with sugar and red maple trees in the wilds of Dutchess County. Lydia and Robb Turner, the owners, have a long connection to the area and are both involved in all aspects of creation of their superior product. The public is invited to sample the various maple treats and taste the difference—what makes Crown Maple products so special. February and March bring tours and pancake breakfasts, yet this destination is a busy place year-round. The gift shop is beautiful, with many unique items. This is a great place to introduce older children to food production!

Culinary Institute of America (845-452-9600; www.ciachef.edu), Route 9, Hyde Park. Open year-round, except for vacation periods the last two weeks in July and December. Free. Founded in 1946 as a place where returning veterans could learn useful culinary job skills, the school is today regarded as a premier training institute for those in the food-service and hospitality industries. The grounds of the institute—housed in a former Jesuit seminary—provide visitors with a sweeping view of the Hudson River. Public tours are offered Monday at 10 AM and 4 PM; Tuesday through Friday at 4 PM. Reservations are required (call 845-451-1588), and the cost is $6. The courtyard has a fine display of carved pumpkins for Halloween and ice sculptures in winter, and autumn usually offers a culinary festival that is lots of fun, as visitors can sample the wares and watch the chefs at work. After breakfast or lunch, take the time to walk around the campus, which overlooks the river.

Hyde Park Railroad Station (845-229-2338; www.hydeparkstation.com), 34 River Road, Hyde Park. (Located at the foot of the hill that is formed by West Market Street and River Road, off Route 9.) Open year-round, Monday 5–9 PM; Saturday, Sunday, and holidays noon–5. Free. This railroad station was built in 1914, based on a design shown at the Pan American World Exposition of 1898, although trains passed through the region during the 19th century. The building was nearly demolished in 1975, when the Hudson Valley Railroad Society acquired the station and set about restoring it. Almost 40 years later, the station is on the National Register of Historic Places and houses exhibits that tell the story of the area's railroads and history. Model trains run throughout the building, and there are always ferro fans on board to answer your questions. A nice stop along historic Route 9.

CULINARY INSTITUTE OF AMERICA IN HYDE PARK

Dutchess County Tourism

Old Rhinebeck Aerodrome (845-752-3200; www.oldrhinebeck.org), 9 Norton Road, Red Hook. Open early June through mid-October, daily 10–5:30; weekend air shows Saturday and Sunday at 2 PM. Admission fee. Viewing stands for the air show are outside, so dress appropriately. One of the most unusual history museums around, the aerodrome is the site for air shows, displays, and demonstrations of aeronautic history. But the finely restored airplanes (or copies with original engines) are not earthbound—they are frequently taken for a spin over the Hudson Valley or used in a make-believe dogfight. Fokkers, Sopwiths, and Curtiss airplanes are

Dutchess County Tourism

OLD RHINEBECK AERODROME IN RED HOOK

found in the museum, which offers guided tours. During weekend air shows, daring men and women reenact flights from the pioneer and Lindbergh eras, complete with nefarious villains, beautiful damsels, and brave fighter pilots. Open-cockpit biplane rides in a 1929 craft are available during the week by appointment only. Picnic tables, snack bar, and gift shop.

The Richard B. Fisher Center for the Performing Arts at Bard College (845-758-7900; www.fishercenter.bard.edu), 60 Manor Avenue, Annandale-on-Hudson. (Cross the Kingston-Rhinecliff Bridge, and at the first traffic light make a left onto County Route 103. Drive north for 3.5 miles.) Open year-round; check website for schedule of events. For seven weeks in early July through mid-August every year, Bard Summerscape presents continual performances of opera, music, theater, dance, films, and cabaret, making this an ideal time to visit. Experience music and dance performances in the East Coast's only Frank Gehry–designed performing-arts center, which opened in 2003. This unique and controversial venue, an architectural wonder, is worth a visit for all travelers to Dutchess County, even just to see the exterior. There are two theaters: One has 900 seats (the Sosnoff Theater) and is primarily for professional performances, and the other has 200 seats (Theater Two) and is used by students in Bard's dance and theater programs (see *Entertainment—Theater & Dance*). This performance facility celebrates Bard College's advocacy of the arts. With this remarkable space (the acoustics are phenomenal), Bard will be better equipped to fulfill its commitment to making the arts central to education. Despite the fact that art outside the commercial realm has suffered increasingly in recent years, the aesthetic sphere is vital to freedom and individuality. This building, as a performance space and a work of art in itself, is a statement of the college's mission that the arts are essential to humanity and will endure despite difficult times.

Wing's Castle (845-677-9085; www.wingscastle.com), 717 Bangall Road, off County Route 57, Millbrook. Open Memorial Day weekend through Labor Day, Wednesday through Sunday noon–4:30; after Labor Day through October, weekends only. Admission fee. An intriguing site, the "castle" has been under construction for more than 40 years, and work is still in progress. Salvaged materials have gone into the towers, crenellations, cupolas, and arches—don't be surprised if a Victorian birdbath turns up as a sink or a cauldron as a bathtub. A couple of performance events are held here during the summer, and children especially will enjoy a castle tour and meeting interesting owners Peter Wing and his wife, Toni. This is a must-see for travelers interested in architecture and anomalies!

FOR FAMILIES **Fun Central** (845-297-1010; www.fun-central.com), 1630 Route 9, Wappingers Falls. Open year-round Monday, Tuesday, and Thursday 3:30–9; Friday 3:30–11:30; Saturday 10 AM–midnight; Sunday 10 AM–9 PM. This multiactivity indoor and outdoor recreational facility, with miniature golf, bumper boats, an arcade, virtual-reality roller coaster, and laser tag, is a great place to stop if you are traveling with children. At night, teenagers hang out here in large numbers; it's best to go earlier in the day with younger children.

Kids Kingdom Indoor Play Center (845-471-7529; www.kidskingdompc.com), 36 Firemens Way (off Route 55), Poughkeepsie. Open Monday through Friday 9–6; Wednesday and Friday until 8; Saturday and Sunday 10–6. This is an indoor play center with activities for children between the ages of one and nine. There

THE RICHARD B. FISHER CENTER FOR THE PERFORMING ARTS AT BARD COLLEGE

Dutchess County Tourism

Dutchess County Tourism

WING'S CASTLE IN MILLBROOK

are four padded areas specifically for toddlers, a sandbox, spiral slide, air hockey, and ball pits. This is a great place to let kids indulge on a rainy day!

Mid-Hudson Children's Museum (845-471-0589; www.mhcm.org), 75 North Water Street (at the waterfront, close to the train station), Poughkeepsie. Open Tuesday through Saturday 9:30–5; Sunday 11–5. Open until 8 PM on the third Saturday of the month; free admission 5–8 PM on those days. This hands-on museum features permanent and changing exhibits that focus on the sciences and the arts. Children ages 2–12 will enjoy these educational displays, some of which include a horizontal rock climbing wall, a huge play structure of the heart and lungs, and science on wheels that includes a bicycle gyroscope and giant bubble machine. There is also a StarLab planetarium and Hudson River tides water-play table.

Rainbow's End Butterfly Farm and Nursery (845-832-6749; www.rainbowsendfarm.biz), 13 Rainbow's End, Pawling. Open Memorial Day weekend through Labor Day, weekends 11–4. This wonderful 96-acre farm and breeding center for butterflies welcomes visitors to walk and picnic among the butterflies. Make sure to visit the "flight house," where a variety of monarchs, painted ladies, and black swallowtails reside. Kids may hold Gatorade "lollipops" (Q-tips soaked in the juice) that attract the butterflies to drink right from their hands. The Flutter-Buy Shop has caterpillar kits, jewelry, books, homemade honey, and maple syrup. Patricia and Cornelius du Plessis, a retired couple, own the farm with their three daughters. This educational detour will delight both parents and children.

Splash Down Beach and Adventure Island Family Fun Center (845-896-6606; www.splashdownbeach.com), 16 Old Route 9, Fishkill. Open May through September, daily 10–7, but check website for extended weekend hours, as they vary depending on the season. The multiactivity water park here includes a wave pool, bullet bowl, half pipe, water slides, shipwreck island, and a 700-foot river for

Dutchess County Tourism
SPLASH DOWN BEACH AND ADVENTURE ISLAND FAMILY FUN CENTER IN FISHKILL

the adventurous, as well as Bob the Builder splash works for the youngest visitors. Adventure Island offers indoor and outdoor amusements, including an arcade. This is a great place to go on a sweltering summer day.

Stony Kill Environmental Education Center (845-831-1617; www.stonykill.org), 79 Farmstead Lane (off Route 9D), Wappingers Falls. Grounds are open year-round, daily sunrise to sunset. Part of a 17th-century estate owned by Gulian Verplanck, this nature center was later used as a farm. Today Stony Kill is fulfilling its mission to provide agricultural and natural-history programs to the public. The trails are relatively short (the longest is 2 miles), and there are places to study pond life, deciduous forests, swamps, and fields. The bird observation area is a great place to view migrating and native birds, and special events and family-oriented workshops are held throughout the year. The trails and grounds are open sunrise to sunset for hiking, fishing, birding, and snowshoeing.

Trevor Zoo (845-677-3704; www.trevorzoo.org), 131 Millbrook School Road, Millbrook. Open daily 8:30–5. Admission fee. Started as a teaching zoo in 1936 with the hope that children would better appreciate wildlife if they were familiar with it, the zoo is now a 4-acre site accredited by the American Zoological Association, offering close-up views of more than 80 types of animals, both exotic and indigenous. Red-tailed hawks, coatis, otters, red pandas, wolves, and alpacas are only some of the zoo's residents. There is a self-guided nature walk through the zoo.

HISTORIC HOMES **Franklin Delano Roosevelt Home** (845-229-9115; 1-800-FDR-VISIT; www.nps.gov/hofr), 4097 Albany Post Road (Route 9), Hyde Park. Open year-round, daily 9–5. Admission fee. Your first stop, the visitors center, offers an orientation film as well as a café (open April through October, daily 10–4), with refreshments of all kinds. Here you can purchase tickets to tour the home, and they include admission to the library and museum. If you would like to tour Val-Kill, the Vanderbilt Mansion, and Top Cottage, tickets to tour these sites are available for sale here as well.

The Victorian house, embellished with Georgian touches, was the boyhood home of Franklin Delano Roosevelt. Here Eleanor and Franklin raised their family, entertained heads of state, and shaped world history. The site includes the house, the first presidential library, rose garden, and the site of the Roosevelts' graves. In the house itself, once jokingly called the Summer White House by Roosevelt, family memorabilia, including photos, antiques, and the possessions of Franklin's iron-willed mother, Sara, are displayed. Don't forget to stop at the gravesite and rose garden (exquisite in June). A visit to the FDR Home is a must for any visitor to Dutchess County.

Dutchess County Tourism

FRANKLIN DELANO ROOSEVELT HOME IN HYDE PARK

Locust Grove, the Samuel Morse Historic Site (845-454-4500; www.morse historicsite.org), 2683 South Road (Route 9), Poughkeepsie. Open April through December, daily 10–5; January through March, Monday through Friday 10–5. Grounds are open 8 AM until dusk, weather permitting. Situated along an old stagecoach route, this 150-acre site known as Locust Grove was the summer home of Samuel Morse. An artist and scientist who changed the way the world communicates (he invented the telegraph and Morse code), he purchased the country residence in 1847 and under the tutelage of architect Alexander Jackson Davis began to transform the house into an Italianate villa with extensive gardens. The house boasts a four-story tower, a skylighted billiard room, and a false stone exterior. Throughout the house decorative items (including china and a then-elegant and new fabric known as denim), furniture, art, and paintings by John James Audubon can be enjoyed. The formal gardens, walking trails, and wildlife sanctuary offer a lovely setting in which to spend an afternoon. The site includes a network of trails that cover 3 miles through a diverse habitat teeming with wildlife as well as a variety of trees (and wildflowers in season). If you have the time, take a walk on one of the many trails formerly used by wagons and horse-drawn carriages that have been restored. The visitors center, where tours begin with a 10-minute orientation film, distributes a map/trail guide, and the paths are marked with arrowed plaques corresponding to the brochure descriptions. Most are an easy walk. The visitors center also contains the Morse Gallery, with paintings and sculptures by Samuel Morse, as well as his patent model for the telegraph and a display on telegraphic communication.

Madam Brett Homestead (845-831-6533), 50 Van Nydeck Avenue, Beacon. Open April through December, second Saturday of the month 1–4; group tours by appointment only. Admission fee. When Catheryna and Roger Brett moved to the area now known as Beacon in 1708, they built a homestead of native stone, graced with scalloped cedar shingles and sloping dormers. The house is one of the oldest in Dutchess County and was the center of a 28,000-acre estate. During the Revolutionary War, the homestead was believed to have been a storage place for military supplies as well as a stopping point for such luminaries as Washington, Lafayette, and the Baron von Steuben. The house remained in the family until 1954, when it was purchased by the Daughters of the American Revolution. Today there are 17 rooms of furnishings, porcelain, paintings, books, and tools. The house offers visitors a look back to the time when there were lodgings for slaves, and what is now the front door was the rear: As the town grew around the house, the main street formed at the back of the building, so the doors were switched for the convenience of callers. There was even a well accessible from inside the house—a major convenience in the 18th century. During the summer months, stroll through the herb and formal gardens, which are quite beautiful.

Mills Mansion, Staatsburgh State Historic Site (845-889-8851; www.nysparks.com), 75 Mills Mansion Road, Staatsburg. Open April through October, Tuesday through Saturday 10–5; Sunday 11–5. November and January through March, Saturday and Sunday 11–4; December, Thursday through Sunday 11–4 for holiday tours, but call to confirm hours. Admission fee. One of the grand old Hudson River estates, the Mills Mansion has its origins in the 18th century, when Morgan and Gertrude Lewis built a home on the site. The house was destroyed by fire in 1832 and was rebuilt by Ruth Livingston Mills in 1896. Rooms were gilded and plastered, with ornamental balustrades, ceilings, and pilasters. The size of the rooms is still overwhelming, as are the furnishings: dining tables that take 20 leaves; carved, gilded, and floral furniture in the style of Louis XIV, XV, and XVI;

LOCUST GROVE IN POUGHKEEPSIE

Dutchess County Tourism

Dutchess County Tourism

MILLS MANSION, STAATSBURGH STATE HISTORIC SITE

and many fine paintings and elaborate tapestries. Incredibly, the house was used primarily as an autumn retreat and then infrequently the remainder of the year. There is a wonderful museum store on-site, and popular annual events include free outdoor summer concerts, an herb festival, a Celtic festival, an antique car show, and a Gilded Age Christmas. This is one historic site where access to the Hudson River is only a short walk away. It's an easy stroll, so if the weather is good, make sure to follow the path down to the water after the house tour. There are several miles of walking trails on the land surrounding this site (see *To Do—Hiking*).

Montgomery Place (845-758-5461; www.hudsonvalley.org), County Route 103 (River Road, off Route 199), Annandale-on-Hudson. Open May through October, Thursday through Sunday 11–4. Visitors may take a self-guided tour of the grounds, but the house may only be seen by tour. Admission fee. A magnificent, Classical Revival–style mansion, Montgomery Place was once the home of Janet Livingston Montgomery, wife of the Revolutionary War general Richard Montgomery. Begun in 1802 and completed three years later, the mansion is the centerpiece of an estate that includes waterfalls (don't miss the stream tumbling down to the Hudson River), footbridges, gardens, and Catskill Mountains views. The building was remodeled in the 1840s and 1860s by the great architect Alexander Jackson Davis and was home to the Livingston family until 1985. Purchased and restored by Historic Hudson Valley, the mansion reflects the family's history rather than one specific era. Gilbert Stuart portraits, Persian tile chairs, Czechoslovakian chandeliers, family china, and rare books are only some of the treasures to be seen on a house tour. Walking the grounds (all 434 acres), visitors can enjoy watching ships on the Hudson and seeing the variety of trees on the property. The 200-plus-year-old arboretum has some wonderful specimen trees.

Mount Gulian Historic Site (845-831-8172; www.mountgulian.org), 145 Sterling Street, Beacon. (Take Route 9D north of I-84 for 0.3 mile, turn left into the Hudson View Park apartments, and then make a left onto Lamplight Street, which becomes Sterling Street, and go to the end of the road.) Open May through October, Wednesday through Friday and Sunday 1–5. Admission fee. This 44-acre Dutch homestead was the family seat of the Verplancks, prominent Hudson Valley farmers, and offers a place to learn about domestic and agricultural life in the 18th and 19th centuries as it unfolded along the river. Visitors will see a unique Dutch barn that dates from the 1740s. Mount Gulian was constructed between 1730 and 1740; during the American Revolution it was the headquarters of General von Steuben, who is credited with molding the colonial troops into a fighting force. The house was also where the Society of the Cincinnati was formed in 1783, a fraternal organization for officers that is still in existence. A visit to Mount Gulian includes a tour of the house and the English formal gardens, which have been restored to their former glory; the gardens' history was recorded by James Brown, an escaped slave who worked in them from 1829 to 1868. Special events are held throughout the season; check website for a schedule.

Top Cottage (845-229-9115), 7097 Albany Post Road (Route 9), Hyde Park. Open May through October, daily 10–5. Admission fee. (Note that shuttle bus tours leave from the visitors center at the FDR Home and Library, where tickets must be purchased to go to this site.) This hilltop retreat that FDR designed for himself provided a tranquil place for him to get away after he left office. During his third and fourth terms, the cottage was used as a private meetinghouse for political purposes: forging essential relationships with Winston Churchill and King George VI of Great Britain, among others. It is interesting to see how the cottage was designed to accommodate a wheelchair and meet Roosevelt's physical needs. First opened to the public in 2001, the cottage has been restored to its original appearance during Roosevelt's time. There are displays of memorabilia and photographs throughout the site.

Val-Kill, Eleanor Roosevelt National Historic Site (845-229-9115; www.ervk.org), Route 9G, Hyde Park. Open May through October, daily 9–5; November through April, Thursday through Monday 9–5. Admission fee. This is the only National Historic Site dedicated to the memory of a first lady. Val-Kill was a favorite spot for Roosevelt family picnics; in 1924 FDR deeded the land to Eleanor for a personal retreat. A Dutch-style stone cottage was built (it is now a conference center), and an existing building was converted into a factory, in keeping with Eleanor's efforts to encourage rural economic development. The factory was later remodeled into a house, which now holds the museum. The small furniture factory was adjacent to the cottage shared with Eleanor Roosevelt's friends, Nancy Cook and Marion Dickerman. The three women met in the early 1920s working for the League of Women Voters. They shared a dedication to politics, education, and progressive reform that motivated their interest in creating Val-Kill Industries, a social experiment that embraced the revival of handicraft traditions to supplement income in an agricultural economy. In this way, young people might choose to remain in the area instead of seeking work in the cities. The economic strains of the Depression put an end to the business in 1937. Visitors can learn more about this experiment, tour the cottage, and enjoy a film biography about Eleanor Roosevelt, *First Lady of the World,* as well as walk the trails on the 180-

Dutchess County Tourism

VAL-KILL, ELEANOR ROOSEVELT NATIONAL HISTORIC SITE IN HYDE PARK

acre site. Ongoing lectures, seminars, and community programs center around Eleanor Roosevelt's concerns, including solutions to pressing social problems, and an exploration of contemporary values. Call for a schedule of events and changing exhibits.

Vanderbilt Mansion National Historic Site (845-229-9115; www.nps.gov/vama), Route 9, Hyde Park. Open year-round, daily 9–5. House is open by tour only, although the grounds, gardens, and excellent gift shop are open free of charge. (I suggest stopping here even if you don't have time to spare for the house tour. The views of the Hudson River are spectacular!) Admission fee. This imposing Beaux Arts mansion was used by Frederick Vanderbilt and family as a spring and fall residence. A fine example of Gilded Age living in the 19th century, the mansion was the focus of a large Hudson River estate and was built at a cost of $600,000—a fortune at that time. Lavish furnishings, fine art, and decorative items from around the world are on view throughout the spacious rooms (the living room is 30 feet by 50 feet); visitors can also stroll pathways and take in the breathtaking river panorama. The restored formal Italian gardens feature a reflecting pool, terraces, and a pergola and loggia

VANDERBILT MANSION NATIONAL HISTORIC SITE

Dutchess County Tourism

with three levels of annuals, perennials, and roses; they should not be missed on a visit to the mansion. The wonderful gift shop on the premises is filled with a terrific selection of books and souvenirs. The **Music in the Parks** program (see *Special Events*) is held on the mansion grounds Wednesday nights at 6:30 during July and August. The concerts are free and open to the public. In the event of rain, the concerts are held at Haviland Middle School Auditorium, Route 9G, in Hyde Park.

Wilderstein (845-876-4818; www.wilderstein.org), 330 Morton Road, Rhinebeck. Open May through October, Thursday through Sunday noon–4; December, weekends only 1–4. Admission fee. The history of this country seat begins in 1852, when Thomas Suckley purchased this riverfront site and commissioned an architect to build an Italianate villa. He named the property Wilderstein (wild man's stone) in reference to a Native American petroglyph by a cove on the property. For more than 150 years and three generations, Wilderstein was owned by the Suckley family. It is filled with their furniture, paintings, antiques, and other effects, which attest to the lively social history of the estate and the family's relationship to the Hudson Valley. The main-floor rooms were designed by J. B. Tiffany, and Calvert Vaux was responsible for the landscape design. An intricate network of drives, walks, and trails winds throughout the property, so make sure to explore a few of them when you visit. This site is listed on the National Register of Historic Places; it's a gem, and it will intrigue both scholars and those interested in life in the region during the 19th century.

VANDERBILT MANSION NATIONAL HISTORIC SITE IN HYDE PARK

Dutchess County Tourism

Dutchess County Tourism

WILDERSTEIN IN RHINEBECK

MUSEUMS The Center for Curatorial Studies and Hessel Art Museum of Bard College (845-758-7598; www.bard.edu/ccs), 33 Garden Road (off Route 9G), Annandale-on-Hudson. Open year-round, Wednesday through Sunday 1–5. Free. Founded in 1860 as a men's school, today Bard College is a coeducational institution known for its emphasis on the creative arts. In 1992 this 9,500-square-foot exhibition space opened at Bard to house the college's permanent collection, the core of which is the Marieluise Hessel Collection, with 1,000 works of painting, sculpture, photography, and video from the 1960s to the present. Hessel founded the center with a generous gift to the college, and the building contains a museum and research library as well as the college's master's program in curatorial studies. Hessel's goal, to support the creation of a place for study of late-20th-century arts, was realized, and the museum's changing exhibits encourage experimental approaches to the contemporary visual arts. Student shows are presented in the winter and spring; museum shows take place in the summer and fall. After visiting the museum, take a stroll to two lovely centerpieces of the campus: the Hudson River estate houses Blithewood and Ward Manor. There are gardens and a Victorian gatehouse nearby, as well as the Fisher Center for the Performing Arts (see *To See*), which make Bard College a nice stop any time of year.

Dia:Beacon (845-440-0100; www.diaart.org), 3 Beekman Street, Beacon. Open year-round: mid-April through Columbus Day, Thursday through Monday 11–6; the rest of the year, Friday through Monday 11–4. The museum is located off I-84 and Route 9D. Follow signs to the railroad station. Admission fee (members and children under 12 free). In 2003 this 240,000-square-foot museum, on a 31-acre site along the banks of the Hudson River (adjacent to 90 acres of riverfront parkland and the Beacon railroad station), opened its doors to the public. Housed in a restored printing facility built in 1929 by Nabisco, the expansive light-filled galleries are illuminated almost entirely by natural light, displaying the large-scale works in Dia's renowned collection of American art of the 1960s and 1970s. Since 1974 Dia Art Foundation has become internationally recognized as one of the world's most influential contemporary-art institutions. The name "Dia," taken from the Greek word meaning "through," was chosen to suggest the foundation's role in enabling extraordinary artistic projects that might not be realized without financial assistance. Dia's permanent works include art by Joseph Beuys, Dan Flavin, Donald Judd, Agnes Martin, Richard Serra, and Andy Warhol. The art of this period often represented a radical departure in practice from conventional work, and much of it was large-scale. In addition to holding one of the world's foremost collections of work by artists who came of age in the 1960s and 1970s, Dia maintains long-term site-specific projects in the American West, Manhattan, and elsewhere. Modern-art aficionados will particularly enjoy this museum; most people will enjoy the structure itself, which is as interesting as the art within its walls.

Franklin D. Roosevelt Presidential Library & Museum (1-800-FDR-VISIT; www.fdrlibrary.marist.edu), 4079 Albany Post Road (Route 9), Hyde Park. Open April through October, daily 9–6; November through March, daily 9–5; research library year-round, Monday through Friday 9–5. Admission fee. The museum has both permanent and changing exhibits that reflect the impact both Eleanor and Franklin Roosevelt had on their times and world events during the first half of the 20th century. Visitors will enjoy detailed displays on the lives and careers of the Roosevelts, as well as an array of interactive exhibits. Walking through this museum is like taking a historic tour of the first 50 years of the 20th century; the site is a must-visit for World War II buffs (see FDR Home under *Historic Homes*). Also on the site are FDR's boyhood home and the gravesites of both Eleanor and Franklin. The museum shop at the Henry A. Wallace Visitors Center (named for FDR's first vice-president) should be your first and last stop.

Van Wyck Homestead Museum (845-896-9560), 504 Route 9 (at the junction of Route 9 and I-84), Fishkill. Open June through October, Saturday and Sunday 1–4, and by appointment. Admission fee. Guides in period costume escort visitors through the Dutch Colonial house, built in 1732 by Cornelius Van Wyck and untouched by any changes after a 1757 addition. During the Revolution, the house served as a depot and courtroom, and it is also believed to have been the inspiration for the setting of James Fenimore Cooper's *The Spy*. The homestead is furnished with 18th-century pieces, and visitors can examine artifacts recovered from surrounding archaeological sites, see several Hudson Valley portraits, and enjoy changing exhibits and events.

Vassar College Francis Lehman Loeb Art Center (845-437-5632; www.fllac.vassar.edu), 124 Raymond Avenue, off Route 44/55, Poughkeepsie. Open Tuesday through Saturday 10–5; Sunday 1–5. Free. When Matthew Vassar founded the college in 1861, he not only broke new ground by making it a women's college, but he also made it the first college to have an art gallery and museum. The gallery's permanent collection consists of more than 16,500 pieces, including Hudson River School landscapes, Whistler prints, a large photography collection, European coins, armor, and sculpture; it spans the history of art from ancient Egypt to contemporary America. Shows and exhibits change on a regular basis, and after enjoying the art, visitors can walk around the campus, with its lakes, gardens, amphitheater, and rare trees. Docent-led tours by appointment only—call 845-437-7745. Stop in at the chapel to see the Tiffany windows. Also on the campus is the **A. Scott Warthin Museum of Geology and Natural History** (845-437-5540; Ely Hall, open Monday through Friday 9–5, when the college is in session; at other times by appointment), which houses a large collection of mineral, gem, and fossil exhibits.

After visiting Vassar, a drive through the city of **Poughkeepsie,** with its several historic districts, is worthwhile. **Clinton House** (845-471-1630), 549 Main Street, is the headquarters of the Dutchess County Historical Society (www.dutchess historicalsociety.org), where visitors can see exhibits of local history. They are open by appointment only. They also maintain the **Glebe House** (845-471-1630), 635 Main Street, which dates from 1767 and has been restored to represent a typical home of the late 18th and early 19th centuries (open by appointment only). At 185 Academy Street you will discover **Springside National Historic Site** (845-454-2060; www.springsidelandmark.org), which offers tours by appointment only. Even if you don't take the tour, however, walk the 20 acres of carriage roads on this site, the work of America's first native-born landscape architect, Andrew Jackson Downing, and the last surviving example of his work. Go south off Montgomery Street to reach Garfield Place, one of the most beautiful streets in the city. It was a residential area in the 1850s, and the huge homes have been kept up ever since. The houses, which span several periods, boast turrets, towers, cupolas, and characteristic Hudson River decorative bracketing. Academy Street from Montgomery to Holmes Street is still a gracious residential area with ornate Victorian houses, as is the Union Street Historic District (cross Market Street and continue down Union to Grand Street). In the 1760s Union was a path to the river, and later it was the German-Irish area of town. Notice the cast-iron details on the brick-and-clapboard buildings. This area is now the Little Italy of Poughkeepsie. Lower Mansion Avenue, off North Bridge Street, has fine examples of 19th-century architecture, although there are many modern buildings, as well.

SCENIC DRIVES In Dutchess County almost any drive is a scenic one. Even the Taconic Parkway, which is now more than 50 years old, offers more of a country drive than a trip on a major highway, and there are commanding views of distant mountains and lovely vistas along its length. The roads of this region are well marked, both with direction and historic-site signs, and the county publishes a series of detailed, self-guided driving tours that are keyed to roadside markers. (Call Dutchess County Tourism to request the brochure: 845-463-4000; 1-800-445-3131.)

Don't be afraid to follow the back roads of the county on your own with the assistance of a good map. The following are just a few suggestions of roads that will take you through farmland and villages and along the river. Route 9 is the old stagecoach road that once was the main route to Manhattan; there are many restorations and historic sites along this road, but these days it can be clogged with traffic, particularly during rush hour and on Saturday. Route 9G takes you past old homes and gracious stone walls. Route 44/55 catches up with the Taconic, which is, despite being a parkway, a lovely road to travel. Route 199 runs from east to west toward Connecticut, and the views are more like New England than New York.

WALKING TOURS Beacon. Nestled between the majestic Hudson Highlands and the Hudson River, the city of Beacon is being reborn. Beacon is in the midst of a renaissance, which includes the opening of Dia:Beacon museum, the renovation of the Riverfront Park and Beacon Landing, and an explosion of shops, galleries, and restaurants springing up on Main Street. At one time the city was accessible by rail, steamboat, ferry, and trolley, and Beacon became a hot spot for people from the city looking for a change of scenery. In 1900 a group of local businesspeople formed the Incline Railway Association to erect a cable railway to the top of Mount Beacon. The railway—a monument to the ingenuity of the engineers of the day—was built on a steep grade of 65 percent and transported passengers to the summit at 1,150 feet. Opened in 1902, the railway carried 60,000 passengers during its first season. At the top was the Beacon Crest Hotel and a casino that offered breathtaking views; both were destroyed by fire in 1932 and were never rebuilt. Mount Beacon was the most popular day-trip destination in the Hudson Valley at the turn of the 20th century, and more than 3 million people rode the rail in its 75 years of operation. Today, Mount Beacon park is again welcoming visitors. During the post–World War II years, the economy of the city went into decline, but in the early 1990s restoration efforts began. Artists have now settled in the city, and with the arrival of Dia:Beacon, the community has new energy and life as a creative center.

Walk up and down Main Street, anchored by historic districts featuring numerous architectural treasures that are home to antiques shops, boutiques, and tony eateries. Try to visit on a **Second Saturday** of the month, when there are art openings, readings, and musical performances throughout the city. **Riverfront Park** offers picnic areas and fishing access; the **Beacon Landing** is the 23-acre waterfront property managed by Scenic Hudson that is being revitalized. A former city library, designed by Richard Morris Hunt, the **Howland Cultural Center** (845-831-4988; www.howlandculturalcenter.org), 477 Main Street, features a decorative exterior, brickwork, and a grand interior crowned by ornate wood vaulting. It is open Thursday through Sunday 1–5 or by appointment. **Hudson Beach Glass** (845-440-0068), 162 Main Street, is a three-story firehouse that has been converted into a gallery complete with its own glassblowing studio. They are open daily 11–6.

After walking around town on a hot summer day, it is imperative to make your last stop **Zora Dora's Paleteria** (a Mexican term for a place to buy gourmet ice pops), at 201 Main Street. Here you will find amazingly imaginative popsicle creations. The ice cream is made with organic milk from a Dutchess County farm, and the fruits used are from local orchards and berry patches. There are usually at least 35 flavors of "paletas" from which to choose, and all are refreshing—and delicious. If you crave something with sugar and aren't in the mood for a cold treat, visit the **Alps Sweet Shop,** 269 Main Street, where they have been making chocolate candy since 1922. Kahlúa truffles, chocolate-covered Oreos, and butter crunch are just a few of the handcrafted confections offered here to satisfy a sweet tooth.

Millerton. An idyllic Victorian village with sophisticated shops in a beautiful rural setting, this hamlet is best explored on foot. **Oblong Books** (518-789-3797), 26 Main Street, an oasis in the heart of town since 1975 and renowned for its eclectic selection of books and music, is a great place to start your walking tour. There are several antiques shops, a glassworks, and an array of interesting places to explore.

Millerton is one of my favorite places in the region, and I strongly suggest travelers visit the village and wander along Main Street, as well as bike or walk along the rail trail, with an access point in the middle of town. Some of my favorite shops are **Terni's** (518-789-3474) and **Little Gates Company Wine Merchants** (518-789-3899). After shopping, stop in at **Irving Farm Coffee House** (518-789-6540) or **Harney & Sons Fine Teas & Tea Room** (518-789-2100) for whichever drink you prefer. Both serve high-quality products. Millerton also has one of the most interesting department stores in the Hudson Valley, **Saperstein's Department Store** (518-789-3365), where you will find a huge selection of casual clothing for the entire family at exceedingly reasonable prices. Don't pass by without going in. The store is reminiscent of a bygone era, perhaps because it has been in the same family for three generations.

Red Hook. The town was possibly named when Henry Hudson anchored off its shore in October 1609, and the crew noted the brilliant red sumac and Virginia creeper that covered the hooklike peninsula of Cruger's Island. Another theory is that the name became attached to the town from the red-painted barns at Tivoli, then called Hoffmans' Mills, once part of Rhinebeck. The early population of the area was concentrated in Red Hook, once known as Hardscrabble, and Tivoli. The location contributed to the growth of water-powered mills, wool processing factories, fishing, and river transport in the 18th century. The 19th century was when dairy and fruit farms sprang up, tool and tin making burgeoned, and tobacco processing thrived. The railroad was built in the 1850s, and freight (and tourists) traveled largely by train until the early 20th century. The population has more than doubled from 4,500 in 1955 to about 10,000 at the start of the 21st century, when an influx of people was drawn by the technology and electronics industries. Make sure to visit **Mansion Row;** the old Fraleigh Store (now the **Lyceum Theater**), built in 1875; and the **Tobacco Factory,** at the corner of Tobacco Lane and Broadway (the main street). At the intersection of Cherry Street and North Broadway is the **Elmendorph Inn** (circa 1760), listed on the National Register of Historic Places, a Federal-style structure with a Dutch gambrel roof. One of the two earliest buildings in the village, it was a former stagecoach stop and tavern as well as the site of the town's first kindergarten. Saved from the wrecking ball through a community effort, the inn has a working kitchen fireplace and a reconstructed beehive oven. (Open by appointment only for tours; call 845-758-5887.)

Rhinebeck. This village is rich in architectural delights, and a walk through town can make the history of families like the Roosevelts, Livingstons, and Beekmans come alive. The Beekman Arms, in the center of town, is one of the oldest inns in the United States (see *Lodging*); across the street, the corner department store is housed in a Civil War–era building. The post office was reconstructed in 1938 under the direction of Franklin Delano Roosevelt; it is a replica of a 1700 Dutch house and contains murals by local artists. If you amble down Route 9 and along the side streets, you will discover Gothic Revival homes, Georgian-style churches, and houses with mansard roofs, arched windows, and Second Empire touches. Make sure not to miss Montgomery Row on your walk. There are over 20 stores, restaurants, and interesting places in this section of Rhinebeck's historic downtown. On East Market Street in back of **No Sugar** (where you will find beautiful women's clothing), there are also a number of small shops and eateries and a terrace area, a great place to enjoy a drink at one of the cafés.

If you are interested in discovering more about Rhinebeck's past, make sure to stop at **The Museum of Rhinebeck History** (845-871-1798), located in the Quitman House, 7015 Route 9. They are open to the public June through October, Saturday and Sunday 2–4. The collection of gifts to this museum includes letters, books, military gear, journals, clothing, furniture, photographs, toys, and other artifacts that tell the story of daily life in the community through the centuries. Annual exhibits focus on different aspects of life in town and have included the violet industry and the antebellum years.

Tivoli. This lovely, tranquil town is filled with historic buildings. The **Watts De Peyster Hall** (fireman's hall) in the center of town was built in 1898 and given to the village by a local landowner, John de Peyster, who was a fireman in New York City while he attended Columbia College in the 1840s. At one time the hall contained a courtroom and community meeting rooms; today it houses the Tivoli Free Library and provides administrative offices for the village government. De Peyster's house, the original carriage house and entrance to the Rose Hill estate built in 1860, named for the family's ancestral home in Scotland, is now a private residence and may be seen from Woods Road. The town got its name from a Frenchman, Peter de Labigarre, who bought land on the waterfront in the 1790s. He wanted to design the town with a central square in the European style, but the project went bankrupt, and he had to abandon the plan. A plaque on the brick wall at the end of Friendship Street marks the location of his home, named Le Chateau de Tivoli; he had envisioned an ideal community named after Tivoli in Italy.

WINERIES AND DISTILLERIES **Cascade Mountain Winery & Restaurant** (845-373-9021), 835 Cascade Mountain Road (off Route 82A—watch for signs), Amenia. Open Saturday and Sunday 11–5, or by appointment. This respected winery, which offers tours and tastings, has won accolades from both oenophiles and connoisseurs of fine food. There is a wonderful restaurant on the premises that serves lunch May through October.

Clinton Vineyards & Winery (845-266-5372), 450 Schultzville Road, Clinton Corners. Open for tours and tastings April through December, Thursday through Monday noon–6, or by appointment. There are limited hours during the winter months, so call ahead. This small, picturesque, family-run winery specializes in award-winning seyval blanc, champagne, and dessert wines.

Hillrock Estate Distillery (518-329-1023), 408 Pooles Hill Road, Ancram. Open year-round on Saturday for tours and tastings by appointment only. Solera aged bourbon, crafted using grains grown on the property, and single malt whiskey are featured at this establishment, which opened to the public in 2012. Owner Jeffrey Baker and master distiller David Pickerell, who spent 14 years at Maker's Mark, have partnered to bring Dutchess County its first distillery.

Millbrook Vineyards & Winery (845-677-8383; 1-800-662-WINE; www.millbrookwine.com), 26 Wing Road, Millbrook. Open for tours and tastings September through May, daily noon–5; June through August, daily 11–6. They have the largest 100 percent vinifera vineyard in the Hudson Valley region. Production follows French techniques. They offer chardonnay, pinot noir, and cabernet wines. There are summer concerts, special events, and art exhibits here, so check the website to see what's happening if you are planning to visit the winery. There is also a delightful café serving lunch overlooking the vineyards during the summer months. The second Saturday in November, the winery hosts a **"Sip & Sign for the Holidays"** (see *Special Events*) event featuring 15–20 local authors autographing their books for visitors. The event is free and open to all.

Oak Summit Vineyard (845-677-9522), 372 Oak Summit Road, Millbrook. Open for tours and tastings March through December by appointment only. (Note that the fee for the tour is $35 per person.) John and Nancy Bruno will be glad to take visitors through their beautiful boutique winery producing only pinot noir from grapes grown on their 6-acre vineyard. This is a small operation: Approximately 150 cases (1,750 bottles) are produced annually.

✷ To Do

BALLOONING The primary season for a hot-air balloon trip is April through October, but flights are available year-round, weather conditions permitting. **Blue Sky Balloons** (845-831-6917), 99 Teller Avenue, Beacon, organizes balloon festivals as well as flights and lessons. Flights are always within two hours after sunrise or two hours before sunset. This company uses only FAA-certified pilots and balloons, and has more than 30 years of experience.

BICYCLING **The Harlem Valley Rail Trail** (518-789-9591; www.hvrt.org). Two paved sections of this 20-mile rail trail are open, and the Dutchess County section, about 8 miles, runs from Amenia to Millerton. There is access to the bike trail in both towns: in Millerton, Railroad Plaza, across from the gazebo; in Amenia, at the Mechanic Street parking lot.

Hyde Park Trail (845-229-8086), Route 9, Hyde Park. Open daily dawn to dusk. Part of the Hudson River Greenway, this 13-mile trail runs from Mills Mansion to Norrie Point, and between the Vanderbilt Mansion, the FDR Home, and Val-Kill (Eleanor Roosevelt's home). Bicycling is permitted on the 1.5 miles between the FDR Home and Val-Kill only.

Mid-Dutchess Trailway (845-486-2925). This 12-mile bike path runs from Hopewell Junction north to the city of Poughkeepsie.

Mills-Norrie State Park (845-889-4646), off Route 9, Staatsburg. Open daily dawn to dusk. This 1,000-acre state park offers several bicycle paths, which are easily accessed from the entrance to the park off Route 9.

Wilbur Boulevard Trailway (845-451-4100), Poughkeepsie. This trailway runs along Wilbur Boulevard in the city and town of Poughkeepsie. The paved length is 1.2 miles.

The following state highway corridors in Dutchess County have been designated as part of a regional system of state bike routes: **Route 9D, Route 52, Route 82, Route 199,** and **Route 308.** While this system of state bike routes is intended to provide safe bicycling facilities, it is imperative to be extra cautious when bicycling on these roads. For further information on the best bicycling in the county, contact the **Mid-Hudson Bicycle Club** (www.midhudsonbicycle.org) in Poughkeepsie. They have a wealth of information about both road and mountain biking; they also sponsor social events and an annual group ride. The **Dutchess and Beyond Bicycle Club** (845-454-1190; www.fredinhv.com), 170 Creek Road, Pleasant Valley, also offers weekend bicycle rides.

For those interested in renting mountain bikes and road bikes, there are a few places to contact: **Beacon Cycles** (845-765-0366), 176 Main Street, Beacon; **Bikeway** (845-463-7433), 1581 Route 376, Wappingers Falls; and **Wheel and Heel** (845-632-3050), 2658 East Main Street, Wappingers Falls. The **Rhinebeck Bicycle Shop** (845-876-4025), 10 Garden Street, Rhinebeck, rents mountain bikes with wide tires that are good for touring the village.

BOAT CRUISES If you want to spend an afternoon on the Hudson River relaxing on a tour boat, passing elegant old estates, and being dazzled by autumn's painted trees, your best bet is to head across the river to Newburgh or Kingston (see *Boat Cruises* in "Orange County" and "Ulster County"). However, there are a few options to explore in Dutchess County.

Empire Cruise Lines (315-934-4157; www.empirecruiselines.com), 29 North Water Street, Poughkeepsie. They run several sightseeing, lunch, and dinner cruises from May through October. The 60-foot double-decked boat *Mystere* leaves from Poughkeepsie, and the variety of outings may be found by checking their website. The boat is a relative newcomer to the Hudson River boating scene, having started in business in Dutchess County in 2011. Dinner cruises run approximately two and a half hours; Sunday brunch and lunch cruises are about two hours.

Hudson River Sloop *Clearwater* (845-265-8080; www.clearwater.org), 724 Wolcott Avenue, Beacon. Call Monday through Friday 9–5 to find out dates, times, and locations of the sloop, as well as public sail schedule.

***River Rose* Tours and Cruises** (845-562-1067; www.riverrosecruises.com), Poughkeepsie and Newburgh docks. The *River Rose* is a Mississippi-style paddle wheeler offering sightseeing cruises, dinner cruises, Sunday brunch excursions, and charters. There's an open upper deck and a fully enclosed, climate-controlled main deck. Call for a schedule. Departures are from Newburgh, across the Hudson River from Beacon.

Shadows Marina Water Taxi (845-986-9500; www.shadowsmarina.com), 176 Rinaldi Boulevard, Poughkeepsie. Open Memorial Day weekend through mid-October, Friday through Sunday, every hour from 3 PM–midnight. Since the water taxi is open, the schedule may vary due to weather conditions. A Coast Guard–licensed crew operates the water taxi, taking travelers on a 20-minute trip to the Newburgh Waterfront. The round-trip fare is approximately $25 per person.

FARMERS' MARKETS, FARM STANDS, AND PICK-YOUR-OWN FARMS June's ripe strawberries, summer blueberries, and jewel-like raspberries are three of the most popular crops in Dutchess County. But the harvest doesn't end with the berries: There are apples, asparagus, and big-bellied pumpkins for picking later in the season. Farm stands sprout like corn along the back roads; many are small, homey places where fresh cider and doughnuts lure you inside. Pick-your-own farms often have roadside signs indicating which crop is ready for harvest. For your own comfort, bring along a hat, sunscreen, and a container for the pickings, although you can buy a bucket or boxes at the farms. Harvest times vary with the weather and the temperature, so call before you go. Farmers' markets are usually held on weekends; call the county Cooperative Extension Service, Monday through Friday 8:30–4:30, for information (845-677-8223; 2715 Route 44, Farm & Home Center, Millbrook).

Public Farmers' Markets

Arlington (845-559-0023), Vassar College Campus, Raymond and Collegeview avenues, Poughkeepsie. Open June through October, Thursday 3–7.

Beacon (845-838-4338), Beacon Train Station, 1 Ferry Plaza, Beacon. Open May through mid-November, Sunday 10–4. A winter market is held December through April, indoors in the same location, Monday 10–4.

Fishkill (845-897-4430), Main Street Plaza (Route 52). Open July through October, Thursday 9–3.

Hyde Park (845-229-9111), Hyde Park Drive-In, Route 9. Open June through October, Saturday 9–2.

Millbrook (845-677-4304), Front Street, Millbrook. Open May through October, Saturday 9–1.

Poughkeepsie Farmers Market (845-473-1415), Pulaski Park, Washington Street. Open June through October, Friday 2–6. It's run by the Poughkeepsie Farm Project, and all the produce is organic. The park is just across the street from the entrance to the Walkway Over the Hudson.

Rhinebeck (845-876-7756), 23 Market Street, Rhinebeck. Open May through mid-November, Sunday 10–2.

Organic Produce

Community Supported Agriculture (CSA) projects bring fresh—and often organic—produce directly to consumers. Shareholders pay in advance for a portion of the farm's seasonal production to cover the farmer's costs. In return they get a

FARM STANDS BECKON WITH CIDER AND DOUGHNUTS.

Dutchess County Tourism

weekly portion of the farm's produce. The following are a few such farms: **Poughkeepsie Farm Project** (845-473-1415), and **Sisters Hill Farm** (845-868-7048) in Stanfordville. **Sprout Creek Farm** (845-485-9885), 34 Lauer Road, Poughkeepsie, has a creamery and market, as well as a variety of programs open to the public, including a summer camp. The Poughkeepsie Farm Project is occasionally open to the public for tours. If such an outing is of interest, do call them to make arrangements for a visit.

A couple of places where travelers can pick up organic produce are **McEnroe Organic Farm Market** (518-789-4191), Routes 22/44 in Millerton, which is open daily year-round, and **Green Horizons Organic Farm** (845-855-5555), South Dingle Road in Pawling, which is open April through September for pick-your-own vegetables and pumpkins in season.

Pick-Your-Own & Farm Stores

Greig Farm (845-758-1234), 223 Pitcher Lane, Red Hook (off Route 9G, 3 miles north of town; follow signs), has acres of fields that are available for self-harvesting, as well as a wonderful farm market. Berries, beans, apples, pumpkins, and peaches are only some of the seasonal treats; you will also find a winery, greenhouse, and extensive herb and cut-your-own flower gardens on the site. This is one of the largest and most popular stops for pick-your-own in the county, and visiting all the farm has to offer could take a couple of hours if you spend time in the fields, as well. Open May through October.

Also in Red Hook is **Montgomery Place Farm Market** (845-758-6338), at the junction of Routes 9G and 199, open June through October, where there is a good selection of fruits and vegetables in season. A conveniently located roadside stand by the Kingston-Rhinecliff Bridge, open May through December, is **Migliorelli Farm Market** (845-757-3276), at the corner of River Road and Route 199, Rhinebeck. They offer homemade products in addition to apples, berries, pumpkins, squash, and other vegetables, depending on the time of year you stop by. Also in nearby Rhinebeck is **Wonderland Farm** (845-876-6760), 191 White Schoolhouse Road, which has pumpkins for picking in late September and October, and Christmas trees in November and December.

In the southern part of the county, be sure to stop at **Fishkill Farms** (845-897-4377), 9 Fishkill Farm Road, Hopewell Junction, where you can pick cherries, blueberries, raspberries, strawberries, and peaches during spring and summer, and apples and pumpkins in the fall. The market offers homemade baked goods, plus freshly pressed cider and doughnuts in season. There's live entertainment and children's activities on weekends in autumn, as well as hayrides, and hay bales for the kids to play on. This is a terrific stop, particularly for those traveling with children. In nearby Wappingers Falls is **Secor Farms** (845-452-6883), 63 Robinson Lane, open June through August and the month of October, which has pick-your-own strawberries, which they are known for, as well as apples, berries, and pumpkins in autumn. The kids will enjoy going on a hayride here, as well.

In Poughkeepsie, there are a few places worth visiting. **Adams Fairacre Farm** (845-454-4330), 765 Dutchess Turnpike, is a fantastic farm market/supermarket with a lovely gift shop and garden center. Just behind Adams, in the same parking lot, is the **Pastry Garden** (845-473-5220), 749 Dutchess Turnpike, which has some of the best eclairs and baked goods—don't miss this spot, especially if you have a sweet tooth! In Pleasant Valley, visit **Wigsten's Farm Market** (845-235-7469), 1096 Salt Point Turnpike, which is open June through October for picking your own fruits or vegetables, depending on the season. They have an array of home-baked goods and local gourmet products, as well.

Barton Orchards (845-227-2306), 63 Apple Tree Lane, off County Route 7 (the Beekman Poughquag Road), in Poughquag, is open June through December for pick-your-own crops, including berries of all kinds, apples, pumpkins, Christmas trees, and vegetables. This is a wonderful place to visit, especially with children; autumn hayrides, and special events throughout the season. **Battenfeld & Son** (845-758-8018), 856 Route 199, Red Hook, has been renowned for decades as the place to go for those colorful anemones and Christmas trees in season. A family operation for several generations, they are open to the public daily 9–6 for flowers. **Hahn Farm** (845-266-5042), 1331 Netherwood Road, Salt Point, has a store on the premises where they sell meat, chicken, eggs, and other products from their farm. Do call for hours, however, since they vary with the season. And make sure to attend the Hahn Harvest Festival on October weekends! **Terhune Orchards** (845-266-5382) is also in Salt Point, at 761 North Avenue. They are one of the oldest apple farms in the county, and visitors can enjoy picking their own fruit after a hayride up to the orchard during the autumn months. **Ronnybrook** (518-398-6455), Prospect Hill Road, Pine Plains, now has their own store at the farm, open daily 9–5, selling their well-known yogurt, butter, and chocolate milk, as well as other milk products from their dairy farm. Ronny is usually there overseeing the operation, and you'll see his contented cows grazing as you drive up the pastoral road to the farm.

GOLF Several courses are open to the public in Dutchess County. Hours change with the season, and courses may be more or less crowded, depending on the time of year and time of day. Most are open from April through mid-November. There is sometimes a waiting list during the summer months. Do call ahead to reserve a tee time, particularly on weekends. Just about all the courses open at 6 AM on weekends and 7 AM weekdays.

Beekman Country Club (845-226-7700), 11 Country Club Road, Hopewell Junction. This 27-hole championship course has first-rate facilities that include a clubhouse, driving range, putting green, pro shop, cart rental, and restaurant. There are special rates for junior golfers. Do call a week in advance for a tee time.

Casperkill Golf Club (845-463-0900), 2320 South Road, Route 9, Poughkeepsie. This 18-hole championship golf course was designed by Robert Trent Jones Sr. There is a clubhouse here as well as a driving range, putting greens, pro shop, lessons, cart and club rental, and snack bar.

College Hill Golf Course (845-486-9112), 149 North Clinton Street, Poughkeepsie. This nine-hole course is inexpensive and has junior rates; good for novice golfers.

Dinsmore Golf Course (845-889-4071), 5371 Albany Post Road (Route 9), Staatsburg. This 18-hole course is the second-oldest golf course in the country. There is a clubhouse, pro shop, putting green, and restaurant. The views of the Hudson River and Catskill Mountains are wonderful here, especially when the leaves are off the trees!

Dutchess County Tourism

CASPERKILL GOLF CLUB IN POUGHKEEPSIE

Dutcher Golf Course (845-855-9845), 135 East Main Street, Pawling. This nine-hole course is the oldest public course in America. There is a pro shop, putting green, and snack bar; cart and club rentals.

Fishkill Golf Course (845-896-5220), 387 Route 9, Fishkill. There is a nine-hole course, driving range, and miniature golf course here, as well as a pro shop, practice greens, and restaurant. Club rental available.

Harlem Valley Golf Club (845-832-9957), Wheeler Road, Wingdale. This nine-hole course is a good place for novice golfers.

James Baird State Park Golf Course (845-473-6200), 280 Club House Road, Pleasant Valley. This 18-hole championship course designed by Robert Trent Jones Sr. has a clubhouse, driving range, putting green, pro shop, lessons—and reasonable prices.

The Links at Union Vale (845-223-1000), 153 North Parliman Road, Union Vale. This 18-hole links-style course is quite challenging. There is a clubhouse, driving range, putting green, pro shop, and restaurant on the premises. Lessons and cart rental available.

McCann Memorial Golf Course (845-454-1968), 155 Wilbur Boulevard, Poughkeepsie. This 18-hole championship course also has a driving range, putting greens, pro shop, snack bar, and fine restaurant on the premises. Lessons and cart rentals available.

Red Hook Golf Club (845-758-8652), 650 Route 199, Red Hook. This 18-hole championship course, with clubhouse, putting and chipping green, driving range, pro shop, and Lucchaela's restaurant on the premises, also offers lessons and cart and club rentals. Soft spikes required.

Vassar Golf Course (845-473-9838), Vassar College Campus, 124 Raymond Avenue, Poughkeepsie. This nine-hole course is inexpensive and great for beginners. There are junior and senior rates; club and cart rentals available.

HIKING **Appalachian Trail** (www.appalachiantrail.org/newyork). Thirty miles of the AT pass through southeastern Dutchess County. Within the county there are 4,000 acres of protected parkland with hiking, backpacking, snowshoeing, cross-country skiing, and five overnight use areas. Look for trailheads—marked by AT trail crossing signs—at the following locations: Route 52, 4 miles east of the Taconic Parkway, with parking on the north side of the road; Route 55, west of Pawling, near the Route 292 intersection, with parking just west of the trail crossing; Route 22, north of Pawling, between Route 68 and the DOT parking area, north of Route 68 and Hurds Corners Road. Free. Open year-round.

Dutchess Rail Trail Park (845-298-4600). There are three phases of this approximately 11-mile paved linear park that are open to the public, and the park is continually growing. Phases I and III cover 8 miles from Route 82 in Hopewell Junction to Old Manchester Road in LaGrange. Phase II is a 2.4-mile path from Morgan Lake to Overocker Road in the town of Poughkeepsie. The park is ideal for walking, biking, running, and rollerblading.

Edward R. Murrow Park (845-855-1131), Lakeside Drive and Old Route 55, Pawling. Open May through August, daily 10–7. Admission fee. There are several hiking trails on this 86-acre site, which also has a lake with small beach for swimming, restaurant, and picnic pavilions.

Harlem Valley Rail Trail (518-789-9591). There are 20 miles of scenic paved trail, linking villages and parks on the rail bed from Amenia and Millerton to Copake Falls in Columbia County. There is access to the trail at Railroad Plaza in Millerton and in Amenia on Mechanic Street. Free. Open year-round.

Hyde Park Trail (845-229-9115). There are 8.5 miles of hiking trails connecting several parks and historic sites. Bikes are not permitted, and access is behind the FDR Presidential Library. Free. Open year-round.

Mills-Norrie State Park (845-889-4646), off Route 9, Staatsburg, has 1,000 acres of woodlands with hiking trails, marina, boat launch, picnic areas, and a golf course; it's also near Mills Mansion (see *To See—Historic Homes*). Free. Open year-round.

Mount Beacon Park (845-473-4440). Both the parking area and trailhead are located at the intersection of Route 9D and Howland Avenue in Beacon. The short hike to the top of Mount Beacon offers fantastic views of the highlands and Hudson River. This is considered the northern gateway to the Hudson Highlands. Visitors will also see remnants of the world-famous incline railway, once the steepest of its kind anywhere; it operated from 1902 until the late 1970s. Free. Open year-round, daily dawn to dusk.

Pawling Nature Reserve (914-244-3271), Quaker Lake Road, Pawling. This 1,000-acre reserve has miles of hiking trails amid mountains, fields, woods, and ponds. It is seemingly undiscovered, and its trails are underutilized. It is a wonderful destination for birders. Nearly 80 avian species use the area's diverse habitat for nesting or foraging. Rare plant species found within the reserve include soapwort, gentian, yellow wild flax, scarlet Indian paintbrush, and walking fern. In the reserve's gorge, Duell Hollow Brook cascades down the rocks, one of several ravines that allow for cooler microclimates supporting hemlock/northern hardwood forests, known as "hemlock cathedrals." Free. Open year-round.

Stissing Mountain Fire Tower (518-398-5069), 532 Hicks Hill Road, Stanford, has an elevation of 1,492 feet. The 90-foot lookout tower is reached by following a hiking trail from the base of the mountain, the second-oldest mountain in the Western Hemisphere. Incredible views of three states, along with an interesting piece of local history: the fire tower, a structure that has nearly disappeared from the face of the Hudson Valley. Enjoy watching eagles, hawks, and vultures in flight. Open year-round; free.

Thompson Pond Preserve (914-244-3271), Lake Road, 1.2 miles from Route 199, Pine Plains. Open year-round; free. After climbing Stissing Mountain, check out this multiacre reserve with its fields, woods, and pond areas.

Wilcox Park (845-758-6100), 1639 Route 199, Stanfordville. Open year-round, this 615-acre site has the amenities of a larger park, along with hiking trails suitable for a family outing. Free park entry.

HORSEBACK RIDING **Calypso Farm** (845-266-4664), 25 Seelbach Lane, Staatsburg. This equestrian center offers lessons, training, and a children's summer-riding program. They are open year-round by appointment only.

Cedar Crest Farm (518-398-1034), 2054 Route 83, Pine Plains. Open year-round, Tuesday through Sunday 8:30–5. This equestrian center offers lessons in show jumping, cross-country, and dressage to riders of all abilities.

The Southlands Foundation (845-876-4862), 5771 Route 9, Rhinebeck. Open year-round, but call in advance to schedule lessons. There is a summer riding program and summer camp here, but no trail rides. The equestrian farm is located on 200 acres overlooking the Hudson River.

Western Trail Riding (845-463-2880), 263 Kidd Lane, Tivoli. They are open year-round here for trail riding by appointment if your party consists of one or two people. The horses are gentle, and the ride will be tailored to your ability.

Willowbrook Farm (845-266-4522), Willow Lane, Clinton Corners. Open by appointment only. A professional staff offers training, lessons, and boarding.

KAYAKING **Atlantic Kayak Tours** (845-889-8461), 1 Norrie Way, Staatsburg. Available late May through mid-September, Saturday and Sunday 10–4 or by appointment. They rent kayaks and organize excursions at the Norrie Point Paddlesport Center in Staatsburg. This is a great way for both beginners and more experienced kayakers to get out on the Hudson River.

Mountain Tops Kayak Tours (845-831-1997), 144 Main Street, Beacon. This company is the official outfitter at Scenic Hudson's Long Dock Park kayak launch on the Hudson River. They rent kayaks by the hour and also provide guided tours for groups of four or more. Metro North has partnered with Scenic Hudson: Manhattan residents may take one-day all-inclusive kayaking getaways by going to Grand Central Station, riding the train to Beacon, then walking to the nearby river center kayak launch.

The River Connection (845-229-0595), 9 West Market Street, Hyde Park, is an excellent place to go if you're new to kayaking and don't have equipment. They organize outings on the Hudson and offer classes for beginners as well as advanced students. I went on one of their trips and found it to be an amazing experience, particularly just before sunset—a new way to experience the river!

SWIMMING **Bard College Stevenson Gymnasium** (845-758-7531), off Route 9G, Annandale. Open daily year-round, but call before you go. Admission fee. This indoor, six-lane, 75-foot-long swimming pool is a great place to go for those who enjoy doing laps. It is open to the public for day use, but memberships are also available. Men's and women's locker rooms with saunas; fitness center; squash courts; outdoor tennis courts.

Edward R. Murrow Park (845-855-1131), Lakeside Drive and Old Route 55, Pawling. Open May through August, daily 10–7. Admission fee. This 86-acre park has a wonderful lake with a small beach; perfect for young children.

Taconic State Park, Rudd Pond Area (518-789-3059), County Route 62, Millerton. Open Memorial Day weekend through Labor Day, daily 11–6. Admission fee per vehicle. There is a small beach area; a good place for young children. The pond is 8 feet deep in the swimming area. There is fishing, rowboat rentals, a picnic area, and bicycling.

Wilcox Park (845-758-6100), 1639 Route 199, Stanfordville. Open Memorial Day weekend through Labor Day, weekends 10–7. Admission fee per vehicle for non–Dutchess County residents. This man-made lake (6–7 feet deep) is lovely and offers a good-size beach where you can relax with lots of shade nearby. Hiking trails surrounding the lake provide an easy walk after your swim. This park is nice for bicycling, as well.

ZIP LINE TOURS **Big Bear Ziplines** (1-888-947-2294; www.bigbearziplines.com), 817 Violet Avenue, Hyde Park. Open year-round, Friday through Sunday; tours leave at 9:30 AM and 1:30 PM, with a minimum of two people. Monday through Thursday tours, by appointment only, with a minimum of four people. Most tours are between 8 and 10 participants. Located on 50 acres of woodlands, this is the place to zip through the woods on a three-hour adventure. The eight zip lines (ranging from 30 feet high and 200 feet long to nearly 200 feet high and 1,400 feet long) take you on a course where fire truck ladders are climbed and Tarzan-like vines are swung from. The weight requirement is 80–250 pounds, and those under the age of 15 must be accompanied by an adult (someone over the age of 18). Closed-toe shoes are a must. The cost is approximately $100.

✷ Winter Sports

CROSS-COUNTRY SKIING Dutchess County was made for cross-country skiing, with low hills that slope down toward the river, open meadows turned liquid silver by moonlight, and secret paths that cross streams and disappear into the pines. Many of the area's trails are maintained by towns and villages, and most are quiet. The following state and county parks offer cross-country skiing during the winter months. Since the weather is often exceedingly changeable, do call ahead to check conditions.

Ferncliff Forest (845-876-3196), Mount Rutsen Road, Rhinebeck. Open daily dawn to dusk. Free. This 200-acre park is a gem and less crowded than some of the other parks in the county.

James Baird State Park (845-452-1489), 14 Maintenance Lane, Pleasant Valley. Open daily dawn to dusk. Free. Some 600 acres, including several miles of scenic wooded trails.

Mills-Norrie State Park (845-889-4646), 9 Old Post Road (off Route 9), Staatsburg. Open daily dawn to dusk. This 1,000-acre state park offers several wooded trails for skiing, some of which have Hudson River views. The park also has picnic and sledding areas.

Taconic State Park, Rudd Pond Area (518-789-3059), County Route 62, Millerton. Open daily 8 AM–dusk. Parking fee. There are 225 acres here with several trails.

Wilcox Park (845-758-6100), 1639 Route 199, Stanfordville. Open Monday through Friday 9–4. Free. This is a wonderful place for winter hiking and walking. There are 615 acres here with some lovely trails that go around the lake; they are not marked, however.

ICE SKATING Mid-Hudson Civic Center (845-454-5800; www.midhudson civiccenter.org), 14 Civic Center Plaza, Poughkeepsie. Open year-round. The McCann Ice Arena at the civic center provides hockey and figure skating, as well as public skate sessions for the community. Public skating is usually Monday, Tuesday, and Friday noon–2, and Saturday and Sunday 2–4. There are rentals available, as well as a snack bar. Parking in the adjoining civic center garage is free if you get your parking ticket validated after skating. Check the website to confirm the schedule, as it may vary during the summer months.

✷ Green Space

Beatrix Farrand Garden at Bellefield (845-229-9115), 4097 Route 9, Hyde Park. Open May through October, daily dawn–dusk. These gardens were planted in 1912 by Beatrix Farrand, one of the first women to become a landscape architect in America. The garden is thoughtfully constructed with an array of colorful flowers. After seeing this garden, it is only a short walk next door to the rose garden at the Franklin Delano Roosevelt Home (see *To See—Historic Homes*). There are 28 different varieties of roses here. It is also the burial site of both FDR and Eleanor Roosevelt.

BEATRIX FARRAND GARDEN AT BELLEFIELD IN HYDE PARK

Dutchess County Tourism

Buttercup Farm Audubon Sanctuary (518-325-5203), Route 82, south of Pine Plains, open daily dawn to dusk, offers 640 acres of diverse habitats with rolling fields and open grasslands. There are 6 miles of trails, and over 80 species of birds have been observed here, including great blue herons, wood ducks, and bobolinks.

Fishkill Ridge Conservation Area (845-473-4440), Fishkill. (Take 52 west, off Route 9, through town and make a left on Maple Avenue; at the end, turn right and cross the bridge.

Make a left onto Old Town Road, then a right on Sunnyside Road, and follow to the end. Bear left, then right, and continue up the hill to the parking area.) This 1,900-acre area of the ridge, the northern gateway to the Hudson Highlands, is filled with wildlife and offers stunning views of the Hudson River and surrounding Catskills. There are excellent trails, as well, which connect to Hudson Highlands State Park (see *To Do—Hiking & Outdoor Activites* in "Putnam County") and Mount Beacon.

Hudson River Research Reserve (845-758-7010), Tivoli Bay, Annandale-on-Hudson. Located on the Bard College campus (and the Tivoli Bays Wildlife Management Area), this preserve has 1,700 acres that can be hiked (there are six trails) or enjoyed as part of the various public programs that are offered throughout the year. Call for information on guided canoe trips, organized walks, and other events, or stop in at the visitors center adjacent to the Tivoli Free Library on Broadway (the main street) in Tivoli between 10 and 2 on Saturday (hours vary during the week, so call before you go). Be aware that hunting, fishing, and trapping are permitted in season in this wildlife management area. On two Saturdays each month, May through October, there is canoe and kayak access to Tivoli North Bay. It is recommended to call before going, however.

Hyde Park Trail (845-473-4440), Hyde Park. Trailheads are at both the FDR Home and Vanderbilt Mansion at the intersection of East Market Road and Route 9. This 8.5-mile trail system runs along the Hudson River and links three National Historic Sites—the Vanderbilt Mansion, the FDR Home, and the Eleanor Roosevelt National Historic Site (Val-Kill)—with Hyde Park's Riverfront Park. There are five trail sections, and bicycling is permitted only on the 1.5-mile unpaved Val-Kill loop.

Innisfree Garden (845-677-8000), 362 Tyrrel Road (1.75 miles from the Taconic Parkway overpass on Route 44; make a right onto Tyrrel Road), Millbrook. Open May through October, Wednesday through Friday 10–4; Saturday, Sunday, and holidays 11–5. Admission fee. Inspired by the Eastern cup garden, or three-dimensional image composed of natural elements, these individual "garden pictures" draw the attention to a particular object, setting it apart by establishing an enclosure around it. Following the tradition of Asian artists, garden founder Walter Beck used natural formations as well as terraces, walls, and paths to keep specific areas in "tension," believing that moving rocks or plants only an inch or so would destroy the effect. Visitors can stroll these public gardens and enjoy this visual laboratory and garden notebook. There is a picnic area for use by visitors; no pets are permitted, and there is very limited handicapped access.

Institute of Ecosystem Studies (845-677-5343; www.caryinstitute.org), 2801 Sharon Turnpike, Millbrook. Open April through October, Monday through Saturday 9–6; Sunday 1–6. There are nearly 2,000 acres of nature trails and plant collections at this educational and research facility. Public ecology programs, perennial gardens, and a tropical greenhouse are highlights. These lovely grounds are a great stop if you are traveling with older children. Do check the website for programs scheduled.

Peach Hill Park (845-298-4600), 34 Edgewood Road, Poughkeepsie. Open year-round, daily dawn to dusk. It's a lovely park located off Salt Point Turnpike near the town of Hyde Park. There are 157 acres here with several marked trails. It is also the highest elevation in the town of Poughkeepsie.

Dutchess County Tourism

INSTITUTE OF ECOSYSTEM STUDIES IN MILLBROOK

Quiet Cove Riverfront Park (845-298-4600), Route 9, Poughkeepsie. This 27-acre riverfront park is a favorite place among local residents, and it's open to the public year-round, daily dawn to dusk.

Poet's Walk Romantic Landscape Park (845-473-4440), County Route 103, Red Hook. (Cross the Kingston-Rhinecliff Bridge heading east; turn left at the first traffic light—River Road. The entrance to the park is 0.6 mile farther on the left.) This 120-acre park offers magnificent views of the Hudson River, Kingston-Rhinecliff Bridge, and Catskill Mountains. There are 2 miles of trails, along with rustic cedar pavilions—and benches—when you want to rest and take in the scenery. This is a wonderful place to stop and take a walk while touring Dutchess County by car.

Walkway over the Hudson (845-454-9649; www.walkway.org), between Highland in Ulster County and Poughkeepsie in Dutchess County. A landmark railroad bridge has been transformed into a 1.25-mile linear park and trailway. There is now public access to the Hudson River's scenic landscape for pedestrians, hikers, joggers, and bicyclists. When it's complete, the walkway will connect with a network of rail trails, parks, and communities. Interestingly, the cost of removing the bridge would have been over twice the cost of preserving it! Eventually restaurants will be built on both sides of the bridge. Check the website for information about special events on the walkway.

WALKWAY OVER THE HUDSON JOINING THE CITY OF POUGHKEEPSIE AND HIGHLAND IN ULSTER COUNTY

Dutchess County Tourism

Wethersfield Estate and Gardens (845-373-8037), 214 Pugsley Hill Road, off County Route 86, Amenia. Formal gardens open June through September, Wednesday, Friday, and Saturday noon–5; house by appointment only. This 10-acre formal garden created by Chauncey D. Stillman (1907–1989) is arranged in the classical style, like the Italian villas of the 17th century. It is a garden of scenic views and statues, bursting with colorful flowers. There is an east garden, cupid fountain, arbor vitae arch, and allee, as well as cutting, water, and inner gardens; a knot garden south terrace; pine terrace; peacock walk; belvedere; and rune stone (designed from a ninth-century Swedish original). Stillman's house is a Georgian-style Colonial, with the highest point on the property offering panoramic views of the Catskills to the west and the Berkshires to the north. It is filled with his collection of antiques, paintings, sculptures, and fine furniture. Stillman, an early conservationist, ran one of the first estates in Dutchess County to use soil-and-water-conservation farming techniques. He constructed 12 ponds for irrigation and prevention of soil erosion, rotated crops on contour strips, reforested, and employed organic farming methods. Today both field crops and livestock are raised, and the farm carries on the tradition of conservation. Stillman's interests went beyond agriculture and horticulture and extended to horses. He had a good-size stable on the property and acquired 22 carriages, which he had restored; most date from 1850 to 1910 and can be seen by appointment, along with the interior of the house. Although these gardens are only open limited days and hours, they are worth seeing if you enjoy horticulture.

✷ Lodging

Northwestern Dutchess County (Red Hook, Rhinebeck, Rhinecliff, Staatsburg, Hyde Park, Tivoli)

Beekman Arms (845-876-7077), 24 West Market Street, Rhinebeck 12572. ($$) The oldest inn in America, the Arms is steeped in history and antiques. Located on the main road in town; shops and restaurants are just outside the door. There are 23 rooms, all with private bath. If you want a quieter place—a restaurant and tavern are downstairs (see *Dining Out*)—ask about the Delamater Inn, a gingerbread fantasy that dates from 1844 and is operated by the Beekman Arms. Children welcome. Open year-round. There are also motel-like accommodations behind the inn where pets are permitted. Additionally, the Old Firehouse (the original firehouse of Rhinebeck), with exposed brick walls and high ceilings, is available to guests. Another option is The Townsend; it has four modern deluxe rooms, each with a king-size bed and gas fireplace.

Belvedere Mansion (845-889-8000), 10 Old Route 9, Staatsburg 12580. ($$$) *Belvedere* means "beautiful view," and there is a wonderful one from this restored Greek Revival mansion overlooking the Hudson River with the Catskill Mountains as a backdrop. In addition to the lavish accommodations in the main house, a separate carriage house facing the mansion also offers rooms, with individual entrances and private bath. Each room has a unique character and is decorated with antiques and American folk art. Additions to this wonderful complex are the Hunt Lodge, with luxurious rooms reminiscent of an Adirondack-style camp, and the Zen Lodge; its rooms are stunning in their simplicity. During the winter months a hearty country breakfast is served fireside in the main dining room. In warmer weather breakfast is served alfresco in a pavilion gazebo overlooking the fountain and pond. There is also an inground pool and tennis courts. Open year-round.

The Bird's Nest (845-757-4279), 21 Clay Hill Road, Tivoli 12583. ($) Enjoy a private two-bedroom apartment with a full kitchen, bath, and large deck. A full breakfast will be delivered to your door in the morning. The decor here is simple, clean, and adequate, and the rates are exceedingly reasonable. There is no minimum stay required. Open March through November.

The Bitter Sweet Bed & Breakfast (845-876-7777), 470 Wurtemburg Road, Rhinebeck 12572. ($$) This 1770 Dutch Colonial situated on 150 acres has seven rooms, all with private bath and air-conditioning and filled with antiques. A full breakfast is served. Children over the age of five welcome. Open April through December.

Delamater Inn (845-876-7077), 6433 Montgomery Street (Route 9), Rhinebeck 12572. ($$) This romantic country inn is located in the heart of town. There are seven separate buildings, and four are historic structures. Walk to the restaurants and shops when staying in any of the 50 rooms, all with private bath, air-conditioning, phone, refrigerator, and TV, and 29 with fireplaces. There are five suites (each with a bedroom, separate sitting room, and fireplace), and five rooms have kitchenettes. Continental breakfast is served. Children are welcome. Open year-round.

The Grand Dutchess (845-758-5818), 7571 Old Post Road (North Broadway), Red Hook 12571. ($$) This Italianate mansion built in 1874 is located on 1 acre and is within walking distance of the shops and restaurants in town. There are five rooms, all with private bath. A full breakfast is served, and children over the age of six are welcome. Open April through December.

Hideaway Suites (845-266-5673), 439 Lake Drive, Rhinebeck 12572. ($$) Enjoy secluded elegance in the middle of a forest. The three suites and three guest rooms all have private bath, king-size beds, air-conditioning, TV, and phone. Most have a fireplace, Jacuzzi, wet bar, and private deck. Located 1 mile from the Omega Institute. Open year-round.

Journey Inn Bed & Breakfast (845-229-8972), One Sherwood Place, Hyde Park 12538. ($$) Situated directly across from the entrance to the Vanderbilt Mansion and grounds (where guests can easily take a morning walk or run), this comfortable, cozy B&B is chock-full of fascinating memorabilia from the travels of the owners. There are two master suites, one with a king-size bed, and five bedrooms, all with private bath. Children over the age of nine welcome. Open year-round.

Le Petit Chateau Inn (845-437-4688), 39 West Dorsey Lane, Hyde Park 12538. ($$) This European-style inn built in 1900 is located on a beautiful wooded 40-acre estate. A lovely pond adjacent to the inn is home to ducks, great blue herons, and turtles. Each of the four renovated rooms is named after a famous French wine region, and a basket of wine and food from France greets guests upon arrival. Innkeeper Valerie Hail makes everyone feel comfortable. She is assisted by students from the nearby Culinary Institute of America. Visitors may enjoy wine-related travel videos and a CD collection of the wine world. The inn is a good choice for oenophiles, who should inquire about the wine seminars given here. All rooms have a private bath, fireplace, king- or queen-size bed, cable TV, air-conditioning, and wireless Internet access. Children are welcome. Open year-round.

The Madalin Hotel (845-757-2100), 53 Broadway, Tivoli 12583. ($$$) The charming village of Tivoli was once known as Madalin, and this historic hotel, dating back more than 100 years, was the town's hub. Since May 2006 the Madalin is once again just that—the first place visitors to Tivoli should stop. Step back in time during a stay in one of the beautifully renovated rooms (there are 11), each with king- or queen-size bed, private bath, air-conditioning, flat-screen TV, and wireless Internet access. Guests will feel comfortable yet pampered in this classy oasis, which is at the top of my list for special getaways in the region. The restaurant downstairs, Madalin's Table (see *Dining Out*), with its rich colors, tin ceilings, and oak bar, is where a sumptuous continental breakfast is served in the morning. Make sure to have both lunch and dinner here during your stay: The food is excellent and moderately priced. Open year-round.

Olde Rhinebeck Inn (845-871-1745), 340 Wurtemburg Road, Rhinebeck 12572. ($$$) Listed on the National Register of Historic Places, this early American farmhouse, built before the Revolutionary War by Dutch Palatine settlers, retains many of its original architectural details, including hand-hewn chestnut beams and wide-plank floors. The four rooms, each with its own charm, combine authentic touches with the modern amenities. One room offers a Jacuzzi and private balcony overlooking the spring-fed pond. The large suite has a queen-size canopied bed with adjoining sitting room. All rooms have private bath, satellite TV, air-conditioning, refrigerator, plush terry-cloth robes, and fresh-cut flowers. Full gourmet breakfast. A two-night minimum stay required on weekends. Children not permitted. Open year-round.

Red Hook Country Inn (845-758-8445), 7460 South Broadway, Red Hook 12571. ($$) There are eight rooms with private bath, and a carriage house, in this 160-year-old Federal-style house, converted to a charming inn. A couple of rooms have fireplaces and whirlpool baths. Guests are welcome to enjoy the movie library, in-room coffee service, hair dryers, bathrobes, chocolates, and fresh flowers. The owners, Nabil and Pat, are genuinely warm and hospitable, and go out of their way to make everyone comfortable. A full breakfast is served. Children are welcome. Open year-round.

The Rhinecliff Inn (845-876-0590), 4 Grinnell Street, Rhinecliff 12574. ($$) There are nine lovely rooms with river views in this country hotel, adjacent to the Amtrak railroad station. All have private baths and balconies, whirlpool tubs, air-conditioning, and cable TV. There's a bar/restaurant downstairs. Recommended for heavy sleepers, as the trains do pass by throughout the night!

Veranda House (845-876-4133), 6487 Montgomery Street (Route 9), Rhinebeck 12572. ($$) This charming Federal house built in 1845 was once a farmhouse, and for almost a century it served as a church parsonage. Located in the Rhinebeck Village Historic District, three blocks from the center of town, it features five cozy rooms, all with private bath. The Rose Room, with its queen-size four-poster bed and lacy canopy, is my favorite. Guests are invited to enjoy the library, TV, VCR, and living room with fireplace. The terrace overlooks the garden and is a nice place to relax in the warm-weather months. Children over 12 are welcome. Open year-round.

Whistlewood Farm (845-876-6838), 52 Pells Road, Rhinebeck 12572. ($$) This distinctive B&B is also a working horse farm, located on 40 acres with miles of walking trails through beautiful woodlands. Animals abound here. The living room has a stone fireplace and a view of the paddock area, and there are antiques, including a player piano, throughout the house. A hearty farm breakfast with home-baked muffins, breads, and jams is served daily. The four bedrooms have private bath with Jacuzzi, and private patio; two cottages have fireplaces, and one has a hot tub. Guests may use the entire house. Note that the owner offers deeply discounted rates during the week (Monday through Thursday nights) to single travelers. Children and pets are welcome. Open year-round.

Southwestern Dutchess County (Beacon, Fishkill, Poughkeepsie)

Alumnae House, the Inn at Vassar College (845-437-7100), 161 College Avenue, Poughkeepsie 12603. ($$) This beautiful Tudor-style inn has 20 rooms, 13 with private baths. Seven rooms share two baths. Open year-round.

Botsford Briar B&B (845-831-6099), 19 High Street (between Tompkins and Beekman streets), Beacon 12508. ($$) There are five rooms, all with private bath, in this beautifully restored 1889 Queen Anne Victorian; the design is by the same architect who redesigned Wilderstein in Rhinebeck. The B&B was used as a set location for the film *Nobody's Fool,* starring Paul Newman. A deck, built in 2008 by the innkeeper, offers panoramic views of the Hudson River. Since the location is close to both Main Street and the Metro North train station, this is a good choice for those who don't have a car and plan on exploring Beacon on foot. A continental breakfast is served in your room; TV, air-conditioning, and high-speed Internet service round out the amenities. Open year-round.

Courtyard by Marriott (845-485-6336), 2641 South Road, Poughkeepsie 12601. ($$) There are 149 spacious rooms in this moderately priced hotel, located in the heart of the city's largest shopping area. Enjoy all the modern amenities, including indoor pool, whirlpool, exercise room, and high-speed Internet access. A sumptuous breakfast buffet is available every morning. An ideal place for families. (Note that the hotel is also next to Locust Grove Historic Site, which has wonderful walking paths for those who enjoy morning exercise outdoors!)

Hilton Garden Inn (845-896-7100), 25 Westage Drive, Fishkill 12524. ($$) There are 111 rooms in this hotel, at the junction of Route 9 and I-84. All have high-speed Internet access, refrigerator, microwave, and coffeemaker in addition to the usual hotel amenities. There is an indoor pool, fitness center, and 24-hour business center (with fax, computer, and photocopy machine). Children welcome. Open year-round.

Mount Beacon Bed & Breakfast at Wolcott Manor (845-831-0737), 829 Wolcott Avenue, Beacon 12508. ($$) In this 1911 Colonial Revival home at the foot of Mount Beacon, there are three rooms, one with a fireplace; all have wireless Internet, cable TV, and air-conditioning. There is also an in-ground pool, and breakfast is served in the dining room. High ceilings, hardwood floors, and period furniture make this a lovely place to stay. Open year-round.

Poughkeepsie Grand Hotel (845-485-5300), 40 Civic Center Plaza, Poughkeepsie 12601. ($$) There are 200 rooms in this conveniently located, full-service hotel/conference center, which was totally renovated in 2008. A restaurant and bar are on the premises, as well as a covered garage with plenty of free parking for hotel guests. Open year-round.

The Residence Inn (845-896-5210), 14 Schuyler Boulevard, Fishkill 12524. ($$) Part of the Marriott hotel chain.

There are 139 suites here, each with the usual modern amenities, as well as fireplace and kitchen. A continental breakfast is served. An outdoor pool, whirlpool, and exercise room are on the premises (passes to nearby All Sport Fitness Center are given to all guests). Children welcome. Open year-round.

The Residence Inn (845-463-4343), 2525 South Road, Poughkeepsie 12601. ($$) This 2004 addition to the Marriott chain offers the choice of studios, one-bedroom suites, or two-bedroom suites with separate living and sleeping areas, fully equipped kitchen with full-size appliances, cable TV, air-conditioning, and high-speed Internet access. Facilities include a heated indoor pool, whirlpool and exercise room, and an indoor game room with pool table. Complimentary hot breakfast buffet. This hotel is located in the heart of Poughkeepsie's business district; a particularly good choice for business travelers and those with children.

The Roundhouse at Beacon Falls (845-765-8369), 2 East Main Street, Beacon 12508. ($$$) There are three beautifully restored buildings making up the hotel/restaurant (see *Dining Out*) complex here, which opened in 2012. The Roundhouse has 14 spacious, modern rooms and two penthouse suites with views of Beacon Falls. The Mill offers 42 rooms with views of the falls and Mount Beacon. The accommodations are pricey, but this is a welcome addition to the city. Children welcome. Open year-round.

Swann Inn (845-831-6346), 120 Howland Avenue, Beacon 12508. ($$) Originally built in 1866, this cozy B&B is located at the base of Mount Beacon. There are five rooms, each with its own distinctive character; four have private bath. A full breakfast is served to guests. Innkeepers Neil Caplan and his wife, Darlene, offer a wealth of knowledge about the area. Open year-round.

Willow Lake Cottages (914-475-5254), 4 Willow Lake Drive, Fishkill 12524. ($$$) There are four different types of houses on a 5-acre lake on this property. Each house sleeps six, is fully furnished, and has a kitchen; all are air-conditioned. This is a good choice for families or groups who enjoy hiking, boating, fishing, and swimming. It is also ideal for a family reunion. Children and pets welcome.

Central Dutchess County (Millbrook)

A Cat in Your Lap Bed & Breakfast (845-677-3051), 62 Old Route 82 and the Monument, Millbrook 12545. ($) There are two barn studios here with private bath, king-size bed, and fireplace. The garden studio is a little smaller but also charming. The village of Millbrook is within walking distance. A hearty breakfast is served, and these elegant accommodations come at reasonable prices. Open year-round.

Millbrook Country House (845-677-9570), 506 Sharon Turnpike, Millbrook 12545. ($$) The four guest rooms in this delightful 1808 center-hall Colonial, all with private bath and central air-conditioning, are decorated with many 18th-century Italian antiques and paintings. Imported linens are featured on all the beds, which adds a nice touch, and guests can spend time around any of the several fireplaces. The wonderful gardens (both flower and herb) are filled with modern sculptures, a nice counterpoint to the antiques. Guests will enjoy a full gourmet breakfast with homemade jams and syrups; the omelets use herbs from the garden during the summer months. Breakfast is served anytime at your convenience between 7 and 10. Afternoon tea is available between 4 and 5. Those interested in art and antiques will particularly appreciate a stay here. Reduced midweek rates available. Children over the age of 10 welcome. Open year-round.

Eastern Dutchess County (Amenia, Millerton)

Simmons' Way Village Inn (518-789-6235), 53 Main Street (Route 44), Millerton 12546. ($$$) Built originally as a modest merchant's home in 1854, the Village Inn was remodeled in 1892 into an elegant Victorian by the new bank-president owner; it now boasts nine rooms filled with down pillows, fine linens, antiques, and canopied beds, and all have private bath. Enjoy a full gourmet breakfast in your suite, in the dining room, or on the front porch. There is a fine restaurant, **Number 9,** on the premises, as well, which serves dinner Tuesday through Saturday (see *Dining Out*). Children are welcome. Open year-round.

Troutbeck Inn & Conference Center (845-373-9681), 515 Leedsville Road, Amenia 12501. ($$$) This English country estate on 600 acres is an executive retreat during the week, but on weekends it's a relaxed getaway. Fronted by sycamores and a brook, the slate-roofed estate has leaded-glass windows, walled gardens, antiques, and an outdoor pool and tennis courts. The 42 rooms and 6 suites, all with private bath and 9 with fireplace, are beautifully decorated. Note that there are no television sets in any of the guest rooms. Not recommended for children. Open year-round.

✷ Where to Eat

DINING OUT

Northwestern Dutchess County (Tivoli, Red Hook, Rhinebeck, Staatsburg, Hyde Park)

Arielle (845-876-5666), 51 East Market Street, Rhinebeck. ($$) Open for lunch and dinner daily noon–9; Sunday brunch 11–4. This cozy eatery opened in 2008, serving excellent bistro fare including entrées like skate, bronzini, pan-seared salmon, pork Milanese, and steak and frites. The dessert menu has crème brûlée and other treats.

Aroi Thai Restaurant (845-876-1114), 55 East Market Street, Rhinebeck. ($$) Open for lunch Thursday through Monday 11:30–3; dinner served daily 5–9. This Thai restaurant serves well-prepared curry and noodle dishes, as well as daily specials. The two-course lunches for $9 are a real bargain, and I highly recommend visiting then. Desserts are interesting and tasty. The pumpkin custard is my favorite. The homemade ice cream flavors include lychee, ginger, and Thai iced tea. Children welcome.

Belvedere Mansion (845-889-8000), 10 Old Route 9, Staatsburg. ($$$) Open for dinner Thursday through Sunday 5:30–9. There are great views from the dining room in this historic mansion, a particularly wonderful place to dine in the warm-weather months when you can walk the property before your meal. There is Black Angus fillet, Alaskan king salmon, and rack of lamb; the menu has a French accent. This restaurant is a great choice for a special occasion. The bar is a romantic spot to enjoy cocktails before dinner.

Culinary Institute of America (845-471-6608), Route 9, Hyde Park. ($$) Hours vary. There are five restaurants at this world-famous culinary institution, where the food is prepared and served by the students under the guidance of world-class chefs. Except for weekdays at St. Andrew's Café and the Apple Pie Bakery Café (see *Eating Out*), reservations are essential and should be made several weeks in advance; the wait is usually well worth it. All CIA restaurants are closed Sunday, for three weeks during the summer months, and the week between Christmas and New Year's Day. American Bounty Restaurant and St. Andrew's Café serve lunch Tuesday through Saturday 11:30–1 and dinner 6–8:30 when school is in session. You might be able to have lunch at either of these restaurants without a reservation, so do check when you arrive for a visit. Menus change seasonally and use the freshest ingredients available. **American Bounty Restaurant** offers the best in the way of American regional cuisine: Try smoked turkey with black-pepper pasta and cream, then a Mississippi Riverboat for dessert. Visitors are served in a comfortable dining room. **Caterina d'Medici Restaurant** is now located in the newest venue, **Colavita Center for Italian Food and Wine,** which specializes in Northern Italian food like tricolor pasta diamonds with prosciutto. The menu features the culinary traditions of various regions of Italy, and the decor is reminiscent of the architecture and landscape of Tuscany. There are six dining areas, including a formal dining room with Venetian chandeliers, and the Al Forno room, with a casual antipasto bar, open kitchen, and wood-fired ovens. Most of the time it is possible to have lunch in the Al Forno room without a reservation between 1 and 6. **The Bocuse Restaurant** opened in 2013 and features contemporary international cuisine. **St. Andrew's Café** is less formal and offers healthful dishes that are delicious as well, like grilled salmon fillet with tomato-horseradish sauce and chocolate-bread-pudding soufflé for dessert. This restaurant is family friendly and offers an array of selections that will appeal to youngsters. **Apple Pie Bakery Café** (845-905-4500), open Monday through Friday 7:30–5, is a great place to stop for lunch or a midday snack. The salads, sandwiches, cakes, pies, and breads are first-rate.

Flat Iron (845-758-8260), 7488 South Broadway, Red Hook. ($$) Open for dinner Wednesday through Saturday 5:30–9:30. An upscale addition to the rather basic dining options in Red Hook arrived in 2008. Offering oysters, lobster bisque, burgers (served on an English muffin with caramelized onion, oven dried tomatoes, Boston lettuce, and shoestring fries), grilled organic king salmon, dry-aged rib eye steak, and rack of lamb. Not suggested for children.

Gigi Trattoria (845-876-1007), 6422 Montgomery Street (Route 9), Rhinebeck. ($$) Open for lunch and dinner daily 11:30–9; Friday and Saturday until 10. Hours change slightly in the winter months. A casual restaurant featuring Hudson Valley Mediterranean cuisine, with an emphasis on local ingredients in season. Skizza bianca (white pizza with mozzarella and goat cheese, figs, pears, sweet red onion, and fresh arugula, topped with white truffle oil) is a unique creation, so do try it. Other popular choices are the pastas made on the premises, and

CATERINA D'MEDICI RESTAURANT AT THE CULINARY INSTITUTE

Dutchess County Tourism

the 32-ounce rib eye steak served with Tuscan fries. For dessert there is excellent cheesecake with caramel sauce or lemon brûlée with cranberries.

Hana Sushi (845-758-4333), 7270 South Broadway, Red Hook. ($) Open for lunch Friday 11:30–2:30; dinner Tuesday through Thursday 5–9; Friday and Saturday until 10. This is a small, unpretentious eatery in a tiny strip mall. The rolls, tempura, and other Japanese specialties are consistently fresh and well prepared. The service is always friendly, and prices are less than those at other sushi spots in the area.

Le Petit Bistro (845-876-7400), 8 East Market Street, Rhinebeck. ($$$) Open for dinner Thursday through Monday 5–10. This charming, intimate French bistro is a great place to stop for dinner on a special occasion; the food and service are consistently excellent, and everything is prepared to order. All entrées are served with a fresh mixed salad. Excellent wine list. Not recommended for children.

Liberty Public House (845-876-1760), 6417 Montgomery Street, Rhinebeck. ($$) Open for lunch and dinner Monday through Thursday noon–11; Friday noon–2 AM; Saturday 11 AM–2 AM; Sunday 11–11. Located in the historic Starr Building, next door to Upstate Films, this restaurant has two dining areas, a cozy sports bar, and a nightclub downstairs with live entertainment on weekends. One of the dining rooms is decorated with a 48-star American flag and engravings from the Civil War. In the warm weather food is served on the patio, where the outdoor bar is actually a 23-foot sailboat surrounded by bar stools and picnic tables. The surroundings are unusual, and the hearty, eclectic American fare includes something for everyone. Offerings include grass-fed beef burgers with freedom fries, matzo ball soup, and crispy duck, to name just a few popular dishes. Desserts are all homemade and delicious.

The Local (845-876-2214), 38 West Market Street, Rhinebeck. ($$) Open Tuesday through Saturday 5:30–10. Enjoy international cuisine in an informal yet elegant renovated farmhouse. The name sums up most of the fare here, including an array of healthy, interesting dishes prepared with an imaginative flair by a Culinary Institute–trained chef. Some of the entrées include grilled sea scallops, cedar planked wild king salmon, duck "two ways," and pork scaloppine. There are small plates like phyllo-wrapped goat cheese, Asian chicken dumplings, and pretzel-crusted crab-claw cakes. Oysters come raw, broiled, or fried. It's also a wonderful place to have a drink at the bar with a snack like pickled quail eggs or Japanese-style popcorn!

Madalin's Table (845-757-2100), 53 Broadway, Tivoli. ($$) Open for dinner Wednesday through Sunday 5–10. Since opening in the spring of 2006, this restaurant, located in the renovated historic Madalin Hotel (see *Lodging*), has become popular with both local residents and travelers to the region—and for good reason. The romantic turn-of-the-20th-century atmosphere transports diners back in time. Attention to detail is evident throughout this establishment: The decor includes tasteful artwork, tin ceilings, rich colors, and beautiful wooden floors. The contemporary American cuisine, expertly prepared by a Culinary Institute chef, blends seasonal fresh ingredients in wonderfully imaginative ways, transforming standard favorites into satisfying creations at reasonable prices. The cornmeal-crusted calamari and house-made mozzarella are a couple of tempting appetizers. A generous portion of grilled skirt steak is served with caramelized onion marmalade. I thoroughly enjoyed dining on the roasted Pacific halibut served on a bed of creamy soft polenta, broccoli rabe, and roasted red peppers. Make sure to save room for the excellent homemade desserts, including gelatos and sorbets. The flourless chocolate torte with caramel sauce and vanilla ice cream is first-rate. Tea drinkers are in for a treat with the variety of imported selections from the owner's Tivoli Tea Company. A tavern room with a lovely oak bar offers several beers on tap as well as a decent selection of wines and single-malt Scotches. Children will be accommodated; in the warm-weather months there is outdoor dining on the spacious veranda. A wonderful addition to the dining scene in Tivoli!

Market Street (845-876-7200), 19 West Market Street, Rhinebeck. ($$) Open Monday through Thursday 5–10; Saturday and Sunday 11–11. Gianni Scappin has created a wonderful venue where you can enjoy a dozen types of tasty Neapolitan-style pizzas at the pizza bar, have a drink and appetizer at another bar, or sit in the main room and dine on baked salmon, roasted natural baby chicken, Berkshire pork chop, or local aged sirloin. There is also an array of interesting sides, as well as pasta dishes and daily specials. I love their lasagna with green noodles. Everything is prepared to perfection, and the service is first-rate.

Max's Memphis Barbecue (845-758-6297), Route 9, Red Hook. ($$) Open Tuesday through Sunday 5–10. Max's Southern regional cooking is based on family recipes and includes traditional barbecue dishes like Memphis John's barbecue pulled pork plate and Big Mike's famous slow-smoked pork ribs. There are crabcakes, baked cedar plank salmon, barbecued chicken, and a veggie sampler from a menu sure to appeal to just about everyone at this lively restaurant. Children welcome.

Mercato (845-758-5879), 61 East Market Street, Red Hook. ($$) Open for dinner Wednesday through Sunday 5–10. This Italian restaurant serves rustic fare in a simple atmosphere with a busy bar. The chef is part of the Buitoni family, renowned for its pasta. The imaginative pasta selections are recommended, but there are also grilled fish, poultry, and meat entrées.

Osaka (845-876-7338), 18 Garden Street, Rhinebeck; and 74 Broadway, Tivoli (845-757-5055). ($$) Closed Tuesday; otherwise open for lunch Monday through Friday 11:30–2:30; dinner served Monday through Thursday 4:30–9:30, Friday and Saturday until 10:30; Sunday 3–9. Eat in or take out from this first-rate, informal Japanese restaurant at two locations in Dutchess County. The sushi is some of the best to be had in the Hudson Valley. The grilled fish daily special and chicken teriyaki are excellent. They are accompanied by soup or salad. There is also a chef's special lunch box of the day for those considering picnic fare. A seat at the bar offers a great view of the sushi chefs at work. Children welcome.

Panzur Restaurant & Bar (845-757-1071), 69 Broadway, Tivoli. ($$) Open for dinner Tuesday through Saturday 5:30–10; late-night menu on Friday and Saturday 10–midnight. Named after chef-owner Rei Peraza's late grandfather, Panzur's contemporary Spanish cuisine is first-rate. It is the kind of place to go for a light dinner including charcuterie and cheese along with a bottle of wine. They cure their own sausages, and the produce is sourced from local farms. Enjoy an array of imaginative tapas, or opt for one of the larger plates that include hanger steak, lamb shank, roasted chicken, and rainbow trout. You won't be disappointed, but be prepared for something different.

Portofino (845-889-4711), 57 Old Post Road, Staatsburg. ($$) Dinner is served daily, except Monday, from 4 in this moderately priced Northern Italian restaurant, which also features Continental specialties. The town of Staatsburg, 5 miles south of Rhinebeck, is a quiet hamlet tucked away from the bustle of Route 9, and this restaurant is worth a stop when passing through the area. A popular place with local residents.

Rhinecliff Hotel Restaurant & Bar (845-876-0590), 4 Grinnell Street, Rhinecliff. ($$) Open for dinner Wednesday through Sunday 5–10:30; Sunday brunch 11–4. This restaurant/hotel (see *Lodging*) is housed in a renovated 1850 building, and the restaurant boasts a mahogany bar and 90-foot wraparound porch. The pine and hemlock floors have been refinished, and the brasserie restaurant serves local, seasonal produce and regional American cuisine. It's only a short walk from the Amtrak train station. The wine list is impressive, and the hotel's restaurant is a good place to stop for a drink, particularly in the warm-weather months. There is often live jazz during brunch and live entertainment during the summer months.

Santa Fe (845-757-4100), 52 Broadway, Tivoli. ($$) Open for dinner daily, except Monday, 5–10. Enjoy traditional Mexican favorites like tacos and enchiladas in a festive atmosphere. The goat cheese in the quesadillas is locally made. Children welcome. Great margaritas with a number of tequilas from which to choose.

Terrapin (845-876-3330), 6242 Montgomery Street, Rhinebeck. ($$) Bistro open for lunch and dinner daily 11:30–11; Friday and Saturday until midnight. Dining room open for dinner daily 5–9. There are actually two restaurants (together they seat 150) housed in one building here—a large, informal bar/bistro and a more formal restaurant with a spacious dining room. A former Baptist church that dates from the 18th century, the cathedral-ceilinged structure has been completely renovated. The New American cuisine featured in the dining room fuses Asian, Southwestern, and Italian flavors. For those who prefer lighter fare, try the innovative bistro menu, with organic-beef burgers, free-range chicken wings, fresh salads, and a create-your-own sandwich option. Children welcome.

The Tavern at the Beekman Arms (845-876-1766), 6387 Mill Street, Rhinebeck. ($$) Open daily for lunch 11:30–4; dinner 4–9; until 10 Friday and Saturday. Sunday brunch 10:30–3:30; dinner 3:30–9. This Hudson Valley institution is housed in the oldest inn in America (see *Lodging*) and dates from 1766. Weekend brunch is particularly good. Children welcome.

Southwestern Dutchess County (Poughkeepsie, Wappingers Falls, Hopewell Junction, Fishkill, Beacon)

Aroma Osteria (845-298-6790), 114 Old Post Road, off Route 9, Wappingers Falls. ($$) Open for dinner daily, except Monday, 5–10, until 11 Friday and Saturday; Sunday 4–9. Lunch served Tuesday through Saturday 11:30–2:30. The rustic Italian cuisine is served in a lovely country setting. There is an extensive wine list and many wines by the glass. The meal begins with rustic bread and olive oil. The antipasti of bruschetta al pomodoro and steaming Prince Edward Island mussels in a broth of extra-virgin olive oil, garlic, and fresh herbs are fine appetizers. Everything is prepared to order. Children welcome.

Artist's Palate (845-483-8074), 307 Main Street, Poughkeepsie. ($$) Open for lunch and dinner Monday through Friday 11–9; dinner only on Saturday 5–10; closed Sunday. This contemporary bistro is housed in an enormous renovated space with a high ceiling, exposed brick walls, dark-wood floors, soft lighting, and an open kitchen. The restaurant is also an art gallery with a bar featuring an affordable wine list and about two dozen wines by the glass. The menu changes every two weeks and includes only what is freshest and in season. The fare is absolutely wonderful at dinner, and lunch is quite good and a bargain for what you are served. I enjoyed an enormous grilled chicken salad with the freshest produce on a summer afternoon. There is also Kobe burger on onion brioche. Make sure to sample the lobster mac and cheese either as an appetizer or entrée. This restaurant is reason enough to venture into downtown Poughkeepsie. Adjoining the restaurant is **Canvas,** which opened in 2012, featuring small plates and accompanying wines. (See *Eating Out.*)

Beech Tree Restaurant (845-471-7279), 1 Collegeview Avenue, Poughkeepsie. ($$) Open for lunch and dinner Tuesday through Saturday 11:30–10; Sunday brunch 11:30–3; dinner 3–10. This is a popular place with both local residents and the Vassar College community. Entrées like grilled shrimp over asparagus risotto with roasted red peppers, or house smoked spare ribs with sweet lime barbecue sauce and new potato salad, are served with a small salad. Brunch selections are imaginative and include crème Anglaise French toast with raspberry-maple syrup; eggs may be accompanied by Jugtown Mountain no-nitrate bacon or rabbit ginger sausage. The bar is a busy place on Friday nights.

The Blue Fountain (845-226-3570), 940 Route 376, Hopewell Junction. ($$) Open Tuesday through Friday 11–10; Saturday 4–11; Sunday 2–9. The Italian American cuisine here includes the standard steaks, seafood, chicken, and veal dishes. My favorites are the *zuppa di pesce*—an enormous platter of shrimp, mussels, clams, scallops, sole, and calamari over linguine—and the steak au poivre. Fresh bread is always accompanied by a serving of roasted red peppers in herbed olive oil. The dining room tables all have a view of a huge fountain. The Marinaro brothers, who operate this establishment, owned a restaurant in the Bronx for many years. There is a good-size children's menu, and families are welcome. Excellent value.

Brasserie 292 (845-473-0292), 292 Main Street, Poughkeepsie. ($$) Open for lunch Monday through Friday 11:30–3; dinner Monday through Saturday 5:30–10; Sunday brunch noon–4; dinner 4:30–8. Enjoy steak tartare, steamed mussels, crispy duck confit, and a full raw bar in this delightful brasserie. The decor includes oversized mirrors, a tin ceiling, red leather booths, and lots of white tile. This is another lively addition to Poughkeepsie's expanding restaurant row.

Brothers Trattoria (845-838-3300), 465 Main Street, Beacon. ($–$$) Open daily 11–10. A tradition in Beacon for the past 15 years, this is a good place to go for pizza and pasta as well as standard Italian favorites, particularly if you are traveling with children. The renovated dining room is lovely, with an informal yet elegant atmosphere and classy decor. Children's menu available.

Bull & Buddha (845-337-4848), 319 Main Street, Poughkeepsie. ($$) Open for lunch Tuesday through Saturday 11:30–2:30; dinner 5–10, Friday and Saturday until 11; Sunday brunch noon–4, with live jazz every week. Closed Monday. An enormous 2,000-pound hand-carved Tibetan Buddha sits peacefully in the center of this fine Asian fusion restaurant, which combines a sushi bar, American steakhouse, and tapas eatery. The menu includes items like pad thai, steamed mussels, and Korean barbecue short ribs. There are eight types of hot and cold sake, as well as some unusual cocktails like a Thai martini. The wine list is decent, and a large selection of beers is offered.

Cafe Amarcord (845-440-0050), 276 Main Street, Beacon. ($$) Open for lunch Tuesday through Sunday noon–3; dinner 5–10; Friday and Saturday until 11. The lobster macaroni and cheese, bacon and blue cheese stuffed burger, and salmon cake sandwich are all favorite choices of mine on the lunch menu. Dinner entrées are pricey, however, and include shellfish stew, sirloin fiorentina, pork chop, and rabbit.

Catalano's Pasta Garden (845-227-7770), 985 Route 376, Brookmeade Plaza, Wappingers Falls. ($$) Open Monday 4–9; Tuesday through Thursday 2–9; Friday and Saturday noon–10; Sunday 1–10. Since 1991 this restaurant has specialized in Italian home cooking, with veal, chicken and seafood dishes, as well as homemade pastas. Family owned and operated with an informal cozy atmosphere, this is the place to go for comfort food Italian-style. Children welcome.

Crave (845-452-3501), 129 Washington Street, Poughkeepsie. ($$$) Open for dinner Tuesday through Saturday 4–10; Sunday 3–9. Three Culinary Institute graduates opened this restaurant in 2009, bringing a touch of Manhattan to Poughkeepsie. In fact, they are located just under the Walkway Over the Hudson. The contemporary American cuisine is excellent, and entrées include coffee ancho rubbed filet mignon, rabbit gnocchi (from a local rabbit farm), and seafood pasta. The honey lavender crème brûlée is phenomenal. In the warm weather, enjoy patio dining. This is a great place for a special occasion.

Il Barilotto (845-897-4300), 1113 Main Street, Fishkill. ($$) Open Monday through Saturday for lunch 11–2:30; dinner 5–10; until 11 Friday and Saturday. Closed Sunday. Enjoy Italian cuisine with a contemporary flair in this trattoria and wine bar, housed in a historic 1870 brick building with a romantic ambience and old-world charm.

Ice House on the Hudson (845-232-5783), 1 Main Street, Poughkeepsie. ($$) Open daily noon–9. Only a short walk from the train station, the historic Ice House is now a beautifully restored restaurant on the Hudson River. The lunch and dinner fare includes wraps, paninis, fish-and-chips, chili, an array of salads, grilled chicken BLT, and much more. Enjoy watching the boats go by while dining alfresco in the summer months. The restaurant opened in 2012 and is becoming a popular place to have a drink or light meal after exploring the Walkway Over the Hudson. Children welcome.

Le Chambord Inn & Conference Center (845-221-1941), 2737 Route 52, Hopewell Junction. ($$$) Open for lunch Monday through Friday 11:30–2:30; dinner daily 6–10; Sunday 3–9. French nouvelle and classical cuisine served in an elegant atmosphere. The baked French onion soup with imported Swiss cheese is a popular first course. Dinner entrées include châteaubriand for two carved tableside, imported English Dover sole with herbs of Provence, and grilled soy-marinated Atlantic salmon with dill remoulade. The "wine jail" features more than 600 selections, some dating from the 1920s, to complement your meal. The sommelier will help you to make a choice if you like. Not recommended for children.

Mary Kelly's Restaurant (845-765-8874), 37 Lamplight Street, Beacon. ($$) Open for lunch and dinner daily 11–10; Friday and Saturday until 11. (Happy hour Monday through Friday 4–7 PM.) This cozy Irish pub filled with booths is located in a brick building near the Hudson River and offers a variety of craft beers. The fare includes pub standards like bangers and mash, corned beef and cabbage, shepherd's pie, and fish-and-chips, as well as wings, nachos, and quesadillas. On Sunday diners may enjoy a full Irish breakfast all day.

Max's on Main (845-838-6297), 246 Main Street, Beacon. ($$) Open for lunch and dinner daily 11:30–10; Friday and Saturday until 11. All the American favorites are served up in hearty portions at reasonable prices here. Enjoy steaks with garlic whipped potatoes, seafood pasta, or beer-battered fish-and-chips. A specialty of the house is chicken breast Santa Fe (marinated and grilled with jack cheese, avocado, and pico de gallo, and served over rice). Children welcome.

O'Sho (845-297-0540), 763 South Road, Poughkeepsie. ($$) Open for lunch Monday through Friday 11:30–2:30; dinner served daily 5–9:30. Hibachi-style chicken and steak are the specialty, but the sushi is also very good. Dine in an elegant Japanese-style steakhouse. Delightful atmosphere. Children welcome.

The Roundhouse at Beacon Falls (845-440-3327), 2 East Main Street, Beacon. ($$$) Open for lunch and dinner daily 11:30–9; Friday and Saturday until 10. Enjoy contemporary American cuisine accompanied by craft beer and fine wine overlooking the falls on Fishkill Creek and Mount Beacon. This restaurant opened in 2012, and it's a wonderful addition to the city.

Sapore Steakhouse (845-897-3300), 1108 Main Street, Fishkill. ($$) Open for lunch Monday through Friday noon–3; dinner daily 5–10. This Manhattan-style steakhouse serves first-rate filet mignon, porterhouse for two, and sirloin entrées, as well as game dishes, including ostrich, venison, and elk. The wine cellar is enormous, with more than 350 different selections. This restaurant was opened in December 2004 by the owner of Il Cenacolo and Cena 2000, both in Newburgh (see *Dining Out* in "Orange County").

Shadows on the Hudson (845-486-9500), 176 Rinaldi Boulevard, Poughkeepsie. ($$) Open Monday through Thursday 11:30–10; Friday and Saturday until 11; Sunday brunch 11–2. This impressive restaurant with both indoor and outdoor seating offers spectacular views of the Hudson River. In fact, you feel as though you are on an enormous cruise ship when dining here. There are seafood dishes, a raw bar, and several different steak and chicken entrées. If you don't have time to dine here, do stop for a drink and take in the fantastic views! Children welcome.

Sukhothai (845-790-5375), 516 Main Street, Beacon. ($$) Open daily 11:30–9:30, until 10:30 Friday and Saturday. Sukhothai was the name of the first capital city of ancient Siam; it also means "dawn of happiness." This charming 50-seat restaurant, housed in a building that dates back to 1818, features exposed brick walls decorated with Thai art. Chef-owner Chira Rabenda and her husband offer a full menu of authentic Thai cuisine in a relaxing, informal atmosphere. For an appetizer, make sure to try the satay (grilled marinated chicken on a skewer served with peanut sauce). Entrées include a choice of several curry dishes as well as a large selection of imaginative fish, chicken, beef, and vegetable dishes, all accompanied by jasmine rice. (There are detailed descriptions of each for those unfamiliar with Thai cuisine.) From traditional dishes like pad thai (a stir-fried noodle dish that is excellent here) to more exotic selections, everything is prepared to order using the freshest ingredients. Children are welcome.

Northeastern Dutchess County (Millerton, Pine Plains, Millbrook, Amenia)

Aurelia (845-677-4720), 3299 Franklin Avenue, Millbrook. ($$) Open after Labor Day through the end of May, Thursday through Sunday noon–9; Friday and Saturday until 10. June through Labor Day, open daily, except Tuesday. This charming Mediterranean restaurant offers a full menu of paninis, burgers, BLTs, salads, and pasta for lunch. Dinner includes grilled fish, short ribs, lamb chops, risotto, and several specials. During the summer it's nice to dine alfresco on the large patio; in the winter, enjoy the cozy atmosphere with a table by the large fireplace.

Charlotte's Restaurant (845-677-5888), Route 44, Millbrook. ($$$) Open for dinner Wednesday through Friday 5–10; for lunch and dinner Saturday and Sunday 11:30–10. Call for winter (November through April) hours. Housed in a 200-year-old converted church, this restaurant, formerly Allyn's, changed hands in 2006. Enjoy American cuisine with a French accent served in two dining rooms—one is elegant, the other more informal. An intimate, cozy bar and large fireplace add to the relaxed country atmosphere. The emphasis is on fresh, local items as well as game in season. New York strip loin steak with pommes frites and mélange of vegetables, and ratatouille or shrimp penne a la vodka, are a couple of popular entrées from the autumn menu. Make sure to save room for dessert. A few tantalizing selections include warm brownie sundae, pumpkin cheesecake with maple bourbon cream, and pear and cherry crisp served with brown sugar crème fraîche. There is outdoor dining in the warm weather months in a charming patio area.

52 Main (518-789-0252), 52 Main Street, Millerton. ($$) Open Tuesday through Thursday 4–10; Friday and Saturday noon–11; Sunday noon–10. ($) This casual tapas and wine bar specializes in small plates that use local products. Two of my favorite dishes here are the spinach and garlic chickpea puree with pita chips and the Kobe beef sliders with red onion confit and Cabrales cheese. You can order fights of wine, something I recommend, and taste a variety of drinks with the various small plates. Don't skip the classic chocolate chip and coconut cookies for dessert!

La Puerta Azul (845-677-AZUL), 2510 Route 44, Millbrook. ($$) Open for lunch and dinner daily 11:30–10; until 11 Friday and Saturday. Enjoy fine authentic Mexican cuisine in a colorful, festive atmosphere. Everything here is homemade, including all the sauces, chips, and tortillas. The diverse menu features a taco bar, fajitas, an array of tempting specialties, and several offerings of lighter fare (even burgers). They serve guacamole tableside, which aficionados of this appetizer should not pass up. A terrific place to go for drinks, with 80 different wines to choose from as well as 40 different beers available (12 on tap). There are intimate private dining rooms and a spacious bar/lounge with a tequila humidor serving 60 varieties of this Mexican treat.

Les Baux (845-677-8166), 152 Church Street, Millbrook. ($$) Open Wednesday through Monday for lunch noon–3; dinner 5–9. Named after Les Baux, a picturesque, medieval village in France, with narrow streets filled with ruins and stone houses, this cozy bistro is run by a Frenchman who worked at a fine restaurant in Les Baux. For lunch or a light dinner, there is a variety of wonderful salads; the onion soup and steamed mussels are superb. For dinner, the French comfort food offered includes grilled sirloin steak, rack of lamb, salmon fillet with mustard sauce, fillet of sole, and pork tenderloin. The restaurant opened in 2003 and quickly became popular with Millbrook residents.

Manna Dew (518-789-3570), 54 Main Street, Millerton. ($$) Open for dinner Wednesday through Monday 5–10. Open late every night for drinks, desserts, and cheese. The excellent modern American cuisine here is sprinkled with international favorites as well. Only the freshest local ingredients are used here: They have a good-size garden in back of the restaurant and use their own vegetables in the summer months. On Friday and Saturday nights there is live jazz, folk, and blues, but call to confirm the performance schedule. A delightful restaurant with an informal atmosphere—and one of my favorites.

Number 9 (518-592-1299), 53 Main Street, Millerton. ($$) Open Tuesday through Saturday 5:30–10. Located in the Simmons' Way Village Inn (see *Lodging*). The New American menu with French and Austrian touches is filled with inventive cuisine from a chef who has worked at some of Manhattan's finest restaurants. The offerings continually change, and almost everything is created from farm-fresh local ingredients. The choices range from crispy black sea bass and hanger steak to Wiener schnitzel and build-your-own burger. Don't skip dessert here: The pumpkin soufflé and dark chocolate molten cake with pistachio ice cream are truly amazing.

Serevan Restaurant (845-373-9800), 6 Autumn Lane (Route 44), Amenia. ($$) Open for dinner Thursday through Monday 5–10. This is the place to savor the exotic flavors of Middle East and Mediterranean cuisine, in a relaxing atmosphere with an open kitchen and fireplace. The name comes from Lake Serevan in Armenia. A signature dish is the pan-seared branzino with cumin-scented hummus, lemon, and fresh dill. The lamb with apples, cardamom, and steamed couscous is a house specialty. In warm weather, enjoy garden dining. Children welcome.

Stissing House Restaurant & Tavern (518-398-8800), 7801 South Main Street, Pine Plains. ($$) Open for dinner Thursday through Sunday 5:30–10; Saturday and Sunday brunch noon–3. Housed in a historic structure that has been a tavern for more than 100 years, this establishment offers American regional cuisine in an informal, relaxed atmosphere. Their thin-crust wood-fired-oven pizza is excellent. (I loved the one with truffle oil, something I had never had on pizza before—it was phenomenal.) Every entrée is prepared to order, beautifully presented, and delicious, whether you order a burger or grilled salmon. Children welcome.

Southeastern Dutchess County (Pawling, Wingdale, Poughquag)

Il Compare (845-832-3411), 34 Old Route 22, Wingdale. ($$) Open for dinner Wednesday through Saturday 5–10; Sunday 4–9. Enjoy regional Italian favorites in a casual country setting. The varied menu features everything from veal parmigiana, chicken marsala, and *zuppa di pesce* to filet mignon, fresh Chilean sea bass, and halibut. The calamari is first-rate. Desserts change weekly, but the tiramisu, a house specialty, is always available. Outdoor dining on the terrace in the warm-weather months. Children's menu.

The Lodge (845-832-7477), 3115 Pleasant Ridge Road (County Route 21), Wingdale. ($$) Open Thursday through Saturday 5–10. Formerly known as Guidetti's restaurant, this enormous stone building is located on 24 pastoral acres on a century-old estate. The Continental cuisine with an Italian flair includes steaks, seafood, and pasta dishes, as well as several specials.

McKinney and Doyle Fine Foods Café (845-855-3875), 10 Charles Colman Boulevard, Pawling. ($$) Open for lunch Tuesday through Friday 11:30–3; dinner Wednesday through Saturday 5–9:30; Sunday 5–9; Saturday and Sunday brunch 9–3. This old-fashioned, high-ceilinged storefront café has exposed brick walls, a mix of booths and tables, and lots of local memorabilia in the decor. The eclectic cuisine includes such unusual treats as grilled shrimp with Thai peanut sauce over angel-hair pasta, and breast of duck with peppercorns and applejack-soaked figs. An excellent bakery operates out of the café, so don't skip dessert. Sour cream apple pie and raspberry linzer torte are just a couple of the tempting creations.

Rambler's Rest (845-478-2223), 2578 Route 55, Poughquag. ($$) Open daily 11–10 (bar open until 2 AM). This neighborhood Irish pub serves up traditional favorites like shepherd's pie along with steak and seafood entrées in an informal atmosphere. Children are welcome.

EATING OUT

Northwestern Dutchess County

Antonella's Restaurant (845-229-1200), 4246 Albany Post Road (Route 9), Hyde Park. ($$) Open Tuesday through Sunday 11–10. Wonderful thin-crust and Sicilian pizza are served up here, as well as all the Italian specialties. Save room for the cannolis for dessert! Terrific family restaurant with authentic home cooking.

Bread Alone Bakery & Café (845-876-3108), 45 East Market Street, Rhinebeck. ($) Open daily 7 AM–6 PM; dining room open daily 8–4. The homemade soups, hearty sandwiches, and terrific breads offered here make this informal eatery a renowned stop among locals for breakfast, lunch, or take-out. Needless to say, the desserts are wonderful. Children welcome.

Bread & Bottle (845-758-3499), 7496 South Broadway, Red Hook. ($) Open Tuesday through Thursday and Sunday noon–9; Friday and Saturday noon–10. Closed Monday. This interesting combination bakery/wine bar specializes in artisan breads, paninis, salads, and antipasti boards (meat, cheese, or vegetable), along with cake, cookies, and brownies for dessert. There is an extensive wine list, several beers on tap, and live music on weekends. New in 2012, its delightful contemporary atmosphere is attracting a diverse clientele.

Calico Restaurant & Patisserie (845-876-2749), 9 Mill Street, Rhinebeck. ($$) Open for lunch Wednesday through Saturday and Sunday for brunch 11–2. Dinner served Wednesday through Saturday 5–8. This cozy spot is great for an elegant lunch. I recommend the smoked salmon with capers and the chicken-salad sandwich. The pastries are excellent. Children welcome.

Cranberry's at Tilley Hall (845-229-1957), 1 West Market Street, Hyde Park. ($) Open daily, except Monday, 7–4. This hub of Hyde Park serves baked goods, light lunches, and coffee and tea in a cozy café atmosphere. Owner Kathy Larson is always there to make sure the light fare here is prepared to your liking. The menu also offers a range of lunch items, including tuna salad over a garden salad, turkey Cobb salad, chili, French onion soup au gratin, hummus with fresh vegetables in a wrap, and a Reuben sandwich. Children welcome.

Eveready Diner (845-229-8100), Route 9, Hyde Park. ($) Open Sunday through Thursday 7 AM–1 AM; Friday and Saturday 24 hours. This retro 1950s-style diner is difficult to miss when traveling along Route 9 in Hyde Park. The Food Network featured their delicious pancakes (my favorite menu item), but this community oasis is known locally for its comfort food, particularly dishes like meat loaf and mashed potatoes or macaroni and cheese. Make sure to order apple pie, apple crisp, or applesauce, all made on the premises with fruit fresh from the owner's orchard. Soups are hearty and tasty, as well. Children's menu.

Garden Street Café (845-876-2005), 24 Garden Street, Rhinebeck. ($) Open Monday through Saturday 10–4. Located at Rhinebeck Health Foods, this cheerful eatery serves up healthful fare to eat in or take out. There are tasty soups, salads, burritos, wraps, sandwiches, shakes, and organic juices. After shopping in town, this is a quiet place to relax and refresh.

Historic Village Diner (845-758-6232), 7550 North Broadway, Red Hook. ($) Open daily 6 AM–9 PM. Housed in a Silk City dining car, made in New Jersey from the 1920s to the '50s, this village landmark has been a local oasis for decades. If you want lunch or dinner, try a few of the house specialties, which include the half-pound Black Angus burger, the Silk City Special (grilled turkey with bacon), or the roast turkey with stuffing. Breakfasts are hearty and quite good, too. Children welcome.

Holy Cow (845-758-5959), 7270 South Broadway, Red Hook. ($) Open year-round, Monday through Saturday 11–10; Sunday until 9. The line can be long here on hot summer nights for a good reason: They have some of the best soft-serve ice cream you will find anywhere. The prices are super inexpensive, too. If you have a craving for a sundae, shake, or cone, this is the place to go. There are myriad toppings to choose from as well. Those traveling with children shouldn't miss this place!

Hyde Park Brewery (845-229-8277), 514 Albany Post Road, Hyde Park. ($) Open Monday and Tuesday from 4 PM; Wednesday through Saturday 11–10; Sunday brunch 11–2 and dinner 4–10. They brew their own beer here (approximately 1,000 barrels per year), and there are six different kinds to choose from, both light and dark varieties. (Notice the huge bags of malt barley stacked by the restrooms.) The fare includes creative international specials at reasonable prices. My favorite menu item is the vegetarian pita sandwich, which is grilled portobello mushrooms layered with mozzarella, roasted red peppers, and pesto mayo. A great stop for lunch, it's conveniently located across the road from the home of FDR. Children welcome.

J & J's Gourmet Cafe (845-758-9030), 1 East Market Street, Red Hook. ($) Open Monday through Friday 7–4, Saturday until 5. Summer hours are slightly extended. Jen Stokes, a Culinary Institute graduate, and her husband own and operate a cheerful, spacious café where a hearty breakfast, lunch, or early supper may be enjoyed. The Hudson Valley club sandwich, Mediterranean wrap, roast beef club, mac and cheese, and barbecued chicken are just some of the offerings. There is something for everyone here, including vegetarians and vegans. Children welcome.

Luna 61 (845-758-0061), 55 Broadway, Tivoli. ($) Open for dinner daily, except Wednesday, 5–9; Sunday brunch 9:30–4. The organic vegetarian cuisine here includes an eclectic mix of flavors using the freshest ingredients. The salads, chili, and veggie burgers are wonderful. Sandwiches are offered on the dinner menu (a couple of choices are falafel or PLT, a vegetarian rendition of BLT substituting portobello mushrooms for bacon and dressed with wasabi mayonnaise). There is a café atmosphere here that makes this a wonderful stop for those seeking healthful, tasty cuisine. Organic beers and wines. Children welcome.

Matchbox Café (845-876-3911), 6242 Route 9, Rhinebeck. ($) Open Wednesday through Monday 9:30–8. Everything in this small, cozy eatery is prepared to order by chef-owner Sam Cohen. The fries and onion rings, a house specialty, are hand-cut and twice fried for extra crispness. There are eggs, breakfast nachos, French toast, burgers, and grilled chicken or veggie sandwiches, to name just some of the offerings. Make sure to save room for dessert. Cohen's Bakery in Manhattan is renowned for having some of the best cookies in the city, and they're now available in Rhinebeck. I can attest to the fact they are special—and filling!

Rusty's Farm Fresh Eatery (845-758-8000), 5 Old Farm Road, Red Hook. ($) Open for lunch and dinner daily 11–8; Friday and Saturday until 9. There is something for everyone here, from vegans to carnivores, and all the food is prepared using local ingredients. A 35-seat eatery with a casual atmosphere, Rusty's has fresh salads, wraps, paninis, grass-fed burgers, and subs. Owner Rusty's motto is "eat good, feel good." The prices are exceedingly reasonable for the high quality here.

Salvatore's Original Pizza (845-758-1111), 7588 North Broadway, Red Hook. ($) Open daily 11–11. Pizza aficionados will appreciate this eatery, where you can find terrific New York–style thin-crust, Sicilian, and gluten-free pizza. I suggest trying Grandma's Pizza, the house specialty. Calzones, stuffed rolls, sandwiches, pastas, salads, and heros are also available. A great spot for informal family dining.

Samuel's (845-876-5312), 42 East Market Street, Rhinebeck. ($) Open daily 8–6. In July and August until 8 weekdays; 10 on weekends. This small confectionery and coffee shop is the perfect place to enjoy a cup of high-quality coffee, tea, or hot chocolate after browsing the stores in town. The cookies and biscotti are delicious. Children will be delighted by the attractively displayed penny candy and gourmet jelly beans. There is also a variety of truffles, hand-dipped chocolates, and sugar-free sweets.

Taste Budd's Chocolate and Coffee Café (845-758-6500), 40 Market Street, Red Hook. ($) Open daily 7 AM–9 PM. The fare here includes sandwiches, soups, wraps, veggie burgers, and lots of vegan options. Capital City Coffee Roasters coffee is served here, and there is a list of more than 50 different caffeinated and decaf teas. The baked goods (muffins, scones, and vegan desserts) are baked on the premises, and some of the other pastries are obtained locally. A gathering place for Bard students, with an atmosphere reminiscent of a 1960s coffeehouse. Children welcome.

Tavola Rustica in the Courtyard (845-876-6555), 51 East Market Street, Rhinebeck. ($) Open Wednesday through Sunday 10–5. This is the perfect place to stop for a drink, dessert, or light lunch after walking around town. There are sandwiches, salads, and all kinds of Italian specialties. Many of the items are sourced locally, and everything is prepared meticulously. There is a warm, inviting atmosphere, and alfresco dining in the warm weather months. Delightful!

2 Taste Food & Wine Bar (845-233-5647), 4290 Albany Post Road (Route 9), Hyde Park. ($) Open for dinner Tuesday through Sunday 5:30–10. Owners Hallie Quinones Katz and Faith Cuccia opened this 63-seat eatery in 2011 with executive chef Stephen Smrcina, formerly of the renowned Old Drovers Inn. There is steak, salmon, crabcakes, burger with smoked Gruyère on a Kaiser roll, vegetarian dishes, and a small-plates menu. Most items are sourced locally. The wine and beer flights are a wonderful way to sample different drinks with the various plates. Desserts are made daily on the premises and shouldn't be ignored. Try the hazelnut mousse or chocolate terrine with strawberries. A welcome addition to the Hyde Park dining scene!

Two Boots (845-758-0010), 4604 Route 9G, Red Hook. ($) Open daily, except Tuesday 11:30–9. The two boots referred to are Italy and Louisiana and this eatery features informal Cajun-Italian fare (pizza, salads, pasta, catfish, jambalaya, and more) in an informal atmosphere with funky folk art décor. First opened in the East Village of Manhattan in 1987 by two filmmakers who loved pizza, beer, and New Orleans specialties, there are now another fifteen Two Boots restaurants throughout New York City, as well as in Baltimore, Jersey City, Los Angeles, and Nashville.

Southwestern Dutchess County

Amedeo's Brick Oven Pizzeria (845-343-4563), 476 Lauer Road, LaGrangeville. ($$) Open Monday through Saturday 11–10; Sunday 3–9. The authentic Neapolitan pizza served here (no slices, just pies) is some of the best in the region, and local residents have been patronizing the restaurant since 1989. High-quality ingredients and crispy crust distinguish their specialty, and although the pizza is pricier than what you will find at most local eateries, it's definitely worth it. In addition to brick-oven pizza and calzones, there are soups, salads, antipasto, calamari, and pasta dishes. Diners will enjoy the informal atmosphere with an open kitchen; a great family destination.

A Perfect Landing Café (845-677-5010), 30 Airway Drive, LaGrangeville. ($) Open for breakfast and lunch Thursday through Sunday 7:30–3. Perfectly ordinary fare, but it's served at the Sky Acres Airport, where diners can watch planes arrive and depart. A fun place to take small kids or just hang out!

Apple Pie Bakery Café at the Culinary Institute (845-905-4501), 1946 Campus Drive (off Route 9), Hyde Park. ($) Open Monday through Friday 7:30–5. Enjoy fine, fresh soups, salads, sandwiches, and pizzas at exceedingly reasonable prices in this eatery, where students in baking and pastry arts programs run the show. It's a wonderful stop for breakfast or lunch, as well as take-out. Children welcome.

Babycakes (845-485-8411), 1–3 Collegeview Avenue, Poughkeepsie. ($) Open Tuesday through Saturday 8 AM–10 PM; Sunday 8–4. Closed Monday. Located near the Vassar College campus, this popular eatery gets extremely busy at lunchtime. They are known for their burgers, salads, and signature sandwiches, including enticing offerings like the portobello eggplant wrap, BLT on ciabatta bread, and mozzarella pesto melt. Breakfast choices include omelets, brioche French toast, and tofu Tex-Mex (salsa, peppers, and soy cheese in a flour tortilla). There is live music on Friday and Saturday nights.

Beacon Falls Café (845-765-0172), 472 Main Street, Beacon. ($) Open Monday 11:30–4; Thursday and Friday 11:30–9; Saturday 10–9; Sunday 10–4. Closed Tuesday and Wednesday. This informal American bistro serves a particularly good brunch. The pancakes, frittatas, and bananas Foster French toast are recommended. There are salads, Reubens, and panini for lunch; the bacon blue burger is delicious. Portions are on the large side.

Café Bocca (845-483-7300), 14 Mount Carmel Place, Poughkeepsie. ($) Open Tuesday through Sunday 8–8. Chef-owner Erik Morabito's lively café is truly a hub of the community. All the Italian favorites are available here—pizza, pasta, paninis, eggplant or chicken parmigiana, and more—at reasonable prices. Even if you just want a coffee, this is a good choice, and it is located close to the Walkway Over the Hudson. There is often entertainment on weekends, and Erik makes everyone feel welcome. Some of the best cannoli and sfogliatelle you will ever have is next door at **La Deliziosa Pastry Shoppe** (845-471-3636), 10 Mount Carmel Place, a throwback to another era. So make sure to stop in for dessert. You won't be disappointed! They have been in business for decades.

Caffè Aurora (845-454-1900), 145 Mill Street, Poughkeepsie. ($) Open Monday 10–5; Tuesday through Thursday 8:30–6; Friday and Saturday 8:30–7. This café offers the ambience of Little Italy—located in the quaint, quiet Mount Carmel area of downtown Poughkeepsie. Enjoy cannoli, eclairs, butter cookies, and probably the best cappuccino and espresso in the county. In warm weather, have dessert at the outdoor tables and listen to the regulars speaking animatedly in Italian. This neighborhood café is one of the best things about Poughkeepsie! Children welcome.

Crumb Bakery (845-765-8080), 157 Main Street, Beacon. ($) Open Thursday through Monday 9–4; Sunday 10–3. Two Culinary Institute graduates opened this bakery in 2010, and the cakes and pies are first-rate. They expanded to include a café. Breakfast, lunch, and brunch offerings include egg sandwiches on handcrafted breads, hearty soups, and fresh salads. Vegan and vegetarian options are always included on the menu. There is outdoor dining in the warm-weather months.

Cup and Saucer Tea Room (845-831-6287), 165 Main Street, Beacon.

($) Open Monday and Wednesday 11–3; Thursday through Sunday until 5. Closed Tuesday. There are seasonal high teas, and reservations must be made in advance. This Victorian tearoom, decorated with teatime accessories throughout, serves up hot grilled sandwiches, veggie and grilled chicken salads, quiche, soups, and desserts. A specialty of the house is the portobello club sandwich.

DD's Pizza (845-452-1754), 300 Hooker Avenue, Poughkeepsie. ($) Open Wednesday through Monday 11–5. For some of the freshest pizza you can find in the county, head to Dominick's place. He and his brothers are always behind the counter in the open kitchen, preparing your pizza before your eyes—and their mother is always in the back, helping out. I enjoy the salads here (always made to your order, never in advance). It's truly a family business, and the decor hasn't changed since they opened over 30 years ago. Children welcome.

El Charrito (845-471-6193), 26 Academy Street, Poughkeepsie. ($) Open daily 10–9. You will find authentic Mexican food at exceedingly reasonable prices in this simply decorated eatery. The three women cooks serve up fantastic Mexican home-cooked meals—tacos, enchiladas, and quesadillas are just a few of the offerings. This is definitely the place to go for some of the best Mexican food to be had in the Hudson Valley. It's also a great stop for families with young children.

Ella's Bellas Gluten-Free Bakery (845-765-8502), 418 Main Street, Beacon. ($) Open Tuesday 8–2; Wednesday through Saturday 8–4; Sunday 10–3. The treats here are both healthy and delicious, and you won't be able to tell everything is gluten-free, so indulge!

Gino's Restaurant (845-297-8061), 1671 Route 9, Wappingers Falls; in Lafayette Plaza, 1.6 miles south of the Galleria. ($) Open daily, except Monday, noon–10. Enjoy Italian-style home cooking in this family-owned and family-operated casual dining spot. They offer a range of pizzas, pasta dishes, heros, and sandwiches in addition to Italian favorites like lasagna, veal parmigiana, calamari, and many more. Children welcome.

Homespun Foods (845-831-5096), 232 Main Street, Beacon. ($) Open Monday through Friday 11–5; Saturday and Sunday 8–5. This is a great laid-back spot for breakfast or a quick lunch. Offerings at lunchtime include pulled pork quesadilla, shrimp and sweet potato muffaletta, smoked trout salad, and black bean burger.

Julie's Restaurant (845-452-6078), 49 Raymond Avenue, Poughkeepsie. ($) Open Monday and Thursday 7 AM–8 PM; Tuesday, Wednesday, Friday, and Saturday until 3; Sunday 8–2. Julie and her husband serve up wonderful breakfast wraps (try the Vassar or Greek wraps, my favorites) along with pancakes, omelets, and great oatmeal. Lunches include burgers, salads, sandwiches, and soups accompanied by homemade macaroni salad or coleslaw. This is a popular local spot with a loyal following. Children welcome.

Kavos (845-473-4976), 4 North Clover Street, Poughkeepsie. ($) Open Monday and Wednesday through Friday 11–8:30; Saturday noon–8:30; Sunday noon–7. Closed Tuesday. This cheerful eatery serves Greek specialties, including excellent pork and chicken gyros made with no processed meats or added preservatives. Enjoy fresh salads, tabouli, tzatziki, and baklava for dessert. There is outdoor dining during the warm-weather months.

Lola's Café (845-471-8555), 131 Washington Street, Poughkeepsie. ($) Open Monday through Friday 7–4. There are some wonderful variations on the usual sandwich selections here. Tropical curried-chicken wrap and marinated portobello-mushroom panini are just a couple of the intriguing selections offered for lunch. This is a good stop if you're planning to pick up take-out for a picnic or just want to grab something quickly.

Longobardi's Restaurant & Pizzeria (845-297-1498), 1574 Route 9, Wappingers Falls, in Imperial Plaza. ($) Open daily 11:30–9:30. This informal eatery is a perfect stop for lunch or dinner when shopping on Route 9. One of my favorite dishes here is the grilled chicken salad; I also like their *pasta e fagioli* soup. They offer the full range of Italian favorites, including pizza, pasta, and calzones, as well as seafood, veal, and eggplant dishes. Everything is prepared to order. Children's menu.

Maya Café & Cantina (845-896-4042), 448 Route 9, Fishkill. ($$) Open daily 11 AM–midnight; Saturday and Sunday brunch 11–3. Live music on Friday and Saturday nights. Authentic Mayan cuisine (from Guatemala and the Yucatan region of Mexico) served in a colorful, upbeat ambience. Adorning the walls are striking murals hand-painted by local artists. In addition to tacos, enchiladas, and quesadillas, there is always a variety of interesting specials. The red snapper marinated with fresh lime and topped with olives, jalapeños, tomatoes, and cilantro is a house specialty. Another dish to try is the boneless pork marinated in orange juice with Mayan spices and slow cooked in banana leaves. Save room for the chimi banana dessert (cheesecake and banana wrapped in a tortilla, deep-fried, then drizzled with caramel, chocolate syrup, and whipped cream). And don't forget to order one of their phenomenal margaritas! Children's menu.

Palace Diner (845-473-1576), 294 Washington Street, Poughkeepsie. ($) Open daily 24 hours. This well-established gathering place near Marist College, just off Route 9, has been a mainstay of the community. It's popular for lunch among local attorneys and politicians. In addition to the usual diner fare, there are Greek and international dishes, as well as an array of daily specials. The portions are generous, and the desserts are quite good. Children welcome.

Paula's Stone Cottage Wine Bar (845-896-9463), 1158 Main Street, Fishkill. ($$) Open Tuesday through Saturday 5–midnight; Sunday 4–10. This wine bar opened in 2011 and has become a gathering place for oenophiles, artists, and musicians. There are usually over 50 wines available by the glass, and an assortment of small plates including olives, cheese, fruit, and focaccia. Outdoor seating in the garden is available in warm weather.

Poppy's (845-765-2121), 184 Main Street, Beacon. ($) Open Thursday through Monday noon–8. If you love burgers (even if you are a vegetarian and want a veggie burger), this is the place to go. The beef comes exclusively from Kiernan Farm in Gardiner (Ulster County) and is 100 percent grass fed. There are several toppings to choose from, and you can design your burger just the way you want it. The fries are done to perfection. Those traveling with children, take note!

Rosticceria Rossi & Sons (845-471-0654), 45 South Clover Street, Poughkeepsie. ($) Open Monday through Friday 7:30–6; Saturday 8–5. Closed

Sunday. This fantastic deli/eatery has all the imported Italian goodies you can imagine, and they serve up some of the best sandwiches in the county. Everything is made fresh before you, and there is outdoor seating in warm weather. Avoid the lunch hours if you don't want to wait on line!

Saigon Café (845-473-1392), 6A LaGrange Avenue, off Raymond Avenue near Vassar College, Poughkeepsie. ($) Open Monday through Saturday for lunch 11:30–3; dinner 5–9:30; Sunday 5–9. This is a casual dining spot that has Vietnamese cuisine, and it's quite good. Try the Imperial rolls with shrimp, fresh mint, and cilantro. There is an excellent selection of chicken, beef, seafood, and vegetarian dishes. For those who have never dined on Vietnamese cuisine, this is a good place to try it.

Soul Dog (845-454-3254), 107 Main Street, Poughkeepsie. ($) Open Thursday through Saturday 11–8. You can enjoy a variety of hot dogs, including preservative-free and vegetarian varieties, as well as chili, soup, sides, desserts, and gluten-free items made on the premises. A new take on the hot dog experience!

Taco Gold (845-471-3223), 553 Main Street, Poughkeepsie. ($) Open daily 8 AM–9 PM. This informal Mexican restaurant features excellent food at rock-bottom prices. There are tacos, enchiladas, and several Mexican specialties, as well as *tortas* for dessert. The daily specials are a good value. Children are welcome.

Tiramisu (845-227-8707/4877), 810 Route 82, Hopewell Junction. ($) Open daily 10–10; dinner begins at 4. This family-oriented eatery features brick oven–baked pizzas of all kinds, terrific pasta dishes, and the excellent chicken Tiramisu ($16.95), which includes chicken breast, roasted red peppers, onions, and artichokes accompanied by pasta in a light marinara sauce. Relaxed, informal atmosphere. Children are welcome, and the reasonable prices are hard to beat.

Tomato Café (845-896-7779), 1123 Main Street, Fishkill. ($) Open Monday through Friday 11–9; Saturday 8 AM–10 PM; Sunday 8–4. This terrific café has an enormous menu with imaginative creations to please just about any taste. There are eggplant cakes, a specialty of the house (fantastic and highly recommended), wings, salads, sandwiches, pizzas, calzones, and pastas. Everything is prepared to order, and the portions are generous. A great family dining spot!

Vintage Café (845-440-3005), 512 Main Street, Beacon. ($) Open Wednesday through Friday 9–2; Saturday and Sunday 9–3. This old-fashioned café with vintage decor will transport you back to an earlier era (at least while eating breakfast or lunch!). The eclectic menu includes muffins, scones, pancakes, grilled peanut butter and banana sandwich, quiche, beef stew, turkey and avocado wrap, and mushroom risotto. The prices are exceedingly reasonable; note that they take cash only.

Northeastern Dutchess County

Babette's Kitchen (845-677-8602), 3293 Franklin Avenue, Millbrook. ($) Open Monday and Wednesday through Saturday 7–6; Sunday 8–5. This eatery has some of the best healthful gourmet sandwiches, salads, soups, wraps, coffee, tea, and baked goods in the region. It's my favorite place to eat in Millbrook, and the owner, Beth, prepares everything to order. Children are welcome, and prices are reasonable for the high quality.

Coyote Flaco Mexican Bistro (845-605-1200), 82 Tompkins Road, Verbank. ($) Open Sunday through Thursday 11:30–9; Friday and Saturday until 10. Located near Millbrook, this informal eatery specializes in authentic Mexican cuisine. The menu includes quesadillas, nachos, enchiladas, fajitas, and tapas, to name just some of the offerings. Their margaritas are excellent. Children are welcome.

Happy Days Café (845-677-6244), Washington Hollow Plaza, 2517 Route 44, Millbrook. ($) Open for breakfast, lunch, and dinner daily 7 AM–9 PM. This is a fun place to take kids. The decor is 1950s, and the food is American favorites: burgers, wraps, steak, and seafood.

Harney's Tea Room (518-789-2121), 13 Main Street, Millerton. ($) Store is open Monday through Saturday 10–5; Sunday 11–4. Tea Room is open Monday through Saturday 11–4; Sunday noon–3. Harney's Tea Room is a lovely eatery—part of the store where you can purchase literally hundreds of fantastic loose teas. My favorite, the cinnamon spice tea, is excellent either iced or hot. There is always something brewing to be sampled. The day I enjoyed lunch there, the Tea Room restaurant was serving farm country soup, two salads, and about eight intriguing sandwich selections served on whole wheat or white baguettes, baked fresh daily. A couple of the sandwich choices were roast beef, cheddar cheese, house horseradish sauce, and radish slices, or smoked turkey, cheddar, tomato, whole grain mustard, and baby spinach. The sandwiches were reasonably priced. There is even peanut butter and jam for the little ones.

Irving Farm Coffee House (518-789-2020), 44 Main Street, Millerton. ($) Open Monday through Thursday 7–5; Friday 6 AM–8 PM; Saturday 7 AM–10 PM; Sunday 8–5. There are breakfast sandwiches, frittata of the day, granola and yogurt, waffles, fresh baked muffins, scones, and pastries for breakfast. Also enjoy curried chicken salad sandwich, roast turkey sandwich, the great Santini panini, quiche, soup, and salads. They even serve wine and beer at this coffeehouse, which brews some of the best coffee you will find just about anywhere in the Hudson Valley. This eatery is a hub of Millerton, and Meryl Streep and other local celebrities have been spotted here.

Lia's Mountain View (518-398-7311), 7685 Route 82, Pine Plains. ($) Open for lunch and dinner daily, except Monday, 11:30–9; Sunday 4–9. Italian home cooking combined with a lovely view of the mountains. Try spiedini, white pizza, calzones, and the excellent desserts. Wednesday is pasta night, and on Thursday there are complete dinner specials at very reasonable prices. Children welcome.

Millbrook Diner (845-677-5319), 224 Franklin Avenue, Millbrook. ($) Open daily 6 AM–9 PM. This small diner is a local hangout renowned for their club sandwiches, Reubens, burgers, and wraps. The fare is simple yet hearty. Kids will be comfortable here.

Red Devon Market Cafe (845-868-3175), 108 Hunns Lake Road, Bangall. ($$) Open Thursday through Monday 8–4. (Dinner is served in the restaurant Friday and Saturday 6–9:30 and Sunday 5–8.) The café serves a variety of sandwiches and salads made from the finest locally sourced organic ingredients. The baked goods are excellent. This is a good place to get take-out for a gourmet picnic as well. Although thefarm-to-table dinners are only served Friday through Sunday, they are first-rate. Executive Chef Sara Lukasiewicz, a Culinary Institute graduate, has made Red Devon a landmark of fine dining in Dutchess County.

Taro's (518-789-6630), 18 Main Street, Millerton. ($) Open for lunch and dinner Tuesday through Sunday 11:30–9; dinner Monday 4:30–9. First opened in 1989, this basic, informal Italian eatery serves grinders (subs), calzones, eggplant Florentine, pastas of all kinds, pizza (Sicilian, white, and New York style), as well as 23 types of gourmet pizzas and over a dozen kinds of fresh salads. The portions are huge, and the prices are exceedingly reasonable. They accept cash and checks only—no credit cards. Children welcome.

Vineyard Grille & Café at Millbrook Winery (845-677-8383), 26 Wing Road, Millbrook. ($) Open Memorial Day weekend through mid-October, Saturday and Sunday noon–3. This covered pavilion surrounded by vineyards is a lovely place to stop for lunch if you're driving through the countryside around Millbrook. The menu includes burgers, grilled chicken sandwiches, salads, desserts, and, of course, wine by the glass. Make sure to take a tour while you are there since their wine is some of the best in the region.

Wild Hive Farm Cafe (845-266-5863), 2411 Salt Point Turnpike (take Salt Point exit off Taconic Parkway and travel a half mile east), Clinton Corners. ($) Open Thursday 5:30–9; Friday 8 AM–9 PM; Saturday and Sunday 8–4. This bakery-café offers a full line of baked and milled products. Their rosemary garlic loaf and raisin walnut bread are both favorites of mine. There are local grains, organic meats, dairy products, honey, and maple syrup, as well as food-related events. Like a beehive, the place is bustling with activity, particularly on weekends!

Southeastern Dutchess County

Beekman Square Restaurant (845-223-3401), 2515 Route 55, Poughquag. ($) Open for breakfast, lunch, and dinner daily 6 AM–6:30 PM. Early in the day enjoy three-egg omelets, chocolate-chip or banana-walnut pancakes, cinnamon-raisin French toast, or Belgian waffles at this neighborhood restaurant, which specializes in international cuisine. Their French onion soup, grilled chicken Caesar salad, terrific quesadillas, focaccia sandwiches (they make their own breads here), and Beekman Square burger (with bacon, onions, mushrooms, and cheese) are my favorites for lunch. Bourbon Street ribs marinated in homemade light barbecue sauce, as well as steaks, broiled fish, and pasta, are all reasonably priced. Children welcome; there is a children's menu.

Heinchon's Old Farmhouse and Ice Cream Parlor (845-878-6262), Route 22 near Aikendale Road, Pawling. ($) Open daily noon–10; closed during the winter months. Since 1923, this local ice-cream parlor has been dishing out treats from a yellow farmhouse. The original dairy produced milk for Pawling homes, and in 1987 they started producing ice cream. There are dozens of flavors and toppings here, including Hudson Harvest (vanilla churned with local raspberries, whole almonds, and chocolate chips) as well as Mud Pie (coffee ice cream with fudge ripple and Oreo cookies). There are waffle cones, cups, thick shakes, egg creams, and sundaes. The ice cream is produced at the old dairy farm just a mile away from the eatery. Outdoor tables here are a nice place to sit and relax with a sweet treat. Children will love this place!

✷ Entertainment

Dutchess County offers an enormous amount of theater, dance, and stand-up comedy, and the choices keep growing. So after you have enjoyed an excellent repast at one of the region's fine restaurants, enjoy some first-rate entertainment.

THEATER & DANCE **Bardavon 1869 Opera House** (845-473-2072; www.bardavon.org), 35 Market Street, Poughkeepsie. Open year-round. First named the Collingwood Opera House, this elegant concert hall was constructed in 1869 and is the oldest continuously operating theater in New York State. The dramatic dome ceiling has sheltered everything from movies and rock concerts to ballet and dramatic theater. Mark Twain, Frank Sinatra, Sarah Bernhardt, John Phillip Sousa, and Al Pacino are among the entertainers who have performed on the 816-square-foot stage. After being added to the National Register of Historic Places in 1978, the Bardavon has undergone more than $3 million worth of renovations. It is the perfect place to enjoy a symphony, drama, musical, old-time movie, contemporary musician, or comedian. It's worth checking the website to see what is being showcased when you'll be visiting Dutchess County.

Center for Performing Arts at Rhinebeck (845-876-3080; www.centerforperformingarts.org), Route 308, Rhinebeck. Open year-round. Call for a performance schedule. This multipurpose cultural and education center features dramatic plays, musicals, dance, concerts, lectures, staged readings, and workshops. There are children's shows, as well. Check the website for a performance schedule.

Cocoon Theatre (845-876-6470; www.cocoontheatre.org), 6384 Mill Street (Route 9), Rhinebeck, is a nonprofit educational arts organization presenting drama and dance performances suitable for all ages year-round. Check the website for a full schedule.

County Players Falls Theatre (845-298-1491; www.countyplayers.org), 2681 West Main Street, Wappingers Falls. Four or five productions are offered annually by this community-theater group. The work usually consists of traditional Broadway fare. The theater is large, the seats are comfortable, and the production I attended was light entertainment well done.

Fisher Center for the Performing Arts at Bard College (845-758-7900; www.fishercenter.bard.edu), 30 Campus Road, Annandale-on-Hudson. Internationally distinguished performing arts center, designed by renowned architect Frank Gehry, has two theaters offering music, opera, drama, and dance performances (see *To See*). There are tours of the Sosnoff Theater Monday through Friday at 2.

Kaatsbaan International Dance Center (845-757-5106; www.kaatsbaan.org), 120 Broadway, Tivoli. Open year-round. This performance center for all types of dance as well as a working retreat center is dedicated to the growth, advancement, and preservation of professional dance. Located in a renovated space on a spectacularly scenic 153-acre setting (a former horse farm) overlooking the Hudson River and Catskill Mountains, Kaatsbaan—Dutch for "playing field"—presents an array of multiethnic dance companies. The former Callendar House farm, developed by the Livingston family in the 18th century and turned into a horse farm by the Osborne family, is now home to three dance studios, one of which serves as a 160-seat public theater. The historic barns and cottage were designed at the turn of the 20th century in the shingled Arts and Crafts style. There are open rehearsals here in addition to workshops, world premieres, and performances. Check the website for a complete schedule.

Powerhouse Theater at Vassar College (845-437-7235; www.powerhouse.vassar.edu), Summer Theater at Vassar College, 124 Raymond Avenue, Poughkeepsie. June and July only, Tuesday through Saturday 8 PM; Saturday and Sunday 2 and 8. Admission fee. Each summer since 1985, New York Stage and Film, in conjunction with Vassar, has presented new plays premiered in a professional-theater venue. The name is derived from the actual powerhouse on the Vassar campus, built in 1912 to accommodate the college's changeover from gas to electric power. In 1973 the original structure was reinvented as a black-box theater and renamed the Hallie Flanagan Davis Powerhouse Theater, in memory of the legendary dramatist who created the Experimental Theater at Vassar College. Past productions have been of excellent quality and have featured the likes of Juliana Margulies, Kyra Sedgwick, David Strathairn, Jill Clayburgh, and John Heard, to name some of the actors who have been a part of this dynamic venue. The Powerhouse Theater also offers free outdoor Shakespeare. Don't miss seeing a production here if you are in the Dutchess County area during the summer months. Check the website for a detailed schedule of performances.

River Valley Rep Theatre (845-575-3133; www.rivervalleyrep.com), Marist College Nelly Goletti Theatre (located on the third floor of the Student Center building), 3399 North Road, Poughkeepsie, is a professional company in summer residence at Marist since 2009. The season usually runs from mid-June through mid-August, and high-quality comedic and dramatic productions are offered in a beautiful theater. Check the website for a complete schedule.

MISCELLANEOUS VENUES Art along the Hudson celebrates the arts in Beacon and Poughkeepsie every month, the second Saturdays of the month in Beacon and ArtHop Tours on the third Saturday of the month in Poughkeepsie, when art galleries and cultural venues feature art openings, receptions, music, and theatrical events. Sister cities Kingston and Newburgh observe the first and last Saturdays respectively.

Bananas Comedy Club (845-462-3333; www.bananascomedyclub.com), Clarion Hotel, 2170 Route 9, Poughkeepsie. Shows are usually Friday at 8 and 9:30 PM; Saturday 8 and 10:30 PM. See live stand-up comedy with performers from television, films, Las Vegas, and Atlantic City in this hotel nightclub that draws a good-size local following.

The Chance (845-471-1966; www.thechancetheater.com), 6 Crannell Street, Poughkeepsie. This downtown nightclub showcases national musical acts, including rock 'n' roll, country, R&B, and blues. There is usually entertainment on weekend evenings, but check the website in advance for the schedule. Showtimes vary.

Drive-In Movie Theaters: Hyde Park Drive-In (845-229-4738), 4114 Albany Post Road (Route 9), Hyde Park. This theater has been open since 1949 and is located on 12 acres with a full-service snack bar and radio sound. They are open every night, April through September, and Tuesday is bargain day (when the $8 adult admission is reduced to $5). **Overlook Drive-In** (845-452-3445), 126 DeGarmo Road, Poughkeepsie, is owned by the same company as the Hyde Park Drive-In and is also open every night April through September.

Rhinebeck Chamber Music Society (845-876-2870; www.rhinebeckmusic

.org), 6436 Montgomery Street, Rhinebeck. Concerts are held at the Church of the Messiah in town every month from October through May. Check the website for dates and times. String quartets and chamber ensembles are featured.

Towne Crier Café (845-855-1300; www.townecrier.com), 130 Route 22, Pawling. Open Wednesday through Sunday evenings, this club presents live folk, jazz, blues, and zydeco artists, with an array of performers, theater, vaudeville, and children's concerts. At press time, it was announced that this beloved music venue, in business since 1972, is going to be moving to 381 Main Street, Beacon, in the summer of 2012. The phone number will remain the same; their website will have the new hours of operation and a full schedule of events.

Upstate Films (845-876-2515; 1-866-FILM-NUT; www.upstatefilms.org), 6415 Montgomery Street (Route 9), Rhinebeck. Open year-round. There are two to three films daily in the two theaters here (matinees on holidays, weekends, and some Fridays), and you won't find the usual mall offerings. Provocative international cinema is featured, including foreign, independent, documentary, and animated films. Guest speakers appear regularly—filmmakers, scholars, and critics—often to discuss their work after it is screened. This is a local treasure, especially in these days of mostly meaningless commercial movies. Upstate has a large local following, so get there early since the theaters are rather small.

✷ Selective Shopping

ART & CRAFTS CENTERS/GALLERIES **Albert Shahinian Fine Art** (845-876-7578), 22 East Market Street (third floor), Rhinebeck. This gallery has changing exhibitions and specializes in the work of Hudson Valley artists. Open Thursday through Saturday 11–6, Sunday noon–5, and by appointment or chance.

Arrowsmith (845-677-5687), 3788 Route 44, Milllbrook. Open daily, except Tuesday and Sunday, 10–5:30. This is one of the few remaining places to purchase custom steel furniture, lamps, and other accessories made at their own forge. They also operate a gift shop at 3275 Franklin Street in Millbrook.

Barrett Art Center (845-471-2550), 55 Noxon Street, Poughkeepsie, exhibits distinguished Hudson River School and other American artists.

Blue Cashew Kitchen Pharmacy (845-876-1117), 6423 Montgomery Street, Rhinebeck. Open daily 11–6, until 7 on Saturday. This gem of a store offers some of the most distinctive items you can imagine, along with the classics in cutlery, cookware, tools and gadgets, barware, and small appliances. Sean and Gregory have assembled a terrific array of items that will delight cooks and bakers of all stripes!

Calsi's General Store (845-373-7735), Main Street, Wassaic. Open Monday through Friday noon–5; Saturday and Sunday 8–5. There is everything you could possibly imagine in this general store—grocery items; dairy products; organic vegetables; whole grains; livestock feed for sheep, horses, and llamas; seaweeds; vitamins; sugarless cookies and chocolates; herbs; soaps; and goose eggs (March through June). Sharon Kroeger, the proprietor, serves local consumers as well as bicyclists traveling around nearby Rattlesnake Mountain!

Country Thistle (845-635-8642), Key Food Plaza, 1600 Main Street (Route 44), Pleasant Valley. Open Monday through Saturday 10:30–5:30; Thursday until 7. Closed Sunday. There are wonderful cards and gifts in this lovely emporium that combines traditional and contemporary items. Owner Susan Holland took over this shop in 2008 and has made interesting changes, creating a great place to find just the right unusual gift. No need to go to the mall!

Cunneen Hackett Cultural Center (845-486-4571; www.cunneen-hackett.org), 12 Vassar Street, Poughkeepsie, has theater, dance, and art shows on its annual schedule. The center is housed in two restored Victorian buildings, and regional art and artists are usually featured.

Gilmor Glassworks (518-789-6700; www.gilmorglass.com), 2 Main Street, Millerton, is open daily 10–5. Their handblown glass has been made at this working studio since 1977. Enjoy watching the bowls, ornaments, vases, and special pieces being created before your eyes. Check the website for the glassblowing schedule.

Howland Cultural Center (845-831-4988; www.howlandculturalcenter.org), 477 Main Street, Beacon, sponsors exhibits, concerts, and workshops year-round in a late-19th-century building designed by famed architect Richard Morris Hunt.

Hudson Beach Glass (845-831-3116), 162 Main Street, Beacon. Open Monday through Saturday 10–6; Sunday 11–6. There are four artists whose hand-cast glass, using an ancient process, is exhibited here. Both sculptural and functional objects are on display and for sale.

Hunt Country Furniture (845-832-6522), 16 Dogtail Corners Road, Wingdale. Open year-round, Monday and Wednesday through Saturday, 10–5; Sunday noon–5. You will find all kinds of handcrafted wood furniture here. Webatuck (as this site was known) was once a village of artists' studios and workshops along the Ten Mile River. Today visitors will enjoy the lovely locale of this shop once bustling with several craftspeople.

J. E. Heaton Jewelers (845-677-1500), 3297 Franklin Avenue, Millbrook. Open Wednesday through Saturday 10–5; Sunday 1–5. They sell estate and fine jewelry here, and some of the antique pieces are quite unusual. Make sure to stop in when you are walking around town!

Millbrook Variety (845-677-6085), 45 Front Street, Millbrook. Open Monday through Saturday 7–6. This is the place to stop for homemade ice cream, party supplies, great gifts, greeting cards, office supplies, and books about the Hudson Valley. There is something to please everyone in this delightful emporium! Owner Diane Moretti is always on the premises to help you find just the right gift.

Mill Street Loft (845-471-7477; www.millstreetloft.org), 45 Pershing Avenue, Poughkeepsie, is a multicultural arts-educational center that sponsors shows, workshops, and a unique art camp for kids.

No Sugar (845-876-6040), 47 East Market Street, Rhinebeck. Open daily 11–7. This wonderful boutique specializes in the latest clothing styles for women, children, and babies, as well as shoes and all kinds of accessories. Monique, the owner, has a terrific eye for selecting just the right items that are flattering on any figure!

Paper Trail (845-876-8050), 6423 Montgomery Street, Rhinebeck. Open Monday through Saturday 11–6; until 5 on Sunday. Serine Hastings and Maureen Missner have the best cards you will find just about anywhere. In addition there are beautiful invitations, wrapping paper, gift books, and dozens of unique items that will delight just about anyone. This is a must-stop in the busy village of Rhinebeck!

Phoenix Pottery (845-855-5658), 34 Coulter Avenue, Pawling, is open by appointment only. Wheel-thrown stoneware for the kitchen and a choice of everything from lamps to mugs in an array of glazes. Classes offered for both adults and children.

Pure Mountain (845-876-4645), 23 East Market Street, Rhinebeck. Open daily, except Tuesday, 10–6. Enjoy a free "tasting tour" of various balsamic vinegars and olive oils that will transport you from the vineyards of Italy through the olive groves of Spain, California, Chile, and beyond. Family owned and operated by cousins Zak and Charlie, there are over 30 varieties of oils and vinegars, something to please every taste.

Steel Plant Studios at Marist College (845-575-3000, ext. 2308), Beck Place, Poughkeepsie. Open Monday through Saturday noon–5. There are excellent changing exhibits at this art gallery located on the campus of Marist College. It is definitely worth a stop.

Sugar Plum Boutique (845-876-6729), 71 East Market Street, Rhinebeck, is open daily 10–6, with unique sterling and gemstone jewelry as well as clothing from England and California, all at great prices.

Tivoli Artists Co-Op (845-757-2667), 60 Broadway, Tivoli. Open Friday 5–9; Saturday 1–9; Sunday 1–5. There are changing monthly exhibits by the 40 artists that belong to this co-op. If you are in Tivoli on a weekend, make sure to stop in.

Winter Sun & Summer Moon (845-876-3555), 12 East Market Street, Rhinebeck. Open Monday through Saturday 10–5; Sunday 11–4. They carry distinctive shoes, women's clothing, jewelry, craft items, and natural makeup and skin care products in these two adjoining shops on the main shopping street in town. While there are several places to visit in Rhinebeck, don't pass up this one!

AUCTIONS AND ANTIQUES

Lovers of antiques and collectibles will have a field day in Dutchess County, where it seems that every village and hamlet boasts a selection of fine antiques shops. Clocks, vintage clothing, fine china, Hudson River School paintings, and rare jewels are all waiting for a home, and it's easy to spend an afternoon looking for that one-of-a-kind treasure. The search is made even easier at antiques centers that offer a cluster of dealers under one roof and regular hours year-round.

The Annex Antiques and Accessories (845-758-2843), 23 East Market Street, Red Hook, is filled with Victorian and country furniture, jewelry, collectibles, and Americana. **George Cole Auctions, Inc.** (845 758 9114; www.georgecoleauctions.com), 7578 North Broadway, also in Red Hook, holds auctions every Saturday beginning at 5 PM.

Beekman Arms Antique Market & Gallery (845-876-3477), Route 9, is a multidealer antiques emporium located behind the Beekman Arms Hotel (see *Lodging*); open daily 11–5. **Hammertown** (845-876-1450), 6240 Montgomery Street, Rhinebeck, and 3201 Route 199, Pine Plains (518-398-7075), has country wares, folk art, and primitives. Farther south at the **Hyde Park Antiques Center** (845-229-8200), 4192 Route 9, Hyde Park, there are more than 50 dealers and a large range of specialty collectibles and antiques. They are open daily 10–5. **Hopewell Antiques Center** (845-

221-3055), 876 Route 82, Hopewell Junction, offers 21 dealers in one store, and they are open year-round, daily 11–5. **Hudson Valley Auctioneers** (845-831-6800; www.hudsonvalleyauctioneers.com), 432 Main Street, Beacon, conducts auctions of fine European and American antiques year-round. Check their website for a schedule.

Going east in the county, the **Ole Carousel Antique Center** (845-868-1586), 6208 Route 82, Stanfordville, offers a large collection of books, records, and miniatures. In Millbrook there are two centers: the **Millbrook Antiques Mall** (845-677-9311), 3301 Franklin Avenue, has many dealers of 18th-century furniture; the **Millbrook Antiques Center** (845-677-3921), 3283 Franklin Avenue, has nearly 50 different "mini shops." These shops are all open Monday through Saturday 11–5; Sunday noon–5. **Millerton Antiques Center** (518-789-6004), 25 Main Street, Millerton, has 36 dealers under one roof. They are open daily, except Wednesday, 10–5 with extended hours on the weekends.

✷ Special Events

March: **Railroad Exposition** (845-297-0901), Mid-Hudson Civic Center, 14 Civic Center Plaza, Poughkeepsie. There are trains galore here, along with vendors and exhibitors from all over the Northeast.

Last Sunday in April, Memorial Day weekend, July 4th weekend, first weekend in August, Labor Day weekend, Columbus Day weekend, and first Sunday in November: **Stormville Airport Antique Show & Flea Market** (845-221-6561; www.stormvilleairportfleamarket.com), 428 Route 216, Stormville, features more than 600 vendors with antiques, collectibles, arts and crafts, and apparel—new merchandise as well as old treasures are to be found here. Free. This event is held rain or shine from dawn to dusk.

May: **Antique Car Show and Swap Meet** (845-876-4001; www.rhinebeckcarshow.com), Dutchess County Fairgrounds, Route 9, Rhinebeck. Admission fee. This is one of the largest weekend car shows in the Northeast, including hot rods and custom vehicles on Saturday and pre-1977 unmodified antique/classic cars on Sunday. There is a car corral and swap meet, handcrafts building, and food court. **Rhinebeck Antiques Show** (845-876-4001; www.rhinebeckantiquesfair.com), Dutchess County Fairgrounds, Route 9, Rhinebeck. Admission fee. Saturday 10–5; Sunday 11–4. There are nearly 200 exhibitors, with an emphasis on furniture, folk art, decorative accessories, vintage jewelry, clothing, and clocks. Wide range of prices. **Mid-Hudson Balloon Festival** (845-831-6917), Waryas Park and other sites, Main Street, Poughkeepsie. Free, but there is a fee for rides. Hot-air balloon flights are given morning (6 AM) and evening (6 PM), weather permitting. This is nice family entertainment, with rides for the kids and a variety of vendors. This annual event is sponsored by the Dutchess County Regional Chamber of Commerce. **Music in the Parks** (845-229-8086; www.dutchesstourism.com), at both Vanderbilt National Historic Site in Hyde Park and Staatsburgh State Historic Site in Staatsburg. From Memorial Day weekend through August, there is a series of free outdoor concerts. This is the time to get the blankets and lawn chairs, pack a picnic, and enjoy the evening overlooking the Hudson River with the sounds of the area's fine bands. Check the website for a schedule.

June: **St. Anthony Street Festival** (845-454-0340), 11 Mount Carmel

Place, Poughkeepsie. Our Lady of Mount Carmel parish kicks off the summer season with this festival of plentiful Italian food, live music, children's activities, and games of chance. Free. Thursday through Sunday evenings 5–midnight.

July: **Bard Summerscape** (845-758-7900), Bard College, Annandale-on-Hudson. This performing-arts festival includes music, dance, opera, and film. It runs from early July through mid-August, so call for a schedule of events.

August: **Hudson Valley Bottle Show** (845-221-4259), Elks Club, 29 Overocker Road, Poughkeepsie. Admission fee. Open 9–3. Bottle dealers from throughout the Northeast display and sell a wide variety of antique, collectible, rare, and unusual bottles and Depression glass. **Dutchess County Fair** (845-876-4001; www.dutchessfair.com), County Fairgrounds, 6550 Spring Brook Avenue, Rhinebeck. Held toward the end of the month, Tuesday through Sunday 10 AM–midnight. Admission fee. For the biggest—and some say the best—county fair in the Hudson Valley, a stop at this event is in order. The fairgrounds include large display buildings, show arenas, a racetrack, food stands, and more. Plenty of livestock is displayed, and name entertainment is offered. The colorful, noisy midway attracts all ages, and the rides will please the adventurous and the not-so-adventurous alike.

September: **Hudson River Valley Ramble** (518-473-3835; www.hudsonvalleyramble.com). More than 140 guided walking, hiking, kayaking, biking, and equestrian events are held in 10 counties during the third weekend in September. There are several sites in Dutchess County with planned activities, including Stony Kill, Harlem Valley Rail Trail, the Poet's Walk, Tivoli Bays, Pawling Trail, Appalachian Trail, and Stissing Mountain. Check the website for a schedule of events and locations. **Celtic Day at Mills Mansion** (845-889-8851), 75 Mills Mansion Road, Staatsburg. Admission fee. Open 11–5. This Celtic celebration on the Hudson includes pipe bands, Celtic music, dance workshops, sheepdog herding, clan tent displays, and food.

DUTCHESS COUNTY FAIR

Dutchess County Tourism

Hudson Valley Wine Festival (845-658-7181; www.hudsonvalleywinefest.com), Dutchess County Fairgrounds, 6550 Spring Brook Avenue, Rhinebeck. Admission fee. Open Saturday 11–6; Sunday 11–5. There are several wine tastings, gourmet delicacies, farmers' markets, cooking demos, and live music at this annual celebration of the region's wines. There are also Finger Lakes wineries in attendance. **Art Studio Views** (845-876-7578; www.artsnortherndutchess.org). Visit the private studios of over 25 Dutchess County artists; most are rarely open to the public. The studios are open on Saturday and Sunday of Labor Day weekend. Check the website for hours and further details.

Mid-September through October: **Hahn Farm Fall Festival** (845-266-5042; www.hahnfarm.com), 1331 Netherwood Road, Salt Point, is held every weekend mid-September through October, Saturday and Sunday 11–5. Children will enjoy the hayrides, corn maze, pony rides, and all kinds of family fun at this annual harvest celebration. Artisans will demonstrate spinning and weaving and sheep shearing. The pumpkins for sale are always plentiful, and they come in orange, white, and warty varieties! Make sure to check the website for a schedule of special events.

October: **Crafts at Rhinebeck** (845-876-4001), Dutchess County Fairgrounds, 6550 Spring Brook Avenue, Rhinebeck. Admission fee. Open Saturday 10–6; Sunday 10–5. This juried crafts show has more than 350 artists, who work in glass, wood, leather, ceramics, metal sculpture, and jewelry. There is a specialty food section, wine tasting, music, hayrides, and children's activities. **Rhinebeck Antiques Fair** (845-876-4001), Dutchess County Fairgrounds, 6550 Spring Brook Avenue, Rhinebeck. Admission fee. Open Saturday 10–5; Sunday 11–4. See nearly 200 exhibitors of furniture (both formal and country), folk art, jewelry, and quilts at this annual gathering. **NYS Sheep & Wool Festival** (845-876-4001), Dutchess County Fairgrounds, 6550 Spring Brook Avenue, Rhinebeck. Admission fee. Open Saturday 10–5, Sunday until 4. See 175 vendors, including wool artists, culinary displays, spinning and weaving demonstrations, and sheep and alpaca sales. **Gem & Mineral Show** (845-454-5800), Mid-Hudson Civic Center, 14 Civic Center Plaza, Poughkeepsie. Admission fee. Open Saturday and Sunday 11–5. There are usually around 30 dealers at this annual show, which features gemstones, minerals, fossils, fluorescent minerals, and jewelry. There are museum-quality specimens from New York State Academy of Mineralogy. **Gathering of Old Cars** (845-889-8851), Staatsburgh State Historic Site, 75 Mills Mansion Road, Staatsburg. Admission fee. Open 11–4. This get-together for antique autos at Mills Mansion, sponsored by the Red Hook Car Club, is a wonderful way to visit this site and enjoy its marvelous location on the Hudson River. **Beacon Sloop Club's Pumpkin Festival** (845-831-6962), Metro North train station, 1 Ferry Plaza, Beacon. Free. Open noon–6. Enjoy music, environmental displays, food, and pumpkins at this riverfront festival.

November: **Sip & Sign for the Holidays with Hudson Valley Authors** (845-677-8383; www.millbrookwine.com), Millbrook Winery, 26 Wing Road, Millbrook. Free. Held the second Saturday in November 1–4, this festive event provides a rare opportunity to meet 15–20 famous authors who will sign their books for holiday gifts—and personalize them however you like. There are gourmet snacks to accompany Millbrook's fine wines.

December: **Historic Hyde Park Christmas Celebration and Open House** (845-229-9115), Vanderbilt Mansion, Route 9, Hyde Park. This delightful annual event is usually held the first weekend in December. An array of activities, music, refreshments, phenomenal cookies, and gorgeous holiday decorations delight visitors at the open-house festivities that continue throughout the month of December. For anyone with young children, this is a must! **Sinterklaas in Rhinebeck** (845-758-5519), an old Dutch tradition in the Hudson Valley, is an amazing festival held throughout the town on the first Saturday in December. Do not miss this celebration if you have young children—or even if you don't! There are parades, performances of all kinds, open houses, a children's starlight parade, art exhibits, Dutch treats, and, of course, Santa Claus. Dutchess County resident Jeanne Fleming has been coordinating this expanding event since the 1980s.

Also, a number of tree lightings, parades, and open houses take place at the historic sites and great estates throughout the county during December. Do check the website of the Dutchess County Promotion Agency (www.dutchesstourism.com) for a complete list of these events if you are visiting during the holiday season.

Putnam County 11

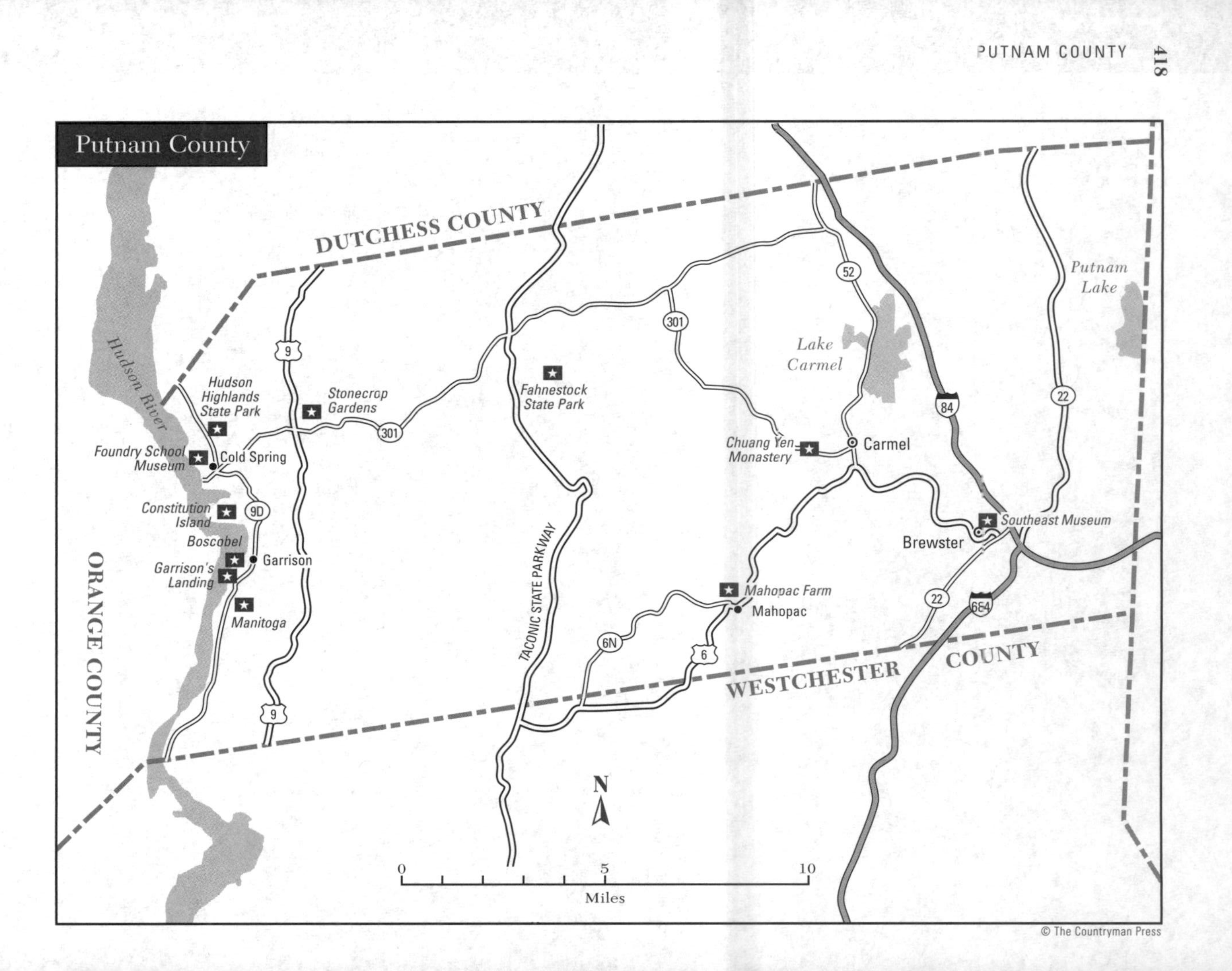
Putnam County
DUTCHESS COUNTY
ORANGE COUNTY
WESTCHESTER COUNTY
Hudson River
Hudson Highlands State Park
Foundry School Museum
Cold Spring
Constitution Island
Boscobel
Garrison's Landing
Garrison
Manitoga
Stonecrop Gardens
Fahnestock State Park
TACONIC STATE PARKWAY
Chuang Yen Monastery
Carmel
Lake Carmel
Putnam Lake
Southeast Museum
Brewster
Mahopac Farm
Mahopac
9
9D
301
52
84
22
684
6
6N
N
0
5
10
Miles
© The Countryman Press

PUTNAM COUNTY

One of the gateways to the Hudson Highlands, Putnam County offers splendid river views, lots of outdoor entertainment, and a chance to see small-town America before it disappears. In Cold Spring the tiny shops and riverside gazebo are charming reminders of a more leisurely past. Up north, the Federal mansion called Boscobel (which came within hours of being demolished) has been restored to its former elegance. A spring walk through the gardens there offers thousands of flowers in full color, blooming with scent. There are also acres of wetlands, lakes, forests, and meadows in Putnam, beckoning the hiker, walker, and nature lover. A very different outdoor environment was created at Manitoga, where industrial designer Russel Wright constructed Dragon Rock, a unique home built into the wall of a quarry. In Putnam you can drive along rustic roads, smell apple blossoms, see houses that date from before the Revolution, stop at an art gallery, or just laze away an afternoon watching the Hudson. Route 9D from the Bear Mountain Bridge goes past many historic areas. Route 9 is the old Albany Post Road and has been in constant use for more than two centuries. Just an hour from Manhattan, Putnam County can seem a century away, with a pace and a grace all of its own.

GUIDANCE **Putnam County Visitors Bureau** (845-225-0381; 1-800-470-4854), 110 Old Route 6, Building 3, Carmel 10512; www.visitputnam.org.

GETTING THERE *By car:* Interstate 84, Route 684, the Taconic State Parkway, and Routes 9 and 9D all go through the county.

By train: **Metro North** (Harlem and Hudson lines) stops in Brewster, Garrison, and Cold Spring.

MEDICAL EMERGENCY **Putnam Hospital Center** (845-279-5711), Stoneleigh Avenue, Carmel.

✷ Villages

Cold Spring. This lovely river town was founded in the 18th century and, according to local folklore, got its name from George Washington's comment on the water found at a local spring. Cold Spring received an economic boost in the 19th century when it became the site of one of the largest iron foundries in the United States. The town's West Point Foundry produced everything from weapons to some rather unusual furniture, some of which can be seen at the Tarrytown home of Washington Irving in Westchester County.

On Main Street you can visit "antiques row," where many dealers own or share shops that specialize in everything from rare books and vintage clothing to knick-knacks and brass beds. The best way to explore the village is to wander up and down Main Street. There are some shops that should not be missed: **Art & Antiques Downtown & Gallery, Cold Spring Antiques Center, The Country Goose, Reigning Dogs & Cats Too,** and **Payning by Caryn.** If you continue down Main Street to the railroad tracks, you will find a plaque commemorating Washington's visit. The bandstand here was constructed for riverside concerts—now it provides a wonderful place to look across the river to Storm King Mountain, which, true to its name, is the center of many storms. At the corner of Main and West streets, follow West Street south to Market to see the Chapel of Our Lady. This one-room Greek Revival chapel was built in 1834 for workers at the foundry; it is the oldest Roman Catholic church in the region and was one of the most popular subjects for painters and artists of the Hudson River School. The chapel looks across the river, but you may have to wait to get in on weekends because it's popular for weddings.

Garrison. The Landing, which overlooks the Hudson River at the railroad station, is the town's hub. Walk down to the riverside gazebo, which was used as the set for the filming of *Hello, Dolly!* The Landing is also home to the Garrison Art Center (845-424-3960; www.garrisonartcenter.org), which holds exhibits, auctions, workshops, and special events, including an art fair, throughout the year. The center is open Tuesday through Sunday 10–5.

✷ To See

Chuang Yen Monastery (845-228-4287; www.baus.org), 2020 Route 301, Carmel. Open year-round, daily 9–5. The monastery houses the largest Buddhist statue in the Western Hemisphere, as well as many other unique shrines, statues, and pieces of art. The library has more than 70,000 books, the majority of them Buddhist texts. A morning meditation session and seminar is held every Sunday, followed by a vegetarian lunch. Visitors are welcome to participate.

Foundry School Museum of the Putnam Historical Society (845-265-4010; www.pchs-fsm.org), 63 Chestnut Street, Cold Spring. Open March through December, Wednesday through Sunday 11–5. Admission fee. The original Foundry School served the children of Irish immigrants and apprentices who were employed at the West Point Foundry; today the 1820 building is a small museum. The exhibits offer a look at local history, including the Civil War artillery weapons (the Parrott gun was developed by a West Point officer) that were constructed here, and there are also small collections of paintings and furniture. There is even a horse-drawn cutter, once owned by Julia Butterfield, who is said to have received the sleigh from the tsarina of Russia. The **West Point Foundry Preserve** is past the museum, at the south end of Chestnut Street and Route 9D (at bridge). This 87-acre landscape is listed on the National Register of Historic Places. The restored wetlands here may be viewed from a short loop trail that follows Foundry Brook.

An exciting future lies ahead for this public park since it has been selected to participate in a new federal program involving green landscape design, construction, and management, the Sustainable Sites Initiative (SITES). The goal is to develop a world-class outdoor museum dedicated to the ironworks' role in America's emergence as an industrial superpower. Soon the park will be part of this national effort to create sustainable landscape and revolutionize the way public spaces are created.

Putnam Art Council Belle Levine Art Center (845-278-0230; www.putnamartscouncil.com), 521 Kennicut Hill Road, Mahopac. Open year-round, Tuesday through Friday 9–3; Sunday 1–4. Fee charged for workshops. This cultural organization has a gallery with annual and changing exhibits, as well as workshops in visual and performing arts for children and adults. Concerts, lectures, and special events are offered throughout the season.

Southeast Museum (845-279-7500; www.southeastmuseum.org), 67 Main Street, Brewster. Open April through December, Tuesday through Saturday 10–4. Suggested donation. This Victorian-style building houses a small museum with an eclectic local collection. There are permanent exhibits on the Borden Dairy Condensory (condensed milk was developed by a Putnam County resident), the construction of the Croton Water System (a project remarkable for engineering innovations), the American circus, Harlem Line Railroad, and a large collection of minerals from local mines. Local history is also a focus of this museum.

HISTORIC HOME Boscobel Restoration (845-265-3638; www.boscobel.org), 1601 Route 9D, Garrison-on-Hudson. Open April through December, Wednesday through Monday 9:30–5. Admission fee. Standing on a bluff overlooking the Hudson River, the country mansion known as Boscobel looks as if it had spent all of its 200 years in peace and prosperity. But appearances can be deceiving. Statesman Morris Dyckman, a Loyalist of Dutch ancestry, began building the mansion in 1805 for himself and his wife, Elizabeth Corne Dyckman, and their family. But he died before it was completed. Designed in the Federal style, Boscobel was furnished with elegant carpets, fine porcelain, and furniture from the best workshops in New York. The house remained in the family until 1888; from then on it had various owners, including the federal government. In 1955 the government decided it no longer needed Boscobel, and the house was sold for $35 to a contractor, who stripped it of many of its architectural details and sold them off. Local people were so incensed that they tracked down the sections that had been sold; they salvaged and restored the other parts of the house, and, finally, purchased land on which to reerect the building. Today visitors to Boscobel will see the house as it was, complete with elegant staircase, fine decorative objects, and period furniture made by New York craftspeople. (It is requested that visitors wear broad-heeled walking shoes to tour the home, which helps to preserve the floors and rugs.) There is now an exhibition gallery at Boscobel featuring paintings by Hudson River School artists Frank Anderson, Samuel Colman, Jasper Cropsey, David Johnson, Rhomas Rossiter, and John Ferguson Weir. Changing exhibits are planned throughout the season.

Boscobel's grounds are enchanting, as well. At the Gate House you can see the home of a middle-class family of the era and explore the Orangerie, a 19th-century greenhouse. In spring and summer the gardens at Boscobel blaze with thousands of flowers, including tulips, daffodils, roses, pansies, and wildflowers. Special events are held all season, such as a rose festival, concerts, candlelight holiday tours, and workshops in horticultural and American crafts. From mid-June to

August, there is the annual Hudson Valley Shakespeare Festival, with several different plays performed on the grounds in a tent (call 845-265-9575 or check www.hvshakespeare.org for schedule).

HISTORIC SITES **Carmel Historical Center** (845-628-0500), 40 McAlpine Avenue, Mahopac. Open March through November, Sunday 2–4 and by appointment. Free. An interesting stop for history buffs, the center was donated by a general of the Civil War. Displays include a general store, an exhibit on local history, and decorative accessories of the period. A large collection of local newspapers is housed here as well.

Old Southeast Church (845-279-7429), Route 22 (Old Croton Turnpike), Brewster. Open June to Labor Day, Sunday 2–5. Free. Founded in 1735 by Elisha Kent, this is the church that most of the tenant farmers of the area attended in the 18th century; the present building was built in 1794. Guides in period dress take visitors through the structure.

✷ To Do

FARMERS' MARKETS, FARM MARKETS, AND PICK-YOUR-OWN FARMS Putnam may not be a large county, but from spring through fall there are a few places to pick your own crops and weekly farmers' markets where organic meats, fruits, vegetables, and breads are available for purchase. Travelers will also find local honey, maple syrup, and wine to take home, delicious reminders of the bounty of the Hudson Valley.

Farmers' Markets

Brewster (914-671-6262), 208 East Main Street (Routes 22 and 6), Brewster. Open mid-June through mid-November, Wednesday and Saturday 9–2.

Cold Spring (845-265-3611), 44 Chestnut Street (Route 9D), Cold Spring. Open May through October, Saturday 8:30–1:30.

Putnam Valley (845-528-0066), 729 Peekskill Hollow Road (Tompkins Corners Methodist Church), Putnam Valley. Open mid-June through September, Friday 3–7.

Farm Markets, Pick-Your-Own Farms, and Places of Interest

Green Chimneys Farm (845-279-2995, ext. 383), 400 Doansburg Road, Brewster, is open year-round, Saturday and Sunday 10–3, and offers organically grown vegetables raised by the students of the Green Chimneys School.

Maple Lawn Farm Market (845-424-4093), 2461 Route 9, Garrison, is open daily March through December and stocks seasonal produce, baked goods, cider, and Christmas trees.

Niese Maple Farm (845-526-3748), 146 Wiccopee Road, Putnam Valley. Open year-round, Wednesday through Friday 10–4; Saturday and Sunday 9–4. Since 1892, seven generations of the Niese family have been producing maple syrup and honey on this farm. During March through November there are pancake breakfasts and lunches on weekends.

Philipstown Farm Market (845-265-2151), 3091A Route 9, Cold Spring, offers fruit, vegetables, flowers, imported foods, and Christmas trees in season; open March through December, daily 8–7.

Ryder Farm (845-279-4161), 400 Starr Ridge Road, Brewster, has 125 acres of organically grown raspberries on its pick-your-own family farm, in operation for more than 200 years. Open May through November (call for hours since the season is weather dependent).

Salinger's Orchards (845-277-3521), 230 Guinea Road, Brewster, has a wide selection of local fruit and vegetables; a cider mill and bakery offer tempting treats to visitors. They produce about 3,000 fruit pies every year baked in a glass-enclosed kitchen at this market. Make sure to take one home: There are apple, blueberry, strawberry, and peach. All are delicious, and the price is exceedingly reasonable. Open year-round, daily 9–6.

Saunders Farm (845-424-3150), 853 Old Albany Post Road, Garrison. Open year-round by appointment. They specialize in certified Angus beef at this 140-acre cattle farm. Every year for a few weeks in October there is an outdoor sculpture exhibition on the farm with approximately 60 large works of art. Some hang from trees, and others are scattered throughout the open fields: They are all for sale. This creates an unusual outdoor museum, and it's worth a stop.

Tilly Foster Farm (845-228-4265), 100 Route 312, Brewster. Open year-round, daily 10–4. A picturesque 200-acre farm, this educational resource is open free to the public for picnics, hiking, and fishing. There are tours of the farm one day each month, May through October; call for information. This is a nice place to visit if you are traveling with children.

GOLF The lush greens of Putnam County golf courses lure golfers of all abilities. You may want to call before you go since some of the courses are semiprivate and might have special events scheduled. All charge fees for use and cart rentals.

Centennial Golf Club (845-225-5700), 185 Simpson Road, Carmel. Open daily April through November. Enjoy a 27-hole, Larry Nelson–designed course; practice facilities; and world-class services.

The Garrison (845-424-3604), 955 Route 9D, Garrison, is open April through November, daily 7–7.

Highlands Country Club (845-424-3727), Route 9D, Garrison, is open April through December, daily 7–6.

Putnam National Golf Club (845-628-4200), 187 Hill Street, Mahopac, has 18 holes and is 6,750 yards in length. Open April through November, daily 7–6.

Vails Grove Golf Course (845-669-5721), 230 Peach Lake Road, Brewster, has nine holes. The course is open to the public April through November, weekdays 7:30–6, weekends after 12:30.

HIKING & OUTDOOR ACTIVITIES **Clarence Fahnestock Memorial State Park** (845-225-7207), 1498 Route 301, east of the Taconic Parkway, Carmel. Open year-round. Free. This 14,000-acre park consists of swamp, lake, forest, and meadow and was assembled through donations of land from private and state organizations. Several hiking trails, including part of the Appalachian Trail, wend in and out of the park; there are also fishing ponds, Canopus Beach, boat rentals, and ice-skating areas. The Fahnestock Winter Park section offers approximately 10 miles of cross-country ski trails as well as a snowshoe area with marked trails. Visitors may rent both skis and snowshoes. Fees are charged for boats and for swimming, and you must bring your own equipment for fishing. The park also sponsors performing-arts programs and has provisions for camping, although you must call ahead to make reservations. The park's marked 1.5-mile Pelton Pond Nature Trail follows the perimeter of a pond formed when an old mine shaft was dammed. You can picnic in this area or watch the woods from a small pavilion. Hikers will want to look for the 8-mile stretch of Appalachian Trail that crosses the park, the Three Lakes Trail—with its varied wildflowers and views—and Catfish Loop Trail, which cuts through the abandoned settlement once known as Dennytown. Since many of these trails cross one another, you should look for signs and trail blazes along the main park roads, which include Route 301, Dennytown Road, and Sunk Mine Road. If you plan to go fishing in the park, you will need a state license. When you visit, be sure to stop at the park headquarters first, where you can pick up a list of special events (some nice programs for children are offered in summer) and free trail maps and fishing guides. Some facilities are accessible to the disabled.

Hudson Highlands State Park (845-225-7207), Route 9D, Cold Spring. Open year-round, daily sunrise–sunset. There are approximately 6,000 acres in this enormous park. However, a few particularly scenic hiking trails meander through the eastern portion of the Highlands, in Putnam. The Breakneck Ridge Trail begins just north of the tunnel on Route 9D, 2 miles north of the village of Cold Spring. Look for the white blazes. The Washburn Trail begins on Route 9D, 1 mile north of Cold Spring, passes an abandoned quarry, then rises steeply before reaching the summit. This trail ends at the beginning of the Notch Trail (blue blazes). The White Rock/Canada Hill Trail begins where the white-blazed part of the Appalachian Trail crosses Route 9 (at the junction of Route 403). Where the AT turns left to ascend the ridge, follow the yellow blazes, which end at the Osborn Loop (blue blazes). Continue to the junction with the Sugarloaf South Trail (red blazes). A side trip to the top of Sugarloaf South offers great views up the river to West Point. The Osborn Loop turns south along the western flank of the mountain, then turns uphill to reach its southern terminus at the Appalachian Trail. Follow north along the ridge, and descend to the junction with the Carriage Connector. This loop is about 6.5 miles long; if you include the side trip up Sugarloaf South, add another mile.

Lake Gleneida Walking Trail (845-808-1994). This 1-mile unpaved trail around Lake Gleneida begins at the intersection of Route 301 and Fowler Avenue in Carmel. There are trail markers, three benches, and several footbridges along the path. It's an easy walk and is recommended for families with young children since it should only take a half hour.

Manitoga/Russel Wright Historic Site & Nature Sanctuary (845-424-3812; www.russelwrightcenter.org), 584 Route 9D, Garrison. Open May through October for house and landscape tours. Reservations are required for tours, which are given Monday through Friday at 11 and on Saturday and Sunday at 11 and 1:30. Call ahead November through March since hours are by appointment only during those months. Admission fee. The name of this center is taken from the Algonquian word for "place of the spirit," and the philosophy of Manitoga lives up to its name. Here people and nature are meant to interact, and visitors are encouraged to experience the harmony of their environment. The center was designed by Russel Wright, who created a 5-mile system of trails that focus on specific aspects of

©tarawingphotography.com

MANITOGA/RUSSEL WRIGHT HISTORIC SITE & NATURE SANCTUARY IN GARRISON

nature. The Morning Trail is especially beautiful early in the day, the Spring Trail introduces the hiker to wildflowers, and the Blue Trail wanders over a brook and through a dramatic evergreen forest (the trail system hooks up with the Appalachian Trail). You will find a full-size reproduction of a Native American wigwam, which was constructed with traditional methods and tools. The site is used as an environmental learning center, and many special programs are offered here. There are public programs in art, poetry, photography, and botany, along with guided nature walks and concerts. You can visit Dragon Rock, the grass-walled cliff house built by Wright. Manitoga is a place where human design and the natural world reflect and inspire each other.

Manitou Point Preserve (845-473-4440), Mystery Point Road, Garrison. (Take Route 9D north for 2 miles from Bear Mountain Bridge. Make a left on Mystery Point Road. Entrance is at the dead end.) This 136-acre retreat once belonged to the Livingston family. Enjoy 4 miles of lush trails that wind through Manitou Marsh, past woods and the Cooper Mine Brook ravine, along the banks of the Hudson. You will pass the restored Livingston mansion, which is now the national headquarters for Outward Bound and not open to the public.

Taconic Outdoor Education Center (845-265-3773; www.nysparks.com), Clarence Fahnestock Memorial State Park, 75 Mountain Laurel Lane, Cold Spring. Free. This state-run center is situated on 300 acres and holds classes and workshops year-round for groups and organizations. There are four public program days annually. Call for exact dates. Boat, swim, fish, or just stay overnight in one of the park's cabins and enjoy the experience at **Highland Lodge** (reservations for camping required).

Other parks include **Pudding Street Multiple Use Area** (845-256-3000), Pudding Street, Putnam Valley; **California Hill Multiple Use Area** (845-256-3000),

©tarawingphotography.com
MANITOGA/RUSSEL WRIGHT HISTORIC SITE & NATURE SANCTUARY

Gordon Road, Kent; **White Pond Multiple Use Area** (845-256-3000), White Pond Road, Kent; **Big Buck Mountain Multiple Use Area** (845-256-3000), Farmers Mills and Ressique Road, Kent; **Ninham Mountain Multiple Use Area** (845-256-3000), Gypsy Trail and Mount Ninham Road, Kent; and **Cranberry Mountain Wildlife Management Area** (845-256-3000), Stagecoach Road, Patterson.

KAYAKING Hudson Valley Outfitters (845-265-0221; 1-866-TO-KAYAK; www.hudsonvalleyoutfitters.com), 63 Main Street, Cold Spring. Open Monday through Friday 11–6; Saturday and Sunday 9–6. If you want to head out on the Hudson River, this is the place to contact. Owner Teri Barr leads a variety of river trips to Constitution Marsh, Bannerman's Castle, and Little Stony Point. Paddle through scenic marshland filled with plants and wildlife. Stop for lunch at a hidden waterfall. Some trips combine hiking. There is something to suit everyone here, and equipment is provided. Reasonable prices.

✷ Winter Sports

ICE SKATING Brewster Ice Arena (845-279-2229; www.brewstericearena.com), 63 Fields Lane, Brewster (near the intersection of I-84 and I-684). There are two Olympic-size indoor ice rinks here that offer public skates as well as hockey and figure-skating sessions. Lessons and rentals are available. The outdoor batting cages operate from April through October. A bar and restaurant are on the premises. Check the website for current schedule information.

SKIING Thunder Ridge Ski Area (845-878-4100; www.thunderridgeski.com), 50 Thunder Ridge Road, Patterson. Open December through March (weather permitting), Monday through Friday 10–9; Saturday 9–9; Sunday 9–5. They have 30 trails here and six lifts (three chairs, a T-bar, and three magic carpets) servicing several gentle slopes. This is an excellent place to introduce young children to the sports of skiing and snowboarding. There are also some challenging advanced trails for experienced skiers as well as a terrain park. They offer night skiing every day but Sunday, and the temperatures here are more moderate than at other areas at higher elevations. Lessons are available at the ski school. A cafeteria and rental services are on the premises.

✷ Green Space

Thousands of acres of Putnam County are dedicated to public use and outdoor education. Most parks are free, but some charge use fees for special events, camping, and swimming; activities include nature studies, birding, hiking, walking, ski touring, and boating.

Constitution Marsh Nature Preserve (845-265-2601; www.constitutionmarsh.org), Indian Brook Road, access off Route 9D, 0.25 mile south of Boscobel in Garrison. Trails are open daily, but visitors must make reservations if they would like a tour. A National Audubon Society haven for nature lovers who enjoy birding along the river and spotting rare wildflowers in spring. There is a boardwalk to make viewing easier and a self-guided nature tour.

Graymoor (845-424-3671; www.graymoor.org), 1350 Route 9, near Route 403, Garrison. Open year-round, daily 10–5. Free. Founded by the Episcopal Church in 1898, this historic site is home of the Franciscan Friars of the Atonement. Today the site is an ecumenical retreat center, with nature trails and access to the Appalachian Trail.

Stonecrop Gardens (845-265-2000; www.stonecrop.org), 81 Stonecrop Lane, off Route 301 (2.7 miles east of Route 9), Cold Spring. Admission fee. Open April through October, Monday through Friday, and on certain Sundays, 10–5. This 63-acre tranquil refuge set above the village of Cold Spring and surrounded by the Hudson Highlands is the former home of Anne and Frank Cabot. There are 12 acres of magnificent gardens, including woodland, water, rock, and grass gardens. According to the British-born director, several student interns live and work at Stonecrop each year to learn gardening techniques. Summer is the time to see the ferns as well as the wisteria pavilion, which overlooks the pond garden, and the enclosed flower garden is bursting with color during the warm-weather months. There are also bamboo groves and foliage throughout the fall. Don't miss the horticultural rarities on display here, like the *Gunnera manicata,* the largest herbaceous plant in the world, native to Brazil. Every season has something beautiful to offer, so remember to call in advance if you are a garden aficionado.

✷ Lodging

Some of the following inns offer special packages for extended stays or midweek visits. Call for reservations and rate information.

The Garrison (845-424-3604), 2015 Route 9, Garrison 10524. ($$$) A truly special resort in the Hudson Highlands, with several historic stone structures and magnificent views of the Hudson River at every turn. There are currently four luxurious rooms available for overnight guests. At this ideal place for a romantic getaway, visitors will enjoy a first-rate golf course, full-service spa, and fine dining (see *Dining Out*) on the premises. You will be transported back to another era, yet with all the modern amenities. Open year-round.

Heidi's Inn (845-279-8011), 1270 Route 22, Brewster 10509. ($) This quiet, simple, comfortable inn has 40 rooms, all with private bath, 13 with kitchenette. A continental breakfast is included with the reasonable room rates. They are open year-round.

Hudson House Inn (945-265-9355), 2 Main Street, Cold Spring 10516. ($$$) The second oldest continuously operating inn in New York State, Hudson House is completely restored and filled with antiques. In addition to quaint bedrooms, there is a cozy lounge, river views, and an exquisite garden. Thirteen rooms with private bath; two suites. A full breakfast is served. Children welcome. Open year-round.

Pig Hill Inn (845-265-9247), 73 Main Street, Cold Spring 10516. ($$) This Georgian brick town house is a most unusual place to stay. Each guest room is furnished in a different style, and most have a fireplace—and if you fall in love with the rocking chair or anything else in your room, you can buy it. Nine rooms with private bath (two have Jacuzzi tubs). There is a gift shop on the first floor. Open year-round.

Plumbush Inn (845-265-3904), 1656 Route 9D, Cold Spring 10516. ($$) Now you can stay at this restaurant on an 1867 estate. Period furnishings fill the rooms, and, of course, the food is quite good (see *Dining Out*). Three rooms with private bath. Open year-round; continental breakfast served. Somewhat pricey for what is offered. Older children only.

✷ Where to Eat

DINING OUT Abruzzi (845-878-6800), 3191 Route 22, Patterson. ($$) Open for lunch and dinner daily 11:30–9. This casual eatery features well-prepared and beautifully presented Italian American specialties ranging from tasty pizzas and tortellini to filet mignon and red snapper. Known for their imaginative pasta creations, this family-oriented trattoria offers something for everyone. The grilled pork chops with escarole and cipollini (tiny onions) is delicious. Children's menu.

The Arch (845-279-5011), 292 Route 22, Brewster. ($$$) Open for lunch Wednesday through Friday noon–2:30; dinner Wednesday through Saturday 6–10. Sunday brunch and lunch served noon–2:30; dinner 2:30–8. An elegant, intimate spot filled with antiques and separated into three small dining rooms with fireplaces and lots of airy windows. The chef specializes in Continental cuisine with a French touch. The menu changes seasonally; game is the specialty in fall. Reservations and jackets for men are required.

Cathryn's Tuscan Grill (845-265-5582), 91 Main Street, Cold Spring. ($$) Open for lunch and dinner noon–10:30; Sunday brunch noon–3. The Northern Italian cuisine here is first-rate, and so is the wine list. Dine alfresco, in a gardenlike setting. Fantastic homemade pastas, fine grilled fish, and hearty beef selections.

Dish (845-621-3474), 947 South Lake Boulevard, Mahopac. ($$) Open for lunch Tuesday through Saturday noon–3; dinner daily, except Sunday, 5–9; Friday and Saturday until 10. There are only a couple of dozen seats in this bistro/wine bar with a casual atmosphere. They serve up a range of choices, from shrimp and chorizo on garlic toast, Mediterranean platter, and a cheese board for starters, to organic roasted chicken, grilled hanger steak, and grass-fed burgers for entrées. The bar offers a nice selection of beers and wine. There is outdoor dining in the warm weather.

Holy Smoke (845-628-9795), 241 Route 6N, Mahopac. ($) Open Tuesday through Sunday 11:30–9; until 10 Friday and Saturday. Barbecue aficionados will be delighted with the baby back ribs, pulled pork, Texas brisket, and other smoked meats in this casual eatery. For those who don't indulge, there are steaks, burgers, salads, and fish entrées. Sides include creamed spinach and sweet potato fries. There are 30 craft beers on tap but only a couple of wine selections, so be forewarned! Children's menu.

Hudson House Restaurant (845-265-9355), 2 Main Street, Cold Spring. ($$) Open for lunch daily 11:30–3; dinner 5–9; Sunday brunch 11–3; dinner 4–9. Winter hours may vary, so do call ahead. Country touches fill this charming 1832 landmark building, and the dining rooms have Hudson River views. Specialties include steaks and cedar plank salmon. Desserts are superb. Children's menu.

Jaipore Royal Indian Cuisine (845-277-3549), 280 Route 22, Brewster. ($) Open daily for lunch noon–3; dinner 5–10; on Sunday only buffet is available. Enjoy a variety of Indian dishes (salads, breads, vegetables, soups, chicken, lamb, and vegetable curries are just some of the choices) in a historic mansion that dates from 1856. Originally the home of a county judge, it became the residence of Mrs. Henry Ward Beecher in 1887. In the 1920s the building was a speakeasy and in the 1980s a topless bar. The buffet (available at lunch) is a bargain and offers diners the opportunity to taste a little of everything.

Le Bouchon (845-265-7676), 76 Main Street, Cold Spring. ($$) Open daily noon–9:30. This brasserie/café is owned by a native of France's Alsace region. A couple of the tempting offerings include prosciutto-wrapped trout with Basque vegetables, and sea scallops with morel and pencil asparagus. Diners may enjoy a variety of imaginative dishes, from salmon strudel and escargot to three types of mussels and salad niçoise.

Marco (845-621-1648), 612 Main Street, Mahopac. ($$) Open for dinner Wednesday through Saturday 5–9; Friday and Saturday until 10. The contemporary American cuisine here changes seasonally. Game dishes are a specialty of the house, and this is definitely the place to order one of the ostrich, antelope, buffalo, or boar selections on the menu. The wild Alaskan salmon broiled with lobster mashed potatoes in a veal glacé (thick brown sauce) garnished with leeks and chives is one of my favorites. Try the chocolate bomb for dessert, with its liquid chocolate center and double vanilla bean ice cream topped with berries. Marco, the chef-owner, is especially passionate about his dessert creations.

Plumbush Inn (845-265-3904), 1656 Route 9D, Cold Spring. ($$) Open Wednesday through Sunday for lunch noon–3; dinner 3–8. A restored home, complete with antiques and cozy paneled rooms. Both dining rooms have fireplaces and candlelight. During the summer, dine on the spacious porch overlooking the grounds. The rustic American cuisine includes selections like venison stew, grilled fillet of tuna with risotto, and free-range chicken with spinach and feta. Not recommended for children.

Ramiro's 954 (845-621-3333), 954 Route 6, Mahopac. ($$) Open Tuesday through Thursday 4–10; Friday and Saturday noon–11; Sunday noon–9. This delightful bistro with a full bar, fountain, and open kitchen serves first-rate Latin American cuisine. A spiral staircase leads upstairs to a more formal dining room and art gallery. The soups, corn cakes, and empanadas are just a few of the appetizers. Beef short ribs, fresh seafood, and enchiladas are offered as entrées. According to *New York Times* reviewer M. H. Reed, the chef "balances textures and flavors subtly and brilliantly; his seasonings lead diners through a sequence of tastes that surprises and delights—fiery, fruity, smoky rich, sweet, sour." The restaurant opened in 2011 and has found a devoted clientele.

Rick's Seafood (845-621-2489), 545 Route 6, Mahopac. ($$) Open daily for lunch 11:30–4; dinner 4–9. Sunday dinner only. This comfortable restaurant with nautical decor is also a fish market. Enjoy coconut-crusted mahimahi, horseradish-crusted Chilean sea bass, and cod oreganato, to name only a few of the wonderful creations here. The fresh fish and shellfish selections are plentiful. Don't pass up the soups. A couple of favorites of mine are the butternut squash lobster bisque and crab corn chowder. BYOB (no corking fee charged at this time). Not recommended for children.

Riverview Restaurant (845-265-4778), 45 Fair Street, Cold Spring. ($$) Open Tuesday through Sunday for lunch noon–3; dinner 5:30–10. The contemporary American cuisine here is hearty, and the place is popular with locals. There is wood-fired brick-oven pizza, a specialty of the house, as well as pasta, salads, steaks, seafood, and burgers. Enjoy the river view while dining on the terrace, weather permitting.

Rraci's Ristorante Italiano (845-278-6695), 3670 Route 6, Brewster. ($$) Open for dinner Tuesday through Sunday 5–10. There are terrific salads and homemade pasta dishes here, along with filet mignon, crabcakes, and daily fish specials. The flagstone patio in the back of the restaurant offers a nice place to dine, with potted plants and green umbrellas at the tables, in the warm weather months.

Tavern at the Highlands Country Club (845-424-3254), 955 Route 9D, Garrison. ($$) Open for dinner Thursday through Sunday 5:30–10. The American cuisine here features organic meats and chicken, as well as local produce. Enjoy steaks, rack of lamb, grilled fish, seafood, salads, and hearty soups; the menu reflects seasonal changes. They have a large garden at the Valley at Garrison (their sister restaurant) and grow most of their vegetables and salad greens in the summer months.

Terrace Club (845-621-5200), 825 South Lake Boulevard, Mahopac. ($$) Open Wednesday through Saturday noon–10; Sunday 11–9. Located on scenic Lake Mahopac, this casual, comfortable restaurant and bar has a large outdoor deck for warm-weather dining. The chef worked at X2O Xaviars in Yonkers, and the cuisine reflects his creative flair. Some of the popular entrées here are coconut shrimp, filet mignon, and tuna and salmon parfait. There are always interesting pasta dishes on the menu. Desserts are wonderful and should not be missed. The wine list is reasonably priced, and there is a decent selection. This restaurant offers excellent value for the money; the lakeside views are enchanting year-round.

Thai Elephant 2 (845-319-6295), 2693 Route 22, Patterson. ($$) Open Tuesday through Thursday 11–10; Friday and Saturday until 11; Sunday noon–10. Housed in an old Colonial-style building with dark wood paneled walls and a fireplace, this Thai restaurant serves a variety of soups, currys, and pad thai. There are several choices for vegetarians, including ginger tofu and eggplant basil tofu.

Valley at the Garrison (845-424-3604), 2015 Route 9, Garrison. ($$$) Open for dinner Thursday through Saturday 5:30–9; Sunday brunch 11–2:30. Contemporary American cuisine featuring the freshest seasonal ingredients from Hudson Valley artisan farmers. The dining room overlooks the Hudson River, and there are magnificent views of the surrounding mountains and West Point. Outdoor dining in the warm-weather months. Signature dishes are the roasted striped bass, steamed baby clams, Asian-barbecued pork chop with bok choi and Thai basil, and spice-crusted rack of lamb with tomato confit, grilled asparagus, and butter bean puree. The food is truly spectacular here; make sure to have one of their terrific dessert creations to end your meal.

EATING OUT **Cold Spring Depot Restaurant** (845-265-2305), 1 Railroad Avenue, Cold Spring. ($) Open daily for lunch 11–4; dinner 4–10. A casual restaurant housed in a restored train station where, to the delight of rail fans, trains still pass by several times a day. Burgers and fries are hearty, and there are wraps, ribs, and steaks. Children welcome.

Foundry Café (845-265-4504), 55 Main Street, Cold Spring. ($) Open Monday, Tuesday, Thursday, and Friday 6:30–3; Saturday and Sunday 8–5. Closed Wednesday. Naturally healthy foods (low fat, whole grain, and tasty) are the specialty here, prepared in the spirit of regional America. Homebaked goods and hearty soups are prepared fresh daily.

The Freight House Café (845-628-1872), 609 Route 6, Mahopac. ($) Open Monday through Friday 7–5; Saturday 8–4. Closed Sunday. Located in a building constructed in 1872 as a railroad storage facility, this spacious, informal café is decorated with old prints, photographs, antiques, and books. It's a great spot to relax and enjoy hearty fare, including the all-day-long breakfast, a bowl of homemade soup, a veggie wrap, or filet mignon steak sandwich with caramelized onions. A family-run business with a friendly vibe. You can watch your meal being prepared in the large open kitchen.

Gino's (845-628-1911), 597 Route 6, Mahopac. ($) Open Tuesday through Saturday for lunch 11:30–4; dinner 4–9. Sunday dinner only. This is the place to go for home-cooked Southern Italian specialties, from hearty portions of lasagna and manicotti to linguine with clam sauce and baked ziti. Their homemade whole-wheat pizza and pasta is excellent, and so are the focaccia sandwiches (grilled eggplant, chicken, or portobello mushroom). Children's menu.

Kitch n' Kaffe (845-621-3535), 985 Route 6, Mahopac. ($) Open year-round, Monday through Friday 9–7; Saturday and Sunday 10–6. This coffee bar/kitchenware store located in a mall offers thousands of products for the home chef, including kitchen tools, cookware, books, and specialty foods. In addition to drinks, muffins, cookies, and brownies are just some of the treats offered here.

Papa John's Pizzeria & Restaurant (845-265-3344), 2510 Route 9, Garrison. ($) Open daily 11–10. This family restaurant, featuring pizza, pasta, sandwiches, and fantastic calzones, is patronized by local residents who enjoy simple, decent Italian food at reasonable prices.

Red Rooster Drive-In (845-279-8046), 1566 Route 22, Brewster. ($) Open Sunday through Thursday 10 AM–11 PM, Friday and Saturday until 1 AM. This old-fashioned, immaculate drive-in with wonderful outdoor eating area (there's even lots of shade) is housed in an A-frame decorated with red-and-white stripes topped with a huge ice-cream cone. The kids will love the burgers, hot dogs, fish-and-chips, and fries. For the more health conscious, there is a charbroiled chicken breast sandwich on the menu. The milk shakes are one of the best items here, making this a great snack stop. The miniature golf course on the premises is owned and operated by the restaurant. Fast food with cachet!

The Stadium (845-734-4000), 308 Route 9, Garrison. ($) Open Monday 4–10; Tuesday through Sunday noon–10. Having a meal here is like dining in a sports museum! The decor consists of glass cases throughout the restaurant displaying thousands of sports memorabilia items from football, baseball, basketball, and hockey. A family restaurant, it houses one of the largest private collections of sports items in the country, including Mickey Mantle's triple crown, the first ever Heisman trophy, and several hall of fame plaques. The food is basic American fare and includes steaks, burgers, seafood, meat loaf, pasta, and chicken entrées served up in an ambience that will delight sports lovers of all ages. There is a game room on the premises, as well as 22 TVs. Children are welcome.

Texas Taco (845-878-9665), Route 22, Patterson. ($) Open daily 11–8:30. In business since the 1960s, this unique Tex-Mex restaurant has a talking parrot that lives out back. Owner Rosemary Jamison is from Texas and started out with a pushcart in front of New York's Plaza Hotel. The chili dogs, franks and chips, and burritos are delicious. This one is worth going out of the way for! Rosemary says Diane von Furstenberg has been her "fairy godmother." When the landlord was going to sell the building that houses the restaurant, Rosemary was going to go out of business. Diane came to the rescue by purchasing the building simply because she loves this unique eatery and didn't want to see it disappear.

✷ Entertainment

Brewster Theater Company (845-598-1621; www.brewstertheatercompany.org), 26 Prospect Street, Brewster. This theater offers both drama and comedy year-round with productions like *The Glass Menagerie* and *Blithe Spirit,* as well as works by new playwrights. Check the website for a full schedule.

Philipstown Performing Arts (845-424-3900; www.philipstowndepottheatre.org), 10 Garrison Landing (at the train depot), Garrison. The performance schedule here runs throughout most of the year and offers musicals, drama, comedy, and youth productions. Check the website for a full schedule.

✷ Special Events

January: **Winterfest** (845-265-3773), Outdoor Education Center, 75 Mountain Laurel Lane, Cold Spring; 11–4. Free. Enjoy a pancake breakfast, nature walks, crafts, and winter sports at this annual festival, which is wonderful for young children.

March: **Sap to Syrup Maple Sunday** (845-265-3773), Outdoor Education Center, 75 Mountain Laurel Lane,

Cold Spring; 9–noon. Free. Watch demonstrations of tapping trees and boiling and producing syrup. There is also a pancake breakfast.

May: **Mother's Day Tea** (845-265-3638), Boscobel Restoration, 1601 Route 9D, Garrison. Admission fee. Celebrate the holiday at this lovely site overlooking the Hudson River with the gardens in full bloom.

June: **Snapping Turtle Walk** (845-265-3638), Boscobel Restoration, 1601 Route 9D, Garrison. In early June female turtles crawl up the steep banks from their habitat in Constitution Marsh to lay their eggs. The program at Boscobel features live turtles from the marsh and a guided walk around the grounds to look for female turtles. The program begins promptly at 7:30 in the morning. **Hudson Valley Shakespeare Festival** (845-265-9575/7858), Boscobel Restoration, 1601 Route 9D, Garrison. Reservations required. Call for specific productions and prices.

July: **Summer Sunset Music Series,** at the bandstand on Main Street, Cold Spring. Free. Enjoy jazz, folk, rock, etc. **Annual Putnam 4-H Fair** (845-278-6738), Veterans Memorial Park, Gipsy Trail Road, Carmel. Friday through Sunday 10–6. Admission and parking free. This is a true country fair, featuring animals, exhibits, entertainment, and food. **Tri N' Du** (845-247-0271), Veterans Memorial Park, 201 Gipsy Trail Road, Carmel. This triathlon takes place on a Sunday beginning at 8 AM in the park. Participants will swim 0.25 mile, bike 14 miles, and run 3 miles. It's fun to cheer on the racers even if you're not taking part!

August: **Garrison Art Center Annual Fine Arts and Crafts Fair** (845-424-3960), Garrison's Landing Riverfront Park, 23 Garrison's Landing, Garrison; 10–5. Suggested donation of $5 for adults. Shop at 70 vendors on the Hudson River. **Daniel Nimham Intertribal Pow Wow** (845-225-0381; 1-800-470-4584), Veterans Memorial Park, Gipsy Trail Road, Carmel; 10–5. Admission and parking free. Enjoy Native American singers, dancers, crafters, foods. **Tour de Putnam Cycling Festival** (845-225-0381), Veterans Memorial Park, 201 Gipsy Trail Road, Carmel. This Sunday event runs 8:30–3 and begins and ends in the park. It is designed by cyclists for cyclists, and participants choose 15-, 30-, 50-, 75-, or 100-mile routes and loops that run throughout Putnam County.

September: **Big Band Evening and Sunset Picnic** (845-265-3638), Boscobel Restoration, 1601 Route 9D, Garrison; 6–8. Admission fee. Bring a picnic supper and enjoy the views of the Hudson River, then dance to the music of a 20-piece jazz orchestra, re-creating the swinging sound of the big-band era. Reservations required. **Annual Brewster Founder's Day Street Fair** (845-279-2477), Main Street, Brewster; 10–4. Free. Enjoy rides, family entertainment, vendors, food.

December: **Traditional Candlelight Tours** (845-265-3638, ext. 115), Boscobel Restoration, 1601 Route 9D, Garrison; 5–8. Admission fee. Go on a candlelight tour of Boscobel, decorated for the holidays. Reservations required.

Westchester County

12

Westchester County Tourism & Film

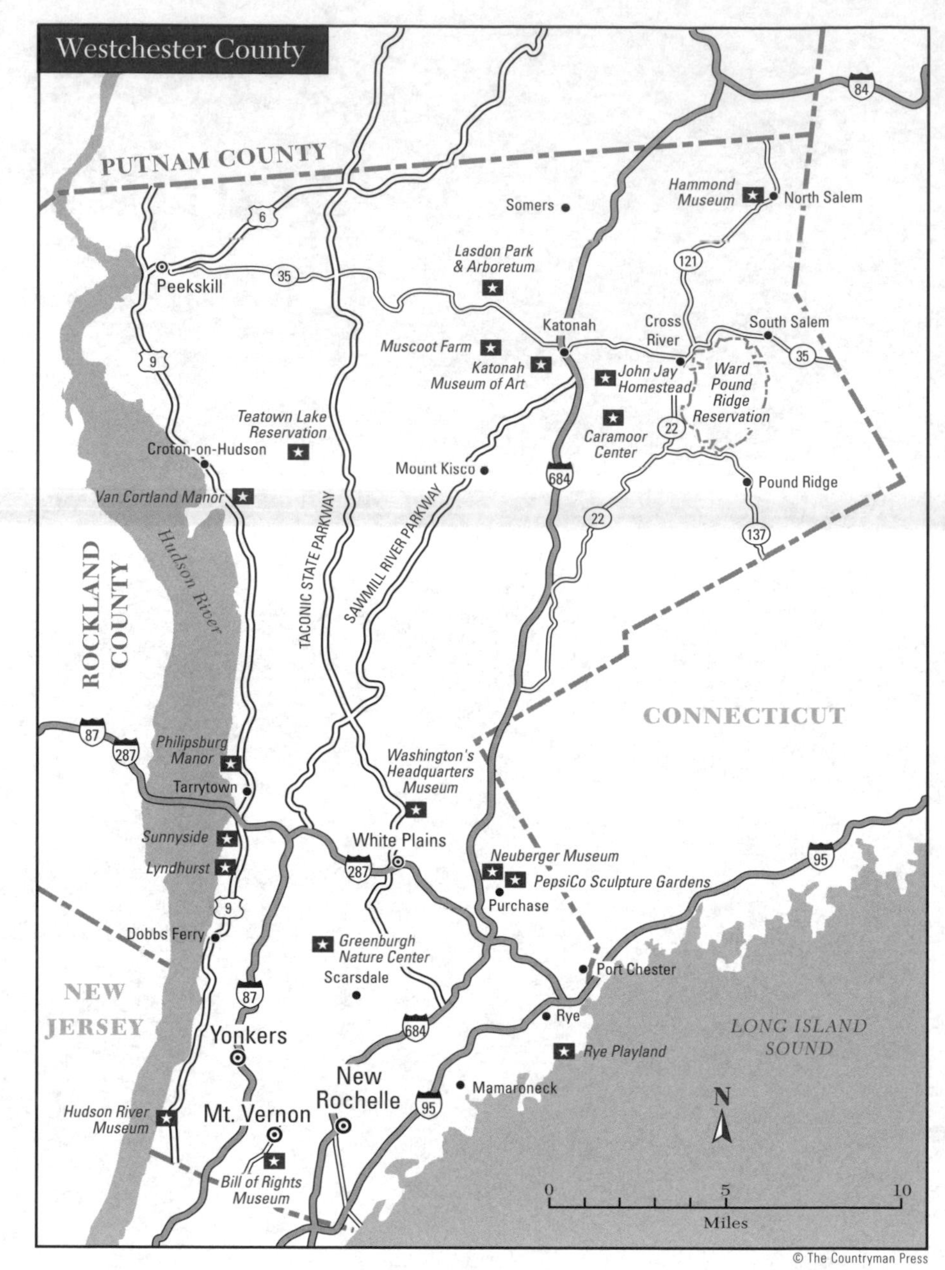
Westchester County
PUTNAM COUNTY
ROCKLAND COUNTY
CONNECTICUT
NEW JERSEY
LONG ISLAND SOUND
Hudson River
Peekskill
Somers
North Salem
Hammond Museum
Lasdon Park & Arboretum
Katonah
Cross River
South Salem
Muscoot Farm
Katonah Museum of Art
John Jay Homestead
Ward Pound Ridge Reservation
Teatown Lake Reservation
Caramoor Center
Croton-on-Hudson
Mount Kisco
Pound Ridge
Van Cortland Manor
TACONIC STATE PARKWAY
SAWMILL RIVER PARKWAY
Philipsburg Manor
Tarrytown
Washington's Headquarters Museum
Sunnyside
Lyndhurst
White Plains
Neuberger Museum
PepsiCo Sculpture Gardens
Purchase
Dobbs Ferry
Greenburgh Nature Center
Scarsdale
Port Chester
Rye
Rye Playland
Yonkers
New Rochelle
Mamaroneck
Mt. Vernon
Hudson River Museum
Bill of Rights Museum
N
0
5
10
Miles
84
6
35
121
9
22
684
137
87
287
95

WESTCHESTER COUNTY

Home of the unexpected: Westchester—which calls itself the Golden Apple—can be a nature preserve, a riverfront mansion, a 17th-century Dutch house tucked just off the old Post Road, or a bustling shopping district. The county has made extraordinary attempts to preserve both its history and its natural environment. Although Westchester borders New York City, it is an area replete with parks and nature preserves that offer an enormous selection of children's activities and special events for visitors. Washington Irving described the enchantment of Westchester in his short stories, immortalizing Tarrytown and the Headless Horseman. On historic Route 9 visitors will be awed by the Gothic castle called Lyndhurst and the working Dutch mill at Philipsburg Manor. From the Pinkster Festival in spring to December's candlelight tours of historic sites, Westchester is fun to visit year-round.

GUIDANCE **Westchester County Office of Tourism** (914-995-8500; 1-800-833-WCVB), 148 Martine Avenue, Suite 104, White Plains 10601; http://tourism.westchestergov.com.

GETTING THERE *By car:* Westchester is accessible from I-87, I-95, Route 684, and Route 9.

By bus: **Adirondack Trailways** (1-800-858-8555) offers service to various towns in Westchester from the Port Authority in Manhattan. The **Bee-Line System** (914-813-7777) offers countywide bus service with more than 55 routes and express service to Manhattan.

By train: **Amtrak** (1-800-872-7245) provides service from New Rochelle to stations on the Boston–Washington Northeast corridor. There is service from Croton-Harmon and Yonkers to upstate New York, Montreal, Chicago, and points west. **Metro North** (1-800-METRO-INFO) operates commuter trains with 43 station stops in Westchester on three lines. There is daily service to Grand Central Station in Manhattan, as well as to points north.

By air: **Westchester County Airport** (914-995-4860; www.westchestergov.com/airport) offers scheduled airline and charter services and corporate flights.

MEDICAL EMERGENCY **Hudson Valley Hospital Center** (914-737-9000), 1980 Crompond Road, Cortlandt Manor.

White Plains Hospital Medical Center (914-681-0600), Davis Avenue at East Post Road, White Plains.

Northern Westchester Hospital Center (914-666-1254), 400 East Main Street, Mount Kisco.

Phelps Memorial Hospital Center (914-366-3590), 701 North Broadway, Sleepy Hollow.

✷ To See

GARDENS **Donald M. Kendall Sculpture Gardens at PepsiCo Headquarters** (914-253-2001), 700 Anderson Hill Road, Purchase. Open year-round, daily dawn–dusk. Free. Here, on 168 acres, visitors will see 45 large sculptures by Rodin, Giacometti, Nevelson, Moore, and Noguchi. Carefully landscaped with paths, reflecting pools, and fountains, the gardens (filled with trees, shrubs, and herbaceous plants) bloom from early spring until fall. Picnicking is permitted.

Hammond Museum and Japanese Stroll Garden (914-669-5033; www.hammondmuseum.org), 28 Deveau Road, off Old Route 124, North Salem. Open May through October, Wednesday through Saturday noon–4. Admission fee. This small Asian arts museum with a 4-acre Japanese-inspired garden offers a chance to step back into the Edo period of Japanese history. Created by Natalie Hays Hammond in memory of her parents, these gardens actually are 13 small landscapes, including a Zen garden, as well as many species of trees and flowers (cherry, katsura, quince, azalea, peony, and iris, among others). Each section is beautifully appointed and has a symbolic meaning: In the reflecting pool, for example, five water lilies represent humanity, justice, courtesy, wisdom, and fidelity. The museum displays a mix of art, antiques, and collectibles, but it is the gardens that

DONALD M. KENDALL SCULPTURE GARDENS AT PEPSICO HEADQUARTERS IN PURCHASE
Westchester County Tourism & Film

Westchester County Tourism & Film

HAMMOND MUSEUM AND JAPANESE STROLL GARDEN IN NORTH SALEM

must not be missed. The **Silk Tree Café** on the grounds serves refreshments and lunch Wednesday through Saturday noon–3.

The Lady Bird Johnson Demonstration Garden at the Native Plant Center (914-606-7870; www.nativeplantcenter.org), Westchester Community College, 75 Grasslands Road, Valhalla. Open year-round, daily dawn to dusk. This center informs visitors about the importance of low-maintenance native plants, which support birds, bees, and butterflies. The 2-acre demonstration garden consists solely of plants and wildflowers indigenous to the northeastern United States. Designed for summer and fall color; no pesticides or fertilizers are used in the garden.

Lasdon Park and Arboretum (914-864-7268), 2610 Route 35, Somers. Open year-round, daily 8–4; until 6 Memorial Day weekend through Labor Day. This lush 243-acre park has a 30-acre arboretum with a formal azalea garden, a magnolia and lilac collection, a rare native American-chestnut grove, and a dwarf conifer collection of pines, spruces, firs, and cypress. Another feature is the Chinese garden with plant species native to China, including cherry trees and butterfly bushes. There is a plant shop on the premises.

Pruyn Sanctuary Butterfly and Hummingbird Garden (914-666-6503), 275 Millwood Road (Route 133), Chappaqua. Open year-round, daily from dawn to dusk. Guided group tours are available by appointment. A 92-acre parcel of protected open space, this garden features more than 125 types of annual and perennial flowering plants selected to be food or nectar plants for butterflies and hummingbirds, including asters, irises, lavender, lilies, and snapdragons. A drip

Westchester County Tourism & Film

LASDON PARK AND ARBORETUM IN SOMERS

pool attracts birds. More than 25 species of butterflies and moths and two dozen species of birds are drawn to the garden. Plants have identification labels.

September 11th Memorial Garden at Kensico Dam Plaza (914-328-1542), 1 Bronx River Parkway, Valhalla. Open year-round, daily dawn to dusk. There is a garden of shrubs and perennials surrounding *The Rising,* Westchester County's memorial to those who lost their lives on September 11, 2001. The garden was designed with a wooded, natural appearance as a backdrop to the memorial. Both native and nonnative species were used in the garden itself. This moving tribute is worth a stop, if you are in the area.

Stone Barns Center for Food and Agriculture (914-366-6200; www.stone barnscenter.org), 630 Bedford Road, Pocantico Hills. Open year-round, Wednesday through Sunday 10–5; farm tours Saturday and Sunday 11:30–4. This educational center—which is located on the 4,000-acre Rockefeller estate—thrives on its natural production of locally grown food. Prior to dining, visitors have an opportunity to tour the grounds that produce what they are eating. Visitors may then indulge in delicacies devoid of fertilizers, pesticides, and herbicides in the center's renovated cow barn, which hosts the **Blue Hill Restaurant** (914-366-9600), open Wednesday through Sunday for dinner 6–9; Sunday for lunch 11:30–2:30. Reservations are required. ($$) Here visitors may relax and dine on American cuisine featuring local, seasonal ingredients, including fresh fish, organic chicken and beef, and a wide variety of Hudson Valley products. Those in a hurry can experience home-grown goodness in the ambience of the **Blue Hill Café,** located in the public courtyard, a perfect stop for a light lunch or refreshments. The café is open year-round, Wednesday through Sunday 10–4:30. The Stone Barns Center is a unique learning experience for Hudson Valley travelers yet also offers a culinary experience that reconnects consumers to the natural world.

Untermyer Park and Gardens (914-377-6429), 945 North Broadway (Route 9), Yonkers. Open year-round, daily dawn to dusk. This historic grand Beaux Arts garden was created in the early 20th century by attorney Samuel Untermyer. The extensive grounds offer breathtaking Hudson River views. Renovated architectural elements such as a Greek-style amphitheater, fountains, and canals characterize the grounds. The gardens feature annuals, perennials, and a large collection of indigenous trees and shrubs.

HISTORIC HOMES **Caramoor Center for Music and the Arts** (914-232-5035; www.caramoor.com), 149 Girdle Ridge Road, Katonah. Open year-round, but hours vary with the season; check website for a schedule. Admission fee. Built in the 1930s by lawyer and banker Walter Tower Rosen, this 117-acre estate was meant to be the setting for Rosen's magnificent collection of fine art from Europe and the Orient. The house itself was created by combining entire rooms (55 in all) from European villas with an American "shell." The result is a unique, magical building that provides an architectural tour of the world in a few hours. Rosen's bedroom, for example, was taken from an Alpine cottage; in his wife's room is a headboard made for Pope Urban VIII; the music room is from a 16th-century Italian villa; portions of the outdoor theater are from the south of France. Throughout the house are thousands of breathtaking pieces of priceless needlework, tapestries, porcelain, furniture, and art, some of which date from the Middle Ages and China's golden age. Tours are offered, and lectures are given by art historians who

STONE BARNS CENTER FOR FOOD AND AGRICULTURE IN POCANTICO HILLS

Westchester County Tourism & Film

illustrate their talks with pieces from the collections. Don't miss the exquisite gardens at Caramoor, where fine statuary is set among evergreens and flowers. Caramoor is also the site of a world-renowned music festival, which is presented each summer (see *Special Events*). The Venetian Theater is a showcase in itself and was built around 15th-century Venetian columns; operas and concerts take center stage on warm evenings, while chamber concerts are offered in the Spanish Courtyard. Concertgoers are allowed to picnic on the grounds before shows.

Horace Greeley House and New Castle Historical Society (914-238-4666; www.newcastlehistoricalsociety.org), 100 King Street, Chappaqua. Open year-round, Tuesday through Thursday and Saturday 1–4. Free. A crusading editor of the *New York Tribune,* presidential candidate in 1872, foe of slavery, and a women's-rights advocate, Greeley lived here during the summer months from 1864 through 1872. There is a guided tour of the furnished house, which has been restored in keeping with the era and is listed on the National Register of Historic Places. Exhibits focus on the history of New Castle and this famous native son, with a collection of Greeley family furniture, memorabilia, papers, and books. The period perennial and herb gardens include unusual species indigenous to the area and plants once used for medicinal purposes. Museum gift shop on the premises. The Chappaqua Antiques Show has been held here every year since 1976 (see *Special Events*).

Jasper F. Cropsey Home and Studio (914-478-1372), 49 Washington Avenue, Hastings-on-Hudson. Open weekdays by appointment only. Free. Although you have to call in advance to view this site, it is well worth the extra effort. Cropsey was a member of the Hudson River School of painters as well as an architect (he designed part of the New York City railroad system), and his Gothic home has about 100 of his works, including paintings, sketches, and studies. The furniture spans those styles that appealed to the Victorian taste, and the artist's studio is part of the tour. Maintained by a private foundation, the site also offers visitors a short video about Cropsey's life and times.

John Jay Homestead (914-232-5651; www.johnjayhomestead.org), 400 Route 22, Katonah. Open year-round, daily 10–4. Admission fee. This 18th-century farmhouse was home to five generations of Jays. As president of the Continental Congress, first chief justice of the Supreme Court, minister to Spain, and foreign affairs secretary, John Jay—the most famous member of the family—held some of the most influential appointments in the new country's government. He retired to this homestead in 1801, and the house reflects the changes wrought by his descendants. Family portraits grace the walls, and the kitchen has an impressive beehive oven along with the hearth. Various styles of furniture and decorative items can be viewed, and the tour adds an

JOHN JAY HOMESTEAD IN KATONAH
Westchester County Tourism & Film

interesting dimension to America's early years. The homestead also hosts special events.

Kykuit (845-631-8200; www.hudsonvalley.org), 381 North Broadway, Sleepy Hollow. Tours begin from Philipsburg Manor. Open May through October, daily, except Tuesday, 9–5. Admission fee. Tours are two hours in length and are not recommended for children under the age of 12. John D. Rockefeller, the founder of Standard Oil, delegated the task of building Kykuit, his home, to his son, John D. Rockefeller Jr. The neoclassical country house and its gardens were completed in 1913, and Kykuit remains one of the finest and best-preserved Beaux Arts homes in America. Governor Nelson Rockefeller lived here from 1960 to 1979. The gardens contain masterpieces by Henry Moore, Alexander Calder, and Louise Nevelson, and there are special tours that focus on the landscapes around the estate. The house is furnished with antiques, fine ceramics, and paintings; a coach barn contains vintage automobiles and carriages.

Lyndhurst (914-631-4481; www.lyndhurst.org), 635 South Broadway (Route 9), Tarrytown. Open April through October, Tuesday through Sunday 10–5; November through March, weekends 10–3:30. Admission fee. The term *Gothic Revival* may bring to mind castles, turrets, and crenellations, but it won't prepare a visitor for the wealth and magnificence of Lyndhurst. Built in 1838 for William Paulding, a former New York City mayor, the house and grounds were enlarged by the Merritt family. Lyndhust was later owned by the notoriously wealthy Jay Gould. Much of the furniture, paintings, and decorative accessories are original to the mansion, which was owned by the Goulds until 1961, when it was given to the National Trust. The rooms are sumptuous, and many are decorated in "faux" material—a substance made to resemble something else. Ironically, in the case of marble,

KYKUIT IN SLEEPY HOLLOW

Westchester County Tourism & Film

Westchester County Tourism & Film

LYNDHURST IN TARRYTOWN

imitating it with wood and paint often cost more than real marble would have (some of the mineral "marble" was actually limestone quarried at Sing Sing prison). Each room is filled with rare furniture, artwork, and decorative pieces: Tiffany glass and windows are outstanding highlights. Outside in the gardens are magnificent roses, a children's playhouse, a conservatory with brick paths, and nature paths among the dozens of different trees, ferns, and plantings.

Van Cortlandt Manor (914-271-8981; www.hudsonvalley.org), 525 South Riverside Avenue, Croton-on-Hudson. Open April through October, Thursday through Sunday 10–5; November and December, weekends only 10–4. Closed January through March. Admission fee. This manor originally consisted of 86,000 acres of land. The main floors of the present manor house were built in 1748; the house remained in the Van Cortlandt family until the middle of the 20th century. As supporters of the American Revolution, the Van Cortlandts were hosts to such luminaries as Washington, Franklin, and Lafayette. Inside the house there is a blend of styles and periods, reflecting the history of the family. One of the most impressive items is the fowling gun, a huge firearm that was fired into a flock of birds and reduced hunting time considerably! Outside, the gardens beckon flower lovers, and the Long Walk—a brick path that leads to the **Ferry House,** a nearby inn and tavern—wanders by well-maintained flower beds and herb gardens. Special events are held throughout the year, with the Great Jack-O'-Lantern Blaze (see *Special Events*) and demonstrations of 18th-century crafts among the most popular. The Ferry House has been restored and furnished with Hudson Valley pieces, and it offers a rare look into the social life of the colonial period. Notice the familiar white-clay pipes—they were for rent, with the ends broken off for each new smoker. The Ferry House is open for tours, as well.

Washington Irving's Sunnyside (914-591-8763; www.hudsonvalley.org), 1 West Sunnyside Lane (off Route 9), Irvington. Open April through October, daily, except Tuesday, 10–5; November and December, weekends only, 10–4. Closed January through March. Admission fee; grounds pass can be purchased at a reduced rate. Washington Irving once referred to his home as being "as full of angles and corners as an old cocked hat," and indeed the charming, wisteria-draped home of the author of *The Legend of Sleepy Hollow* and *Rip Van Winkle* is an original. Irving purchased the small estate in 1835 and soon began to remodel it, adding weathervanes, gables, and even an Oriental-style tower. There is much locally made furniture, and some furnishings from Irving's time, including his desk and many of his books, remain. The kitchen was considered a modern wonder: A large hot-water heater was fed from the nearby pond by a gravity-run system. Every year Sunnyside is lovingly decorated for the holiday season, and candlelight tours are held (see *Special Events*) that recall Irving's pleasure at seeing his home bustling with relatives and guests. The grounds are carefully attended and overlook the Hudson River and the railroad tracks; Irving made a deal with the railroad, allowing it to pass through his land if trains would stop to pick him up for the trip to New York. You can stroll along the paths, picnic near the Little Mediterranean (a pond), watch the swans, see the icehouse and root cellar, and visit the "necessary."

HISTORIC SITES **Lighthouse at Sleepy Hollow (also known as the Tarrytown Lighthouse and Kingsland Point Lighthouse)** (914-366-5109), 299 Palmer Avenue, Sleepy Hollow. Tours (fee) are offered from mid-April through mid-October, Sunday 1–3. This cast-iron tower dates back to 1883 and

VAN CORTLANDT MANOR IN CROTON-ON-HUDSON

Westchester County Tourism & Film

Westchester County Tourism & Film

WASHINGTON IRVING'S SUNNYSIDE IN IRVINGTON

was operational until 1961, when navigational lights on the Tappan Zee Bridge made it obsolete. Twelve light keepers and their families resided in the five-story structure, and on the tour visitors will learn what their lives were like. There is plenty of parking in Kingsland Point Park, where the tours begin.

The Marble School (914-793-1900), 388 California Road, Eastchester. Open by appointment. Admission fee. Although you have to make arrangements with the Eastchester Historical Society to visit this site, if you are interested in seeing a school of the past, by all means go. Built of locally quarried "marble" (actually limestone), the school is furnished in the style of the 19th century, with many antique toys and games still available for playtime. A good collection of children's books from the past is also contained in the society's archives.

Old Dutch Church and Burying Grounds (914-631-1123; www.olddutchburyingground.org), 42 North Broadway (Route 9), Tarrytown. There are cemetery tours every Sunday at 2, Memorial Day weekend through October. At other times of the year, by appointment only. Free. One of the oldest churches in New York State, this stout stone building was erected in 1685 and is still used, albeit infrequently, for services. Surrounding the church is the fascinating Sleepy Hollow Cemetery, where visitors can read old Dutch and English tombstones. Washington Irving is buried here (his grave site is a National Historic Landmark), and the cemetery was reputed to be the spot where a headless Hessian ghost resided, giving rise to *The Legend of Sleepy Hollow.*

Philipsburg Manor (914-631-3992; www.hudsonvalley.org), 381 North Broadway, Sleepy Hollow. Open April through October, daily, except Tuesday, 10–5 (closing time is 4 in November and December). Closed January through March. Admission fee. Once the center of a 17th-century estate of more than 50,000 acres, Philipsburg Manor was founded by Frederick Philipse, an immigrant Dutch carpenter. The manor was in the middle of a bustling commercial empire, which included milling and trading concerns. For almost a century the Philipses were respected colonists; then the family fled to England as Loyalists during the Revolution, and their landholdings were broken up, which is why they are not as well-known as other prominent colonial families.

Tours of the manor begin in the basement, where the dairy and slave cooking quarters are, rather than through the front door. Some of the rooms feature reproductions of period pieces that can be touched. The front hall contains documents like the 1750 house inventory—and advertisements for runaway slaves. At the two-story stone house and office building, the rooms have been restored to their earlier simplicity. The house was not the main residence of the family, so it was not furnished lavishly, but there are several bedrooms, a kitchen, and the counting office to explore. The mill, still run by waterpower, continues to grind meal for the kitchen (you can purchase the flour in the gift shop) and turns out 500–1,000 pounds of flour annually. The resident miller explains the intricacies of a millwright's job, how waterpower turns corn into flour, and so on, all the while working the dusty, noisy machinery.

Outside by the barn and the outbuildings, where costumed guides go about the business of working a small farm, vignettes depicting life at the time are acted out. They show that the North, too, depended on slavery for economic survival. In *Trying Times,* a pair of interpreters play Albert the overseer, at his desk in the main house, and Susan, the enslaved woman, who supervised the dairy operations. Their

OLD DUTCH CHURCH AND BURYING GROUNDS IN TARRYTOWN

Westchester County Tourism & Film

Westchester County Tourism & Film

PHILIPSBURG MANOR

dramatic conversation, where Susan seeks permission to visit a family member who had been sold, expresses some of the complexities of their relationship and reveal negotiations that might very well have gone on at the time. This site has not shied away from the ugly, yet realistic, aspects of early American culture; children will understand more about slavery from such dramatic enactments. A clear sense of how America came together on the backs of different cultures is communicated at this site—which is rare anywhere. I commend Philipsburg Manor for their progressive approach to colonial history and hope other sites follow their lead. Special events are held throughout the year, so check the website for a complete schedule (see *Special Events*).

MUSEUMS Hudson River Museum and Glenview Mansion (914-963-4550; www.hrm.org), 511 Warburton Avenue, Yonkers. Open year-round, Wednesday through Sunday noon–5. There are planetarium shows on Saturday and Sunday only at 12:30, 2, and 3:30. Admission fee. When financier John Bond Trevor built a 19th-century mansion called Glenview on a rise overlooking the Hudson River, he probably never envisioned it becoming a museum, but when the house was purchased by the city of Yonkers, luckily for us that is what happened. Period artwork, clothing, furniture, and decorative accessories are displayed throughout the mansion; the museum is located in a separate wing and contains science and art exhibit areas. Hudson Riverama includes permanent galleries containing Hudson River–themed artwork. There is a terrific museum shop, a favorite stop with visitors. The Andrus Planetarium (the only public planetarium in the area and one of the few in the Northeast) can take you on a journey through the universe. The planetarium offers shows on weekends, and there are special events at this site throughout the year, so it is best to check the website for a complete schedule.

Westchester County Tourism & Film

HUDSON RIVER MUSEUM AND GLENVIEW MANSION IN YONKERS

Hudson Valley Center for Contemporary Art (914-788-7166; www.hvcca.com), 1701 Main Street, Peekskill. Open Saturday and Sunday noon–6 or by appointment. This 12,000-square-foot museum contains changing exhibits and is a hub in Peekskill for the arts community. It is known as a venue for experimental art, and a visit here may include a video presentation and sculpture exhibit. Check the website for special programs, as there are a variety offered year-round.

Katonah Museum of Art (914-232-9555; www.katonahmuseum.org), 134 Jay Street, Katonah. Open Tuesday through Saturday 10–5; Sunday noon–5. Admission fee. This lively teaching museum was founded in 1953 to display the best art of the past and present, and foster arts education. There are exhibits by museum members, an annual local studio tour, and changing displays, which may range from a look at the creations of fashion designers to Navajo rugs or modern art. Special events and shows are held year-round, and the museum is well worth a stop. There is also an outdoor sculpture garden.

Neuberger Museum of Art (914-251-6100; www.neuberger.org), Purchase College Campus, 735 Anderson Hill Road, Purchase. Open Tuesday through Sunday noon–5. Closed national holidays. Admission fee is waived on the first Saturday of every month. Masterpieces of modern art by Avery, Hopper, O'Keeffe, Pollock, and others are displayed in several galleries at this extraordinary teaching museum. There is also an important collection of African art, and selections from Nelson Rockefeller's collection of ancient art are exhibited. An outdoor sculpture area with works by Henry Moore, Andy Goldsworthy, and Alexander Liberman should not be overlooked. This is one of Westchester County's finest cultural resources, with changing exhibitions annually. The museum offers lectures, workshops, tours, performances, and concerts throughout the year. There is a gift shop and café on the premises.

KATONAH MUSEUM OF ART

Westchester County Tourism & Film

Ossining Urban Cultural Park Museum (914-941-3189), 95 Broadway, Ossining. Open year-round, Tuesday through Saturday 10–4. Ossining was once renowned as the home of

Sing Sing prison, and this museum features replicas of prison cells as well as a model of the Old Croton Aqueduct and other exhibits about the town's history. Those particularly interested in the prison will find this stop worthy.

Peekskill History Museum (914-736-0473; www.peekskillmuseum.com), 124 Union Avenue, Peekskill. Open year-round, Saturday 1–4. Free. This local-history museum is housed in the Herrick House, one of Peekskill's most famous Victorian houses. The museum features three permanent exhibits that reveal how well-to-do New Yorkers lived in "the country": the Ladies Victorian Bedroom, the Mario Boyle Children's Room, and the Peekskill Stove Collection, plus other artifacts relating to the city's history, including some Revolutionary War cannons. After visiting the museum, visit the **Peekskill Artist District Open Studios** (914-734-1894) and see how painters, sculptors, and photographers have moved to the downtown area, encouraging a renaissance in the city (see *Special Events*).

Westchester County Tourism & Film

NEUBERGER MUSEUM OF ART IN PURCHASE

ST. PAUL'S CHURCH NATIONAL HISTORIC SITE

Westchester County Tourism & Film

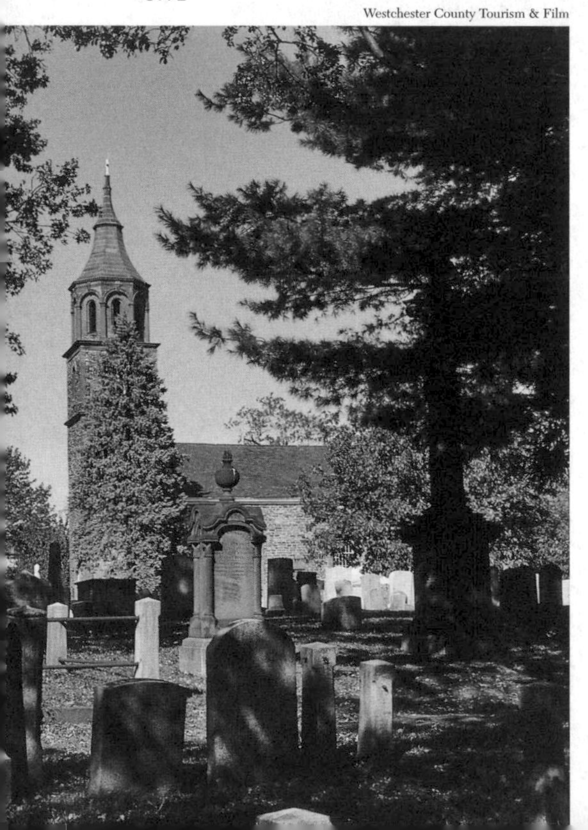

St. Paul's Church National Historic Site (914-667-4116; www.nps.gov/sapa), 897 South Columbus Avenue, Mount Vernon. Open year-round, Monday through Friday 9–5; second Saturday of the month, noon–4. Free. Few people realize that the 18th-century libel trial of John Peter Zenger led directly to the establishment of the Bill of Rights in 1791; fewer still know that this all took place in Mount Vernon, and that an unusual site preserves the story. Begin your visit with a tour of St. Paul's Church, which was founded in 1665 (the present building dates from 1763). The church has a highly carved bishop's chair from 1639 as well as one of the oldest working church organs in the country. You will also see the Freedom Bell, sister of Philadelphia's Liberty Bell and cast at the same time in the same London foundry. At one time the church was used as a courthouse during the week, and lawyers, including Aaron Burr, presented their cases here. The museum is located in the former carriage house and has exhibits that recall America's drive to guarantee essential freedoms. Displays include historic dioramas and panels, and papers and prints that describe America's historic dedication to individual rights. There are self-guided sections of the museum; guided tours are available, as well.

Somers Historical Society and Museum of the Early American Circus (914-277-4977; www.somersny.com), 335 Route 202, Somers. Open year-round, Thursday 2–4, or by appointment. This unusual museum is located in the historic Elephant Hotel, probably the only hotel in the world built in memory of an elephant. Recalling the birth of the American circus in the 18th century, the hotel was erected by showman Hachaliah Bailey (a distant relation of the Bailey of Barnum & Bailey), who acquired the second elephant to be brought to America in 1805. Called Old Bet, the elephant journeyed with Bailey up and down the eastern seaboard as part of a traveling menagerie until it was shot by a suspicious farmer in Maine. Today the former hotel houses a museum full of circus memorabilia, posters, photographs, a miniature big top, and exhibits of local history.

Square House Museum (914-967-7588; www.ryehistory.org), 1 Purchase Street, Rye. Open year-round, Tuesday through Friday 9–4; Saturday 10–3. Admission fee. This 1760 Federal farmhouse and tavern once hosted George Washington, and today the five restored rooms offer a fascinating look at 18th-century life. In the tavern room, visitors learn that the term *bar and grill* derives from barkeepers having secured a wooden covering over the bar at night to avoid having the liquor stolen. In the kitchen a beehive oven (the interior was shaped like an old-fashioned bee skep) is still used by museum staff. There was also an early medical office in the building, and you'll discover that the barber, who was also the surgeon, would wrap bloody cloths around a stick to indicate that he was open for business—the origin of the striped pole still used by barbers today.

SOMERS HISTORICAL SOCIETY AND MUSEUM OF THE EARLY AMERICAN CIRCUS
Westchester County Tourism & Film

Yorktown Museum (914-962-2970; www.yorktownmuseum.org), 1974 Commerce Street, Yorktown Heights. Open year-round, Tuesday and Thursday 11–4; Saturday 1–4; or by appointment. Free, but donations are accepted. A unique collection of dollhouses and miniature landscapes depicting Victorian homes, street scenes, and stores is on display, as are exhibits of Mohegan Indian life and furnished period rooms circa 1750–1850, railroad memorabilia, and local history.

WINERIES, BREWERIES, AND DISTILLERIES **Prospero Winery** (914-769-6870), 134 Marble Avenue, Pleasantville. (Located off exit 27 of the Saw Mill River Parkway.) Open Sunday, Tuesday, and Wednesday noon–5; Thursday and Friday noon–7; Saturday 11–6. Free. Tony and his wife, Silvana, opened a fruit stand in 1973, and in 1999 they opened this winery on the same site. Visitors can taste a variety of wines in the tasting room: cabernet sauvignon, chardonnay, merlot, zinfandel, and more.

StilltheOne Distillery (914-217-0347), 1 Martin Place, Port Chester. Tours by appointment only. Made with pure honey, the Comb Vodka, Comb 9 Gin, and Comb Blossom Brandy produced at this distillery are all served at fine restaurants. It's an interesting operation, and the name refers to the lengthy marriage of the owners, the Pelham Manor couple who opened the distillery in 2011.

A note to beer lovers: **Captain Lawrence Brewing Company** (914-741-2337), 444 Saw Mill River Road, Elmsford, is open Tuesday through Friday 4–7 for tastings; tours are given at 1, 2, and 3 on Saturday only. This craft brewer produces several award-winning beers on the premises.

✷ To Do

BICYCLING If bicycling is your passion, plan to take part in **Bicycle Sundays** (May through September, except holiday weekends, 10–2), when the Bronx River Parkway is closed to vehicular traffic. Call 914-864-PARK and request trail maps for the Bronx River Pathway, North County Trailway, South County Trailway, Briarcliff-Peekskill Trailway, and Old Croton Aqueduct State Historic Park, which have free bike paths that are open year-round. In-line skating is also welcome in most of these areas. To obtain trail maps online, check the website www.westchestergov.com/parks.

Briarcliff-Peekskill Trail (914-864-PARK). This county-owned linear park runs 12 miles from the town of Ossining to the Blue Mountain Reservation in Peekskill.

Bronx River Pathway (914-864-PARK). This 807-acre park extends 13.2 miles in three distinct segments. It is excellent for road biking, hiking, and walking.

North County Trailway (914-864-PARK). There are 22 miles of county-owned trail, running from Mount Pleasant north to the Putnam County Line in Yorktown.

Old Croton Aqueduct State Historic Park (914-693-5259). This level, 26-mile trail from Croton Dam south to Van Cortlandt Park in the Bronx passes through 11 towns and offers striking panoramas of the Hudson River at several points. The trail follows the route of the aqueduct, which carried water to New York City from 1842 to 1955. Most of this structure lies beneath the trail and has been designated a National Historic Landmark.

South County Trailway (914-864-PARK). This 5.2-mile county-owned trail runs from Hastings to Elmsford.

Rivertowns Tourism (914-591-7600, ext. 230; www.rivertownsny.org) is a great source for bikers and walkers. Their website suggests several paths along the Hudson River in Dobbs Ferry, Hastings-on-Hudson, Tarrytown, and Sleepy Hollow. **Endless Trail Bikeworx** (914-674-8567) in Dobbs Ferry offers day-trip packages

Westchester County Tourism & Film

BRONX RIVER PATHWAY

from Manhattan that include a round-trip train ticket to Dobbs Ferry as well as lunch at a restaurant stop. **Westchester Cycle Club** (www.westchestercycleclub.org) organizes over 1,000 bicycle rides for members throughout the county every year, on weekends as well as during the week. The minimal annual membership fee also entitles bike enthusiasts to access a library of 600 Westchester County bicycle routes to plan independent trips. The website includes information on joining the club and all membership benefits.

BOAT CRUISES **Hudson Highlands Cruises** (845-534-7245; www.hudsonhighlandscruises.com). On the last Saturday of the month from May through October, the excursion boat *Commander* offers a three-hour narrated cruise to the Hudson Highlands, leaving Peekskill at 12:30 PM from Riverfront Park, passing West Point, Fort Montgomery, Garrison, Constitution Island, and the Bear Mountain Bridge. Advance reservations required.

New York Sailing School (914-235-6052; www.nyss.com). Open April through November for sunset sails, Tuesday through Sunday nights, departing from New Rochelle at 6:30. Do bring a picnic dinner and drinks. Overnight cruises are available, with sleeping accommodations on the vessel. Call for information and reservations.

Trinity Cruise Company (914-589-7773; www.trinitycruisecompany.com), Charles Point Marina, 5 John Walsh Boulevard, Peekskill. Open mid-May through October, Thursday through Sunday. The *Evening Star* offers narrated sightseeing cruises on the Hudson River as well as sunset cruises. Check the website for a complete schedule and reservations.

FARM STANDS AND PICK-YOUR-OWN FARMS Even though Westchester is more built up than many other Hudson River counties, farm stands provide fresh local produce during the summer and fall harvest seasons. Farmers' markets are held in many towns, and they are a great way to sample the bounty of the county!

Cabbage Hill Farm (914-241-2658), 115 Crow Hill Road, Mount Kisco, seeks to increase public awareness about sustainable agriculture through an educational working farm. They conserve rare and endangered breeds of animals here. On the first Friday of every month, the 175-acre farm is open to the public (or by appointment). Make sure to see the greenhouses; one has an aquaponics operation where greens are grown year-round and are fed entirely from the fish tank water. The other greenhouse contains flowers and herbs, all organically grown. Crops are fertilized using compost made from the farm animals. A fascinating farm where a number of rare heritage breed animals may be seen.

Harvest Moon Farm & Orchard (914-485-1210), 130 Hardscrabble Road, North Salem, offers tours. You can pick apples in the fall or shop at the stand year-round, where you will find fresh vegetables, jams, and other treats. The store is open daily 9–6, and there is apple and pumpkin picking in season daily 10–5. This is a popular place with local residents, and they have first-rate produce.

Hilltop Hanover Farm (914-962-2368), 1271 Hanover Street, Yorktown Heights, consists of 187 acres with forest, pastureland, and buildings that date back to the 1600s, when the Underhill family owned the property. Children will enjoy the animals, and just about everyone will like hiking the trails here. They are open May through October, daily 10–4; the rest of the year, Tuesday through Friday 10–4.

Stone Barns Center for Food & Agriculture (914-366-6200), 630 Bedford Road, Pocantico Hills, has a farm market and farm store open to the public year-

HILLTOP HANOVER FARM IN YORKTOWN HEIGHTS

Westchester County Tourism & Film

round, Wednesday through Sunday 10–5. The center welcomes visitors to "unleash their inner farmer." The public is invited to participate in a farm-to-table program, enroll in an herbal infusions class, attend a farm-policy lecture, join their toddler in the little farmers program, or talk with the farmers. The public may also tour the historical architecture at the center. Programs and activities change monthly with the weather and the seasons. There are programs here to suit just about anyone's interest at this wonderful venue.

Stuart's Fruit Farm (914-245-2784), 62 Granite Springs Road, Granite Springs, is open April through October, daily 9–6; November and December, daily 9–5; closed January through March. They sell a large selection of fruits and vegetables in season. You can also pick your own peaches, pears, apples, and pumpkins here.

Westchester Greenhouses (914-693-2935), 450 Secor Road, Hartsdale, is open year-round, daily 9–6. They offer plants, fresh produce, cider, jams, and honey.

Wilkens Fruit and Fir Farm (914-245-5111), 1335 White Hill Road, Yorktown. Open August through mid-December, daily 11–5. Pick your own apples and peaches in season Saturday and Sunday 10–4:30. Choose and cut Christmas trees after Thanksgiving through mid-December, 10–4.

The following **farmers' markets** are popular with local residents and visitors to the county. Try to visit at least one on your travels through Westchester.

Chappaqua Farmers' Market (914-478-8068), St. Mary's Church, 191 South Greeley Avenue. This bustling year-round market is held outdoors May through November and indoors December through April, Saturday 9–1:30. There is organic produce from Stone Barns, baked goods, cooking demonstrations, and more.

Hartsdale Farmers' Market (914-993-1507), Train Station Plaza. Late June through October, Saturday 9–2. Visit here for seasonal produce and flowers, home-baked breads and pastries.

Hastings-on-Hudson Farmers' Market (914-923-4837), Maple Avenue (next to the library). Mid-June through mid-November, Saturday 8:30–2. They sell wine, organic produce, breads, pastries, cut flowers, potted plants, and poultry.

Larchmont Farmers' Market (914-923-4837), Metro North parking lot off Chatsworth Avenue, June through mid-December, Saturday 8:30–2.

Lewisboro-Katonah Farmers' Market (914-923-4837), Route 121 at John Jay High School, Cross River, June through November, Saturday 8:30–2.

New Rochelle Farmers' Market (914-923-4837), South Division Street and LeRoy Place. From the end of June to late November, every Friday 8–3, you will find all kinds of fruits and vegetables in season, as well as home-baked breads, pies, jams, and doughnuts.

Ossining Farmers' Market (914-923-4837), Main and Spring streets. Mid-June through mid-December, Saturday 8:30–2. Enjoy organic produce, cheeses, meats, wines, breads, pastries, cut flowers, honey, and jams.

Peekskill Farmers' Market (914-737-2780), Bank Street. Mid-June through mid-November, Saturday 8–2. Produce, dairy items, poultry, baked goods, plants, herbs, soaps, and bath products, in addition to live entertainment.

Pleasantville Farmers' Market (914-923-4837), Memorial Plaza, off Manville Road. June through October, Saturday 8:30–1, they offer organic produce, wine, breads, cider, eggs, pastries, and cut flowers.

Rye Farmers' Market (914-923-4837), parking lot on Theodore Freund Avenue, June through November, Sunday 8:30–2.

Tarrytown Farmers' Market (914-923-4837), Patriot Park, 125 North Broadway (Route 9). Mid-June through November, Saturday 8:30–2, there is organic produce, honey, eggs, wine, flowers, and potted plants, and musical entertainment to enjoy as you stroll around.

White Plains Farmers' Market (914-422-1411), 255 Main Street. May through mid-November, Wednesday 9–4, you will find organic produce, baked goods, plants, and more.

Yonkers Farmers' Market (914-963-3033), St. John's Courtyard, 1 Hudson Street. Early July through October, Thursday 9–4. The offerings here include fresh produce, bakery items, homemade jams, and a flea market.

FOR FAMILIES **The Cliffs** (914-328-ROCK), 1 Commerce Park, Valhalla. Open year-round, Monday through Friday 10–10; Saturday 9–8; Sunday 10–6. Admission fee. This indoor rock climbing and fitness facility features over 13,000 square feet of climbing suitable for all ages and ability levels.

Funfuzion at New Roc City (914-637-7575; www.funfuziononline.com), 19 LeCount Place, New Rochelle. Open daily, including holidays, 11–9. Admission fee. This enormous indoor entertainment complex features six amusement venues. Kids can create their own fun experiences that incorporate video games, rides, glow in the dark bowling, miniature golf, pool, go-karts, and more.

Muscoot Farm (914-864-7282; www.muscootfarm.org), 51 Route 100, Somers. Open year-round, daily 10–4. Free, but there are workshops on the premises that charge a fee. A showplace for the farming techniques of the 19th century, this 777-acre interpretive farm offers a look at life in a bygone era. It was built in 1885 by a pharmacist (*muscoot* means "something swampy" in a local Native American language), and visitors today can view a variety of farm animals and displays of vintage farm equipment, tour historic farm buildings, and enjoy hayrides on Sunday May through October. Muscoot also has a series of trails that wind through ferns and wildflowers, along which animals and an amazing number of birds make their homes; there are ponds, wetlands, and meadows to explore, as well.

THE CLIFFS IN VALHALLA
Westchester County Tourism & Film

Playland (914-813-7010; www.ryeplayland.org), 1 Playland Parkway (off I-95), Rye. Different sections of the

Westchester County Tourism & Film

MUSCOOT FARM IN SOMERS

park are open year-round, although hours vary widely during the season, so call ahead. Open mid-May through Labor Day and weekends only in the month of September. Admission fee. A true old-fashioned amusement park and National Historic Site, Rye's Playland is an architectural gem. Built in 1928, this was the first amusement park constructed according to a complete plan where recreational family fun was the focus. Fortunately, the park's family atmosphere and art deco style are still here to be enjoyed. Set on the beaches of Long Island Sound, Playland offers a famous 1,200-foot boardwalk, a swimming pool, gardens, a saltwater boating pond (paddleboats can be rented), a beach, and, of course, there are 50 rides and an amusement area. Seven original rides are still in use: Among them are the carousel (with a rare carousel organ and painted horses), the Dragon Coaster (a rare wooden roller coaster), and the Derby Racer (horses zip around a track). Fireworks and special entertainment, including free musical revues, go on all summer; in winter the three ice-skating rinks at Playland are open to the public (see *Winter Sports—Ice Skating*).

PLAYLAND IN RYE

Westchester County Tourism & Film

GOLF Westchester is famous for some prestigious professional golf tournaments hosted in the county. Five county-owned courses are open to the public:

Dunwoodie (914-231-3490), 1 Wasylenko Lane, Yonkers, is an 18-hole, par-70 course with pro shop, driving range, snack bar, and restaurant. **Maple Moor** (914-995-9200), 1128 North Street, White Plains, is an 18-hole, par-71 course with pro shop, snack bar, and restaurant. **Mohansic** (914-862-5283), 1500 Baldwin Road, Yorktown Heights, is an 18-hole course, par 70, with pro shop, driving range, snack bar, and restaurant. **Saxon Woods** (914-231-3461), 315 Mamaroneck Road, Scarsdale, is an 18-hole, par-71 course with pro shop, restaurant, and locker rooms. **Sprain Lake Golf Course** (914-231-3481), 290 East Grassy Sprain Road, Yonkers, is an 18-hole course, par 70, with pro shop, snack bar, and restaurant.

Semiprivate golf courses include **Doral Golf Club** (914-939-5500), 975 Anderson Hill Road, Rye Brook, 9 holes, par 35; and **Lake Isle Town Park** (914-961-3453, ext. 206), 660 White Plains Road, Eastchester, 18 holes, par 70.

HIKING There are more than 40 county-owned parks in Westchester, and the county's **Department of Parks, Recreation and Conservation** (914-864-PARK) can provide an extensive list of places to hike. These are my favorite spots, but do refer to the *Green Space* section in this chapter for additional areas that should not be overlooked.

Franklin D. Roosevelt State Park (914-245-4434), 2957 Crompond Road, off the Taconic Parkway, Yorktown Heights, is open year-round, daily 8 AM–dusk and has hiking and cross-country ski trails, a huge outdoor pool that is accessible to the disabled, and boating on Mohansic Lake and Crom Pond.

Indian Brook Assemblage of The Nature Conservancy (914-244-3271), Mount Holly Road, Lewisboro, is really a collection of smaller parks and preserves maintained by The Nature Conservancy. Lakes, waterfalls, ponds, and trails form a perfect getaway for the outdoors lover, and the hiking ranges from a leisurely walk to a challenging climb.

Marshlands Conservancy (914-835-4466), 220 Boston Post Road, Rye. Marked trails take the hiker through fields and woods and along the seashore. This is a great spot for birders, and a small nature center offers exhibits on the natural history of Long Island Sound.

More hiking is found at the **Mianus River Gorge** (914-244-3271), Mianus River Road, Bedford, and along the **Old Croton Aqueduct** (914-693-5259), Route 129, to the Croton Dam Plaza. The latter hike is a total of 30 miles, but both hikers and cyclists can follow as much or as little of the trail as they want. Stop at the plaza spillway, which was considered an engineering marvel in its day. **Westchester Wilderness Walk** (914-241-6346), Upper Shad Lane, Pound Ridge, is part of the Westchester Land Trust and includes 150 acres of woodlands, streams, and somewhat rugged terrain. There are four hiking loops that meander through 6 miles of trails here. The terrain is somewhat challenging on a couple of the trails.

KAYAK TOURS **Atlantic Kayak Tours** (914-739-2588; www.atlantickayaktours.com), 1 Annsville Circle, Cortlandt Manor. This is the only on-water full-service canoe and kayak center on the lower Hudson River. It's housed in the Annsville Creek Paddlesport Center. You can rent canoes and kayaks here as well as take lessons. Guided tours are offered from May through October.

Westchester County Tourism & Film

KAYAKING

SWIMMING Those who want to go to the beach can enjoy the one at **Playland Park** in Rye (914-813-7000; see *For Families*). There are some other nice beaches, as well:

Blue Mountain Reservation Beach (914-862-5275), Welcher Avenue, Peekskill, has beaches, a pool, and extensive recreation areas.

Croton Point Park and Beach (914-862-5290), 1A Croton Point Avenue, Croton-on-Hudson, overlooks the Hudson River and has special events during the summer months. There is also a swimming pool, recreation hall, and playing fields.

Osceola Beach and Picnic Grounds (914-245-3246), 399 East Main Street, Jefferson Valley, is a good place to go with small children. Snack bar, picnic tables, family atmosphere.

Spruce Lake at Mountain Lakes Park (914-669-5793), 201 Hawley Road, North Salem. This lake is open Saturday, Sunday, and holidays only from Memorial Day weekend through Labor Day. There is a nice sandy beach and picnic area, which makes this a good place to go with young children. Rowboats and canoes are available for rental by advance reservation.

✷ Winter Sports

CROSS-COUNTRY SKIING Westchester County offers a large number of places to cross-country ski when the weather cooperates. For information on ski conditions, clinics, and workshops, call 914-864-PARK before you go. The following places offer marked trails:

Blue Mountain Reservation, Welcher Avenue, Peekskill; **Cranberry Lake Preserve,** 1609 Old Orchard Street, North White Plains; **Lenoir Preserve,** Dudley

Street, Yonkers; **Marshlands Conservancy,** 220 Boston Post Road, Rye; **Mountain Lakes Park,** 201 Hawley Road, North Salem; **Saxon Woods Park,** 315 Mamaroneck Avenue, White Plains; **Ward Pound Ridge Reservation,** Routes 35 and 121, Cross River.

ICE SKATING Since schedules vary from month to month, do call the ice rinks for hours. Make sure to specify if you are interested in figure skating, ice hockey, public sessions, or freestyle time. There are three indoor rinks at Playland (see *To Do—For Families*) and at the following locations:

Ebersole Ice Rink (914-422-1348), Lake Street, White Plains. There are public skating sessions every day here for both ice hockey players and figure skaters.

Edward J. Murray Memorial Skating Center (914-377-6469), 348 Tuckahoe Road, Yonkers, is open daily for figure skating, speed skating, and ice hockey.

Hommocks Ice Rink (914-834-1069), 130 Hommocks Road, Larchmont, is open October through mid-June. Call for hours.

Ice Hutch (914-699-6787; www.rinktime.com), 655 Garden Avenue, Mount Vernon. The indoor ice rink here opened in 1997 and offers public skating year-round, as well as specific sessions for ice hockey and figure skating. There is a pro shop and concession on the premises. Check the website for a full schedule.

Playland Ice Casino (914-813-7059), 1 Playland Parkway, Rye, is open from late September through late May. There are three indoor rinks offering freestyle, adult, and children's sessions.

Westchester Skating Academy (914-347-8232), 91 Fairview Park Drive, Elmsford, has 2 NHL-size ice rinks with classes and rentals. Open year-round; call for hours.

✷ Green Space

Westchester County may be a bustling area for big business and corporate headquarters, but you will also find dozens of lovely public parks and outdoor facilities throughout the region.

Blue Mountain Reservation (914-862-5275), Welcher Avenue, Peekskill. Open year-round. Situated in the northwestern part of the county, this recreation area has a large lake for swimming in the summer and ice skating during the winter. There are facilities for hiking, fishing, and picnicking. Camping is available in the Trail Lodge, which has a dining hall and large fireplace.

Colonial Greenway (914-864-PARK). This 15-mile unpaved trail goes through New Rochelle, Mamaroneck, Eastchester, and Scarsdale. No bicycles are permitted here, and it is ideal for hiking or walking. Dogs are permitted if they are leashed. Some of the areas encompassed by this greenway are Saxon Woods, the Hutchinson River Pathway, Twin Lakes County Park, Ward Acres, and the Leatherstocking Trail.

Cranberry Lake Preserve (914-428-1005), 1609 Old Orchard Street, off Route 22, North White Plains. Open year-round, Tuesday through Sunday 9–4. This lovely preserve consists of 190 acres of unspoiled wetlands and hardwood forests. The park has a 5-acre lake with trails and boardwalks, so visitors can observe life in an aquatic habitat. You will also find cross-country ski trails and hiking. A small lodge offers interpretive programs and seasonal exhibits. There is also a summer ecology program for children as well as a rock quarry at the preserve.

Croton Point Park (914-862-5290), Croton Avenue (off Route 9), Croton-on-Hudson. Open year-round. This park is located along the banks of the Hudson River and features a pool, canoe-launching area, recreation hall, and ball fields. The location is ideal for fishing, hiking, and picnicking. Cabins, lean-tos, and facilities for tents and trailers are also available. On 504-acre Croton Point Park, the largest peninsula on the Hudson River, there are exhibits on local flora and fauna in the **Croton Point Nature Center** (914-862-5297), as well as displays on local and Native American history.

Greenburgh Nature Center (914-723-3470), 99 Dromore Road, off Central Avenue, Scarsdale. Open year-round, daily, except Friday, 9:30–4:30. Situated on 32 acres, this innovative nature center offers visitors a chance to explore several environments, including woodlands, a vineyard, orchards, and cultivated gardens. More than 30 different species of trees can be found in the preserve, along with wildflowers, ferns, and a host of songbirds. At the center's museum, see a Nunatak, an Inuit word meaning "hill of stone"; more than 100 animal exhibits; descriptive displays that explain some of the area's natural history; and a glass beehive. You can also pick up maps here to use on the self-guided nature walks. Many special events are held at the nature center, from concerts on the lawn to art exhibits.

Marshlands Conservancy (914-835-4466), 220 Boston Post Road, Rye. Open year-round. There is an environmental education center with changing exhibitions and four saltwater aquaria at this 173-acre wildlife sanctuary. The unique character of the conservancy lies in the diversity of habitats preserved within its boundaries, including woods, fields, freshwater ponds, a salt marsh, and shore. Paths throughout the conservancy lead to these points of interest.

Rockefeller State Park Preserve (914-631-1470), 125 Route 117, Pleasantville. Open year-round, daily 7 AM–sunset. Find a variety of habitats here, including wetlands, woodlands, meadows, fields, and a lake. Miles of hiking trails, which during the winter become cross-country ski trails, will delight outdoors lovers, and for horseback riders, there are beautiful bridle paths. The visitors center hosts exhibits of local and historical interest. This preserve is truly a county treasure, private land opened to the public through the generosity of the Rockefeller family.

Rye Nature Center (914-967-5150), 873 Boston Post Road, Rye. The grounds are open daily dawn to dusk. The nature center is open daily, except Sunday, 10–4. A small nature center (less than 50 acres), this is a nice stop if you are traveling with children. The museum has exhibits of local plants and animals, and there are some mini exhibits about nature. Take the 2.5-mile walk, described in a guide you can pick up at the museum. Picnic area available to visitors.

Scenic Hudson Park at Irvington (845-473-4440). From I-287, exit 9, take Route 9 south for 1.6 miles. At the light turn right onto Main Street and continue to the end. Make a right on North Astor Street, a left on Bridge Street, cross the railroad tracks, and continue bearing to the left. The park is on the right, past Bridge Street Properties. This 12-acre site, with views of the Manhattan skyline, the Palisades, and Tappan Zee Bridge, is continually being transformed into parkland. Scenic Hudson Land Trust saved the area from development. There is a promenade, small boat launch, and ball fields.

Teatown Lake Reservation (914-762-2912), 1600 Spring Valley Road, Ossining. Take exit 134 off the Taconic, and then follow Grant's Lane to Spring Valley Road. Open daily year-round; museum open Tuesday through Sunday 9–5. Free. This 834-acre reservation has marked nature walks and 15 miles of hiking trails, a museum, and outdoor exhibits. Wildflowers are abundant here in the spring, with more than 230 species native to the area on a 2-acre island. Guided tours of the island are offered April through September. Visitors can enjoy viewing waterfowl and other animals at a large lake; inside the museum are live exhibits of local animals and plants.

Ward Pound Ridge Reservation (914-864-7317), Routes 35 and 121, Cross River. Open year-round, daily 8–dusk. Parking fee. Ward Pound Ridge is the largest park in Westchester, covering more than 4,300 acres. There are 35 miles of trails for cross-country skiing, sledding, hiking, and horseback riding. There are also several places to go fishing and to picnic. You can easily spend a day here. Year-round, on Saturdays there are often nature programs for children and families at the Trailside Nature Museum (open Tuesday through Saturday 9–4).

ROCKEFELLER STATE PARK PRESERVE IN PLEASANTVILLE

Westchester County Tourism & Film

Weinberg Nature Center (914-722-1289), 455 Mamaroneck Road, Scarsdale. The nature trail here is open year-round, daily from dawn to dusk. The Trailside Museum is open after Labor Day through May, Monday, Wednesday, and Friday 10–5; Tuesday and Thursday 10–2. June through Labor Day, Monday through Friday 9–5. This sanctuary is home to a range of birds and wildlife, with a meadow, orchard, butterfly and hummingbird garden, Japanese-style Zen meditation garden, and outdoor Native American village. The Trailside Museum shows exhibits and offers educational programs focusing on the local environment and its wildlife, archaeology, and Native American culture. A great place to take children!

Westmoreland Sanctuary (914-666-8448), 260 Chestnut Ridge Road, Mount Kisco. Open year-round, dawn to dusk. Museum open Monday through Saturday 9–5; Sunday 10:30–5. Free, but fees are charged for some workshops and special events. The sanctuary is an active site, with more than 7 miles of walking and hiking trails, wildlife displays, and exhibits of local natural history. There are workshops, lectures, and events all year, including seasonal hikes, birdsong identification walks, Earth Day celebrations, even a search for the first ferns of spring! An excellent site for a family visit.

✱ Lodging

BED & BREAKFASTS Westchester County is home to many conference centers and fine hotels, which offer visitors everything from saunas and spas to fine dining. Visitors who prefer B&B establishments will have difficulty finding one. Due to the restrictive zoning regulations in most Westchester communities, such businesses are rare. After extensive research, I discovered only the following places in the county that fit into this category.

Alexander Hamilton House (914-271-6737), 49 Van Wyck Street, Croton-on-Hudson 10520. ($$) This Victorian house dates from 1889 and has eight luxurious rooms; two have Jacuzzis, and five have fireplaces. The bridal chamber is on the third floor and has a king-size bed, skylights, and pink-marble fireplace. All rooms have private bath, TV, telephone, and high-speed Internet access

Crabtree's Kittle House (914-666-8044), 11 Kittle Road, Chappaqua 10514. ($$) This 200-plus-year-old building has been an inn since the 1930s, when it attracted film stars like Henry Fonda and Tallulah Bankhead. One of the only inns in Westchester, the Kittle House is moderately priced for the area. A full breakfast is served, and children are welcome. There are 13 rooms with private bath, telephone, cable TV, and high-speed Internet access. Guests can enjoy the fine restaurant on the premises, as well (see *Dining Out*).

HOTELS AND CONFERENCE CENTERS The following full-service hotels and conference centers welcome individual guests as well as groups.

The Castle on the Hudson (914-524-6366), 400 Benedict Avenue, Tarrytown 10591. ($$$) Only 25 miles north of Manhattan, perched in splendor on 10 hilltop acres overlooking the majestic Hudson River, is this establishment—an authentic castle and one of the oldest and grandest historic landmarks in the region. The main tower rises 75 feet, the highest point in Westchester County. Built between 1897 and 1910 by the son of a Civil War general, the Castle has changed little in the last 100 years. Much of the hewn-oak girders, beams, woodwork, and some of the furniture were brought over from Europe. The innkeepers are European, and the service is excellent. Today a luxury inn, gourmet restaurant (the Equus; see *Dining Out*), and special-events facility, this is one of the most magical, romantic spots anywhere. The accommodations include 26 rooms and 5 enormous suites that range from 750 to 900 square feet. For a special occasion, ask for the tower suite—it is magnificent and has fantastic views of the river and mountains; I will always remember my stay there. Spacious living rooms, working fireplaces, and luxurious bathrooms are standard. Each suite includes color cable TV, in-room fax, and minibar, and most have a fireplace. Open year-round.

Courtyard by Marriott (914-631-1122; 1-800-589-8720), 475 White Plains Road, Tarrytown 10591. ($$) This relatively small (139 rooms), moderately priced hotel offers a Jacuzzi and pool where guests can relax, as well as a scenic courtyard. The Courtyard Café serves breakfast daily.

Crowne Plaza (914-682-0050; 1-800-PLAINS-2), 66 Hale Avenue, White Plains 10601. ($$) This hotel, with 400 guest rooms and an indoor pool, whirlpool, sauna, and exercise room, also has a restaurant on the premises where guests can get breakfast, lunch, and dinner daily.

Doral Arrowwood (914-939-5500; 1-866-241-8752), 975 Anderson Hill Road (exit 8E off I-287), Rye Brook 10573. ($$$) This full-facility resort of 374 rooms is located on 114 wooded acres. You will find a nine-hole golf course, indoor-outdoor pools, tennis and squash courts, along with a sauna and Universal gym. The atrium dining room is a multilevel restaurant that overlooks the grounds and gardens, and serves excellent food. Weekend packages are available during the spring and summer. Children are welcome.

Doubletree Hotel (914-631-5700; 1-800-222-8733), 455 South Broadway, Tarrytown 10591. ($$) There are 246 rooms in this full-service hotel, with an indoor swimming pool and all the amenities, including a restaurant on the premises. This is a great location if you plan to visit the historic sites along Route 9. Open year-round.

Hampton Inn (914-592-5680; 1-800-HAMPTON), 200 Tarrytown Road, Elmsford 10523. ($$) There are 156 rooms in this moderately priced hotel. A fitness room and outdoor pool are available to guests, and a deluxe continental breakfast is served 6–10. Open year-round.

Hilton Westchester (914-939-6300; 1-800-HILTONS), 699 Westchester Avenue, Rye Brook 10573. ($$) This

THE CASTLE ON THE HUDSON IN TARRYTOWN

Westchester County Tourism & Film

Westchester County Tourism & Film

DOUBLETREE HOTEL LOBBY IN TARRYTOWN

hotel has 445 guest rooms, indoor and outdoor pools, saunas, whirlpool, tennis courts, and an exercise room. The restaurant **Tulip Tree** serves casual, inexpensive fare.

The Inn on the Hudson (914-739-1500; 1-800-526-9466), 634 Main Street, Peekskill 10566. ($$) This moderately priced inn has 53 guest rooms, an outdoor pool, and a restaurant on the premises. A continental breakfast is served 5:30–9:30. Open year-round.

La Quinta Inn & Suites (914-273-9090; 1-800-444-8888), 94 Business Park Drive, exit 3 off I-684, Armonk 10504. ($$) This renovated 140-room hotel has an exercise room, as well as complimentary shuttle service to and from Westchester County Airport. A restaurant is on the premises.

Renaissance Westchester Hotel (914-694-5400), 80 West Red Oak Lane, White Plains 10604. ($$$) This 347-room full-service hotel has an indoor pool, sundeck, whirlpool, sauna, exercise room, and tennis and volleyball courts. Located on 30 wooded acres. There are nice dining facilities in **80 West Restaurant** overlooking the grounds. Special weekend rates.

Tarrytown House Estate and Conference Center (914-591-8200; 1-800-553-8118), 49 East Sunnyside Lane, exit 9 off I-287, Tarrytown 10591. ($$) There are 212 rooms here in this beautiful, completely renovated castlelike structure. Guests can enjoy indoor and outdoor pools, a fitness center, racquetball, sauna, Jacuzzi, and tennis courts. Breakfast, lunch, and dinner are served to guests.

Westchester Marriott (914-631-2200; 1-800-882-1042), 670 White Plains Road, exit 1 off I-287 or exit 9 off I-87, Tarrytown 10591. ($$$) The hotel has 444 guest rooms, an indoor pool, sauna, whirlpool, and fitness center. **The Harvest Grill** serves breakfast only; **Ruth's Chris Steakhouse** serves excellent porterhouse steaks in an elegant atmosphere every evening from 5. There is also a sports bar, the **Pub,** on the premises. The location is excellent, close to many of the historic attractions in Tarrytown.

✷ Where to Eat

Westchester is fortunate to have hundreds of eateries, in all price ranges and to please all tastes. I only wish I had the time and money to sample all of them—a daunting task. The following were selected from my personal experience traveling throughout the county; they are only some of the fine choices available. Since the county is large, restaurants in the *Dining Out* section are grouped by geographic area (northwest, northeast, central, southwest, and southeast). Don't be afraid to try the broad spectrum of places—ranging from Indian and Thai to Italian and American—that can be found in this restaurant-intensive region of the Hudson Valley!

DINING OUT

Northwestern Westchester (Including Peekskill, Croton, Ossining)

Birdsall House (914-930-1880), 970 Main Street, Peekskill. ($$) Open Monday through Wednesday 12–12; Thursday through Saturday noon–1 AM; Sunday 11 AM–midnight. This renovated 1940s tavern, with black-and-white checked floor, several red leather booths, and enormous mahogany bar, serves an excellent selection of craft beers. The chef here, a graduate of the Culinary Institute, worked at Chez Panisse in Berkeley, California. His creative cuisine includes such interesting offerings as nachos with sweet and spicy mango salsa over pulled pork, black beans, cheddar cheese, and sour cream with blue tortilla chips, and garlic shrimp skewers with ratatouille. There are also burgers and fried chicken for the less adventurous. Prices are surprisingly reasonable.

Churrasqueira Ribatejo (914-941-5928), 39 Spring Street, Ossining. ($) Open every day, except Tuesday, 11–10 for lunch and dinner. This family-run Portuguese diner, an informal eatery where you can watch your food being prepared on an open grill, is a real find. The barbecued chicken (or meat) and spicy shrimp with rice and fresh vegetables are piled high on the plate, and the prices here are difficult to beat. The fresh fish (red snapper) and steaming clams in garlic broth are my favorite dishes. For a quick take-out choice (and there's a lot to choose from), go with the homemade cod cakes. Children welcome.

Division Street Grill (914-739-6380), 26 North Division Street, Peekskill. ($$) Open daily, except Tuesday, for lunch 11:30–4; dinner from 5. Live jazz on Friday and Saturday nights. Contemporary American cuisine served in an intimate atmosphere in the city's artist district. The work of local painters decorates the walls. An imaginative take on the standard offerings. Try the first-rate pan-seared tuna in a soy buerre blanc, or goat cheese and herb-encrusted rack of lamb. For dessert, there is banana chocolate chunk bread pudding, which is wonderful. Homemade chicken fingers will delight the kids!

Gleason's (914-402-1950), 911 South Street, Peekskill. ($) Open Monday through Wednesday noon–10; Thursday through Saturday noon–midnight. Located in a historic building with high-gloss wood floors, pressed-tin ceilings, and vintage movie posters adorning the walls, this is the place to go for hearty food at affordable prices. The name is a tribute to Jackie Gleason, a resident of the area in the early 1960s. The specialties here are flatbreads and artisanal pizzas. Most are amazingly imaginative and tasty, and seasonal ingredients are used. There are also pasta dishes, a number of daily specials, soups, and salads. Don't skip dessert, since the tiramisu is excellent—they make their own ladyfingers.

Hudson at Haymount House (914-502-0080), 25 Studio Hill Road, Briarcliff Manor. ($$) Open Tuesday through Saturday 5:30–10; Sunday brunch 11:30–2:30; dinner 5–8. Located in a century-old Southern-style mansion with gorgeous Hudson River views (formerly Maison Lafitte French restaurant), this contemporary American restaurant features imaginative entrées using the freshest local ingredients. A few of the offerings include gnocchi with prosciutto and lobster, roast cod with tomato-rhubarb compote, and smoked beef short ribs. All desserts, as well as ice creams and sorbets, are homemade and excellent. The spacious wood and marble bar is set off in a separate room with a less-expensive tavern menu that includes items like burgers and pasta. This is a delightful place to enjoy a relaxing repast, particularly during the summer months.

India House (914-736-0005), 199 Albany Post Road, Montrose. ($$) Open daily for lunch 11:30–2; dinner 5–10. Lots of greenery surrounds this attractive restaurant. The dining rooms are decorated to resemble a colorful, handmade tent, with walls hung with antique tapestries. Tandoori lamb, chicken, and shrimp dishes are the specialty. The vegetarian entrées are excellent, and everything can be prepared from mild to very hot and spicy—just let the server know your preference. Children welcome.

Iron Horse Grill (914-741-0717), 20 Wheeler Avenue, Pleasantville. ($$$) Open for dinner Tuesday through Saturday from 5. Located around the corner from the Jacob Burns Film Center (see *Entertainment*) in the renovated waiting room of the Pleasantville train station, this establishment specializes in contemporary American cuisine in elegant surroundings. A favorite appetizer of mine is the tuna sashimi with seaweed. Entrées include breast of duck with rhubarb chutney, rack of lamb with polenta, and fillet of yellowtail sole, all creatively presented. Outdoor dining on the patio in the warm-weather months. The prix fixe menu offers excellent value. Good wine list with moderately priced selections.

Ocean House (914-271-0702), 49 North Riverside Avenue, Croton-on-Hudson. ($) Open for dinner Tuesday through Saturday 5–10. This cozy restaurant, a former diner dating from the early 20th century, serves up hearty seafood and fresh fish of all kinds. The clam chowder is phenomenal, and so is the fish stew. No reservations are taken, and BYO wine or beer. Good value. Children welcome.

Quiet Man Public House (914-930-8230), 18 North Division Street, Peekskill. ($$) Open Tuesday through Sunday noon–10; bar open until 4 AM. This traditional Irish pub allows customers to pull their own pints of Guinness or select from over a dozen beers on tap. There are traditional offerings like soda bread, fish-and-chips, shepherd's pie, and bangers and mash, as well as burgers, chili, and beef stroganoff. Enjoy outdoor dining here during the warm weather months and savor the tastes of Ireland!

Squires (914-762-3376), 94 North State Road, Briarcliff Manor. ($) Open Monday through Saturday 11:30–10; Sunday 4–9:30. This informal pub, located in a strip mall, has been in business for over 40 years . . . and for good reason. Their Kobe beef burgers are simply excellent—charcoal grilled perfectly so that they remain rare on the inside. There are also buffalo chipotle burgers, cheeseburgers, and an array of choices for toppings. This unpretentious eatery is worth a detour if you're a burger aficionado!

Twelve Grapes Music & Wine Bar (914-737-6624), 12 North Division Street, Peekskill. ($$) Open Tuesday through Saturday for dinner from 5:30; Saturday and Sunday brunch 11–3. Late night menu on weekends. New American cuisine by a Culinary Institute graduate featuring imaginative appetizers and light entrées. Do try the mushroom ravioli and margarita pizza; both were quite good. There is live music Thursday through Saturday, as well as at Sunday brunch (jazz, blues, and contemporary rock).

Umami (914-271-5555), 325 South Riverside Avenue, Croton-on-Hudson. ($) Open for dinner Sunday through Thursday 5:30–10, Friday and Saturday until 11. Pronounced oo-MAH-mee, the word refers to an amino acid present in various acidic foods that gives them a more complex taste. Diners in this intimate, simply furnished eatery will enjoy citrus flavors and interesting food combinations. The imaginatively prepared international cooking features specialties like coconut lime soup with chicken, shrimp, or vegetables; mini tacos with seared tuna guacamole and wasabi-laced sour cream; Peking duck quesadilla; or Thai-style curry. Try the Blue Pig ice cream for dessert. This restaurant opened in 2002 and has a dedicated local following. Reasonable prices for healthful, delicious creations.

Yama Sushi (914-941-3100), 1914 Pleasantville Road, Briarcliff Manor. ($) Open daily for lunch 11–3; dinner 5–10. This tiny, simple Japanese restaurant offers excellent sushi and sashimi. The rolled sushi has little rice and lots of fish, making it particularly tasty. Teriyaki, tempura, noodle dishes, and daily specials (make sure to ask about them) are also offered, but this is the place to go for sushi lovers!

Zephs' (914-736-2159), 638 Central Avenue, Peekskill. ($$$) Open Thursday through Sunday at 5:30 for dinner. Set in a reclaimed factory building, Zephs' serves American cuisine with a fresh twist. Choices may include Moroccan lamb, potato-crusted salmon, tomato tart, salt and pepper squid, fresh fruit cobblers, mud cake, and rich custards. Many of the herbs are grown by the owners, and summer diners can enjoy the outdoor patio area. Reservations are necessary.

Northeastern Westchester (Including North and South Salem, Katonah, Mount Kisco, Pound Ridge, Chappaqua)

Bacio Trattoria (914-763-2233), 12 North Salem Road, Cross River. ($$) Open for lunch Tuesday through Saturday 11–3; dinner Tuesday through Thursday 5–9:30, Friday and Saturday until 10; Sunday 12:30–9. This intimate restaurant, featuring Mediterranean cuisine, has a large outdoor patio for alfresco dining in the summer months; there is a relaxed leisurely pace about the service. The grilled calamari is excellent, and so is the white-bean soup and roasted-vegetable ravioli with walnut sauce. Lemon risotto with grilled scallops, and monkfish fillet in cherry tomato and garlic sauce, are also popular here. For dessert try the apple pie à la mode. Moderately priced wine list. Children's menu.

The Barn and Farmhouse at Bedford Post Inn (914-234-7800), 954 Old Post Road (Route 121), Bedford Village. ($$$) There are two restaurants here: The Barn is casual and serves brunch Monday through Friday 8–2 and Saturday and Sunday 9–3, and dinner Monday and Tuesday 5–8:30. The Farmhouse is open for dinner Wednesday through Sunday 5:30–9:30. When this restaurant first opened in early 2008, in a historic property, it was the topic of lots of conversation in the county: The celebrity co-owner is Richard Gere. The contemporary American cuisine is excellent and imaginative despite some of the pretension here, with just about everything served coming from local purveyors. The café-style main room has old beams that give the feeling of a barn. There is a small outdoor patio for dining in the warm-weather months.

The Blue Dolphin Ristorante (914-232-4791), 175 Katonah Avenue, Katonah. ($) Open daily, except Sunday, for lunch 11–3; dinner 5–10. This family-owned and family-operated Italian restaurant housed in a dinerlike building is a mainstay in town. Don't miss the ziti Blue Dolphin, fried calamari, and excellent soups. The prices are exceedingly reasonable, and the service is friendly. A wonderful choice for those traveling with children.

Crabtree's Kittle House (914-666-8044), 11 Kittle Road, Chappaqua. ($$$) Open for lunch Monday through Friday noon–2:30; dinner served daily 5:30–10; Sunday brunch noon–2:30. The American cuisine here has Italian, French, and Asian influences. The menu changes daily, but the excellent roasted free-range Hudson Valley chicken with black truffles is a specialty of the house. There is an award-winning wine cellar here. The pastry chef suggests the Alsatian cheesecake with huckleberry sauce—one of his favorites. Live jazz on Friday and Saturday nights.

Kira (914-765-0800), 575 Main Street, Armonk. ($$) Open for lunch Monday through Saturday 11:30–3; dinner 3–10; Sunday noon–10. This traditional Japanese restaurant offers sushi, sashimi, tempura, and some wonderful Pan-Asian dishes. I enjoyed the fantastic sashimi deluxe. Those who prefer hot entrées should sample the Malaysian red curry with chicken. Although this restaurant is located in a strip mall and the ambience isn't anything special, the fish is always fresh.

La Camelia (914-666-2466), 234 North Bedford Road, Mount Kisco. ($$) Open for lunch and dinner daily, except Monday, noon–9:30. One of the best Spanish restaurants you will find anywhere in the county, La Camelia is located in a landmark 150-year-old building. Northern Spanish cuisine is the specialty and includes gazpacho, shrimp Catalan, squid with angel-hair pasta, and homemade desserts. Children welcome.

La Cremaillere (914-234-9647), 46 Bedford Road, Banksville. ($$$) Open for lunch Thursday through Saturday noon–2:30; dinner Tuesday through Saturday 6–9:30; Sunday 1–8. This renowned classic French restaurant offers a beautiful country setting in which to enjoy entrées like châteaubriand, duck, and rack of lamb. Excellent wine list. Reservations suggested. Not recommended for children.

Lalibela (914-864-1343), 37 South Moger Avenue, Mount Kisco. ($$) Open Tuesday through Friday for lunch 11:30–4; dinner 4–9:30; Saturday and Sunday 12:30–10:30. Ethiopian cuisine is served on a large central tray lined with flatbread for scooping the food that is usually stewed. Knives and forks are available here by request, but it's more fun to have the communal experience of eating with one's hands. There are several kinds of fresh salads, vegetable and lentil dishes, as well as chicken and beef stews. The dishes are subtly spiced, and it's fun to order a few different entrées. The waitstaff will be pleased to assist with selections.

Le Chateau (914-533-6631), 1410 Route 35, South Salem. ($$$) Open daily, except Monday, for dinner at 6; Sunday brunch noon–3. This French restaurant with old-world charm is situated on 32 wooded acres and offers magnificent sunset views and lavishly decorated dining rooms. House specialties include châteaubriand béarnaise for two, or roasted sea scallops with asparagus tips and vermouth truffle coulis. There is Grand Marnier soufflé for dessert. This is a perfect choice for a special occasion; Le Chateau is elegant, and the cuisine and service are first-rate.

Le Fontane (914-232-9619), 137 Route 100 (corner of Routes 100 and 139), Katonah. ($$) Open Tuesday through Friday for lunch 11:30–3 and dinner 5–10; Saturday and Sunday noon–9:30. Traditional Southern Italian cuisine featured on seasonal menus with all the usual favorites. Indoor as well as alfresco patio dining. The fixed-price lunch and dinner menu is a bargain. They've been around for 25 years and are a mainstay in town.

Moderne Barn (914-730-0001), 430 Bedford Road, Armonk. ($$) Open for lunch Monday through Friday noon–2:30; dinner Monday through Thursday 5–10; Friday and Saturday until 11; Sunday brunch noon–2:30; dinner 5–9. The outstanding contemporary American cuisine here has Mediterranean influences enhanced by locally sourced seasonal produce. A few of the entrées include peppercorn tuna, seafood risotto, and beefsteak with a choice of sauces, but there are also burgers, pasta, and thin-crust pizzas. Attention to detail is evident in every dish. The dining space, a renovated furniture barn, features booths with long banquettes and seats 200, yet has a festive, welcoming atmosphere. A separate bar serves a number of wines by the glass.

Myong Gourmet (914-241-6333), 487 Main Street, Mount Kisco. ($$) Open daily for lunch 11–4; dinner daily, except Sunday, 5–10. The Asian fusion/American cuisine here is difficult to describe. There are Korean dishes like barbecued short ribs and bim bop (brown rice with vegetables topped with a fried egg), as well as lamb sliders, lobster shooters, and ricotta basil ravioli. The small café is perfect for a quick snack, and a large dining room accommodates those who want a larger repast.

NEO World Bistro and Sushi Bar (914-244-9711), 69 South Moger Avenue, Mount Kisco. ($$) Open for lunch Monday through Saturday 11:30–3; dinner Monday through Thursday 4:30–10; Friday and Saturday until 11; Sunday 1–9:30. The combined flavors of the East and West meet here. For example, there is a sushi tortilla filled with tuna, salmon, cilantro, and guacamole. A tangy seafood bouillabaisse is prepared with chili aioli. There is a full range of sushi and sashimi, of course, as well as chicken crêpes for lunch. Try the green tea crème brûlée for dessert!

Nino's (914-533-2671), 355 Smith Ridge Road, South Salem. ($$) Open for lunch and dinner daily noon–10. This simple restaurant serving Northern Italian cuisine is run by five brothers. Try the fried calamari and grilled veal chops. The Dover sole with lemon, white wine, and garlic is another of my favorites from the extensive menu. And save room for one of the treats from the multitiered dessert cart. Not recommended for children.

North Star (914-764-0200), 85 Westchester Avenue, Pound Ridge. ($$) Open for dinner daily 5:30–10.

High-quality American cuisine is served in a relaxed atmosphere featuring rich colors, antique wood beams, and low lights. The entrées include trout, halibut, oysters on the half shell, filet mignon with a choice of rubs, as well as interesting pasta selections and salads. Make sure to save room for dessert here. There is live music on Wednesday, Thursday, and Sunday evenings. On Tuesday, wine bottles are half price.

121 Restaurant (914-669-0100), 2 Dingle Ridge Road, North Salem. ($$) Open daily for lunch 11:30–2:30; dinner 5–10. This is the best kind of neighborhood restaurant. They serve creamy potato leek soup, crisp fried calamari, wood-fired oven pizzas, ribs, roasted chicken, pasta, and sandwiches served with steak fries. Do try a side of the truffle-scented French fries! There's live music on occasion and fixed-price dinners at various times of the year.

Purdy's Farmer and the Fish (914-617-8380), 100 Titicus Road, at the junction of Routes 116 and 22, North Salem. ($$) Open for lunch Monday through Saturday noon–3; dinner Monday through Thursday 5:30–11, Friday and Saturday 5:30–midnight, Sunday 5:30–10. This renovated 18th-century homestead has beamed dining areas around a central stone chimney. The 5 acres in back of the restaurant are used as gardens where all kinds of vegetables and herbs grow in season. Fish is the specialty of the house here, including a tiered seafood tower for two. A raw bar with well-chilled oysters, clams, shrimp, scallops, and lobsters is at the entrance. Everything is fresh and beautifully presented with an array of interesting garnishes. If you are a lobster lover, this is the place to order it!

Restaurant North (914-273-8686), 386 Main Street, Armonk. ($$$) Open for lunch Tuesday through Friday noon–2:30; dinner Tuesday through Thursday 5–9:30; Friday and Saturday until 10:30; Saturday brunch 11–2:30. Closed Sunday and Monday. The menu changes daily at this farm to table, slow food restaurant, reflecting what is fresh and in season. The walls here are cream colored and the bar is white marble, adding to the spare, sophisticated ambience. The owner was formerly chef at the renowned Tavern in Garrison. Some of the fancy food here is hit and miss, but the homemade pumpernickel rolls, tuna tartare over avocado, and venison loin with foie gras dirty rice are memorable. Be aware that the restaurant can be extremely noisy when it is crowded. There is outdoor dining in the warm weather.

Spoon (914-238-1988), 415 King Street, Chappaqua. ($$) Open Monday through Saturday for lunch 11:30–3; dinner 4:30–10; Sunday 4:30–10. The Asian fusion offerings include many Japanese dishes, featuring an array of rolls and excellent sashimi. There are also dishes like pork loin, seafood udon, Asian duck with pancakes, baby back ribs, and chocolate truffle cake for dessert.

Vox (914-669-5450), 721 Titicus Road, North Salem. ($$) Open for lunch Thursday and Friday noon–2; dinner Wednesday and Thursday 6–9, until 10 Friday and Saturday; Sunday 1–8. Enjoy contemporary American cuisine with a French touch in this lovely country inn. Comfortable chairs and beautifully appointed tables grace the dining room, and the dinner menu includes such treats as filet mignon with tarragon-scented béarnaise, grilled yellowfin tuna, and duck "two ways." For those who desire lighter fare, the Vox burger is an imaginative variation on a classic. Don't skip the chocolate ribbon cake if you want dessert. Excellent wine list.

Central Westchester (Including White Plains, Larchmont, Scarsdale, Hartsdale Area)

Anna Maria Italian Restaurant (914-833-0555), 18 Chatsworth Avenue, Larchmont. ($$$) Open Tuesday 5–10; Wednesday and Thursday 11:30–10, Friday and Saturday until 11; Sunday 11:30–9. Closed Monday. This comfortable, welcoming family restaurant specializes in Italian comfort food. There is a wide variety of offerings, including fried calamari, pumpkin mascarpone ravioli, rigatoni Bolognese, and hanger steak, to name just some of the varied dishes on the menu. Anna Maria Santorelli was born in Naples, Italy, and is always at the restaurant, making sure patrons are well served.

Bellota at 42 (914-861-3226), Ritz-Carlton Westchester, One Renaissance Square, White Plains. ($$) Open Tuesday and Wednesday 5–10; Thursday 5–10:30; Friday and Saturday 5 PM–1 AM. Closed Sunday and Monday. Bellota is a restaurant within a restaurant (see the 42 Restaurant listing in this section) and includes a bar and lounge with dramatic views of the city from the 42nd floor of the Ritz-Carlton. *Bellota* means acorn, and in Spain pigs eat them, producing a delicious ham that is served here. The first-rate tapas are the specialty on the Spanish- and Portuguese–influenced menu. A couple of the offerings include baby lamb chops and ceviche.

BLT Steak (914-467-5710), 221 Main Street, White Plains. ($$$) Open for dinner daily 5:30–10:30. This is a reinvention of the classic American steakhouse, specializing in aged, perfectly prepared meats and fresh seafood. T-bone steak, short ribs, lamb shank, Dover sole, and roasted chicken are some of the entrées offered here. There is an excellent selection of wines by the glass. Not recommended for children.

China White Noodle Bar (914-437-9700), 578 Anderson Hill Road, Purchase. ($$) Open daily for lunch 11:30–2:30; dinner 5–10:30. There are large white paper lanterns lighting the dining room here, and, as the name suggests, everything is white. The Cantonese dishes include steamed shrimp dumplings, crisp pork spare ribs, Peking roast duck with mu shu pancakes, and chicken chow fun. The bar is busy and serves up a number of exotic cocktails. This is a fun place to dine, and children are welcome.

The 808 Bistro (914-722-0808), 808 Scarsdale Avenue, Scarsdale. ($$) Open daily noon–11. The international fare in this informal dining spot includes gnocchi, duck, mushroom risotto, roast chicken, and skirt steak. There is something for every taste, and most offerings are both healthful and tasty. Children welcome.

42 Restaurant (914-761-4242), One Renaissance Square, White Plains. ($$$) Open daily, except Sunday, for lunch noon–3; dinner 5–10. This restaurant is located on the 42nd floor (South Tower) of the Ritz-Carlton Hotel, the highest building between Albany and Manhattan. The 22-foot-tall windows offer panoramic views of New York City, the Long Island Sound, and the Hudson River. There's a 3,600-bottle wine cellar as well. This first-rate restaurant serving New American cuisine draws many diners for the amazing venue, but the fare is superior as well.

Harrys of Hartsdale (914-472-8777), 230 East Hartsdale Avenue, Hartsdale. ($$$) Open daily for lunch 11:30–3; dinner 3–10:30; Saturday and Sunday brunch 11–3. This steakhouse is also known for its raw bar, which offers shrimp, lobster, crabmeat, and clams. I could dine at least twice a week at the oyster bar, which serves at least six types of oysters (which vary seasonally); Harrys sells more than 3,000 oysters a week. In addition, steaks, chicken, pasta, and fish entrées are served. This is a great place to try tuna and salmon tartare . . . and creamsicle cake for dessert. Family atmosphere—children are welcome.

Lucky Buddha (914-495-3365), Thornwood Town Center, 1008 Broadway, Thornwood. ($$) Open Monday through Saturday for lunch 11:30–3; dinner 3–10:30; Sunday 1–10. A large Buddha statue at the entrance here welcomes guests to the restaurant, featuring a bar, sushi station, and grill room with hibachi-style grills. There are lots of comfortable black leather booths in the main dining room and a large menu of Chinese and Thai specialties. While sushi is a favorite choice among diners, there is pad thai and several wok-grilled dishes. This is a fun place to go with a large group who enjoy sharing dishes. The lunch specials are a great bargain.

Lusardi's (914-834-5555), 1885 Palmer Avenue, Larchmont. ($$) Open for lunch and dinner daily noon–10:30. The Northern Italian cuisine here has a Mediterranean accent; it's served in an informal atmosphere. Enjoy veal Martini, homemade pasta stuffed with spinach and porcini mushrooms, or artichoke salad with arugula, Parmesan cheese, and diced cherry tomatoes. Children welcome.

Meritage (914-472-8484), 1505 Weaver Street, Scarsdale. ($$) Open for dinner daily 6–10. This simple restaurant, located in a strip mall, attracts a predominantly local clientele for a reason—the New American fare is consistently good. The duck confit, crab and avocado salad, and pan-roasted halibut were all prepared to perfection. The pastas are made on the premises, and most of the ingredients are local and organic. The desserts are quite good here, too, so indulge.

Mulino's (914-761-1818), 99 Court Street, White Plains. ($$) Open Monday through Friday for lunch 11:30–4; dinner 4–11:30; Saturday dinner only 5–midnight. The Northern Italian cuisine here is quite good, and the tables look out on a courtyard garden with waterfalls. This is the gathering place of several politicians in Westchester County, White Plains being the county seat, and the location of the restaurant is in the downtown area. Enjoy rack of lamb, veal chop, and fresh fish, including Dover sole, and save room for the tempting desserts. Children are welcome.

Mythos (914-747-2122), Thornwood Town Center, 1006 Broadway, Thornwood. ($$) Open daily 11–10. Greek specialties like taramosalata, tzatziki, pastitsio, spanakopita, and moussaka are served in a family-friendly atmosphere. The walls are covered with photographs of well-known tourist sites in Greece, and there are several cozy booths. Appetizers and salads are offered in generous portions, and one can easily make a meal from them. There are entrées like grilled lamb chops and a seafood platter for those who prefer more basic fare, but make sure to try the Greek dessert galaktoboureko (custard in phyllo with cinnamon and honey)!

Pete's Saloon (914-592-9849), 8 West Main Street, Elmsford. ($$) Open daily 11:30–midnight. This informal eatery with a busy bar serves classic American favorites, including a variety of burgers, steaks, sandwiches, and salads. The stuffed pork chops and lemon chicken are two popular entrées.

There are several bottled beers available, as well as 10 beers on tap. There is entertainment two nights a week starting at 10:30 PM.

Plates (914-834-1244), 121 Myrtle Avenue, Larchmont. ($$) Open for lunch Tuesday through Friday noon–3; dinner Tuesday through Sunday 5–10. Closed Monday. This charming contemporary American restaurant with Asian, French, and Italian influences is located across the street from the train station and has a lovely intimate dining room. The chef is devoted to local ingredients and makes his own pasta and smokes salmon on the premises. The bottomless barbecue, all-you-can-eat pulled pork, ribs, and brisket from the restaurant's smoker, is offered on Sunday. There is seared duck with passion fruit glaze, scallops with roasted vegetables, as well as burger made from grass-fed beef topped with raw milk cheddar cheese.

Ray's Café (914-833-2551), 1995 Palmer Avenue, Larchmont. ($$) Open for lunch and dinner daily 11–10. This Chinese restaurant serves Shanghai-style cuisine. The crispy shrimp with honey walnuts is excellent, as is the sesame chicken. You can also order crispy or steamed whole fish, prepared to order the way you like it. Children welcome.

Watercolor Café (914-834-2213), 2094 Boston Post Road, Larchmont. ($$) Open daily 11–11. This restaurant derives its name from the decor: watercolor paintings by local artists. The contemporary American cuisine includes such intriguing dishes as hoisin-barbecued chicken, grilled shrimp over angel-hair pasta served with basil cream sauce, and pecan-crusted salmon. Live music on Tuesday through Saturday nights; call to check the schedule.

Za'Za (914-472-4005), 753 Central Park Avenue, Scarsdale. ($$) Open Monday through Thursday 4–10; Friday and Saturday 11:30–11; Sunday noon–9:30. A full-service, family-friendly Italian restaurant with several pasta dishes, gnocchi, veal parmigiana, and double-cut pork chop, Za'Za's pizza is what keeps devotees returning here. The wood-burning oven is imported from Italy, and the crust is always done to perfection on the dozens of varieties of pizza offered here.

Southwestern Westchester (River Towns: Tarrytown, Irvington, Hastings, Dobbs Ferry)

Blue Hill at Stone Barns (914-366-9600), 630 Bedford Road, Pocantico Hills. ($$$) Open for dinner Wednesday and Thursday 5–10, until 11 Friday and Saturday; Sunday brunch 11:30–2. The motto here is "find the shortest, simplest way between the earth, the hands, and the mouth." Located on an 80-acre working farm with gardens, greenhouses, and barns, this center for food and sustainable agriculture celebrates the produce of the Hudson Valley, much of it raised organically on-site. Many items that diners will consume, they can see growing before entering the restaurant, which is housed in spacious renovated stone barns. Fish and meats are braised, poached, or roasted delicately and include entrées like red snapper with caper-almond sauce or braised bacon and roasted pig. Desserts include molten chocolate cake and passion fruit soufflé. The food, wine list, and service are excellent, and the ambience is truly special.

Buffet de la Gare (914-478-1671), 155 Southside Avenue, Hastings-on-Hudson. ($$$) Open for lunch Thursday and Friday noon–2; dinner Tuesday through Saturday from 6. Enjoy classical French cuisine in a relaxing ambience. Everything here is prepared to order, and the desserts should not be passed up. The fine reputation of this establishment, long a favorite with local residents, has spread throughout the county.

Equus Restaurant at the Castle on the Hudson (914-631-3646), 400 Benedict Avenue, Tarrytown. ($$$) Open daily for lunch noon–2; dinner 6–9:30. This is one of the most romantic spots in the region, located in a castle constructed 100 years ago. The restaurant has several elegantly appointed rooms as well as an enclosed veranda with magnificent views of the Hudson River. The Oak Room is constructed of wood brought from Germany. The excellent imaginative cuisine is French with Japanese influences and features local ingredients in season. Save room for the beautifully presented and mouthwatering desserts.

Half Moon (914-693-4130), 1 High Street, Dobbs Ferry. ($$$) Open for dinner daily 5–10. Every part of this restaurant offers spectacular views of the Hudson, and in the warm weather months there is outdoor seating, making this a desirable place to dine year-round, so do make a reservation. Fresh fish and seafood are specialties here, and there is a large menu from which to choose. The Chart House occupied this space for years before Half Moon arrived in 2008.

Harper's Bar and Restaurant (914-693-2306), 92 Main Street, Dobbs Ferry. ($$) Open for lunch Tuesday through Friday 11:30–3; dinner Tuesday through Sunday 5:30–10; Saturday and Sunday brunch 11–3. The standard American favorites here are made with locally sourced ingredients. Some of the offerings on the dinner menu include goat cheese ravioli, risotto, grilled rainbow trout, crispy duck, and grilled pork chop. The restaurant looks like a 19th-century tavern with dark wood tables and leather banquettes. The chef owns the Meritage in Scarsdale and has worked at La Panetiere in Rye, so expect fine fare but in a casual atmosphere.

Harvest on Hudson (914-478-2800), 1 River Street, Hastings-on-Hudson. ($$$) Open for lunch Monday through Friday noon–2:30; dinner Monday through Thursday 5–10, Friday and Saturday until 11, Sunday 5–9. This huge Tuscan villa–style building at the edge of the Hudson offers wonderful views of the river as well as their own herb and vegetable gardens. The eclectic contemporary American cuisine includes ahi tuna seared and served with rice, wasabi vinaigrette, and seaweed salad, as well as an array of pastas, quail, sea scallops, and steak entrées. There are covered and open patio areas for alfresco dining in the warm-weather months. Live entertainment on some Friday nights 9 PM–1 AM. The sorbets and gelato are highly recommended. The drinks here are expensive, however.

Horsefeathers (914-631-6606), 94 North Broadway, Tarrytown. ($$) Open daily 11:30–10 for lunch and dinner. One of the first "grazing" restaurants in the county, Horsefeathers continues to offer great café food like burgers, steaks, and overstuffed sandwiches and wraps. The atmosphere is casual and comfortable, and children are welcome.

Juniper (914-478-2542), 575 Warburton Avenue, Hastings-on-Hudson. ($$) Open Sunday and Tuesday 10–3; Wednesday through Saturday 10–10. Closed Monday. Adventurous diners will get great value for their money at this informal open-kitchen restaurant, and reservations are strongly suggested. The decor is blue, brown, and eggshell, with place mats on bare wood tables. The cuisine is eclectic French, with dishes like asparagus salad, mushrooms on polenta, escargots with garlic flan, hanger steak, and burger made with ground brisket.

Mima Wine Bar (914-591-1300), 63 Main Street, Irvington. ($$) Open Monday through Saturday 5–11; Sunday 4–9. Reservations recommended. Fine Italian home cooking is the mainstay at this popular restaurant. And there are 22 wines by the glass here. Handmade pasta with shrimp, arugula, fresh basil, and sweet onion; pan roasted chicken with soft polenta, spinach, and leeks; Hudson Valley trout, stuffed with capers, olives, onion, and tomato, with lemon pressed olive oil; and wild salmon are some of the fine entrées offered.

MP Taverna (914-231-7854), 1 Bridge Street, Irvington. ($) Open daily for lunch noon–3; dinner 5–10, until 11 on Friday and Saturday; Sunday 5-9. This restaurant is housed in a former warehouse near the Hudson River, and there is an outdoor dining area for the warm weather months. Renowned chef Michael Psilakis, who owns Greek restaurants in Manhattan, opened this wonderful brasserie in Westchester in 2012. There are soaring ceilings, old wood beams, and large mirrors. The upscale comfort food is simple and fresh, and there are several grilled fish, chicken, and lamb entrées from which to choose. The gyro-spiced beef sliders are popular, and so is the Greek paella filled with shellfish and spicy lamb sausage. Orzo replaces rice in this classical dish. Don't pass up the baklava for dessert!

Orissa (914-231-7800), 14 Cedar Street, Dobbs Ferry. ($$) Open for lunch Tuesday through Friday and Sunday noon–3; dinner Tuesday through Thursday and Sunday 5–10; Friday and Saturday until 11. Closed Monday. This contemporary Indian restaurant serves tasty original entrées like grilled shell steak rubbed with Indian spices and a fennel-infused rack of lamb. Traditional curry dishes and chicken tikka masala, as well as samosas, are also well prepared. There is always a reasonably priced prix fixe multicourse dinner on the menu.

Red Hat on the River (914-591-5888), One Bridge Street, Irvington-on-Hudson. ($$) Open for lunch Monday through Friday noon–3; dinner daily 5–10. This relaxed restaurant is located along the Hudson River, and from their terrific rooftop bar one can see the Tappan Zee to the right and the Manhattan skyline to the left. Formerly part of the Lord and Barnham factory complex that manufactured greenhouses, the Red Hat is literally only a few feet from the Hudson when dining alfresco. I stumbled upon this terrific restaurant and enjoyed a burger done to perfection with a house salad that was fresh and perfectly presented. The grilled salmon was excellent. The desserts are worth sampling as well.

River City Grille (914-591-2033), 6 South Broadway, Irvington. ($$) Open daily for lunch 11:30–4:30; dinner Monday through Thursday 4:30–10, Friday and Saturday until 11; Sunday 4–9. This eclectic family-friendly place serves American comfort food along with Mediterranean-style cuisine and offers an imaginative children's menu. Whether you are interested in pasta and steak or prefer Maryland crabcake and grilled leg of lamb with artichoke hearts, tomatoes, olives, and feta, there is something here to please. Vegetarians will find a number of offerings as well. This is a good solid neighborhood restaurant.

Santa Fe (914-332-4452), 5 Main Street, Tarrytown. ($$) Open Monday through Thursday 4:30–9:30; Friday and Saturday noon–10:30; Sunday noon–9. You can get steak, chicken, shrimp, and even swordfish fajitas at this colorful Mexican dining spot. For taco lovers there is a make-your-own taco basket, and diners are served chicken or beef; beans, rice, and peppers; and other fixings from which they can create their own meal. One of the most unusual and delicious dishes is the shrimp and crab enchiladas with blue corn tortillas. Children are welcome.

Santorini Greek Restaurant (914-631-4300), 175 Valley Street, Sleepy Hollow. ($) Open Monday through Saturday 11–10; closed Sunday. This wonderful welcoming restaurant features delicious homemade Greek specialties at fantastic prices. The moussaka was done to perfection, as were the chicken souvlakis. A Santorini platter offers a few different specialties of the house. Greek salad or soup is included with all entrées. Servings are generous, and the baklava is like ambrosia. Children welcome.

Sazan (914-674-6015), 729 Saw Mill River Road, Ardsley. ($$$) Open for lunch Monday through Saturday noon–2:30; dinner daily 5:30–10. There are dozens of small plates and appetizers at this Japanese restaurant, and ordering a variety of them is a great way to sample the range of offerings here. A sushi bar seats eight and divides the restaurant into two dining rooms. Noodle dishes are hearty, and there is a tasting menu of four dishes and dessert for $36.

Sunset Cove (914-366-7889), 238 Green Street (the Washington Irving Boat Club), Tarrytown. ($$) Open for lunch Monday through Saturday 11:30–3; dinner daily 5–11; Sunday brunch 11:30–3. During the winter months, closed on Sunday and Monday. The views of the Hudson are wonderful, especially if you dine outdoors on the large sweeping patio at the river's edge at sunset. The sun goes down behind the Palisades in full view of the Tappan Zee Bridge, while boats pass by. If you opt to have a light meal, try the calamari or clams on the half shell. Entrées that are quite good are the Moroccan chicken with polenta, rack of lamb with Gorgonzola, and grilled salmon. For dessert, the pecan tart or Sunset sundae are good bets. Children welcome.

Sushi Mike's (914-591-0054), 146 Main Street, Dobbs Ferry. ($$) Open for lunch weekdays 11:30–3; dinner Monday through Friday 4:30–10, Saturday until 11; Sunday 3–10. In addition to the expected sushi, sashimi, and teriyaki dishes of Japanese restaurants, there are several unusual offerings here. Try the grilled yellowtail cheek (*hamachi kama*), *negitoro* (finely chopped yellowtail and mild Japanese leek), or Sushi Mike's Roll. The Fantastic Roll is huge, wrapped in white seaweed, and filled with salmon, tuna, yellowtail, flying fish roe, avocado, and vegetables. For dessert there is mochi, a sweet rice paste that has ice cream in the center. Children welcome.

The Tap House (914-337-6941), 16 Depot Square, Tuckahoe. ($$) Open Monday through Wednesday 11:30–10; Thursday through Saturday 11:30–11; Sunday brunch 11–3:30; dinner 3:30–10. This renovated pub with lots of brass, leather, and wood features 10 beers on tap and an open kitchen in its center. The front barroom is usually bustling, while the rear dining room offers a quieter venue to dine. The American cuisine features entrées that include grilled fish, crisp-skinned duck confit, roasted chicken, and wonderful salads and burgers. The chef, formerly at La Cremaillere, adds imaginative touches to all the entrées and desserts.

X20 Xaviars on the Hudson (914-965-1111), 71 Water Grant Street, Yonkers. ($$$) Open for lunch Tuesday through Friday noon–2; dinner 5:30–10. Dinner only on Saturday and Sunday 5–10. Sunday brunch noon–2. The arrival of this restaurant is probably one of the most exciting culinary additions to Yonkers in decades. Chef-owner Peter X. Kelly, who owns three Rockland County restaurants, has preserved a century-old crumbling pier to bring a wonderful dining option to the city waterfront. The ambience is magical, particularly at night with close-up views of the Hudson. Lunchtime diners have a view of the Palisades. Although the inspired cuisine is international (there's a sushi bar here as well), the steak, chicken, and fish are topped with imaginative garnishes depending upon what is in season. At brunch diners have a choice of only two dishes. Splurge and have dessert—it's memorable!

Zuppa (914-376-6500), 59 Main Street, Yonkers. ($$) Open for lunch Monday through Friday 11:30–3:30; dinner Monday through Thursday 5–10; Friday and Saturday 5–11; Sunday 5–9. Live music on Tuesday evening. Enjoy relaxed dining at this spacious, comfortable restaurant and bar, located by the waterfront area of Yonkers. The renovated *Gazette Press* factory building provides a wonderful ambience for this elegant establishment, which boasts a plethora of imaginative Italian dishes, including perciatelli pasta with lobster and roasted garlic or porterhouse steak with oyster mushrooms. Diners may choose from a wide variety of international wines, as well as an outstanding selection of desserts, including a heavenly slice of warm chocolate cake topped with vanilla ice cream.

Southeastern Westchester (Including Eastchester, Mamaroneck, New Rochelle, Port Chester, Rye)

Alba's (914-937-2236), 400 North Main Street, Port Chester. ($$$) Open for lunch Monday through Friday noon–3; dinner Monday through Thursday 5:30–10, Friday and Saturday until 11. Closed Sunday. The restaurant has a large elegant dining room with Oriental-style rugs throughout and a separate bar and lounge area. Fine traditional Northern Italian cuisine is offered here, with a variety of al dente pasta dishes as well as veal, chicken, seafood, and steaks. Beware that it can get noisy here on busy nights. Not recommended for children.

Alvin & Friends (914-654-6549), 49 Lawton Street, New Rochelle. ($$) Open for dinner Wednesday through Saturday 5:30–11; Sunday brunch 11:30–3; dinner 5–9. Enjoy excellent Southern contemporary and Caribbean cuisine in a comfortable restaurant surrounded by colorful paintings on the walls (the work of owner Alvin Clayton). Raymond Jackson, the chef, worked with Emeril Lagasse in New Orleans and brings creative touches to the offerings here. Some of the dishes on an intriguing menu are curry crab and corn chowder, scallop ceviche, cornmeal fried oysters, sugarcane pork chop, jerk-rubbed duck, and chicken-fried tofu. The menu changes seasonally and uses an array of fresh local ingredients.

Bayou (914-668-2634), 580 Gramatan Avenue, Mount Vernon. ($$) Open for lunch and dinner daily 11:30–11. The Cajun Creole cuisine includes stuffed pork chops, jambalaya, gumbo, and mudbugs (boiled crawfish). For those who prefer less-adventurous fare, steak, sandwiches, and burgers are offered as well.

Casa Brusco Ristorante & Wine Bar (914-346-5170), 219 Main Street, Eastchester. ($$) Open for lunch daily, except Monday, 11:30–3; dinner Tuesday through Saturday 4–11, Sunday until 10. Live music Tuesday evenings. The Italian cuisine here includes selections like antipasti, carpaccio of filet mignon, and whole-wheat pasta with chopped roasted vegetables. There are several wood-fired-oven pizza selections and several wines by the glass. All the fine desserts are made in-house; do try the tartuffo or warmed apple torta with vanilla ice cream. Enjoy a comfortable atmosphere and attentive service with consistently fine food.

Cienega (914-632-4000), 179 Main Street, New Rochelle. ($$) Open for lunch daily 12:30–3:30; dinner Wednesday through Sunday 4–11; Sunday brunch 11–4. Live music (usually a jazz quartet) on Thursday 7–11. If you are not familiar with Latin cuisine, this upscale restaurant with a sophisticated ambience is a great place to try it. The striped bass may be coated with a plantain crust or be accompanied by sautéed spinach with pine nuts, cranberries, and flavorful red vinegar. There is lots of attention paid to presentation here, as well. Make sure to order the deconstructed Key lime dessert.

Club Car (914-777-9300), 1 Station Plaza, Mamaroneck. ($$$) Open for lunch Friday and Saturday 11:30–3; Sunday brunch 11–3; dinner Tuesday and Wednesday 5–10, Thursday until 11, Friday and Saturday until midnight, Sunday until 9. The 19th-century Mamaroneck train station has been meticulously renovated and transformed into a classy dining venue with exposed brick walls, dark wainscoting, and crystal chandeliers. The specialties of the house include beef classics—filet mignon and T-bone—as well as a nice selection of fish dishes. Hamburgers may be topped with caramelized onions, cheese, bacon, or foie gras. There is an extensive raw bar menu, pasta, chicken, and braised pork shank. This is a place to keep in mind to celebrate a special occasion.

Coromandel Cuisine of India (914-235-8390), 30 Division Street, New Rochelle. ($$) Open daily for lunch noon–2:30; dinner 5–10. Authentic Indian cuisine is served in an atmosphere of Indian decor and music. The menu features tandoori specialties as well as classical Indian curries and vegetable fritters. There is an exotic dessert consisting of frozen milk with cashews, raisins, and saffron, which should be tried if you have never sampled it.

Da Giorgio (914-235-2727), 77 Quaker Ridge Road, New Rochelle. ($$) Open for lunch Tuesday through Friday noon–3; dinner Tuesday through Saturday 5–10, Sunday until 9. Closed Monday. Located in the Quaker Ridge Shopping Center, this cozy restaurant specializes in fine traditional, yet creative, Italian cuisine. The calamari pocco pazzo, a salad specialty of the house, combines arugula, banana, and avocado topped with ginger citrus vinaigrette. There are more than a dozen pasta dishes to choose from, along with several veal and risotto selections. A place to enjoy classical dishes prepared with an interesting twist. Not recommended for children.

Eastchester Fish Gourmet (914-725-3450), 837 White Plains Road, Scarsdale. ($$$) Open for lunch Thursday and Friday 11:30–2:30; dinner Sunday through Thursday 5–9:30, Friday and Saturday until 11. Nautical decor adorns this classic fish and seafood restaurant a few doors away from the Eastchester Fish Market. An array of consistently first-rate dishes are imaginatively prepared with interesting fruit, vegetable, and herb reductions that complement the fish. To start, try jumbo crabcake with pickled sweet red pepper or tuna and salmon carpaccio with pear, ginger, and lime. Enjoy swordfish with black olive butter as an entrée, or Dover sole with sweet anise. Piano music on weekends. Children welcome.

Elia Taverna (914-663-4976), 502 New Rochelle Road, Bronxville. ($$) Open Monday through Saturday 11:30–10, Sunday until 9. This warm, inviting Greek restaurant serves first-rate salads, grilled lamb chops, spanakopita, and moussaka, as well as dishes like grilled octopus and sautéed rabbit. The chicken souvlaki platter is a popular entrée. There is high-quality Greek food here at affordable prices, and families are welcome.

Emilio (914-835-3100), 1 Colonial Place, Harrison. ($$$) Open for lunch Tuesday through Friday noon–2:30; dinner Tuesday through Saturday 5:30–10:30; Sunday 5–9. This regional Italian restaurant is housed in a Colonial-style house; entering the large main dining room, you can't help but notice the huge antipasto table. Fresh pasta, made on the premises daily, is excellent. The spinach lasagna and wild-mushroom ravioli are my favorites. The menu changes seasonally, and in the winter months there are interesting game dishes from which to choose. Children welcome.

Haiku (914-337-5601), 56 Pondfield Road, Bronxville. ($$) Open Sunday through Thursday 11–10, until 11 Friday and Saturday. This Asian bistro serves wonderful soups (try the seafood or miso) and salads (calamari is my favorite), as well as a mix of seasonally varied Chinese, Japanese, Thai, Vietnamese, and Malaysian dishes. Their fresh king crab sushi roll is superb, as are all of the sushi offerings (generous with the fish and light on the rice). Try the seafood specials and the pad thai, which is prepared perfectly. The grilled rack of lamb, coconut shrimp, and steak teriyaki are popular with local patrons. I love the Malaysian-style curry with seafood (it also comes with chicken or vegetables). Children welcome.

Kraft (914-337-4545), 104 Kraft Avenue, Bronxville. ($$) Open for lunch Monday through Friday 11:30–3:30; dinner Monday through Saturday 3:30–10; closed Sunday. This neighborhood restaurant offers an informal atmosphere with timber beams, soft candlelight, and a large, inviting bar. It's a fine choice for modern American cuisine with a Mediterranean touch, whether you desire light fare or a full dinner: Both are equally creative. Mussels in curry sauce, salmon carpaccio, and seared tuna wasabi or beef kebab on a bed of rice pilaf are just some of the tempting choices here. The penne pasta with cubes of lamb, yogurt, cucumber, and garlic was unusual and delicious. Dessert includes banana crème brûlée and light berry napoleon. Nice wine list.

La Panetiere (914-967-8140), 530 Milton Road, Rye. ($$$) Open for lunch Tuesday through Friday and Sunday noon–2:30; dinner daily 6–9:30. Housed in a building that dates from the 1800s, with a Provençal interior featuring exposed beams, stucco walls, and a huge grandfather clock, this is one of the finest French restaurants in the county. Appetizer specials include warm oysters with leeks, duck terrine with truffles and pistachios, and fresh foie gras; entrées include squab, venison, and Dover sole filled with puree of artichokes. A six-course prix-fixe menu is available and is a good value. This is a place to go to celebrate a special occasion.

Le Provencal Bistro (914-777-2324), 436 Mamaroneck Avenue, Mamaroneck. ($$) Open for lunch Monday through Friday and weekend brunch noon–3; dinner daily 6–10. Enjoy home-style cooking found in French bistros. There is excellent foie gras, along with comfort foods like lamb sirloin and chicken with lentils and carrots. For dessert, enjoy chocolate-mousse cake or biscotti. Children welcome.

Modern Restaurant and Pizzeria (914-633-9479), 12 Russell Avenue, New Rochelle. ($) Open daily 10 AM–10:30 PM. One of the oldest pizza parlors in the county; the original brick oven here was built in the early 20th century and is still in use. An old-fashioned Italian family restaurant serving pasta, chicken, steaks, and seafood, but it's best to go for the pizza!

Nouveau Sushi (914-921-9888), 17 Purdy Avenue, Rye. ($$) Open for lunch every day, except Sunday, 11:45–3; dinner served Monday through Thursday 5–10 and until 11 weekend nights. This unassuming Japanese dining spot features excellent sushi, sashimi, and tempura dishes, along with fusion creations that are particularly flavorful and worth trying. Don't miss the sorbet for dessert. Children welcome.

Pollo a la Brasa Misti (914-939-9437), 110 North Main Street, Port Chester. ($) Open daily, except Tuesday, 8 AM–10 PM. Authentic Peruvian food is served in this no-frills restaurant with a largely immigrant clientele. The name of the restaurant is also one of the popular entrées, chicken served with rice and salad, a mainstay in Peru. Make sure to get dessert here: They are all homemade and delicious.

Q Restaurant and Bar (914-933-7427), 112 North Main Street, Port Chester. ($) Open daily noon–9:30. Hearty Midwestern-style barbecue fare is served at long, crowded tables in a bustling atmosphere at this informal family restaurant. Enjoy Texas barbecued brisket, pork ribs, chicken wings, and sausage smoked on the premises. Food is brought out on paper-lined trays after orders are taken up front on arrival—and paid for in advance. Meals are accompanied by fresh corn bread, biscuits, and a choice of two sides (coleslaw, potato salad, baked beans, or collard greens). The Texas no-bean chili is made with brisket and flavored with cinnamon; hamburgers are offered for those who don't indulge in barbecue. Kids love to watch their meal being prepared in the glassed-in kitchen.

Rosa's La Scarbitta Ristorante (914-777-1667), 215 Halstead Avenue, Mamaroneck. ($$$) Open for dinner Sunday through Thursday 6–10; Friday and Saturday until 11. Chef Rosa Merenda and her husband, Angelo, will usually greet patrons and recommend particular dishes to order. The cuisine is authentic Italian, in the style of Bari, where the chef hails from, and it won't disappoint. The burrata appetizer (house-made cheese) is excellent, and so is the ravioli stuffed with porcini mushrooms and truffles in a Gorgonzola cream sauce. Homemade gnocchi is made with ricotta, rather than potatoes, and is light and melts in your mouth. Grilled bronzino and osso buco are done perfectly. Dining here is often pricey; not recommended for children.

Scalini Osteria (914-337-4935), 65 Pondfield Road, Bronxville. ($$) Open Monday through Saturday for lunch noon–3; dinner 5–10; Sunday brunch 11:30–2:30; dinner 2:30–9. The fare at this intimate romantic trattoria is regional Italian specialties. The clams and mussels fra diavolo, grilled calamari with chopped vegetables, and pasta with wild boar sausage are a few of my favorite dishes here. The menu changes seasonally, and grilled fish entrées are always offered. Make sure to dine alfresco on the courtyard patio in warm weather; it's absolutely delightful.

Seaside Johnnie's (914-921-6104), 94 Dearborn Avenue, Oakland Beach, Rye. ($$) Open April through October, Monday through Saturday 11–4, Sunday until 3 for lunch; dinner menu available all day until 11 every night, Friday and Saturday until midnight. Enjoy magnificent views of Long Island Sound from the dining room, and in warm weather dine on the large open terrace, where you can watch the seagulls and take in the fresh salty air. There are cherrystone clams, steamers, fried calamari, barbecued ribs, and grilled swordfish, which are all prepared decently. Stick with ice cream for dessert. Children welcome.

Sonora (914-933-0200), 179 Rectory Street, Port Chester. ($$) Open for lunch Tuesday through Friday noon–3; dinner daily 5–10. Lush Southwestern colors and rich woods abound at this warm, inviting restaurant, featuring Latin American regional cuisines. The unusually creative menu is organized by geographic region. Quesadillas melt in one's mouth; they're filled with lobster and avocado, then drizzled with crème fraîche. The paella surrounds a whole lobster and is generously filled with clams, mussels, sea scallops, and enormous shrimp on a bed of rice. Succulent roasted chicken is accompanied by lobster mashed potatoes. It's worth going out of your way to dine here; the extraordinary preparation makes all the difference.

Underhill's Crossing (914-337-1200), 74½ Pondfield Road, Bronxville. ($$) Open daily 11:30–10. The eclectic Asian-fusion cuisine ranges from pizza, sandwiches, and burgers to veal, lamb, and salmon entrées. Every dish is prepared to order. Open since 1994, this restaurant is popular with local residents.

EATING OUT There are hundreds of terrific informal eateries dotting Westchester County. Due to space considerations, it is impossible to list them all. I have selected about 25 of my favorites to feature in this section. The idea is to offer a somewhat varied selection. I'm sure as you travel the county you will discover many others to your liking.

Bean Runner Café (914-737-1701), 201 South Division Street, Peekskill. ($) Open Sunday through Wednesday 8–6; Thursday 8–8; Friday and Saturday 8 AM–11 PM. This vibrant hub of the community combines a café, music venue, and art gallery. Enjoy a full breakfast menu with vegetarian and gluten-free options. For lunch, paninis, wraps, soups, salads, and mouthwatering desserts are offered. A big attraction here is the live music on Friday and Saturday nights (jazz, blues, reggae, and more). There is a children's playroom on the premises, making this a good place for families to stop for refreshments.

Black Cow Coffee Company (914-495-3727), 7 Wheeler Avenue, Pleasantville and 64 Maple Street, Croton-on-Hudson. ($) Open Monday through Wednesday 5 AM–8 PM, Thursday and Friday until 10 PM; Saturday 6 AM–10 PM; Sunday 7–6. Hours vary slightly at Croton-on-Hudson location. The superior coffee here will delight aficionados of the beverage. There are assorted baked goods, including scones, muffins, pastries, and cookies, as well. If you are in need of a shot of caffeine, these community coffeehouses are the places to recharge.

Blue Pig (914-271-3850), 121 Maple Street, Croton-on-Hudson. ($) Open Tuesday through Saturday 11–8; Sunday noon–8. Closed Monday. Winter hours vary. Their homemade ice cream, with flavors like cinnamon walnut and espresso Oreo, is made daily from scratch using local milk. The hot fudge and whipped cream are also made fresh from high-quality ingredients. No preservatives or fillers will be found in anything created here, and the superior flavors are a testament to the purity of the products. Their ice cream sandwiches are made with chocolate chip cookies and brownies. The offerings here are the best ice cream treats in the county, and they may be enjoyed alfresco on the lovely garden patio.

Café at Mariani Gardens (914-273-3083), 45 Bedford Road, Armonk. ($) Open daily 9–3. After a stroll through the beautiful flower gardens here, a lovely shaded patio is an inviting place to enjoy breakfast or lunch. The seasonal menu includes omelets, pancakes, crêpes, poached salmon, and paninis. For dessert enjoy fruit salad, gelato, or sorbet.

Cravings Eats and Treats (914-944-4622), 549 North State Road, Briarcliff Manor. ($) Open Monday through Friday 9–5, Saturday until 4. Enjoy reasonably priced, hearty homemade soups, sandwiches, paninis, frozen yogurt, and an array of fresh baked goods at this eatery. Diners can create their own salads as well. There are also cookbooks and food-related items for sale.

Epstein's of Hartsdale (914-428-9668), 387 North Central Avenue, Hartsdale. ($) Open daily 9–9. There aren't many authentic kosher Jewish delis left, but this is the place to find enormous corned beef, pastrami, or freshly roasted turkey sandwiches. For over 40 years, this mainstay in Hartsdale has been offering all the classics, including matzo ball soup, knishes filled with spinach or potato, and more.

Frank Pepe Pizzeria Napoletana (914-961-8284), 1955 Central Park Avenue, Yonkers. ($) Open daily 11:30–11. This casual pizzeria with a large open kitchen serves up thin-crusted pies (no slices) from coal-fired ovens. Their signature pizza—freshly shucked clams with white sauce and no cheese—is unusual and delicious. The prices are low; beer and wine are served as well.

Growlers Beer Bistro (914-793-0608), 25 Main Street, Tuckahoe. ($) Open Tuesday through Friday 4–10; Saturday and Sunday 1–11. The craft beer list here is huge, and the food is particularly good. A seasonally inspired menu usually includes items like gumbo, pulled pork sandwich, rosemary chicken burger, smoky baby back ribs, and Growler burgers, made with a blend of beef, pork, and veal. The tasty fries are topped with bacon, parsley, and Parmesan cheese. On weekends it can get very noisy, so be forewarned.

Henry's on the Hudson in the Peekskill Inn (914-737-0515), 364 Main Street, Peekskill. ($$) Open April through November, daily 11:30 AM–close. Overlooking the Hudson River on a cliff, this is a great place to go and watch the sunset or relax on a summer evening. Large light-fare menu, full bar, and mouthwatering desserts.

Kathleen's Tea Room (914-734-2520), 979 Main Street, Peekskill. ($) Open Monday through Thursday 11–5, Friday and Saturday until 7; closed Sunday.

This is the perfect place to stop for tea for two (or one) after visiting Peekskill's artist studios. Their scones are excellent, and you will feel transported to another time—and place!

La Tulipe Desserts (914-242-4555), 455 Lexington Avenue, Mount Kisco. ($) Open Tuesday through Saturday 7:30–6:30; Sunday 8–2. Closed Monday and for two weeks in January and August. You will feel transported to a European patisserie when you see the phenomenal marzipan fruits, handmade truffles, lemon tartlets with meringue cones, and other tempting treats displayed here. The young owner hails from Holland, where he studied baking; he also went to school in Paris to learn his craft. The finest ingredients are used in all the creations in this unassuming oasis of desserts. A rare find, and definitely worth a stop if you are in the area.

Lazy Boy Saloon (914-761-0272), 154 Mamaroneck Avenue, White Plains. ($) Open daily 11:30 AM–2 AM. This neighborhood gathering place, truly an ale house, has been serving up several microbrews along with bottled beers (there are over 400 in total to choose from!) since 1994. Unlike many places that focus on beer, Lazy Boy has organic meats and decent chicken hot wings on the menu.

Little Kabab Station (914-242-7000), 31 East Main Street, Mount Kisco. ($) Open Monday through Saturday 10–10, but closed between 3 and 4; Sunday 10–9. This tiny 10-seat eatery is designed for take-out, but the menu is surprisingly large. Everything is prepared to order with fresh ingredients, and the tandoor roasted kebabs, curries, and biriyanis are delicious. Do try one of the Indian rolls if you are in the mood for a quick snack.

Manna Foods (914-946-2233), 171 Mamaroneck Avenue, White Plains. ($) Open Monday through Friday 9–6; Saturday 9–5. Closed Sunday. This organic café, located in a health food store, serves up fresh homemade treats like zucchini gumbo, taco veggie burgers, vegetarian chicken Parmesan, and an array of salads and sandwiches made to order. The fresh-pressed vegetable juices, herbal teas, and yogurt shakes make this a great summer stop; there is also outdoor dining on the patio.

Paulie's (914-773-0003), 14 Marble Avenue, Pleasantville. ($) Open daily, except Sunday, 4 PM–2 AM. There is the usual bar food served up here—burgers, wings, salads—but it's a popular place to go for drinks and relax.

Pony Express (914-769-7669), 30 Wheeler Avenue, Pleasantville. ($) Open daily 11–8. Enjoy organic (no trans-fat) fast food—sliders, burritos, hot dogs, even fries—at this informal eatery. If you won't patronize McDonald's, try this healthy alternative.

The Tavern at Croton Landing (914-271-8020), 41 Riverside Avenue, Croton-on-Hudson. ($) Open Tuesday through Saturday 11:30–10; Sunday 10–10. Thursdays and Sundays are wing nights, and the fresh chicken wings here are tasty as well as a bargain. All the sauces and blue cheese dips are made fresh. Of course, there are burgers, thin-crust pizza, salads, and pasta on the menu as well. Local residents know about this place and frequently indulge!

Temptation Tea House (914-666-8808), 11A South Moger Avenue, Mount Kisco. ($) Open daily 11–10. The tea here is excellent—and pricey (average per pot cost is $6–8). You can also order by the cup; make sure to try one of their homemade sweet items to accompany your beverage.

Three Dogs Gluten-Free Bakery (914-762-2121), 510 North State Road,

Briarcliff Manor. ($) Open Tuesday through Saturday 8–5; Sunday 9–1. There are cookies, muffins, and breads here, and the prices are reasonable. While much of the business is wholesale, there are a couple of tables, and it's a great place to find a gluten-free snack.

Treat Station (914-788-4141), 21 South Division Street, Peekskill. ($) Open Tuesday through Sunday 11–7; closed Monday. This model-railroad emporium will take you back to your childhood with its amazing selection of old-fashioned candy. There are atomic fireballs, rock candy, dots on paper, and more to delight children of all ages. A great place to stop in for party items, or to treat yourself.

Walter's Hot Dogs (no phone), 937 Palmer Avenue, Mamaroneck. ($) Open daily 11:30–6. There's a pagoda with a sign that spells out WALTER'S selling hot dogs, which *Gourmet* magazine named "the best in the country" several years ago. The recipe for perfection, created by founder Walter Warrington, keeps locals coming back for singles and doubles (two on one bun). A must-stop for aficionados of this American classic.

Winery at St. George (914-455-4272), 1715 East Main Street, Mohegan Lake. ($) Open Wednesday 6:30–10 PM; Thursday through Saturday 5:30–10 PM. This picturesque abandoned stone church, now a tasting room, serves several wines made from cabernet franc, seyval blanc, and noiret grapes grown at Hilltop Hanover Farm in Yorktown Heights. The accompanying snack menu includes a cheese plate, vegetarian steamed dumplings, pâté, organic sesame noodles, sliced duck breast, and antipasto. There are pastries for dessert, as well as coffee, tea, and sodas. There is live music on Wednesday nights.

✷ Entertainment

Arts Exchange (914-428-4220; www.artswestchester.org), 31 Mamaroneck Avenue, White Plains. Free. There are changing art exhibits year-round featuring the work of local artists. Live@ Arts Westchester is a performance series showcasing live jazz, music, readings, and other events. A full schedule of film, children's events, and theater throughout the county is offered on the website.

Bendheim Performing Arts Center (914-472-3300, ext. 403; www.jccmw.org), 999 Wilmot Road, Scarsdale. This theater, with more than 200 seats, offers a distinctive entertainment experience—musical and theatrical performances, comedy acts, lively lectures with leading intellectuals, and a wide variety of children's programs.

Caramoor Center for Music and the Arts (914-232-5035; www.caramoor.org), 149 Girdle Ridge Road, Katonah. This Katonah Landmark (see *To See—Historic Homes*) is home to the annual Caramoor International Music Festival, one of the top five outdoor festivals in the country (see *Special Events*). For six weeks every summer the two outdoor theaters here are filled with music created by the world's best classical, operatic, and jazz artists. There are other performances in the warm-weather months; check the website for a complete schedule.

Emelin Theatre (914-698-0098; www.emelin.org), 153 Library Lane, Mamaroneck. Founded in 1972, this theater offers exceptional entertainment in 11 different series, including theater, family programs, classical music, folk, jazz, holiday performances, klezmer, bluegrass, children's offerings, film, and lectures. Check the website for a complete schedule of performances.

Hudson Stage at Pace University (914-271-2811; www.hudsonstage.com), 235 Elm Road, Briarcliff Manor. This is the home of the Hudson Stage Company, an Actor's Equity company, producing several original plays and staged readings throughout the year. Check the website for a complete schedule.

Jacob Burns Film Center (914-747-5555; www.burnsfilmcenter.org), 364 Manville Road, Pleasantville. If you will be in the area, check out this three-screen theater that features foreign, independent, documentary, and classic films. There are retrospectives, film festivals, and special series offerings year-round. The historic theater, which dates from 1925, closed its doors in 1987, but thanks to Friends of the Rome Theater, it reopened in 2001. Close to 3,000 memberships were sold within the first two months, and the cinema has become a cultural phenomenon, drawing moviegoers from all over the county. Two of the three theaters collaborate with the Film Society of Lincoln Center, and the advisory committee includes Martin Scorsese, Ang Lee, Glenn Close,

JACOB BURNS FILM CENTER IN PLEASANTVILLE

Westchester County Tourism & Film

Westchester County Tourism & Film

PERFORMING ARTS CENTER IN PURCHASE

Susan Sarandon, and Richard Gere. You do not have to be a member to attend a movie; check the website for a schedule.

Performing Arts Center (914-251-6200; www.artscenter.org), SUNY Purchase, Anderson Hill Road, Purchase. There are five theaters here that offer more than 70 events annually in dance, classical music, jazz, and more. Call or check the website for a schedule.

Tarrytown Music Hall (914-631-3390; www.tarrytownmusichall.org), 13 Main Street, Tarrytown. This national landmark dates from 1885. The 840-seat theater has Queen Anne, Victorian, and art deco elements, and it is home to the Jazz Forum Arts Series, comedy, dance, children's performances, classical and folk music, and musical theater. Check the website for a schedule of events.

Westchester Broadway Theatre (914-592-2222; www.broadwaytheatre.com), One Broadway Plaza, Elmsford. Enjoy popular musical revivals in this intimate dinner theater, where all 450 seats have a great view of the 30-by-35-foot stage. Before the show, enjoy a three-course meal served at your table. This is the longest-running year-round Equity theater in the state of New York.

Westchester Community College (914-606-6262; www.sunywcc.edu), 75 Grasslands Road, Valhalla. A mixture of musical, dance, and theatrical performances are offered here, as well as a film series. Check the website for a schedule of events.

Westchester County Center (914-995-4050; www.countycenter.biz), 198 Central Avenue, White Plains. There is a 100-seat Little Theatre in this multipurpose facility, as well as a 12,800-foot exhibit hall, with changing shows throughout the year. Check the website for a schedule of events.

Westco Productions (914-761-7463; www.westcoproductions.org), 9 Romar Avenue, White Plains. Since 1979 this nonprofit organization has been producing and presenting musicals, comedies, dramas, and live professional children's theater. The two major venues used are the Rochambeau Theater in White Plans and the Irvington Town Hall Theatre in Irvingon. Make sure to get on their mailing list if you are interested in theatrical productions in the area.

WESTCHESTER BROADWAY THEATRE IN ELMSFORD

Westchester County Tourism & Film

White Plains Performing Arts Center (914-328-1600; www.wppac.com), 11 City Place, White Plains. This 410-seat state-of-the-art theater opened in 2003 as part of the revitalization program for the city. Classic Broadway musicals, dance performances, children's entertainment, and family-oriented drama are all here. Check the website or call for complete schedule.

Yorktown Stage (914-962-0606; www.yorktownstage.org), 1974 Commerce Street, Yorktown Heights. This 550-seat regional theater offers professional musical productions and plays. There are children's events, opera, and dance offered here. Check the website for a schedule.

* Selective Shopping

Westchester County is often synonymous with shopping. The county has many charming downtown shopping districts in villages like Briarcliff Manor, Pleasantville, Chappaqua, Mount Kisco, Bedford, and Katonah. The best way to see the interesting small boutiques, bookstores, and specialty shops is to wander through these towns at a leisurely pace. The following selection of antiques stores, auctions, and shopping centers is by no means comprehensive but rather is intended as a guide to discovering the shopper's paradise that exists in the county.

ANTIQUES AND AUCTIONS In Cross River, don't miss the **Yellow Monkey Antiques** (914-763-5848), 792 Route 35, with 8,000 square feet

Westchester County Tourism & Film

WESTCHESTER COUNTY CENTER IN WHITE PLAINS

of elegant European country furniture and accessories like glassware, china, and linens, plus custom design services. They are open Tuesday through Saturday 10–5:30; Sunday noon–5:30.

In Hastings-on-Hudson, there is **Riverrun Rare Book Room** (914-478-1339), 12 Washington Avenue, open daily 11–4, with more than 200,000 books in categories ranging from Shakespeare and James Joyce to history, travel, art, and poetry. There are 10,000 American fiction titles alone. Used- and rare-book aficionados won't want to miss this wonderful store.

WHITE PLAINS PERFORMING ARTS CENTER

Westchester County Tourism & Film

In Larchmont, **Designer's Corner** (914-834-9170), 2085 Boston Post Road, specializes in fully restored vintage and antique chandeliers, sconces, and lamps as well as antique furniture and accessories. Open Tuesday through Saturday 11–5:30. **Dualities Antiques and Art, Inc.** (914-834-2773), 2056 Boston Post Road, has paintings, sculpture, fine porcelain ceramics, glass, silver, and decorative objects. They have been in business for over 30 years and are open Monday through Saturday 10–5.

In North Salem, **Union Hall General Store** (914-485-1550), 2 Keeler Lane, opened its doors in 2012. Their hours are Monday through Friday 6 AM–7:30 PM; Saturday and Sunday 9–4.

This spacious shop is housed in a historic building, formerly an art gallery, and still has wonderful artwork adorning the walls. It's a delightful place to shop or just to stop for a fine coffee, hot soup, or a gourmet breakfast wrap. The unusual gift items and food products are intriguing and will strike just about everyone's fancy! Owner Jane Beltz has created a terrific hub for the community.

In Tarrytown, there are several antiques shops along Main Street. **Belkind Bigi Antiques Ltd.** (914-524-9626), 21 Main Street, has both antiques and contemporary furniture and gifts. They are open Tuesday through Sunday noon–5. Also on Main Street is **Michael Christopher Antiques** (914-366-4665), 29 Main Street, open Wednesday through Sunday noon–5.

In Peekskill, **Bruised Apple Books** (914-734-7000), 923 Central Avenue, is an amazing place, especially for bibliophiles, with over 50,000 books and plenty of room to browse. They buy, sell, and trade all kinds of used, out of print, and rare books, records, CDs, and movies. Don't miss this shop if you are in Peekskill! They are open Monday and Tuesday 10–6, Wednesday through Saturday 10–8; Sunday noon–6.

Pound Ridge is a wonderful place to find antiques. Two of my favorite places are **All Your Yesterdays** (914-764-3063), 34 Westchester Avenue, open Wednesday through Sunday 11–5, with 19th- and 20th-century American, European, and Oriental furniture, paintings, pottery, glass, clocks, dolls, toys, quilts, folk art, and Americana. Across the street is **Antiques & Tools of Business & Kitchen** (914-764-0015), 65 Westchester Avenue, open daily 11–5, and stocked with all kinds of things for the barn, kitchen, and workplace. You will find medical items, furniture, kitchen gadgets, cookware, sheet music, bottles, saddles, woodstoves, wagon wheels, and more. There is an outdoor antiques market the second Sunday of every month.

There is one major auction service in the county, **Clarke Auction Gallery** (914-833-8336; www.clarkeny.com), 20 North Avenue, Larchmont, and they hold auctions year-round on Sunday at 2. Check the website or call to confirm.

SHOPPING CENTERS **Cross County Shopping Center** (914-968-9570), 8000 Mall Walk, Yonkers. Open daily 10–9:30. This is the county's largest mall, with more than a million square feet of space across several buildings joined by a promenade. There are more than 70 stores here.

Empire State Jewelry Exchange & Flea Market (914-939-1800), 550 Boston Post Road, Port Chester. Open year-round, Friday noon–8; Saturday and Sunday 10–6. This exchange/flea market has more than 150 vendors with new merchandise.

Vernon Hills Shopping Center (914-472-2000), 700 White Plains Road, Eastchester. Several upscale stores; hours vary with the establishment. This is not an enclosed mall but an outdoor shopping center.

The Westchester (914-683-8600), 125 Westchester Avenue, White Plains. There are more than 100 fine stores in this 830,000-square-foot mall, featuring upscale amenities like valet parking, bronze sculptures, and marble and carpeted floors.

✱ Special Events

March: **Hudson Valley Restaurant Week** (914-232-6538; www.hudsonvalleyrestaurantweek.com). From Sunday through Friday, midmonth, nearly 100 restaurants throughout the region participate in offering a three-course lunch for $16.09 and a three-course dinner for $26.09—a celebration of the culinary treasures in the Hudson Valley. The meals are a bargain and a good way to try eateries you don't normally frequent.

April: **Sheep to Shawl** (914-631-8200), Philipsburg Manor, 381 North Broadway, Sleepy Hollow. Admission fee. Scottish border collies exhibit their sheepherding skill, plus you can enjoy shearing, wool dyeing, and cloth-weaving demonstrations at this annual spring event.

May: **Annual Flower Festival** (914-965-4027), Philipse Manor Hall State Historic Site, 29 Warburton Avenue, Yonkers. Free. There are plant and flower sales, arts and crafts, and music at this festival welcoming the spring season. **White Plains Cherry Blossom Festival** (914-422-1336), Ternure Park on Lake Street, White Plains. Free. Asian-influenced activities and entertainment amid the flowering cherry blossom trees: origami workshops, Taiko drummers, tea ceremonies, and karate exhibitions. **Pinkster** (914-631-8200), Philipsburg Manor, Sleepy Hollow. Admission fee. A multicultural festival re-creating an African American celebration of spring in colonial times with music, dance, food, and revelry. **Blessing of the Animals** (914-669-5033; www.hammondmuseum.org), Hammond Museum & Japanese Stroll Garden, 28 Deveau Road, North Salem. Held on the first Sunday in May, rain or shine, this colorful tradition at the museum begins with a bagpiper leading a procession into the garden for a blessing of the animals by a Native American leader, a rabbi, a Catholic priest, a Zen Buddhist priest, and an interfaith min-

THE WESTCHESTER

Westchester County Tourism & Film

ister. Participants are asked to have their pets on a leash or in a crate. The festivities usually begin at 2 PM, but check the website for the schedule.

May and September: **Crafts at Lyndhurst** (914-631-4481), Lyndhurst Historic Site, 635 South Broadway (Route 9), Tarrytown. The crafts shows are usually held the third weekend of May and the third weekend of September, Friday and Sunday 10–5; Saturday 10–6. Admission fee. This spectacular crafts fair has become a Westchester tradition for more than 25 years. Craftspeople from across the country participate—potters, jewelers, fiber artists, and glassmakers. There is a children's tent with activities, so parents can shop in the huge tents unimpeded. Food vendors offer an array of delicious treats. Be sure to get there early and beat the crowds.

June: **Great Hudson River Revival** (1-800-67-SLOOP), Croton Point Park, 1A Croton Point Avenue, Croton-on-Hudson. Admission fee. This weekend-long riverside festival of music, art, and environmental activism is held to support the work of the historic sloop *Clearwater.* Enjoy performances by well-known musicians in addition to founder and folk legend Pete Seeger. **Juneteenth Parade** (914-737-3400) is held on a Saturday afternoon in mid-June. Admission fee. This is the oldest and longest-running African American celebration in U.S. history marking the date when the nation's last slaves learned slavery had been abolished. In addition to the parade (it usually begins on Park Street at 2 PM), there are gospel, rap, and other performances, as well as dozens of food vendors, in a festival at Riverfront Park. Call for further information. **White Plains Outdoor Arts Festival** (914-422-1336), Tibbets Park, White Plains. Free. An outdoor showcase of the work of fine artists, craftspeople, jewelers, and sculptors from the region. Performances, demonstrations, and a variety of fare. **Tarrytown Street Fair** (914-631-1705), Main Street, Tarrytown. Free. Outdoor festival with food, crafts, and an array of vendors. **Peekskill Artist District Open Studios** (914-734-1894), downtown Peekskill. Free. Visitors can meet more than 35 artists in their studios and see an array of artwork on the first Friday of the month until 9 PM. Guided tours of galleries, art studios, and residential lofts in and around the growing downtown art district are available as well.

Mid-June through mid-August: **Caramoor International Music Festival** (914-232-1252), Caramoor Center for Music and the Arts, 149 Girdle Ridge Road, Katonah. Admission fee. This internationally renowned outdoor music festival features symphonic and chamber music, opera, jazz, and pops. Picnicking is allowed on the magnificent grounds.

July: **Fourth of July Fireworks: Mamaroneck** (914-777-7784), Mamaroneck Harbor; **New Rochelle** (914-654-2086), Five Island Park; **Playland** (914-813-7000), Rye; **Yonkers** (914-377-6450), City Recreation Pier. **Independence Day Festivities** (914-591-8763), Sunnyside, Tarrytown. Admission fee. Celebrate July 4th in 19th-century style, with a pie-judging contest, town ball game, slack-rope walkers, and juggling. Picnicking on the grounds is permitted.

August: **Peekskill Celebration** (914-736-2000), Peekskill Riverfront Green and downtown. Free. This citywide event includes a sailing regatta, environmental exhibits, kids' fun tent, fireworks over the Hudson River, kayak trips, arts and crafts, carnival rides, a car show, and more. The ice-cream social downtown features horse-and-buggy rides, high tea, Victorian homes tours, an ice-cream-eating contest, croquet, and storytelling.

September: **Church Tower Walk** (914-667-4116), St. Paul's Church National Historic Site, 897 South Columbus Avenue, Mount Vernon. Friday at 3. Free. Visitors may enjoy a guided tour up the wooden staircase in the 230-year-old church tower, which leads to the historic 1758 Freedom Bell, cast in London at the same foundry that produced the Liberty Bell of Philadelphia. **Armonk Outdoor Art Show** (914-273-9706), North Castle Community Park, Armonk. Admission fee. This juried art show and sale of fine art includes works in oil, acrylic, and watercolor, as well as photography, sculpture, and mixed media.

October: **Tarrytown Halloween Parade** (914-631-8389), Broadway to Patriot's Park. Free. People of all ages parade down Broadway in costume, and the array of floats will delight just about anyone. **Teatown Fall Festival** (914-762-2912), Teatown Lake Reservation, 1600 Spring Valley Road, Ossining. This family festival includes fun, food, music, hayrides, storytelling, pumpkin carving, and birds of prey demonstrations. **Great Jack-O'-Lantern Blaze** (914-631-8200), Van Cortlandt Manor, 525 South Riverside Avenue, Croton-on-Hudson. This amazing festival celebrating Halloween includes pumpkin carving and creating those amazing jack-o'-lanterns for the holiday season. Call for exact dates.

November: **Chappaqua Antiques Show** (914-238-4666), West Orchard Elementary School, 25 Granite Road, Chappaqua. Held the first weekend in November, Saturday and Sunday 10–6. This show has become a tradition in Chappaqua, with more than 50 vendors from around the Northeast; it also offers an opportunity to tour a historic home. **Turkey Scavenger Hunt** (914-723-3470), Greenburgh Nature Center, 99 Dromore Road, Scarsdale. Admission fee. Turkey token hunt along the nature trails, followed by refreshments; a perfect outing for those with young children. **Thanksgiving Day Parade** (914-632-5700), North Avenue to Main Street, New Rochelle. Free. This is the county's largest parade, held on the Saturday before Thanksgiving, with 18 marching bands, 15 floats, and more than 1,000 marchers. The festivities begin at 10 AM.

December: **Classic Toy Trains Display** (914-788-4141), 21 South Division Street, Peekskill. Free. This mesmerizing collection of original Lionel trains from the 1940s and 1950s is on permanent display at Treat Station, the old-fashioned candy shop here. However, during the month of December, train buffs and children will be delighted with the holiday decorations, and it's definitely worth a stop if you are in the area. The store is open daily, except Monday, 11–7. **Frosty the Snowman Parade & Holiday Lighting** (914-273-2420; www.armonkchamberofcommerce.com), Armonk. Free. Steve Nelson had the village of Armonk in mind when he composed his famous song and fairytale about Frosty the Snowman in 1949. The celebration is held on the second Saturday afternoon in December with cars decorated in holiday lights and Santa ringing the siren from the Armonk fire department's oldest engine. After the parade, Frosty pushes the lever that lights the Christmas tree, menorah, crescent moon, and star in the village park. Check the website for the schedule of children's activities throughout the day before the parade. **Holiday Candlelight**

Evenings (914-631-8200), Sunnyside, Van Cortlandt Manor, 525 South Riverside Avenue, Croton-on-Hudson. Admission fee. Enjoy special holiday tours of these candlelit historic sites on weekend evenings in December, with caroling and hot cider around the bonfire. Call for exact times. **Fairy Tale Evenings at Lyndhurst** (914-631-4481), 635 South Broadway (Route 9), Tarrytown. The elaborately decorated mansion is a sight to behold during weekend evenings in December; enjoy live music, hot cider, and dessert treats in a festive atmosphere. Call for exact times.

INDEX

A

A. Scott Warthin Museum of Geology and Natural History, 366
A Tavola, 163–64
Above the Clouds, 52
Abruzzi, 428
accommodations. *See* lodging; *and specific accommodations and destinations*
Accord: events, 184–85; lodging, 155; sights/activities, 121, 129–30, 134, 137–38, 139, 141
Accord Bicycle Service, 134
Adair Vineyards, 130
Adams Antiquarian Books, 195
Adams Fairacre Farm (Lake Katrine), 139
Adams Fairacre Farm (Poughkeepsie), 373–74
Adelphi Café, 305
Adelphi Hotel, 290, 296–97
Adirondack Inn, 298
Adirondack Trailways, 39, 113, 193, 223, 255, 284, 437
Adventure Island Family Fun Center, 356–57
Agnello's, 31
agriculture. *See* farms
air shows, at Old Rhinebeck Aerodrome, 353–54
airplane tours, 52, 132, 323
airports. *See specific airports*
A.J. Snyder Estate, 117
Alain's Bistro, 27
Alapaha Golf Links, 140
Albany, 255–79; dining, 268–74; emergencies, 256; entertainment, 275–76; events, 277–79; information, 255; lodging, 266–68; map, 254; shopping, 276–77; sights/activities, 256–65; traveling to, 255–56
Albany Civic Theater, 275
Albany County Hockey Training Facility, 264
Albany Devils, 264
Albany Heritage Area Visitors Center, 256–57
Albany Hilton, 266
Albany Institute of History and Art, 257
Albany International Airport, 114, 223, 255–56, 284, 313
Albany JazzFest, 279
Albany Mansion Hill Inn, 266
Albany Marriott Hotel, 266
Albany Medical Center, 256
Albany Memorial Hospital, 256
Albany Pine Bush Discovery Center, 257–58
Albany Pump Station, 273
Albany Symphony Orchestra, 275
Albany Trolley, 258
Alba's, 478
Albergo Allegria Bed & Breakfast, 240
Albert Shahinian Fine Art, 409
Alexander Hamilton House, 463
All Your Yesterdays, 489
Allen, Woody, 19
Allis Trail, 58
Alpine Endeavors, 145
Alpine Osteria Bed & Breakfast, 158
Alps Sweet Shop, 367
Al's Sport Store, 200
Altamura Center for Arts and Culture, 247
Alternative Baker, 166–67
Alumnae House, 385
Alvin & Friends, 478
Amedeo's Brick Oven Pizzeria, 400
Amenia: dining, 396; lodging, 387; sights/activities, 329, 369, 370, 376, 381–82
American Bounty Restaurant, 388
American Glory BBQ, 335
American Gothic Antiques, 249
American Indians. *See* Native Americans
American Revolution: Bicentennial Trails, 23; Fort Montgomery Historic Site, 48; Knox's Headquarters, 46; Minisink Battleground Memorial Park, 85; Mount Gulian Historic Site, 361; New Windsor Cantonment, 46, 76; reenactments (encampments), 21, 76, 188, 287, 310; Saratoga National Historical Park, 287, 310; Stony Point Battlefield, 17, 21; Washington's Headquarters, 48–49
Amphitheatre (Greene County), 227
Amtrak, 113, 223, 255, 313, 351, 437
amusement parks. *See* Playland
Ancram, 321; sights/activities, 324, 325, 327, 328, 329, 331, 369
Ancramdale, 330; dining, 340
Andes, 194; dining, 209, 212;

events, 217; lodging, 205; shopping, 215–16; sights/activities, 195, 200
Andes Antiques & Art, 215
Andes Farmers' Market, 200
Andes Hotel, 205, 209
Andrus Planetarium, 448
Angel Wing Hollow Bed & Breakfast, 334
Angelo's 677 Prime, 268
Angel's Bed & Breakfast, 266
Ann Street Gallery, 73
Anna B. Warner Memorial Garden, 46
Anna Maria Italian Restaurant, 472
Annandale-on-Hudson: events, 413; performing arts, 354–55, 407; sights/activities, 360, 364, 377–78, 380, 407
Annex Antiques and Accessories (Red Hook), 411
Anthony Dobbins Stagecoach Inn, 60
Anthony Wayne Trail, 23
Antique Palace Emporium (Liberty), 107
antiques: Andes, 215–16; Austerlitz, 345; Callicoon, 107–8; Chappaqua, 492; Cold Spring, 420; Columbia County, 344–45; Cross River, 487–88; Delhi, 216; Deposit, 216; Ferndale, 108; Gardiner, 182; Greenwood Lake, 73; Hastings-on-Hudson, 488; High Falls, 182; Hillsdale, 345; Hopewell Junction, 411–12; Hudson, 344–45; Hunter, 249; Hurley, 182; Hyde Park, 411; Kingston, 182; Larchmont, 488; Liberty, 107, 108; Middletown, 73; Millbrook, 412; Montgomery, 73; New Baltimore, 249; New Lebanon, 345; New Paltz, 182; North Salem, 488–89; Nyack, 35; Philmont, 345; Phoenicia, 182; Pine Bush, 73, 182; Pound Ridge, 489; Red Hook, 411; Rhinebeck, 412, 414; Roxbury, 216; Saugerties, 182; Stanfordville, 412; Tarrytown, 489; Tuxedo, 73; Walton, 217; Westchester County, 487–89; Windham, 249; Wurtsboro, 106
Antiques & Tools of Business & Kitchen, 489
Antiques at Rick's Barn, 216
Antiques Center of Callicoon, 107
Antoine McGuire's Oyster & Ale House, 27
Antonella's Restaurant, 397
Appalachian Trail, 57, 376, 423, 424
Apple Bin (Ulster Park), 137
Apple Greens Golf Course, 141
apple orchards. *See* farms
Apple Pie Bakery Café, 388, 401
Apple Pond Farm and Renewable Energy Education Center, 84
Applegate Farms, 139
Applewood Orchards, 55
Applewood Winery, 50
Arch, The (Brewster), 428
Arden: historic sites, 45
Ardsley: dining, 477
Arenskjold Antiques Art, 344
Arielle, 387
Ariel's Vegetable Farm, 292
Arkville: dining, 210, 212, 213; lodging, 206; shopping, 215; sights/activities, 196, 198, 199, 203
Arkville Bread & Breakfast, 212
Arkville-Bikeville-Hikeville-Snowville, 199
Armadillo, 159
Armonk: dining, 469, 470, 471, 483; events, 492; lodging, 465
Armonk Outdoor Art Show, 492
Armstrong's Elk Farm, 226
Arnell's Gift Center & Fine Antiques, 73
Aroi Thai Restaurant, 387
Aroma Osteria, 391–92
Aroma Thyme Bistro, 166
Arrow Park, 58
Arrowhead Maple Syrup Farm, 139, 184
Arrowsmith, 409
Art along the Hudson, 408
Art Café of Nyack, 31–32
art galleries: Columbia County, 345–47; Delaware County, 215–16; Dutchess County, 409–11; Greene County, 249–50; Orange County, 73–74; Ulster County, 182–84. *See also specific galleries*
Art House (Sugar Loaf), 73–74
Art Omi, 314, 347
Art on Lark, 278
Art Society of Kingston, 182–83
Artist's Palate, 392
Artists' Soapbox Derby, 187
Arts Alliance of Haverstraw, 19
Arts Council of Rockland County, 17
Arts Exchange (White Plains), 485
Arts Upstairs (Phoenicia), 184
Ashford Cottage, 60
Ashokan Reservoir, 129, 132, 140
A.S.K. Gallery, 183
Athens: dining, 242, 243; events, 251; sights/activities, 228, 229, 230, 233
Athens Lighthouse, 225
Athens Street Festival, 251
Athos Restaurant, 268
Atlantic Kayak Tours, 135, 377, 458
auctions, 74, 182, 198, 345, 411–12, 489
Audrey's Farmhouse Bed & Breakfast, 154
Auntie El's Farm Market, 22
Aurelia, 395
Austerlitz: events, 347; shopping, 345; sights/activities, 320, 328, 329
autumn foliage, 53, 85, 196, 237, 427
Awosting Lake, 146, 149
Axtell Antiques, 216

B

Baba Louie's, 339
Babe's, 27
Babette's Kitchen, 404
Babycakes, 401
Bacio Trattoria, 468
Back Yard Bistro, 65
Backstage Studio Productions, 175
Backwater Bar & Grille, 335
Bailey's Café, 309
Bailiwick Ranch, 233
Baker's Tap Room, 99
Bakery, The (New Paltz), 172
bald eagles, 81, 86, 108, 132; Eagle Institute (Barryville), 83–84
Baldwin Vineyards, 50, 130
Ballard's Honey, 201
ballooning, 52, 323, 370, 412
Ballston Spa: events, 310; sights/activities, 285, 292, 293
Bananas Comedy Club, 408
Banchetto Feast, 27
Bangall: dining, 405
Banksville: dining, 469
Bannerman Island, 53, 55
Bard College: Fisher Center, 354–55, 407; Hessel Art Museum, 364; Stevenson Gymnasium, 377–78
Bard Summerscape, 413
Bardavon 1869 Opera House, 407
Barking Dog Antiques, 182
Barn and Farmhouse at Bedford Post Inn, 468–69
Barn Antiques (Hillsdale), 345

Barn Dance (Pine Island), 77
Barneche, 179
Barneche Vacation Rental, 158
Barnsider, The (Albany), 268
Barnsider Tavern (Sugar Loaf), 71
Barrett Art Center, 409
Barryville: dining, 99, 100, 103, 104; lodging, 95, 97; sights/activities, 55, 83–84, 88, 92
Barthels Farm Market, 137
Barton Orchards, 374
baseball, 21, 218
Basement Bistro, 241–42
Basha Kill Wildlife Management Area, 94
BashaKill Vineyards, 87
Basia Designs, 179
Basilica Hudson, 345
basketball, 48, 264
Batcheller Mansion, 290, 298–99
Battenfeld & Son, 374
Battle of Saratoga Anniversary and Encampment, 310
Bavarian Manor Country Inn, 237–38, 242
Bavarian Summerfest, 250
Baxter House River Outfitters & Guide Service, 91
Bayou (Mount Vernon), 478
beaches. *See* swimming
Beacon, 367; dining, 392–95, 401–4; entertainment, 408, 409; events, 414; lodging, 385–86; shopping, 410, 412; sights/activities, 352, 358–59, 361, 364–65, 367, 370, 371, 372, 376, 377; traveling to, 351–52
Beacon Cycles, 371
Beacon Falls Café, 401
Beacon Institute for Rivers and Estuaries, 352
Beacon Landing, 367
Beacon Riverfront Park, 367
Beacon Sloop Club's Pumpkin Festival, 414
Bean Runner Café, 482
Bean's Place, 339
Bear Café, 159
Bear Creek Landing Family Sport Complex, 226
Bear Creek Restaurant (Hunter), 245
Bear Mountain Inn, 24, 25
Bear Mountain State Park, 21, 23–24; ice skating, 59; swimming pool, 58
Bear Mountain Zoo, 48
Bear Spring Mountain Campground, 200
Bear Spring Mountain State Park, 204
Bearsville: dining, 167; lodging, 154; shopping, 183–84
Bearsville Theater, 175
Beatrix Farrand Garden, 379
Beaverkill Angler, 90
Beaverkill Creek: fishing, 90–91, 201–2
Beaverkill Trout Hatchery, 91
Beaverkill Valley Inn, 158
Bedford Post Inn, 468–69
Beebe Hill State Forest, 328
Beech Tree Restaurant, 392
Beekman Arms, 382, 391
Beekman Arms Antique Market & Gallery, 411
Beekman Country Club, 374
Beekman Square Restaurant, 406
Beekman Street Bistro, 301–2
Bee-Line System, 437
Bee's Knees, The, 346
Beff's, 273
Belkind Bigi Antiques Ltd., 489
Bell House Bed & Breakfast, 332
Bella Rose Café, 32
Belleayre Beach, 146
Belleayre Mountain: cross-country skiing, 147; hiking, 141–42; skiing, 148
Belleayre Mountain Fall Festival and Concerts, 188
Belleayre Music Festival, 175–76, 186–87
Bellota at 42, 472
Bell's Café, 245
Bellvale: dining, 67–68
Bellvale Farms Creamery, 71
Belvedere Mansion, 382, 387
Bendheim Performing Arts Center, 485
Benedictine Hospital, 114
Benji & Jakes, 102
Benmarl Winery, 130
Bernie's Holiday Restaurant, 98
Berry Farm (Chatham), 325
Best Western Nyack on Hudson, 25–26
Bethel: dining, 99, 100; lodging, 96; performing arts, 105; shopping, 108; sights/activities, 82–83, 87, 89, 93, 94
Bethel Woods Center for the Arts, 82–83, 105
Beth's Café, 245–46
Betsy Ross Park, 23
Betty Acres Farm Stand, 200
Bevier House, 122–23
Bibliobarn, 195
Bicentennial Trails, 23
Bicycle Depot (New Paltz), 134
Bicycle Sundays (Westchester), 452
bicycling: Albany, 262; Columbia County, 323–24; Delaware County, 198–99; Dutchess County, 370–71; Greene County, 228; Rockland County, 21; Saratoga Springs, 290; Sullivan County, 88; Ulster County, 132–34; Westchester County, 452–53
Big Band Evening and Sunset Picnic, 433
Big Bear Ziplines, 378
Big Buck Mountain Multiple Use Area, 426
Big Indian: dining, 165–66; lodging, 159
Big Pond (Andes), 200
Bike Plattekill Mountain Resort, 199
Birchcreek Retreat, 158
Bird House Inn, 208
Bird-On-A-Cliff Theatre Company, 177
Bird's Nest, 382–83
Birdsall House, 466
bird-watching: Columbia County, 324, 329; Delaware County, 203; Dutchess County, 357, 376, 379; Greene County, 226, 233; Putnam County, 427, 439–40; Rockland County, 25, 94; Sullivan County, 83–84; Ulster County, 121, 127, 149; Westchester County, 458, 461, 462. *See also* bald eagles
Bistro Brie & Bordeaux, 242
Bistro Lilly, 65
Bistro To Go, 167
Bitter Sweet Bed & Breakfast, 383
Black Cow Coffee Company, 482–83
Black Creek Forest Preserve, 142
Black Dirt Farming Region, 50, 55–56
Black Horse Farms, 229
Black Rock Forest, 57, 58
Blackhead Mountain Lodge and Country Club, 231
Blauvelt: activities, 23; dining, 33
Blessing of the Animals, 490–91
Blooming Hill Organic Farm, 55–56
Bloomington, 130–31, 184
Bloomville: dining, 213; shopping, 216; sights/activities, 201, 204
BLT Steak, 472
Blu Fig New City, 32
Blu Fig Stony Point, 32
Blue Bee Café, 212

Blue Cashew Kitchen Pharmacy, 409
Blue Dolphin Ristorante, 469
Blue Finn Grill & Sushi, 68
Blue Fountain, 392
Blue Hill at Stone Barns, 440–41, 474
Blue Hill Golf Course, 22
Blue Horizon Diner, 102
Blue Mountain Reservation, 459, 460
Blue Pig, 483
Blue Plate, 335
Blue Sky Balloons, 370
Blue Sky Bicycles, 290
Blueberry Festivals, 187, 347
bluegrass festivals, 217–18, 250, 310, 347
Bluestone Grill, 213
BMG Gallerie, 183
boat cruises: Albany, 262; Dutchess County, 371; Greene County, 228; Orange County, 52–53; Ulster County, 134–35; Westchester County, 453
boating: Greene County, 228–29; Saratoga Springs, 291. *See also* canoeing and kayaking
Bocuse Restaurant, 388
Boehm Farm, 229
Bog Meadow Nature Trail, 295
Boiceville: lodging, 153; shopping, 179
Boitson's, 159–60
Bombay Grill Indian Cuisine, 27
Bombers Burrito Bar, 273
Bongiorno's, 268
Bop to Tottom, 179
Borden's Pond Preserve, 328
Boscobel Restoration, 421–22, 433
Botsford Briar B&B, 385
Bovina Center: dining, 213; lodging, 207; shopping, 215
Bowman Orchards and Farm Store, 292
Braden Brook, 144
Bradstan Country Hotel, 95
Brandywine, 242
Brasserie 292, 392
Bread & Bottle, 397–98
Bread Alone (Kingston), 167; (Woodstock), 167
Bread Alone Bakery & Café (Rhinebeck), 397
Brewster: dining, 428–30, 432; entertainment, 432; events, 433; lodging, 428; sights/activities, 421–23, 426
Brewster Founder's Day Street Fair, 433
Brewster Ice Arena, 426
Brewster Theater Company, 432
Briarcliff Manor: dining, 467–68, 483–85; entertainment, 486
Briarcliff-Peekskill Trail, 452
Brick House (Montgomery), 43–44
Brick Museum (Haverstraw), 19
Bricktown Inn (Haverstraw), 26
bridges. *See* covered bridges
Bridle Hill Farm, 92
Brigade of the American Revolution Spring Encampment, 76
Brimstone Hill Vineyard, 50, 130
Brio's, 175
Broken Spoke Stables, 204
Bronck Museum, 224
Bronx River Parkway, 452
Bronx River Pathway, 452
Bronxville: dining, 480, 481–82
Brother Bruno Pizza & Restaurant, 102
Brotherhood Winery, 50
Brothers Trattoria, 392–93
Brovetto Dairy and Cheese House, 200–201
Brown Derby, 268
Bruised Apple Books, 489
Brunswick Bed & Breakfast, 299
Bryant Farms, 325
Buffet de la Gare, 474–75
Bull & Buddha, 393
Bull's Head Inn, 66
Bully Boy Bar, 29
Bunbury's Coffee Shop, 32
Buona Fortuna, 98
Burgoyne, John, 259, 310
Burning of Kingston Reenactment, 188
Burroughs, John, 129; Homestead, 196–97
Buttercup Farm Audubon Sanctuary, 379
butterflies, 89, 356, 439–40, 462
Butterfly Botanicals, 89
Buttermilk Falls Inn & Spa, 154–55; dining, 164–65
Buttermilk Falls Park, 23
Byebrook Farm, 201
Byrdcliffe Arts Colony, 115–16, 183
Bywater Bistro, 164

C

Cabbage Hill Farm, 454
Cable Lake, 91
Cadet Chapel (West Point), 48
Cafe Amarcord, 393
Café at Mariani Gardens, 483
Café Bocca, 401
Café Capriccio, 268–69
Café Fiesta, 69
Café Le Perche, 339–40
Café Mezzaluna, 167
Café Mio, 172
Café Pitti, 69
Café Portofino, 27
Caffè Aurora, 401
Caffè Italia, 269
Caffè Lena, 305, 309
Cairo, 227; activities, 231, 233; events, 250–51; lodging, 238
Caldwell House Bed & Breakfast, 60
Caleb Street's Inn, 238
Calico Restaurant & Patisserie, 398
California Hill Multiple Use Area, 425–26
Callendar House, 407
Callicoon: dining, 101; emergencies, 82; events, 108–9; lodging, 98; shopping, 107–8; sights/activities, 84, 89–90, 92, 94
Callicoon Canoe Regatta, 109
Callicoon Center, 84, 90
Callicoon Flea Market, 107–8
Calsi's General Store, 409
Calypso Farm, 377
Ca'Mea, 333, 335–36
Cameo's Restaurant, 242
Camillo's at the Crossroads, 66
Camp Shanks World War II Museum, 20
Campbell Hall: dining, 66; sights/activities, 44–45, 56
Canaan: activities, 327, 331; dining, 335
Canada Hill Trail, 424
Canal Towne Emporium (Wurtsboro), 106
Candido's Old World Italian Restaurant, 214
Candlelight Tours, 348, 433, 492–93
Canfield Casino, 285
Cannonsville Reservoir, 201
canoeing and kayaking: Columbia County, 324–25; Delaware County, 199–200; Dutchess County, 377; Orange County, 54–55; Putnam County, 426; Saratoga Springs, 291; Sullivan County, 88; Ulster County, 135–36, 144–45; Westchester County, 458
Canterbury Brook Inn, 63
Cantina (Andes), 209
Cantina (Saratoga Springs), 305
Capital District Apple Festival & Craft Fair, 279

Capital District Garden & Flower Show, 277–78
Capital District Scottish Games, 279
Capital Hills at Albany, 263
Capital Holiday Lights in the Park, 279
Capital Region Health Park, 256
Capital Repertory Theatre, 275
Capitol Building, 260
Capriccio Saratoga Restaurant/Café, 302
Captain Jake's Newburgh, 63–64
Captain Lawrence Brewing Company, 452
Captain Schoonmaker's Bed & Breakfast, 155
car shows, 412
car travel (driving): Albany, 255; Columbia County, 313; Delaware County, 313; Duchess County, 351; Greene County, 223; Orange County, 39; Putnam County, 419; Rockland County, 17–18; Saratoga Springs, 283; Sullivan County, 81; Ulster County, 113; Westchester County, 437. *See also* scenic drives
Caramoor Center for Music and the Arts, 441–42, 485
Caramoor International Music Festival, 491
Carl's Rip Van Winkle Motor Lodge, 238
Carmel: emergencies, 419; events, 433; information, 419; sights/activities, 420, 423, 424
Carmel Historical Center, 422
Carol's Woodstock Country Inn, 151
Carriage House Inn (Bovina Center), 207
Carriage House Inn (Saratoga Springs), 298
Carrie Haddad Gallery, 346
Casa Brusco Ristorante & Wine Bar, 479
Cascade Mountain Winery & Restaurant, 369
Cascades, The (Hudson), 340
Casey Joe's Coffeehouse, 212
Casperkill Golf Club, 374
Castle on the Hudson, 463, 475
Cat in Your Lap Bed & Breakfast, A, 386
Catalano's Pasta Garden, 393
Catamount Adventure Park, 315–16
Catamount Ski Area, 331
Caterina d'Medici Restaurant, 388
Catherine's, 66
Cathryn's Tuscan Grill, 428
Cat'n Around Catskill, 250
Catskill: dining, 243–46; entertainment, 248; events, 250; lodging, 238; shopping, 249; sights/activities, 224–25, 227–33; traveling to, 223
Catskill Animal Sanctuary, 120
Catskill Art Society, 104
Catskill Center for Conservation and Development, 203
Catskill Chocolate Café, 246
Catskill Creek, 230
Catskill Distilling Company, 87, 99
Catskill Equestrian Center, 233
Catskill Fly-Fishing Center and Museum, 83, 108
Catskill Forest Preserve, 149, 202–3
Catskill Golf Club, 231
Catskill Harvest Gourmet Market & Garden Center, 102–3
Catskill Mountain Country Store & Restaurant (Windham), 229, 246, 248–49
Catskill Mountain Foundation (Hunter), 247–48
Catskill Mountain Foundation Farm Market and Café (Hunter), 230, 246
Catskill Mountain House (Greene County), 232
Catskill Mountain Railroad, 121
Catskill Mountain Sugar House (Grahamsville), 106–7
Catskill Mountain Thunder Motorcycle Festival, 251
Catskill Outdoor Education Corps, 203, 205
Catskill Outfitters, 200
Catskill Region Farmers' Market, 229
Catskill Regional Medical Center, 82
Catskill Rose, 151, 160
Catskill Scenic Trail, 199, 203, 204
Catskill Seasons Inn, 160
Catskill State Fish Hatchery, 91
Cauliflower Festival, 218
Cave Mountain Brewing Company, 227–28
Cedar Crest Farm (Pine Plains), 377
Cedar Grove (Catskill), 224–25
Cedar Rapids Kayak and Canoe Outfitters, 88
Celtic Day at Mills Mansion, 413
Cena 2000, 64
Centennial Golf Club, 423
Center for Curatorial Studies, 364
Center for Performing Arts at Rhinebeck, 407
Center for Photography at Woodstock, 116, 183
Center Square-Hudson Park Historic District, 261–62
Central Valley: dining, 67; golf, 56
Central Valley Golf Club, 56
Century House Historical Society, 117
Cereghino Smith Winery, 130–31
C.H. Evans Brewing Company, 273
Chace-Randall Gallery, 215
Chalet Fondue, 242
Chamber of Commerce of the Nyacks, 17
Chance, The (Poughkeepsie), 408
Chappaqua: dining, 469, 471; events, 492; lodging, 463; sights/activities, 439–40, 442, 455
Chappaqua Antiques Show, 492
Chappaqua Farmers' Market, 455
Charlotte's Restaurant, 395
Chateau and Tudor Rooms, Saugerties Bed & Breakfast, 151–52
Chateau Belleview, 242
Chateau Hathorn, 67
Chatham: dining, 335, 336, 337, 341; entertainment, 343; events, 347–48; lodging, 331–32; shopping, 345, 346; sights/activities, 323–29
Chatham Bed & Breakfast, 331
Chatham Brewing Company, 323
Chatham Farmers' Market, 326
Cheese Barrel, The, 213
Cheese Louise!, 167
Cherry Hill, 258–59
Chester: dining, 66; entertainment, 72; lodging, 61
Chestnut Tree Inn, 299
Chez Grand'mere, 116
Chianti Il Ristorante, 302
Chichester: lodging, 158; shopping, 179
Children's Museum: Poughkeepsie, 356; Saratoga, 284
China White Noodle Bar, 472
Chocolate Bar, 340
Chocolate Mousse Café &

Bakery, 103
Chowderfest, 309
Christman's Windham House Country Inn and Golf Resort, 231, 240
Christmas trees, 56, 90, 139, 229, 373–74, 422, 455
Chuang Yen Monastery, 420
Church, Frederic Edwin: Olana, 319–20, 348
Churchill House Bed & Breakfast, 334
Churrasqueira Ribatejo, 466
Cider Mill Inn, 60
Cienega, 479
Circle A Stables, 204
Circle W General Store, 246
Circular Manor, 299
Circus, Museum of the Early American, 451
City Mouse, Country, 216
City of Kingston Kayak Tours, 135–36
Civile's Venice on the Hudson, 27–28
Clarence Fahnestock Memorial State Park, 423–24, 425
Clark House Bed & Breakfast, 239
Clarke Auction Gallery, 489
Claryville: sights/activities, 86, 89, 91, 142, 147
Classic Country (East Chatham), 346
Classic Toy Trains Display, 492
Claverack: dining, 340; farms, 325
Claverack Creek, 326–27
Claverack Food Mart, 340
Clearview Vineyard, 51
Clearwater, 118, 371, 491
Clearwaters Distinctive Gifts, 74
Clermont State Historic Site, 317–18, 330, 347
Cliffs, The (Valhalla), 456
Climax: farms, 229, 230
Clinton Corners: dining, 406; sights/activities, 369, 377
Clinton House (Poughkeepsie), 366
Clinton Shops (Montgomery), 73
Clinton Vineyards & Winery (Clinton Corners), 369
Clouds, 181
Clove Acres Riding Academy, 58
Clove Furnace, 45
Club Car, 479
Club Helsinki Hudson, 336, 343
Coach House Players, 178
Cochecton: dining, 100–101; farm, 89; lodging, 96
Cocoon Theatre, 407
Coffee Beanery, 167
Coffee Creation (Narrowsburg), 103
Cohen's Bakery, 172
Cohotate Preserve, 233
Colavita Center for Italian Food and Wine, 388
Cold Spring, 419–20; dining, 428–31; events, 432–33; lodging, 428; sights/activities, 420, 422, 424–27; traveling to, 419
Cole, Thomas, 224, 244; National Historic Site, 224–25
College Hill Golf Course, 374
Colonial Golf Club (Tannersville), 231
Colonial Greenway, 460
Colonial Motel (Grand Gorge), 207
Colonie, 263; dining, 272
Colonie Center, 276
Colonie Riverfront Bike-Hike Trail, 262
Colony Café (Woodstock), 116, 176
Columbia Civic Players, 343
Columbia County, 313–48; dining, 335–42; emergencies, 314; entertainment, 343–44; events, 347–48; information, 313; lodging, 331–35; map, 312; shopping, 344–47; sights/activities, 314–31; traveling to, 313–14
Columbia County Airport, 314, 323
Columbia County Chamber of Commerce, 313
Columbia County Council on the Arts, 313
Columbia County Fair, 347
Columbia County Lodging Association, 331
Columbia County Museum, 314, 318–19
Columbia County Tourism, 313
Columbia Land Conservancy, 328; Country Barbecue, 347
Columbia Memorial Hospital, 224, 314
Comedy Works, 275
Commander, 52, 453
Commodore's, 69
Community Playback Theatre, 178
Community Supported Agriculture (CSA), 372–73
Confetti Ristorante & Vinoteca, 28
Congers: dining, 29; sights/activities, 22, 23, 25
Congregation of the Sons of Israel, 18
Congress Park, 284–85, 288, 295
Conscious Fork, 71–72
Constitution Island, 45–46
Constitution Marsh Nature Preserve, 427, 433
Copake, 331; dining, 336–37
Copake Auction, 345
Copake Country Club, 327, 336–37
Copake Falls, 324, 327, 329, 330
Copper Hood Retreat and Spa, 158–59
Coquito's, 67
corn festivals, 115, 187
Corner, The (Eldred), 103
Cornetta's Restaurant and Marina, 28
Corning Preserve, 262
Corning Riverfront Park, 260–61, 264
Corning Tower Observation Deck, 265
Cornwall: dining, 63–65, 70–71; emergencies, 40; lodging, 60–61, 62; shopping, 74; sights/activities, 41–42, 52, 55–58
Cornwallville, 226
Coromandel Cuisine of India, 479
Cortlandt Manor: emergencies, 437
Cosimo's on Union, 69–70
Cottage Restaurant (East Chatham), 340
Couch Court, 18
CounterPoint Music and Arts Festival, 176
Country and Farm Bed & Breakfast (Accord), 155
Country Corner Café (Saratoga Springs), 305
Country Emporium, Ltd. (Walton), 217
Country Heritage Antique Center (Pine Bush), 73, 182
Country Inn (Krumville), 164
Country Squire Bed & Breakfast (Hudson), 332
Country Suite Bed & Breakfast (Windham), 240
Country Thistle, 409–10
county fair: Columbia, 347; Delaware, 218; Dutchess, 413; Orange, 76–77; Saratoga, 310; Ulster, 187
County Players Falls Theatre, 407
Courtyard by Marriott (Albany), 266; (Kingston), 152; (Poughkeepsie), 385; (Saratoga Springs), 297; (Tarrytown), 463–64
covered bridges, 86, 195–96

Coxsackie: dining, 244, 247, 248; lodging, 238; sights/activities, 224, 228, 230, 233
Coxsackie Antique Center, 249
Coxsackie Guest House, 238
Coyote Flaco Mexican Bistro, 404–5
Coyote Ridge Stables, 144
Crabtree's Kittle House, 463, 469
Crafts People (West Hurley), 179
Craftsmen's Gallery (Phoenicia), 182
Cragsmoor, 150–51
Cranberry Lake Preserve, 459, 460–61
Cranberry Mountain Wildlife Management Area, 426
Cranberry's at Tilley Hall, 398
Crandell Theatre, 343, 348
Crave, 393
Cravings Eats and Treats, 483
Crawford (David) House Museum, 44
Creek Locks Bed & Breakfast, 155
Creo, 269
Crescent Wrench Café, 214
Crimson Sparrow, 336
Crispell (Polly) Cottage, 115
Cromwell Manor Inn, 60–61
Cropsey, Jasper, 421
Cropsey (Jasper F.) Home and Studio, 442
Cross County Shopping Center, 489
Cross River: dining, 468; shopping, 487–88; sights/activities, 455, 460, 462
Cross Roads Café, 212
Cross State Bicycle Tour, 278
cross-country skiing: Columbia County, 330–31; Delaware County, 205; Dutchess County, 378–79; Greene County, 234–35; Saratoga Springs, 295; Sullivan County, 93; Ulster County, 147–48; Westchester County, 459–60
Crossgates Mall, 276–77
Crossroads Brewing Company, 228
Croton Point Nature Center, 461
Croton Point Park and Beach, 459, 461, 491
Croton-on-Hudson: dining, 467, 468, 482–83, 484; events, 491, 492–93; lodging, 463; sights/activities, 444, 461
Crown Maple Syrup, 352–53
Crowne Plaza (White Plains), 464
Crowne Plaza Hotel & Conference Center (Suffern), 26
cruises. *See* boat cruises
Crumb Bakery, 401
Crystal Inn, 67
Crystal Spa, 288–89
Cub Market and Deli, 167
Cucina (Woodstock), 160
Cuddebackville, 59, 74
Culinary Institute of America, 353, 387–88, 401
Cunneen Hackett Cultural Center, 410
Cup and Saucer Tea Room, 401–2
Curtiss House, 322
Cutting Garden, 107

D

Da Giorgio, 479
DA/BA, 336
Daily Grind, 273
Dallas Hot Wieners, 167–68
Daly's Coffee Bar, 246
dance, 77, 275, 407; National Museum of Dance, 285–86
Dancing Angel Cottage, 152
Dancing Cat Saloon, 99
D'Angelo's Bed & Breakfast, 209
Dango Fitzgerald's Irish Pub, Steakhouse & Sports Bar, 305
Daniel Nimham Intertribal Pow Wow, 433
Danny's Restaurant, 212
Danske Hus, 241
Davenport Farms, 137
David Crawford House Museum, 44
Day to be Gay in the Catskills, 109
DD's Pizza, 402
Debbie's Kitchen, 273–74
DeBruce, 91, 93; lodging, 95
DeBruce Country Inn on the Willowemoc, 93, 95
Deep Notch, 227
Deer Mountain Inn, 239, 242–43
Deerfield, 155
Dee's Tiques & Train Shop, 216
Deising's Bakery & Coffee Shop, 168
DeJohn's Restaurant & Pub, 269
Delamater Inn, 383
Delaware & Hudson Canal Historical Society & Museum (High Falls), 118
Delaware & Hudson Canal Park (Cuddebackville), 59
Delaware and Ulster Railride, 196
Delaware Arts Center, 104
Delaware Community Center, 108, 109
Delaware County, 193–219; dining, 209–14; emergencies, 193–94; entertainment, 214–15; events, 217–19; information, 193; lodging, 205–9; map, 192; shopping, 215–17; sights/activities, 194–205; traveling to, 193
Delaware County B&B Association, 205
Delaware County Chamber of Commerce, 193, 198, 201, 217, 218
Delaware County Fair, 218
Delaware County Historical Association, 194–95
Delaware County Sheriff, 193
Delaware Delicacies Smokehouse, 216
Delaware River, 81; canoeing and kayaking, 54–55, 88, 199–200; fishing, 90, 91, 201–2; rafting, 88; Riverfest, 109
Delaware Trading Post, 215
Delaware Valley Arts Alliance, 104
Delaware Valley Chamber Orchestra, 106
Delaware Valley Hospital, 194
Delaware Valley Opera, 105–6
Delhi, 197; dining, 209–10, 212; emergencies, 194; events, 218–19; information, 193; lodging, 207–8; shopping, 215, 216; sights/activities, 200–203, 205; traveling to, 193
Delhi College Golf Course, 202
Delhi Farmers' Market, 200
Deli Central (Stony Point), 32
Demarest Hill Winery and Distillery, 51
Demming-Latrelle House, 19
Denning Point State Park, 352
Deposit: lodging, 208; shopping, 216
DePuy Canal House, 164
Designer's Corner (Larchmont), 488
Desmond Hotel & Conference Center, 266
Destino Cocina Mexicana, 336
Devil's Path, 232
DeWint House National Shrine, 20
Deyo House, 124
Dia:Beacon, 364–65, 367
Diamond Mills Hotel, 152
Diamond Mills Tavern, 160

Diamond Notch, 233
Didier Dumas, 32
Diehl Farm, 89
Digrazia Tree Farm, 139
Dines Farms, 230
dining. *See specific dining establishments and destinations*
Dinsmore Golf Course, 374
Dionysos Italian Restaurant, 243
Dish, 428–29
Division Street Grill, 466
Dobbs Ferry: bicycling, 452–53; dining, 475, 476, 477
Doctorow Center for the Arts, 248
Don Baker Farm, 326
Donald M. Kendall Sculpture Gardens, 438
Donskoj & Company Gallery, 183
Doral Arrowwood, 464
Doral Golf Club, 458
Dorsky Museum of Art, 119–20
Doubletree Hotel (Tarrytown), 464
Dover Plains, 352–53
downhill skiing. *See* skiing
Downing Film Center, 54
Downsville, 197, 198; dining, 210, 213; emergencies, 194; events, 217–18; lodging, 208; sights/activities, 200
Downsville Covered Bridge, 195
Downsville Diner, 213
Doyle Antiques, 344
dp An American Brasserie, 269
Dr. Davies Farm, 22
Dream Catcher Lodge, 208
Dressel Farms, 137
driving. *See* car travel; scenic drives
Drowned Lands Swamp Conservation Area, 328
Druthers Brewpub, 305
Dry Goods (Saugerties), 179
Dualities Antiques and Art, Inc., 488
Dubois Fort, 124
Dumond House, 115
Dunwoodie Golf Course, 458
Duo Japanese Restaurant and Lounge, 302
Duo's, 168
Durham: lodging, 241; sights/activities, 230, 233. *See also* East Durham
Dutch Ale House, 168
Dutch Apple Cruises, Inc., 262
Dutch Garden (New City), 23
Dutcher Golf Course, 375
Dutchess and Beyond Bicycle Club, 370
Dutchess County, 351–415; dining, 387–406; emergencies, 352; entertainment, 406–9; events, 412–15; information, 351; lodging, 382–87; map, 350; shopping, 409–12; sights/activities, 352–82; traveling to, 351–52
Dutchess County Airport, 352
Dutchess County Fair, 413
Dutchess County Historical Society, 366
Dutchess County Regional Chamber of Commerce, 351
Dutchess County Tourism Promotion Agency, 351
Dutchess Rail Trail Park, 376
Dutchman's Landing, 248

E

Eagle Crest Golf Club, 292
Eagle Institute (Barryville), 83–84
Eagle Weekend Watching, 108
eagles. *See* bald eagles
Earlton: dining, 241–42
Earth Day at Rogowski Farm, 76
Earth Foods, 340
East Branch Café, 212–13
East Durham: activities, 226–27, 233, 251; events, 250
East Durham Annual Irish Music Festival, 250
East Kill Trout Preserve, 230
East Meredith: dining, 210–11; events, 217; lodging, 208; sights/activities, 195, 201
East Mountain Tree Farm, 139
East Side Recreation Field, 295
East Windham, 232, 237, 241, 245
Eastchester: dining, 479; shopping, 489; sights/activities, 446, 458, 460
Eastchester Fish Gourmet, 479–80
Easter Egg Hunt, 108
Eastern Mountain Sports Climbing School, 145
Eastern New York Dressage and Combined Training Association, 309–10
eating. *See specific establishments and destinations*
eba Dance Theatre, 275
Ebersole Ice Rink, 460
Ecce Bed & Breakfast, 95
Eddy's Restaurant, 168
Edgwick Farm, 56
Edward Hopper House, 19–20
Edward J. Murray Memorial Skating Center, 460
Edward R. Murrow Park, 376, 378
Egg, The (Albany), 264, 275
Egg's Nest, 172
80 West Restaurant, 465
88 Charles Street, 66
808 Bistro, 472
1850 House & Tavern (Rosendale), 155, 168, 174
Eisenhower Hall Theatre, 48, 72
El Bandito, 32
El Charrito, 402
El Loco Café, 274
El Mariachi, 270
El Paso Winery, 131
Elda's On Lark, 269
Eldred: dining, 99, 103
Eldred Preserve Resort, 92, 94, 99
Eleanor Roosevelt National Historic Site, 361–62, 370, 380
Elena Zang Gallery, 183–84
Elia Taverna, 480
Ella's Bellas Gluten-Free Bakery, 402
Ellenville: dining, 166, 172–73; emergencies, 114; events, 187, 189; lodging, 159; performing arts, 178; sights/activities, 132, 137, 141
Ellenville Regional Hospital, 114
Elm Rock Inn, 155
Elmendorf House (Hurley), 115
Elmendorph Inn (Red Hook), 368
Elmsford: dining, 473–74; entertainment, 486–87; lodging, 464; sights/activities, 452, 460
Elsie's Luncheonette, 71
Emelin Theatre, 485
Emeline Park, 19
emergencies: Albany, 256; Columbia County, 314; Delaware County, 193–94; Dutchess County, 352; Greene County, 223–24; Orange County, 40; Putnam County, 419; Rockland County, 18; Saratoga Springs, 284; Sullivan County, 82; Ulster County, 114; Westchester County, 437–38
Emergency One Urgent Care and Diagnostic Center, 114
Emerson Country Store, 117
Emerson Resort and Spa, 117, 152, 166
Emiliani Ristorante, 160
Emilio, 480
Eminence Road Farm Winery, 87
Empire Cruise Lines, 371

Empire State Jewelry Exchange & Flea Market, 489
Empire State Plaza, 255, 257, 264–65; events, 277, 278, 279; farmer's market, 262–63; ice skating, 264
Empire State Plaza Farmers' Market, 262–63
Empire State Railway Museum, 118
Enchanted Balloon Rides, 52
Enchanted Manor of Woodstock, 152–53
Endless Trail Bikeworx, 452–53
entertainment: Albany, 275–76; Columbia County, 343–44; Delaware County, 214–15; Dutchess County, 406–9; Greene County, 247–48; Orange County, 72–73; Putnam County, 432; Rockland County, 34–35; Saratoga Springs, 307–9; Sullivan County, 104–6; Ulster County, 175–78; Westchester County, 485–87
Epstein's of Hartsdale, 483
Equus Restaurant, 475
Erie Trail, 23
Escarpment Trail, 232
Esopus Creek: fishing, 139–40; kayaking, 135; tubing, 146–47
Esopus Indians, 114, 123
Esopus Meadows Lighthouse, 142
Esopus Meadows Point Preserve, 142
Esperanto, 305–6
Evening Star, 453
events: Albany, 277–79; Columbia County, 347–48; Delaware County, 217–19; Dutchess County, 412–15; Greene County, 250–51; Orange County, 76–77; Putnam County, 432–33; Rockland County, 35–36; Saratoga Springs, 309–10; Sullivan County, 108–9; Ulster County, 184–89; Westchester County, 489–93. *See also specific events*
Eveready Diner, 398
Evolve Design Gallery, 183
Executive Mansion, 259
Exposures Gallery, 74

F

Fable, 210–11
Fabulous Furniture, 179
factory outlets, 75–76
Fahnestock Memorial State Park, 423–24, 425
Fairlawn Inn, 239
Falcon Ridge Folk Festival, 347
fall foliage, 53, 85, 196, 237, 427
Family of New Paltz Turkey Trot, 189
Fantasy Balloon Flights, 52
Farm & Garden Market (Jeffersonville), 90
Farmer's Little House (Thompsonville), 95–96
farmer's markets: Albany, 262–63; Andes, 200; Arlington, 372; Beacon, 372; Bethel, 89; Brewster, 422; Callicoon, 89; Campbell Hall, 56; Catskill, 229; Chappaqua, 455; Chatham, 326; Cold Spring, 422; Cross River, 455; Delhi, 200; Fishkill, 372; Goshen, 56; Halcottsville, 200; Hartsdale, 455; Hastings, 455; Hudson, 326; Hyde Park, 372; Jeffersonville, 89; Kinderhook, 326; Kingston, 136; Larchmont, 455; Liberty, 89; Middletown, 56; Millbrook, 372; New Paltz, 136; New Rochelle, 455; Nyack, 22, 36; Ossining, 455; Peekskill, 455; Piermont, 35; Pleasantville, 456; Poughkeepsie, 372; Putnam Valley, 422; Rhinebeck, 372; Roscoe, 89; Rosendale, 136; Rye, 456; Saratoga Springs, 292; Saugerties, 115, 136; Stuyvesant, 326; Tarrytown, 456; White Plains, 456; Woodstock, 136; Yonkers, 456
Farmer's (Driving) Range Golf Course, 328
Farmer's Wife, The, 340
farms (stands and pick-your-own): Albany, 263; Columbia County, 325–26; Delaware County, 200–201; Dutchess County, 371, 372–74; Greene County, 229–30; Orange County, 55–56; Rockland County, 21–22; Saratoga Springs, 291–92; Sullivan County, 89–90; Ulster County, 136, 137–39; Westchester County, 453–55
FASNY American Museum of Firefighting, 314–15
Fat Lady Café, 99
Father's Day Concert, 278
Fed On Lights, 181
Ferncliff Forest, 378
Ferndale: information, 81; shopping, 108
Ferndale Antiques Marketplace, 108
Fernwood Restaurant and Bistro, 243
Ferry House (Croton), 444
festivals. *See* events; *and specific festivals*
Fiber Flame, 179–80
Fiddler's Flea Market, 108
Fields Sculpture Park, 314, 346
52 Main, 395
Film Columbia, 348
Fins and Grins, 231
Firefighting Museum, 314–15
Firemen's Field Days, 217
Firemen's Home, 314–15
Fireside Steak Pub, 28
First Care Walk-In Medical Center, 114
First Night, 265, 310
Fish Creek Marina, 291
fish hatcheries, 91
Fisher Center for the Performing Arts, 354–55, 407
fishing: Catskill Fly-Fishing Center and Museum, 83, 108; Columbia County, 326–27; Delaware County, 201–2; Greene County, 230–31; Rockland County, 22; Saratoga Springs, 292; Sullivan County, 90–92, 108–9; Ulster County, 139–40. *See also* ice fishing
Fishkill: dining, 393, 394, 403, 404; lodging, 385–86; sights/activities, 356–57, 365, 372, 375, 379–80
Fishkill Farms, 373
Fishkill Golf Course, 375
Fishkill Ridge Conservation Area, 379–80
Fisk House Bed & Breakfast, 207
Fitches Bridge, 195–96
Flat Iron, 388
Fleischmanns: dining, 210; lodging, 206
Fletcher Gallery, 183
Flour Patch, The, 213
Flour Power Bakery, 103
Flower Festival (Yonkers), 490
Floyd & Bobo's Bakery and Snack Palace, 103
fly fishing. *See* fishing
Fly-Fishing Center and Museum, 83, 108
football, 48
Forestburgh: lodging, 96; theater, 105
Forestburgh Playhouse, 105
Forno Bistro, 302
Forsyth Nature Center, 121
Fort Constitution, 46
Fort Delaware Museum of Colonial History, 84–85

Fort Montgomery: lodging, 63
Fort Montgomery Historic Site, 48
42 Restaurant (White Plains), 472
Foundry Café, 431
Foundry School Museum, 420
Four Mile Point Preserve, 233
Four Winds Farm, 137
Fox Hill Bed and Breakfast, 156
Fox Ridge Christmas Tree Farm, 56
Francis Lehman Loeb Art Center, 365–66
Frank Guido's Port of Call, 246
Frank Pepe Pizzeria Napoletana, 483
Frankie & Johnny's/Nardi's, 102
Franklin, 194; events, 218; theater, 214
Franklin D. Roosevelt State Park, 458
Franklin Delano Roosevelt Home, 357, 370, 380
Franklin Stage Company, 214
Franklin's Tower, 270
Fred J. Johnston Museum, 118
Fred's Place Restaurant & Bar, 168
Freehold: art galleries, 249; dining, 244; golf, 231
Freelance Café and Wine Bar, 28
Freer House, 124
Freight House Café, 431
French Woods Golf & Country Club, 202
Friends of Music, 214
Frisbee (Gideon) Homestead, 194–95
Frogs End Tavern, 66
Front Porch Café & Martini Lounge (White Lake), 99–100
Front Street Guesthouse, 332–33
Frost Valley YMCA, 142, 147
Frosty the Snowman Parade & Holiday Lighting, 492
Frozendale, 189
Fruition Chocolate, 175
F&S Tube and Raft Rental, 147
Full Circle Antiques, 217
Full Moon Resort, 159
Fun Central, 355
Funfuzion at New Roc City, 456

G

Gabrielle's (Stamford), 211
Gabriel's Café (Kingston), 168–69
Gaby's Cafe, 172–73
Gadaleto's Seafood Market & Restaurant, 173
Gaffney's, 306, 309
Gallery at R&F, 183
Garden Cathay, 141
Garden Club Tea (Ellenville), 189
Garden Street Café, 398
Gardiner: dining, 165, 172; lodging, 156; shopping, 182; sights/activities, 125, 132, 133, 137–39, 143, 145, 147, 150
Gardnertown Farms, 58
Garlic Festival, Hudson Valley, 187
Garnerville Arts and Industrial Center, 19
Garrison, 420; dining, 430–32; entertainment, 432; events, 433; lodging, 427–28; sights/activities, 421–25, 427
Garrison, The, 423, 427–28, 431
Garrison Art Center Annual Fine Arts and Crafts Fair, 433
Gasho of Japan, 67
Gathering of Old Cars, 414
genealogy, 224, 322
Genesis Gallery, 184
George Cole Auctions, Inc., 411
George Washington Masonic Historic Site, 20
Gerard's River Grill, 100
Germantown: dining, 341; events, 347, 348; shopping, 346; sights/activities, 317–18, 325, 330
Germantown Variety, 346
Geyser Lodge Bed & Breakfast, 299–300
Ghent: dining, 342; events, 347; sights/activities, 314, 316, 323, 325, 327; theater, 343
Ghent Playhouse, 343
Gideon Frisbee Homestead, 194–95
Gideon Putnam Resort and Spa, 297, 302
Gigi Trattoria, 388–89
Gilded Otter Restaurant & Brewery, 173
Gilligan's on the Hudson, 32
Gillinder Glass, 75–76
Gilmor Glassworks, 410
Gino's (Mahopec), 431
Gino's Restaurant (Wappingers Falls), 402
Gippert Farm, 137
Giulio's, 28
Gleason's, 466–67
Glebe House, 366
Gleneida Lake, 424
Glenford: lodging, 152
Glenmere Mansion, 61, 66
Glenview Mansion, 448
gliding, 93, 132
Global Home (Jeffersonville), 107
Global Palate, 164
Gloria Dei Episcopal Church, 227
Glorie Farm Winery, 131
Golden Ginza, 160–61
Golden Guernsey, 96
Golden Harvest Farms, 326
Goldsmith Denniston House, 61
golf: Albany, 263; Columbia County, 327–28; Delaware County, 202; Dutchess County, 374–75; Greene County, 231; Orange County, 56–57; Putnam County, 422–23, 423; Rockland County, 22–23; Saratoga Springs, 292–93; Sullivan County, 92; Ulster County, 140–41; Westchester County, 457–58
Gomez Mill House, 44, 123
Good Samaritan Hospital, 18
Goold Orchards, 263, 279
Goshen: dining, 62, 65–66, 71; information, 39; lodging, 60; sights/activities, 40–41, 56, 57
Goshen Courthouse, 39
Goshen Farmers' Market, 56
Goshen Gourmet Café, 71
Goshen Harness Racing Museum and Hall of Fame, 40–41
Goshen Historic Track, 41
Governor Nelson A. Rockefeller Empire State Plaza. *See* Empire State Plaza
Grahamsville: maple products, 106–7
Grand Dutchess, 383
Grand Gorge, 197, 204; lodging, 207
Grand Union Motel, 298
Graney's Stout, 274
Graymoor, 427
Grazhda, 227
Grazin', 340
Great Freedom Adventures, 324
Great Hudson River Revival, 491
Great Jack-O'-Lantern Blaze, 492
Greek Festival, 189
Greeley (Horace) House, 442
Green Acres Golf Club, 140
Green Chimneys Farm, 422
Green Cottage, 180
Green Horizons Organic Farm, 373

Greenburgh Nature Center, 461
Greene County, 223–51; dining, 241–47; emergencies, 223–24; entertainment, 247–48; events, 250–51; information, 223; lodging, 237–41; map, 222; shopping, 248–50; sights/activities, 224–37; traveling to, 223
Greene County Council on the Arts, 249
Greene County Historical Society, 224
Greene County Historical Society Tour of Homes, 250
Greene County Promotion Department, 223, 230, 250
Greene County Sheriff's office, 223
Greene County Youth Fair, 250–51
Greene Room Players, 248
Greenport: sights/activities, 319–20, 324–25, 329
Greenport Conservation Area, 329
Greens at Copake Country Club, 336–37
Greenstein Piano Collection, 248
Greenville: golf, 231; lodging, 238–39
Greenville Arms 1889 Inn, 238–39
Greenwood Lake, 59, 63
Greig Farm, 373
Grey Fox Bluegrass Festival, 250
Grossinger Country Club, 92
Grotto of Our Lady of the Mountain, 227
Growlers Beer Bistro, 483
Guest House (Livingston Manor), 96
Guesthouse at Holy Cross Monastery, 156
Gypsy Wolf Cantina, 169

H

H. Houst & Son, 116, 181
Hacienda Restaurant, 71
Hahn Farm, 374; Fall Festival, 414
Haiku, 480
Haines Falls: activities, 227, 228, 235, 237
Halcottsville: farmer's market, 200; lodging, 206
Half Moon, 475
Halloween Parades, 36, 492
Halls Mills Covered Bridge, 86
Hambletonian House, 61
Hamden, 196, 197, 203; dining, 211
Hamden Covered Bridge, 196
Hammertown, 411
Hammond Museum and Japanese Stroll Garden, 438–39, 490–91
Hampton Inn & Suites (Albany), 266–67; (Elmsford), 464; (Saratoga Springs), 297
Hamptonburgh: golf, 56
Hana Sushi, 389
Hanah Mountain Resort & Country Club, 202, 205–6
Hancock: dining, 211, 213; golf, 202; lodging, 208; shopping, 216
Hancock Golf Course, 202
Hancock House, 208, 213
Hand and Hoe, The, 22
Hand Melon Farm, 291–92
Handmade and More (New Paltz), 181
Hanford Mills Museum, 195, 217
hang gliding, 93, 132
Hanofee Park, 93
Happy Days Café, 405
Hardwood Hills Golf Course, 202
Harlem Valley Golf Club, 375
Harlem Valley Rail Trail, 323–24, 329, 331, 370, 376
Harmony Hill Lodging and Retreat Center, 208
harness racing, 41, 92
Harness Racing Museum and Hall of Fame: Goshen, 40–41; Saratoga, 286
Harney & Sons Fine Teas & Tea Room, 368, 405
Harper's Bar and Restaurant, 475
Harriman State Park, 21, 23–24
Harriman State Park Beaches, 58
Harrison: dining, 480
Harrison Center B&B, 207
Harrys of Hartsdale, 472–73
Hartsdale, 455; dining, 472–73, 483
Hartsdale Farmers' Market, 455
Harvest Café, 173
Harvest Festivals, 118, 217, 279, 374
Harvest Maple Festival, 279
Harvest Moon Farm & Orchard, 454
Harvest on Hudson, 475
Harvest Spirits, 322
Harvey Mountain State Forest, 329
Hasbrouck House (New Paltz), 124
Hasbrouck House (Newburgh), 48–49
Hastings-on-Hudson: dining, 474–75; shopping, 488; sights/activities, 442, 452, 455
Hastings-on-Hudson Farmers' Market, 455
Hats Off to Saratoga Music Festival, 310
Hattie's Restaurant, 306
Haverstraw, 19; dining, 27–29, 31–34; lodging, 26
Haverstraw Brick Museum, 19
Hawk Watch, 24, 36
Hawk's Nest, 50, 86
Hayes, Helen, 18
Headless Horseman Hayrides, 187
Hecht, Ben, 18
Heidi's Inn, 428
Heinchon's Old Farmhouse and Ice Cream Parlor, 406
Henry Hudson Planetarium, 256
Henry's at Buttermilk Falls Inn, 164–65
Henry's on the Hudson in the Peekskill Inn, 483
Hensonville: dining, 244–45
Heritage Trail, 57
Hessel Art Museum, 364
Hi Ho Home Market, 182
Hickory, Dickory Dock, 35
Hickory BBQ and Smokehouse, 169
Hidden Antiques, 217
Hidden Cellar, 165
Hidden Inn (South Kortright), 211
Hidden Meadow Farm, 233
Hideaway Suites (Rhinebeck), 383
High Angle Adventures, 145
High Falls: dining, 164, 172, 173; lodging, 155, 158; shopping, 180, 182, 184; sights/activities, 118, 129–30, 138, 141, 142–43
High Falls Mercantile, 180
High Rock Park, 288–89, 292
Highland: dining, 165, 173; emergencies, 114; lodging, 156, 157; performing arts, 178; sights/activities, 132–33, 137, 138, 141
Highland Manor Bed and Breakfast, 156
Highland Mills: dining, 69; sights/activities, 51, 58
Highland Springs Farm, 216
Highlands Country Club, 423, 430
Highlands Trail, 58
Highmount: lodging, 158
hiking/walking: Albany, 260–62, 264–65; Columbia County, 321–22, 328–30;

Delaware County, 202–3; Dutchess County, 367–69, 376–77, 379–82; Greene County, 231–33, 237; Orange County, 57–58, 59–60; Putnam County, 423–26, 427; Rockland County, 23–25; Saratoga Springs, 289–90, 295–96; Sullivan County, 85, 94–95; Ulster County, 141–43, 149–51; Westchester County, 458, 460–63. *See also specific trails*
Hillhaven Farms, 201
Hill-Hold, 44–45
Hillrock Estate Distillery, 369
Hillsdale: dining, 337, 338; lodging, 332; shopping, 345, 346; sights/activities, 315–16, 331
Hillsdale House, 337
Hilltop Hanover Farm, 454
Hilton Garden Inn (Fishkill), 385; (Newburgh), 61
Hilton Pearl River, 26
Hilton Westchester, 464–65
Historic Cherry Hill, 258–59
Historic Village Diner (Red Hook), 398
Historic Walton Theatre, 214
Historical Society of Rockland County, 17, 20
HITS-on-the-Hudson Horse Shows, 144
Hi-Way Drive-In, 248
Hobart: activities, 204; bookstores, 195
Hobart Book Village, 195
hockey, 48, 264
Hoffman House Restaurant, 161
Hogan's Family Diner, 32–33
Hogan's General Store and Restaurant, 212
Holiday in the Village of Saugerties, 189
Holiday Inn (Albany), 267; (Kingston), 153; (Orangeburg), 26
Holiday Inn Express (Albany), 267
Holiday Mountain Ski Area, 93
Holmquest Farm, 325
Holocaust Museum & Study Center, 20–21
Holy Cow, 398
Holy Cross Monastery, 156
Holy Smoke, 429
Home Goods (Margaretville), 216
Home Made Theater, 307
Homespun Foods, 402
Hommocks Ice Rink, 460
Honest Weight Food Co-op Cafe, 274
Honored Guest Bed & Breakfast, 332
Honor's Haven Resort and Spa, 141, 159
Hook Mountain State Park, 18, 21, 24
Hooley on the Hudson, 187
Hopewell Antiques Center, 411–12
Hopewell Junction: activities, 374, 376; dining, 392, 393–94, 404; shopping, 411–12
HopHeads Craft Beer Market & Tasting Bar, 173
Hopper, Edward, 18, 449; House, 19–20
Horace Greeley House, 442
Horse & Hounds, 96
horse racing: Saratoga Springs, 293–94, 309–10. *See also* harness racing
horse shows, 144
horseback riding: Columbia County, 330; Delaware County, 204; Dutchess County, 377; Greene County, 233; Orange County, 58; Saratoga Springs, 293; Sullivan County, 92–93; Ulster County, 143–44; Westchester County, 461, 462
Horsefeathers, 475
Horseshoe Inn Bar & Grill, 309
hospitals. *See* emergencies; *and specific hospitals*
hot springs, in Saratoga Springs, 287–89
hot-air ballooning, 52, 323, 370, 412
Hotel Indigo, 267
hotels. *See* lodging; *and specific hotels and destinations*
Howland Cultural Center, 367, 410
Hudson, 321–22; dining, 335–42; emergencies, 224, 314; entertainment, 343–44; events, 347–48; information, 313; lodging, 332–34; shopping, 344–47; sights/activities, 314–15, 321–23, 325–27; traveling to, 313–14
Hudson, Henry, 255, 313, 351, 368
Hudson Area Library Association, 322
Hudson at Haymount House, 467
Hudson Beach Glass, 367, 410
Hudson City Books, 322, 346
Hudson Farmers' Market, 326
Hudson Highlands Cruises, 52, 453
Hudson Highlands Nature Museum, 41–42
Hudson Highlands State Park, 424
Hudson House (Nyack), 33
Hudson House Antiques (Hudson), 344
Hudson House Inn (Cold Spring), 428
Hudson House Restaurant (Cold Spring), 429
Hudson Merchant House, 333
Hudson Opera House, 343
Hudson River: fishing, 139–40, 230–31; kayaking, 54–55, 135–36, 144–45, 377, 426, 458. *See also* boat cruises
Hudson River Adventures, 52–53
Hudson River Cruises, 134–35
Hudson River Maritime Museum (Kingston), 118
Hudson River Museum (Yonkers), 448
Hudson River Research Reserve, 380
Hudson River School, 223, 224–25, 237, 257, 319, 365–66, 409, 421, 442
Hudson River Valley Ramble, 413
Hudson River Water Taxi, 135
Hudson River Way, 260–61
Hudson Sailing, 135
Hudson Stage at Pace University, 486
Hudson Street Café, 70
Hudson Valley Arts Center, 346
Hudson Valley Auctioneers, 412
Hudson Valley Authors, 414–15
Hudson Valley Bottle Show, 413
Hudson Valley Center for Contemporary Art, 449
Hudson Valley Dessert Company, 169
Hudson Valley Garlic Festival, 187
Hudson Valley Hospital Center, 437
Hudson Valley Outfitters, 426
Hudson Valley Pedal, 279
Hudson Valley Pottery Trail, 129–30, 184
Hudson Valley Rail Trail, 132–33
Hudson Valley Resort, 141
Hudson Valley Restaurant Week, 76, 489–90
Hudson Valley Shakespeare Festival, 422, 433
Hudson Valley Wine Festival, 414
Hudson-Athens Lighthouse, 225

Hudson-Chatham Arts Walk, 348
Hudson-Chatham Winery, 323
Huggins Lake, 200
Huguenot Historical Society, 123–24
Huguenot Path, 124
Huguenot Street Stone Houses, 123–24
Hull-O Farms, 230, 241
Hunt Country Furniture, 410
Hunter: dining, 243–47; entertainment, 247–48; events, 250, 251; lodging, 239–40; shopping, 249; sights/activities, 226, 227, 230, 231, 233–36; traveling to, 223
Hunter Mountain: dining, 244, 246; events, 250, 251; hiking, 232; lodging, 239–40; skiing, 235–36
Hunter Mountain Expeditions and Sports Center, 231
Hunter Mountain Hotel and Spa, 239–40
Hunter Mountain Skyride, 234
Hunter Mountain Zipline Adventure, 233–34
Hunter Village Square, 246, 249
Hunting Tavern Museum, 195
Hurds Christmas Tree Farm, 139
Hurley, 114–15; events, 186, 187; shopping, 180, 182, 184; sights/activities, 125, 142–43, 145, 154, 179
Hurley Corn Festival, 115, 187
Hurley Country Store, 180
Hurley Patentee Manor, 125
Hurley Rail Trail, 142–43
Hurley Reformed Church, 115, 187
Hurley Stone House Day, 114, 186
Hurleyville: dining, 102; sights/activities, 84, 92
Hyde Park: dining, 387–88, 397–401; entertainment, 408; events, 412, 415; lodging, 383; shopping, 411; sights/activities, 353, 357, 361–63, 365, 370, 372, 376–80
Hyde Park Antiques Center, 411
Hyde Park Brewery, 398–99
Hyde Park Drive-In, 408
Hyde Park Railroad Station, 353
Hyde Park Trail, 370, 376, 380

I

Ice Carnival (Livingston Manor), 108
Ice Caves, 151
ice fishing, 94, 331
Ice Harvest Festival at Hanford Mills, 217
ice hockey, 48, 264
Ice House on the Hudson, 393
Ice Hutch, 460
ice skating: Albany, 264; Dutchess County, 379; Orange County, 59; Putnam County, 426; Saratoga Springs, 295; Ulster County, 148–49; Westchester County, 460
Ice Time Sports Complex, 59
Ichabod Crane School House, 319
Il Barilotto, 393
Il Cenacolo, 64
Il Compare, 397
Il Fresco, 28
Il Portico, 28
Il Tesoro, 66
In2Retro, 108
Independence Day celebrations, 109, 186, 250, 278, 310, 347, 491
Independent Helicopters, 52
India House (Montrose), 467
Indian Brook Assemblage, 458
Indian Grill (Kingston), 161
Indian Head Canoes, 88
Indian Head Mountain, 232
Indian Hill, 58, 59–60
Indy 7, 118
information: Albany, 255; Columbia County, 313; Delaware County, 193; Dutchess County, 351; Greene County, 223; Orange County, 39; Putnam County, 419; Rockland County, 17; Saratoga Springs, 283; Sullivan County, 81; Ulster County, 113; Westchester County, 437
inns. *See* lodging; *and specific inns and destinations*
Inn at Ca'Mea, 333
Inn at Green River, 332
Inn at Hudson, 333
Inn at Lake Joseph, 96
Inn at Saratoga, 297
Inn at Stone Ridge, 156
Inn at Stony Creek, 61
Inn at Tamayo, 153
Inn at Twaalfskill, 156
Inn at Vassar College, 385
Inn Between, 210
Inn on South Lake Bed & Breakfast, 267
Inn on the Hudson, 465
Inner Wall (New Paltz), 146
Innisfree Garden, 380
Institute of Ecosystem Studies, 380
International Celtic Festival, 251
International Pickle Festival, 189
Irish American Heritage Museum, 258
Irish festival, 250, 251
Iron Forge Inn, 67–68
Iron Horse Grill, 467
Irving, Washington, 437, 446; Sunnyside, 445
Irving Farm Coffee House, 368, 405
Irvington, 445; dining, 476
Ivy Rock Farms, 58

J

J & J's Gourmet Cafe, 399
Jack's Irish Pub at Caitlin Gardens, 72
Jack's Oyster House, 270
Jackson's Old Chatham House, 337
Jacob and Anthony's American Grille, 302–3
Jacob Blauvelt House, 20
Jacob Burns Film Center, 486
Jaipore Royal Indian Cuisine, 429
James Baird State Park, 378; golf course, 375
James Cox Gallery, 184
James Vanderpoel House, 314, 318
Jan Van Deusen House, 115, 182
Jane Bloodgood-Abrams Studio, 183
Jasper F. Cropsey Home and Studio, 442
Java Grande, 103
Java Love Coffee Roasting Company, 103
Jay (John) Homestead, 442–43
jazz festivals, 279, 310, 433
J.E. Heaton Jewelers, 410
Jean Claude's Bakery & Dessert Café, 72
Jean Hasbrouck House, 124
Jean Turmo Ltd., 116, 180–81
Jefferson: sights/activities, 200–201, 204
Jeffersonian Bed & Breakfast, 96
Jeffersonville: dining, 101, 102, 107; events, 109; lodging, 96, 97–98; sights/activities, 89, 90, 92
Jenkins (Robert) House, 322
Jenkins-Leuken Orchards, 137
Jenkinstown Antiques, 182
Jennie Bell Pie Festival, 187
Jerry's Three River Canoe Corporation, 88
Jesters Comedy Club, 72
Jewett, 227

Jewett Center, 227
JMW Auction Service, 182
John Burroughs Homestead, 196–97
John Davis Gallery, 346
John Jay Homestead, 442–43
Johnny D's, 70
John's Harvest Inn, 68
Johnson (Lady Bird) Demonstration Garden, 439
Johnston Museum, 118
Jones Farm Country Store, 74
Joshua's Restaurant, 161
Journey Inn Bed & Breakfast, 383
Juckas Stables, 58
Julie's Restaurant, 402
July 4th celebrations, 109, 186, 250, 278, 310, 347, 491
Jumel Mansion, 290
Juneteenth Parade, 491
Juniper, 475–76
Justin's, 270
Justus Asthalter Maple Syrup, 107

K

Kaaterskill Falls, 232, 237
Kaaterskill High Peak, 232
Kaaterskill Inn, 238
Kaatsbaan International Dance Center, 407
Kaatskill Mountain Club, 236, 239, 244
Kabinett &Kammer, 215–16
Kaleidoworld, 117
K&K Equestrian Center, 233
Kanwit, Roy, 315
Kaplan's Egg Farm, 90
Karcher's Country Kottage, 216
Karma Road, 173
Karmabee, 180
Kate's Lazy Meadow Motel, 153
Kathleen's Tea Room, 483–84
Katonah: dining, 469, 470; entertainment, 485; events, 491; sights/activities, 441–43, 449, 455
Katonah Museum of Art, 449
Kauneonga Lake: dining, 99, 100, 102, 103
Kavos, 402
kayaking. *See* canoeing and kayaking
Kayderosseras Creek, 283
Kedem Royal Winery, 131
Keegan Ales, 131
Keepers of the Flag B&B, 208–9
Kelder's Farm & U-Pick, 138
Kenco, 145
Kendall Sculpture Gardens, 438
Kendon Antiques, 344
Kennedy Dells Park, 23
Kenoza Lake, 90, 91, 94–95
Kensico Dam Plaza, 440
Kerhonkson: events, 187; sights/activities, 134, 138, 139, 141, 143, 184
Khan's Mongolian Garden, 33
Kiamesha Lake, 90, 91
Kids Kingdom Indoor Play Center, 355–56
Killoran House, 19
Kinderhook, 321; dining, 339; lodging, 334; sights/activities, 314, 318–19, 321, 324, 325, 326, 330
Kinderhook Creek, 327, 329
Kinderhook Farmers' Market, 326
Kings of Old Antiques, 249
Kingsland Point Lighthouse, 445–46
Kingston, 125–26, 128–29; dining, 159–63, 167–72; emergencies, 114; events, 185–89; information, 113; lodging, 152–53; performing arts, 175, 177, 178; shopping, 178–80, 182–83; sights/activities, 118, 121, 122, 125–31, 134–36, 139, 140, 144–45, 146, 148; traveling to, 113–14
Kingston Airport, 114
Kingston City Reservoir, 140
Kingston Farmers' Market, 136
Kingston Heritage Area Visitors Centers, 125–26
Kingston Hospital, 114
Kingston Point Beach, 146
Kingston Point Park, 144–45
Kira, 469
Kirkside Park, 205, 218
Kitch n' Kaffe, 431
Kittatinny Canoes, 55, 88
Kittatinny Zip Line, 88
Kiwanis Ice Arena, 148–49
Kleinert/James Arts Center of the Woodstock Guild, 176
Klein's Kill Fruit Farm, 326
Klyne Esopus Museum, 118–19
Knaub's Farm, 89
Knickerbocker Ice Festival, 36
Knickerbocker Lake, 330
Knox's (Henry) Headquarters, 46
Koo Koose Farmers' Market, 200
Korean Arts Village, 100
Kortright Creek Creamery, 201
Kowawese Unique Area, 60
Kraft (Bronxville), 480
Kraus Farm Antiques & Vintage, 108
Krause's Homemade Chocolates, 115
Krisco Farms, 56
Krumville: dining, 164
Kutsher's Resort, 92, 93
Kykuit, 443
Kyoto Sushi, 161

L

La Bamba, 33
La Cabana, 210
La Camelia, 469
La Cascada, 29
La Conca D'Oro, 243
La Cremaillere, 469
La Deliziosa Pastry Shoppe, 401
La Florentina, 169
La Panetiere, 480–81
La Perla Restaurant, 270
La Petite Cuisine, 72
La Puerta Azul, 395–96
La Quinta Inn & Suites (Armonk), 465
La Serre Restaurant, 270–71
La Tulipe Desserts, 484
Lady Bird Johnson Demonstration Garden, 439
LaGrange, 376
LaGrangeville: dining, 400–401
Lake Gleneida Walking Trail, 424
Lake Huntington: events, 109; lodging, 98
Lake Isle Town Park, 458
Lake Katrine: dining, 162, 168; farm, 139
Lake Ridge Restaurant (Round Lake), 303
Lake Superior State Park, 94
Lake Taghkanic State Park, 329, 331; bicycling, 324; cross-country skiing, 331; fishing, 327; hiking, 329; swimming, 330
Lake View House (Newburgh), 64
Lalibela, 469–70
Lander's River Trips, 54–55, 88
Landmark Inn, 68
Lansing's Farm Market, 263
Lanterna Tuscan Bistro, 29
Lanza's Country Inn, 96, 103
Larchmont: dining, 472, 473, 474; shopping, 488, 489; sights/activities, 455, 460
Larchmont Farmers' Market, 455
LARKfest, 279
Lasdon Park and Arboretum, 439
Last Bite, The, 173
Last Chance Antiques and Cheese Café, 246–47
Late Bloomer Farm & Market, 56
Latin Fest, 278–79

Latin Star Restaurant, 33
Lazy Boy Saloon, 484
Lazy Pond Bed & Breakfast, 96
Lazy Swan Golf & Country Club Village, 140
Le Bouchon, 429
Le Canard-Enchaine, 161
Le Chambord Inn & Conference Center, 393–94
Le Chateau, 470
Le Fontane, 470
Le Petit Bistro, 389
Le Petit Chateau, 383
Le Provencal Bistro, 481
Leeds: events, 251; information, 223; lodging, 238
Leeds Irish Festival, 251
LeFevre House, 124
Legend of Sleepy Hollow (Irving), 445, 446
Legends by Candlelight, 348
Lenoir Preserve, 459–60
Les Baux, 396
Levity Live Comedy Club, 34
Levon Helm's Rambles, 176
Lew Beach: lodging, 158
Lewisboro-Katonah Farmers' Market, 455
Lia's Mountain View, 405
Liberty: dining, 102–4; events, 109; information, 81; lodging, 96; shopping, 107–8; sights/activities, 86, 88, 89, 92, 93
Liberty Bell Drop, 109
Liberty Bike Trail, 88
Liberty Chamber of Commerce, 81
Liberty Diner & Restaurant, 103–4
Liberty Public House, 389
Liberty View Farm, 137
Lick, 340
lighthouses, 115, 128, 134–35, 142, 225, 445–46
Liliandloo, 346
Lindenwald, 319
Links at Union Vale, 375
Lipperas' at the Chatham House, 337
Little Bake Shop, 33
Little Bear Chinese Restaurant, 161–62
Little Gates Company Wine Merchants, 368
Little Kabab Station, 484
Little Pond, 200
Live at the Falcon, 176
Livingston Manor: dining, 103; entertainment, 104; events, 108–9; lodging, 96; sights/activities, 83, 86, 90–91
Lloyd, 133
Local, The (Rhinebeck), 389
Local 111, 340–41
Local Pub & Teahouse (Saratoga Springs), 306
Loch Sheldrake, 92, 105
Lochmore Golf Course, 92
Locust Grove (Poughkeepsie), 358
Locust Grove Farm (Milton), 139
Locust Lawn (Gardiner), 125
Lodge, The (Wingdale), 397
Lodge at Rock Hill, 96–97
Lodge at the Emerson Resort, 117, 152
lodging: Albany, 266–68; Columbia County, 331–35; Delaware County, 205–9; Dutchess County, 382–87; Greene County, 237–41; Orange County, 60–63; Putnam County, 427–28; Rockland County, 25–26; Saratoga Springs, 296–301; Sullivan County, 95–98; Ulster County, 151–59; Westchester County, 463–66
Lola's Café, 403
Lombardo's, 271
Long Eddy: winery, 87
Longfellow's Inn & Restaurant, 303
Longobardi's Restaurant & Pizzeria, 403
Lori's Creative Café, 169–70
Loughran House, 128
Love Bites Cafe, 170
Loveapple Farm, 325
Lucky Buddha, 473
Lucky Chocolates, 181
Lucky Dog Cafe, 211
Lumberjack Festival, 217
Luna 61, 399
Lusardi's, 473
Luykas Van Alen House, 314, 318–19
Luzon Station, 100
Lyceum Theater, 368
Lycian Centre, 72
Lyme disease, 141, 328
Lyndhurst Historic Site, 443–44; events, 491, 493
Lyonsville Sugarhouse and Farm, 139, 184
Lyrical Ballad, 290

M

McCann Memorial Golf Course, 375
McCullers, Carson, 18
McEnroe Organic Farm Market, 373
McGuire's, 271
Mac-Haydn Theatre, 343
Machu Picchu Peruvian Restaurant, 64
McIntosh Auction Service, 198
McKinney and Doyle Fine Foods Café, 397
Madalin Hotel, 383–84, 389–90
Madalin's Table, 389–90
Madam Brett Homestead, 358–59
Maestro's at the Van Dam, 306
Magnanini Farm Winery, 131
Magoya, 66
Mahalo, 249
Mahayana Buddhist Temple, 227
Mahopac: dining, 428–31; sights/activities, 421, 422, 423
Mahwah River: fishing, 22
Main Course (New Paltz), 173
Main Street Diner (Valatie), 341
Maine Black Bear Restaurant, 210
Major Welch Trail, 23
Mama Maria's Restaurant, 211
Mama Theresa's, 64
Mamaroneck: dining, 479, 481, 485; events, 491; theater, 485
MAMBO! Mission Style Burritos, 247
Mamoun's Restaurant, 274
Manitoga, 424–25
Manitou Point Preserve, 425
Manna Dew, 396
Manna Foods, 484
Mansion, The (Saratoga Springs), 300
Mansion Historic District (Hudson), 261
Mansion Ridge Golf Club, 56
Maple Hill Farms, 230
Maple Lawn Farm Market, 422
Maple Moor Golf, 458
Maple Room, The, 213
Maple Shade Farm, 201
maple syrup, 107, 139, 184–85, 279, 352–53, 432–33
Maplecrest, 249
Maples Farm, 56
maps: Albany, 254; Columbia County, 312; Delaware County, 192; Dutchess County, 350; Greene County, 222; Orange County, 38; Putnam County, 418; Rockland County, 16; Saratoga Springs, 282; Sullivan County, 80; Ulster County, 112; Westchester County, 436
Marble School, 446
Marbletown, 122–23
Marcello's Ristorante, 29
Marché at 74 State, 271
Marco, 429
Margaretville, 197, 198; dining, 210, 213–14; emergencies,

194; events, 217, 218; lodging, 205–6; shopping, 215, 216; sights/activities, 198, 202, 204; theater, 214; traveling to, 193
Margaretville Hospital, 194
Margaretville Mountain Inn, 206
Maria's Bazaar, 170
Mariner's Harbor, 162
Mariner's-on-the-Hudson, 173–74
Mario's, 337
Marist College, 408, 411
Mark Gruber Gallery, 184
Mark Vail Auction Services, 74
Market Street (Rhinebeck), 390
markets. *See* farmer's markets
Marlboro: dining, 165, 174; entertainment, 176; sights/activities, 44, 123, 131–32, 138, 144
Marriott Courtyard (Saratoga Springs), 297
Marshlands Conservancy, 458, 460, 461
Martin Van Buren National Historic Site, 319
Martin Van Buren Park, 324
Mary Kelly's Restaurant, 394
Masonville: activities, 202, 203; dining, 214; shopping, 217
Masonville General Store, 214, 217
Matchbox Café, 399
Mathilda, 118
Matthewis Persen House, 125
Matthew's on Main, 100–101
Maverick Concerts, 176–77
Max London's, 303
Max's Memphis Barbecue, 390
Max's on Main, 394
Maya Café & Cantina, 403
Meadowgreens Golf Course, 327
Meadowlark Farm, 61
Meadowood Inn, 206
Meadows Golf Center, 202
Medway Reservoir, 230
Meissner's Auctions, 345
Memories, 108
Mercato, 390
Meredith Dairy Fest, 217
Meritage, 473
Messina's Italian Restaurant, 243
Metro North, 39, 113–14, 351, 419, 437
Mexican Radio, 337
Mezza Notte Ristorante, 271
Mianus River Gorge, 458
Michael Christopher Antiques, 489
Michelangelo's Restaurant, 101
Michele's Lakeside 55, 100
Michie Stadium, 48
Middletown: activities, 52, 56–59; dining, 68–69, 72; emergencies, 40; entertainment, 73; events, 76; shopping, 73, 76
Middletown Farmers' Market, 56
Mid-Dutchess Trailway, 370
Mid-Hudson Balloon Festival, 412
Mid-Hudson Bicycle Club, 370
Mid-Hudson Children's Museum, 356
Mid-Hudson Civic Center, 379
Midtown Grill, 209
Migliorelli Farm (Mount Tremper), 137
Migliorelli Farm Market (Rhinebeck), 373
Military Academy, U.S. (West Point), 47–48; Constitution Island, 45–46; entertainment, 48, 72; golf, 57; lodging, 62–63
Mill Restaurant & Tavern, 165
Mill Road Acres, 263
Mill Street Loft, 410
Millbrook: dining, 395–96, 404–6; events, 414–15; lodging, 386–87; shopping, 409, 410, 412; sights/activities, 355, 357, 369–70, 372, 380
Millbrook Antiques Center, 412
Millbrook Antiques Mall, 412
Millbrook Country House, 386–87
Millbrook Diner, 405
Millbrook Inn (Pond Eddy), 100
Millbrook Variety, 410
Millbrook Vineyards & Winery, 369–70
Millbrook Winery, 406, 414
Millerton, 367–68; dining, 395, 396, 405–6; lodging, 387; shopping, 410, 412; sights/activities, 370, 373, 376, 378, 379
Millerton Antiques Center, 412
Millrock Restaurant, 243
Mills Mansion, 359–60, 413
Mills-Norrie State Park, 370, 376, 378–79
Milton: dining, 164–65; farm, 139; lodging, 154–55, 157
Mima Wine Bar, 476
Minard Farms, 138
Minisceongo Creek, 22
Minisink Battleground Memorial Park, 85
Minnewaska Lodge, 156
Minnewaska Mountain Bike Festival, 185
Minnewaska State Park, 149–50; bicycling, 133; cross-country skiing, 147; hiking, 143, 149–50; swimming, 146
Miracle Mile, 215
ML Gifts & Accessories, 35
Mod Restaurant (Hudson), 341
Modern Restaurant and Pizzeria (New Rochelle), 481
Moderne Barn, 470
Mohansic Golf, 458
Mohawk Hudson Bikeway, 262, 264
Mohegan Lake: dining, 485
Mohonk Mountain House, 126–27, 150, 156–57; cross-country skiing, 147–48; golf, 141; hiking, 143; horseback riding, 144; ice rink, 149; lodging, 156–57
Mohonk Preserve, 133, 143, 147–48, 150
Mongaup Creek, 91; fishing, 90
Mongaup Falls, 86
Monkey Joe's Roasting Company & Coffee Bar, 170
Monroe: sights/activities, 42, 55–58
Monroe Museum Village, 42
Montgomery: dining, 65–66; shopping, 73, 74; sights/activities, 43–44, 56, 58
Montgomery Place, 360, 373
Monticello: dining, 98–99, 102; sights/activities, 85, 86, 89, 92, 93; traveling to, 81
Monticello Casino and Raceway, 92
Montrose: dining, 467
Moodna Creek Marsh, 55, 60
Morahan Beach, 59
Morgan State House, 267
Morne Imports, 180
Morningside Classic: Bass Season Opens, 108–9
Morse, Samuel: Historic Site, 358
Morsston, 90, 104
motels. *See* lodging; *and specific motels and destinations*
Mother's Day Art & Craft Show, 278
Mother's Day Tea, 433
Motorcyclepedia, 42
Mount Beacon Bed & Breakfast, 385
Mount Beacon Park, 367, 376
Mount Gulian Historic Site, 361
Mount Ivy, 23
Mt. Ivy Café, 33
Mount Kisco: dining, 469–70, 484; emergencies, 438; sights/activities, 454, 462
Mount Merino Manor, 333
Mount Peter, 59

Mount Tremper: dining, 160, 166; entertainment, 177; lodging, 151, 152, 153; sights/activities, 117, 137, 143, 148
Mount Tremper Arts, 177
Mount Utsayantha, 197, 203
Mount Vernon: dining, 478; events, 492; sights/activities, 450–51, 460
Mountain Breeze Miniature Horse Farm, 204
Mountain Brook Inn, 207
Mountain House (Sparkill), 33
Mountain Lakes Park, 459, 460
Mountain Meadows Bed and Breakfast, 157
Mountain Tops Kayak Tours, 377
Mountain Trails X-C Ski Center, 235
Mountain Valley Guides (Cornwall), 55
Mountain Wings, 132
Mountaintop Arboretum, 237
Mountainville: art museum, 43; lodging, 62
Mower's Saturday/Sunday Market, 116
MP Taverna, 476
Mr. Apples Low-Spray Orchard, 138
Mr. Willy's Restaurant, 98–99
Mrs. London's, 306
Mud Creek Environmental Learning Center, 316
Mud Pond, 200
Muddy Acres Farm, 293
Mulino's, 473
Mum Festival, 188–89
Murrow Park, 376, 378
Muscoot Farm, 456
Museum of Rhinebeck History, 369
Museum of the Early American Circus, 451
Museum Village (Monroe), 42
music. *See* entertainment
music festivals. *See* bluegrass festivals; events; jazz festivals; *and specific festivals*
My Linh, 271
My Saddle Brook Farm, 58
Myong Gourmet, 470
Mystere, 371
Mysteries and More, 195
Mythos, 473

N

NACL Theatre, 105
Nanuet: dining, 27
Napanoch: dining, 166; sights/activities, 119, 139
Narrowsburg: dining, 100, 103; entertainment, 104, 105; events, 109; shopping, 106, 107; sights/activities, 55, 84–85, 88, 89
National Bottle Museum, 285, 310
National Museum of Dance, 285–86
National Museum of Racing and Hall of Fame, 286
Native Americans, 24, 35, 85, 258, 313, 363, 425, 461, 462; Daniel Nimham Intertribal Pow Wow, 433. *See also* Esopus Indians; Nyack Indians
nature trails. *See* hiking/walking; *and specific trails*
NEO World Bistro and Sushi Bar, 470
Neuberger Museum of Art, 449
Neversink Farm, 89
Neversink River, 91
Neversink Valley Museum of History and Innovation, 59
New Baltimore: antiques, 249
New Castle Historical Society, 442
New City: dining, 27, 31, 33–34; information, 17; sights/activities, 20, 23
New Forge State Forest, 329
New Jersey Transit, 39
New Lebanon: dining, 337–38; entertainment, 343–44; lodging, 331, 334–35; shopping, 345; sights/activities, 315, 327
New Paltz: dining, 163–64, 165, 172–75; events, 185–89; lodging, 156–57; performing arts, 177, 178; shopping, 178–79, 181, 182, 184; sights/activities, 119–20, 123, 126–27, 129–31, 133, 134, 136–41, 143, 144, 146, 147, 149–50; traveling to, 113
New Paltz Farmers' Market, 136
New Paltz Festival/Institute, 178
New Paltz Golf Course, 141
New Paltz Summer Repertory Theater, 178
New Rochelle: activities, 455, 456, 460; dining, 478, 479, 481; events, 491, 492
New Rochelle Farmers' Market, 455
New Windsor: activities, 52, 56, 58, 60; dining, 64, 65, 70
New Windsor Cantonment, 46, 76
New World Bistro & Bar (Albany), 271–72
New World Home Cooking (Saugerties), 162
New York in Bloom, 277
New York Renaissance Faire, 77
New York Sailing School, 453
New York State Capitol, 260
New York State Military Museum, 286
New York State Museum, 258
New York State Police, 223
New York State Vietnam Veterans Memorial, 264–65
Newburgh: dining, 63–65, 69–70; entertainment, 73; lodging, 61; shopping, 73; sights/activities, 42, 44, 48–54, 56, 58, 59; traveling to, 39–40
Newburgh Brewing Company, 51
Newburgh Waterfront, 53–54
Niese Maple Farm, 422
Night Pasture Horse Farm, 204
Nina (Middletown), 68
9 Maple Avenue (Saratoga), 309
1906 House (Callicoon), 101
Ninham Mountain Multiple Use Area, 426
Nino's, 470
Niskayuna Riverfront Bike-Hike Trail, 262
Niverville: lodging, 334
No Sugar, 368, 410
North Branch: lodging, 97
North County Trailway, 452
North River Charters, 135
North Salem: dining, 471; events, 490–91; shopping, 488–89; sights/activities, 438–39, 454, 459, 460
North Star, 470–71
Northern Dutchess Hospital, 352
Northern Westchester Hospital Center, 438
North-South Lake State Park, 228, 235, 237
Nouveau Sushi, 481
Number 9, 387, 396
Nunzio's Pizza, 306
Nyack, 18; dining, 27, 29–34; emergencies, 18; entertainment, 34–35; events, 18, 36; information, 17; lodging, 25–26; shopping, 35; sights/activities, 19–24; traveling to, 18
Nyack Beach State Park, 21, 24
Nyack Farmers Market, 22
Nyack Hospital, 18
Nyack Indians, 18
Nyack Main Essentials, 33
Nyack Public Library, 18
Nyack Tobacco Company, 35
Nyack Village Theatre, 34

NYS Sheep & Wool Festival, 414

O

Oak Hill Cemetery, 18, 20
Oak Ridge Farm, 93
Oak Summit Vineyard, 370
Oakdale Pond, 327
Oakley's Place, 213
O&W Napanoch Train Station Museum, 119
Oblong Books, 367
Ocean House (Croton-on-Hudson), 467
O'Connor Hospital, 194
Octagon Farm Market, 201
Octagon Motor Lodge, 209
Oktoberfest, 251
Olana, 319–20, 348
Old '76 House (Tappan), 29
Old Bryan Inn, 306
Old Chatham: dining, 337, 341; sights/activities, 316–17, 330
Old Chatham Country Store, 341
Old Chatham Sheepherding Company, 316–17
Old Croton Aqueduct State Historic Park, 452, 458
Old Dutch Church (Kingston), 127
Old Dutch Church and Burying Grounds (Tarrytown), 446
Old Franklin Day, 218
Old Homestead Steakhouse (Monticello), 99
Old Mine Road, 129
Old North Branch Inn, 97
Old Quarry/Rockshelter Trail, 85
Old Red Barn Auctions, 74
Old Rhinebeck Aerodrome, 353–54
Old Schoolhouse Inn (Downsville), 210
Old Southeast Church (Brewster), 422
Olde Hudson, 341
Olde Rhinebeck Inn, 384
Olde Saratoga Brewing Company, 290
Ole Carousel Antique Center, 412
Oliverea Schoolhouse Maple Syrup, 139
Olive's Country Store/Café, 170
One Caroline Street Bistro, 303, 309
121 Restaurant (North Salem), 471
Onion Festival, Orange County, 55, 77
Onteora: The Mountain House, 153
Open Eye Theater, 214
Open House Woodstock, 189
Opera Saratoga, 307–8
Opus 40, 127–28
Oquaga Creek State Park, 203
Orange County, 39–77; dining, 63–72; emergencies, 40; entertainment, 72–73; events, 76–77; information, 39; lodging, 60–63; map, 38; shopping, 73–76; sights/activities, 40–60; traveling to, 39–40
Orange County Antique Fair & Flea Market, 73
Orange County Fair, 76–77
Orange County Onion Festival, 55, 77
Orange County Tourism, 39
Orange Regional Medical Center, 40
Orangeburg: dining, 28; historic site, 20; lodging, 26
orchards. *See* farms
Orchards at Concklin, 22
Ore Pond, 327
Original Christopher's Antiques, 35
Oriole 9, 170
Orissa, 476
Osaka, 390
Osceola Beach and Picnic Grounds, 459
O'Sho, 394
Ossining: dining, 466; events, 492; sights/activities, 449–50, 452, 455, 462
Ossining Farmers' Market, 455
Ossining Urban Cultural Park Museum, 449–50
Otto's Market, 341
Ouleout Valley Cemetery, 194
Our Daily Bread, 341–42
Our Lady of the Snows, 227
OUT Cold Spring Depot Restaurant, 431
Out of the Barn Antiques (Philmont), 345
outlet stores, 75–76
Overlook Drive-In, 408
Overlook Farm Market, 56
Overlook Mountain, 143
Overlook Mountain Bikes, 134
Overlook Observatory, 119

P

Pace University, 486
Pachaquack Preserve, 329
Painter's Tavern, 64
Paisley's Country Gallery, 215
Pakatakan Farmers' Market, 200
Palace Diner, 403
Palace Performing Arts Center, 275
Palaia Vineyards, 51
Palenville: dining, 243, 246; golf, 231; lodging, 239, 240
Palisades Center, 35
Palisades Parkway, 17–18; Tourist Information Center, 39
Pamela's on the Hudson, 70
Pancho Villa's Mexican Restaurant, 247
Panza's on the Lake, 303
Panzur Restaurant & Bar, 390–91
Papa John's Pizzeria & Restaurant, 431–32
Paper Trail, 410–11
Paramount Theatre, 73
Park, The (Middletown), 68
Park Falafel & Pizza, 342
Parksville: dining, 104; lodging, 97; shopping, 107
Parlor Coffee & Teahouse, 342
Parting Glass, The, 306, 309
Pastures Historic District, 261
Pathfinder Farms, 230
Patterson: activities, 426–27; dining, 428, 430–31, 432
Paula's Stone Cottage Wine Bar, 403
Paulie's, 484
Pawling: dining, 397, 406, 409; shopping, 411; sights/activities, 356, 373, 375, 376, 378
Pawling Nature Reserve, 376
Payne Farm, 144
Peaceful Breeze Farm & Alpacas, 89
Peaceful Valley Bluegrass Festival, 217–18
Peaceful Valley Campsite, 200
Peach Grove Inn, 61–62
Peach Hill Park, 380
Peaches Café, 274
Pearl River: dining, 30; farm, 22; golf, 22; lodging, 26
Peekamoose Restaurant & Tap Room, 165–66
Peekskill: dining, 466–68, 482–85; events, 491–92; lodging, 465; shopping, 489; sights/activities, 449, 450, 452, 453, 455, 459, 460
Peekskill Artist District Open Studios, 450, 491
Peekskill Celebration, 491–92
Peekskill Farmers' Market, 455
Peekskill History Museum, 450
Penguin Rep, 34–35
Pepacton Reservoir, 197, 198, 201
PepsiCo Headquarters, 438
Perfect Landing Café, 400–401
performing arts: Albany, 275–76; Columbia County, 343–44; Delaware County, 214–15; Dutchess County,

406–9; Greene County, 247–48; Orange County, 72–73; Putnam County, 432; Rockland County, 34–35; Saratoga Springs, 307–9; Sullivan County, 105–6; Westchester County, 485–87
Performing Arts Center (Purchase), 486
Performing Arts of Woodstock, 178
Persen (Matthewis) House, 125
Pete's Saloon, 473–74
Phelps Memorial Hospital Center, 438
Philip J. Rotella Memorial Golf Course, 22
Philip Orchards, 325
Philip Schuyler House, 287
Philipsburg Manor, 446–48, 490
Philipstown Farm Market, 422
Philipstown Performing Arts, 432
Phillies Bridge Farm Project, 137
Philmont: dining, 338, 340–41; lodging, 333–34; shopping, 345
Phoenicia: dining, 166, 170–71, 175; entertainment, 177, 178; lodging, 159; shopping, 180, 182, 184; sights/activities, 118, 121, 146, 147
Phoenicia Belle, 159
Phoenicia Diner, 170–71
Phoenicia International Festival of the Voice, 177
Phoenix, The (Mount Tremper), 166
Phoenix Pottery (Pawling), 411
Piccolo Paese, 102
Pickle Festival, 189
Piermont, 19; dining, 27– 32; lodging, 26; shopping, 35
Piermont Flywheel Gallery, 19
Piermont Marsh, 25
Pig Hill Inn, 428
Pillars Restaurant, 337–38
Pine Bush: dining, 174; horseback riding, 58; lodging, 62; shopping, 73, 74, 182; wineries, 50, 130
Pine Bush Auction, 74
Pine Bush House, 62
Pine Farm Christmas Trees, 90
Pine Hill: activities, 141–42, 146, 147, 148; lodging, 158; music festival, 175–76, 186–87
Pine Hill Lake, 146
Pine Island: events, 76, 77; farms, 55–56; golf, 56; lodging, 60
Pine Meadow Trail, 23
Pine Plains: activities, 377; dining, 396–97, 405; shopping, 411
Pine View Bakery (Shokan), 171
Pine View Farm (New Windsor), 56
Pinkster (Sleepy Hollow), 490
Pinksterfest (Albany), 255, 278
Pioneer Hills Golf Course, 292
Pitkin Company Refinishers & Antiques, 345
PJ's Bar-B-Q S.A., 306–7
planetariums, 256, 448
Plates, 474
Plattekill Creek, 139
Plattekill Mountain Resort, 199, 204–5
Playland, 456–57
Playland Ice Casino, 460
Playland Park, 459
Pleasant Stone Farm, 72
Pleasant Valley, 375, 378, 409
Pleasantville: dining, 467, 482–83, 484; entertainment, 486; shopping, 487; sights/activities, 452, 456, 461
Pleasantville Farmers' Market, 456
Pleshakov Piano Museum, 315
Plumbush Inn, 428, 429
PM Wine Bar, 338
Pocantico Hills: dining, 474; sights/activities, 440–41, 454–55
Poet's Walk Romantic Landscape Park, 381
Point Breeze Marina, 291
Point Lookout Mountain Inn, 241, 245; gardens, 237
Pollo a la Brasa Misti, 481
Polly Crispell Cottage, 115
polo, in Saratoga Springs, 294
Pomona: dining, 29, 33; sights/activities, 21, 22, 23
Pond Eddy, 88; dining, 100
Pony Express, 484
Poppy's, 403
Port Chester, 452; dining, 478, 481, 482; shopping, 489
Port Ewen, 142
Port Jervis: ballooning, 52; shopping, 75–76
Portofino, 391
Potato Republic Café, 33–34
pottery and ceramics, 106, 129–30, 184
Potuck Reservoir, 230
Poughkeepsie, 366; dining, 392–94, 401–4; emergencies, 352; entertainment, 407–8; events, 412–13; lodging, 385–86; shopping, 409–11; sights/activities, 355–56, 358, 365–66, 370–76, 379–81; traveling to, 351–52
Poughkeepsie Farm Project, 373
Poughkeepsie Farmers Market, 372
Poughkeepsie Grand Hotel, 385
Poughquag: dining, 397, 406; farm, 374
Pound Ridge: dining, 470–71; shopping, 489
Powell Wildlife Sanctuary, 330
Powerhouse Theater at Vassar College, 408
Pratt (Zadock) Museum, 225–26
Pratt's Rocks, 225–26
Prattsville, 225–26; dining, 245–46
Pride of New York Harvest Festival, 279
Pride of the Hudson, 52–53
Prima Pizza, 70
Prime at Saratoga National Golf Club, 303–4
Prospect Hill Orchards, 139
Prospect Restaurant, 243–44
Prospero Winery, 452
Provence, 272
Provident Bank Park/Home, 21
Pruyn Sanctuary Butterfly and Hummingbird Garden, 439–40
Public Restaurant & Lounge (Roxbury), 211
Pudding Street Multiple Use Area, 425
Purchase: dining, 472; entertainment, 486; sights/activities, 438, 449
Purchase College, 449
Purdy's Farmer and the Fish, 471
Pure City, 174
Pure Mountain, 411
Purling: dining, 242; lodging, 237–38
Putnam 4-H Fair, 433
Putnam Art Council Belle Levine Art Center, 421
Putnam County, 419–33; dining, 428–32; emergencies, 419; entertainment, 432; events, 432–33; information, 419; lodging, 427–28; map, 418; sights/activities, 419–27; traveling to, 419
Putnam County Visitors Bureau, 419
Putnam Historical Society, 420
Putnam Hospital Center, 419
Putnam Market, 307
Putnam National Golf Club, 423

Q

Q Restaurant and Bar, 481
Quality Inn & Suites (Albany), 267
Quarryman's Museum, 127–28
Queechy Lake, 327, 331
Quiet Cove Riverfront Park, 381
Quiet Man Public House, 467

R

Raccoon Saloon, 174
rail trails. *See specific rail trails*
Railroad Playhouse, 73
Rails-To-Trails, 88, 203
Raimondo's, 101
Rainbow Golf Club, 231
Rainbow's End Butterfly Farm and Nursery, 356
Ramapo River: fishing, 22
Rambler's Rest, 397
Ramiro's 954, 430
Rams Horn-Livingston Sanctuary, 233
Ray's Café, 474
Reader's Quarry, 180
Real Seafood Company, 272
Red Devon Market Cafe, 405
Red Dot Bar & Restaurant, 338
Red Hat on the River, 476
Red Hook, 368; dining, 388–90, 397–400; lodging, 383, 384; shopping, 411; sights/activities, 353–54, 373, 374, 375, 381
Red Hook Country Inn, 384
Red Hook Golf Club, 375
Red Onion Restaurant & Bar, 162
Red Robin Song Guest House, 334
Red Rooster Drive-In, 432
Reds Restaurant, 244
Redwood Tennis and Swim Club, 58–59
Reel Happy Charters, 231
Reformed Church of Tappan, 19
Reginato Ristorante, 162
Renaissance Faire, 77
Renaissance Westchester Hotel, 465
Renwick Clifton House B&B, 153
Residence Inn (Fishkill), 385–86
Residence Inn (Poughkeepsie), 386
Residence Inn by Marriott (Saratoga Springs), 297
Restaurant North, 471
Restaurant X, 29
restaurants. *See specific restaurants and destinations*
Revolutionary War. *See* American Revolution
Rexford: farms, 292
Reynolds House Inn, 97
Rhinebeck, 368–69; dining, 387–91, 397–400; emergencies, 352; entertainment, 407, 408–9; events, 412–15; information, 351; lodging, 382–85; shopping, 409–11; sights/activities, 363, 368–69, 372, 373, 377, 378; traveling to, 351–52
Rhinebeck Antiques Fair, 414
Rhinebeck Antiques Show, 412
Rhinebeck Bicycle Shop, 371
Rhinebeck Chamber Music Society, 408–9
Rhinebeck Chamber of Commerce, 351
Rhinecliff Hotel Restaurant & Bar, 391
Rhinecliff Inn, 384
Ricciardella's Restaurant, 166
Richard B. Fisher Center for the Performing Arts, 354–55, 407
Rick's Seafood, 430
Rip Van Winkle, 134–35
Rip Van Winkle Bridge, 233, 324
Rip Van Winkle Country Club, 231
Rip Van Winkle Lake, 230
Ritz Theater, 73
River Aviation, Inc., 114
River Brook Farm (Cochecton), 89
River City Grille (Irvington), 476
River Club (Nyack), 29
River Connection (Hyde Park), 377
river cruises. *See* boat cruises
River Gallery (Narrowsburg), 107
River Grill (Newburgh), 65
River Hill Bed and Breakfast (Milton), 157
River Market (Barryville), 104
River Rock Health Spa, 116
River Rose, 53, 371
River Run (Fleischmanns), 206
River Run Restaurant & Bar (Hancock), 211
River Valley Rep Theatre, 408
Riverbank Bar and Grill (Cornwall), 64–65
Riverfest (Narrowsburg), 109
Riverrun Rare Book Room, 488
Riverside Café (Roscoe), 101
Rivertown Film Society (Nyack), 35
Rivertowns Tourism, 452
RiverView Bed & Breakfast (Piermont), 26
Riverview Marine Services, Inc. (Catskill), 228–29
Riverview Orchards (Rexford), 292
Riverview Restaurant (Cold Spring), 430
Roaring Brook Inn, 209
Robert Jenkins House, 322
Roberts' Auction, 198
Robibero Family Vineyards, 131
Rock City Falls: lodging, 300
rock climbing, 145–46
Rock Hill: dining, 98; lodging, 96–97
Rockefeller Empire State Plaza. *See* Empire State Plaza
Rockefeller State Park Preserve, 461
Rocking Horse Ranch, 157
Rockland Boulders, 21
Rockland Center for the Arts, 35
Rockland Coaches, 18
Rockland County, 17–36; dining, 27–34; emergencies, 18; entertainment, 34–35; events, 35–36; information, 17; lodging, 25–26; map, 16; shopping, 35; sights/activities, 18–25; traveling to, 17–18
Rockland County Historical Society, 17, 20
Rockland County Tourism, 17
Rockland House, 101
Rockland Lake Champion Golf Course, 23
Rockland Lake State Park, 25
Rock'n Mexicana, 244
Rodgers Book Barn, 346
Roebling's Suspension Bridge, 85
Roeliff Jansen Creek, 327
Rogers Island, 324
Rogowski Farm, 55, 76, 77
Rolling River Café, Gallery and Inn, 97, 104
Rolling Stone Ranch, 93
Rolling V Transportation Services, 81
Rondout Creek, 138, 139
Rondout Golf Club, 141
Rondout Landing, 118, 134, 135, 163
Rondout Lighthouse, 134–35
Ronnybrook, 374
Roosevelt, Eleanor, 357, 365; National Historic Site, 361–62, 370, 380
Roosevelt, Franklin Delano, 260; Home, 357, 370, 380; Presidential Library & Museum, 365; Top Cottage, 361

Roosevelt Baths & Spa, 289
Roosevelt Ride, 351–52
Roosevelt State Park, 458
Rosa's La Scarbitta Ristorante, 481
Roscoe: dining, 101, 104; information, 81; lodging, 97, 98; shopping, 106; sights/activities, 89–92
Roscoe Chamber of Commerce, 81
Roscoe Diner, 104
Roscoe Little Store, 90
Roscoe Motel, 97
Rosehaven Alpacas, 90
Rosendale: dining, 164, 166, 168, 174; events, 189; lodging, 155; shopping, 184; sights/activities, 117, 129, 133, 136, 145
Rosendale Café, 174
Rosendale Farmers' Market, 136
Rosticceria Rossi & Sons, 403–4
Rotella Memorial Golf Course, 22
Rotterdam Riverfront Hike-Bike Trail, 262
Round Top: entertainment, 247; events, 250; lodging, 238; sights/activities, 226, 231
Round Top Raptor Center, 226
Roundhouse at Beacon Falls, 386, 394
Roxbury: dining, 211, 212–13; entertainment, 214; events, 218; lodging, 206–7; shopping, 216; sights/activities, 196–97, 199, 201, 202, 204–5
Roxbury Arts Group, 214
Roxbury Motel, 206–7
Roxbury Village Inn, 207
Rraci's Ristorante Italiano, 430
Ruby's Hotel, 244
Rudd Pond Area, 331, 378, 379
Rural Residence, 344–45, 346–47
Russ Barber Hot Air Balloon Rides, 323
Russel Wright Historic Site & Nature Sanctuary, 424–25
Russell Brook, 90
Russell's Store, 213, 215
Rusty's Farm Fresh Eatery, 399
Ruth's Chris Steakhouse, 465
Ryder Farm, 423
Rye: dining, 480–81, 482; events, 491; sights/activities, 451, 456–61
Rye Brook: lodging, 464–65
Rye Farmers' Market, 456
Rye Nature Center, 461

S

Sackett Lake Road, 85–86
Saffron Fine Indian Cuisine, 68
Saigon Café, 404
St. Andrew's Café, 388
St. Anthony Community Hospital, 40
St. Anthony Street Festival, 412–13
St. Francis Hospital, 352
St. John the Baptist Ukrainian Church, 227
St. Luke's Cornwall Hospital, 40
St. Patrick's Day Parade, 185
St. Paul's Church National Historic Site, 450–51, 492
St. Peter's Hospital, 256
St. Vincent Millay, Edna, 320, 347
Salinger's Orchards, 423
Salisbury Mills: lodging, 60
Salvatore's Original Pizza, 399
Samascott Orchard, 325
Samba Café, 101–2
Samba Inn, 97
Sam's Point, 151
Sam's Point Preserve and Conservation Center, 150–51
Samuel Dorsky Museum of Art, 119–20
Samuel's, 399–400
Sandy Klempner Antiques & Interiors, 345
Sanfords Horse Farm, 204
Santa Fe (Tarrytown), 476–77; (Tivoli), 391
Santa Fe Uptown (Kingston), 162
Santorini Greek Restaurant, 477
Sap to Syrup Maple Sunday, 432–33
Saperstein's Department Store, 368
Sapore Steakhouse, 394
Saratoga. *See* Saratoga Springs
Saratoga and North Creek Railway, 294
Saratoga Arms, 297–98
Saratoga Automobile Museum, 286
Saratoga Boat Works, 291
Saratoga Casino and Raceway, 293
Saratoga City Tavern, 307
Saratoga County Chamber of Commerce, 283
Saratoga County Fair, 310
Saratoga Farmers' Market, 292
Saratoga Farmstead Bed & Breakfast, 300
Saratoga Film Forum, 308
Saratoga Harness Racing Museum and Hall of, 286
Saratoga Hilton, 298
Saratoga Hospital, 284
Saratoga Jazz Festival, 310
Saratoga Lake, 283, 291, 292
Saratoga Lake Golf Club, 292
Saratoga Mini Golf, 292
Saratoga Monument, 287
Saratoga Motel, 298
Saratoga National Battlefield Park, 310
Saratoga National Golf Club, 292–93, 303
Saratoga National Historical Park, 287, 310
Saratoga Performing Arts Center, 308
Saratoga Race Course, 283, 293–94
Saratoga Sleigh, 300
Saratoga Spa Golf Course, 293
Saratoga Spa State Park, 289, 294–96; events, 310; performing arts, 307–8
Saratoga Springs, 283–310; dining, 301–7; emergencies, 284; entertainment, 307–9; events, 309–10; information, 283; lodging, 296–301; map, 282; sights/activities, 284–96; traveling to, 283–84
Saratoga Springs Heritage Area Visitor Center, 283
Saratoga Springs History Museum, 285
Saratoga Springs Ice Rinks, 295
Saratoga Springs YMCA, 295
Saratoga Wine and Food Festival, 310
Saratoga Winery, 290
Saugerties, 115; dining, 160, 162–63, 167–72, 171; events, 185–89; lodging, 151–53; performing arts, 176; shopping, 178, 179, 181, 182; sights/activities, 120, 127–28, 135, 136, 137, 139, 140, 144, 148–49
Saugerties Antiques Center, 182
Saugerties Artists Studio Tour, 187
Saugerties Farmers' Market, 136
Saugerties Lighthouse, 115, 128
Saugerties Lighthouse Bed & Breakfast, 153
Saunders Farm, 423
Saunderskill Farms, 137–38
Savona's Trattoria, 162
Sawkill Creek, 139–40
Sawkill Family Ski Center, 148
Saxon Woods Golf, 458
Saxon Woods Park, 460
Sazan, 477

Scalini Osteria, 481–82
Scallions, 307
Scandinavian Grace, 180
Scarsdale: dining, 472, 473, 474, 479–80; entertainment, 485; events, 492; sights/activities, 458, 461, 462
scenic drives: Columbia County, 321; Delaware County, 197–98; Dutchess County, 366; Greene County, 227; Orange County, 49–50; Sullivan County, 85–87; Ulster County, 128–30
Scenic Farms Golf Course, 56
Scenic Hudson Park at Irvington, 461
Schauber Stables, 293
Scheuermann Farms, 55
Schimpf Farms, 22
Schlesinger's Steak House, 65
Schnare's Sunset Orchard, 230
Schoharie Reservoir, 201, 230
Schunnemunk Mountain, 58
Schuyler (Philip) House (Stillwater), 287
Schuyler (Philip) Mansion (Albany), 259
Scotts Family Resort at Oquaga Lake, 208
Scribner Hollow Lodge, 240, 243–44
Scrimshaw, 272
Seaside Johnnie's, 482
Secor Farms, 373
Senate House State Historic Site, 128
September 11th Memorial Garden, 440
Septemberfest, 36
Sequoia, 118
Serevan Restaurant, 396
74 State Hotel (Albany), 267, 271
1712 House (Stone Ridge), 157–58
Shadow Mountain Farm Bed & Breakfast, 62
Shadowland Theatre, 178
Shadows Marina Water Taxi, 371
Shadows on the Hudson, 394
Shaker Meadows Bed & Breakfast (New Lebanon), 334–35
Shaker Museum-Mount Lebanon, 315
Shaker Shed Farm Market & Greenhouse (Colonie), 263
Shakers, 278, 313, 315, 344
Shakespeare Festival, Hudson Valley, 422, 433
Shandaken: dining, 160; lodging, 158–59; shopping, 182
Shandaken Theatrical Society, 178
Shandelee Music Festival, 109
Shaupeneak Ridge Cooperative Recreation Area, 143
Shawangunk Country Club, 141
Shawangunk Rail Trail, 133
Shawangunk Wine Trail, 130–32, 189
Sheep and Wool Festival, 347
Sheep to Shawl, 490
Shephard Hills Golf Course, 202
Shinglekill Falls, 233
Shinglekill Grist Mill, 233
Ship Lantern Inn, 165
Ship to Shore Restaurant, 163
Shirley's Restaurant, 307
Sho Chiku Sushi, 29
Shokan: dining, 170, 171, 175; shopping, 180
shopping: Albany, 276–77; Columbia County, 344–47; Delaware County, 215–17; Dutchess County, 409–12; Greene County, 248–50; Orange County, 73–76; Rockland County, 35; Sullivan County, 106–8; Ulster County, 178–84; Westchester County, 487–89. *See also* farmer's markets
Short Line/Coach USA, 39, 81, 351
Sidewalk Bistro, 29–30
Sidney: lodging, 208–9
Sidney Summer Arts and Music Festival, 218
Siena Saints Basketball, 264
Signatures by Candlelight, 209–10
Silent Farm, 62
Silk Tree Café, 439
Silver Canoe Rentals, 54, 88
Simmons' Way Village Inn, 387
Sinterklaas in Rhinebeck, 415
Siro's, 304
Siro's Trattoria at the Lodge, 304
Sissy's Café, 171
Sisters Hill Farm, 373
Sitar, 272
Six Sisters Bed & Breakfast, 300
Sixty One Main Gallery, 216
Skate Time 209, 121
skating. *See* ice skating
Ski Plattekill Mountain Resort, 204–5
Skidmore College: art museum, 286–87
skiing: Columbia County, 331; Delaware County, 204–5; Greene County, 235–37; Orange County, 59; Putnam County, 426–27; Sullivan County, 93–94; Ulster County, 148. *See also* cross-country skiing
Skillypot Antique Center, 182
Sky Acres Airport, 352, 400–401
Sky Top, 150
Skydive the Ranch, 132
skydiving, 132
Skytop Steak House & Brewing Company, 163
Slabsides, 129
Slate Hill: ballooning, 52; dining, 72
Slater Destroyer Escort 766, 258
Slattery's The Landing, 30
Sleepy Hollow: dining, 477; emergencies, 438; events, 490; sights/activities, 443, 445–49, 452
Sleepy Hollow Cemetery, 446
Sleepy Hollow Lighthouse, 445–46
Sleepy Valley Inn, 62
Snapping Turtle Walk, 433
snowboarding. *See* skiing
snowmobiling, 226, 236, 328, 329
snowshoeing, 199, 203, 205, 235, 236, 357, 376, 423–24
Snyder (A. J.) Estate, 117
soaring (hang gliding), 93, 132
Sojourner Truth Ulster Landing County Park, 146
Somers: sights/activities, 439, 451, 456
Somers Historical Society, 451
Something Sweet, 68–69, 72
Sonoma Falls Cider Mill & Country Market, 90, 104
Sonora, 482
Soul Dog, 404
South County Trailway, 452
South Kortright: dining, 211
Southeast Museum, 421
Southfields Furnace, 59–60
Southlands Foundation, 377
Southwestern Grill, 171
Sparkill: activities, 23; dining, 33
spas, in Saratoga Springs, 287–89
special events. *See* events; *and specific events*
Spectrum Theater, 275
Spencer House Bed & Breakfast, 335
Spencertown: entertainment, 343, 347; sights/activities, 315
Spencertown Academy, 343
Spencertown Cottages, 331–32
Sperry's, 304
Spirit of the Hudson, 228
Splash Down Beach, 356–57
Spook Rock Golf Course, 23

Spoon, 471
sports. *See specific sports*
Spotty Dog Books & Ale, 322, 342
Sprain Lake Golf Course, 458
Spring House Commons, 97
Spring Valley: dining, 32; historic site, 20–21; information, 17
Springs Motel, 298
Springside National Historic Site, 366
Sprout Creek Farm, 373
Spruce Lake, 459
Square House Museum (Rye), 451
Square Restaurant (Margaretville), 210
Squash Blossom, 35
Squires, 467–68
Squirrel Corners, 85
Staatsburg: dining, 387, 391; events, 412–14; lodging, 382; sights/activities, 359–60, 370, 374, 376–79
Staatsburgh State Historic Site, 359–60, 412, 414
Stadium, The (Garrison), 432
Stageworks/Hudson, 343
Stair Galleries, 345
Stamford, 197–98; dining, 211; entertainment, 214; lodging, 207; sights/activities, 201–4
Stamford Depot, 199
Stamford Golf Club, 202
Stanfordville: activities, 373, 377, 378, 379; shopping, 412
Stanley Maltzman's Four Corners Art Gallery, 249
State Capitol (Albany), 260
state parks. *See specific parks*
State Street Mansion Bed & Breakfast, 267–68
State University of New York (SUNY). *See* SUNY
Steel House Restaurant & Bar, 163
Steel Plant Studios, 411
Steepletop: House & Gardens, 320, 347
Steinway Book Company, 216
Stella's, 163
Stephen's Antiques, 216
Sterling Forest State Park, 58
Sterling Ridge Trail, 58
Steven E. Greenstein Piano Collection, 248
Stevenson Gymnasium, 377–78
Stewart International Airport, 40, 52, 81–82, 114, 352
Stewart State Forest, 58
Stewart's Department Store, 215
Stillman, Chauncey D., 381–82
StilltheOne Distillery, 452
Stissing House Restaurant & Tavern, 396–97
Stissing Mountain Fire Tower, 376–77
Stockade Tavern, 171
Stockport Flats, 324–25
Stone & Thistle Farm, 201
Stone Arch Bridge Historical Park, 94–95
Stone Barns Center for Food and Agriculture, 440–41, 454–55, 474
Stone Dock Golf Course, 141
Stone Ridge: farms, 137, 139; lodging, 155–58; shopping, 184
Stone Ridge Orchard, 138
Stone Tavern Farm, 204
Stone Wall Acres, 97
Stonecrop Gardens, 427
Stony Creek Farm, 201
Stony Ford Golf Course, 56
Stony Kill Environmental Education Center, 357
Stony Point: dining, 28, 32–33; entertainment, 34; lodging, 26
Stony Point Battlefield, 17, 21
Stony Point Conference Center, 26
Storm King Adventure Tours, 55
Storm King Art Center, 43
Storm King Lodge, 62
Stormville Airport Antique Show & Flea Market, 412
Stoutridge Vineyard, 131–32
Strawberry Festival, 217
Strawtown Café, 34
Stuart's Fruit Farm, 455
Stuyvesant Farmers' Market, 326
Stuyvesant Plaza, 277
Suffern: dining, 29; emergencies, 18; golf, 23; lodging, 26
Sugar Brook Maple Farm, 139
Sugar Loaf: dining, 71; entertainment, 72; lodging, 62; shopping, 73–75
Sugar Loaf Crafts Village, 74–75
Sugar Loaf Village Bed & Breakfast, 62
Sugar Maples Center for Arts and Education, 249
Sugar Plum Boutique, 411
Sukhothai, 394–95
Sullivan County, 81–109; dining, 98–104; emergencies, 82; entertainment, 104–6; events, 108–9; information, 81; lodging, 95–98; map, 80; shopping, 106–8; sights/activities, 82–95; traveling to, 81–82
Sullivan County Area Farmers Market, 89
Sullivan County Community College, 105
Sullivan County Golf and Country Club, 92
Sullivan County International Airport, 82
Sullivan County Museum, Art and Cultural Center, 84, 104–5
Sullivan County Pottery Trail, 106
Sullivan County Visitors Association, 81
Sundance Rappel Tower, 146
Sunfrost, 171
Sunny Hill Resort & Golf Course, 231
Sunny Sail Charters, 228
Sunrise House B&B, 97–98
Sunset Cove, 477
Sunshine Cottage and Pottery Bed & Breakfast, 98
SUNY Delhi: dining, 209–10
SUNY New Paltz: art museum, 119–20; events, 186; theater, 178
SUNY Purchase: performing arts, 486
Super 8 Motel of Nyack, 26
Suruchi, 165
Susan's Pleasant Pheasant Farm, 206
Sushi Mike's, 477
Sushi Thai Garden, 304
Susquehanna River: fishing, 201–2; kayaking, 199–200
Swan Lake, 90, 91
Swan Lake Golf and Country Club, 92
Swann Inn, 386
Swedish Hill Winery, 290
Sweet Sue's, 175
swimming: Columbia County, 330; Dutchess County, 377–78; Orange County, 58–59; Saratoga Springs, 294–95; Ulster County, 146; Westchester County, 459
Swinburne Rink and Recreation Center, 264
Swington Bridge Lake, 91
Swiss Hütte, 338
Swoon, 338
Szechuan King, 171–72

T

Table on Ten Café, 213
Tackamack North Park, 23
Tackamack South Park, 23
Taco Gold, 404
Taconic Orchards, 326
Taconic Outdoor Education Center, 425
Taconic Parkway, 366
Taconic Sculpture Park and Gallery, 315, 347

Taconic State Park, 324, 327, 329–31; Rudd Pond Area, 331, 378, 379
Tacos Marianita, 34
Taghkanic (town), 321, 329; dining, 342
Taghkanic Diner, 342
Taghkanic State Park. *See* Lake Taghkanic State Park
Taliaferro Farms, 137
Tallman Mountain State Park, 25
Tang Teaching Museum and Art Gallery, 286–87
Tannersville: activities, 230, 231, 232, 235, 237; dining, 242, 245–47; lodging, 239
Tannersville Bike Path, 228
Tannery Pond Concerts, 343
Tantillo's Farm Market, 138–39
Tanzy's, 342
Tap House (Tuckahoe), 477–78
Tap New York Craft Beer & Food Festival, 250
Tappan, 19; dining, 28, 29; sights/activities, 20, 23
Tappan (Kittle) Bridge, 196
Tappan Golf Center, 23
Tappan Library, 19
Tappan Zee Theatre, 18
Taro's, 406
Tarry Brae Golf Course, 92
Tarrytown, 437; dining, 475, 476–77; entertainment, 486; events, 491–93; lodging, 463–64, 465; shopping, 489; sights/activities, 443–46, 452, 456, 475
Tarrytown Farmers' Market, 456
Tarrytown Halloween Parade, 492
Tarrytown House Estate and Conference Center, 465
Tarrytown Lighthouse, 445–46
Tarrytown Music Hall, 486
Tarrytown Street Fair, 491
T.A.'s Place, 214
Taste (Albany), 272
Taste Budd's Chocolate and Coffee Café, 400
Taste of New Paltz, 187–88
Taste of the Catskills, 218, 219
Tatiana's Italian Restaurant, 244
Tavern at Croton Landing, 484
Tavern at the 1850 House, 174
Tavern at the Beekman Arms, 391
Tavern at the Highlands Country Club, 430
Tavola Rustica in the Courtyard, 400
Tay Home, 215
Tay Tea Bar, 212
Teal, 135
Teatown Fall Festival, 492
Teatown Lake Reservation, 462, 492
Teddy's Roadhouse Grille, 211
Ted's Restaurant, 102
Temptation Tea House, 484
Temptations, 34
Ten Broeck Mansion, 259
Ten Mile Creek, 230
Tender Land Home, 180
Tennanah Lake Golf & Tennis Club, 92, 98
Terhune Orchards, 374
Terni's, 368
Terrace Club (Mahopac), 430
Terrapin, 391
Terwilliger House, 125, 189
Texas Taco, 432
Thai Elephant 2, 430–31
Thai House, 30
Thanksgiving Day Parade, 492
Thayer Hotel, 62–63
theater. *See* performing arts
Theater Barn (New Lebanon), 344
Thiells: golf, 22
Thirteen Vodka Bar & Lounge, 309
36 Main Street Restaurant & Wine Bar, 174
Thomas Cole National Historic Site, 224–25
Thomas P. Morahan Beach, 59
Thompson House, 241
Thompson Pond Preserve, 377
Thompson-Finch Farm, 325
Thompsonville: lodging, 95–96
Thornwood: dining, 473
Three Dogs Gluten-Free Bakery, 484–85
Thunder Ridge Ski Area, 426–27
Thunderhart Golf Club, 231
Tibetan Buddhist Monastery, 116, 120
Tilly Foster Farm, 423
Time & Space Limited, TSL Warehouse, 344
Times Union Center, 275–76
Timp-Torne Trail, 23
Tiramisu, 404
Tivoli, 369; dining, 389, 390, 391, 399; entertainment, 407; lodging, 382–84; shopping, 411; sights/activities, 377, 380
Tivoli Artists Co-Op, 411
Tiznow, 304
Tobacco Factory, 368
Tomasco Falls, 86–87
Tomato Café, 404
Tomo Sushi, 163
Top Cottage, 361
Torches, 65
Tortillaville, 339
Tour de Putnam Cycling Festival, 433
tourist information. *See* information
Tousey Winery, 323
Town & Country Antiques (Liberty), 108
Town of Colonie Golf Course, 263
Town of Thompson Park, 93
Town Tinker Tube Rental, 147
Towne Crier Café, 409
Tractor Parade, 109
Trailside Museum, Nature Trail, and Zoo (Bear Mountain), 24
Transport of Rockland, 18
Traphagen's Honey, 230
Travelodge (Albany), 268
Travers Festival Week, 310
Tre Alberi, 100
Treasure Box Antiques, 108
Treat Station, 485
Trees of the Woods, 90
Trevor Zoo, 357
Tri N' Du, 433
Trinity Cruise Company, 453
Tri-States Monument, 75–76
Trolley Museum, 122
Trout Pond, 200
Troutbeck Inn & Conference Center, 387, 396
True Food, 34
tubing, 146–47
Tuckahoe: dining, 477–78, 483
Tulip Festival (Pinksterfest), 255, 278
Tumblin' Falls House, 238
Turkey Scavenger Hunt, 492
Turn of the Century Day, 218
Turning Point Café, 30
Turquoise Barn, 216
Turtle Creek Golf Course, 141
Tusten Theatre, 105–6
Tuthill House, 165
Tuthilltown Spirits, 132
Tuxedo: activities, 58, 59–60; shopping, 73
Tuxedo Antiques Center, 73
Tuxedo Ridge, 59
Twelve Grapes Music & Wine Bar, 468
TWG Fabric Outlet, 76
Twilight General Store, 228, 237
Twin Gables of Woodstock, 153–54
Twin Lakes (Hurley), 154
Twisted Foods, 174
Two Boots, 400
Two Henrys, 30
Two Old Tarts Bakery and Cafe, 213
Two Spear Street, 30–31
2 Taste Food & Wine Bar, 400

U

Ulster County, 113–89; dining, 159–75; emergencies, 114; entertainment, 175–78; events, 184–89; information, 113; lodging, 151–59; map, 112; shopping, 178–84; sights/activities, 114–51; traveling to, 113–14
Ulster County Area Transit (UCAT), 114
Ulster County Chamber of Commerce, 113
Ulster County Fair, 187
Ulster County Historical Society, 122–23
Ulster County Tourism, 113, 184
Ulster Park: events, 187; sights/activities, 118–19, 131, 137, 145
Ulster Performing Arts Center, 177
Ultimate Fly-Fishing Store, 216
Umami, 468
Unadilla, 197–98
Underground Railroad, 115, 256, 262
Underhill's Crossing, 482
Undermountain Golf Course, 327
Union Gables Bed & Breakfast, 300–301
Union Hall General Store, 488–89
Union Restaurant & Bar Latino, 31
Union Street Guest House, 333
Union Vale: golf, 375
Unison Arts and Learning Center, 177
Untermyer Park and Gardens, 441
Upstate Films, 409
U.S.S. *Slater* Destroyer Escort-766, 258
Utsayantha Trail System, 203

V

Vails Gate, 46, 76
Vails Grove Golf Course, 423
Valatie, 321; dining, 341; sights/activities, 322, 326–30
Valhalla: entertainment, 487; sights/activities, 439, 440, 456
Val-Kill, 361–62, 370, 380
Van Alen (Luykas) House, 314, 318–19
Van Buren, Martin, 313, 318–19; National Historic Site, 319
Van Cortlandt Manor, 444, 459, 492–93
Van Deusen House, 115, 182
Van Houten Farms, 22
Van Schaack House, 334
Van Winkle's at the Kaatskill Mountain Club, 244
Van Wyck Homestead Museum, 365
Vanderbilt House, 333–34, 338
Vanderbilt Mansion National Historic Site, 362–63, 380, 415
Vanderpoel (James) House, 314, 318
Van's Vietnamese Restaurant, 272
Vantran Covered Bridge, 86
Vasilow's, 345
Vassar Brothers Medical Center, 352
Vassar College: Francis Lehman Loeb Art Center, 365–66; golf, 375; Powerhouse Theater, 408
Vassar Golf Course, 375
Vedder Memorial Library, 224
Veggie Heaven, 34
Velo Wine Bar & Bistro, 31
Velveeta cheese, 55
Veranda House, 384
Verbank: dining, 404–5
Verkeerderkill Falls, 151
Vernon Hills Shopping Center, 489
Vernooy Kill Falls, 143
Vertigris, 345
Vesuvio, 244–45
Veterans Research Center, 286
Vico, 338–39
Victoria Pool (Saratoga Springs), 294–95
Victoria Rose B&B, 208
Victorian River View (Fort Montgomery), 63
Victorian Rose Restaurant (East Windham), 245
Victorian Street Walk (Saratoga Springs), 310
Victory Café, 272–73
Villa Roma Resort & Conference Center, 92, 94, 98
Village Bistro (Tannersville), 245
Village Square Bookstore & Gallery (Hunter), 249
Village Tea Room (New Paltz), 174–75
Vineyard Grille & Café at Millbrook Winery, 406
vineyards. *See* wineries
Vintage Café, 404
Vinum Café, 71
Violette, 163
visitor information. *See* information
Volunteer Firemen's Hall and Museum, 126
Vox, 471–72

W

Walden: dining, 67; horseback riding, 58
walking. *See* hiking/walking
Walkway over the Hudson, 381
Wallkill: lodging, 154, sights/activities, 131, 133–34, 141, 143
Wallkill Golf Club, 57
Wallkill River School & Gallery, 74
Wallkill Valley Rail Trail, 133–34, 143
Wallkill View Farm, 139
Walnut Mountain Park, 88, 93
Walter's Hot Dogs, 485
Walton, 197, 198; dining, 212, 214; emergencies, 194; events, 218; lodging, 209; shopping, 215, 217; sights/activities, 200, 201, 204; theater, 214
Walton Theatre, 214
Waneta Lake, 90, 91
Wappingers Falls: dining, 402, 403; entertainment, 407; information, 351; sights/activities, 355, 357, 371, 373
Ward Pound Ridge Reservation, 460, 462
Warner House, 45–46
Warner Memorial Garden, 46
Warthin Museum of Geology and Natural History, 366
Warwick: dining, 67–68, 71–72; emergencies, 40; farms, 55, 56; lodging, 60–63; skiing, 59; wineries, 50, 51
Warwick Farmers' Market, 56
Warwick Valley Bed & Breakfast, 63
Warwick Valley Winery and Distillery, 51–52
Warwickshire Bed & Breakfast, 63
Wasabi (Nyack), 31
Wasabi Japanese Restaurant (Hudson), 339
Washburn Trail, 424
Washington, George, 419, 451; Headquarters (Newburgh), 48–49; Masonic Historic Site, 20
Washington Irving Inn (Hunter), 240, 247
Washington Park, 262, 265, 278–79
Washingtonville: dining, 71; winery, 50
Wassaic, 329, 409
water parks, 226–27, 356–57

Water Street Antiques Center, 182
Water Street Market, 181
Watercolor Café, 474
Waterfall House, 240
Waterstone Inn, 63
Watts De Peyster Hall, 369
Wawaka Lake, 206
Webster's Corner, 266
Weed Orchards, 138
Weekend Chamber Music for All Time Summer Festival, 109
Weinberg Nature Center, 462
West Branch House Bed and Breakfast, 207–8
West Branch Preserve, 203
West Coxsackie: dining, 244, 247
West Kill Falls, 233
West Kortright Centre, 214–15
West Lebanon: lodging, 334
West Nyack: farms, 22
West Point, 47–48; Constitution Island, 45–46; entertainment, 48, 72; golf, 57; lodging, 62–63
West Point Foundry Preserve, 420–21
West Point Golf Course, 57
West Point Museum, 48
Westchester Broadway Theatre, 486–87
Westchester Community College, 439, 487
Westchester County, 437–93; dining, 466–85; emergencies, 437–38; entertainment, 485–87; events, 489–93; information, 437; lodging, 463–66; map, 436; shopping, 487–89; sights/activities, 438–63; traveling to, 437
Westchester County Airport, 437
Westchester County Center, 487
Westchester County Office of Tourism, 437
Westchester Cycle Club, 453
Westchester Greenhouses, 455
Westchester House Bed & Breakfast, 301
Westchester Mall, 489
Westchester Marriott, 465–66
Westchester Skating Academy, 460
Westchester Wilderness Walk, 458
Westco Productions, 487
Western Riding Stables, 330
Western Trail Riding, 377
Westmoreland Sanctuary, 462–63
Wethersfield Estate and Gardens, 381–82
Wheel and Heel, 371
Wherehouse, 70
Whispering Pines Bed & Breakfast, 158
Whistlewood Farm, 384–85
White Cloud's Beaverkill Fly-Fishing School, 90–91
White Goose, 345
White Lake, 91; dining, 99–100; lodging, 95
White Plains: dining, 472, 473, 484; emergencies, 438; entertainment, 485, 487; events, 490, 491; information, 437; lodging, 464, 465; shopping, 489; sights/activities, 456, 458, 459, 460
White Plains Cherry Blossom Festival, 490
White Plains Farmers' Market, 456
White Plains Hospital Medical Center, 438
White Plains Outdoor Arts Festival, 491
White Plains Performing Arts Center, 487
White Pond Multiple Use Area, 426
White Rock/Canada Hill Trail, 424
White Stone Café, 342
White Wolf Restaurant & Lounge, 166
Whitecliff Vineyard and Winery, 132
Whitewater Willie's Raft and Canoe Rentals, 88
Wigsten's Farm Market, 374
Wilbur Boulevard Trailway, 370
Wilcox Park, 377, 378, 379
Wild and Scenic River Tours and Rentals, 54
Wild Blueberry & Huckleberry Festival, 187
Wild Hive Farm Cafe, 406
Wild Rose Inn Bed & Breakfast, 154
Wilderstein, 363
Wildfire Grill, 66–67
Wildflower Cottage, 63
Wildlife Education Center (Cornwall), 41–42
Wilkens Fruit and Fir Farm, 455
Wilklow Orchards, 138
Willow, 119, 122, 184
Willow Lake Cottages, 386
Willowbrook Farm, 377
Willowemoc Creek, 83, 86, 91; fishing, 90
Wilson M. Powell Wildlife Sanctuary, 330
Wilson State Park, 143, 148
Winchell's Pizza, 175
Windham: dining, 242, 243–46; entertainment, 248; events, 250; lodging, 240–41; shopping, 248–50; sights/activities, 227–28, 229, 231, 232, 236–37
Windham Chamber Music Festival, 248
Windham Country Club, 231
Windham Fine Arts, 250
Windham Mountain: bicycling, 228; skiing, 236
Windham Mountain Outfitters, 228
Windham Vineyard & Winery, 228
Winding Brook Country Club, 327–28
Winding Hills Park, 58
Wine Bar (Saratoga Springs), 304–5
Wine Bar & Bistro (Albany), 274
wineries: Columbia County, 322–23; Dutchess County, 369–70; Greene County, 227–28; Orange County, 50–52; Saratoga Springs, 290; Sullivan County, 87; Ulster County, 130–32; Westchester County, 452
Winery at St. George, 485
Wing Fling, 185
Wingdale: dining, 397; golf, 375; shopping, 410
Wing's Castle, 355
Winnie's Jerk Chicken & Fish, 339
Winter Clove Inn, 238
winter sports. *See* cross-country skiing; ice fishing; ice skating; skiing; snowmobiling; snowshoeing
Winter Sun & Summer Moon, 411
Winter WonderLARK, 279
Winterfest, 432
Wintje Farms, 325
Winwood the Mountain Inn, 241
Wishing Well Restaurant, 309
Wolcott Manor, 385
Women's Health & Fitness Expo, 185
Women's Studio Workshop, 184
Wonderland Farm, 373
Woodbury Common, 75
Woodchuck Lodge Historic Site, 196–97
Woodland Trail, 85
Woodridge, 88, 90
Woodstock, 115–16; dining, 159–61, 163, 167, 169–72; events, 185–86, 189; lodging, 151–54; performing arts,

175–78; shopping, 116, 179–84; sights/activities, 116, 120, 122, 134, 136, 143; traveling to, 113–14
Woodstock Artists' Association, 183
Woodstock Farm Animal Sanctuary, 122
Woodstock Farm Festival, 136
Woodstock Festival Site, 82–83
Woodstock Film Festival, 177
Woodstock Framing Gallery, 183
Woodstock Guild, 176, 183
Woodstock Historical Society Museum, 116
Woodstock Inn on the Millstream, 154
Woodstock Mountain View Guest House, 154
Woodstock Museum, 116
Woodstock Playhouse, 177
Woodstock Wonderworks, 116
Woodstock/New Paltz Art and Crafts Fair, 185–86
Woody Guthrie, 118
Woody's, 70–71
Woody's Country Kitchen, 212
Would Restaurant, The, 165
Wreath Fineries at 12 Wineries, 189
Wright, Frank Lloyd, 332
Wright, Russel: Historic Site & Nature Sanctuary, 424–25
Wright Farms, 139
Wright Gallery, 183
Wulff, Lee, 83
Wulff School of Fly-Fishing, 91
Wunderbar & Bistro, 342
Wurtsboro: information, 81; shopping, 106; sights/activities, 87, 93, 94
Wurtsboro Airport, 82, 93
Wurtsboro Board of Trade, 81

X

X20 Xaviars on the Hudson, 478
Xavier's at Piermont, 31

Y

Yaddo, 296
Yama Sushi, 468
Yanni Restaurant & Café, 175
Yellow Bird Gallery, 54
Yellow Monkey Antiques, 487–88
Yoast Mabie Tavern, 19
Yobo, 65
Yonder Farms, 326
Yonkers: dining, 478, 483; events, 490, 491; shopping, 489; sights/activities, 441, 448, 456, 458, 460
Yonkers Farmers' Market, 456
Yono's, 273
Yorktown Heights: entertainment, 487; sights/activities, 451–52, 454, 458
Yorktown Museum, 451–52
Yorktown Stage, 487
Youngsville: lodging, 97; shopping, 107; sights/activities, 90, 93
Yulan Country Store, 104
Yum Yum Noodle Bar, 172

Z

Zadock Pratt Museum, 225–26
Za'Za, 474
Zeeh's Tree Farm, 139
Zephs', 468
ziplines, 88, 233–34, 378
Zona Rosa, 67
Zoom Flume Water Park, 226–27
zoos, 24, 48, 357
Zora Dora's Paleteria, 367
Zuppa, 478